QUENTIN COOPER & PAUL SULLIVAN

M·A·Y·P·O·L·E·S, M·A·R·T·Y·R·S & M·A·Y·H·E·M

366 days of British customs, myths and eccentricities

BLOOMSBURY

DEDICATIONS

Paul dedicates this book to Gill, who enabled him to work without starving, and whose love and support staved off the otherwise inevitable insanity.

Quentin would like to thank the many friends and strangers who continue to make him giggle, dance, or sandwiches.

The authors and publisher have endeavoured to ensure that the information in this book is accurate and up-to-date. Although they cannot accept responsibility for errors, the publisher would welcome suggestions for amendments for inclusion in future editions of this title.

The expression Country Living is the trade mark of The National Magazine Company Limited and The Hearst Corporation, registered in the UK and the USA, and other principal countries of the world, and is the absolute property of The National Magazine Company Limited and The Hearst Corporation. The use of this trade mark other than with the express permission of The National Magazine Company or The Hearst Corporation is strictly prohibited.

First published in 1994

This paperback edition first published in 1995 by Bloomsbury Publishing Plc
2 Soho Square
London W1V 6HB

Copyright © 1994 by Quentin Cooper and Paul Sullivan

The moral right of the authors has been asserted

A copy of the CIP entry for this book is available from the British Library

ISBN 0 7475 2206 5
10 9 8 7 6 5 4 3 2 1

Typeset by Hewer Text Composition Services, Edinburgh
Printed in Britain by Cox & Wyman Ltd, Reading, Berks

CONTENTS

INTRODUCTION

'Custom, then, is the great guide of human life'
David Hume, *An Enquiry Concerning
Human Understanding* (1748)

'*The EVERY-DAY BOOK, by its abundant information, and chronological arrangement, is a
storehouse of continuous instruction and amusement for persons of all ages, in all ranks of society.*

*1. It is a HISTORY OF THE YEAR – for it is a History of Every Day in the Calendar –
Day by Day
2. It is a PERPETUAL GUIDE TO THE YEAR – not to any one Year in particular, but to
Every Year.
3. It is a COMPLETE DICTIONARY OF THE ALMANAC – for the Daily Use and
Information of Every Person who has an Almanac, and desires a Key to it.
4. It is the EVERY-DAY BOOK OF PLEASURE AND BUSINESS – of Parents and
Children – of Teachers and Pupils – of Masters and Servants.*'

These bold assertions were made by William Hone some 170 years ago, in the introduction to his
excellent and enormous *Every-Day Book*. We would say much the same about *Maypoles, Martyrs
& Mayhem* if we had even one vertebra of his brass neck. But we have been guided by the same
principles as Hone: as well as mapping over 400 current and continuing customs, we have put
emphasis on the more neglected corners of history, seeking out humorous and downright odd
stories which chart the course of the year.

What emerges is an ever-shifting 12-month cycle which, for many people, is no longer familiar.
Strawberries all year round, identical high streets nationwide, central heating (it's not all bad news)
– seasonal and regional variations continue to be papered over as Britain is redesigned to fit in with
the gaudy minimalism of the global village. But, fortunately, it has been a botched job – here and
there traces of the old vibrant colour scheme peek through, and occasionally entire stretches of the
underlying pattern can still be glimpsed.

It is these unique deviations from the increasingly omnipresent norm which first inspired us to
write this book. There are ancient rites, rituals and celebrations still going on, somewhere in
Britain, almost every day of the year. Superstitions still thrive, with countless regional and local
variations. And even where everything active is long gone, almost every village, hill and stream
seems to have its own story to tell – either a legend, or a piece of often overlooked history. Putting
these into chronological order not only reveals the flow of events through the seasons, it also means
that for any given time of the year it is easy to see what is happening where, and whether it is worth
going along. The various symbols used in the text are as follows:

© *A custom or event that is alive and kicking, with spectators – or even participants – welcome*

◉ *Still going on, but it is either a largely private affair, or so irregular that attending could
prove tricky*

☼ *Weatherlore: something to watch out for on the day, and then prove to be accurate or
otherwise*

♀ *There are lots of long-gone ghosts and monsters in the book, but this symbol is used only if a
place is still said to be haunted, or is regularly visited by strange creatures*

▥ *Something relevant to the day, and which can still be seen*

◉ *Divination: only used if the particular method of peering into the future can be carried out at
home, and does not involve ridiculous ingredients or the ritual sacrifice of close relatives*

Where there is a place ⅲ or event © which can be visited, the entry includes the location of the nearest town with a tourist information centre. While the vast majority of customs in this book will take place on or near the date on which they are listed, the tourist information centres are generally the best place to find out the precise date and timing of the event in any given year. We would be mad men indeed if we believed that there were no anomalies in this book – it is a feature of many customs and traditions that they continue to shift and change.

The single biggest headache for anyone attempting to set out the ceremonies and traditions of Britain in chronological order is what to do with the moveable feasts which take place on wildly different dates from year to year. While it is straightforward enough to put an event which is held 'on the third weekend of May' – or whenever – on an appropriate day within the relevant month, the more erratic festivals are a little more problematic. Chinese New Year has been put on 31st January, Purim on 26th February, and Diwali on 10th November. But the biggest moveables span several days – or even weeks – and scores of separate events, and so have been given their own sections. Lent, Easter, Whitsun and Rogationtide are each between the months which they straddle. Harvest can be found between August and September. In using the book to find out what is happening on any given day, it is worth scanning these between-the-months sections, along with moveable festivals in the surrounding week. The Appendix gives the exact timing of Easter, Chinese New Year and all the other major moveables up to and including the year 2000.

Throughout the book there are frequent references to the 'Old' Calendar. In 1752 Britain was brought into line with the rest of Europe by losing 11 days. Many old customs steadfastly resisted this change, and continued to be celebrated on their 'Old' dates. 'Old' May Day is therefore on 12th May; whereas 'New' May Day is where everyone expects it, on 1st May. Adding a further layer of chaos, the mathematics frequently went awry, with some 'Old' and 'New' dates separated by ten or twelve or even thirteen days. For more details of this gloriously confusing calendar change see 29th February.

This book would not have been possible without the assistance of many helpful souls up and down the country. We have listed as many as possible in the acknowledgements; but special mention must be made of Marlene Sullivan – Paul's Mum – for work above and beyond the cost of a huge phone-bill; Harry Cooper – Quentin's Dad – for proof-reading the whole thing; and to the tireless graft of the inestimable Morag McFarland. Without Morag and her skills at extracting information there would be no '*Maypoles, Martyrs & Mayhem*'.

Quentin Cooper and Paul Sullivan, Stoke Bruerne, June 1994.

P.S. No matter how strange they seem, every myth, legend, ghost, divination and story in the book is a genuine practice or belief. Apart from one.

JANUARY

1st January
New Year's Day/Ne'er Day

First-Foot, First-Football

New Year is a minefield of superstition. There is plenty of good luck to be garnered, but one foot wrong – first or otherwise – and ill-fortune, the evil eye, death, plagues of carnivorous geese and worse await. From Manchester comes a warning about being over-zealous in enforcing these traditions. A man once walked into a pub in the city and asked for whisky on credit. Giving money in the form of cash or credit on New Year's Day is considered very bad luck, but as the date was Monday January 2nd, the man felt that he was entitled to his whisky. The barman refused, pointing out that as New Year's Day had fallen on a Sunday, the Monday was the carried-over holiday and so counted as January 1st, taboos and all. One thing led to another, and during the ensuing brawl the barman was stabbed to death. The discreditable drinker was sent to the gallows.

© It is unlucky to give credit, or cause someone to be in your debt, at New Year. But to give unconditionally brings unbridled good fortune, and this is the basis of **first-footing**. The correct first-foot steps are made by a man – usually tall and dark, but that varies enormously up and down the country – who should arrive after midnight carrying symbols of warmth, wealth and food. A favourite combination is coal, salt and cake – sometimes known as *handsel*. Ideally the Footer should be an outsider, and he should be entertained when he has finished symbolicking around.

Twigs of evergreen are recommended first-footing items too; and, for fishing communities such as Dundee, a red herring. If the Footer – also known as Lucky Bird in Yorkshire, and **Quaaltagh** on the Isle of Man – fails to bring anything, expect a miserable year. The best quaaltagh is a person born foot-first; while the worst quaaltagh is a spaagah, a splay-footed man.

© A favourite Scottish first-footing drink was the het pint, a mixture of beer, whisky, sugar and eggs – the night before and the following breakfast all in one. At Lanark in Strathclyde the drink has been institutionalised at the **Het Pint Ceremony**, held this morning at the District Council Offices. In 1662 money from a 'Mortification' – in this case the interest on three debts owing to the council – was used to send five poor boys to Lanark Grammar School, and for other pious causes. From this charity arose the tradition of providing a large glass – a Scots pint used to be the equivalent of three English ones – of mulled ale for the *'decayed burgesses'* of the town. These days this is taken to mean local pensioners, who get £1 as well as their pint at the ceremony.

© Those seeking bucketfuls of good luck have to drag themselves away from the first-footing fun to ensure that they get the **Cream of the well**. This is the first water drawn from the well at the beginning of the year. It brings fabulous wealth and happiness to the household. Obsessives have been known to camp overnight by wells: queuing for Harrods' sale is a contemporary version of this custom. The one who wins the Cream – or Flower – sprinkles hay or petals on to the surface of the water, to let late-comers know that the well has been de-Flowered, and to placate the resident water-spirit. The Cream stays free of impurities all year.

In the north of England, notably at the three wells at Wark in Northumberland, the Cream bestowed magical powers. Drink some and you could fly and travel through keyholes. In Scotland, lonely women were in luck if they won the Cream. One mouthful, and they would be married within 12 months.

A macabre Highland custom involved taking a cupful of water from the **Dead and Living Ford** – a common name for streams regularly crossed by funeral parties. On New Year morning they had to drink from the water, and sprinkle some around the homestead without letting the cup touch the ground. All exits and vents were then sealed, and juniper was set alight in the house. When asphyxiation was imminent, the doors and windows were flung wide, and everyone coughed a lot. This was purification by fire and water. Similarly, in South Wales until early this century, it was customary to be visited by singing youths sprinkling newly-drawn water on everything and everyone indoors. For this anti-social behaviour they expected cash rewards.

All year, evil and diseases (particularly one known as smut) were prevented from crossing the threshold by twisting hawthorn into a globe-shape, seasoning it with cider, and hanging it in the kitchen. Today was the day to remove the old globe and put a new one in its place. The old one then had to be placed on a pile of burning straw and carried across the fields to the family dump. If the flames blew out en route then a poor year for crops lay ahead. Two chief areas for this **Burning the Bush** ceremony were at Brinsop and Birley Court, both near Hereford. In Worcestershire, a crown of blackthorn twigs took the place of the hawthorn.

© A revived and composite version of Burning the Bush now takes place near the old water mill at Putley, just outside Ledbury in Hereford and Worcester. Shortly after midnight on New Year's Day 13 bonfires are lit – a ring of 12 small ones and a larger central pyre – using a blazing straw-stuffed hawthorn globe on the end of a long pole. The globe is then thrown on to the central bonfire, and while it burns fresh hawthorn is cut and made into a second sphere. It is doused with cider, and later singed in the dying embers of the main fire. The crowd chants '*Old Ci-der*' nine times on a note so low that it would trouble most baritones, and the luck-bringing globe is then taken away to hang in the kitchen at the water mill until the next year's ceremony.

© At Symondsbury near Bridport in Dorset the local mummers choose this evening to assail the pubs with their play and songs – see December 26th for more on mumming.

© At Kirkwall, on Mainland, Orkney, street football breaks out at 10 am on Ne'er Day (there is also a warm-up game on Christmas Day), starting with the Boys' Game in front of the cathedral at the Mercat Cross. The main contest, the Men's Game, begins at 1 pm, and can last up to seven hours. The teams are the Uppies versus the Downies: a common distinc-

tion in street games, referring to the upper and lower parts of the town. The pitch for the **Ba' Game** spans most of the town, from the castle to the harbour, and the game involves about 120 players. The cork-filled leather ball is later presented to the player who has been named man of the match.

▥ Also on the Mainland at Birsay near Twatt, the **Stone of Quoyboyne** nips to the Loch of Boardhouse as the Hogmanay bells ring out and goes for a quick dip. And on the next island up, Rousay, the stone called **Yetnasteen** walks down to Loch Scockness for a Ne'er Day drink. Neither stone has ever made it to the Kirkwall Ba' Game. To discourage people from checking up on these superstitions, it is said that should you stumble upon either stone in mid-wander, you will die on the spot.

2nd January

A Year's Supply of Weather

Edinburgh held the **Powderhall New Year Pedestrian Handicap** today and yesterday, a whole range of speed-walking races performed according to 'The Rules Governing Pedestrianism'. An 1843 contest matched '*the veteran Townsend*' – a man in his 50s – against a teenager called Pet. The distance was nine miles, worked out as 31 circuits of the stadium. The race did not finish until long after dark, and Pet won by 50 yards. Perhaps Townsend lost because, as one newspaper report put it, he had '*more signs of a victualling department*' – one of the best euphemisms for fatness yet devised. Powderhall continued to be a precinct for pedestrianism until well into this century. But in 1957, in spite of local outcry, the local council turfed over the track. As a small consolation, Powderhall remains Edinburgh's main venue for speedway and greyhound-racing.

● Hubberholme in North Yorkshire holds a **candle auction** for the Poor's Pasture at *The George*. This custom, called the **Landletting**, used to take place on New Year's Day, but has since moved to the first Monday of the year to discourage huge Bank Holiday crowds – only a handful of visitors are allowed to attend. Bidding for this 16-acre piece of land begins at 8 pm, only becoming serious about four hours later when a pin stuck in the burning candle is about to fall, thus ending the auction, with the land going to the person who last bid. The origin of the candle auction is unknown. Some sources claim that it is 1,000 years old, others say it is little more than 100. Whatever, the vicar is always the auctioneer, and the money raised from selling the Poor's Pasture goes to the needy of the parish. For the rest of the year there is a tradition of keeping a candle alight in the bar during opening hours. The pub changed hands early in 1994, but the new owners say they will continue to stage the annual wick's-end auction.

A similar custom used to take place in January at the villages of Broadway and Upwey in Dorset. Broadway held its bidding on the instructions of the 15th-century will of one John Gould. The Parish Meadow was auctioned while a one-inch candle burned, the bids ceasing when it sputtered out. The candle was balanced on the blade of a knife, and in 1892 there was mild disgruntlement when it fell over and went out before a decent price had been reached. But custom is custom, and someone got the land for a one-off bargain price that year.

☕ In terms of **weather**, it is said that the first three days of the year reflect the prevailing conditions over each of the next three months. For those who prefer their forecasting longer-range, in some areas it is believed that the pattern extends even further, so that the first 12 days of January set the tone for the entire year. But today has a significance all of its own, as anything that happens in the heavens on the 2nd determines the climatic conditions across September. It is possible for all these separate bits of weather-lore to co-exist, but only if February and September always end up with the same weather.

3rd January

Knaves in the Nave

Today in 1804 at **Wellington Barracks** in London, somewhere between the eighth shiver and the tenth yawn, the man on sentry duty saw a woman. That in itself would have been unusual enough given the time and the place. But this was not just another jogger getting an early start. She was headless, and rose from the ground two feet away from the sentry, surrounded by a misty cloud.

The spooked soldier told his colleagues, and was a chief witness when the increasing incidents of haunting were later investigated. The sentry told the court hearing that he saw clearly the woman's dress, red-striped with spots between the lines. Her favourite haunt was between the canal and St James's Park. Accompanying the manifestations, there were also strange noises at the windows of one of the barracks' houses. One witness said that they had heard the ghost call out in a weak voice '*Bring me a light!*'

✟ The sad truth, which emerged at the trial, was that a sergeant had murdered his wife on that spot several years before, cutting off her head and throwing her into the canal. Any ghost worth its salt would go a-haunting after that, and the apparition is still intermittently sighted, but only by soldiers based at the barracks. Over the passing years the phantom has also proved a useful device for explaining away glimpses of women being sneaked in or out of the barracks for some off-duty canoodling.

Once a pan-European bout of madness, **The Feast of Fools** is now tragically defunct. It was a riotous parody of church and monastic procedure, and was undertaken by the monks and clergy themselves. Always more popular on the continent, in the Middle Ages The Feast of Fools also had a decent foothold in Britain. The participants danced naked in the church, sang dirty songs, brayed like donkeys during a spoof service, ate sausages or black pudding before the altar in parody of Mass, burned old sandals in place of incense, broke wind, gambled, swore, and drank themselves silly. A Mock Bishop – the Abbot of Misrule – acted as scurrilous MC for these proceedings. It was the most audacious of all the 'letting off steam' traditions, turning the normal austerity of clerical life on its head, and lasting most of the first week of January.

Only the most senior and/or devout of monks objected to these religiously dubious outrages – for many young men monastic life was not a calling, but a desperate or forced career move. At their peak many monasteries were like overcrowded boarding schools, and occasional outbreaks of ritualised excess, such as the Feast of Fools, were grudgingly tolerated as it was thought they lessened the likelihood of random riots and general unrest.

▦ The authorities eventually clamped down. By the 15th century the feast was already in terminal decline in Britain, though it lasted until the mid-1700s in remote corners of Europe. Its origins lay in the Roman winter feasts of Saturnalia and the Calends of January. One of the hotbeds for Foolish Feasting was at the now picturesquely ruined 12th-century Quarr Abbey, near Ryde on the Isle of Wight in Hampshire.

4th January

We Plough the Fields and Natter

The road from Abingdon to Oxford is now known as the A34. It used to be known less prosaically, and more alarmingly, as a hang-out for **highwaymen**. The risky bit for travellers was the stretch through Bagley Woods, the sort of place where the Sheriff of Nottingham's men always get waylaid in Robin Hood films. On 4th January 1783, one Mr Blewitt was set upon in the middle of the woods by two highwaymen who offered to relieve him of his belongings.

In a burst of courage, Blewitt opted to stay seated and not deliver anything. He challenged the robbers to shoot at will, and spurred his horse away in a hail of bullets. One shot went through the brim of his cap, but Blewitt galloped home otherwise unscathed. Such encounters and escapes were not everyday 18th-century occurrences, in spite of the apparent evidence of old movies and historical fiction. Blewitt's brush with bandits was so unusual that he became a celebrity. He spent the rest of his days on the dinner-party circuit repeating his tale, deploying his punctured hat as an applause-garnering prop.

William Burgess was hanged at Taunton Gaol, Devon, today in 1859. His wife had died in 1857, and he shirked his paternal duties afterwards. Two of his three children, Tom and Emma, were sent away to work on the land, leaving only the youngest daughter, Anna, in his care. Burgess was still unhappy. He felt that the weekly half a crown which she cost him was too much to spend on a child. So he killed Anna at a remote spot on Exmoor, covering his ground afterwards with lame excuses, saying that she had gone away for unspecified reasons to visit unspecified relatives. When suspicions began to grow, he disinterred the corpse and threw it down a well at Wheal Eliza's disused mine.

☦ The detective work of local Parson Thornton, backed up by a ghostly glow that local people saw over the well, eventually brought the crime to light. Sure enough, poor Anna was discovered down the deep, flooded shaft, and her supernaturally assisted retrieval sealed Burgess' fate. The ghostly light was so pleased with the outcome that it left the well alone and moved to Anna's grave at Simonsbath, where it is still sometimes seen.

The introduction of a huge plough to dig furrows deep enough for the growing of parsnips does not seem folklorically promising. However, on the Channel Islands it meant party-time. The parsnip plough arrived on the scene in the 18th century, and was so massive that it needed 16 or more oxen to pull it. No single farm had that kind of oxen clout, and so neighbours had to pool their beasts. This rapidly became an excuse for a day or two of feasting and socialising as the oxen team did the rounds of all the parsnip fields. The accompanying merrymaking, drinking, chatting and guzzling became known as *Le Grand' Querrue* – the big plough – and took place on all the Channel Islands until the early 19th century.

5th January
Twelfth Night/
Old Christmas Eve

Curried Faggots

Jesus' uncle, **Joseph of Arimathea**, made his contacts with Britain through trading in tin. It was a pragmatic start to what became a religious pilgrimage. Legend fills in the gaps, saying that Joseph later sailed to these shores and founded the first British church. His retinue followed him to Glastonbury, and at Weary-all Hill he rested and thrust his staff into the ground. It sprouted and became a thriving thorn tree. Glastonbury has never looked back.

🌳 The **Glastonbury Thorn** was so holy that it flowered on Christmas Day. In the 17th century Oliver Cromwell's men thought it all highly idolatrous, and they chopped the thorn down. During this puritanical pruning, one of the men accidentally chopped his leg off, a crippling piece of divine retribution. A stone marks the site of the original thorn, but a cutting somehow survived the attack, and, replanted in the grounds of St John's church, it continued to bloom at Christmas. After the change in the calendar in 1752, crowds gathered on December 25th to see if the thorn would still flower on cue. '*To their great disappointment, there was no appearance of its blowing.*' So everyone trooped back 11 days later – when Christmas would have been if the calendar had not been changed (logically this makes today Old Christmas Day, but for some reason an extra day's delay crept in, and January 5th became known as Old Christmas Eve, with tomorrow Old Christmas Day). On January 5th 1753, the thorn did indeed bloom, and ever since it has regularly flowered today, or failing that some time between new and old Christmas. It also usually manages a second burst of buds in the spring. A cutting is given to the reigning monarch to decorate the royal table on Christmas Day. Botanists support the story to a certain degree, averring that the species of thorn in question has its roots in the Middle East, and flowers twice a year, given the right conditions.

⏸ There are similar fickle Christmas-flowering holy trees up and down the country, including ones at Quainton in Buckinghamshire, Tedstone Delamere in Hereford and Worcester, and Queen Mary's College at St Andrews in Fife, all of them thorns; while the one at Cadnam, near Southampton in Hampshire, was an oak, just to be different.

It is a traditional source of uncertainty, but in strict terms **Twelfth Night** is the evening before Twelfth Day. Known as Auld Yule in Scotland, most of today's celebrations revolved around **wassailing**. This was a ceremonial, convivial toast, drunk originally from a huge wassail-bowl – a highly decorative punch-bowl. The word *wassail* is Saxon, meaning literally 'be hale and cheery', an early form of *cheers*. The correct response to the toast is '*Drinc hale!*'
© Wassailing occurred throughout the Christmas season, culminating on Twelfth Night. It came in two distinct guises. The Visiting Wassail involved travelling from door to door with song, greeting and muddy boots, and an embedded plea for food and drink. The best surviving example is at **Curry Rivel** near Taunton in Somerset, where the wassailers carry an ash faggot around the village today, starting around 6 pm. At 10.30 pm the revellers return to the *King William* pub, where the oldest man present throws the faggot on to the fire (see December 24th for more on the ash faggot).

The second, more esoteric, form of wassailing involved ceremonially honouring various plants and creatures. Apple-trees were wassailed to ensure a good crop (see January 16th and 17th). Bees were wassailed to make them produce lots of honey. And cattle were individually wassailed to keep them healthy. This last custom was particularly popular in Hertfordshire. There, the best of the cattle each received a specially-baked **cow cake** with a hole in the middle. The wassailers descended on the beast singing:

Fill your cups my merry men all!
For here's the best ox in the stall;
Oh he is the best ox, of that there's no
  mistake,
And so let us crown him with the Twelfth
  Cake!

The cake was then hooked over one of the animal's horns, and stayed there until it was tossed to pieces or fell apart. The ox-wassailers – all of them men – then danced home, to find themselves locked out. This was all part of the ritual. In some versions, they had to guess what the women indoors had at the end of a long stick before they were allowed in. The object would be something obvious, but if the men failed to figure out what, it was clear that they were too drunk or boisterous to gain admission, and were left to calm down in the damp night air.

In Somerset, the beasts enjoyed Old Christmas as a holiday. Horses were not allowed to do any work today, and all the animals found special titbits sneaked into their feeding troughs. Salted herring, apparently, is what cows secretly crave.

Twelfth Night was a great time for **bonfires**. There were usually 13 at a major location, one for each of the Twelve Nights, plus a thirteenth **Judas Fire**, which was always extinguished during the proceedings. At Brough in Cumbria the fire was mobile, as large burning holly and ash branches were carried through the streets accompanied by a band and fireworks. The occasion was known as **Holly Night**, and bits of the charred wood were gathered by the crowds for luck.

6th January
Twelfth Day/Old Christmas Day/Epiphany/Uphalieday

Swaying with the Boggans

Some 700 years ago Lady Mowbray was riding between Haxey and Westwoodside on January 6th when the wind blew the red hood from her head. Thirteen labouring men immediately gave rumbustious chase over the muddy furrows. The man who retrieved the hood was so shy that he passed it on to another of the labourers, who returned it to Lady Mowbray with great courtesy. She dubbed them 'Fool' and 'Lord' respectively, and gave 13 half acres of land so that the chase could be re-enacted every year in the form of a game. In a puff of apocrypha, **Haxey Hood** was born.

© The Hood still takes place at Haxey in Humberside today, Old Christmas Day. The improbable story is one explanation for the ancient Rugby-cum-Rollerball game today between Haxey and Westwoodside, and for the thirteen red-clad Boggans who are officials at the event – including a Lord and Fool. Players and watchers gather at the stone near Haxey church, to hear a speech from the Fool which explains that two and a half bullocks have been killed for the occasion, and ends with the words: '*House agen house, town agen town; if tha meet a man, knock 'im down, but don't 'urt 'im!*' The Fool is then symbolically 'smoked' from his position with damp straw behind the stone. In 1957 the straw was not damp enough, and the smoked Fool caught fire.

After this the Lord Boggan, with his wand of thirteen willow withies bound with thirteen more, leads everyone into the remaining half-acre of the original thirteen. Ten sacking 'hoods' are tossed in the air, and youthful participants try to get them past the Boggans: if they do they can claim 50p.

Preliminaries over, the **Sway Hood** – a coil of thick rope bound with leather – is produced and thrown up. Then battle begins. The aim is to get the Hood to the home pub in either Haxey or Westwoodside. The ensuing scrum, the Sway, has been known to destroy not just fields and hedges, but stone walls and household contents.

Some 1932 reportage gave a splendid description of the Sway: '*Down he would go, all among the broccolies . . . and for some time there would be a seething mass of bodies among the greens.*' Needless to say, not everyone looked kindly on the Hood – over to our 1832 correspondent: '*This usage, which originated in the remote ages of ignorance and barbarism was celebrated on Monday . . . to the disgrace of our country and despite the "march of intellect".*' But, after all, as they say in the village, 'There is no law in Haxey on the 6th.'

In years gone by the Hood was roasted briefly on a spit in the winning pub, and basted with hot ale which was then consumed. This, along with the bullock references in the speech, the recommencement of ploughing on Plough Monday (the one after the 6th), and the fact that 'hood' in this context may be the Viking word *huid*, meaning a head, all suggest that this is a pagan fertility ritual. The bull was sacrificed to ensure good crops, and a boisterous spring-awakening game was played with its head. The winning pub gets to keep the hood for the year.

If the 6th is a Sunday, the Hood is held the day before. The authors found this out the hard way, after a frosty and fruitless six-hour round-trip on Sunday 6th January 1991.

After the first stroke of midnight today, the normally calm waters of **St Anne's Well** at Aconbury near Hereford bubble frantically, and blue smoke rises from the aquatic depths. This alleged spectacle indicates that magic is in the air: the first bucketful drawn from the well afterwards has medicinal value, and is especially good for the eyes.

Being the far limit of all the Christmas festivities, today was often the last chance to party before long winter labours. There was a glut of Twelfth Day fancy-dress, known as **Guisering** – from the same root as the word 'disguise' – and its practical virtue was that it afforded a degree of camouflage for miscreants who might regret everything in the morning. In Cornwall the word mutated from 'guisering' to the even more entertaining 'goose-dancing'.

Twelfth Night Cake – called **Uphalieday** cake in Scotland – featured heavily in the festivities. Deep in the mix it contained a pea and a bean, and the lucky recipients became the King (bean) and Queen (pea) for the occasion. If a male split a pea or a female bit into a bean, they had to have an immediate sex-change. Twelfth Night Cake died out only this century, under the pressure of the now ubiquitous Christmas cake.

◉ A different species of Twelfth Night Cake makes its annual appearance at the Theatre Royal, Drury Lane, London, tonight. In

1794, the will of cook-turned-actor Robert Baddeley stipulated that a cake be made in his honour and eaten in the Green Room of the theatre. He left £100 for this purpose, and the current actors, in full stage make-up, still raise their glasses and slices of the **Baddeley Cake** in memory of Robert tonight. The cake is accompanied by punch in an antique silver punch-bowl, presented to the Theatre in 1963, which links in neatly with yesterday's Twelfth Night wassail-bowl traditions.

◉ Christianity is not entirely forgotten. **Epiphany** marks the arrival of the Three Magi and their eccentric gifts. At St James's Palace in London today, frankincense and myrrh are carried to the altar-rail by the Queen's proxy during the church service. These days the gold has been replaced by a handful of fivers, and the money is handed out to pensioners afterwards – modern-day stand-ins for the more ill-defined traditional beneficiaries, the poor. Until the reign of George III, the Monarch handled the goods in person. But poor mad George was not up to it. Royalty has stayed away ever since.

◉ Not everyone celebrates Christmas on Christmas Day. When the Gregorian calendar was introduced in 1752 and 11 days were skipped, many stuck to the Old Calendar for their feasts and traditions. As time passed only a few rural areas held out, and even they tended to cave in for the big festivals. The one exception is isolated Foula, west of Shetland, which still celebrates, Christmas today – the inhabitants call it **Yule**. Presents are handed out, and there is a special meal of salt-smoked mutton (*reetsit*), potato soup and a Yule bread made with caraway seeds. The men go for a walk along the cliff tops, shooting at tin cans and balloons, and everyone ends up at the same house for a party – the island has a population of less than 100. Newcomers to Foula have brought the conventional Christmas with them, so children on the island have become accustomed to two celebrations. On Christmas Day they open parcels sent by mainlanders – known as '25th-ers' – and at Yule they receive gifts from family and friends on Foula. It is made clear to the children that after Santa has sorted out the rest of the world on December 25th, he makes a special trip to the island on the 6th. Foula also has its New Year's Day – called Newer Day – on January 13th.

7th January
St Distaff's Day/St Brannoc's Day

The Undead Cow

More than almost any other saint, 6th-century **Brannoc** makes a good case for being named patron saint of the surreal. He sailed from Wales to Devon in a stone coffin. When he arrived at what is now Braunton, he decided that a sow suckling its piglets was the divine sign that he had been seeking on the vexed issue of where to found a church. So he shooed the pigs on, built his church on the spot, and set about converting the locals. It helped that he was a supernatural vet, coming up with miracle cures for all their sick animals. It also helped that he was the first in the area to have the latest hi-tech farming gadgetry – the plough. Using a couple of wild deer to pull it, he instructed large chunks of Devon in how to till the soil.

Brannoc used some divine bovine intervention after a jealous neighbour stole his milking cow, killed it, chopped it up, and turned it into stew. When Brannoc found out, he gently called to the cow by name. The animal pulled itself together, jumped out of the cauldron, and plodded home to several more years' good service.

🏛 St Brannoc is buried in Braunton church, Devon. The sow and her litter and several of his best animal miracles are shown in various carvings in the church.

St Brannoc was odd, but he was real. Today's other saint, St Distaff, is a long piece of wood. A distaff is a cleft staff used for spinning flax – work that was so much the province of women that 'distaff' came to mean women's work in general, and then became a term for the female side of a family. Today was known as **St Distaff's Day**, as this was when women returned from the long Christmas break to check their staffs and other equipment before resuming the drudgery of full production tomorrow. An old saying does its best to sum the mood up: '*On St Distaff's Day neither work nor play.*' The men often livened up the day by trying to burn small sections of the flax, while the women, in turn, lurked behind doors with buckets of water in order to soak the saboteurs. The poet Robert Herrick stretches the rhyme a smidgeon when he describes this larking about in his *Hesperides* of 1648:

Bring in pails of water, then
Let the maids bewash the men,
Give St Distaff all the right;
Then bid Christmas sport Good-night!
And next morrow, everyone
to his own vocation.

In the regions where Plough Monday was important, however, St Distaff's was shifted to the same date – the Monday after the 6th. It was a sly way of extending the season that little bit further.

© In Greece, fishermen bless the seas each Epiphany (January 6th) to ensure rich catches in the year ahead. On the afternoon of the Sunday nearest Epiphany two areas of Britain with strong Greek Orthodox communities – Hastings in Sussex and Margate in Kent – stage parades and their own **Blessing the Sea** services. During the Hastings service a large flower-decked church cross is dipped into the sea three times. At Margate they go a stage further, and the golden cross is thrown into the icy waters. A young boy, very often a relative of the priest, then dives into the sea to retrieve it.

8th January

Devout-Manoeuvred

The year 871 was the **Year of Battles** – nine in all – none of which resolved the stalemate between the Wessex Saxons and the invading Vikings. On January 8th, King Ethelred and his brother, soon-to-be-King Alfred, trudged wearily to their next fixture at Ashdown, near Streatley in Berkshire. Mid-way through the Saxon's dawn Mass, approaching Vikings were spotted. If the Wessex troops hurried they could secure their positions. But pious Ethelred insisted on finishing Mass, and this delay gave the Vikings complete command of the battle-field: a huge tactical advantage.

Ethelred seemed destined to go down in history as the King who died through excessive prayer. But this Ethelred was not Unready – the one who was given that nickname ('Unready' meaning 'without council') was Ethelred II, a century later – and he led his Wessexmen to a historic against-all-odds victory, personally killing a Viking king and two jarls, or chiefs. The site of the set-to was marked by a lone hawthorn tree, and 200 years later in the Domesday book this naked thorn –

or **Nachededorn** in the language of the time – had given its name to the battle. Today the site is home to a whole clump of hawthorns, originally nurtured, perhaps, by the gore of combat.

Catherine of Aragon, Henry VIII's first divorcee, died a prisoner today in 1536 at Kimbolton Castle, Cambridgeshire. Her ghost used to haunt the castle, but has not been seen for centuries. Catherine's major mark on tradition was to popularise lace-making while getting herself confused with St Catherine – see November 25th.

⛪ At the site of Ampthill Castle in Bedfordshire, where Catherine stayed during the divorce wrangling, a Cross was erected in her memory in 1773. It is still possible to make out Hugh Walpole's ode to Catherine etched on its base. During the 1980s there was a brief fad for treasure-hunt books, and the most popular of these was Kit Williams' *Masquerade*. The tip of the shadow cast by Catherine's Cross on the Summer Solstice marked the spot where his treasure – a golden hare – was buried.

The Sunday after January 6th is **Plough Sunday**, a religious pause before the riotous last-fling of Plough Monday, after which the new working year could begin in earnest. For as long as there have been farmers it has been recognised that the plough is *the* symbol of life and prosperity, nonpareil:

The King he governs all, the Parson pray for all,
The Lawyer plead for all, the Ploughman pay for all and feed all.

Sayings such as this, and songs like *The Saucy Ploughboy* and *We're All Jolly Fellows That Follow The Plough* make ploughing seem prestigious, and fun. But it was back-breaking drudgery, and by the 1870s many in the fields were singing ballads such as *Come All You Bold Fellows*, which celebrated the Labourers' champion Joseph Arch:

Come all you bold fellows that follow the plough,
Either hedging or ditching or milking the cow;
The time has arrived and the Union flag waves
We won't be kept down like a lot of white slaves.

© There has been a widespread revival of Plough Sunday blessings, with many churches across the land seizing on the ceremony as a colourful crowd-pleaser. The blessing at Goathland in North Yorkshire acts as a preface to the sword dancing on the following Saturday (see January 13th). Today's high-profile services take place in the Cathedrals at Chichester in West Sussex and Exeter in Devon. Ploughs are the star guests on these occasions. At Flamstead near Luton in Hertfordshire, local farmers take part in a short play during the 9.30 am Plough Sunday service at St Leonard's, and are given lines to read, including:

Before the soil can be broken, or the seed sown, or the green corn grow, or the grain be reaped, or the bread baked, or the people be fed, we must plough the field.

▥ © The priest then lists all the farms in the area – many of which no longer exist – including Cheverells, Gibraltar and Puddephats. A blue and red painted plough is kept in the church all year round, and is dragged up to the altar for the service. At Cawston near Norwich a 'The Plough' inn-sign hangs on the walls of St Agnes' church, over a plough. Today the plough used to be dragged round the village accompanied by appeals for money, and was blessed at the church altar. Now no-one can be found to heave it around, and during the 10 am service today the plough is blessed where it lies in one of the church aisles.

9th January
St Fillan's Day

Mock Jagger

Today in 1684 John Evelyn recorded in his diary his visit to the fair in London. There were the usual merchants, sideshows, beer and food stalls, as well as horse-racing and a bull-bait. Evelyn refers to other 'lewd' entertainments, '*so that it seemed to be a Bacchanalian triumph*'. Unusually, the fair lasted a whole month. Even odder, it was held on the Thames. This was an opportunistic **Frost Fair**, held while the river was under thick ice. Fires were lit without fear, and a heavy printing press was set up, churning out souvenir sheets bearing the legend '*Printed on the River Thames, being frozen*'.

The last half-hearted attempt at hosting a Frost Fair was in 1820, when the Thames froze with more than five feet of ice. The old London Bridge had conspired in these fairs, making the water more sluggish and prone to freezing. Once it was replaced with a bridge that let the river flow, the tradition of frost fairs sank, never to resurface.

Today is 8th-century **St Fillan's Day**. As part of their therapy, lunatics were often taken to the valley of Strathfillan, near Tyndrum in Central Region. They were immersed in **St Fillan's Pool**, his Bell was placed on their heads, and they were left tied up in the ruined chapel, where the saint is buried. In the morning, if the 'patients' had managed to loosen their bonds, they were cured. This unscientific practice continued well into the 19th century.

▥ Pittenweem, near Anstruther in Fife, is Pictish for 'place of the cave', and the cave in question belonged to St Fillan: it can still be seen in the town, with its well and altar. Once, writing in the dark, Fillan's arm emitted a torch-like glow, enabling him to continue his scribblings. The saint has another magical well, which is at its most potent in August – see August 4th for the details.

For a once widespread custom, it is surprising that so few **Plough Monday** celebrations remain. Across the country, the Monday after the 6th was marked by processions and extortion. The **Plough Jags** – also known as Plough Jacks/Bullocks/Stots/Witches, according to the location – sang their way through the streets with a plough or mock-plough, demanding donations. Refusal led to the householder's lawn or front step being 'jagged' – ploughed up. The man collecting the cash wore outlandish costume: fixed details included a bullock's tail, and often a hat made from a fox. Many of these all-male collecters opted for drag, in which case they were called *Bessie*. Occasionally non-payment was inadvertent. At Winterton in Lincolnshire last century, a woman opened her door to be confronted by a man dressed as a sheep. She was so terrified that she refused to come out. The Jags promptly destroyed her garden.

Many places had **Plough Plays** to accompany all this. These were Mumming plays with the age-old theme of life, death and resurrection. They starred a weird array of characters who announced themselves with a loud '*Here come I . . .!*', before ritually abusing and assaulting each other. At Revesby, Lincolnshire, the climax came when Pickle Herring and his brothers Ginger, Blue and Pepper Breeches locked their sham swords around the Fool's neck, and jumped away in mock-decapitation, claiming that they had killed him:

> . . . *And here he lies in all his purple gore,*
> *And we are afraid he will never dance more.*

The Fool then leaped up to refute it. In other versions a doctor appeared on the scene to cure the dead man. He would claim to cure:

> *Hipsy, pipsy, palsey, and gout,*
> *Pains within and pains without,*
> *Heal the sick, and cure the lame,*
> *Raise the dead to life again.*

This was often rounded off with '*If this man has 19 diseases in him, I will cure 21!*'

Confusingly many Plough Plays, such as the one which survived into this century at Hibaldstow, Lincolnshire, have neither a plough nor plot. Characters simply appear, speak a few garbled lines, and then ask for money. The First World War saw the end of almost all these theatricals. There is a poignant line in the Winterton play:

> *I'm a recruiting serjeant arrived 'ere just*
> *now;*
> *My orders are to 'list all that follow cart and*
> *plough.*

In real life, they did; and that was the end of the Plough Jags. One Dorset village did manage to resurrect their local Plough Play in 1938. It was a huge success, but an ill-timed one – the next year war killed it off for the second time.

© A Plough Play was successfully reinstated in 1986 at Hinckley in Leicestershire, after being banned in the mid-19th century. Plough Bullocks and Molly Dancers make a musical tour of local villages, though their more destructive instincts are kept in check these days. In 1993 one participant commented: '*We celebrate Plough Monday in the traditional way . . . We do not, however, follow the old custom of ploughing up drives when we are not greeted in the true spirit.*' They leave that job to the gas board.

In areas where there were no plays or parades, Plough Monday was the cue to resume work. If the ploughboy managed to rise before the maids of the house on the Monday morning, he was given a **chicken** on Pancake Day. Alternatively, he could claim his chicken on returning home from work that day if he managed to shout '*Cock in the pot!*' before the maid could shout '*Cock on the dunghill!*'. If the ploughboy got his cry in first, the maid was said to have 'lost her cock'. Indeed.

10th January

Straw Bear Fields c/w Penny Gain

Today was the low point for the humble **penny**. On January 10th 1828, the Bank of England issued its lowest ever denomination bank-note, promising to pay the bearer on demand the sum of one penny. The penny coin had been in trouble for some time. The old silver penny fizzled out in the reign of Charles II (1649–85). In 1797 it reappeared in a new copper guise, but immediately became associated with the lowly side of life: penny broadsides and penny-dreadfuls which peddled songs and tacky stories; penny shows at fairs; and penny pots of bad beer. The term 'penny pots' became synonymous with the spots accumulated by desperate drinkers.

The tarnished image of the penny was restored on another January 10th. On this day in 1840, the Penny Black stamp was introduced. Since 1680 a postal service had existed within a ten-mile radius of London, but now there was a national Penny Post. This gave the penny piece a new sheen of respectability, and started a trend that wrecked many a boy's adolescence: fickle hormones manifesting as a desire to hunch over a Stanley Gibbons catalogue while holding a pair of tweezers.

A favourite use of the penny – lobbing it into a well and making a wish – has in the late 20th century extended to include almost any body of water, be it ornamental pond or shopping-precinct fountain. This custom harks right back to the origins of coinage. To the Celts, the head was the home of the soul and the life-force, and so when coins had the ruler's head stamped on them, they were thought to carry some of the power of the head itself. Throwing heads into wells was a favourite pre-Christian pastime – a way of adding to the magic of the well-water – and coins were an admirable, less messy substitute.

In the Fens, the day after Plough Monday (*i.e.* the Tuesday after the 6th) was **Straw Bear Tuesday**, an excuse to extend the holiday period for yet another day. The Straw Bear was a man covered entirely in straw, with a straw tail and a huge conical sheaf over his head. He did not resemble a bear. Restrained on a rope, the bear danced or just clowned around. His antics were often just an eccentric thank-you for the money collected the previous day, and an excuse for a colourful pub-crawl.

© The Straw Bear was still going strong at Whittlesey in Cambridgeshire early this century, and has been revived there – looking as impressively weird as ever – as part of the Whittlesey Straw Bear Festival of folk music and dance, held on the second weekend of January.

Despite the name, it is unlikely that the Straw Bear derives from the dancing or baited bears which were once a common feature at fairs and wakes. A more probable source is hinted at by the fact that at Holton-le-Clay in Lincolnshire the Plough Monday performers had a **straw man** in their midst, dressed in the same unorthodox manner as the Cambridge-shire Bear. Across Europe straw men – either real men covered in straw, or figures made from straw – were usually associated with Shrove Tuesday, when they were ritually sacrificed. If the straw man was an effigy, it was burned; if a living man, he was symbolically despatched only (except in *The Wicker Man*, the finest and daftest of all films drawing on British legends and superstition, in which virgin po-liceman Edward Woodward becomes a human sacrifice, burned alive inside a massive man-shaped wicker cage).

11th January

Tom Hardy and the Hearty Tom

This was the day, in 1928, when **Thomas Hardy** died. In his novels, short stories (notably *Wessex Tales*) and poems, he re-corded many folk-beliefs and customs of the 19th century. The most famous of these include the wife-selling in *The Mayor of Casterbridge* and the drunken Harvest Home supper in *Far From the Madding Crowd*.

▥ Hardy's death has acquired its own legend. Hardy's parish church at Stinsford in Dorset and Westminster Abbey both laid claim to his remains. The deal was that Stinsford got his heart, while Poet's Corner got the rest. The heart was duly removed, but before it could be buried Hardy's cat ran in, and ran out again taking the heart with it. The carve-up is true,

but there is little evidence to support the heart-attack cat. The organ was buried, as intended, on top of the skeleton of Hardy's first wife. Later the tomb was reopened and the ashes of his second wife were scattered on top.

Hardy's gloom, doom and tomb-strewn novels were a product of his own beliefs – '*I have been looking for God 50 years and I think if he had existed I should have discovered him.*' Each year thousands go to see Hardy's tomb, and one theory is that the cat burglar was invented and perpetuated by a disgruntled Stinsford cleric, annoyed at such a heathen man's attracting so many visitors to his church.

The **Heanor Runner** was born today in 1825, at Heanor, Derbyshire. Christened Edward Stainsby, he had achieved only limited success as a crab salesman when fate took a hand. At a sports meeting a group of runners asked him to hold their extraneous clothes. He did, joining in the race at the same time. Despite the extra burden, he won comfortably and never looked back, becoming the Alf Tupper of his day. As well as victories gained entirely under his own steam, Stainsby also excelled as a donkey jockey. It was said that his legs were so long and powerful that he could grasp the donkey between his thighs and run to give it a rest.

January 11th is 'Old' New Year's Eve in Scot-land (but not England – see March 24th), and at Burghead near Elgin in Grampian they cele-brate with the **Burning the Clavie** fire festival. 'Clavie' comes from the Gaelic word *cliabh*, meaning a basket. The festival is thought to be of mixed Druidic and Norse origin. A herring barrel is sawn in half, making a wide bucket, and nailed on to a long salmon-fisherman's pole, the Spoke. A herring cask is broken up and fitted underneath the bucket, becoming a cage through which the Clavie-carrier sticks his head. All the items used must be either given or borrowed, not bought; and the specially-forged, iron-free nail that secures the bucket is driven into the wood with a stone, hinting at a truly ancient, pre-Iron Age origin, no matter what later additions have made of the event. The bucket is filled with wood and tar, and a Clavie King torches it with burning peat.

© The fun commences at 6 o'clock sharp. Only members of old local families are allowed to construct and carry the Clavie. It is hot, strenuous and dangerous work – an early burns night – and everyone takes turns. If anyone stumbles, it means bad luck for the whole town. Led by the Clavie King the fiery trophy is carried up Doorie Hill and inserted in a stone holder, from which vantage point the burning contents are thrown down the hillside. The crowd scramble to catch a piece of the hot stuff, as it bestows colossal prosperity and protection against evil.

12th January

The Crab-Fish-Goose Tree

The dubiously named Captain Bytheway astounded the world on this day in 1807 by discovering the mythical **Goose Tree**. Upstart naturalists were just beginning to challenge long-held beliefs about the barnacle goose's origins. Bytheway's find proved that the scientists were wrong, and that the wonderful old stories were true – these geese sprang from barnacles, the black and white shellfish, and the shellfish were the fruit of a tree. He had located the goose trees mainly on Orkney, with a few also found on Piel Bar, at Walney Island near Barrow-in-Furness in Lancashire. As expected, the tree was covered in barnacles, from which the unformed goose eventually emerged, feet-first, before dropping into the water and slowly assuming proper goose dimensions.

A whole branch of spurious biology developed. Some researchers challenged Bytheway's findings, claiming that the trees did not spontaneously sprout the barnacles, but were invaded by crab-like worms which hardened into shell-fish before metamorphosing into partially formed geese. What encouraged these not entirely rigorous approaches to the goose's life-cycle was that as long as the goose was classified as fish or fruit, it could be eaten during Lent.

Long before Bytheway's discovery, the barnacle goose was a key feature of Lent's lean cuisine because of its supposed origins. In the face of 19th-century scientific scepticism, his find meant that theoretically fasting monks and other pious types were able to keep goose on their menus with a clear conscience. The barnacle-goose myth may have originated in the Jewish homelands. There, the bird appears during summer, and people wondered where it had sprung from. The tree-myth was concocted, and the goose was diagnosed as a fruit; although some argued that it was a reptile and a monstrosity. The argument as to whether the creature was

kosher raged for several centuries. As usual, when enough people want to believe something, the extent to which it is true becomes largely irrelevant.

◕ ◎ In Dyfed the festival of *Hen Galan* is celebrated today in the Cwm Gwaun region near Fishguard in Dyfed. In the morning children go marching and singing through the streets and countryside, begging for *calennig*, gifts. In the evening is a *noson lawen*, a feast of good food and beer at local farmhouses, serenaded by story and song. These parties are private; but the *Hen Galan* **service at Llandysul church, near Cardigan in Dyfed, is more accessible. The delights here include a local style of singing called** *pwnc* **chanting, which is the forerunner of pwnc rock. Or so says Captain Bytheway.**

☟ A bit of *Hen Galan* sunshine has its downside:

If on 12th January the sun shine,
It foreshadows much wind.

13th January
St Mungo's Day/
St Hilary's Day

Marry, Mungo and Merlin

The mother of 7th-century **St Kentigern** was a virgin. Not everyone believed her though, including the man who had been hoping to marry her. Enraged, he threw the pregnant woman from the top of a hill near Haddington in Lothian. She survived the fall, and so he recaptured her and set her adrift in an oarless coracle on the Firth of Forth. She came to rest, unharmed, at Culross in Fife, and gave birth to Kentigern.

Kentigern's spiritual mentor at Culross was St Serf. When Serf's pet robin was accidentally killed, Mungo said a few magic words and restored it to life. It was Serf who suggested that Kentigern take on the name **Mungo** – meaning 'Good Friend'.

The holiest man of the time was old Fergus of Kernach. It was believed that he would not die until he had met the saviour of the kingdom of Strathclyde (an area including all of modern Strathclyde plus most of Cumbria). When Mungo popped round to take his vows, Fergus took one look at him and promptly died. Mungo put Fergus' body in a cart, tied two wild bulls to it, and told them to follow God's will. They trotted to a nice quiet spot where Mungo decided to build a church. The place where Fergus was buried is now the site of Glasgow Cathedral.

Mungo/Kentigern is one of the great legend-accumulating saints. He encouraged adultery by rescuing a queen who had given her husband's ring to a handsome soldier. The king spotted the ring when he chanced upon the sleeping soldier whilst out hunting. He retrieved it, and angrily threw it into the Clyde. Then – just in case it had only been a ring that looked like his – he asked if he could inspect the Queen's jewellery. Realising that no ring might well mean no head, the Queen summoned Mungo. Mulling the problem over, Mungo ordered a salmon – brain-food. When he tucked in, there in its mouth was the ring. The Queen dodged retribution, and ever since then Glasgow's arms have featured a fish with a ring in its mouth.

The saint also bumped into **Merlin** just before the wizard died three times. In Scots legend, Merlin is wilder and hairier than he is elsewhere in Celtic legend, and is identified with the prophet Lailoken. Merlin was raving mad when he ran into Mungo, driven over the edge by guilt and angst. He had recently been the cause of a huge battle – at Arthuret in Cumbria – and had experienced a blinding vision in which a voice from the skies had condemned him to spend the rest of his days as a woodland hermit. Merlin begged Mungo to give him the sacrament, as he knew that he would soon die a triple death. Mungo obliged, and they went their separate ways. Later that day Merlin was set upon by shepherds, who beat him with cudgels, and threw him into the Tweed where he was impaled by an underwater stake. Beaten, drowned and transfixed, the body of Merlin is said to be buried under a thorn-tree in a Tweed-side meadow just below the church at Drumelzier near Peebles in the Borders.

Mungo himself, like Fergus, is buried at Glasgow Cathedral. If he ever returns, the lot of one of Scotland's few **werewolves** will improve. According to the folk ballad *Kempion*, a sorceress in Wormie Wood turned her daughter into a repulsive sea-monster. Only when passing hero Kempion gallantly kissed the monster three times did it turn back into a slime-free woman. As punishment, the wicked step-mother was turned into a werewolf and sentenced to stay that way '*Till St Mungo come o'er the sea*'.

☙ This is also 4th-century **St Hilary's Day**. In Sussex his – yes, *his* – day is supposed to be the coldest of the year. A solitary piece of historical evidence backs up this theory – in 1205 a famously severe frost began on the 13th, and the freeze did not abate until March 22nd.

St Hilary's is also the first day after Christmas on which you are allowed to marry, according to tradition.

© Goathland near Whitby in North Yorkshire has its **Sword Dancing** on the Saturday after Plough Monday (the one after the 6th) – it is amazing how far you can stretch the Christmas season if you put your mind to it. The participants are the Plough Stots, male mummers and dancers who used to stot their stuff on the Plough Monday itself until the weekends came to dominate our social lives and the celebrations were moved to the Saturday. Two teams of Stots perform a series of dances around the village from 9.30 am, each ending with the flexible long-swords interlocked in star-shapes, all great fun to watch. They round things off with a slap-up meal, the *Stot Rosh*, and then throw a barn dance for all comers.

The sword-dancing was revived early this century. Local historians scoured old records to ensure that the traditional words and dance patterns were recreated authentically. Boys in the village learn the dances at the age of six. Perhaps, here in the 1990s, it is time to give the girls a chance too?

14th January

2001: A Drake Oddity

On this day in 1674 Bleaklow Hill in Derbyshire was particularly bleak. Sudden horizontal snow and zero visibility. A couple from nearby Hope fell victim to the weather and disappeared. They were not discovered until the following May, and to save fuss and effort they were simply buried where they lay. Whizz forward nearly 30 years, and the tale of their icy death and shallow hillside graves has become a bar-room favourite. So someone decides to see if the story is true. The deceased are discovered, disinterred, and found to be fair-skinned and unrotted. After this, **corpse-watching** becomes a local sport in Hope and the surrounding area, with hundreds visiting the exposed grave to prod the bodies preserved in the peat-moss.

After 20 years of the bizarre custom, the repeatedly-exposed fair flesh is looking decidedly less healthy. The woman's leg has come off in a posthumous struggle with a manhandler, and she is beginning to decay. A descendant of one of the deceased belatedly arranges for the bodies to be given a decent burial in Hope churchyard. A year later they are exhumed for one last peep. Surprise surprise: they have rotted.

☿ The 14th is said to be either the coldest or the wettest day of the year: take your pick. Since yesterday also claims to be the coldest day, the only way for both bits of **weatherlore** to be true, is for today to take the soggy option.

◉ At All Souls College, Oxford, this is **Mallard Day**. All residents of the college are involved in the 'Gaudy', a raucous midnight hunt, and scour the building and grounds in search of a mallard. Hunt saboteurs need not stir, as in five centuries nothing has ever been caught – the hunters are seeking not just any unlucky duck, but a mythical **giant mallard**. Led by a man called the Chief Mallard, everyone carries long staves and wears Mallard medals depicting the Chief, his men, and a duck on a stick. Their Mallard Song has the chorus:

> Oh by the blood of King Edward!
> It was a swapping, swapping mallard.

The verses strongly suggest parody rather than ancient tradition, eg:

> The Griffin, Bustard, Turkey, Capon,
> Let other hungry mortals gape on,
> And on their bones with stomachs fall hard,
> But let All Souls men have their Mallard.

Archaeologists suggest that the game derived from the name William Mallard, found on a 14th-century seal discovered in the 1600s; but the more likeable (if less likely) story is that the annual hunt came about after a gigantic mallard flew from a drain under the foundations while the college was being built in 1437. The Gaudy soon came into disrepute. In 1632 Archbishop Abbot likened the noise and chaos to a scene of war, adding: 'Civil men should never so far forget themselves under pretence of a foolish mallard as to do things barbarously unbecoming.' Eventually spoilsport pressure against this annual disruption became so great that the Mallard Hunt was downgraded to a once-a-century event: it is next due in 2001.

15th January
St Ceolwulf's Day

God Shave the King

On this day in 1838 the trial of five Glasgow **cotton spinners** came to an end. During their 1837 strike a blackleg worker had been shot in the back. Although the judge decided to acquit the accused men of murder or conspiracy to murder, he did not like the cut of their jib, and so sentenced them to seven years' transportation somewhere unpleasant. Their official crime was noted down as Illegal Activities, mainly picketing. The sense of frustration and injustice resulted in a swiftly penned broadside ballad that became a nationwide underground hit. Many concurred with a line from the song:

> Whigs and Tories are united, we see very
>   plain,
> To crush the poor labourer it is their daily
>   aim.

There was such an outcry at the fate of the condemned spinners, both in Scotland and England, that the authorities actually began to listen. After being held for two years in Woolwich, the Glasgow Five were released.

The 15th is the feast-day of **St Ceolwulf**. He was King of Northumbria from 729 to 737, reigning during the life of Bede, who dedicated his epic Ecclesiastical History to him in 731. Like most historians, Bede found the past easier to tackle than the uncertainties of the present. Towards the end of his tome he notes: 'Both the onset and course of Ceolwulf's reign were filled with so many grave disturbances that it is quite impossible to know what to write about them or what the outcome will be.'

In the year of Bede's dedication, 731, Ceolwulf was deposed and abducted. To prevent him from resuming the throne, his captors hit on the novel device of shaving Ceolwulf's head. Forcibly tonsuring him effectively made him a monk, and no monk could sit on the throne. This barber-ous deed did not have the desired effect. As soon as Ceolwulf got free, he ruled exactly as before, only with much less hair.

But the haircut apparently made the King think. In 737, of his own free will, Ceolwulf abdicated, opting for the monastic life at Lindisfarne in Northumberland. The monks were overjoyed: Ceolwulf brought with him a considerable wealth, and the already important monastery was now able to enjoy limitless beer, wine and mead along with the usual milk and water. After his death, Ceolwulf shifted about a bit. He was buried at Lindisfarne, but was moved to Norham-on-Tweed, Northumberland, in 830. Demand for his relics became so great that the church authorities went one stage further than his former persecutors and removed Ceowulf's entire head, sending it to the cathedral at Durham.

✟ Since Georgian times there has been an insidious custom of sneaking up on traditions and antiquities, hitting them on the head with a sharp reference number, and sticking them in a museum. That wonderful, melancholy graveyard of societies and usage, the British Museum, opened its doors for the first time today in 1759. Its headquarters were originally at Montague House in Bloomsbury, the present building not being started until 1823. By 1880 this distilled version of civilisation had already acquired a ghost – a phantom scholar complete with book – but these days he is seldom sighted. Perhaps he finds the nearby British Library a more appropriate haunt.

16th January
Old Twelfth
Night/St Sigebert's Day/St
Fursey's Day/St Henry's Day

Hat Fulls, Cap Fulls, Three Bushel Bag Fulls

A handful of minor saints jostle for prominence today. St Sigebert was King of East Anglia but gave it all up to enter a monastery. Later, when Penda of Mercia invaded the kingdom in 638, Sigebert's former subjects knew that there was only one man capable of repelling the occupying army. They marched on the monastery, grabbed their ex-king and forced him to ride into battle to help the men's morale. Now a man of peace, reluctant leader Sigebert opted to carry a stick instead of a spear or sword. This stacked the odds in favour of Penda's troops,

and Sigebert's wood-wielding army came to a sticky end.

Sigebert lived around the same time as, and briefly met, another of today's saints, the Irish mystic St Fursey. On one occasion Fursey claimed to have been taken from his body and given a tour of Heaven, attending a concert by the Heavenly Choir. Three days later he had another vision; but this time he was assailed by demons, who taunted him with his own sins. An angel then intervened and showed him a vision of the Earth as a dark valley gradually being eaten away by four separate forest fires – the devouring flames of Falsehood, Covetousness, Discord and Cruelty. All those guilty of lighting these fires, he was told, would suffer in their flames after death. When Fursey at last returned to Earth, he came with the angelic message that '*The Saints will go from strength to strength*', which pleased the Church. And certain football fans.

St Henry of Coquet Island, Northumberland, was another visionary. He sought a hermit's life by setting up home on the bleak sea-bound rock. But such was his fame that Coquet Island developed a brisk trade in daytrippers, with Henry's followers rolling up to seek wisdom, blessings and general benevolence. On one occasion he admonished an austere visitor after reading his mind and discovering that the man had refused his wife's sexual advances during Lent. Henry died in 1127, and his remains were buried at Tynemouth Priory.

© ☻ Apple-wassailing had all but died out early this century. But it is now back in fashion, with revived January wassails today – Old Twelfth Night – at Much Marcle near Ledbury in Hereford and Worcester, brought back in 1988 with help from cider-makers Westons; and at Norton Fitzwarren just outside Taunton in Somerset, sponsored by Taunton Cider. Norton's by-invitation-only wassail starts at 9.15 pm. The oldest surviving appletree wassailing is at nearby Carhampton – see tomorrow. It is no coincidence that the words used to woo the trees in the Norton orchard are almost identical to those belted out at Carhampton:

> *Old Apple Tree we wassail thee and hope*
> *that thou wilt bear,*
> *For Lord doth know where we shall be till*
> *apples come another year;*
> *To bloom well and to bear well, so merry let*
> *us be,*

> Let every man take off his hat and shout out
>   to thee, Old Apple Tree.
> Old Apple Tree, we wassail thee, and hope
>   that thou wilt bear,
> Hat fulls, cap fulls, three bushel bag fulls,
> And a little heap under the stairs.

The last three lines are shouted, just to make sure the trees wake up.

The Monday after the 12th (Old New Year) was **Handsel Monday** in Scotland, a day of feasting and fraternity which fizzled out 100 years ago. Handsels were gifts given by the richer to the poorer. Or so went the theory; but in a template for continuing inequalities in the education system, the pupil who gave the biggest handsel to the teacher was King (or Queen) for the day and could grant a school holiday. At least it meant that the children could join in the Handsel Monday fun. To reap maximum luck all Handsel money received on the day should be spat upon and placed in an empty pocket.

Whisky, plum-pudding, steak pie, goose and pig's-head were among the day's delicacies, as were treacle sandwiches bought at the Handsel Monday street markets. In mainland Scotland, the speciality of the day was *powsowdie*, sheep's-head broth; whilst on the island of Islay, Strathclyde, it was time to have a breac, have a buntat: *Buntat' Breac* was a mutton stew washed down with whisky and porter served today by the landowner. On top of all this there were various sports and dances, and a spot of very late first-footing.

Some areas enjoyed it so much that they did it all again on the following day. Handsel Tuesday was also known as **Roking Day**, after the *rokes*, or spinning wheels, which were brought out for the first time in the new year on this day, making it a Scottish version of St Distaff's Day – see January 7th.

17th January
Old Twelfth Day/
St Antony of Egypt's Day

Ascetic Acid

At Pitminster in Somerset two sons were set to share the family estate when their father died. But when the will was read out, the younger brother got everything. As a small consolation

he allowed his big brother to have a few clapped-out bits of the farm: one old donkey, one decrepit ox and one ancient, overgrown orchard.

The older brother was sanguine in the face of such meanness. He rubbed magic herbs into the ox to revive it, and then mulled some cider and wassailed the oldest of his apple trees. This attention so pleased the spirit of the orchard, the Apple Tree Man, that it advised him to '*Take and look under this gurt diddicky root of ours*'. The man understood tree lingo, and delved under the roots. There he found an enormous pot of gold, the lost treasure long rumoured to be buried on the farm.

The younger brother had also been seeking this treasure, and little suspecting that it had been unearthed, he planned to recover it. He knew that on Christmas Eve all the animals talked to each other, and he felt sure that if he eavesdropped on the creatures they would let slip the location of the treasure. But when the day came, he discovered that he had become the laughing stock of the livestock – a talking tree had already spilled the beans; the wronged brother was now a rich man; and all his cruel sibling rivalry had been for naught.

The above story is still told in Somerset to show the value of wassailing, which still takes place on the 5th, but mainly on the 16th, and today, Old Twelfth Day.

© At sunset tonight in **Carhampton**, near Minehead in Somerset, **wassailers** issue from *The Butchers' Arms* pub and approach the tree known as the Old Apple Tree in the adjoining orchard. Cider-soaked toast is put into the tree for the robins, and cider is poured around the tree's roots. Then comes the song (almost word for word the same as the one sung at Norton Fitwarren – see yesterday) which serves politely to request a good crop. The tree is then given three cheers, and shotguns are fired through its branches, to ensure that it shrugs off its winter blues and starts putting out some greenery. The very popular Carhampton wassailing was given a secure future when the owners of the pub bought the Old Apple Tree's orchard.

The 4th-century St Antony is usually depicted with a pig in attendance. It was common to call the runt of a pig-litter *Tantony* in his honour, and to refer to someone overly servile as a St Antony Pig. But the saintly swineherd is probably apocryphal: Antony's hog-emblem comes from the Order of Hospitallers of

St Antony, founded in 1100 to treat people and animals suffering from **St Antony's Fire**. More properly known as ergotism, it is a condition contracted by eating mouldy rye – LSD is a synthetic version of this mould, which may explain why hermits and saints are so prone to visions. The blood of kittens was the drastic cure for ergotism; but it was also believed that all it took to combat the disease was a bell worn around the neck. By special decree the hospital's outpatient pigs, complete with neck-bells, were allowed to roam the streets, and this distinctive sight eventually led to pigs – and bells – becoming St Antony's symbols.

18th January
St Ulfrid's Day

Choppers, Ghostly and Otherwise

Descended from a line of Vikings converted to Christianity in England, 11th-century **Ulfrid** decided that it was only fair to spread the word back in the land of his forefathers. Off he went in high spirits to Sweden, where the Norse gods still held sway. He had heard all the tales of saints smashing heathen idols, or converting pagan temples into Christian altars. So, when he confronted a statue of Thor, Ulfrid made a brief speech about idolatry, and proceeded to hack Thor to pieces with an axe. The watching locals were gripped by a religious fervour. Sadly, it was the wrong religion. Incensed at what they saw as sacrilegious vandalism, the crowd beat Ulfrid to death and threw him into a bog. He came, he Thor, he conked out.

Supernatural sightings these days can be divided into two main groups: ghosts, and UFOs. These categories are normally mutually exclusive, but in 1973–4 a ghostly Unidentified Flying Object haunted the skies of northern England. Sometimes solid, sometimes not so solid, it took the form of a **Phantom Helicopter**, and was regularly spotted and heard in the Cheshire and north-east Derbyshire area. Every new late-night flight gained it fresh coverage in the local papers. It enjoyed a couple of spins around Hillhead Quarry south of Buxton in Derbyshire, put in a stint near Macclesfield in Cheshire, and buzzed the midnight Mam Tor hang-gliders near Edale in the Peak District.

Throughout January 1974 it was tracked by police, and events culminated in headlines in *The Derbyshire Times* on January 18th. The last sighting was when the helicopter landed at Goostrey in Cheshire – very close to Jodrell Bank's two radio telescopes, which must have helped with the tracking.

The initial theory that it was joy-riders in a real helicopter was dented when police and journalists failed to uncover any firm evidence of flights or landings, and witnesses were repeatedly unable to capture the craft on film. Such a lack of hard facts has only strengthened the case of those who claim that what they saw was a phantom helicopter. It has even been suggested that it may be the ghost of one which exploded when it flew into a hill in the Peak District in the 1960s – even though there are no records of any such crash.

© The **Up Helly A'** at Scalloway, Shetland, is always timed to fall 11 days before the main Lerwick conflagration, which is on the last Tuesday of the month. This means that the boom in local torch sales in Scalloway is on either the second or third Friday in January. For the lowdown on Up Helly A', see January 28th.

19th January
St Wulfstan's Day

Stone the Crozier

Helen Duncan was the last person to be charged under the 1735 Witchcraft Act. She was arrested on January 19th 1944, and accused of obtaining confidential military information by unknown means – she had 'predicted' the sinking of a ship – and of pretending to conjure the dead. Her seances had been held in The Master Temple Psychic Centre, a room over a Portsmouth chemist shop. Crowds had paid to see Helen commune, often through her parrot-medium, Bronco.

Helen was great at manifesting ectoplasm, which was described as a thick snake, or else as '*living snow*'; though her detractors claimed that it was all a sleight-of-hand trick with cheesecloth. One witness even offered to show how easy it was to swallow and regurgitate cloth; but the judge refused to let the demonstration take place. The court found Helen guilty, and she was sent to prison for nine months.

After her release, she returned to the phantom fray. In 1956 the police raided one of her seances while she was in deep trance, and Helen collapsed. She later died, and although the official cause was diabetes, her followers blamed the ecto-trauma.

© Every year on or around the 19th there is a memorial service in the crypt of Worcester Cathedral, in honour of **St Wulfstan**, whose feast-day this is, and whose tomb is in the crypt. The annual pilgrimages to his tomb died out early in the 18th century, but the service keeps his spirit alive in the city.

While he was Bishop of Worcester – both before and after the Norman Conquest, a unique Saxon achievement – Wulfstan was once accused of being unworthy to hold his post. To argue his case, Wulfstan planted his crozier into the shrine of Edward the Confessor at Westminster Abbey and said that if he was guilty as charged, the crozier could be pulled out again. Various people tried to shift the stick, but it was stuck fast. Wulfstan then effortlessly drew the crozier out of the shrine himself, and was proclaimed innocent. If only he had tried the same trick with a sword and a stone he could have gone for a promotion.

Soon after Wulfstan's death so many miracles and cures began happening at his tomb that William Rufus – son of William the Conqueror – had the whole thing coated in gold and silver. A century later Wulfstan's cult was enormous; **King John** counted himself one of the saint's biggest fans. John was certain that come Judgement Day Wulfstan was a saint with the key to the executive washroom. He also thought that Oswald was a good saint to keep in with. So since the two saints' tombs were near each other in Worcester cathedral, King John opted to be buried between them, as a way of increasing his chances of a happy-ever-after-life.

🕮 Hero worship from such an anti-hero may have had its downside for the saint. John died in 1216 and, as he had requested, was given a tomb abutting Wulfstan's. In the same year a sizeable levy from a French prince led to some severe cash-flow problems. It is unclear whether John's devotion had served to tarnish Wulfstan's reputation, or whether it was just an act of financial desperation, but the saint's opulent shrine was stripped to pay the bill. Fortunately, the reaction to this rash downgrading of a much-loved saint was such that an even more magnificent shrine was hastily constructed. John's tomb, with its original figure of the king in Purbeck marble – the oldest royal effigy in England – can still be seen in Worcester Cathedral. When it was opened in 1797 the body inside was found wrapped in the remains of a monk's cowl.

20th January
St Agnes' Eve/St Vigean's Day

Stag Night in the Underworld

St Agnes' Eve is a favourite night for the **Cwn Annwn** to cock a leg. They are spectral Welsh hounds – literally 'The Hounds of the Underworld'. Believed to be the souls of the damned, they shun physical contact with mortals, but to hear their portentous howling means that doom, death, and/or disaster are imminent.

A notable exception to this rule befell Pwyll, Prince of Dyfed. According to a story in the ancient collection of Celtic folk-tales, *The Mabinogion*, Pwyll was hunting with his dogs when he spotted the Cwn Annwn out for a bite to eat. Their bright coats glowed in the traditional colour scheme of faerie animals: white with red ears. When the hell-hounds pulled down a stag, Pwyll set his own dogs on to the fallen beast, and they chased off the Annwn pack. Enter a very disgruntled Arawn, King of Annwn. He declared that he would persecute Pwyll to the equivalent of a hundred such stags, unless Pwyll agreed to swap lives with him for a year and a day, and also to kill his greatest enemy. The Prince of Dyfed agreed, and, magically transformed into an Arawn-look-alike, he trotted off to lord it over the Celtic Underworld.

On Pwyll's 366th day down under, Arawn's elusive greatest foe finally showed up. The netherworld looked set for a mighty contest. But Pwyll dispatched the enemy with one blow, and was returned to Dyfed. Arawn had been similarly impressive during his stint as doppelganger Prince; and when he returned to Annwn he was impressed to find that while Pwyll had slept with his Queen for a year, he had left her unmolested. Such was his gratitude that he agreed to an eternal pact between the two kingdoms, and Pwyll became known as the Head of Annwn.

👁 St Agnes' Eve is a fine night for **divination**. Take some barley grains and sow them under an apple tree, chanting:

Barley, barley, I sow thee
That my true love I might see;
Take thy rake and follow me.

The wraith of your future bedfellow will then appear, complete with rake.

Alternatively, eat a **salted herring** before bed-time and your lover-to-be will thoughtfully appear with a glass of water during the night. More complicated, but supposedly more reliable is the **dumb-cake** ceremony. After fasting all day, the cake must be made and eaten in complete silence. Once baked, take a slice, walk to bed backwards; and – as long as you have not fallen downstairs and wound up in casualty – you should dream about the love of your life-to-be. See Christmas Eve for other variations on the dumb-cake routine.

In his poem *The Eve of St Agnes*, published in 1820, John Keats gives young hopefuls a less complicated option:

. . . supperless to bed they must retire,
And couch supine their beauties, lilly white;
Nor look behind, nor sideways, but require
Of Heaven with upward eyes for all that they
desire.

A fair used to be held today at St Vigean, near Arbroath, Tayside, in honour of the 7th-century Irish abbot, **St Vigean**. Legend insisted that the church at St Vigean was built over a subterranean lake, and that every time Communion was held there the congregation risked plummeting to a watery grave. This fear of the nave going naval became so great that from 1699 to 1736 the service was abandoned. Finally, the minister decided to challenge the superstition and held Communion by himself, while the villagers watched from a safe distance. When he failed to go for a terminal swim, the parishioners decided that the place must be safe, and normal service was resumed.

21st January
St Agnes' Day

Giant with a Bleeding Heart

Bolster was an amorous **Cornish giant**. When St Agnes appeared in his vicinity in the 4th century, he fell head over heels in love – grim news for Agnes, as Bolster was so big that he could plonk one of his heels on Carn Brae and the other on St Agnes' Beacon, a span of six miles. There was no getting away from him; but Agnes kept rejecting his over-sized overtures, not because of the logistical problems of congress between beings of such differing dimensions, but because Bolster was already married.

Agnes devised a plan that was cunning, brutal, and messy. She told Bolster to prove his love for her by filling a hole in the ground at Chapel Porth near Truro with his blood. Besotted, he eagerly opened a vein and watched his life-blood ebb away. For hours he bled, not realising that the hole led directly to the sea and could never be filled. When he was near death Agnes booted him over the edge and into the water.

⛏ Wrath's Hole at Chapel Porth in Cornwall can still be seen, and the red-stained rocks around it were supposedly coloured by Bolster's blood. From nearby St Agnes' Beacon, it is possible on a clear day to see the towers of 31 churches.

It may bolster giant-lovers to know that Agnes, saint and murderess, also died violently. A 13-year-old girl who refused to marry a Roman soldier, she was put in an asylum, and then tied to a stake to burn. The fire would not light; but there was no escape – she was stabbed through the throat with a sword, in 350 AD. Agnes is a patron saint of virgins, and her exploits in Cornwall are thought to derive from a folk memory of a pre-Christian pre-Agnes heroine.

Thanks to some accidental Latin punning – *Agnus Dei* translates as 'lamb of God' – St Agnes' symbol is a sheep, and the 21st has become a traditionally good day for blessing all things woollen. Do not name your children after this saint, though. It is said that people called Agnes always go mad. Attempting to duck this curse may account for the trend in the 1960s and 1970s – particularly in Scotland – for those christened Agnes to flip their names to Senga.

👁 Predicting the identity of **future lovers** is still possible on the 21st, despite the main fixture on St Agnes' Eve. Eat nothing all day, and then chant the following:

Sweet Agnes work thy fast,
If ever I be to marry man,
Or even man to marry me,
I hope him this night to see.

If you are afflicted with visions of Ronald McDonald or Bernard Matthews then the starving option is clearly not having the desired effect. Instead, you could try saying the Paternoster (the Lord's Prayer) whilst sticking pins in your sleeve: this should lead to the required dream, without your having to skimp on supper. Another alternative is to sprinkle rosemary and thyme with water three times, bung them in your shoes, place the shoes on either side of the bed and say:

St Agnes, that's to lovers kind,
Come ease the troubles of my mind.

Warning: if the affair is to be passionate, the wraith of the hunk-to-be will give chase up the stairs, tearing the diviner's clothes off one by one until the bed is reached.

22nd January
St Vincent of Saragossa's Day

Swallow Your Pride, Lust, Gluttony Etc.

St Vincent died on this day in AD 304. In prison he was starved and then ordered to make sacrifices to dubious gods. He refused, and was taken to the rack. After a brief stretch he was semi-roasted on a grid-iron, and then left in the stocks to die. And his reward for this terrible suffering? He is remembered as the patron saint of **drunkards**.

☼ Vincent's association with excessive drink may derive simply from having '*vin*' at the start of his name. This is fortified by some spurious **weatherlore**:

If on St Vincent the sky is clear,
More wine than water will crown the year.

This means dry weather and lots of wine pouring down parched throats. Similarly:

If St Vincent's has sunshine,
One hopes much rye and wine

is on much the same tack with good news for rye crops as well. A sunny St Vincent's also presages a windy year. And for those who like their weather in detail:

Remember on St Vincent's Day,
If that the sun his beams display,
Be sure to mark his transient beam,
Which through the casement sheds a gleam,
For 'tis a token bright and clear
Of prosperous weather all the year.

When Thomas Baker of Kellingham near Goole in Humberside died, **burying cakes** were often made for his wake, on this day in 1833. Such cakes or biscuits were often given to guests before funerals, served with a glass of wine. This, and the broader concept of the funeral meal, is a vestigial survival of **sin-eating**, where the transgressions of the deceased are digested by the guests. This allows the soul to float to Heaven, free from the hindering, weighty ballast of sin. As recently as last century sin-eating was sometimes carried out explicitly, and it was common to hire people to take on this task. An official sin-eater was usually a poor woman in genuine need of food. Bread, cake and ale were passed to her over the corpse, along with a coin for her — and the dead's — troubles. This symbolically transferred all the sins to the sin-eater.

◉ The Suffolk game of **Dwile Flonking** became a country-wide craze in the late 1960s, after it featured on the TV programme *It's A Square World*. A match today in 1967 between Beccles and Bungay got massive press coverage, with much made of the game's eccentric 'Waveney Rules of 1585'. The fielding team form a circle (girter) and dance round one member of the opposition (the flonker). He holds a stick (driveller) on the end of which is a cloth (dwile) soaked in ale (flonk). When the music stops the flonker flings the dwile and tries to hit the girter, scoring points depending on which bit of their body is struck. Failure to score incurs a penalty — the flonker must rapidly drink six pints. In 1967 Beccles lost 16–1. Games are still staged intermittently — notably at the *Farmer's Boy* pub at Kensworth in Bedfordshire — but the 1585 rules are almost certainly a hoax, and dwile-flonking can more realistically be traced back all the way to 1966 when a Suffolk printer invented it to liven up a charity fête.

23rd January

It's a Wonderful Death

1570 saw the beginning of a bad patch for the **Earls of Moray**. The First Earl, James Stewart, was the natural son of James V – also Stewart – and had become the Scottish Regent after helping to ease out Mary Queen of Scots (who was responsible for assuming the French spelling of the family surname, *Stuart*). He was not a universally popular choice, and while riding through Linlithgow today he was shot in the stomach. He got off his horse, walked regally to his lodgings, and died.

His son-in-law, also called James Stewart, became the Second Earl of Moray. His even more violent death is remembered in the maudlin Scottish ballad, *The Bonnie Earl of Moray*, and in a gory painting of his hacked corpse, which can still be seen at Darnaway Castle near Forres in Grampian. According to the ballad the Second Earl was the first love of Anne of Denmark, the Scottish queen. This did not please her husband, King James VI (another James Stewart – or, rather, Stuart – and soon to be James I of Great Britain). He sent Moray's old enemy, the Earl of Huntly, to arrest him. Huntly and his men were not interested in taking prisoners – they set fire to Moray's residence in North Queensferry, and when he ran out, hair aflame, their swords and daggers finished him off. James VI was so angry with Huntly for having exceeded his orders that he sentenced him to one whole week's imprisonment in Edinburgh Castle.

Charles Kingsley the novelist died today in 1875. He resurrected Hereward the Wake (for the real Hereward see June 29th) and delivered him back to the national consciousness via his book of that name; and his works such as *The Water Babies* provided saccharine folk tales for the Victorian palate. He also gave rise to the ludicrously named Devonshire seaside resort Westward Ho!, exclamation mark and all, named after another Kingsley novel. There is a fine marble statue of Kingsley at nearby Bideford – where he wrote *Westward Ho!* – and the town also boasts an even more memorable memorial, a bust of 19th-century Bideford worthy J.R. Pine-Coffin.

The final 12 days of January reflect the general mood of the 12 months ahead – yes, yes, the same was said about the first 12 days of the month too. There is a whole barnful of January **weatherlore**, most of which suggests that if the month is fine, the rest of the year will be lousy:

A January Spring is worth nae-thing.

Jack Frost in Janiveer
Nips the nose of the nascent year.

If you see grass in January,
Lock your grain in granary.

And go easy on the chickens. Remember that:

If one but knew how good it were
To eat a hen in Janiveer,
He would not leave one the flock
For to be trodden by the cock.

24th January

Cock and Bulldog

Today in 1838 Bevil Blizard, 'The Last Necromancer of Winchcombe', died at Oxenton, Gloucestershire, aged 94. Blizard freely admitted that his powers derived from a Satanic pact. People came to him for advice and fortune-telling, and he was thought to be very wise, if a little eccentric. On one occasion he was mowing grass, when he suddenly screamed something about chickens, and dashed off. His scythe carried on mowing, alarming his neighbours who feared that he had sub-contracted the mowing to the Grim Reaper. But when Blizard the wizard returned he explained that he had received a vision of his chicken coop being plundered, and after casting a quick scythe-alive spell, he had got back just in time to ward off the intruders.

In spite of his Satanic claims, Blizard seemed to go to limbo rather than Hell after his death. He has been repeatedly spotted posthumously wandering around Winchcombe church. Winchcombe was the capital of the old Kingdom of Mercia, which may account for the fact that Blizard is only one ghost among many. These include multiple monks at the ruined Abbey, and a lone monk who hovers two feet above the ground in a hollow near the cemetery.

Winston Churchill died today in 1965. He came – partly through tenacity and loquacity, partly through sheer physical resemblance – to embody that spirit of patriotism and parochialism known as **British Bulldog**. This phrase gained such currency in the 1940s that British

Bulldog became the new nationwide name for an ancient schoolyard game. Over the centuries, and across the country, it had previously been known by a variety of titles. The most widespread of these was the no-nonsense *Cock*, which no longer seemed entirely appropriate for something played by young children. British Bulldog is still almost a compulsory precursor to male adolescence; but for the uninitiated, the players run from one end of the allotted field to the other, while a lone mercenary tries to collar one of their number. Once caught, the victim must join the catcher; and so it goes on until everyone is caught. It all seemed somehow less aimless at the time . . .

� It is said that the blue tit starts singing on January 24th. Should its cry sound like *'pincher!'* – today or at any other time – it means cold weather lies ahead.

25th January
Burns Night/St Dwynwen's Day/Feast of the Conversion of St Paul

Simmer Gently, Then Drown

There was once a glittering city surrounded by hills in what is now rural North Yorkshire. St Paul (or in other versions of the story Christ, or a witch, or an unnamed beggar transformed into an angel of death) visited it one day to find out how Christian its citizens were. Dressed as a beggar, he went from door to door seeking alms. Several thousand slams and swear-words later, he reached a hillside cottage. The poor resident Quaker family invited him to share their food, and to sleep there. Later that night their guest was overheard mumbling in the vernacular:

Simmerwater rise, Simmerwater sink,
And swallow up all but this,
Where they gave me bread and cheese and
summat to drink.

The following morning Paul had gone, and the Quaker's house was on the shore of a new lake – the whole town had been drowned.
ⅲ And that is the origin of Semerwater in Wensleydale in North Yorkshire, a beautiful spot with or without submerged city. If you look into the lake when the weather is calm, you can see the walls and roofs of the old town. So they say.

☺ On the Feast of St Paul's Conversion, good weather means a great year ahead, and rain indicates an average sort of year. Thick clouds or fog are harbingers of pestilence and dearth; but worst of all are high winds and thunder, which presage war and death.

ⅲ St Dwynwen, or Dwyn, shares this feast-day with Paul. Despite having been an avowed celibate, she is Wales' patron saint of lovers. Dwynwen once prayed that all true loves should be either successful in their passions, or else be able to forget romance altogether. A visit to her shrine at Llanddwyn island on Anglesey was a must for all couples, and her nearby well contained fish whose movements were said to indicate the destiny of those who looked inside. Dwynwen's name was also invoked to cure sick animals or find lost cattle, and her shrine was regularly attended by ailing livestock. Dwynwen is commemorated by a cross on the island, near the remains of her church.

© The 25th is Burns Night, great news for haggis-toasters everywhere. Many malt-teasers at Burns and Caledonian Societies go through the time-honoured motions tonight, and across Scotland there are countless public events. The first Burns Night was held by the poet's friends in 1801, though it did not become widespread until 1859. The general format is supper, followed by speeches, followed by songs.
ⅲ Robert Burns was born today in 1759 into a family of poor farmers at Alloway, Strathclyde, and his birthplace is now the Burns Museum. His work drew on his Classical education, combined with a knowledge of local landscape, song and legend. He revitalised or in some cases simply appropriated folk songs, and many of his poems are riddled with divinations, witches, ghosts and superstitions. Wine, women and song were the loves of his life. Under the influence of at least one of these Burns spent the night snoring in the rain at a roadside in 1796. Days later, he died of rheumatic fever.

26th January
St Tortgith's Day/
Australia Day

G'day for a Party

It is tough at the forefront of devoutness. In Essex, Barking nun **St Tortgith** was so zealous in her faith that she was visited with a painful wasting disease. Strength, on a spiritual level, is supposedly made greater in weakness. And so Bede in his *Ecclesiastical History* notes that, '*Under the providence of our Redeemer (the disease) caused her distress for six years in order that any traces of sin . . . might be burned away in the fires of prolonged suffering.*' All Tortgith seemed to get out of it was a vision of her friend, Ethelburga, the Mother of the convent, shining brighter than the sun, and being drawn up to Heaven on bright golden cords. Days later, the soon-to-be-saint Ethelburga died. Tortgith then lost the use of her limbs and voice; but three years later she had another vision of Ethelburga. Despite the disease, her powers of speech returned, and she was able to talk with the hallucination. Witnesses wrote down Tortgith's side of the conversation and sent it to Bede. The chat concerned the precise timing of Tortgith's death – which came, as promised, in 681.

◉ **Australia Day** is commemorated with an invitation-only bash at Australia House, London, today. There used to be a service for all comers, at St Martin's-in-the-Fields, but this event has now lapsed. There are still numerous unofficial celebrations in flats and bedsits all the way from Earl's Court to Shepherd's Bush; although to appreciate the more subtle cultural nuances of these upfront, outback, down-under knees-ups, it helps if you are an Australian.

The event commemorates the 'discovery' of the continent and its suddenly second-class natives. But this was also the day when, in 1788, the first penal colony was set up with a shipload of transports who landed at Botany Bay. **Transportation** of criminals to Australia was looked upon as a godsend by the authorities, who had been short of space since losing the American colonies. It was eventually phased out by the Australian states between 1840 and 1868, but not before a batch of gloomy ballads had appeared on the broadside-seller's platter. The song *Australia* gives the reason for one man's misfortune:

I fell in with a damsel, she was handsome and gay,
I neglected my work more and more every day,
And to keep her like a lady I went on the Highway,
And for that I was sent to Australia.

With a few words changed, the same song had already done the rounds as *Virginia*, when it bemoaned the iniquities of transportation to America; but this remix was an even bigger hit. The most popular song of this genre was *Botany Bay*, which has a dirge-like chorus along the lines of:

Son, oh son, what have you done,
You're bound for Botany Bay!

Transportation was not the exclusive preserve of mass-murderers and political agitators: it was a punishment doled out for the most petty of offences. Along the canal network it was not uncommon to see signs warning: '*The punishment for tampering with these works is transportation.*'

27th January

The Big Sleep

After a miserable life, **Jane Puckering** died on this day in 1652, aged 19. As the young, lame, sick heiress to the Warwick Priory house and grounds, she was bundled off by evil scheming executors to live with a stranger, Sir David Cunningham, who was related to one of the will's executors – one who stood to gain a good deal 'should the child fail'. The unscrupulous men then siphoned off as much of Jane's assets as they could, and only when Jane's mother managed to get the attention of the House of Lords did the law leap in and return the girl to the Priory. But her troubles were not over. She was later abducted by a man called Walsh while walking in Greenwich Park, Kent, and sent to Dunkirk. This was a den of vagabonds in those days, one of whom – Walsh himself – forced Jane to marry him.

But by now Ms Puckering was a celebrated distressed damsel, and the English law sent human bloodhound Magdalen Smith to track her down. Eventually, returned for a second time to her home at the Priory, her marriage was declared null and void. So what did her loving mother do? In spite of the girl's manifestly ill health, she married her daughter off to one Sir John Bate, and Jane died horribly in childbirth.

🏛 Warwick Priory can still be seen, at Richmond . . . in Virginia, USA. In 1925 a rich American came up with the highest bid at the auction and had the whole lot shipped over and re-erected stone by stone. Priory Park in Warwick is the original site of the building. Manipulated in life and spoilt for choice in death, the only-to-be-expected ghost of Jane has not been seen at either site.

Today in 1698 **Samuel Clinton** woke up feeling refreshed. He had slept with only one interruption since August 17th of the previous year – a total bed time of 151 days. The one swift break had come on November 19th, when he stirred just long enough to demand bread and cheese, then dozed off again. While he slumbered, his household in Timsbury near Midsomer Norton in Avon became a flurry of activity, as servants and friends attempted to rouse Clinton. Their many unsuccessful wakey-wakeys included sticking pins into Clinton's arm, and injecting smelling salts up his nose.

☼ The prolonged singing of **thrushes** this month – particularly from an exposed branch of a tree or the top of a building – indicates terrible storms to come, which is quite appropriate given the missel-thrush's alternative name, storm-cock. However, should Shakespeare's '*throstle with his note so true*' sing at sunset – at any time of year – it means that the next day will be fine. *Jeremy Joy* is yet another name for the missel-thrush, meaning 'January joy'.

28th January

Burning your Boats

More than just a top-notch sailor, **Sir Francis Drake** was a remarkable myth-magnet. Even before his death on this day in 1596, he was said to have sold his soul in order to gain his skills at sea, and to be the commander of a legion of demons. When Admiral Nelson later threatened to eclipse his nautical fame, it became rumoured that he was in fact a reincarnation of Drake.

When the Spanish Armada was sighted off Plymouth Hoe in Devon in 1588, Drake did not just calmly finish his famous game of bowls and set off to sea. Some versions of the story say that he called for a hatchet and stick, and began hacking off slivers of wood. They flew into the water, where they were transformed into fireships, routing the first efforts of the Spanish before any English sailors had lifted a finger. He also called in some friends – a coven of witches – at Devil's Point, near Devonport. Together with Drake they whipped up storms that wrecked many of the Spanish ships.

🏛 On another occasion Drake decided that Plymouth could do with a decent water supply. He rode to Dartmoor and muttered magic words over a spring, which then cantered along behind him as he rode back home, leaving behind a channel which can still be seen running from Dartmoor to Plymouth.

🏛 While Drake was enjoying an extended stay in the Antipodes, his wife back home decided that he was probably dead, and so prepared to marry another man. Just as she was about to say 'I do', her extra-marital efforts were thwarted by one of Drake's demon-helpers. It raced across the world to its master's side and spilled the beans. Drake then fired a cannon through the earth, and was such a mean shot that it popped out between the would-be bride and groom, effectively deterring them. The globe-bisecting cannonball is at Combe Sydenham Hall near Minehead, Somerset.

🏛 Buckland Abbey near Plymouth, Drake's former home, is now a museum. **Drake's drum** can be seen there. Legend has it that Drake will return when England needs him most, and that all it will take to summon him is the sound of this drum. Independently of Drake it also sounds at time of war, playing a supernatural drum solo. The most notable phantom roll came just before the German surrender at Scapa Flow in 1919. Such was the din on the flagship of the British fleet that a formal search was undertaken. Even though all the crew were accounted for, nothing was found.

♱ While he waits to be summoned, a ghostly Sir Francis, inside a black carriage pulled by headless horses, rides at the head of the Wild Hunt on Dartmoor. To see it is an omen of death.

🏛 ♱ On his deathbed today in 1547 **Henry VIII**, the father of the Church of England, repented his religious revolution with the words: '*All is lost! Monks, monks, monks!*' His mark on the nation's customs is typically self-centred. A chair at Allington Castle, Kent – now in Maidstone Museum – was avoided by all women who wished to duck the King's advances. According to a curious inscription on its back, Henry was entitled to a kiss '*from everie ladie thott settes downe in itt*'. For a man married six times, this smacks of desperation. Henry's ghost is more elusive than those of some of his Queens, but is sometimes heard as an invisible bulk which drags its legs in the cloisters at Windsor Castle.

© The last Tuesday in January witnesses **Up Helly A'** – meaning 'end of the Holy days' – at Lerwick, Shetland. These days the festival centres on a music-fuelled procession of 500 or so men dressed as Vikings and led by the Guiser Jarl. They carry a mock Viking longship and flaming torches. At the harbour, rockets are fired and the torches are thrown onboard the launched vessel to make a ship-pyre, while the song *The Norseman's Home* is belted out. It is then time for dancing and drinking at each of the town's 13 public halls. Up Helly A' is a boisterous but non-rowdy affair. As a policeman commented at the 1991 bash: '*It's no' like ye'd get in Caithness.*' Lerwick parish only appeared in 1700, so the revelry is not that old; though it is likely that the original inhabitants were celebrating in a genuinely traditional manner, remembering their Norse forebears. The festival marks the end of the great winter festival, Yule. The Lerwick fire-fest is the biggest of several such events across Shetland between January and March – there are also burnings at Scalloway (11 days earlier, on the second or third Friday in January); Girlsta; Northmavine; Cullivoe on Yell; and Brae.

29th January

God's Cool Rut-Time

Herne's Oak in Windsor Park, Berkshire, was replanted on this day in 1906. The original was felled in the reign of George III (1760–1820). It is the place where **Herne the Hunter** likes to hang out. Herne is a form of Cernunnos, a Celtic horned god of the Underworld; but local legend begs to differ. It is said that as a mortal man, Herne placed himself between a charging stag and Henry VIII, receiving dreadful wounds and royal favour at the same time. Henry made Herne his chief huntsman; but that caused jealousy in the ranks. Slanderers eventually made Henry sack Herne, and the man went and hanged himself from the oak. Like the man in the *Thor* Marvel comics, he was transformed into an ancient god. With antlers, black beard, giant girth and huge black horse, he has been blasting on his horn ever since.

Herne crops up in Harrison Ainsworth's novel *Windsor Castle*; and in *The Merry Wives of Windsor* Shakespeare makes use of the legend: Falstaff, conned into dressing up as Herne, begins to feel something of the god's powers as his lust rises. He scorns the god Jove, and says: '*For me, I am here a Windsor stag; and the fattest, I think, i' the forest: send me a cool rut-time, Jove, or who can blame me to piss my tallow?*' Herne also made regular, mystical, appearances as a deus-ex-arborea in the 1980s ITV series, *Robin of Sherwood*.

✞ The last encounter with Herne is said to have been as recent as 1962. A London teddy boy was visiting friends in Windsor, and during a walk in the Park he found a horn, which he proceeded to blow. Aware of the legend, his friends scarpered. The Londoner then heard baying dogs and thundering hooves. He was chased through the Park, and his friends insisted that they heard the twang and thud of a well-aimed arrow. Their visitor was dead. But it was a great way to go – a teddy boy pursued by an ancient god. Herne is still said to haunt the Park all through the winter, appearing at midnight near the oak. It is advisable not to tamper with his horn.

When a person dies, their clock is supposed to 'die' at the same moment. This idea inspired the song *My Grandfather's Clock*; and heads nodded sagely when the **House of Lords clock** stopped at the death of George III today in 1820. Not all clocks were so punctually punctilious, and it was common for them to be forcibly stopped for the period between death and burial, and covered with a cloth.

✞ It is rare for anyone to attempt **talking to ghosts**. Spirits usually retain ethereal silence, occasionally moaning, or uttering ominous pronouncements. But for a human to try to break the verbal ice is almost unheard of. It happened, though, in the middle of what was described as '*the most famous case of haunting since the Society of Psychical Research was formed*'. On this day in 1884, Rosina Despard of Pittville Circus Road, Cheltenham, Gloucestershire, spoke to a ghost that had been seen many times in the previous two years. The black-draped form was thought to be the wraith of a previous occupant, Imogen Swinhoe. The ghost gasped when Rosina addressed her, but was unable to answer, although Rosina thought its face contorted with the effort. Normally ghosts harass the living, but Rosina continued with the role-reversal, regularly attempting to touch the spirit or engage it in smalltalk. By 1890 the ghost had had enough, and vanished. But in the 1950s it reappeared, a few houses further down the same street, and it is still sometimes seen there.

30th January

Calf, Cod, Pike and Pigeon

Pittenweem in Fife was not the place to be in 1705. A boy named Morton accused his neighbours of witchcraft, and everyone believed him. On January 30th, after fleeing her tormentors, innocent suspect Janet Bornfoot was beaten, tied up, tortured, stoned, crushed with rocks, and finally squashed under a sledge. Morton's later exposure as a psychopathic religious liar was no consolation for the likes of Ms Bornfoot.

Charles I was beheaded on this day in 1649 at Whitehall, his forfeit for having lost the Civil War. The charge that legally brought about the execution claimed that the King '*hath had a wicked design totally to subvert the ancient and fundamental laws and liberties of this nation*'. Several portents had also predicted his demise.

When Bernini's bust of the King arrived at Chelsea Palace, a hawk with a dead pigeon clutched in its talons flew overhead, and the blood spattered the bust's throat. As omens go, this is on the grim side. Charles' head soon rolled, and the bust later perished in a fire. It led to the less-than-catchy saying, '*He who is sprinkled with pigeon's blood will never die a natural death*'. Just in case the earlier message had not got through, the top of Charles' staff fell off during his trial: a sure sign that his own top was soon to follow.

During the Commonwealth Charles I was remembered on January 30th at the Calves' Head Club feast. The calf's head was a symbol of idiocy, and several were served, all in different jocular contexts to represent Charles' various policies. There was also a cod's head on the table, to represent the King himself, and a pike with small fish stuffed into its mouth to represent Tyranny. After the feast the hagiographical book *Eikon Basilike*, published before the execution and starring Charles and the Divine Right of Kings, was ceremonially burned. A toast was then raised '*To those worthy patriots who killed the tyrant!*' The feast led to them saying '*There are many ways to serve a calf's head*', meaning that there are several ways to reveal your follies.

After the Restoration the Calves' Head Club was unsurprisingly disbanded, and Charles' death-day was kept instead as a religious observation. Fasting and humiliation were amongst its uplifting themes; though there were no approaches to the Pope, either then or later, for official canonisation. Despite this, The Feast of Charles was still a popular pseudo-religious event until it was suppressed in 1859, and several churches are still dedicated to the non-saint 'Charles the Martyr' – the oldest are at Peak Forest near Buxton, Derbyshire; Tunbridge Wells, Kent; Falmouth, Cornwall; Newtown, north of Shrewsbury, Shropshire; and Shelland near Stowmarket, Suffolk.

In a rare example of the instant custom, within minutes of Charles' execution, handkerchiefs soaked in his blood – or claiming to be soaked in his blood – were doing the rounds, and were thought to have great power as cure-alls.

© There are several short services in London today to commemorate Charles, including the laying of wreaths beneath both his statue in Whitehall and his bust at the Banqueting House – the scene of his decapitation. Very appropriate considering that the King's last word before the block was '*Remember*'.

♀ As a memory-jogger, Charles is also one of the classic headless ghosts, wandering around Marple Hall in Greater Manchester.

31st January
Bridget's Eve

Get Rich Fast Food

Guido Fawkes was executed on this day in 1606. On his way to the scaffold, propped up by his warders, he looked like one of the rougher Guy Fawkes effigies, having undergone some severe torture. There were no firework speeches from the man. He asked for forgiveness, and faced his fate. He was hung, drawn and quartered – not burned. The final irony was that this all took place outside the buildings that were supposed to have been destroyed by the Gunpowder Plot.

On the Isle of Man, **Bridget's Eve** was observed tonight. At sunset householders stood outside with armfuls of rushes and invited the saint/god in for a spot of B&B. The correct words, translated from Manx, were '*Bridget, Bridget, come to my house tonight. Open the door for Bridget and let Bridget come in.*' The rushes were then strewn on the floor to make Bridget – or Bride, as she was also known – a bed. Father Christmas-like, she had to be in several places at once to bless the houses and to bring luck and fertility. The ritual was known as **Laa'l Breeshey**.

Calculation of the **Chinese New Year** is based on the moon, and is therefore moveable. Twelve animals take it in turn to watch over the year and exert their own particular idiosyncracies: the dragon, for example, brings rain, and the monkey showers mischief on the land; while the ram engenders a dangerous global tendency towards brinkmanship, with fingers poised over red buttons.
© In London's Chinatown the New Year celebrations are a ragbag of traditional Chinese motifs: the Lion Dance and Dragon Dance parades being the most celebrated. There are also firecrackers, musicians, martial artists, and an array of traditional food. The most dangerous item on this menu is the sweet dumpling: its sugar can retain much heat, and reckless guzzlers have been known to die afterwards, fried from the inside.

Places with a sizeable Chinese population – notably Manchester and Glasgow – will stage their own New Year bash, the date usually falling in late January or early February. Thoughts of the Old Country are uppermost: the event marks an annual assertion of identity in what is, historically speaking, a foreign land. But celebrants must not relax so much that they lose their vigilance: there are various formalities to observe. There must be no cleaning as this washes away good luck: a belief which has English parallels. Similarly, the notion of clearing all debts and lending no money at New Year is common to both cultures. No scissors or blades either, as they will tear your luck for the coming year.

Back on the festive dining table, the Chinese revel in puns. A dried vegetable called *faat-choi* is eaten because its name puns on 'get rich'. Lotus has an imbedded gag of 'sufficiency all year'; and fish are guzzled with the digestible play on words 'wealth to spare'. The latter must not be eaten on New Year's Day itself, in accordance with the flesh-free Buddhist diet – no matter that meat is uppermost for the rest of the year. The Buddhist notion is that nothing with a soul must be eaten. Unfortunately for the oyster, it has been judged soulless, and can be slurped freely.

Children can look forward to new clothes for the festival, and red envelopes of lucky money. Red is a colour full of luck for the Chinese: red decorations abound, many with slogans written on them to invoke good luck.

FEBRUARY

1st February

Bride in a Snakeskin Habit

Eyes peeled for **oystercatchers** in Scotland – their arrival signals the imminent outbreak of Spring. They traditionally time their fly-past for February 1st, **Bride's Day**. Hence in Gaelic oystercatchers are *Gille Brighde*, 'Bride's Servant'.

This particular bride is high on the old and borrowed, low on the new and blue. Officially a Christian saint, she moonlights as a Celtic goddess and a minor Scottish snake. For starters Brigid, aka Bride (pronounced *bree-der*, as in the top ones who recommend Pedigree Chum), was an Abbess of Kildare who died in 525 and rapidly gained promotion to Saint. The known facts of her life are as follows: she lived in Kildare, founded a nunnery, became an Abbess, and died. That's it.

Undaunted, legend-makers set to work. Brigid, they decided, had been a great provider – her cows gave milk three times a day and food multiplied when she touched it. She even slaked the thirst of some parched clerics by turning her bathwater into beer – a trick which too many pubs have mastered in reverse. At Conwy in Gwynedd she answered the prayers of locals during a fish-famine, chucking an armful of rushes into the water. At first the locals were understandably unimpressed by this divine intervention; but a few days later the rushes became fish. Since then Conwy fish have been known as sparlings or *brwyniaid*, meaning 'rush-like'.

Her fame snowballed in medieval Ireland, especially when it transpired that despite missing the big event by 500 years she had somehow been the midwife at the birth of Jesus. Brigid/ Bride was soon patron to various groups, including dairymaids, poets, students, blacksmiths and healers. The site of her nunnery became a sacred glade: Gerald of Wales, the 13th-century historian, described 20 nuns guarding an ever-burning fire in the glade, surrounded by bushes past which no man was allowed to venture. All of which seems somewhat over-the-top for a humble holy-woman.

But there are stories of that same everlasting fire blazing for another Bride long before the Christian version donned her wimple. And so St Bride's impressive posthumous social life does make sense: the church had simply boosted its ratings by adapting the pre-existing Celtic cult of Bride to fit their own creed.

This Celtic Bride was the daughter of *Dagda*, 'The Good God', whose ever-filling cauldrons found later echo in Brigid the nun's limitless larder. Inheriting this pantry of plenty from her top-god father, Bride was a symbol of replenishment and fertility. Many wells and springs were dedicated to her, and these waters were the ultimate in prehistoric anti-contraception: one splash on the way past ensured a bonus member of the family nine months later. And good old Bride would even help out during the pregnancy, easing labour pains. Dubbing Brigid the midwife of Mary had in fact been a canny piece of Christian fact-jiggling.

✟ So far our Bride of Frankenstein has been stitched together from random bits of vaguely compatible myth – she is all benevolence and bounty. However, bored with this wholesome image, Bride also turns up as **Queen of the Serpents**. Tonight, near Scalasaig Farm at Glenelg on the west coast of the Scottish Highlands opposite Skye, she emerges from a barrow in snake-form (a popular symbol for goddesses associated with water). In pre-Christian times this area was associated with serpent worship, and Bride, to the anguish of her image-makers, was the local reptilian Queen:

This is the day of Bride
The Queen will come from the Mound
This is the day of Bride
The serpent will come from the hole.

As the last line implies, Bride was not alone in emerging from her lair – her appearance today is the traditional cue for adders to leave their winter nests.

There are traditions today similar to those mentioned on Bride's Eve, January 31st. Barra in the Hebrides has a custom of making 'Bride's Bed' with straw, and shouting: *Bride, come in, your bed is ready!* Bride then leaves her cows and cauldrons at the door and resides within for the coming year, bringing luck and prosperity – and hopefully working wonders with the bath-water too.

Bride was supposed to have gone from Ireland to Man to receive the veil from St Maughold, a 5th-century repentent pirate described, once he was Bishop, as '*a rod of gold, a vast ingot*'. In those days this sort of thing was complimentary.

🔲 Numerous wells and churches bear Bride's name: the best known is St Bride's in Fleet Street, London. Under yet another name – Brigantia – she can be seen carrying a pool cue and a bun in a splendid 3rd-century sculpture at the National Museum of Antiquities in Edinburgh. St Brigid's silver and brass jewelled shoe is in the National Museum, Dublin; and if you are in Bruges with two minutes to spare, her tunic is in the Church of St Donations there.

February 1st was **Imbolc**, one of the old Celtic quarter days (though with the arrival of the Christian calendar the quarter day was realigned to coincide with Candlemas on February 2nd). Celts used to sacrifice **cockerels** at Imbolc: a cheap and plentiful offering which averted the attentions of evil spirits. This ritual death was an extension of one of cocks' roles in life – if they crowed unexpectedly, it was taken as a sign that otherwordly beings were on the prowl. In mythology cockerels are associated with the sun, whose daily rising they herald with much crowing. The sacrifice provided the winter sun with the extra chickens it needed to stoke its fires, ready for the long climb back to its summer zenith.

Borders – crossroads and the junctions of streams especially – have always been thought of as hazy, unstable places where faeries and spirits can gain access. The sacrificial Imbolc cock was often interred, alive, at the point where three streams joined. Wise farmers always kept at least one of their old birds back, for:

He that will have his farm full
Must keep an old cock and a bull.

Primarily Imbolc was the festival of *lambing*. Lambs born at this season can feed on lush spring grass, and are fat enough for market later in the year, providing they survive the inclement February weather.

🌀 On the Isle of Man a snowy or frosty February 1st means that the water supply is not about to run out: '*Bridget's feast-day white, every ditch full*'. Though whether it is to be with rain or with snow, no one is too sure. If it is sunny today, continues the Manx weatherlore, it will snow before May Day – not the most helpful or precise of predictions. It is also said that whichever way the wind blows today, it will keep gusting in that direction until April 30th, the eve of the next quarter day, Beltane.

2nd February
Candlemas

Long Gone John Silver

Candlemas was party-time for Romans everywhere, with candles and torches carried down the streets in honour of goddess-of-the-month, Februa. The Christian version kept the candles, and celebrated the ritual Purification of Mary, 40 days after the birth of Jesus, and the Presentation of the infant at the Temple.

Eventually Candlemas became one of the four Celtic Quarter Days, important junctures in the pastoral year, and the time for numerous fairs. The fair at Radnor Forest in Powys, boasted healer, bone-setter and terminal 19th-century eccentric 'Silver' **John Lloyd**. No fan of money, he would only accept payment in silver buttons, which he sewed onto his coat.

✟ One day Silver John went missing. It was not until the following Candlemas Fair that he was found by a skater on the ice-covered lake, Llyn Hilyn. The skater tripped and saw his frozen face staring back at her from the ice below. As Silver John had been a bone-setter it was deemed bad taste to smash the corpse free and risk breaking its bones. And so the burial had to wait until the thaw. Eternally disgruntled, Silver John still haunts the area around Llyn Hilyn, and the grass of his grave on Great Craigau – in the east side of the forest, in the Harley valley – is said to be greener than the surrounding terrain. He is thought to have been murdered for his silver; but luckily he had passed on his manipulative skills before death, and the family continued as bone-setters for generations. None of which leads comfortably into the vague, still extant, local rhyme:

Silver John is dead and gone, so they came home singing,
The Radnor boys pulled out his eyes and set the bells a-ringing.

🏨 Silver John Lloyd's story and memorial can be seen at the *Forest Inn*, close to Llyn Hilyn, at the junction of the A44 and A481 in the Radnor Forest, west of Llandrindod Wells, Powys.

☕ The traditional end of Winter, this is a big day for bad **rhymes**:

Candlemas Day, put beans in the clay
Put candles and candlesticks all away.

On Candlemas Day if the thorn hangs a drop
Then you're sure of a good pea crop.

If it neither rains nor snows on Candlemas Day
You may straddle your horse and go and buy hay.

On Candlemas Day if the sun shines clear
The shepherd had rather see his wife on the bier.

☕ The 1993 hit comedy film *Groundhog Day* took its title – and its central event – from an old American custom: on February 2nd groundhogs give their yea or nay to the end of winter. This is not a British custom, due to the severe shortage of groundhogs, but in some parts of the country there is a very similar superstition involving **hedgehogs**, as it is maintained that today: '*If a hedgehog casts a shadow at noon, winter will return.*'

3rd February
St Blaise's/St Werburga's Day

The revenge of the talking geese

Today is the feast of **Werburga**, patron saint of the quarter-pounder and daughter of Wulfhere, first Christian King of Mercia. During Werburga's stint at Weedon Abbey in 7th-century Northamptonshire, the countryside fell foul of a flock of ravenous geese, who applied their gizzards to the fields and orchards with such zest that the locals despaired.

Appeals were sent to Werburga, who ordered her men to round up the geese. Formerly unruly, the geese unexpectedly caved in to the demands, apologising for all their culinary crimes. Unfazed by their conversational skills, Werburga forgave and freed them. But the next day they were back, the chief gander complaining that not only had one of his flock gone missing during their brief imprisonment but that, coincidentally, a pile of fresh goose bones had been found in the Abbey kitchen. Knowing his goose to be cooked, the chef admitted guilt. Angry that her trust had been betrayed, Werburga commanded the bones to be brought forth. They instantly became fleshed and feathered, and the digested bird resumed its previous form. Reanimating a dead goose – arguably the ultimate in minor miracles.

Today is also **St Blaise's Day**. Blaise was a 4th-century doctor, whose most spectacular cure involved a child choking on a fish. One touch to the boy's throat and out flew the offending flounder. This sort of thing soon landed Blaise in prison, where he was gratuitously ripped apart with iron rakes. Because these implements resembled the combs used in wool-making, he was adopted as patron saint by macabre woolmakers.

© His memory was also kept ablaze by the mother of the boy with the fishy throat. She lit a candle each year in his memory, which accounts for the candles used in the **Blessing of the Throats** ceremony today at St Etheldreda's Church, Ely Place, London. Two candles are tied together at one end, lit, and touched on each side of the sufferers' throats. The priest says: '*May the Lord deliver you from the evil of the throat and from every other evil.*' The cure is supposed to work.

If you cannot make it to the church, simply touch the afflicted area and command the irritant to: '*Move up and down, in the name of St Blaise*'. Alternatively, you can use the old Saxon method, which involves getting all aggressive and shouting hoarsely: '*I buss the Gorgon's mouth!*'

Bury St Edmunds in Suffolk and Bradford in West Yorkshire were the chief Blaise celebrants from the woollier side of the legend. When the wool trade was in the ascendant in the 18th and 19th centuries, there were grand Blaise processions in the streets. When the trade lagged, Blaise got the blame, and was promptly forgotten.

4th February
St Gilbert of
Sempringham's Day

The outlaw who Mistook His Wife for a Hat

Deformed at birth and barred from knightly pursuits, **Gilbert of Sempringham** founded the only English monastic order, to take his mind off personal problems. He was squire and parson at the same time in Sempringham, Lincolnshire, before getting down to full time pray-as-you-earn monkey business. He founded 13 monasteries, setting the neighbours talking when he established a core house of Seven Devout Women at his Sempringham base. Gilbert championed lepers, the poor, and orphans; and he moonlighted as carpenter, builder and manuscript copier. Thomas Beckett once evaded the King's officers by disguising himself as a Gilbertine – not that it saved him in the end, mind. Gilbert did better, age-wise, than his famous follower, dying a non-agenarian in 1189.

☐ **Loch Mochrum** near Wigtown in Dumfries and Galloway is habitually avoided by ice-skaters. According to local legend the healing loch is incapable of freezing. There are four optimum dates on which to brave the northern tempest and take a paddle in the curative antifreeze. The first Sunday in February is the earliest of the four blue-faced red-letter days, the others being the first Sundays of May, August and November.

St Medana's Well, in the same region, was created when Medana, who was so determined to stay like a virgin, that she flung her eyeballs at a persistent suitor to dissuade him from his affections. She then caused the healing well to spring forth so that she could cure herself and see once again.

© ☐ On the first Sunday in February the **Rocking Ceremony** is held at Blidworth church in Nottinghamshire. The star of the show is the baby boy from Blidworth who was born nearest to the previous Christmas Day. During the morning service, the child is baptised. In the afternoon, he is put into an old wooden cradle which is festooned with flowers and plants. The vicar reads the service, pausing only to rock the cradle and bless its contents. Child and consenting parents are then reunited, the baby is given a blessed bible as a thank-you for his participation, and the whole thing is rounded off with a rousing chorus of that evergreen favourite, *Nunc Dimittis*. The boy's name is later added to the register of Rocking Babies, on the wall in the Baptistry.

The Rocking Ceremony is an old Christian custom linked with Candlemas. It was hit on the head during the 19th century, but made a comeback due to popular demand in 1922. In its original form, it seems to have been a short play, depicting the Presentation of Jesus in the Temple – what survives is a severely pruned version of this biblical story.

Blidworth is near Mansfield, in the middle of what remains of Sherwood Forest. Will Scarlet is said to be buried somewhere in the churchyard, and on Main Street is a house which claims to be the place where **Maid Marian** lived prior to her marriage to Mr Hood. The Marian bit is unlikely, however, as this flower of womankind was actually a hat. Her name originates in a Morris dance, *The Mad Morion*, so called because the principal dancer wore a morion, a brimless round hat. Sorry about that, Robin.

5th February

The Mayor with the Silver Balls

On this day in 1748 at Eyam in Derbyshire Stephen Broomhead, the church **dogwhipper**, died. Every Sunday, brandishing an ash-stick with handy leather thong attachment, Stephen had descended on Eyam Church before the service and hounded the hounds with his whip. It appears that dogs liked nothing better than to spend a leisurely Sunday morning cocking their legs against church pews.

Stephen Broomhead was not a one-off: most parishes had their whippers. Neighbouring Youlgreave has a record in its parish notes stating that a Robert Walton, early in the 17th century, was given one shilling and fourpence for '*whipping y dogges forth of y church in tyme of divine service*'. As for the '*Dog Whipper de Eyam*' (as the death notice styles Stephen Broomhead), he did not perish Hollywood-style in a heroic struggle with a church-going pit-bull terrier, but was dogged by bad weather, '*overlaid in y snow upon Eyam Moor*'.

© On the first Monday after February 3rd, known as Feast Monday, St Ives in Cornwall holds its annual **Hurling the Silver Ball** contest for local children. Game for a lark, the Mayor – who has led a colourful morning procession at 9.45 am on the previous day – gets the ball rolling at the parish church. Fresh from a swift ball-wetting ceremony at the town's Venton Ia well, he throws the silver-coated cork ball to the waiting children at 10.30 am and thus sets the bizarre game in motion. In a combination of pass-the-parcel and pro-celebrity wrestling played along the streets and beaches by children and their menacing elder brothers, the ball changes hands for an hour and a half. At noon the child holding it is given a crown piece – which in recent lean years have been ones minted for the wedding of Charles and Di. At no point does any hurling take place, hence the contest's name. The mugging activities of the elder siblings has led to complaints, though this unfortunate rule of terror is doubtless returning the game to its more robust beginnings.

Originally the hurling was a straightforward match, with St Ives taking on neighbouring Lelant, until the latter village found its team massively outnumbered. The St Ives game continued, a novel early rule saying that all men called John, William or Thomas should be on one side, and all other Christian names on the other.

At 11.30 am, any child who has been mugged by the bullies, or who is simply fed up with the Hurling, can attend the Guildhall for a penny-scramble, thrown by the hyperactive Mayor. And he is back in the fray at 7 pm, kicking off the traditional rugby game which brings the day's frenzied activities to a close.

Feast Day is linked with the dedication of the church to St Ia, whose feast is on February 3rd. Ia – or Ives – was a virgin who arrived in Cornwall after fleeing Irish pursuers, taking to sea in that most unorthodox of vessels, a leaf.

6th February
St Dorothy's Day

Beer and Croquet with the Merry Monarch

Charles II died today in 1685, and is buried in Westminster Abbey. He had already assured himself a place at the forefront of legend during his exile by hanging out in a tree, the event that instigated Oak Apple Day on May 29th. His life ended with a folkloric flourish too. While Charles was visiting the Tower of London, a passing sparrow-hawk became entangled in one of the iron crowns on top of the White Tower. It died there, hanging upside down. The combination of the noble but hara-kiri hawk and the symbolic crown could mean only one thing. Sure enough, the King was under the sod before the week was out.

▥ Colourful tales anchored Charles in the public memory. He once rode to Godmanstone in Dorset to reshoe his horse. He called for ale, but the blacksmith replied that the smithy was unlicensed. The King, pint-pot in one hand and Royal Prerogative in the other, granted a licence on the spot. As soon as Charles had galloped off the blacksmith threw away his anvil, and ever since then the 600-year-old smithy has fulfilled a more lucrative role as *The Smith's Arms* – it claims to be the smallest pub in England, and the Guinness Book of Records agrees.

▥ Charles also inspired the street name Pall Mall – one of the pink bits on Monopoly boards and a famous London thoroughfare. After years of hardship and exile in France, what better way for Charles to celebrate his return than by playing croquet? Or at least **pall-mall**, an alternative version of the game where the ball has to pass through a free-swivelling circular iron ring. After Charles had popularised the game, a 1000-yard-long court was built at St James, and when the site was later paved over Pall Mall was retained as the name of the new street. Until recently *The Freemason's Arms* in Hampstead played a close relative of the game, under the name *mell*, or lawn billiards, on the only pitch in the country dedicated solely to the sport. However, in an unsporting act of desecration the pitch has now been concreted over, though the pub does still have one of only three surviving Old English skittle alleys.

Such was the popularity of the Merry Monarch that long before Charles' death Lord Rochester penned the following touching **epitaph**:

> *Here lies our great and Sovereign Lord*
> *Whose word no man relies on,*
> *He never said a foolish thing*
> *Nor ever did a wise one.*

☕ Today is **St Dorothy** (or Dorothea)'s Day. Scarves and shovels at the ready, for according to folklore: '*Dorothea gives the most snow.*' The 4th-century Dorothy was on such intimate terms with the Divine powers that she was able to order a basket of fruit from Heaven – a gift to a lawyer who had mocked her and challenged her to send him the produce of paradise – which proves that the Lord giveth, and the Lord does takeaway.

7th February

Ghostly Drummer on Ice

With a bit of twilight mist and a sharp eye today, it may be possible to spot the **phantom skating drummer** of Hickling Broad in Norfolk. In life he was an Army drummer, paradiddling and thumb-twiddling on leave during the winter before the Battle of Waterloo. Pleased to have temporarily escaped the all-male company of the Forces, he filled his free time by falling in love with a girl from Potter Heigham. He met her while gliding across the frozen Broad, and it was love at first skate.

There was a problem, however, in the form of the girl's soldier-hating father. The lovers were compelled to meet in secret. Night after February night the young soldier donned his skates and slid off for some holiday-on-ice romance at Swim Coots, an area sandwiched between Potter Heigham and Hickling Broad. Alas, one evening the ice gave way and the swimming coots all sank, the soldier included. ♀ On misty evenings in February the soldier takes his paranormal percussion across the Broad, where he can be seen and heard summoning his lover to a final tryst. Be there at seven o'clock with flask and sandwiches to catch a glimpse. Hickling Broad is now a nature reserve, and skating drummers are a protected species there.

© **Charles Dickens** was born in Portsmouth, Hampshire, on this day in 1812. In an annual ceremony today at 2 pm outside the Charles Dickens school in Southwark, London, the Lord Mayor places a wreath on the author's bust. There are readings from Dickens' works, and re-enactments of scenes from Dickens' books.

Marcley Hill, Hereford and Worcester, is worth a peek. At 6 pm today in 1571 the upland upped and *'roused itself with a roar, and by seven the next morning had walked forty paces'*. The fell walking continued for the next three days, with the 26 acres, complete with hedges, trees and alarmed sheep, moving a total of 400 yards, via the unfortunate Kinnaston Chapel.

Joseph Arch was, according to his enemies, 'the Arch Apostle of Arson'. According to his colleagues he was a man of 'strength and determination' – the virtues needed in order to rally the vast agricultural workforce. Arch held the first labourers' union meeting at Wellesbourne, near Stratford in Warwickshire, on this day in 1872 – the fact that he did not live in a tied house meant that he could not be evicted: an otherwise inevitable consequence of such radicalism. Due to the man's efforts, the labourers finally won the right to vote in 1884, by which time the National Agricultural Labourers Union was well-established.

© 🏛 The tree under which Arch first preached died in 1948, but the spot is still marked, with a commemorative plaque, at the foot of a replacement tree, which was planted in the following year. Every year on February 7th trade union representatives gather at the Wellesbourne tree to pay their respects, after which they tramp to Barford to lay a wreath on Arch's grave.

8th February
St Cuthman's Day

Nevell Say Die

Nevell Norway was murdered on this day in 1840, done in by robbers on the road from Bodmin to Wadebridge in Cornwall. Just another unsolved case in the files of Old Scotland Yard were it not for his brother Edmund, at sea thousands of miles away near St Helena. On the day of the murder Edmund had a vivid dream in which his brother was dragged from his horse and killed. Just a dream, but he recorded details of the imagined attack anyway. He described the site of the crime, and mentioned the pistol which had twice failed to fire before the robbers used it to club Nevell to the ground. Unfortunately, every detail of Edmund's dream turned out to be accurate, and Nevell turned out to be dead.

It always rains when you cut the grass at Steyning, thanks to **St Cuthman**. The precocious child Cuthman roamed around Steyning in West Sussex spreading the Good Word. He stood out from other roving child preachers, for behind him on the end of a sturdy rope he pulled a wheelbarrow containing his paralysed mother.

One day the ruts in the road and the weight

of the invalid mother proved too much for the wheelbarrow. At Penfolds Field it burst apart, much to the amusement of the resident haymakers, who jeered and shouted abuse. Cuthman was so incensed by this that he cursed the field, saying that forever after it would rain when hay was being cut, thus spoiling the crop. Penfolds Field is now covered by the old Steyning Grammar School, which may have hindered this curse; but when the hay-mowers are out there is sometimes a nasty patch of cumulo-nimbus in the corner of the science lab.

〠 Come rain or shine, the historical facts about Cuthman are that he was born at Chidham in Sussex. He preached and cursed in the 7th century, lived in poverty with his mother and later built a tiny wooden church at Steyning which became the site of the present stone structure. The stone that is supposed to have covered St Cuthman's grave is in the wall of Steyning church. Along with lots of other stones.

Colours each have their own significance in folklore. Red was the colour of martyrdom for Catholics – no prizes for guessing why – and was chosen by **Mary Queen of Scots** on the day of her execution at Fotheringhay, February 8th 1587. Just before facing the axe she took off her outer dress, to reveal an under dress of dark red – a move far more memorable than a string of empty last words. The Scots in the audience probably found added poignancy, and not a little irony, in contemplating a line from an old Scottish colour-rhyme: '*Red is brazen with health and strength.*'

〠 A lump in the ground and a single block of rubble is all that remains of **Fotheringhay Castle** in Northamptonshire. The thistles which grow on the site are said to have been planted by Mary to remind her of Scotland.

♀ Mary decided not to haunt Fotheringhay, but reputedly crops up on the stairs of the Talbot Hotel in nearby Oundle, either weeping or gazing out of the windows dressed, for a change, in black. Oundle is also home to the **Drumming Well**, which beats out a supernatural tattoo before events of national significance. It is down Drumming Well Lane, near the Methodist chapel.

9th February
St Teilo's Day

The One-Legged Satanic Marsupial Badger

Today in 1855 across 100 miles of rural Devon, a single straight line of **cloven hoof-marks** appeared after a snow-storm. It was proclaimed that the prints, distinctly non-quadrupedal, had been made by Satan.

Detractors swiftly pointed out that if the tracks were the Devil's, then he either had a very mincing gait or else only one leg, such was the trueness of the single line of prints. Researchers concocted some great theories: the tracks had been made by everything from a one-shoed donkey to a badger; from a group of flightless birds to a kangaroo. The trail went under bushes and over rooftops, gates, walls and haystacks. For one brief stretch it even managed to go through a six-inch-high pipe. At Dawlish a pack of dogs was put on the scent, but at a dense thicket they howled and refused to follow the Devil's tracks any further.

At Woodbury the apocrypha and sulphur mingled further, as the deeply-rutted tracks suggested the use of a heated shoe. There was also doubt as to whether the line of hoof-marks, running from Totnes to Littlehampton, was uninterrupted as originally claimed. Perhaps badgers, hoaxers, limping donkeys, kangaroos and three-toed sloths had each played their part. Surviving pictures of the undeviating line suggest the work of one man and a shod Space Hopper.

Today is **St Teilo's Day**. The waters of his well – now dried up – near Maenclochog in Dyfed, were said to cure **whooping cough**. There was only one drawback: they had to be slurped from Teilo's skull. This strange practice continued into the 20th century using one of the saint's *three* skulls.

〠 Teilo was born at Penally in Dyfed, became Bishop at Llandaff Cathedral in Cardiff, and died back in Dyfed at Llandeilo Fawr. These three places all wanted his remains, and so God was brought in to arbitrate. His solution was to clone the body so that each church had its own dead Teilo. A miracle, or perhaps just a dodgy excuse for a triple set of relics. The three churches, former centres of the Teilo cult (which was limited to Wales and Brittany), are still standing. Down the centuries, the saint's multiple relics went missing piece by piece; but what is claimed to be one of Teilo's skulls recently reappeared. In Hong Kong. After protracted negotiations, on February 9th 1994 there was a special service at Llandaff, at which the skull was installed in its own niche in the cathedral's St Teilo chapel. The reinstated relic is now considered far too precious to be used as a cup.

Incidentally, there are other ways of preventing **whooping cough** without getting out of your skull. Pass the patient under a donkey nine times; or else persuade them to take a ride on the nearest bear. This particular brand of preventative medicine often kept a bear-keeper in sticky buns and honey. Or whatever bears eat.

throwing a **shoe**. Many great civilisations from ancient Egypt onwards enjoyed a pre-marital fling. Throwing the shoe represents the completion of a contract, and this is why shoes are tied to the honeymoon couple's car along with tins and distant relatives.

Treaties and business transactions were all marked by the odour of unleashed feet. It was a sign of respect to the propitiating gods to remove one's shoe. Meanwhile, Saxon sexists received their bride's shoe from her father, and promptly clubbed her over the head with it.

© Early in February, Nesting and Girlsta on Shetland go in for their own spot of **Up-Helly-A'ing**, with parades, boats and would-be Vikings. Details of the main event at Lerwick are given on January 28th.

10th February

Ice Station Woodcock

Meteors, snow-caves and nutcrackers are all in a day's disaster at Impington in Cambridgeshire. The day in question was in 1799, and the disaster befell **Elizabeth Woodcock**, riding home from Cambridge in a blizzard. Half a mile from home the sky was lit up by a falling meteor. The horse bolted, forcing it and Elizabeth to part company dramatically. Unaware of blizzard etiquette, the depressed and dehorsed woman sat down for a quick nap. She awoke to find herself trapped in a snow-cave. All she had with her were a pair of nutcrackers, a bag of nuts, and two pinches of snuff. After nine days of this high-calorie N-plan diet she was rescued, on February 10th. Unfortunately for poor Elizabeth the resultant frostbite finally laid her low in July. She lost all her toes and fingers before she died.

A monument detailing Elizabeth Woodcock's demise can be seen near her grave at Impington churchyard. The nutcrackers are preserved in Cambridge Folk Museum.

In common with the 1st, 3rd, 19th and 21st of this month, today is a **good day for marriage**. This is all according to Andrew Waterman's 1655 Almanac. He advised discerning men that these are the ideal days on which to '*contract a wife, for then women will be fond and loving*'. However, this seems to have been based on nothing more than Waterman's wish to fill a few pages with random dates.

But for those taking the Almanac's advice, credence can be given to the proceedings by

11th February
St Caedmon's Day

The Singing Cowboy of Dark-Age Whitby

St Caedmon was a 7th-century Whitby cowherd who started life with an aversion to singing. At feasts he would beat a retreat as soon as the music started. His neighbours teased and mocked him, all because he could or would not sing. On the verge of personal crisis, Caedmon was saved by a passing angel which sauntered over and suggested that he sing the song of Creation, from day one to Doomsday. This was a tall order, but Caedmon gave it a go, and became the first English Christian poet. The Venerable Bede mentions him in glowing terms.

Sadly, the glow did not extend to capturing Caedmon's prolific output for posterity. Nothing remains other than the legend, a eulogy in Bede's 8th-century *Ecclesiastical History*. He describes how Caedmon would listen to biblical tales and immediately compose an English poem based upon what he had heard. Bede says that Caedmon's poems '*stirred the hearts of many to despise the world*'. Despising the world, for the average Saxon, had the positive connotation of loving the afterlife, looking forward to consolation for the bad times that you were having on earth.

Caedmon's audiences loved him. His big hits *Terrors of the Day of Judgement* and *Horrors of the Pains of Hell* were said to be very hummable. But to the dismay of posterity, Bede quotes only half a dozen lines from the Caedmon canon – a fragment called *The Hymn of St Caedmon* – and nothing else remains. It is certainly one way of escaping the critics. The tradition of translating religious tales into popular song has been popular ever since. Some would argue that Caedmon has a lot to answer for.

◉ The **Trial of the Pyx** is not governed by tides, or the moon, but is still highly moveable according to arcane and impenetrable rules. It takes place sometime in February or March, with the verdict announced at a luncheon sometime in May. Elusive, it is still important, as the trial is the annual independent check on the coins of the realm. The procedure set out by Henry III in 1248 is still closely adhered to today, with 12 jurors – usually Freemen of the Goldsmith's Company or financial wizards from the City – testing how accurately and consistently the Royal Mint is churning out its coins. One coin from every batch minted in the past year is put aside for the ceremony, and these coins are kept in bags of 50 in special Pyx (meaning 'Mint') boxes. The jurors open the bags and choose one coin at random from each. The coin is put into a copper bowl, while the other 49 are placed in a wooden one. It is only the coins in each copper bowl which are taken downstairs to be weighed and thoroughly examined for imperfections. A degree of mechanisation has now been introduced, with some of the coins counted by machine, but this did not prevent a recent near-crisis when one of the coins went missing. After a protracted search, it was eventually discovered in the trouser turn-up of one of the jurors.

The full testing and analysis takes several weeks, and the results are announced at the Pyx Luncheon in May – the Chancellor of the Exchequer, who is officially Master of the Mint, is the main speaker – but it is extremely rare for any serious faults to be found with the Pyx'n'mix coins.

12th February

Nine-Day Queen in Bad Career Move

♰ A ponderous, amorphous, glowing white shape hovers above the ground at the Tower of London today. There is no cause for alarm. It is only the unusually laidback ghost of Lady **Jane Grey**, back for a spot of haunting on the anniversary of her execution at the Tower on February 12th 1554.

Lady Jane's ghost gets her a place in the folklore annals. But she deserved a place anyway on account of being the country's shortest-reigning monarch. After the death of young Edward VI in 1553, the Duke of Northumberland – having strategically married his son to Lady Jane a few weeks beforehand – had her crowned in London, on the authority of the dead king. She was a Protestant, the granddaughter of Henry VIII's sister. The gamble was that people would rally to Jane rather than to the more obvious Catholic heir, Mary, Henry VIII's eldest daughter. Alas, there were to be no Christmas speeches and portrait opportunities with corgis for Lady Jane. Nine days after the crowning she was arrested and Mary was on the throne.

⌂ On the Monday of or after the 12th, **Loch Manaar** between Strathnaver and Strath Halladale near Bettyhill in Highland Region, is on great form for those seeking **healing**. Last century travellers from all over Scotland would make the journey. A sympathetic reporter in an 1877 edition of *The Inverness Courier* describes them as: '*the impotent, the halt, the lunatic and the tender infant.*' They would all hang about in the dark on Sunday until the stroke of midnight – the key time for the Loch's magic. Loch Manaar (also spelt Monaar or mo Naire) is equally effective on the Mondays of, or after the 12th of May, August and November.

The power of the Loch stems from an old woman of Strathnaver who had a pet stone. It was doubly welcome in that it had great powers and ate very little. This enviable lump of geological magic did not go unnoticed in the ranks of the powerful Gordons of Strathnaver. One of them visited the woman and demanded the stone. Not surprisingly she sent him packing with a earful of abuse. At this Gordon took her to the Loch and tried to drown her. The woman, sensing a legend in the air, threw the stone into the water and declared: '*May it do good to all created things save a Gordon of Strathnaver.*' Gordon promptly beat her over the head with a non-magical stone, and as she died she cried out '*Manaar! Manaar!*', which means 'shame'.

☕ In the Highlands, the 12th, 13th and 14th of February are the month's '*Borrowing Days*', said to be on loan from January, and therefore reflecting the weather of the previous month. If they are bright and fine, the farming year will suffer; if they are stormy and miserable, farmers will be celebrating. In fact the weather is usually bad: in Scotland the Days' name, *faoilteach*, came to mean 'lousy weather'.

13th February
Valentine's Eve

Passengers Please Note: Next Service in 50 Years Time

Goodwin Sands, nicknamed 'Calamity Corner' by seamen, is a notorious sandbank five miles off the Kent coast near Deal. No moth was ever lured to lamplight as unerringly as vessels have been lured to Goodwin over the years. Most nautical black spots have just a few hundred casualties to boast of. Goodwin Sands has claimed in the region of 50,000 lives. To give ghostly credence to this ghastly toll, it is claimed that the sands were originally a town called Lomea whose sea-walls were breached in the 11th century. The town has been getting its own back ever since.

On February 13th 1748 *The Lady Lovibond* was passing by. On board were Simon Reed and his new wife Annetta. Sadly, the steersman – one John Rivers – was in love with Annetta too. He drove the schooner onto the fatal sands in a suicidal act of vengeance. *The Lady Lovibond* reappeared 50 years later on February 13th 1798, and again on the same day in 1848, when the local lifeboat was sent on a fruitless rescue mission. It set sail again in 1898, but sources differ as to whether the phantom ship was seen in 1948, which casts a bit of a shadow over the 1998 jaunt.

Goodwin Sands were said to have appeared after the erection of **Tenterden Steeple**; though it is not known why a church steeple – several miles inland – should have such a novel side-effect.

The Nine of Diamonds is **The Curse of Scotland**. One theory says that this tag originated with Sir John Dalrymple, who used the card to show his assent to the **Massacre of Glencoe**. Dalrymple was Secretary of State under William III, who had demanded that the clans bow to England. The MacDonalds failed to comply, and their foes the Campbells hatched a dastardly plot. After the Nine of Diamonds thumbs-up, they went as guests to Glencoe today in 1692 and slaughtered all 38 MacDonalds present.

Some legends say that in divine-ish retribution, the Campbells were led astray on the way home to Fort William by pro-MacDonald faerie pipers. Massacres, however, were quite common amongst the clans. Glencoe seemed particularly despicable simply because it breached the Highland laws of hospitality. Slaughtering the host is the height of bad manners.

⊙ To catch a nocturnal glimpse of your future lover on **Valentine's Eve**, take a hard-boiled egg, remove the yolk, fill the cavity with salt, and eat the robust delicacy in silence before going to sleep, taking no water during the night. Do not forget to rid your mouth of the resultant Satan's Breath before greeting your Valentine the following morning.

The Wednesday of this week, the seventh after Christmas, was **Binding Day** at Portland, Dorset. Locals burgled their neighbours' houses and ransomed the booty, a felony said to commemorate the time when raiders killed the local men and enslaved the women. A few Portlanders managed to hide during the assault and led a successful counter-revolution. It is unclear as to why this incident should be remembered by nicking next-door's silver spoons and CD collection.

14th February
Valentine's Day

Third-Century Martyrs in Sex-Romp Lottery

The early church faced a dilemma. The influence of the Roman **Lupercalia** – a bonanza of beer and benking – was felt throughout the West today, and a new Christian feast of love was needed to oust it. The church decided therefore to rope in an innocent saint, and as **Valentine** was martyred on this day in the 3rd century, he was posthumously volunteered. In fact he was martyred twice today, once as Bishop of Terni, and again a couple of years later as a Roman priest. The two Valentines are probably the same man, but no one knows for certain.

Unfortunately for the church there was not much in Valentine's CV to link him with love-lotteries, fondling, and the other highlights of Lupercalia. So, somewhere along the line ambitious legend-makers knocked Valentine into shape. He was said to have been a man who defied Emperor Claudius II's decree that soldiers were not to marry, as sex sapped their strength. Valentine presided over illicit Christian weddings. Later, during pre-execution incarceration, he fell in love with the jailer's daughter, and as a final farewell he left her a simple message which read 'Your Valentine'. Hogwash of course, but the stuff of legend.

Those were the Christian reasons for celebrating today. But the mood is mirrored in nature too. **Birds** set the scene and choose their mates on this date, something familiar enough to Chaucer in the 14th century when he wrote his *Parlement of Fowles*:

*For this was on seynt Valentynes day
Whan every foul cometh there to chese his
make.*

Poets used this bird-motif for many centuries afterwards, in spite of the obvious evidence to the contrary. But in 1766, whatever coupling instincts the birds had were thwarted by the weather. The Reverend William Cole wrote in his diary on that day: '*Kites and Hawkes fell from the Trees and were carried into the House, their Wings and Feathers being so frozen that they could not gett off.*'

⊚ Still on the subject of **birds**, there is a certain hazard in observing them today. The first fluttering of wings in the morning foretells the nature of your future house-partner. A sparrow means that a woman will marry a poor man but will be happy; a robin denotes a sailor; a dove symbolises money and happiness; and a goldfinch announces happiness and boundless wealth. Happen to spy a passing Andalusian hemipode, however, and you will wed a one-armed dancing bear with a chain of hardware stores and very dangerous parents. Much better to use this shamelessly romantic Exmoor rhyme, which manages to catch the spirit of most of the above:

*This is the day the birds choose their mate
And I choose you, if I'm not too late.*

If you were unlucky enough not to receive a visit from your loved one today, you were known as **dusty**. You were thus swept down with a broom or a handful of straw. No one really knew or cared why – it was sufficient to know that the dusty victim suffered indignity, while the dusters enjoyed inflicting it.

The Valentine **lottery** was a Roman tradition which survived into the 20th century. The names of prospective intimates were placed in a box, and drawn at random by members of the opposite sex. Robert Burns highlights the amorous game in his poem *Tam Glen*:

*Yestreen at the Valentine's dealing
My heart to my mou' gied a sten,
For thrice I drew ane without failing,
And thrice it was written, Tam Glen.*

If lotteries prove too much hassle, remember that the first person you see on Valentine's Day will be your love for the coming year. Family and animals do not count.

In former years the day served as a pretext for some no-nonsense **begging**. Children were up and about before sunrise knocking on doors and shouting '*Good morrow Valentine!*' twice. If they got through this before the bleary-eyed householder could speak, they were entitled to money or Valentine cakes, also known unappetisingly as **plum shittles**. In Norfolk, if this was attempted after sunrise the alms-collectors were said to be 'sunburnt' and were duly told where to stick their shittles.

Not related to Valentine – unless legendmakers care to insert a repentant fish into the apocrypha – is the custom of **Blessing the Nets**. This derives from the old practice of throwing a plaid into the river to placate the water god, and of salting the nets before the fishing season with the same aim in mind. Otherwise – and sometimes regardless of these precautions – the river spirit would claim one life a year.

Such a blessing used to take place in the early hours today at the ancient fishery of Pedwell near Norham-on-Tweed on the England-Scotland border, though it fell into disuse in the late 1980s. The vicar conducted a chilly service, blessing the water, the boats and their would-be contents, both human and piscine. This blessing covered all 38 of the Tweed's ancient fisheries, being a 100-year-old custom which was itself a revival of a lapsed fish-service stretching back into the gills of time. The old prayer asked for '*finest nights to land our fish, sound and big to fill our wish*'. These precautions were understandable. God once took away all the salmon in the river after the locals fished on the Sabbath.

Today used to be the traditional opening of the **eel-season** in the Fens. The name of the main fen town, Ely, means 'the place of eels', after a legend in which an irate St Dunstan turned the sinning monks into eels, whose ancestors still haunt the local waters. These days the one remaining legal eel-catcher on the Ely stretch of the Great Ouse, Mr. Sid Merry, is licensed to catch eels all year round, but prefers not to start until mid-April.

Fishermen used to tie eel skins around their legs to prevent cramp as they fathomed the fens with their fork-headed eel stangs. Eels were a vital part of the fenland economy. South Lincolnshire residents were called **Yellow Bellies** after the colour of the local eels' underbellies. The name now applies to all denizens of the county. Some say that the term came from the jaundiced colour of the local soldiers' regiment; but on the day of reckoning our vote will be with those eels.

15th February
Lupercalia

Sixties' Semi-Ghost

The 1960s – drugs, flower-power, lamentable dress-sense, and suburban **poltergeists**. Stow-on-the-Wold in the Cotswolds probably had its share of the first three; but it excelled in the fourth. The venue was that favourite haunt of creatures from beyond: a post-war semi-detached house. On February 15th 1963 strange puddles appeared on the floor, and not an incontinent cat in sight. Excessive damp is not necessarily supernatural in origin of course; but after ensuing bouts of ripped wallpaper, ghostly wall-writing, gouge-marks on the beds, roving furniture, shredded sheets, and a spectral baby's hand which grew into a man-sized fist, the clues seemed to be pointing that way. The family involved tried, but failed, to exorcise the phantom, and even found that leaving the house did not alleviate the problem – the ghost pursued them on holiday. Eventually they decided simply to accept it as a non-paying co-tenant. After all, the ghost was no more disruptive than the average teenager – there was no physical violence, just a growing account at B&Q.

As for possible origins, on one occasion the usually inarticulate poltergeist explained that it had been a workman who was killed at the building site on February 15th several years earlier. He had gone from one spirit-level to another.

Today used to be **Lupercalia**, a festival of love and bestiality swallowed up in later Valentine's traditions. But after the lotteries and furtive card deliveries of yesterday, the 15th is still a day of emotional reckoning, with new relationships divided into the long-lasting, and the wrong-lusting.

But where oh where are the goats of yesteryear? Lusty Lupercalians liked nothing better than to don the nearest goatskin and run down the streets striking everyone with goat-thong whips. The hides originated from goats which, along with dogs, were sacrificed to the fertile god Lupercus (a Roman version of Pan) for the protection of the flock. This ancient custom was obsolete at the time of Julius Caesar, who promptly revived it. Traditionally the chief celebrations took place at the Lupercal – the spot where the maternal wolf Lupus suckled Romulus and Remus, founders of Rome. But that was too far away for the far-out Britons, and so – like burying towns under volcanic ash – this was one Italian tradition which never really caught on in Britain.

February 15th 1971 was D-Day: Britain went **decimal**. Six brand new coins were successfully introduced, along with various weights and measures which have still not entirely taken over from the old Imperial system. Having 12 old pence in a shilling and 20 shillings in a pound (and 21 in a guinea) had long struck some as a reckless drain on the nation's computational skills. When Isaac Newton was Master of the Mint in 1699 he argued passionately in favour of having 100 pennies to the pound, and complete sets of decimal coins were minted in 1857, 1859 and 1918.

Prior to the 1971 switch-over, there had been only one success for those who thought that Britain should cease to mint Imperials. In 1848 the florin, worth two shillings (10p), was introduced. It had been intended to replace the half crown but support for the old coin remained strong, and both remained in circulation until decimalisation rapidly rendered the half crown – now worth an awkward 12½p – obsolete. The florin got off to a poor start. The first batch omitted the words *'Dei Gratia'*, and became known as the 'Godless florins'.

16th February

Songs in a Miner Key

Not all folklore stems from a time before the Industrial Revolution or from semis in Stow-on-the-Wold (see yesterday). For every ditty about May mornings, sheep and rustic revelry, there are songs about mining disasters, satanic mills, and urban horrors. Mines have an especially rich seam of myths and mysterious tales.

On this day in 1882 an explosion at **Trimdon Grange** Colliery in County Durham killed 68 men. It was commemorated in a song which became the sombre anthem of the mining masses. Full of unashamed doom and gloom, the song's only note of consolation comes in the final lines:

Death will pay us all a visit – they have only gone before;
We may meet the Trimdon victims where explosions are no more.

Casting aside the customary 'Anon' or 'Trad' tag, the author, Tommy Armstrong, had the piece published in his own volume of songs. With 16 children and a huge appetite for beer, he needed all the cash he could get. One of his sons later commented: *'Me Dad's muse was a mug of beer'*. But most of the money went, not into the pockets of mine host, but into Union funds which paid out to widows and orphans affected by industrial disaster.

Far from uncommon, it has been estimated that there was an average of one fatal explosion a year during the lifetime of Armstrong. As official pit-poet he had a responsibility to act swiftly with pen and paper. As the man himself said, if he did not produce the goods folk would say: *'What's wi' Tommy Armstrong? Has someone druv a spigot in him an' let oot all the inspiration?'*

Mining omens abound. If a disaster is imminent, strange sweet-smelling **death-flowers** will bloom underground, prompting the keen-nosed to get to the surface. Similarly, **death-birds** – usually robins or pigeons – found inside the mine are very bad news. There are records of birds found underground just before the Senghennydd Colliery explosion in Mid Glamorgan: more than 400 died, making it one of the worst mining disasters.

No one must whistle in a mine or say the word 'cat'. Being late for work is bad luck too – doubtless a superstition invented by a cunning pit manager. But for those who fancy taking the entire day off, there are certain events to look out for prior to clocking-in. Having your path crossed by rabbits, pigs, birds or people with squints means that you must turn back or else you will soon be working your last shift. Similarly if anyone in the family **dreams** of death, calamity or – bizarrely – broken shoes, the pit-workers in the household must stay home or face another miner disaster.

Many had such death-dreams in October 1966, shortly before a slag heap at the mining village of **Aberfan** in Mid Glamorgan slid on to a school, killing 116 children and 28 adults. All those who had received a premonition of the disaster were later persuaded to go to London, to take part in a television programme hosted by David Frost. Their coach never arrived. One of the passengers had had another premonition, and claimed that the coach was destined to crash if they went to the television studios. A hastily rejigged programme went ahead without them.

17th February
St Finan of Lindisfarne's Day

The Monk with Tunnel Vision

Long before **Lindisfarne** was a fog-bound rock band and a mass-market mead, it was a key centre for Christianity. When its now defunct Northumberland priory got planning permission in the 11th century, the labourers supposedly survived on bread made from air, and wine from a bottomless cup. Earlier, in AD 875, fiery serpents were seen in the sky, forewarning locals of a Viking raid. And earlier still, in the 7th century, the tiny island nearly changed the face of British religion – thanks to today's saint, St Finan.

St Finan, the Bishop of Lindisfarne, battled against the dominance of the church in Rome, favouring his own brand of Celtic Christianity. The Celts had different traditions, calendars and hairstyles, and Finan sought new adherents to his religion. He sweet-talked Oswiu, King of Northumbria, into sending missionaries to the wilderness of the newly-converted south of England. Sadly, the missionaries sent by Oswiu were themselves divided as to which form of Christianity should be practised, and so the pro-Lindisfarne and pro-Rome lobbies began a tug-of-war for the souls of the English.

The church was forced to call a Synod at Whitby in 664 to sort out the conflict. Their verdict came down in favour of Rome – Finan's fair-weather friend Oswiu voted against Lindisfarne, as did Finan's former star pupil St Wilfrid. It was the finish of Finan, and for the next 900 years the church in England remained under Rome's rule. Despite having crossed the church authorities in Rome, Finan still had considerable clout as one of the fathers of the English church, and he was elevated to sainthood after his death, all transgressions forgotten.

✝ **Greystoke Castle** lies near Staunton in Cumbria. In fiction it is the ancestral residence of Lord Greystoke, better known as Tarzan. In reality it is the family home of the Howards. In legend, it has a tunnel running from one of the castle bedrooms to the local church. This passage was the favourite thoroughfare of an errant monk who used it for covert journeys to the bedroom for coyly unspecified activities. But following some quick brick-work by over-zealous workmen, he was sealed en route. Perpetually miffed, the monk now roams Greystoke, habitually favouring February. Appearances are usually quiet and ethereal; but once, when the castle-owner violated the Sabbath, he broke his vow of silence.

Charles Howard had invited a friend to hunt on a Sunday. After a game-pie supper back at the castle the guest retired to his room – the bedroom at one end of the erstwhile passage. No one knows what the monk said to him, but the unfortunate guest was never seen alive again. Charles escaped such divine retribution, though his castle has since been haunted by the ghosts of both the monk and the dead guest.

One of the foremost aristocratic houses in England, the Howards' illustrious name derives, satisfyingly, from the lowly *hogsward*, meaning a keeper of pigs.

February 18th

Last Orders, Please

Today in 1478 the **Duke of Clarence** was given the wine list and chose a vintage death. Officially his capital crime was to have proclaimed the innocence of two men accused of necromancy. Off the record, his offence was to have rather too strong a claim on the throne for Richard III's liking. Whatever, Clarence knew that his time was up, and opted to get it down the neck, rather than in the neck. His favourite tipple was **malmsey**, and the obliging executioners stuffed him head-first into a butt of the stuff. Clarence either drowned, or drank himself into permanent oblivion. Other versions of the story, notably Shakespeare's (in *Richard III*), have Clarence stabbed, then less voluntarily drowned in the butt of malmsey.

Malmsey is the sweetest type of Madeira. Originally a straightforward wine, in later years Madeira's fame, and strength, increased. During a hot 18th-century sea voyage a cargo of the stuff underwent a fabulous chemical change. Relaunched as a fortified wine, Madeira is the only drink to have been invented by a ship.

February, from Candlemas onwards, is the month of **snowdrops**. A bunch left on the kitchen window-sill is said to purify the house. Except in Wales, where snowdrop petals symbolise death.

This notion comes from the story of **King Albion's son**, who fell in love with Kenna, daughter of faerie king Oberon. Distrusting mortals, Oberon banned the suitor from his kingdom. Albion's son retaliated by storming the other world to claim Kenna as his bride. Not all fairy-tales end happily, and the lad was caught and clubbed to death. Distraught, Kenna tried a magical remedy – she applied the herb moly to staunch the wounds and revive her lover. However, when the juice touched the corpse, it transformed it into a bunch of snowdrops. Very decorative, but not much cop as a lover. Allowing for a random sex-change, this is meant to explain why snowdrops have since been known as Fair Maid of February.

Oberon was reluctant to confront the suitor's father because, as a faerie, he was less than three feet high, while Albion was head of a race of Giants. As for **moly**, it is a plant of mythology which has never been conclusively identified. The hottest contender is wild garlic. In Homer, Hermes gives moly to Odysseus to offset the sorcery of Circe. On that occasion it worked.

February colds can be soul-destroying. It is important for someone to say '*bless you*' at each sneeze, or part of the spirit will escape. The only consolation is that sneezing on a Wednesday in Scotland indicates the imminent arrival of an important letter.

Besides trying Lemsip®, nastier February colds can be cured by thrusting rubbed sage or orange peel up the nose. The accompanying chesty cough is tackled by boiled goats' milk and holly bark; while basil clears the blocked head. This may be why Isabella grows the herb in a pot containing her lover's severed head in John Keats' *Isabella and the Pot of Basil*. Meanwhile, at the even less reputable end of the market, cow dung or goose grease rubbed into the chest cure colds, but ruin the bedsheets. For a simple cough, though, make a sandwich of the patient's hair and give it to a dog. If the dog eats it, it eats the cough too.

19th February

Fair, Fire, Fever

In 1888 on this day in darkest Colchester, Essex, a drunkard climbed into a hayloft to sleep off his liquid transgressions. He turned over, spontaneously combusted, and that was that. The many witnesses claimed that the hay around him was untouched by the flames. Relatives probably blamed Charles Dickens for putting the idea into his head: *Bleak House*'s gin-swigging crook – wittily named Krook – randomly bursts into flames, due to what Dickens (bottom of the class in science) diagnoses as a fate *'inborn, inbred, engendered in the corrupted humours of the vicious body itself'*. Dickens believed passionately in the phenomenon of **spontaneous combustion**; but despite whatever happened in Colchester, the case for it is as dodgy as a wet box of Swan Vestas.

☀ Truths and contradictions sweep in a cold front with scattered showers across the February **weather** scene. First:

All the months of the year,
Curse a fair Februeer;

which is just an excuse for an outrageous rhyme. The following verse resigns itself to either rain or snow:

February fill the dyke,
Whether it be black or white.

Then, refuting the snow and ice equation is the assertion:

February brings the rain,

To thaw the frozen lake again.

And there is one sure way of helping that desired rain along. Buy some hives, because:

If bees get out in February,
The next day will be rough and rainy.

There is a possible link between the name of the month and the Latin *febris*, meaning fever – a state all too prevalent at this time of year. Whatever, March offers folkloric cheer, undoing all February's dirty work: *'February fill-dyke, March muck it out again'*. And bear this in mind: *'If in February the midges dance on the dunghill, lock up your food in the chest.'* This is also make or break time for hoggs:

February, an ye be fair,
The hoggs'll mend and nothing pair;
February an ye be foul,
The hoggs'll die in ilka pool.

Just to add confusion, the 'hoggs' in this rhyme are sheep.

A fair was formerly held at Old Deer in Grampian, on the third Thursday of this month. Rumour had it that:

The Fair-day at Auld Deer
Is the warst in a' the year.

Old Deer has an extant fair in mid-July – see July 12th.

20th February

An Unkindness of Ravens

Eager for visions, **St Wulfric** (1080–1154) engaged in the usual prayers and prostrations in his lonely cell at Haselbury Plucknett in Somerset. But he only got into his full stride after resorting to extremes of monastic masochism – wearing chain mail and taking frequent immersions in ice-cold water. His fame was sealed when he unparalysed a friend of King Henry I and then went on to prophesy the king's death, which occurred in 1135.

But Wulfric's posterity was not all based on austerity. He was renowned for gentleness and a love of animals. Local tales told of how Wulfric once moved his bed so as not to disturb a wren and its fledglings which were nesting above him. On another occasion he found a squirrel storing nuts in his only cup, and decided to make another one rather than turf out the intrusive rodent. This all shows a very substantial change of heart, given that the only reported hobbies from Wulfric's pre-monastic life were falconry (killing birds) and hunting-dogs (killing everything else).

In bird-lore, **ravens** are first off the blocks in the nesting season (having chosen their mates on Valentine's Day, of course). Reality concurs a little: ravens are early nesters, though by no means the earliest, and their first young appear about now. They use the same trees every year, and certain trees have had ravens as long as they have had branches. This should make them the bringers of new life, spring, et cetera; but superstition is having none of it: ravens are considered to be birds of ill omen. They may exchange twigs in a tender ritual known as 'the raven's kiss', but in Cornwall their loving cry is transcribed *'Corpse, corpse!'*. In Scotland pre-Grecian 2000, those desirous of lustrous black hair were advised to eat ravens' eggs.

If you hear a raven croaking over your left shoulder, that is really bad luck in Lincolnshire. Luckily, Lincolnshire has no ravens left. The bird is bringer of death and pestilence. This stems from their appearance on battlefields soon after the last blow has fallen. They are the vultures of the north. Equally grim, flocks of ravens mean famine. Shakespeare and Marlowe attest to their ill-omening. In *Macbeth* there are so many grim portents that Lady Macbeth comments *'The raven is hoarse'* after a hard day's croaking. And yet to kill one in Cornwall or Scotland is bad luck, for ravens are the embodiment of King Arthur, no less.

The Norse men were fond of the raven too. Odin had a pair of the birds one on each shoulder, called Hugin and Munin, meaning *mind* and *memory*. The raven is also associated with the Celtic goddess Morrighan, who liked to appear as a raven (or a wolf, or an eel); and with the hero **Bran**, whose head was buried on the site of the Tower of London to protect England from all enemies. *Bran* means 'raven', and the birds in the Tower of London are an echo of the hero-god – they, like him, prevent the city from falling. Bran is unique among Celtic gods in having his life-story cerealised at breakfast-time – in 1993 *Good Morning* bran flakes began to unfold Bran's legend on the back of their packets.

21st February

Rose Encounters of the Absurd Kind

On February 21st 1883, just before new girl Rose was due to start work in the household of the Whites of Worksop, the table in Mrs White's kitchen began to dance. But this was nothing compared to what happened after Rose's arrival. Kitchen utensils followed the girl up the stairs and then flung themselves down again. The violence increased as the days passed, and the cutlery cavalry was soon joined by chunks of torn carpet and hot coals.

Rose protested her innocence, but the excitable crockery continued to shimmy and shatter. Then came the disembodied footsteps and the physical phantom blows to Mr White's person. A clock that had not worked for nearly 20 years struck the hour, jumped in the air and killed itself. Furniture defied upholsterers by breaking apart, and only after a week or so of this mayhem did Mr White have his brainwave. Taking Rose by the ear-lobe he gently ejected her from the house, after apologies and a consolation cup of tea. The **poltergeist** ceased at once, and the bemused human whirlwind pottered away from the pages of history.

▯ The erection of a commemorative stone, along with its downmarket cousin the plaque, is a custom which has gathered pace in recent decades. But such stones seldom mark the sites of suicides. **William Donaghy's commemorative stone** on Dartmoor at Hartland Tor near Postbridge in Devon was erected in 1914 after his body was discovered there on February 21st. Donaghy had fled Liverpool in a deeply depressed state, and it appears that he decided to finish himself off by milling around on bleak, exposed Dartmoor. Donaghy's stone has – as yet – no weird hauntings attached to it.

Anti-monarchists used to cling to the old rhyme:

> *If Chichester steeple fall,*
> *In England there's no King at all.*

But, as every interpreter of oracles knows, you have to think laterally in these situations. On February 21st 1861, **Chichester steeple** fell through the church roof, and there was indeed no king: Victoria was on the throne at the time.

22nd February

Jemima Nicholas Saves Britain

The assault by the Normans in 1066 may be the most famous **invasion of British soil**; but the most recent was that led by an American called Tate on this day in 1797. He landed at Strumble Head near Fishguard (aka Abergwaun) in Dyfed, bringing with him an army of French desperadoes. Tate's plan was to lead a peasant revolt against the landowners. However, his crack troops turned out to be cracked troops – French psychopaths and ex-convicts who promptly set about looting the surrounding countryside in search of alcohol, women, cash and more alcohol. They succeeded in overpowering the tiny, inept local militia, and set up headquarters in a local farm.

Two days later the local women were fed up with the invaders' repeated attempts to make French connections. Led by Jemima Nicholas and all wearing red, they bore down on the troops. As Jemima had hoped, the French soldiers mistook the women's garb for the red cloaks of the British army and fled to Goodwick beach. There the rebels surrendered to the ruthless Lord Cawdor and his men. Jemima, rather than Tate, passed into posterity, and became known locally as 'the General of the Red Army'. An inscribed stone on Goodwick beach marks the spot where the rebels surrendered to Cawdor. Jemima died in 1832, and her grave is in the Church of St Mary, Fishguard.

There are dusty corners of tradition which insist that today is the first day of spring. **Weatherwise** it is important, for if the day is cold there will be ice and misery in the weeks ahead. And if the night of the 22nd is snowy, or clear, or subtropical, or whatever, then these conditions will continue for the next 40 days. If the day is cold and the night is pleasant then there is a clash of superstitions, and Michael Fish will be forced to adjudicate.

In England this is **lambing** time. It is lucky to see the first lamb of the year with its head turned towards you; bad luck if it is looking away. Good luck can be boosted by turning over the loose change in your pockets.

Many prehistoric shepherds' counting rhymes survived into the 20th century – at least until the 1950s, and possibly beyond. They have tantalising echoes in other rhymes recorded around the world, notably those of North American Indians. This leads to the mind-expanding possibility that the herders of Britain and those of the American plains have the same prehistoric linguistic background; though it is possible that the Americans learned the rhymes from early European settlers. An example of a Lincolnshire counting rhyme runs: '*Yan, tan, tethera, pethera, pimp; sethera, methera, hothera, covera, dik; yan-a-dik, tan-a-dik*' and so on ending – unexpectedly – in '*bumfits*'. Every time the equivalent of 20 is reached the shepherd raises a finger, and can thus count to 200 without taking off his socks.

Shepherds were often buried with a tuft of wool in their hands. The practice was recorded as late as 1932 at Alfriston in Sussex. This was not an afterlife memento of their charges, but evidence designed to help convince St Peter that they had the best of excuses for not being regular church-goers.

23rd February
St Milburga's Day

Wenlock and Keyse

Things were tough in the 8th century. Innocent young **Milburga** – later to become Abbess of Wenlock Priory, at Much Wenlock in Shropshire – was riding through sunny Mercia when malevolent pagan vagabonds gave chase with their hounds. For two whole days she was pursued, until she fell bleeding to the ground. Fortunately, her blood seeped into the earth and, naturally, caused a well to spring spontaneously forth. This was enough to baffle the exhausted hounds, who knew a miracle when they saw one, and it allowed Milburga to make good her escape.

An alternative version says that the hounded Milburga fell and hit her head. She asked some nearby barley-mowers for water to clean the wound. '*What water?*' they gamely responded, at which Milburga commanded her horse to strike its hoof against a stone. It did, and water sprang forth.

Whatever its source, St Milburga's Well is still visible close to the church in Stoke St Milborough, near Ludlow in Shropshire.

A silver casket at Wenlock Priory (contents: Milburga's bones) was lost a few hundred years after her death. Only in the 12th century was it rediscovered, when some boys fell through the topsoil and landed amidst Milburga's mildewed remains. The rescued relics rapidly found fame for curing assorted blind people and lepers – it is said that local doctors went out of business for a few decades afterwards. But the relics' most spectacular remedy was effected on a man suffering from a wasting disease. He touched the bones, said a prayer, and vomited up a huge and hideous worm, the rather novel cause of his illness.

Not exactly a law, more a deep-rooted fear of incurring divine wrath, it was customary to reprieve a condemned man if he miraculously thwarted the gallows three times in one session. Not that this happened often. Last century John 'Babbacombe' Lee was accused of killing his employer Emma Keyse in Babbacombe, Devon. He was found guilty, and sentenced to hang by the neck until celebrated on a Fairport Convention record. It was a tough verdict. Lee protested his innocence and spoke of prophetic dreams assuring him that he would not die. The evidence against him included bloodstains on his clothes, the presence of the murder weapon in his room, and the fact that he was known to hate Emma Keyse. Apart from this the police had nothing to go on.

Come the day of execution, February 23rd 1885, the gallows trap-door at Exeter gaol was successfully tested and Lee prepared to swing. But the door failed to open. Retested, it opened perfectly. So again Lee got ready for the drop, and again the trap stayed shut. This whole farce was repeated one more time before the executioners gave up, blaming warped – if fickle – boards. Lee's death penalty was instantly commuted to a long stretch behind bars, and by the time of his release his escape from the gallows had converted him from villain into something of a local hero. John 'Babbacombe' Lee died in America in 1933 – of natural causes.

Fairport Convention recorded their concept album *Babbacombe Lee* – the folk-world equivalent of *Tommy* – in 1971.

24th February
St Matthias' Day

Dousing the Northern Lights

Today in 1716, James Ratcliffe, the last **Earl of Derwentwater**, and Viscount Kenmure of Scotland were beheaded on Tower Hill, London. They had been the joint leaders of an uprising which sought to kick out Hanoverian George I and install the son of James II as King James III. The Jacobites marched south and took Preston. It was a good start, but a bad end,

and they were all arrested there.

Derwentwater and Kenmure were popular heroes of the day, the subjects of various songs, notably Robert Burns' *Kenmure's On and Awa', Willie*; and the ballad *Lord Derwentwater*, often sung to the tune *Derwentwater's Farewell*. In the latter song our man receives the news of his imminent arrest and has nothing but a bad time from then on. One verse notes Derwentwater's violent horse-allergy:

> *He set his foot in the level stirrup and*
> *mounted his bonny grey steed,*
> *The gold rings from his fingers did break and*
> *his nose began for to bleed.*
> *He had not ridden past a mile or two when*
> *his horse stumbled over a stone;*
> *These are tokens, said My Lord*
> *Derwentwater, That I shall never return.*

Sure enough, a few verses later his head and body have parted company. By then Lady Derwentwater had high-tailed it from her holiday home on Lord's Island in Derwentwater, Cumbria. She eluded her foes by climbing a rock known afterwards as Lady's Rake (on Walla Crag at the lake's eastern side), taking the family treasure with her in the hope of ransoming her husband. But it was too late, and when news reached her of his death, she threw the family jewels into the lake. Often sought, they have never been found.

♱ Lord Derwentwater and his men regularly ride in ghostly form around his main home, Dilston, just outside Hexham in Northumberland. **Dilston Castle** itself is haunted by the hand-wringing ghost of his rakish wife, perpetually penitent for having talked her husband into signing up with the rebels.

Tradition states that when Derwentwater was executed, the stream at Dilston Hall ran red, the river Derwent turned into a torrent of vipers, and the sun became the colour of blood. The **aurora borealis** (Northern Lights) may have had something to do with all this. They are still known locally as Lord Derwentwater's Lights, and are said to have been first sighted on the day that he died.

☕ This is **St Matthias' Day**, variously mentioned as the day to start sowing, to '*shut up the bee*'; and to store a few candlesticks for those last dark days before spring. It is also a time of ice. It is said that St Matthias breaks the ice on the 24th, and if he cannot find any then he will make some. So things will either be icy today or else in the immediate future.

25th February
St Ethelbert's Day/
St Walburga's Day

Pagans at the Pearly Gates

Ethelbert (560–616) was king of Kent. His early life as a devout follower of pagan religions did not seem to point to a saintly ending. Even when the first Mediterranean missionaries dropped in on an unsuspecting England at the end of the 6th century, Ethelbert was sceptical. He gave Augustine and his monks an audience in the open air (to stop them employing indoor magic), and soberly accepted their words as being reasonable. Even though he could not bring himself to conform to the new religion, the king allowed his guests to pitch tents in Canterbury and preach to anyone who cared to listen.

Ethelbert was riding high in the king stakes; despite having been defeated in the Battle of Wimbledon in 568, he was popular with his pagan subjects and had no rivals in court. But his wife was a Christian, so it was perhaps inevitable that in 595 Ethelbert should risk everything by becoming the first Christian king in England. Augustine was installed as Archbishop of the English (head office: Canterbury), and within a decade most of Ethelbert's subjects had converted to the new faith. When Ethelbert died, he was, in the words of the Venerable Bede, '*The third English King to hold sway over all southern Britain, but the first to enter the Kingdom of Heaven.*'

The dimensions and interior decor of Heaven remain the subject of much speculation. It is roomy enough, though, to have space for a pagan earth goddess beloved of witches. Read Goethe's *Faust*, or a Dennis Wheatley tale of suburban satanism, and there you will find Walpurgis, alter-ego of **St Walburga**. Today is her feast day. She started life in England, and died today in 779 during missionary work in Germany. Medicinal oil flows perpetually from her tomb at Eichstatt. So far, so saintly; but somewhere down the line Walburga got muddled with the Germanic deity Walborg, and came to be represented by the goddess' symbol, three ears of corn. In this new guise, she was taken on board by revelling witches – both black and white. April 30th, the eve of her alternative festival day, is Walpurgis Night, traditionally a big pagan knees-up across most of mainland Europe.

◉ Still held periodically, either today or else on the nearest Wednesday, the sport of **Larding the Otter** is, tragically, unique to Halpsham in Shropshire. It involves a rugby-type battle in which two teams of 13 fight for possession of the 'otter' – a greased, old-fashioned three-pint leather bottle. If a player manages to get the bottle to his team's end of the 200-yard pitch – which is crossed by a river at one point – a 'holt' is scored, and the otter is re-greased. The winning team receives a fresh salmon. After the presentation of the prize at the *Greyhound* pub, the bottle is filled with beer, and the captain of the winning team has to drain it, standing in midstream on the Otterrock.

Legend says that an otter once stole a gigantic salmon from the kitchens of the long-gone Fulstow Hall – which stood just to the north of the village – and in evading the irate cooks the animal became covered in goose-grease from the recently roasted Sunday lunch. The man who caught the otter in his leather jerkin was awarded the fish, on condition that he re-enacted the kitchen chaos annually. '*To lard the otter*' became proverbial in these parts, meaning to tease someone by setting them an impossible task.

26th February

Fancy Dress Fast

✞ The Old Court House in London was the venue for **Christopher Wren's** death on this day in 1723. His ghost appears and pitter-patters across the first-floor dining room on the anniversary of his demise. His hands also brush against the walls; and on one occasion the ghost evidently had friends round. They were heard exercising the creaky floorboards on the stairs for most of the day. The Old Court House is near Hampton Court on Greater London's western rim. Wren stayed in the former while supervising work on the latter. The house has a second ghost: that of a long-haired boy who, from his attire, appears to have been a 17th-century page.

◉ On the last Friday in February it is **Red Feather Day** at the school named after and founded by the 18th-century Sheriff of London and City MP, Sir John Cass. Staff and pupils go to the nearby church of St Botolph's-without-Aldgate for a remembrance service, wearing red-dyed turkey feathers in their caps or lapels. Sir John was born on February 20th 1661 and baptised at St Botolph's. His life ran smoothly until moments before his death in 1718. As he was writing his last will and testament, Sir John's lungs haemorrhaged, and the blood stained his quill. With the eternal irony of posterity it is this unfortunate hiccup, rather than anything from his healthier heydays, which is remembered in today's service.

◉ Purim is a Jewish festival which hits the streets of Barnet in north London, Borehamwood and Elstree in Hertfordshire, and everywhere with a sizeable Jewish population. Purim takes place mainly behind closed doors. But because part of the ritual involves dressing in outlandish attire, celebrants can be seen doing the shopping or nipping to the Post Office dressed as clowns, Godzilla or Bambi.

The Jewish year is based on a lunar calendar. Purim falls on the moveable 14th of Adar, in late February or early March. Adar is the 12th month of the year, and the partying is encouraged in a traditional saying: '*When Adar begins, joy should be increased.*' But to add to the confusion, there are often 13 months instead of 12, in which case there are two Adars. Purim always falls in the second Adar.

The Book of Esther from the Bible is read at Purim, and the festival is based on the symbolism of that story. The feast itself commemorates escape from persecution, and the confirmation that it is God, and not blind Fate, who dictates the ways of the world. After fasting the night before, chief concerns on the day are extra prayers and trips to the synagogue. The outrageous dress-sense originated as a parody of strict authorities, and a comment on the mysterious ways in which God moves. In *Esther* God is assumed to be the off-stage force directing events and rescuing the Jews, though he is never explicitly mentioned as such. Mock-Rabbis used to be elected at Purim – they have parallels in the Lord of Misrule figure once predominant at various European winter festivals.

It is traditional at Purim to give alms to the poor and send food to needy neighbours. It is also a day for drinking alcohol. 'Purim' means 'a casting of lots', named after the lots which Haman, Persian king and enemy of the Jews, casts in *Esther* to decide when to launch his ill-fated attack. It is a popular feast, but is definitely on the fringe, a kind of folklore festival, though it is said that during the Messianic Age, all Jewish festivals will be abolished, apart from Purim.

27th February

Revving up at Borley

Marie Lairre was walled up in Borley, Essex after an illicit affair with a monk. Alternatively, she was strangled by the lord of the manor. Whichever is true, any ghost could be forgiven its disgruntled haunting after such an ignominious end. Marie was content with harmless manifestations in Borley village, roaming the streets and hanging out with a rather unoriginal coach and headless horses, until 1863, when Reverend H.D. Bull built **Borley Rectory** across one of her favourite routes. Marie decided it was time to up her profile. She began gazing in at the vicar through the window. He responded pragmatically, and bricked up the offending aperture. Soon after this his son, the Revd Harry Bull, inherited the post and the ghost.

Having her right of way impeded, and then being ignored, was too much for Ms Lairre. Ghostly coaches began to race through the rectory walls and out on to the lawn; and Marie, having perfected an expression of dismal woe – eyes closed, mouth agape – appeared at all hours of the day. In 1929 a new rector packed his bags when a flying candlestick bounced off his head. His successor, Reverend Lionel Foyster, witnessed flying objects, plummeting temperatures, and ghostly writing on the walls, apparently calling, in a calligrapher's nightmare of scribble, first for help, and then for '*light, Mass, candles*'.

A 1938 seance at Borley Rectory reported that Marie Lairre had indeed been strangled (in 1667, to be precise), and was buried somewhere near the house. But at the sequel to this seance another ghost interrupted the proceedings like a clumsy railway station announcer. It revealed that its name was Sunex Amures, and that the house would burn down that very night, March 27th. Everyone expected the worst; but the rectory remained flame-free. The following year on February 27th the prediction lurched into belated action: a levitating lamp flung itself to the floor and the rectory was razed. Marie was seen at one of the upstairs windows as the flames danced. Bones were then discovered under the house and given Christian burial. Sunex '11 Months Out' Amures was too embarrassed to comment.

✙ And so it should have ended. But Marie Lairre was ultimately unimpressed by all the action. She still roams the Borley roads when the mood takes her, favouring the month of June.

You too could be like Marie Lairre. For those wishing to make a few additional bows after facing the final curtain, practise those woeful expressions, and when your bucket is about to be kicked, put some **pigeon feathers** under your pillow. You will then roam with the undead, if that's your cup of tea. In Emily Brontë's *Wuthering Heights*, Catherine Earnshaw's ghost refers to this belief, when she says: '*Ah! They put pigeon's feathers in the pillow – no wonder I couldn't die.*' Once someone finds and removes the feathers, your ghosting will end.

28th February
St David's Eve/St Oswald
of Worcester's Day

Dog-Geese from Hell

Today is St David's Eve – the Calendar of Saints does not include 29th February, and so St David's Eve is always on the 28th. In Wales it is one of the favourite nights for the **Cwn Annwn** – hounds of *Annwn*, the Underworld – to take to the skies. Howling and racing across the heavens in dog-form, the Cwn Annwn are actually the souls of the damned, out to hunt more souls for the sin-hungry furnaces of Hell. They do not devour the doomed like spiritual Bonios, but merely portend death for whoever is unfortunate enough to hear them. Sometimes they appear as huge hounds with human heads. They do not fetch sticks or say '*sausages*'.

Their howls are distinctive. From a distance they sound like lamentations and hellish screams, but as the hounds get closer they are reported to sound prosaically like a pack of small beagles with a lone bloodhound baying in its midst. More often than not their cries suspiciously resemble those of migrating geese.

Most pre-Christian religions had hunts similar to the Cwn Annwn. They were led by diverse personages down the ages, from Woden to Francis Drake, as well as the Devil and various faeries. In the 12th century, in a well-documented sighting of the hounds, a huge

pack of black dogs, horses and huntsmen was seen to stretch from Stamford to Peterborough in a medieval traffic jam. The last mass sighting of the wild hunt was near Taunton, Somerset, in 1940. For more on the celestial hunt, see January 20th.

St Oswald – whose feast day is today – had a more diminutive encounter with other worldly denizens whilst engaged in the building of Worcester Cathedral. Despite pushing, pulling, levering, and innumerable tea-breaks, 80 men repeatedly failed to move a certain stone that was vital to the structure. Then someone noticed that a grinning imp was lounging atop the lump of masonry. The workers called for Oswald. The Worcester saint had a word in the imp's ear and it took to its heels. In the space of a sentence, the cathedral was successfully completed.

✙ ☕ ▥ A **ghostly woman in white** opens one of the doors at Hathersage rectory, in the Peak District of Derbyshire, on this night. After this she, er, goes away again. Perhaps she is just checking the **weather** – a clear sky today foretells a good year. Hathersage, by the way, also happens to be the last resting place of **Little John**: his 14-foot-long grave is in the churchyard. He is said to have died here of a broken heart after the death of Robin Hood in Kirklees near Leeds.

29th February
Leap Day

Date with God-Head

This day only comes around every four years, as the Earth inconveniently returns to its starting point after 365.2422 days. A natural tendency to call it 365.25 led to the eventual accumulation of a surplus, even with **Leap Years** in play. To be truly accurate – to get over the discrepancy of 0.0078 days – someone worked out that you must exclude the last year of the century from the Leap Year rule, except when the year number is divisible by 400. In practice, this means that 1700, 1800, and 1900 were not Leap Years, but 1600 was and 2000 will be. By the way, December 31st 2000 is the official last day of the 20th century and the second millenia, but that will not prevent everyone from going completely hog-wild a year earlier.

The Leap Year idea goes right back to the Ancient Greeks, but it took a long time for anyone to cotton on to those extra 0.0078 days that kept creeping in. On the manifest evidence of reliably occurring events such as the longest and shortest days, by 1582 the European calendar was adrift by 10 days. So Pope Gregory XIII consulted the mathematicians and took the radical step of axing those extra days. Catholic countries all joined in; but Britain was unimpressed and thought it a Protestant mootpoint to stick to the **Old Calendar**. For the best part of two centuries Britain remained out of step with Europe.

It was not until 1752 that we adopted the Gregorian version – by which time another day had accumulated, and 11 days were lost to the void of logic. There were a few riots by those who claimed to have been robbed of 11 days of their lives, and, more to the point, 11 days of pay. Indeed the confusion in folklore and customs terms has continued. The 'Old' and 'New' dates for each festival or observance derive from this mess. Hence such peculiarities as Twelfth Night wassailing celebrations taking place on January 16th, or the Scottish island of Foula still celebrating Christmas and New Year according to the Old Calendar. Further confusion arose when some event-organisers calculated for 10 or 12 days instead of 11. Calamity, chaos and confusion.

The 29th – or the entire **Leap Year** – is the time when a woman can propose to a man; but only if she is wearing red petticoats. A man who refuses the proposal must buy the woman a pair of gloves for Easter, or a silk gown – which can only be handed over if the woman flashes the aforementioned loud petticoats. Enlightened tradition-lovers point out that this is a load of old sexist rubbish.

Broad beans are said to grow the wrong way in a Leap Year, according to Nottinghamshire lore; while around Peebles in the Scottish Borders they reckon: '*A Leap Year is never a good sheep year.*'

In Scotland, Leap Years are unlucky, and of all the leaping days, February 29th is the unluckiest. This is linked to the fact that, even if the Bible neglects to mention it, today is Job's birthday. Job once got out of bed on the wrong side and cursed the day that he was born. This curse blighted the day, which is why God only lets it happen every four years. God explained all the apparent injustices of the world to Job after manifesting in his hair. And with an infestation of divinity on your head, you need to be very patient. But no matter how much Godhead & Shoulders he used, Job always had deity hair.

SHROVETIDE

Just before Lent comes **Shrovetide**: the Saturday, Sunday, Monday and Tuesday preceding the fast – four days in which to eat all the soon-to-be-illegal stuff in the pantry. The *Shrove* bit comes from the fact that people used to receive a post-confession blessing – a shriving – to see them through the lean days ahead. The event is moveable, depending on the whereabouts of ever-restless Easter.

Shrovetide gets under way with Quinquagesima Eve. *Quinquagesima* probably comes from the Latin for 'fiftieth', referring to the approximate 50 days until Easter Sunday. In Lincolnshire, Quinquagesima Eve is known as **Brusting Saturday**. The name derives from a thick, crumbly pancake called brusting pudding, which was rustled up by the panful throughout the county. Another Brusting dish was the *gofer*: not an American burrowing rodent on toast, but a type of hot buttered waffle cooked in a special gofer-iron. The same day was **Egg Saturday** in Oxford as, getting in there ahead of the rest of the country, all the students were given decorated eggs.

The next day, Quinquagesima Sunday, is a quiet one in terms of customs and traditions, with the real Shrovetide excesses starting on the Monday. A collop is an egg fried on a thick rasher of bacon, or – in some parts of the country – just the meat itself. **Collop Monday** was the day for guzzling as many as possible; or, in poorer areas, to go begging for collops – they provided the fat for Shrove Tuesday pancakes, and were also a welcome foodstuff. Vegetarians should move to Cornwall, where collops are eschewed rather than chewed. Here the day is **Peasen Monday**, and pea soup is the only thing on the menu.

Across the West Country the Monday evening was one of mischief and vandalism. **Nickanan Night** was its name, and its Nick was definitely of the Old school. Youths went around mutilating doors, unhinging gates, filling unguarded houses with rubbish, dousing passers-by in water and soot – anything or anyone on the streets and not tied down was at risk. All the stolen items were heaped up in a public place, and those whose property found

its way into the pile were not considered unlucky, but negligent. An accompanying rhyme sets the tone of the night:

Nicky, nicky nan,
Give me a pancake and then I'll be gone,
But if you give me none
I'll throw a great stone
And down your door shall come.

In Devon this was **Dappy Door Night**, a PG-certificate version of the Nickanan shenanigans, with gangs of youths engaging in inane tricks such as knocking on doors and running away. There is more of this sort of fun on Shrove Tuesday.

Other general Shrovetide delicacies include doughnuts fried in hog's lard, once a favourite at Baldock in Hertfordshire; and Norwich Coquilles, which were buns in the shape of miniature loaves.

SHROVE TUESDAY

The high water mark of Shrovetide is Shrove Tuesday, now more commonly known as **Pancake Day**, an epic bout of eating and sport. It was also called by several other names, including Bannock Nicht or Brose Tuesday in Scotland, as oatmeal bannocks and brose – a thick savoury broth – featured heavily, along with beef. It was said that if you did not tuck into some beef today your livestock would fail. Another delicacy was the fitness or fastyn cock: a boiled suet and oat dumpling shaped like a chicken.

Fairs were common today, including the oddly named **Saint Rattle Doll Fair** at Crowland in Lincolnshire. The rattling was done by dice, which were used in mass gambling for nuts and oranges. The dolls belonged to some of the accompanying stalls; and the 'Saint' bit was added to give the event a thin veneer of respectability.

And so to **pancakes**. As a by-product of the need for lots of cracked eggs, the preliminary school sport of **egg-shackling** evolved. Each egg was given the name of a 'player', and jiggled in a sieve until only one – the winner – remained whole. The version at St Columb Major in Cornwall was even messier, a game of conkers with a bowl to catch the splattered eggs. Easy, harmless, silly and useful: egg-shackling is an ideal candidate for a Shrove Tuesday revival.

© ☺ Across most of the country, **pancake bells** sounded at 11 am. In Cheshire they were called the Guttit bells, as 'good'-eating competitions were a popular feature of the day. The pancake bell still rings in some places. At Scarborough, the bell is now in the local museum, and its noon chimes summon the townsfolk to the beach; but not to catch fish (see below). The pancake peal also sounds elsewhere in Yorkshire, at Bingley and Richmond. When the pancake bell rings at Darlington in County Durham, the nearby Bulmer's Stone is said to turn round nine times. But since the bell no longer sounds there today, the stone just continues to gather moss. Originally these peals rang out to summon penitents for a pre-Lent shriving or blessing, but it gradually came to be the nationwide signal for each home's pancake-making to begin. Most families now stick to making, tossing and eating pancakes, but some still play a series of games during the cooking. In one version, everyone has to toss their own pancakes and they are forced to eat the results, even if their cake lands on the cat. Alternatively – or simultaneously – you must devour your pancake before the next one has finished cooking. Slow eaters are punished by being thrown into a bush or on to the dung-heap.

The idea of making food and having fun simultaneously was too much for some people. Writing in 1630, one Puritan clearly thought that it was the original recipe for disaster: '. . . *there is a thing called wheaten floure, which the cookes do mingle with water, eggs, spice, and other tragical, magical inchantments, and then they put it by little and little into a frying pan of boiling suet, where it makes a confused dismal hissing, like the Lernean Snakes in the reeds of Acheron, Stix, or Phlegeton . . . a Pancake, which ominous incantation the ignorant people doe devoure very greedily.*'

Fortunately the 'tragical, magical inchantments' survived this onslaught, benefiting from the addition of lemon and sugar. One pancake-related ritual which did seem to have a hint of the occult about it took place at Eton in Berkshire. In 1560 records show that the cook at the college tied his pancake to a crow which had recently hatched its chicks. This appears to have been a one-off act of oddness, but may have had some deeper, darker significance.

© **Pancake races** are now a regular Shrove Tuesday fixture in many towns and villages, but few of these scaled-up egg-and-spoon races date from before the 1960s. There are one or two honourable exceptions. **Olney**, north of Milton Keynes in Buckinghamshire, has supposedly traced its high-street dash back to 1445, when a preoccupied pancaker heard the church bells and rushed to the service, still carrying her pan. The story may not be true, but the race is very old. The town centre is cordoned off, and a bell is rung twice: firstly to order the making of the cakes; and then again at 1 pm to start the race. The distance run is 415 yards, from the Market Square to the church. Competitors must be women over 18 who have been resident for at least three months. They have to wear aprons and bonnets; and must toss the pancakes at least three times during the sprint. The winner receives the dubious prize of a kiss from the verger; and both she and the runner-up are given new prayer-books. Everyone then attends a church service, during which the pans are piled by the side of the altar. In the 1960s, an Olney vicar emigrated to the town of Liberal in Kansas, and imported the pancake race tradition. The two races are now run simultaneously and over the same distance, with a telephone link-up to make sure the transatlantic toss-up runs smoothly.

© The race at **Winster** near Matlock in Derbyshire also goes back hundreds of years. Open to anyone who brings their own pan and pancake, it is run from 2 pm between the Dower House and the Old Market House, with different categories for different ages and sexes, and small prizes for the winners. The demands of the sport are such that Winster has developed its own special racing pancake, not recommended for eating, but tough enough to survive sustained jogging and tossing.

● Not all pancake sports are races. Westminster School in London each year stages the **Pancake Greaze**. The cook, dressed in white, enters the Great Schoolroom with a mace-bearing verger, and tosses a pancake from his pan over a bar 16 feet off the ground. The boys then scramble, and whoever escapes from the brawl with the largest portion is the winner. He is not encouraged to eat the spoils of victory – the pancake has been made from a mix of Polyfilla and horsehair – but the boy is given prize-money of one guinea. Only once this century has the cook's skill failed: in 1934 the pancake stuck on the bar, and a substitute had to be swiftly cooked. But in 1865 a less skilled tosser who missed the bar three times was set upon by the boys, who threw all their schoolbooks at him. The cook retaliated by hurling the monster pan at the assailants, and one of the children suffered a severe head wound.

There were, and are, enough Shrove Tuesday sports to fill a 24-hour edition of *Grandstand*. And most have nothing to do with eggs, flour and milk. This was the big day for **cock-fighting**, with school-children bribing their teachers a cock-penny to abandon lessons in favour of staging their own bird-brainings. In Scotland the master acted as invigilator at the fights, and could claim any cock which fled the arena. These teachers' pets were called **forgers**; and the cash which they generated, together with that which the teacher had been given in cock-pennies, provided a substantial fillip to his annual income. The boy who owned the winning cock – the one still crowing when all the others were dead – was exempt from punishment during Lent, and could confer this privilege on any of his pals by beating them with his cap.

Perhaps even crueller than cock-fighting, and almost as popular, was **cock-throwing**, or cock-squailing. As an old rhyme says:

And on Shrove Tuesday when the bell does ring,
We will go out at hens and cocks to fling.

The bird was tethered, and heavy sticks were thrown at it from a distance. The winner was the first person who concussed the bird and managed to grab it before it regained consciousness. At Brighton fowls were suspended in pots over the street, and pitched at for 2d a go. These cock-throwings were so boisterous that passers-by were occasionally killed by a missile. This, rather than the appalling treatment of the animal, was the reason for the demise of the game.

A Sussex variation was **thrashing the hen**, which required tying a chicken to a man covered in bells. Blindfolded competitors then tried to beat it to death. To the amusement of spectators, by the time the bird had been killed the participants had usually beaten each other black and blue.

In some parts of the country – notably Somerset and parts of the north-west – a less bloodthirsty version of the sport evolved in which men threw at **Lenycocks**, which were in fact daffodils. At Wildboarclough in Che-

shire the game survived until just before the Second World War, although by then the targets were old cotton bobbins, with the chicken stepping in as the prize only.

For close to 1,000 years cock-fighting in all its forms was probably Britain's number one sport. It was popular at all levels of society: James I and Charles II were both devotees, and Henry VIII had a cockpit built at Whitehall for his entertainment. Few seemed to perceive its inherent cruelty, and some of its strongest supporters were among the clergy – at Barnoldby-le-Beck in Humberside the cockpit was in the vicarage garden, and at Wednesbury in Staffordshire the vicar went to extraordinary lengths to show his support (see May 15th for the full story). In the 1840s a Blackburn blacksmith reputedly sold his soul to the Devil in order to have enough cash for gambling on cocks; but he may not have got a good deal, as in 1849 cock-fighting was finally banned in Britain. However, unfortunately, to this day illegal fights continue to be held.

⚏ Cock-fighting goes back at least as far as the Greeks and Romans, and one dubious theory as to why it became so big in England suggests that it stems from the Latin for domestic fowl, *Gallus*, also a nick-name for the French. So *le coq sportif* symbolised the Englishman terrorising the old enemy. A sculpture at Blenheim Palace in Oxfordshire showing a lion attacking a cock is thought by some to be an architectural pun.

Shrovetide football – a mixture of rugby, hurling and soccer – has managed to outlive the chickens. There are 50 or so traditional sites for the game, though only a few matches survive. The game at Chester-le-Street in County Durham lingered until 1932. Over the years Derby grew to expect the annual influx of roistering rowdiness that accompanied its Shrove Tuesday game, but in 1839 there were scenes of unprecedented mayhem. The army intervened, the Riot Act was read and the game ceased to be. After this, only a local bell-rhyme remained:

Pancakes and fritters, say All Saints and
St Peter's,
When will the ball come?, say the bells of
St Alkmun,
At two they will throw, says St Werabo,
Oh very well, says little St Michael.

© There are six notable survivals of the Shrove Tuesday ball. **Sedgefield** near Darlington in County Durham kicks off at 1 pm, with the ball passed three times through a small ring – known as the Bull Ring – on the village green. It is then thrown to the baying pack of anything up to 1,000 players. The 500-yard pitch stretches between the two goals: the old duck pond and a stream. Once a goal has been scored, the ball is manhandled back up the field and passed through the Bull Ring three times, bringing the game to an end. All this can take several hours, and the ball is usually to be found at the bottom of a multi-bodied scrum. The game dates back to the 13th century: only locals participate, and they can draw inspiration from an inscription on the 1923 ball:

When the pancakes you are sated
Come to the ring and you'll be mated
There this ball will be upcast
May this game be better than the last.
God Save the King.

© At **Alnwick** in Northumberland, garlanded goals stand by two bridges roughly 200 yards apart on land known as the Pastures. The ball is brought out with the Duke of Northumberland's piper, the most skilful player on the pitch. With teams 100 or so strong, the game ends when one of the teams has scored two hales – goals – after which the men compete to carry the ball, via the River Aln, to an allotted boundary for a prize. If by midnight the two sides are still on course for a hale-less draw, the ball has to be handed to the local constabulary, and the game is resumed on Ash Wednesday. The game's minimalist rules say that no motorised vehicles may be used in the game, and stipulate that there must be *'no murder, no manslaughter'*.

© **Ashbourne** in Derbyshire starts its game at 2 pm at the traditional Shawcroft site, which used to be a field but is now a car park. The Up'ards, born on one side of the river Henmore, take on the Down'ards, born on the other. The goals are a colossal three miles apart, with several streams in between, and the ball is weighted to prevent it being kicked or thrown too far. It comes as no great surprise to learn that the biggest ever victory was 2–0. Again, if there is no score at the end of the day, the match resumes on Ash Wednesday.

© At **Atherstone** near Nuneaton in Warwickshire, the inhabitants claim that their annual match originated in the reign of King John, when men played with and for a bag of gold. This makes a change from the story put forward about most other mass football games, namely that they began as a kick-about after some great battlefield victory, using the heads of the vanquished enemies as balls. At Atherstone the main road is an important part of the pitch, and so traffic has to be diverted. The game starts at 3 pm, and after 4.30 pm it is legal to deflate the water-filled ball, a rule which could liven up the national game. Whoever is at the bottom of the scrum at 5 pm is the winner: they get to keep the ball and can go round the district collecting money.

© The match at **Corfe Castle** in Dorset takes place after the annual midday meeting of the Ancient Order of Purbeck Marblers and Stonecutters at the Town Hall. Apprentices seeking to join the Order must each bring along a quart of ale, a penny loaf, and 6s 8d (33p). The most recently wed member of the Order must bring along a football, which is then used in a vigorous game on the streets of the town. The pitch used to extend all the way to Owre Quay on Poole Harbour, three miles away, and the match is an ancient means of maintaining the right of way so that local Purbeck Marble can be taken to the port. This route passes through Owre Farm, and even though the Quay is long gone and the match now sticks to Corfe itself, each Shrove Tuesday the farm's owner is still paid a pound of pepper – a literal peppercorn rent – for allowing the Marblers to cross his land.

© The sport at **St Columb Major**, east of Newquay in Cornwall, has been described as *'aerial rugby'*. Officially it goes under the title of **hurling** rather than football, hurling being a very popular sport in old Celtic areas, especially Ireland. The goals are two miles apart, and from 4.30 pm teams of several hundred run through the village's boarded-up streets. The game must be over by 8 pm, and the winner is the first person to score a goal. The small ball is silver-coated, perhaps a relic of sun-worship. To touch it brings good luck; and after the game it is dipped in beer. This becomes 'silver-ale', and whether it brings luck or not it is certainly consumed in vast quantities. Eleven days later, on the second Saturday after Shrove Tuesday, there is a rematch, again at 4.30 pm. Although this is the more recent of the two games, the fact that it is at a weekend means that even more players and spectators attend.

All these games have done well to avoid the fate of the Chester match, which was curbed in 1539 as a result of: *'Some having their bodies brused or crushed; some their arms, heades, or legges broken, and some otherwise maimed or in peril of their lives.'*

Football and cock-fighting were sports that united the nation on Shrove Tuesday. But different corners of the country also had their own peculiar pastimes. Among the strangest was the two-part sport at the Newarke area at the old castle in Leicester. As each game of shinney – a primitive version of hockey – drew to a close, the **Whipping Toms** leaped on to the pitch. These were men with whips assisted by attendants with bells. They attacked the shinney players, who were jeered by the crowd if they did not stand their ground. The Toms could only whip below knee-level, and if a shinney player managed to grab one of the bellmen, they had to stop altogether. It would come as something of a shock if an event with such a violent basis did not regularly climax in brawls and large-scale arrests, and in 1847 it was whipped off the Leicester sporting calendar. It is said to have begun as a commemoration of the driving-out of the Vikings in 1002.

In the absence of people (and chickens), whipping-tops was also a favourite Shrove Tuesday pursuit, as was **knur and spell**. The knur – a small wooden or glass or Wedgwood pottery ball – is tipped or mechanically flipped into the air, and whacked as far as possible by the batsman. There were numerous variations in rules and spelling; and just as all of them were close to extinction, cricketer Fred Trueman helped revive interest when he showcased knur and spell on a 1969 television programme. Now each summer there are usually several games and exhibition matches in the game's last strongholds, the moorlands of Yorkshire and Lancashire.

At Ludlow in Shropshire, the name of the game on Shrove Tuesday was **rope-pulling**. The two teams, the Blue and the Red Knobs, stood between two rivers, and pulled on a thick 36-yard-long rope with knobs at each end. The winner was the first team to dip its knob in the water. The losers could then pay for a rematch, and if they won, there was a decisive third bout. The rope was then sold, and beer was purchased with the proceeds. Feelings ran high; and after regular punch-ups and the occasional improvised lynching had led to several upbraidings, rope-pulling was banned in 1851.

☺ The ropes at Scarborough have survived, but are much more genteel. In former years, this was Ball Day: balls were sold on the streets for football matches, and the beaches were crammed with people playing all kinds of Shrovetide sports. These days the pancake bell rings at noon, summoning thousands of rope-fans to the South Foreshore beach for a mass outbreak of **skipping**. This was the time of year when fishermen repaired their nets, and the skipping seems to have stemmed from the imaginative utilisation of the discarded fishing tackle. The sport made a leap in popularity when a film-crew captured it in 1927, billing it, with slight exaggeration, as an ancient custom. These days anyone can join in: ropes are provided, and the skipping lasts until dusk or an exceptionally high tide.

🎲 With games to be played and pancakes to be eaten, work was out of the question on Shrove Tuesday. At Norton-in-Hales, Shropshire, **bradling** was the penalty for anyone who showed up at factory, forge, field or office. This involved being dragged back and forth over the Bradling Stone on the village green whilst being beaten. The stone can still be seen at the front of the church. For the twin reasons of no-work and no-flesh, it was especially bad for prostitutes to ply their trade today, in spite of patrons who argued that it was a valid sport. Raids were mounted on brothels, and sometimes the inmates were whipped through the streets.

Lack of labour did not mean lack of activity, and everyone was expected to be up and about cooking or playing games. On Shrove Tuesday the last person in the household to rise from their pit suffered a special treat known as the **Bed Churl** – they were thrown into the family midden. Similarly, the last child to arrive at class was called the **Besom Stale**: the poor pupil was hoisted onto a pole or chair and subjected to derision and horseplay as a warm-up for the cock-fighting to come.

👁 For those in a more serious frame of mind, Shrove Tuesday augurs well for all manner of **divinations**. The first pancake of the day should be tossed into the chicken coop. If the cock eats first, it means that you will have many eggs; if the chief hen is first on the scene, it means many chickens. But which came first? Alternatively, if marriage is on your mind, the chickens can help. The number of birds who peck at the pancake represent the number of years left until the big day; though if the cock pecks first, you will marry within the year. In general, giving the first pancake to the chickens is supposed to increase the hens' egg yield.

👁 If eggs are cracked into water today, the shapes they form indicate future events; although there are not many ways of interpreting a white mass with a big yellow blob in the middle. One person should then remove the eggs from the water in silence, and use them to make a bannock or scone. Place it under your pillow, or in your left-foot sock at bedtime, if you wish to dream of things to come. The addition of soot assists in the magic, but wrecks the taste; and if you specifically want to dream about a forthcoming relationship, a ring should be added to the list of ingredients. In Scotland this concoction was the *bannich bruader*, the **dreaming bannock**. Even today dreamers are encouraged to put faith in the all-powerful egg – an advert in the 1994 *Old Moore's Almanack* reveals how readers can use eggs to enhance their finances, health and sex life. Stage one involves sending some money to Folkestone . . .

⊙ **Matrimonial Brose** can be made on Shrove Tuesday too. A ring is hidden in the thick broth, and each time it turns up on someone's spoon, it is returned to the pot. The first person to find it more than once will soon be married.

Today was also the principal date for **church-clipping** – holding hands and circling the church. At South Petherton in Somerset, and Bradford-on-Avon, Warminster and Trow-bridge in Wiltshire, the clipping was preceded by a game of **Threading the Needle**. Couples danced through the streets in meandering lines, each taking it in turn to form an arch through which the others threaded. The game ended at the church, which was usually clipped three times, sunwise. At Trowbridge they used to sing:

> *Shrove Tuesday, Shrove Tuesday, when Jack went to plough,*
> *His mother made pancakes, she didn't know how;*
> *She tipped them, she tossed them, she made them so black,*
> *She put so much pepper she poisoned poor Jack.*

On a final note of violence, Shrove Tuesday was the main time for **lensharding**. Children went from door to door seeking alms; and if none were forthcoming, they showered porches and front gardens with broken crockery. The fun was also known as pansherding or Lent-crocking, giving the day the alternative names Sharp Tuesday or Lincrook Day. The unlikely excuse in the Stour-prefixed villages near Shaftesbury in Dorset was that the lenshard-ing commemorated King Alfred. He arrived in the district and needed to summon an army at short notice, so someone rode through the streets throwing things at the doors. The story seems more plausible as an explanation of how American paper-boys developed their unique delivery style.

Lensharding was most popular in the South West, including the Scilly Isles. In some areas wood was thrown, and there are tales of house-holders with strong doors encouraging children to attack as their missiles provided a welcome addition to the log-pile. Songs accompanied most lenshardings, and even in the more genteel version, known simply as **shroving**, the lyrics unsubtly implied that violence would follow if the singers were not given money or food:

> *Please I've come a-shroving*
> *For a piece of pancake or a little ruckle of cheese*
> *Of your own making.*
> *If you don't give me some, if you don't give me none*
> *I'll rottle your door and away I'll run.*

© Shroving survived longest at East Hendred in Berkshire, Old Milton in Hampshire and Durweston in Dorset. In Durweston, local man Valentine Rickman left money in his 1925 will to pay for the continuance of shroving amongst the schoolboys, and for flowers to be left on his grave. In 1993 the headmistress of the local school decided that the flowers should be given to the living rather than the dead, and children now sing a shroving song as they hand out flowers to passers-by.

© Today at Clovelly, near Bideford in De-von, boys drag cans through the streets and down to the beach at dusk, symbolically driving the Devil into the sea, a task so satisfying that the boys do not feel the need to collect alms as they go. At Gittisham, outside Honiton in the same county, there is a vague threat of linger-ing-with-intent as children go **tip-toeing** from house-to-house in the early evening:

> *Tip, tip, toe, please for a penny*
> *And then we'll go.*

LENT

Lent, in reality, is a surfeit of pancake followed by 40 days of culinary business-as-usual. It is meant to be a fast, a time of constrained eating, stretching from Ash Wednesday to Easter. Above and beyond marking Jesus' stint in the wilderness, Lent was also a seasonal necessity, making a virtue of the fact that there was very little food around at this time of year. The word 'Lent' derives from the old name for March, 'Lenten-tide month', meaning the time when the days lengthen. The fast period itself was known as a *carne vale*, literally a 'farewell to flesh'. Over the centuries 'carnival' has managed an almost 180-degree shift in meaning. The date of Lent is calculated simply by subtracting 40 days from Easter Sunday.

The food rules allow only one proper meal per day, with meat, eggs, dairy produce and wine all off the menu. These constraints made Lent a boom-time for fishmongers. In medieval days **lampreys** were one of the most favoured fish: King John elevated them to luxury status by making lampreys weigh in at two shillings (10p) a gill – a colossal sum in those days.
Mindful of this seasonal fish-dependency, in 1537 John Thake of Clavering, near Saffron Walden in Essex, left a **herring** will. He bequeathed land, the interest from which was to pay for a barrel of red herrings and 720 white herrings to be given to the local poor over Lent. Thake's fishy bequest continued until just before the First World War, when the poor pointed out that they would rather just have the money. The charity continues, but has now been amalgamated with several others in the area. A board with the words of Thake's will can still be seen at the church in Clavering.

Similarly, David Salter of Farnham Royal in Berkshire left herring for the needy, along with two shillings to buy the clergyman a pair of kid-gloves. He could have bought a lamprey with that.

At the back end of Lent in Oxfordshire, children would try to cadge a few alms with the song:

Herrings, herrings, white and red,
Ten a penny, Lent's dead,

Rise, dame, and give an egg
Or else a piece of bacon;
One for Peter, two for Paul,
Three for Jack-a-Lent's all,
Away, Lent, away!

Like all people on diets, those fasting at Lent stretched the definition as to what was and was not permissible to eat. In the Middle Ages whales, dolphins and seals all fell into the fish category. Beavers were also permissible as their underwater lifestyle proved that they were fish. And **barnacle geese** found their way to the table via the great is-it-a-fish-or-a-bird-or-a-crab-or-a-fruit argument, as detailed on January 12th.

Lent **weatherlore** and general **proverbs** abound, from '*Marry in Lent and you'll live to repent*' to the more cheerful '*Dry Lent, fertile year*'. Shrove Tuesday – the day before the fast starts – is the key to the Lent weather: the amount of Shrove sunshine will be echoed on every day of Lent. A thundery Shrove Tuesday means a year of crops and plenty, but lots of wind. It is also vital to beat dogs during Lent, as it was believed that they would otherwise go mad.

THE FIRST WEEK OF LENT

Lent kicks off with **Ash Wednesday**, when nothing white must be worn. The relevant ashes are the ones which were sprinkled on penitent people at today's sombre church services. Curses were read aloud, deriding any unrepentant sinner: the congregation said *Amen* after each curse. As a result Ash Wednesday was known as **Cussing Day**, the one time when the church sanctioned the insulting of neighbours.

After all the sport and fun of Shrove Tuesday, Ash Wednesday is relatively tranquil. But in the Holderness area of Humberside, a few hours were put aside for a round of **Tutt-ball**. This is a version of rounders, with three bases instead of four. The batsman strikes the ball with a hand, and the single bowler-cum-fielder tries to catch it or successfully hit the striker with it as the latter nips round the bases. If the bowler succeeds, he swaps places with the batsman, and so it goes on.

The **marble** season officially opens on Ash Wednesday, lasting through until Good Friday. The lowliest of all marbles are the home-baked clay marradiddles. Up-market traditional marbles include alleys, poppos, barios and stonies. See Good Friday for more on how to lose your marbles.

Having horrified with Shrove tales of thrashed chickens, it is time to introduce the morally acceptable face of the sport. **Aunt Sallys** were straw-stuffed human effigies used for beating and target practice on Ash Wednesday: see August 28th for details of their modern form. In Cornwall the figure was the more sinister **Jack-a-Lent**. He, she or it is a scapegoat figure, possibly based on Judas Iscariot, though probably derived from an old winter god. Jack was dragged through the streets today and ceremonially hanged.

© Foodwise, if you ate pancakes yesterday, then eat some yummy grey peas today and you will have unrelenting Lent luck ahead. But save some peas for Carling Sunday (see Passion Sunday, below). In 1612 Alderman John Norton of London took pity on his fellows in the **Stationers' Company** – evidently suffering after a whole 12 hours of Lent – and left them, in his will, cash to buy beer and buns today. After enjoying their morning snack, the Company, in full formal regalia, process from the Stationers' Hall to the crypt of St Paul's Cathedral, where a special service is held.

The Thursday after Ash Wednesday revels under the wonderful name **Fruttors Thursday**. If you like fritters, then this is the day for you. They were usually currant-stuffed ones. In Lincolnshire the day was **Clerk Thursday**: teachers were locked out of the classroom by their pupils until they granted the school a day's holiday.

© A dazzling combination of football and anarchy, the **Jedburgh Hand Ba' Game** has been played at Jedburgh, Borders, for centuries. It was banned in 1704 on the not unreasonable grounds that: '*There have been sometimes both old and young near lost their lives thereby*.' It only survived by becoming a slightly less murderous game of handball. The game is known as the **Fastern's E'en Ba' Game**, and by rights it should take place on Fastern's E'en – which across most of the country is an alternative name for Shrove Tuesday. But in Jedburgh they insist that Fastern's E'en is in fact the first Tuesday after the first new moon after Candlemas, February 2nd. However, since this almost invariably *is* Shrove Tuesday, Jedburgh's distinction is rather mystifying. In recent years the formula has become even more complicated with the game having shifted two days to Fruttor's Thursday. The Boys' Game begins at noon, with the main game at 2 pm. In theory anyone can play the Ba' Game, but the organisers recommend it only to the strong and stupid.

The ball, decorated with coloured streamers, can be thrown or carried. The windows of all shops and houses are barricaded as the two sides – the Uppies versus the Downies – scramble across street, garden and field, until they end up in the River Jed. Great fun, and even more futile than American football. Locally it is said with ill-concealed glee that the game originated in the Border wars – after the Scots victory at Ferniehirst Castle near Jedburgh, the heads of some of the vanquished English were used as balls for an impromptu kickabout. The whistle was nearly blown on the match in 1849 when strenuous attempts were made to quash the tradition. But the townsfolk won an appeal in the High Court at Edinburgh, and saved the game.

The next day, Friday, used to be Kissing or **Nippy-Hug Day** at Sileby, Leicestershire. The ancient practice involved a ritual to make a new man shudder. Sileby males could exact kisses from the women they met, and if the kiss was refused, they were entitled to pinch the woman's bottom. This dubious custom was reintroduced in the 1970s by the local vicar. Mercifully, it has since died out again. In some areas a similar event took place on Shrove Tuesday, and was known as **Lousing**. A 'loused' girl was supposed to be unofficially betrothed to her seducer.

The first Sunday in Lent used to be fire-festival time on the Channel Islands. Known as the **Dimanche de Brandons**, it originated at the Pointe de Clonque on Alderney. Aldermen and Alderwomen danced round bonfires and then ran back to St Annes with burning sticks. The custom gradually spread to the other Channel Islands, but with only a limited amount of foliage to torch, the custom eventually burned itself out.

MOTHERING SUNDAY

Mid-Lent Sunday, the fourth Sunday in Lent, is **Mothering Sunday**. This was an important holiday long before aggressive guilt-marketing turned it into **Mothers' Day**. Originally the matron referred to was the Mother Church, and today was the time when everyone tried to return to their home-town church. This usually entailed visiting the old folks as well, and the shift from Mother Church to mother was a simple one. It was a holiday for people in service, and they would often come home with gifts for their mothers – cakes or flowers, or discarded clothes from employers.

The idea of having a mid-Lent respite originates in the two traditional church readings of the day. One deals with Old Testament Joseph's banquet for his brothers; and the other concerns that wonderful trick with bread, a few fish, and 5,000 hungry followers. The church called the day *Dominica Refectionis*, the Sunday of Refreshment, and from then on it has been a history of cakes, slap-up lunches and boxes of chocolates. As they say in Northamptonshire:

On Mothering Sunday above all other
Every child should dine with its Mother.

The lurch from the old Mothering Sunday to the current card-manufacturers' profit-margin got its impetus during the Second World War. American servicemen mistook the festivities here for their own Mothers' Day, held on the second Sunday in May. Congress had adopted the Day in 1913 following the rigorous campaigning of Anna Jarvis of Philadelphia, who lost her own mother in 1907 and wanted the whole world to know about it, via church services, the wearing of carnations (red for a living mother, white for a dead one), and cult status for mums across the land. Like many other aspects of America, by the end of the war it had interbred with its British equivalent, sowing the seeds of the current Mothering Sunday/Mothers' Day mutant.

The most famous traditional food of the day is simnel cake, which has resulted in the alternative name **Simnel Sunday**. The words comes from Latin *simila*, a fine flour. *Simenel* was the name given to top-grade white bread. The key centres for baking the cakes were Shrewsbury in Shropshire, Devizes in Wiltshire, and Bury in Lancashire. The general recipe is a rich fruit cake with a strong presence of saffron. In Devizes the cakes were star-shaped and pastryless, and although they looked delicious, a local octogenarian baker recently advised against reviving the recipe, as the cake was '*revolting*'. Bury's are flat and dense; while the Shrewsbury version has a thick, hard crust coloured yellow with the saffron. Just to make it extra hard, the cake is first boiled and then baked. A local story tells of a thankful, short-sighted mother who took her cake and used it as a footstool. In all three towns, and elsewhere, mass-produced and less idiosyncratic simnel cakes are now made all year round.

At the church of All Saints in Leighton Buzzard, Buckinghamshire, there is ancient graffiti on one of the pillars, reputedly showing how this double cooking came about. It depicts mythical bakers **Simon and Nell**. The pair argued about cake-making. One wanted to boil it, while the other insisted on baking. As a compromise they did both, and the first simnel cake was born, named after themselves, Sim + Nell.

Equally unfounded legends link the name with **Lambert Simnel**, one of the pretenders to the throne in the reign of Henry VII late in the 15th century. After Lambert's exposure as a fraud, the cakes in his father's shop window were called Simnels, which became a derogatory term for the produce of a conman baker. The case for this legend is diminished somewhat by evidence that Lambert's dad was a joiner. Appropriately, Lambert Simnel ended his days working in Henry's kitchens.

At Chilbolton, Hampshire, the special delicacy has long been **simnel wafers**. The secret recipe survives in the custody of just one family. But the price of its concealment was that each year on Mothering Sunday the family were obliged to have made enough for the whole village. So in 1956 they quit, and baking the wafers was indefinitely suspended. The last surviving member of the family to have supervised the baking, Tilly Baverstock, died in 1992, leading many to suspect that the custom was over forever. But before she passed away, Tilly had passed the recipe on to a local historian. Unfortunately, the historian almost immediately managed to mislay the priceless secret formula. Only by getting several of Tilly's surviving relatives together was it possible for the recipe to be reconstructed. All this excitement has led to locals speculating that the wafers may soon be back on the Mothering Sunday menu. The same chequered history has dogged the unique and wildly ornate 400-year-old tongs with which the wafers were made. Down the years they have been broken just as the Prince of Wales was due to inspect them, and sold by accident. Until the tongs are back in use making wafers, the villagers hope to put them on display in the church.

On the drink front, a spicy ale called **bragot** was popular in Lancashire, giving the day yet another name: Bragot Sunday. The word comes from the Anglo-Saxon *bragawd*, a kind of spiced mead.

© Feeling a little left out by all these traditons, at Cookham Dean near Maidenhead in Berkshire in 1972 villagers boldly invented their own custom. Mixing the Mothering Sunday church tradition with Shrove Tuesday church clipping, the now popular mock-ancient ritual involves locals forming a ring around the church at 10.30 am, shouting '*Hosanna!*' and having a good revel.

PASSION SUNDAY

Also known as Care, Carle or **Carling Sunday**, this is the week after Mothering Sunday. In the area between Hull and Newcastle, pubs used to serve carlings to customers today. Some still do, and in Teesside they are still sold in supermarkets. Carlings are grey peas – in fact brown or black in colour – soaked, boiled, seasoned, and fried in hog's lard. A legend in Yorkshire says that a ship called *The Carling* was wrecked today in the 1880s, and its cargo of sea-swollen grey peas was washed up in Filey Bay. The pragmatic locals boiled them and served them to their livestock, but then found that a bit of salt and pig fat made them quite palatable. An alternative version from Tyneside says that in the middle of a famine, fate saved the locals from starvation when a storm blew the pea-laden boat up the Tyne.

Grey peas are an imported variety, it is true; but the more likely explanation is that eating peas is a survival of the pagan custom of eating beans in commemoration of the dead: Carling Sunday and the following Care (or Passion) Week are a period of mourning for the imminent death of Christ.

Across the north of England, it was a compulsory drinking day. This fine superstition insists that a certain sum of money, the **Carlin groat**, has to be spent on beer today, or else bad luck will fall. As an added incentive, many landlords laid on a free supply of carling peas. Just as with free bar-snacks today, the peas were usually well-salted to encourage customers to go beyond their groatsworth of booze.

The peas were also eaten at **Care suppers**.

When just a few were left in the pan, the children of the house would each take a pea in turn. Whoever got the last pea – or in some versions a bean hidden amongst the peas – would be the first to marry.

© Alongside the grey peas, **Passion dock** is another traditional Carling Sunday food in Yorkshire. It is made from dock – the plant that cures nettle stings and, say some Yorkshiremen, every other ailment as well – plus onions, oatmeal and nettles. The result is a slack, greenish pudding resembling industrial slurry. Such is its growing popularity that on Carling Sunday in 1971 the Calder Valley held the first Dock Pudding Contest at Hebden Bridge, wallowing in the food's virtues.

Leverington in Cambridgeshire went in for **whirling cakes**, and its feast-day was renamed Whirling Sunday. Legend has it that a Leverington woman was making cakes on Easter Sunday, when a knock came at the door. Aware that baking was not a Sabbath-approved activity, she opened the door cautiously. She was sucked out by a whirlwind, and in the eye of the storm was Satan, who whisked her over the top of Leverington church and away to his own ovens. Whirling Sunday died out in 1860.

PALM SUNDAY

One week after Carling Sunday comes **Palm Sunday**, the sixth one in Lent, and the last before Easter. Most events are on the Sunday itself, but schools at Lanark in Strathclyde used to perform their Palming Parade a day earlier. In the days before teachers had heard of performance-related pay, they still went in for pay-related performance – the parade leader was the child who had given teacher the largest gift at Candlemas, February 2nd. Good training for later life.

Palm Sunday commemorates Christ's entry into Jerusalem on a donkey, when spectators threw palms into the road – the traditional recognition of a returning hero. In Britain palm does not grow; but by giving sallow – **pussy-willow** – the name *English Palm*, the natives had ample substitutes. Sallow is used to decorate churches and houses today, along with other greenery – yew, box, hazel, willow, daffodils. The lent lily is another name for the daffodil, because it blooms at this time of year. These days it is more common to import authentic palm from Spain, usually woven into crosses.

Jesus also revived the fortunes of a barren fig

tree today, zapping it into productivity. So second only to palms, this is a day for figs. In the Cotswolds it is known as **Fig Pudding Day**. Because of the fate of the fig, it was said that any seed planted today would be doubly fruitful. Furthermore, if you walked through your crops straight after Mass today, they would be blessed. At Cheselbourne in Dorset this only worked if the person circling the crops was a woman, and dressed in white.

In Wales the day was called **Flowering Sunday** – *Sul y Blodau*. As Care Week came to a close and the death of Christ approached, all family graves were cleaned and weeded and covered in fresh flowers. The custom lingers on in Glamorgan.

Soon after the Reformation, Protestants were complaining about the Palm Sunday greenery and parades. They claimed that it turned religious observance into '*a May game and a pageant-play*', and there was a huge shift away from the old adage '*He that hath not a palm in his hand on Palm Sunday must have his hand cut off*'.

But plant-waving continues to dominate the day, despite the protests, and despite such events as the **Brighton Stripping** of 1831. Celebrating Sussex crowds devastated fields and hedges around Brighton in their search for fronds of greenery, and drinking and rioting broke out in the streets.

Any vegetation collected today will bring luck as long as it remains inside the family home. At **Our Lady of Nant's Well** in Little Colan, near Newquay in Cornwall, the greenery was thrown into the water, a rite that originated as an offering to the guardian spirit of the well. If the foliage sank, it had been accepted and prosperity was sure to follow; if it floated, the spirit was unimpressed and poverty, or even death, beckoned. At Lady Ann's Well on the Howley Hills near Morley in West Yorkshire, **Fieldkirk Fair** used to take place today. The well water here was said to change colour for the Fair's duration, and had brief but powerful healing properties.

The commonest Palm Sunday well-tradition was the making of liquorice water. Sweets – mainly Spanish liquorice – were mixed with well-water by children to make a sweet drink, and the day was known as **Spanish Sunday** in the Midlands. There were allsorts of liquorice water customs, and one version continued to be observed by children at Lady's Well, in Finstock near Witney, Oxfordshire, as late as the 1960s. Tap-water and commercial sweet drinks whittled away this particular custom, although

the well – which even in droughts has never run dry – is still there.

Hills were as important as wells today. In Wiltshire the game **bandy** – a primitive form of golf – was played up and down the chalk uplands. Near Pewsey in Wiltshire boys used to slide down the slope of Martinsell Hill using the jaw-bones of horses as sledges. Capitalising on today's crowds, there were scores of hill-top fairs, known as **fig-fairs** because of the dried fruit on offer. The largest man-made hill in Europe, **Silbury Hill** near Marlborough in Wiltshire, combined the various elements of the day, with a greenery-clad procession up the hill for a feast of fig cakes, liquorice water and cider. No one knows the secrets of the 4,000-year-old, 130-foot-high mound at Silbury. King Sil is said to sit inside it in golden armour, astride his solid gold horse.

The strangest hill ceremony took place on Pontesford Hill near Shrewsbury in Shropshire. On Palm Sunday large numbers wandered the hill, for a token attempt at **Seeking the Golden Arrow**. After a fruitless search they gathered greenery and settled down for a picnic. There was then a race down to the stream in Lyde Hole. Whoever managed to run downhill in one spurt without falling – almost impossible – could dip the fourth finger of their right hand into the stream, and be sure of marrying the first person of the opposite sex who came their way afterwards. The greenery-gathering and race made up for the fact that quite what the golden arrow was, and why it was being sought, had long been forgotten.

One legend says that a disinherited man will find the arrow and then be able to return to his lawful estates. Another claims that faeries have hidden it, and that an unspecified wrong will be righted once it is found. However, all the tales agree that it will only be detected by the seventh daughter of a seventh son searching just after midnight – in total darkness. It is said that whoever finds it will be able to sit on the **Devil's Chair** which dominates the nearby rock formation, the Stiperstones. Normally, to sit in his chair means death will soon follow. The stones are often shrouded in mist – the well-informed keep their distance, as this means that the Devil is in his chair. The arrow was still being sought in the 1950s; but now both it and the custom have been given up as lost.

Between Spring Hill and Rising Sun Hill near Tysoe in Warwickshire there used to be a horse etched into the red soil of the hillside, said to represent the old horse god Tui. In the 18th century the **red horse** was on land belonging to Simon Nicholls, who also owned the nearby Rising Sun Inn. The ancient site was a traditional Palm Sunday place to visit, and Nicholls had to weed and clear the horse just before the day in order to take advantage of the massive influx of thirsty customers. But one year he impulsively decided that horse-cleaning was peasants' work, and ploughed the thing up. His Palm Sunday trade disappeared and a guilt-riven Nicholls etched a new horse, closer to his pub. But no one fell for that trick. He had single-handedly destroyed a site and a tradition. The Vale of the Red Horse is now under forestry land.

◉   At Kings Caple and Sellack, and formerly at Hentland, all near Ross-on-Wye in Hereford and Worcester, **Pax Cakes** are distributed today after the church service. They are wafers stamped with a picture of the Paschal Lamb, and are individually handed over by the vicar with the words '*Peace and Good Neighbourhood*' – which is also what is written on the cakes. Lady Scudamore financed what was probably already an ongoing custom in 1570, siphoning off some of her income to pay for cakes and ale, which over the years has dwindled into cakes sans ale, and now into the small pax wafers.

The Lord of the Manor of Hundon in Lincolnshire allowed the Lord of the Manor of Caistor to work land at Broughton only if he carried out an annual tenure custom on Palm Sunday. This only explains the bare bones, not the true meaning, of the wonderful **gad-whipping** ceremony at Caistor, south-east of Brigg, Humberside. A representative from Broughton came to the church with an ash whip, five and a half feet long with a thong of over seven feet. He cracked it in the porch three times, and then walked down the aisle. When the minister came to the Second Lesson, the gad-whipper whirled his weapon three times over the anxious man's head, and then kept the whip-stock suspended above him, a leather purse dangling from the wood. The purse contained 24 or 30 silver pennies, later transmuted into half a crown. After the service, whip and purse were taken to the farmhouse at Hundon.

▦   In the 1830s a petition was sent to the House of Commons to stop this irreverent practice, and in 1846 when the Broughton land was sold, the new tenant was not interested in maintaining the gad-whipping. It was revived once after the second World War but is no longer a feature of the Caistor calendar, although the whip – in its long glass case – can still be seen in the church.

The whip-stock used to have pieces of wych-elm tied around it. This was in memory of a boy who had been whipped to death with wych-wood by a man on the Hundon estate. The large thong may be linked with the legend which tells how proto-Saxon Hengist was granted rights to as much land at Caistor – or *Thong Castor* as it was then called – as he could cover with a bull hide. Hengist cut the hide into thin strips and enclosed a vast area. The same legend is said to apply to Thonge in Shropshire, and Thong Castle near Sittingbourne in Kent, as well as in various European mythologies. All that can be said for certain is that the gad-whipping was weird and unique.

©   The Monday following Palm Sunday is the traditional date for **Leasing the White Bread Meadow** at Bourne near Spalding in Lincolnshire. In recent years, the dates have got somewhat woollier, with the prices-for-slices sale now taking place on a convenient day in April. Two boys race up and down a 100-yard road while the bidding takes place. If they manage to get all the way there and back between bids, the auction is over. If not, they run again. In former years the audience received free gin to 'stimulate bidding', and in an enthusiastic year the boys certainly earned their small financial recompense. This was all instigated by Richard Clay, who said in his will of 1770 that rent from the meadow should pay for bread to feed the poor of the Eastgate area of town. After the bidding, everyone sits down to a meal of bread, cheese, onions and beer.

MAUNDY THURSDAY

Maundy or **Shere Thursday** is the day before Good Friday, and is the last day of Lent.

> *On Shere Thursday and all in the morning*
> *They made a crown of thorns for our*
> *   Heavenly King,*
> *And was not that a woeful thing?*
> *And sweet Jesus we'll call him by name.*

Maundy comes from the Latin *mandatum novum*, referring to Christ's 'new commandment' that his disciples should love one another, uttered after he had washed their feet as an example of humility. 'Shere' may be from an old word meaning to clean: altars and churches were scrubbed prior to Easter. Conversely, clothes must not be cleaned today, otherwise you will have 12 months of bad luck. Some etymologies half-heartedly suggest that Shere was when everyone sheared their hair and beards to look nice and neat for Easter.

◉ Monarchs washed the feet of the poor on Maundy Thursday, aping the biblical example. The rite was last carried out by James II, by which time elaborate gifts had been introduced, turning the humble ceremony into the spectacle which survives today. Minted coins and a few pounds – the **Royal Maunds** – are handed out by the Queen or her representative. The service is usually at Westminster Abbey when the year has an odd number, and elsewhere when the year has an even number. If that seems complex, worse is to come: the number of recipients of each sex and the amount they get corresponds to the age of the monarch. On Maundy Thursday 1997, when the Queen is due to have reached her 70th birthday, 70 men and 70 women will each get 70p in Maundy money – made up of silver 1p, 2p, 3p and 4p coins. If the Queen ever gets round to sending herself a telegram, the pensioners will walk away with a whole £1. Fortunately, as these coins are the only silver ones still issued by the Royal Mint, and as they have also been unavailable to the general public since 1909, they are worth considerably more than their face value. A set of one of each coin is currently priced at close to £300 – it is perfectly legal to sell them, and so after the Queen's 70th some pensioners could be well over £2,000 better off.

In the 18th century the gifts were sometimes even more generous. A report of the 1731 proceedings lists the alms as beef, mutton and ale, along with '*undressed, one large old ling, and one large dried cod; twelve red herrings, and twelve white herrings, and four half quarter loaves*', as well as shoes, stockings, wool and linen, leather bags, cash in lieu of the monarch's gown which used to be thrown in as a job lot, plus a foot-washing by the Archbishop of York.

© The Elizabethan **Marvyn Dole** is observed at Ufton Court near Padworth in Berkshire on Maundy Thursday. In 1581 local dogooder Lady Marvyn left money to pay for precisely detailed amounts of wheat and cloth to be given to the local needy, by way of thanking the parishioners who had sent out a search party when she became lost in nearby woodland. The dole has now been updated so that not just the poor but anyone from nearby Ufton Nervet can apply. What is now passed through the back window at Ufton Court consists of 161 loaves of bread – calculated as being the exact equivalent of the amount of wheat set down by Lady Marvyn in her will. The bequest of cloth has been transmuted into the hand-out of several duvet covers.

© There is more benevolence today at Leigh in Greater Manchester. The **Travice Dole** is handed out over the tomb of Henry Travice, in accordance with his will of 1627. Originally 40 people had to walk over his grave, which is inside the church, but this has now been scaled down to a three-person trampling, after the evening service. £10 is divided between Leigh and nearby Atherton and Tylesley, for the local vicars to do with as they see fit.

In the Western Isles of Scotland, fisherfolk know today as **Gruel Thursday**. As recently as last century this was the day for giving offerings to the local **sea god**. And what the sea god wanted, they believed, was gruel and ale. The purpose of the benefaction was to ensure a good seaweed crop for fertilising the land. The fishers' prayer to the gruel sea translates from the Gaelic as:

> *Oh God of the sea, put weed in the drawing wave,*
> *To enrich the ground, to shower on us food;*

which makes a refreshing change from *Our Father*.

MARCH

1st March
St David's Day

The Leek Shall Inherit the Earth

The patron saint of Wales, St David, died today in AD 589, a saintly centenarian. His monastic seat was at Glyn Rhosyn (now the town of St Davids, Dyfed). During the monastery's construction the Irish pagan Boia led a sneak attack on David's holy masons. The pagans were on top until David stepped into the fray, unleashed a fierce volley of proselytising, and converted Boia to Christianity on the spot. Boia's wife was not so easily shaken. Her husband had failed, but she had a secret weapon – her handmaidens. She sent them off, stark naked, to tempt the labouring masons: this was one occasion when women encouraged builders not just to wolf-whistle, but to go the whole hod. Such was David's oratory skills that not a single man wavered or even puckered up, and Mrs Boia's girls left empty-handed. From then on David's fame was assured.

David spent much of his life causing wells to spring forth spontaneously; and he engaged in dramatic landscape gardening when he needed an attention-grabbing preaching-spot at Llanddewi Brefi, east of Aberaeron in Dyfed. The saint stamped his foot next to the church, and the whole area rose up to form a convenient hillock. Ever since, getting the locals to church has been an uphill struggle.

David raised the profile of vegetarianism during his lifetime by subsisting on a diet of leeks and leeks, with a few tasty leeks for pudding. His obsession lasted into the afterlife. When David's spirit visited King Cadwallon's army at Hatfield Moors in South Yorkshire in 633, it was not to offer theological guidance: he had returned to tell the troops to put leeks on their heads, so enabling them to differentiate between friend and foe. Proud veg aloft, the Welsh went on to defeat King Edwin of Northumbria's men.

Since that magical moment at Hatfield, the Welsh have worn **leeks** on St David's Day. This is commemorated in the many leek-related exchanges in Shakespeare's *Henry V* – notably Pistol's threat to Fluellen to '*knock his leek about his pate upon Saint Davy's Day*'; and Fluellen's eventual response of thrusting a leek down Pistol's throat. Daffodils, which are said to first bloom today, are the slightly more chic alternative lapel-wear.

Leeks also play a part in the neighbourly custom of **cymhortha**. Anyone too ill to finish ploughing, must be visited today with a plough, an ox, and a sackful of leeks from which a special stew is prepared. The ensuing meal is wholesome, if a little heavy on the leeks. Besides being high in fibre and iron, leeks are said to drive off evil spirits, and purge the blood – but only if eaten during March.

© **Whuppity Scoorie**, or Stourie, takes place today in Lanark, Scotland. It is a wild custom, with very convoluted origins. For centuries Lanark lads today ran round the church three times, and then fought a rival gang using only their caps as weapons. By the 18th century the rival gang was firmly established as the youth of nearby New Lanark, and the battleground was at Wellgate Head. Caps bloodied, the victors paraded back singing:

> Hooray, boys, hooray! For we have won the
>   day!
> We've met the bold New/Old Lanark boys
>   and chased them doon the brae!

Increasing violence, including stone-throwing and run-ins with the police, led to the caps being replaced – imaginatively – with screwed up paper balls on string. These days at 6 pm there is a special peal of bells, and the Lanark lads run three times sunwise round St Nicholas' church, battering each other with their paper maces. After this the provost and his pals throw £10-worth of coppers for a penny-scramble at nearby Hyndford Place.

The suggested origins are diverse. The clang of bells and the energy of racing and brawling bodies suggest an ancient spring versus winter festival, driving out and pummelling the forces of darkness. Going three times round a sacred object (in this case the church) was a favourite druidic pastime. The best local theory about Whuppity Scoorie is that the area's criminals used to be 'whupped' round the town kirk by the town's children, then paraded down a hill to be 'scoored' – ducked – in the River Clyde. Optimistic etymologists claim that an English prisoner once fled to the church yelling 'Sanctuary!', to which the heartless Scots responded 'Up at ye!' The combination 'Up at ye, sanctuary' is supposed to sound vaguely like 'Whuppity Scoorie'. More plausibly the name comes from the Scots dialect word scoorze, which means 'whirls of (March) dust'. Devils were said to lurk in this dust, ready to blight the crops. The custom was a way of driving them out, as they hate having things thrown at them – caps were particularly effective, as were shoes, knives and mole-hill earth.

On top of all this, there is a Whuppity Stourie faerie tale. A press-ganged farmer left an unfortunate wife with a young child and a pregnant sow. The triumvirate was coping admirably when the sow unexpectedly keeled over and failed to litter. The woman was distraught; but a faerie woman sauntered over and promised to fix things, in exchange for a gift of her choosing. The wife swiftly agreed to the deal. The faerie magically returned the pig to rude health, and then claimed her prize: she wanted the woman's child. The faerie had other business to do, but vowed to return in three days to take the child away.

As fans of Rumplestiltskin know, the way to break such a faerie's power is to discover its name. The wife followed the woman to a quarry and overheard these rash words:

*Little kens our gude dame at hame
That Whuppity Stourie is my name.*

Come the fateful day, the wife toyed with the faerie woman, until the latter grew impatient and called her a 'muckle, ill-faured skelloch'. Outraged, the wife shouted 'Whuppity Stourie!', and the faerie whirled away in a cloud of dust.

A more straightforward and widespread St David's Day custom was **Sweeping the Fleas**. '*If you kill one flea in March, you kill a hundred*,' so they say. It was common to rise before dawn today, fling open a window and shout '*Good morning March!*' The step was then swept very thoroughly to offset flea-invasion. Just to liven things up there was an optional accompanying rhyme:

*'If from fleas you would be free,
On the 1st of March let all your windows
closed be.'*

This dilemma as to whether windows should be flung open or kept closed may have contributed to the demise of the custom.

The one consolation of a flea invasion is that, as those wise folk of Norfolk say, '*Fish are plentiful when fleas are plentiful*'. And they taste better too.

2nd March
St Chad's Day

Wot – No title?

Chad, Bishop of Lichfield, died today in AD 672. One week earlier an angelic band had appeared before him. It was music with a message, and unfortunately for Chad the message was that his time was almost up. Chad was assured of a place in heaven as he was famous for his humility and continence; although he had suffered a lifelong problem with wind.

When the isobars were packed together on the Dark Age meteorological map Chad never had a moment's peace. Tempests and violent gusts of wind terrified the saint, forcing him into prayers and prostrations. But in other respects the elements left him undaunted. At his local well in Stowe he would not only baptise any inquisitive pagan who popped by, but would stand naked in the water, praying. Such behaviour at the back end of a cold February may give clues as to his sudden death.

Many saints' wells are famous for their curative waters. But St Chad's still-visible well in the churchyard at Stowe – despite, or because of, his hours of nude devotion there – is said to be poisonous. His pilgrims could take consolation by visiting Chad's tomb, also at Stowe in Lichfield, Staffordshire. It was shaped like a house, with a hole in the side from which the faithful took dust. They seasoned water with the unsavoury scrapings and used it as a cure-all. Demand for the potion was such that the church exacted a tax from the locals, known as Chad-farthings or Chad-pennies. The cash went towards the upkeep of tomb and building.

☕ In spite of Chad's fear of wind, his day is associated with **beans**:

> *Sow peas or beans on David or Chad*
> *Whether the weather be good or bad.*

Careful, though. **Ghosts** dwell in bean-fields, drawn there by their love of the smell of bean-flowers. Beans themselves can rout persistent witches if spat in their direction. They are also linked with nightmares. Dreams of bean-eating symbolise sickness; dreams of bean-growing represent a forthcoming quarrel; and to sleep in a bean-field is a pathway to certain insanity.

🏛 Footprints embedded in a tombstone at Epworth Rectory, near Scunthorpe in Humberside, are said to have been made by the fire and brimstone boots of **John Wesley**, who died on this day in 1791. A sullen man, he believed that contagious laughter was the work of the Devil. The oak under which Wesley preached his last open air sermon – on October 7th, 1790 – is outside the churchyard at Winchelsea near Rye in East Sussex. There is a fine equestrian statue of Wesley outside the oldest Methodist chapel in Britain, the 1739 New Room in Broadmead, Bristol.

3rd March
St Winnol's Day

The Ghost Who Paid Her Bills

Mrs Webb of Barby, near Rugby in Warwickshire, died at home today in 1851, but remained unsettled. After the funeral her neighbours heard moans, bangs, and the sound of mobile furniture, though the house was empty. Undeterred, plucky tenants the Accletons moved into Mrs Webb's old home. The noises continued, and a wraith-like Mrs Webb appeared before them every day, either shaking her head or smiling, wishing to communicate. The Accletons declined the offer, and so Mrs Webb did her ghostly party-piece, tossing balls of light through the attic trapdoor. The Accletons passed on that one too; but Mrs Webb's heir and nephew saw the light and decided to explore the attic. There among the rubbish, he found a bag of gold and a set of

outstanding bills. One transference of cash later, and everyone was happy. Mrs Webb took her balanced bank-book to everlasting rest and was not seen again.

> *First comes David, then comes Chad,*
> *Then comes Winnol, roaring like mad.*

☕ Probably because no one has heard of him. The roaring is not **St Winnol's** fault, just a spell of traditional lousy weather which coincides with his feast day.

🏛 His contemporaries knew him as Winnwaloe, an abbot from Brittany. Hair shirts and prostrations were his thing. After death his roving relics found their way to England, resting at such diverse locations as Lizard Point in Cornwall, and Norwich in Norfolk, whence the roaring rhyme originates. Winnol had a fish-bell, a marvellous instrument which when rung made all fish in the area come to the saint. Fine when he was beside a stream; bad news for the fish if he was in the middle of the high street. Winnol's other trick was to carry churches – East Portlemouth church near Salcombe in Devon is said to have been lugged there by Winnol, and a screen in the church depicts him shouldering his burden. At the Lizard in Cornwall there are two other churches which celebrate Winnol's lot – at Landewednack and Gunwalloe.

◉ On the first Thursday in March, **Maid's Money** is up for grabs at the Guildhall, Guildford, Surrey. It is won by rolling a dice. This is all down to the will of John How in 1674. The dicing has to be carried out by two worthy serving maids or nannies who have held their jobs for at least two years, and who do not live in an inn or alehouse. They roll for the interest on How's original endowment of £400 (about £12). Formerly there was no second prize. Originally the Parson wanted his invested cash to go to a poor apprentice-boy, or a maid servant if no apprentice proved eligible; but it has now been revamped as the second prize at the Maid's Money event. His endowment was £600, and the interest goes to the girl who comes second in the dice game – so the real winner is the loser.

Even more intriguing – especially for those named Charles – is an old charter from Guildford which declares: '*Whenever the King comes to Lothesley Manor near Guildford, the lord is to present his Majesty with Three Whores*'. Tabloid heaven.

4th March
St Adrian of May's Day

A Rotten Trick

Richard Parsons of Bisley, Gloucestershire, wanted to get his sins out of the way early, and by the age of 19 he had sealed his reputation as drinker, gambler and blasphemer. The drinking was just for show, and his blasphemy was easily achieved with a few colourful phrases and an aversion to churches on Sunday. But it was the gambling at which Richard excelled, especially all-night card schools.

During one routine card orgy through the small hours, Richard fell out with his companions in the discussion of a particular hand. He swore on his own version of events, declaring that he was willing to damn himself to the eternal flames, and that the flesh should rot on his bones if he was wrong. Oh dear. A bruise mysteriously appeared on his thigh, and soon began to fester. Before you could say *Snap!*, he was on his deathbed, the festering having spread all over his body. Belatedly, Richard took himself to the nearest surgeon, who diagnosed a classic case of flesh-rotting-on-the-bones-as-a-result-of-rash-words. There was no cure, and shortly before he shuffled off, witnesses watched Richard as he appeared to play – and lose – a supernatural card-game. Evidently left with the Old Maid in his hand, he fell into a shaking fit and died on March 4th 1766. His eyes would not close, and he was placed in his coffin poker-faced, staring at Satan's hand of eights and aces.

The Isle of May in the Firth of Forth has long been a centre of pilgrimage for anyone who fancies an afternoon's chilly prayer. Place names on the island such as Pilgrim's Haven, Holyman's Road and Angel Stack recall its former religious significance. The priory on the island was dedicated to St Adrian, also known as Hadrian, an Irish missionary who, along with his followers, was slaughtered by passing Vikings on this day in 875. The story was probably little more than a handy fabrication to justify building the priory offshore, where a legal loophole meant that local lords did not need to give planning permission. The island's high cliffs make landing difficult, but in good weather there are regular boat trips from Anstruther in Fife. Most visitors now come not to see the ruined priory, or the earliest Scottish coal-fired warning beacon – which has now been given Ancient Monument status – but for the island's abundant bird life.

Slightly further along the same Firth, the **Forth Rail Bridge** opened today in 1890. Its span of more than one and a half miles made it far and away the longest bridge in Britain, and its 1,700-foot main spans were for decades unsurpassed anywhere in the world. The original design for the bridge, by Sir Thomas Bouch, was dropped and hastily replaced when his bridge over the Tay collapsed in 1879, killing 90 people. The most famous folklore about the Forth Bridge maintains that as soon as the workmen have finished painting it with red oxide, they have to start again at the beginning. Cutbacks have moved this particular story out of the truth category and into that of legend.

5th March
St Piran's Day

Calculated Success

Born in 1707 at Elmton in north-east Derbyshire, **Jedediah Buxton** – Jeddy to his chums – skipped schooling but somehow had a great gift for going forth and multiplying. No calculation was too vast for the man, and it was fortuitous that in addition to his mathematical skills he was able to assess the dimensions of land and buildings by eye alone. His fame spread, and following a trek to London he became a national celebrity.

One of Jeddy's most famous calculations concerned the number of barley-corns that it would take to stretch end-to-end for eight miles. The answer was 1,520,640. His audience were amazed. The fact that the accuracy of the answer was unprovable did not limit their enthusiasm. But Jeddy saved his most poignant sum for the end. He said farewell to everyone in 1772, declaring that, according to his figures, on Thursday next he would be nothing but another prime number on the slide-rule of infinity. On Thursday March 5th, Jeddy died as calculated, and was taken away to his decimal place in heaven.

Tin-miners prayed to **St Piran** today. Piran, a 5th-century hermit, revealed to Cornishmen the secrets of mining. Piran dolls or engravings of the saint were later left at the entrances of tin mines to invoke the blessing of the mine-host.

The hovel that Piran called home was at Perranzabuloe near Newquay, where he first landed in Cornwall; a 7th-century oratory marked the spot. Excavations of the shrine last century uncovered three ancient headless bodies and three skulls. Piran's stance on ritual decapitation remains unclear.

The bodies may be linked with nearby Penhale Sands, where violent storms over the years have revealed other skeletons. This gives credence to a tale which tells how Penhale was once Langarroc, a large town with seven churches. Alas, with the wealth from tin came the inevitable decadence and profane partying. God sent a great storm to bury the town under a sand dune, which is all that remains today. Legend insists that the seven bell towers can still be heard chiming in heavy storms.

🗍 Piran's ruined oratory at Perranzabuloe was uncovered during a storm in 1835. An ugly concrete shell was erected over the site; but sadly, having been built to protect the building, it merely attracted vandals. The shell was smashed, and the oratory disappeared under the sands once again. A stone inscribed with the saint's name now marks the spot, on top of a large mound of sand. Of greater aesthetic appeal is the nearby Celtic cross which marks Piran's original hermitage. The many Cornish villages called Perran-something-or-other are all named after the saint.

6th March
St Baldred's Day

A Load of Old Ballads

The sure way of remaining alive in popular memory is to become the subject of a drinking song. *Widecombe Fair* – with **Uncle Tom Cobbley** borrowing Tom Pearce's mare to take a scrum of his mates to the nearby fair – is one of the most widely-sung of such songs. Cobbley was a real person. The fact that he never borrowed anyone's mare – he was a man with plenty of his own horses, thank you very much – is immaterial when it comes to the posthumous fame which the song has given him. A prosperous yeoman, Tom Cobbley came from Crediton in Devon, where the birth of Pearce and two other characters from the song are also mentioned in the church records. He died on this day in 1794 at nearby Sprayton, aged 96.

✝ Cobbley's chief concern in later life was to ensure that his favourite heirs got their dues at the expense of those who had fallen from favour. His eyesight and hearing were poor, and the will was drawn up several times before the print was large and unambiguous enough to satisfy crotchety Cobbley. Tradition has not given him eternal rest, however, for his ghost still goes a-haunting the roads of Widecombe with the crew of the song, as well as *'Tom Pearce's grey mare and a rattling of bones'*. Tom's consolation is that his is the only name which every singer remembers.

🗍 Tom Cobbley's grave is still visible in the churchyard at Sprayton (though this may in fact be the resting place of Tom's nephew: Tom Cobbley, or Cobleigh, was a popular name in the family); and the fair at Widecombe still takes place – see September 11th.

🗍 There used to be a hazardous stretch of sea between Bass Rock and mainland Lothian, caused by the hidden danger of a rocky reef. This obstacle was removed by 8th-century hermit St Baldred, sole occupant of Bass Rock: with the aid of a mighty prayer he shifted the submerged mass to its present site, on the coast near North Berwick. The rock features St Baldred's Boat and St Baldred's Cradle still dominate the coastline. The town provides boat-trips around Bass Rock.

One enduring custom is the **instant topical song** or poem. In years gone by if a passing pirate vessel was sunk or if someone came to grief in colourful or macabre circumstances, chances were that by the following morning someone would have rattled off a dozen swift stanzas and would be flogging them on street corners – usually adorned with a dreadful woodcut print and a note urging *'To the tune of* The Merry Penguin's Waltz', or whatever. Sometimes the stories were genuinely newsworthy. More often than not the broadsides rehashed old stories. Sometimes a complete non-event would make a bid for posterity. The classic example of this occurred on March 6th 1716. The sunset over Hartington, Derbyshire, was witnessed that night by a desperate ballad-writer, who then tried to get excited about it in print. His seven long verses have the following plot: at dusk over 20 rays of light appeared in the sky, then turned red before being obscured by the clouds. Before you could say 'pleasant but unspectacular sunset' the non-event was in print under the catchy title *'On the Strange and Wonderful*

Sight that was Seen in the Air on March 6th, 1716'.

7th March

Chickens of the Gods

Chickens, especially black chickens, are generally lucky – whether kept, eaten, or seen crossing the road. But those born in March are especially lucky and fertile – '*a chicken in March is eggs for a year*'.

The dawn cock is linked with the pagan sun-god, crowing to disperse evil, and so enabling everyone to go to work without encountering the forces of darkness. Somerset lore declares '*a cock will frighten away the Devil himself*'. In various old songs (such as *The Grey Cock* and *The Wife of Ushers' Well*) the crowing cock is the cue for the undead to cease meddling with the living and return to their graves. Faith in the chicken's powers to ward off evil and illness was such that the unfortunate bird was often buried alive in the foundations of new buildings or at the junction of streams. This tradition continues in some cultures to this day.

Somewhat contrarily, it was also believed that the bird was so sacred that to sacrifice one would offend the gods. An 18th-century collection of sayings called *Protreptics of Iamblichus* asserts '*Nourish a cock but offer it not in sacrifice*'.

The bird's crowing has its downside:

A whistling wife and a crowing hen
Is neither good for god or men.

A whistling wife is a euphemism for a witch, whistling up storms.

An even number of eggs is unlucky; an odd amount is lucky; and curiously a clutch of 13 is the ideal number. But, of course, chickens must not be counted until they have hatched. As she sits brooding, the hen is alleged to say in (chicken) English:

Cuca, cuca, cayit,
I've laid an egg, come ta' it.

Coincidentally, on March 8th 1981 a new world record for the distance flown by a chicken was set, when a Japanese hen called Shorisha flew 310 feet.

None of the above may inspire you to that delicacy of yester-year, **Cock Ale**. This consists of a dead cockerel marinaded in ale and sherry, with sugar, fruit and spices.

There used to be a fair at **Bourne** in Lincolnshire on this day, and if the relatively lacklustre affair was popular then it was perhaps due to the reputation recorded in the rhyme:

Peterborough for pride, Stamford for poor,
Deeping for a rogue, and Bourne for a whore.

At this time of year seeding was likely to be over, ending in **Hopper-Cake Night**. The Hopper was a seed-basket, and the cakes were usually fruit buns dunked in spiced beer (not Cock Ale). After the seeding the children had to repel seed-seeking birds. They had various songs and chants to drive off the vermin, including the terrific:

O you nasty black-a-tops,
Get off my master's radish-tops;
For he's a-coming with his long gun,
So you must fly and I must run;
Hell-o, oo-oo, hell-o, oo-oo.

8th March

The Man who Bleated to Death

In 1828 **sheep-stealing** was punished by transportation or death. Noble Edden from Haddenham, near Aylesbury in Buckinghamshire, thought this a little severe, and so he said nothing when he happened to witness local ne'er-do-wells Tylor and Sewell in the act of swiping a ewe. Unfortunately for all concerned, Edden suffered from Recurring Joke Syndrome. Whenever he saw Tylor or Sewell thereafter, he could not resist bleating like a sheep. At first they smiled too, grateful that he had helped pull the wool over the eyes of the local lawmen. As time passed, Edden found the jape funnier and funnier, but for the sheep-stealers it soon ceased to be a laughing matter. They waylaid Edden and clubbed him to death. Prior to the murder, Noble had received a premonition of some imminent unpleasant deed, and his wife also saw a vision of Tylor wielding the fatal hammer.

After the prophetic Mrs Edden had raised the alarm, the body was discovered; but there was no evidence against the two men. So she invited Tylor to settle matters by touching her husband's corpse – it was long held that any body touched by its murderer would immediately begin to bleed again. Tylor declined the challenge.

Later, in prison for theft, Sewell let slip that Tylor might be linked with Edden's death. Tylor was brought in, but the charges failed to stick. To celebrate his release a euphoric Tylor put ribbons in his hat and danced outside the houses of his accusers.

The murderous Morris man remained free until the hapless Sewell again fell foul of the law after stealing some birds. Sentenced to 14 years' transportation, Sewell tried to lessen his term by revealing how Tylor had murdered Noble Edden. It failed to occur to Sewell that once arrested Tylor would also implicate him in the murder, and that he might end up with a lot more to answer for than bird theft. Condemned by each others' statements, Tylor and Sewell were hanged outside Aylesbury jail on March 8th 1830, before a crowd of 5,000.

✟ Noble Edden still hangs out at the site of his murder: a lane branching from the A418 at Haddenham. There have been regular sightings of his **ghost**, and to meet it brings bad luck.

The quaint custom of **transportation** was used for the pettiest of offences. In 1828 a law stated that if three men carrying at least one heavy stick were found in a wood after dark, the sentence was an automatic 14-year transportation. Punishment through transportation provided a regular source of slave labour in the colonies, including Tasmania, the dreaded Van Diemen's Land. The unfairness of transportation was the subject of an extremely popular 19th-century ballad, *Van Diemen's Land*, first printed soon after the deaths of the Haddenham sheep-stealers in the 1830s and still widely available long after it contributed to the outlawing of transportation in 1853.

9th March
St Constantine's Day

Changing Sex and Species in One Easy Lesson

▥ **St Constantine** was mystic to the point of utter obscurity. He may have been a chieftain, and was possibly martyred on the Kintyre peninsula in Scotland in the 6th century. The only aspect of his life-story that can be stated with any degree of certainty is that he was Cornish, and two places in Cornwall are called

Constantine in his honour – one is near Padstow and the other, south-west of Falmouth, is the site of a granite-walled underground tunnel known as Pixie's Hall.

As the name implies, the hall was believed to be the home of a colony of **pixies**, the sub-species of little people – also known as piskies or pigsies – unique to the West Country. They are unmistakable, dressing in green, with red hair, turned-up noses, pointy ears, and faces that are broader than they are long.

Fond of helping around house and farm, pixies are not averse to stealing, horses being their favourite prey. They also lure travellers from their pathways, but will not interfere with anyone carrying a rowan cross or a hunk of bread. To placate the pixies, hearths should be kept scrupulously clean so that the creatures can dance there, and pails of water should be left outside so that pixie babies can bathe.

Pixies' stranglehold in the west came about after a battle with the faeries, who were driven east of the River Parrett, which flows through Bridgwater in Somerset. The river remains the boundary between the kingdom of the faeries and that of the pixies.

The **mad March hare** gets its reputation from its mating ritual, which, at this time of year, transforms the normally placid males into leaping, fighting, crazed rivals. This dual personality – splitting hares – has led to the hare's sacred status with assorted cults and faiths. Transforming into a hare was supposed to be within the power of witches, aided by the incantation:

> *I shall go into a hare, with sorrow and such and mickle care;*
> *And I shall go in the Devil's name, aye while I come home again.*

Part of the appeal may have been that hares had the legendary ability to change sex without an operation. Cautionary tales exist, however, of hares being shot and human bodies subsequently being discovered with the same fatal wounds. But random pot-shots should hold no fear, as only a silver bullet can kill a witch-hare.

A hare's movements offer insights into the future. Boudicea is said to have unleashed one from her wolfskin vest before a battle with the Romans, to read her fate in its quirky flight. The point was that hares are unpredictable when running. Hence the implicit challenge in the opening line of the hare soup recipe from 1747's wonderfully vague classic *The Art of Cookery*: '*First, catch your hare . . .*'

If a pregnant woman meets a hare it will give the child a hare-lip, unless a friend cuts off some of the would-be mother's clothing as a remedy. Dead hares are mostly beneficial, however: a hare's foot in the left pocket prevents rheumatism. Pepys records in his Diary that a hare's foot cured his problems with wind. Otherwise hare superstitions have little to do with digestion: the animal's goddess-links make hare-consumption akin to cannibalism. Their flesh induces a deep melancholy, even though a meal of hare is supposed to keep you beautiful for exactly one week. But for those still determined to follow *The Art of Cookery's* recipe, it may help to know that once a hare is captive, it will obey you if you ask it to commit suicide.

10th March

The Dogs and Nipples of Satan

On this day in 1890 at Morfa Colliery, near Port Talbot in West Glamorgan, disaster struck. For several days beforehand, the air had been thick with portents and omens. First, the **Red Dogs of Morfa**, a pack of ghostly hell-hounds, ran amok all night. Then a parade of phantom lights known as **corpse-candles** marched through the tunnels. Next, a bloom of invisible but sickly sweet-smelling **death flowers** turned the colliery into a macabre Interflora. To ram the point home, falling earth and screams were heard in the wind. A plague of rats spilled from the mouth of the pit, and a procession of dead miners trooped through the mine, pulling ghostly coal-trams. Incredibly, half the shift still thought the stay-at-homes were being overly superstitious. Pushing past the various apparitions, they went down the mine. There was a subterranean explosion, and 87 died.

🜚 Underground mining began in South Wales in the early 16th century. Where there were once scores of pits, there are now only a few still in full-time operation. The industry's history – and the many mining disasters – are charted at the Welsh Miners' Museum of Coal, which is just up the Afan valley from Port Talbot, in the Afan Argoed Country Park.

☣ If it does not freeze on March 10th, the year will be fertile. If there is ice, then get that bulk order in to Fisons.

March 10th was the edifying **Day of Public Humiliation**, one of the few events instigated by Cromwell's Puritans, who were much fonder of cancelling things. This was humiliation in the sense of restraint and abstinence, when with bowed head everyone was meant to contemplate what a rotten lot was mankind; and to talk about '*the nation's errors of Popery, superstition, heresy, schism and profaneness*'.

The mid-17th-century Puritan regime introduced legislation that matched the Poll Tax on the popularity front. It abolished Christmas and set about removing '*all festivals or Holy-Dayes, heretofore superstitiously used and observed*'. One of its spokespersons, Stubbes, denounced all music as '*a cup of poyson to the world*', and claimed that plays, from Shakespeare to the most rustic mumming play, were '*quite contrarie to the Word of Grace and sucked out of the Devill's teates*'. This may have left Satan questioning his sexuality, but it did not impress the masses. Not surprisingly, the Day of Humiliation did not outlive the ill-fated Commonwealth.

11th March

Six-Pack of Witches' Brew

In 1613 Joan Flower and her daughters Margaret and Philippa worked at **Belvoir Castle** for the Earl and Countess of Rutland. It was no secret that they dabbled in a spot of magic to relieve their lowly lot and feed the cat, Rutterkin. They turned to full-time **witchery** after Philippa was caught pocketing the family spoons at the castle, and all three were collectively sacked.

Black magic and a grudge are a bad combination. Joan enlisted three other witches: the epileptic visionary Anne Baker; Joan Willimott, whose mother had 'blown' an evil spirit into her mouth; and Ellen Green, one of whose familiars was a mole. The hexing sextet then toiled and troubled, causing the Rutlands' youngest sons to die. One of them expired after his glove was pricked with pins and boiled in water. A subsequent ballad outlining the dastardly deeds states meaningfully that the son sickened '*till death his life did change*'.

The witches then made their erstwhile employers sterile; but that was a bad career move. They were ushered before a court in 1618 and made to confess all. Local gossip said that Joan tried to recant, calling for bread and butter and saying '*If I be guilty may it never pass through me!*' She choked on it and died. However, the insidious truth is that one of the most popular ordeals for testing an alleged witch, in the absence of a damning satanic birthmark or a river in which to throw her, was to force a large object down the accused's throat. If she choked – an almost inevitable outcome – she was guilty of witchcraft. Joan's daughters and the other women were hanged on this day in 1618 at Lincoln. The fates of Rutterkin and the demonic mole are not recorded.

In Bottesford Church, north of Melton Mowbray in Leicestershire, Earl and Countess Rutland can be seen on a monument, kneeling with their dead children who, the inscription reads, were '*bewitch'd to death*'. There are many other fine Belvoir tombs in the church's chancel, and the ornate alabaster and wood carvings feature a preponderance of peacocks. Belvoir Castle itself is open to the public, and is pronounced in a way almost completely unrelated to how it is spelt.

© Today is **Penny Loaf Day** in Newark, Nottinghamshire. In 1644, in the middle of the civil war, the mightily named Hercules Clay of Newark dreamed that his house was burning down. The next night he had the same dream, and the following night he dreamed it all again. Enough was enough. Securing his family, he evacuated the house, and was not entirely surprised when it proceeded to burn down. It had been hit by the Roundheads, who at the time were laying siege to Newark. In gratitude for the forewarning, he left £100 to purchase penny loaves, shoes and boots for the poor of Newark, who had to listen to a sermon first. At its 19th-century peak 3,000 loaves were handed out today. This sermon still takes place on or near March 11th, the date of the original almsgiving; but unfortunately the money has run out, and the congregation now leave empty-handed.

12th March
St Gregory the Great's Day

Saint Onion and the Slave Boys

Today in 1847, the *Stamford Mercury* reported the week's outrage at Barrow-upon-Humber, Humberside. George Wray had asked the town crier to announce that he was selling his wife in the market place. Eventually a sailor named Harwood purchased Mrs Wray for a shilling, with three and a half pennies to be paid back later 'for luck'. The former Mrs Wray was said to be happy as she strode off arm-in-arm with her cut-price paramour. The sailor held himself '*with as much coolness as if he had purchased a new coat or hat*'.

Occasionally a **wife-seller** would wind up in court. But such separations were usually agreed by the couple prior to the sale. Until the Act of Divorce 1857, official divorce needed a special Act of Parliament and cost the equivalent of £30,000 in modern terms. Even after 1857 it was too expensive for most people. So unwritten law decided that as long as the sale was announced, the market toll paid, and the wife presented on show with a halter on her neck or waist, the affair would be legal, in an illegal sort of way.

In Thomas Hardy's *The Mayor of Casterbridge* a sailor buys Mrs Henchard from Mr Henchard for the princely sum of five guineas – £5.25. In reality the business was usually settled beforehand and concluded jovially by all concerned in the pub afterwards. And the fee paid was generally a lot lower: a famous sale at the village stocks in Ninfield, East Sussex, had the price fixed at a half-pint of gin. A report at the time noted that the ex-wife '*appeared mightily delighted about the ceremony, and the hopeful pair departed filled with joy and expectation from the happy union*'. The village stocks were made of iron and still survive, with the original whipping-post, near the village church.

Britain's first recorded wife-sale was in 1073. The last is reputed to have been in Northumberland in the dim and distant days of 1972.

◉ Today is **St Gregory the Great's Day**, known fondly in Lancashire as Gregory-gret-Onion. The watery-eyed Saint's nickname stems from the fact that today is the time to sow onion seed and thus ensure a bumper crop. From the resultant onions it is possible to assess the coming winter. A thin skin means it will be mild, a thick skin means wrap up in as many layers as the onion.

Gregory has an important role in British tradition as Father of the Church. A 6th-century Pope in Rome, he saw a brace of beautiful slave-boys and enquired after their place of origin. On hearing that they were from pagan Britain, Gregory declared that it was criminal to leave such a handsome race unbaptized. He liberated the slaves and dispatched his envoy Augustine to Britain, importing the radical new religion of Christianity to these shores in 597.

There are 32 ancient churches in Britain dedicated to Gregory – all acknowledge that he was sage, but none mention his onions.

13th March

Sex with Toads

In 1664 at Lowestoft in Suffolk, Amy Duny accepted the post of childminder to Dorothy Durent's offspring. The child had epilepsy, but such was the mood of the times that Amy was suspected of witchcraft. A supposed wise woman told Dorothy to undo the magic by wrapping the child in a blanket which had earlier been stuffed up a chimney. Anything that then crawled from the blanket had to be burned. Dorothy followed this advice and watched a toad leap out; and when thrown on to the fire it behaved like a firework. The exploding toad was immediately suspected of being Amy's companion in witchery; but if so she must have been a little too familiar with her supposed familiar, as her thighs were visibly scorched when the creature whizzed and banged.

When Amy was put on trial, along with her friend Rose Cullender, the implausible toad story – with all its hideous implications – was the main thrust of the prosecution's case. Amy and Rose were said to have bewitched several other local children, all of whom testified against the women. The judge at Bury St Edmunds believed every word of what was said, and on this day in 1664 he found them guilty as charged. They were hanged three days later. This witch trial set the tone for many other high-credulity, high-venom, low-facts cases across the country, and became a key reference point in the notorious Salem witch trials in Massachusetts, USA, in 1692.

Comets have always been the most potent of portents, the most ominous of omens. But March 13th was the day on which Edmund Halley took the wind from the comet's sails a little. In 1682 he observed a comet and worked out that it had also appeared in 1607 and 1531 – a regular gap of 76 years. He predicted that it would come back in another 76 years. In 1758, bang on schedule, Halley's Comet returned. This left comets no longer the all-powerful cosmological arbiters of doom, but celestial bodies bound by the laws of astrophysics.

The most famous earlier manifestation of Halley's Comet was in 1066, an appearance depicted in the Bayeaux Tapestry. When it appeared, no one was quite sure what it signified. But days later, with England conquered, its meaning became abundantly clear. Some astronomers have also suggested that just over a millenia earlier, Halley's comet was the 'star' which led the wise men to the newborn Christ.

Almost as dramatic, the comet of 1712 was widely thought to herald the end of the world by fire. Londoners took to the Thames, thinking to escape Armageddon by water. Stocks plummeted. Old scores were settled, and firemen surrounded the Bank of England, daring God to do his worst. Recent stockmarket crashes look rather tame in comparison.

Halley's Comet's last appearance, in 1986, was visually disappointing, although it did inspire the hilariously bad nude-alien-vampires-frozen-in-Halley's-comet film *Lifeforce*. Despite this, the comet is still expected to look in on its next visit to our corner of the cosmos, sometime in the year 2062.

Still in outer space, March 13th also saw the discovery of **Uranus** by Sir William Herschel. His 1781 announcement to a friend – 'I've gazed upon Uranus' – led to two long centuries of the same old joke, until the less comical 'your-ann-us' pronunciation was adopted in the 1980s. Coincidentally, on the same day in 1931 Clive Tombaugh discovered Pluto, originally known Hispenis.

14th March

I Byng Mistreated

Charles Charlesworth was born today in 1929, entering folklore as a national celebrity. At the age of four he went hurtling through puberty, sporting a fine beard before the year was out. Over the next four years he began to stagger into old age, so that by the time he was eight he was on his deathbed with white hair and wrinkles. Unruffled, the coroner simply recorded the cause of death as old age.

When facing the firing squad, it is customary to wave a handkerchief when you are ready to be killed. A blindfold is also optional, however. On this day in 1757 on the ship *Monarch*, Admiral Byng opted for no blindfold. The gunmen took aim, but could not bring themselves to shoot him. Not because they were cowards or because he was an innocent man – although there was a strong whiff of scapegoat about his death sentence – but because his piercing stare had unnerved them. Byng reluctantly agreed to be blindfolded, and the execution was finally executed.

Admiral Byng's capital crime was to have fought an indecisive battle against the French off Minorca. The French had gone on to capture the island, and Byng's subsequent court-martial dumped all the blame for the loss on the Admiral, accusing him of incompetence and lack of effort. Anti-Byng feeling ran high, and a series of ballads reviled and ridiculed him, often at great length. These are the last lines of the nine lengthy verses of *An Address, From the Regions Below to Admiral Byng*:

> May the subject who caused this subject so
> foul
> Be hanged, shot, or drowned I wish from my
> soul.

There were those who found Byng's execution and the accompanying mockery rather excessive. They included Voltaire, who in *Candide* concluded that the British periodically shoot one of their admirals in order *'to encourage the others'* – a phrase that has become Byng's unofficial epitaph.

🏛 Byng is buried in the mausoleum at the park in Southill, near Bedford.

Blood-letting was long invoked as a cure for all manner of ailments, and March 14th was believed to be an optimum day for starting a course of treatment. After parting with blood from their right arm during the hours of daylight today, those seeking rude health were advised to wait until April 11th before surrendering some of the contents of their left arm. The final stage came on May 2nd, when a donation from either arm sufficed to end the regimen, and guarantee a full year free from fever, falling gout, sister gout and *'loss of thy sight'*. The same procedure was said to work equally well if started on March 7th, providing the first blood-letting took place at night.

For those interested in blood-letting but unwilling to slice open their own veins, nature provides a handy alternative in the form of the leech. *Hirudo medicinalis* was once an essential in any doctor's bag, as it not only made its own incision, but provided the anaesthetic. Quacks were so keen on prescribing the creatures that 'leech' became a general term for doctors, and their medically unsound practices led to the saying *'Leeches kill with licence'*. But faith in the leech was not entirely misplaced – blood-letting itself may be a dubious treatment, but the worms secrete an anti-coagulant, Hirudin, and surgeons still make use of leeches in some delicate operations to keep the circulation going in small blood vessels.

15th March
The ides of March

Beware the Rides of March

Today is the **ides of March**, ides being a monthly non-event in the old Roman calendar simply denoting the middle of the month (falling on the 15th in some months, the 13th in others). The cry *'Beware the ides of March!'*, though more famous than many traditionally unlucky days or omens, has never had any general connotation of disaster. A soothsayer shouted the warning to Julius Caesar in the eponymous play by Shakespeare, days before the Emperor received fatal multiple entry wounds in the dorsal area. Romans thought the ides a bad day to marry or begin new ventures; but that was all – it was a perfectly good day for Caesaricide. March itself was named after the war-god Mars and was the first month of the Roman year, an appropriate time for a fresh start, or for an imperial game of ide and shriek.

© This is the earliest possible day for the oldest – and oddest – flat race in England, the **Kiplingcotes Derby** just outside Market Weighton, Humberside, held on the third Thursday in March. The four-mile course climbs from 160 to 450 feet above sea-level, crossing fields, a railway bridge and a major road. The derby is thought to have been instigated in 1519 to assess the state of the horses after winter, and shows up in records from the mid-16th-century. Men and women compete: all riders must weigh more than 10 stone, and if they are less than that after the race they are disqualified. It is acceptable for light riders to fill their pockets with heavy objects to make up the weight. They are also disqualified for striking or hindering a fellow contender.

First prize comes from the interest on a sum of £365 deposited in 1618. The runner-up receives a sizeable percentage of the riders' entrance fee; with inflation, this is now almost always larger than the first prize. There is at least one known instance of two riders, way ahead of the field, stopping to haggle, each anxious that the other should come first.

The Derby has thwarted all disasters. Two world wars did not hinder it, and the deep snows of 1947 failed too. On the latter occasion, there was only one plucky entrant, who rode and walked the course in the strange cause of tradition. These days, despite the limited prize-money and the risks of horse-injury on the rugged course, riders come from all over the country to take part in a piece of racing history.

The only thing now endangering the event is the fact that the latest Ordnance Survey maps no longer mark the diffuse settlement of Kiplingcotes. Humberside Council even took down the road signs, but the scattered residents converged in affronted opposition, and new brown and white tourist signs were erected in March 1993.

Kiplingcotes Derby weighs in and finishes in a lane off the A163 between Market Weighton and Middleton-on-the-Wolds. The start is at a sandstone post a mile north of the disused Kiplingcotes railway station. It is almost impossible to see both the beginning and end of the race, although this was achieved in 1956 by a man with a pilot's licence, who after the start jumped into a helicopter and flew to the finishing line.

16th March

Exorcist – the Prequel

On 16th March 1594 at Clayworth near Leigh in Lancashire, roving exorcist Revd John Darrell came into Nicholas Starkie's service, his job being to remedy the demoniacal possession of the household. Only Starkie himself had remained immune during the strange outbreak of the evil eye. Earlier attempts to oust the demons had led to Starkie hiring John Hartlay, a well-known wizard. Hartlay used various spells; his fee increased weekly; but the evil forces lingered. When Revd Darrell arrived, he at once denounced the wizard as a crook, saying that '*Hartlay was conjuror enough to discover the difference between Mr Starkie's table and his own*'. But had Hartlay just ripped off the gullible Starkie, or had his magic added to

the evil infestation? Witnesses claimed that the wayward wizard breathed devils into his victims with his kisses.

When Margaret Byrom of Salford visited the Starkies, she contracted a contagious demon. She said that there was now a small calf inside her, nuzzling at her heart. She had visions of a large, evil-looking black dog, which she inisted was Hartlay in spirit form. To others he was simply a '*designing knave*', and at Darrell's behest he was locked in Lancaster Castle. Darrell and over 30 sidekicks then prayed and fasted alongside the massed ranks of the demoniacally possessed. This intensity of holiness routed the spirits, who exited their human victims leaving wounds and bleeding orifices. They assumed various shapes in their flight, including a hunchback, a man with shoulders higher than his head, a fiery demon . . . and a hedgehog.

All seemed well, but in true cinematic false-ending tradition, the monsters returned and besieged Starkie's house. Square-jawed Darrell won the battle, and the demons cleared off never to return. Hartlay was convicted of witchcraft and hanged. He repented on the scaffold and the rope broke, saving his life. False ending number two. The audience cheered, but he was strung up again, and that was that. Finally, just as the music swelled and the closing credits seemed about to roll, there was a final twist as leading man John Darrell was accused of exorcising spirits to enhance his fame and finances. He was imprisoned, and a law was passed saying that in future no one, not even a clergyman, could cast out demons without a note from his bishop. Local legend still casts Reverend Darrell as the hero – pious and noble but misunderstood. But it may be that he was a brilliant con-man, with a neat line in special effects.

This was the day when England and Wales first tried out a form of government that did not rely on the reigning monarch – effectively the system in operation today. Under Cromwell's Protectorate the House of Lords and the Monarchy were consigned to the scrap heap. The new Commonwealth was run by a Council of State. Its President, empowered on March 16th 1649, was **Judge John Bradshaw** – a key figure in the sentencing of Charles I.

♱ Bradshaw presided wisely over the Commonwealth's brief tenure of power, and died peacefully. Later, as part of the 1660s' Restoration desecrations, his body was disinterred and gibbeted on the express orders of Charles I's vengeful and back-on-the-throne son, Charles II. Bradshaw's ghost now alternates between quietly haunting at Westminster Abbey's deanery, and manifesting in the Manor House at Walton-on-Thames, Surrey.

17th March
St Patrick's Day/
St Withburga's Day

A Box of Snakes, Withburga to Follow

According to a Scottish myth, the patron saint of Ireland, **St Patrick**, was born near Glasgow. He was so holy that the Devil immediately sent witches and demons to kill him. Patrick made a run for it and headed towards Ireland via the Clyde. Unable to cross water, the irate forces of darkness lobbed a mighty rock after him. It missed by miles, but became the huge hump-like hill on which Dumbarton Castle in Strathclyde now stands.

Then again, it has been 'proven' that Patrick was born in old Pembrokeshire – now part of Dyfed; and again at Battersea in London.

Delete all of the above. There is clear historical evidence that Patrick was born in 389 at *Bannavem Taburniae*, a Roman village near Norton, Northamptonshire. His father Calpurnius was a Roman town councillor and deacon who married a Briton. Patrick inherited Christianity from his dad, but did little with it for the first few years. Only when captured at the age of 16 and sold as a slave to an Irish cattle-rancher did he pause to consider how handy it would be to have a decent god behind him. Six years later, when a runaway boulder looked set to crush him but suddenly split at the last second, Patrick realised that he had been given a sign. After a quick reunion with his family, he established a base in Armagh and set about converting Ireland to Christianity.

On his deathbed Patrick wrote his confession – the earliest post-classical biography in Europe – in which he appears as a humble, ill-educated bloke trying his best in the face of adversity. It was left to independent biographers to flesh him out. They told how he once escaped from pagan King Laoghaire O'Neill of Tara by disappearing with his retinue and making the king think that they had all been transformed into deer. Other famous exploits included stuffing all the Irish **snakes** into a box and chucking it into the sea. This brilliant fable

explains at a stroke not only why there are no snakes in Ireland, but why the Irish Sea is so choppy, as the restless snakes want to get out. Less publicised is the fact that at the same time as he cast out the snakes, Patrick banished toads, lizards, and even the bewildered, innocent newt. He cursed ferns, which is why they do not bloom; and meanwhile he did wonders for the image of the **shamrock** – using its three leaves on one stalk to illustrate the nature of the Trinity.

As Patrick's fame spread, there were those who sought to test his faith. A druid cold-bloodedly killed Patrick's charioteer, and then apologised, asking to be forgiven. The druid was sounding out the holy man's stance on the controversial issue of Christian forgiveness. Patrick was personally willing to forgive, but he pointed out that the only true forgiveness could come from Heaven. A sword sent the unfortunate druid there at once for the heavenly verdict. The man should have known better: Patrick, in an early foray, had levitated another druid and then bounced him off the rocks below.

For all the strange beliefs and legends that have risen in his wake, **St Patrick** was no fan of superstition. The popular divination of looking into mirrors to see apparitions was punishable by excommunication under Patrick's law. Meanwhile, as a lasting tribute to his reptile and amphibian banishing trick, it is said that the soil of Ireland can be sprinkled on any garden to rid the lawn of '*venomous worms*'.

Ireland has two surviving Patrick shrines, one containing his bell, another his tooth: both are in the National Museum in Dublin.

Today is also the feast-day of **St Withburga**. In 7th-century East Dereham, Norfolk, she cured a local drought by conjuring up two deer to give never-ending supplies of milk to her nuns. An ill-advised hunter decided to chase the deer one day, but God destroyed him with a bolt from the blue.

St Withburga appears every now and then as that rarest of apparitions, the **dead ghost**. Her incorporeal corpse is seen being carried in an open coffin by monks along the Little Ouse towards Ely in Cambridgeshire. The monks are doing penance for the Bishop of Ely who stole Withburga's body to bring prestige and pilgrims to his own church. But the original grave near St Nicholas' church in East Dereham turned into a **healing well**, ensuring that the town remained her shrine. The well is inscribed with the story of the relic-stealing monks of

Ely, and a ruined chapel next to St Nicholas's now covers the site of Withburga's tomb.

✝ One of the regulars at The Old Ferry Boat Inn at Holywell, just east of Huntingdon in Cambridgeshire, has been dead since the middle of the 11th century. Young Juliet Tewsley hanged herself from a willow tree on this day, having been spurned by her true love, Tom Zoul. She was buried by the River Ouse, and her grave now forms part of the pub's flagstone floor. Every March 17th, known locally as **Juliet Eve**, the inn's patrons gather round to watch the woman rise from the grave, pass through the floor of the pub and drift across the bar and out towards the river. Even though Juliet is seldom seen, it is rare for the Eve to end without one of the drinkers claiming to have felt the ghost's presence.

18th March
St Edward the Martyr's Day

A Peel of Bells

In AD 979 **King Edward** rode to the royal palace at Corfe Gate, on the Isle of Purbeck in Dorset, after doing a few turns round the local forest with his huntsmen and dogs. While the men escorted the hounds back to the kennels, Edward greeted his stepmother Elfthryth, who gave him a cup of wine. The King sat on his horse drinking and doubtless embroidering a tiresome tale of the wild-boar-that-got-away, but he was cut off in full flow when someone reinforced the kick in the wine by surreptitiously stabbing him. Surprised, Edward spurred his horse forward, and slipped from the saddle in his death throes, hanging on by one foot as the steed carried him simultaneously into oblivion and legend. His body could not be found, and the official story went out that the King had suffered a fatal fall while hunting. Meanwhile, ambitious Elfthryth watched her own son Ethelred mount the throne.

Things might have remained as they were had it not been for an outburst of miracles on the road between Corfe and Wareham. Nothing was seen, but to the accompaniment of a sound likened to rustling reeds all manner of wayfarers abruptly found that their ailments had vanished. The blind and deaf had their respective senses restored; cripples hobbled up and then sprinted home in record time. St Dunstan sent some holy gravediggers to investigate, and in a shallow roadside grave they found Edward's punctured body, undecayed and with the tell-tale wound gleaming in the sunlight.

▥ In spite of the circumstantial evidence, no charge was brought against Elfthryth; though she ended her days in repentance as a nun at Wherwell in Hampshire. Edward's pristine remains were taken to Shaftesbury in Dorset, which became a highlight of the pre-Reformation pilgrim circuit. Edward's empty tomb was unearthed at the Abbey there in 1861; but some of his relics have survived, at the Eastern Orthodox church in Brookwood, near Woking in Surrey. Corfe Castle is open to the public.

✝ Edward – after a short delay – now rests in peace, but his horse is still heard trotting around Corfe Castle. Presumably because its grave was never discovered.

© On the third Thursday in March, St Clement Danes Church, Strand, London holds its **Oranges and Lemons Service**. The church is decorated with oranges and lemons, and after the 3.30 pm service the fruits are doled out to children from St Clement Danes Primary School. The bells chime out the old nursery rhyme at 9 am, noon, 3 pm and 6 pm. The church was bombed in the last war, and the bells were rehung in 1957 at a cost greatly in excess of five farthings. The ceremony originated in the Middle Ages, when porters carried oranges and lemons to Clare Market via Clements Inn, where a fruit-toll was paid. The custom fizzled out at the end of the 19th century, only to be revived in its present church-and-children form in 1920. The fruit these days is donated by the city's Danish community, who were involved in the trade from an early stage – they are the 'Danes' in the church's name. The ceremony still contains more vitamin C than any other custom.

19th March
St Joseph's Day

By the Time I Get to Phoenix

By March 19th 1716 the Phoenix was engulfed, not by flames but by snow. On the following day she rose again after being discovered, none the worse for a fast which had lasted five days. **Phoenix** – a 13-year-old girl from Peak Forest, Derbyshire – had sat down at Peaslow near Chapel-en-le-Frith. Then she had been caught in '*the most severe . . . snowing and driving rain that hath been seen in the memory of man*'. Stiff limbs and thirst were her only complaints, and she combated hunger and boredom by resorting to day-dreaming. The story caused great interest, the chief concern being why her parents had opted for such a weird name.

✝ But then Peak Forest was itself weird. Between 1728 and 1754 the vicars there had no superiors, and assumed the grand title 'Principal Official and Judge in Spiritualities in the Peculiar Court of Peak Forest'. The area capitalised on its independence to become another Gretna Green, with the besotted travelling from all over the country to '*Pay, marry, say nothing and go away*' – as the church's motto succinctly put it. One clandestine couple, having spent the evening in nearby Castleton, were murdered in Winnats Pass after a pre-nuptial mugging. They had been boasting in the Castleton pubs about their pocketfuls of cash. Their ghosts still wander the pass in bemusement, and can be heard howling in the wind.

An Act of Parliament came into effect on March 25th 1754, quashing the furtive marital activity at Peak Forest. You can still marry without banns in the village, as long as one of you has lived there for at least 15 days; though Peak Forest Chapel was destroyed in 1880.

Still with marital matters, **Alexander III** of Scotland remarried at Jedburgh Abbey, Borders, in 1285 and had to contend with a gate-crashing skeleton. It danced towards him like an escapee from *Jason & the Argonauts* and thrust its finger to within millimetres of the King's nose. It was an omen of his death, and on March 19th the following year Alexander and his horse plummeted off the cliffs near Kinghorn, Fife.

🏛 An alternative legend says that Thomas Learmont, aka **Thomas the Rhymer** of Erceldoune, predicted the King's death the day before. Thomas was a poet, prophet and weirdo, who had once met the Faerie Queen in the Eildon Hills in the Borders. She dragged him off to spend seven years with her in Elfhame – the Scottish faerieland. It was an epic journey, recounted in the *Ballad of True Thomas*:

For forty days and forty nights he wade
through red blude to the knee,
And he saw neither sun nor moon, but heard
the roaring of the sea.

Thomas was not allowed to speak; but when he eventually got back to the world of mortals he had the gift of prophecy, as well as a tongue that could never lie – a mixed blessing. Thomas eventually returned to the Queen, escorted over the mystic border by a couple of deer, and he still lives in Elfhame as a councillor to the faeries. His tower is at Earlston (Thomas' 'Erceldoune'), near Melrose, Borders.

This is **St Joseph's Day**, an unfavourable day for marriage, at Peak Forest or anywhere else. But anyone *born* today arrives with buckets of good luck. In Scotland a St Joseph's child cannot be shot in battle. And a medal depicting St Joseph has the ability to extinguish fires.

20th March
St Cuthbert's Day/
St Herbert's Day

Misogynist Monster Man Seals His Feet

St Cuthbert sought solitude, but got noise. He set up home on the allegedly uninhabited Farne Islands in Northumberland, but found that he had neighbours – goblins who shrieked and roared all night. Cuthbert exiled them to some of the less desirable offshore rocks, where they rode on goats and continued to wail. Otherwise he got on well with all animals: an enamoured eagle once swooped down and gave the saint a fish. When Cuthbert prayed in the sea, seals often followed him onshore to dry his feet and legs, staying on to be blessed. And on one occasion two sea monsters crept up to Cuthbert while he was at prayer, and asked for a blessing. He complied.

🏛 Angels sought Cuthbert for conversation. One even cured his knee-tumour; though it was a second tumour, on his chest, that finished him off. His great friend **St Herbert**, who lived on an island in Derwent Water, Cumbria, was so alarmed at the prospect of Cuthbert's death that he prayed to be delivered into heavenly bliss on the same day. They both died on March 20th 687, joining each other in saintdom. St Herbert has a surviving cell in a clearing on the Derwent Water island.

Cuthbert's affability did not extend to women. He hated them, especially after a Pictish princess claimed that he was the father of her child. Horrified, Cuthbert prayed for proof of his innocence. The ground opened and swallowed his accuser. Her father then begged Cuthbert for forgiveness, and for the return of his daughter. The saint complied, but only on condition that no woman should come near him again.

🏛 Even in death churches dedicated to Cuthbert were 'men only'. When his body came to rest at Durham, a woman took a short cut through the cemetery and strayed near Cuthbert's tomb. She suffered a fatal stroke. Another woman who sneaked into the cathedral was found the next day having apparently cut her own throat. Despite all this misogyny, Cuthbert was for centuries one of the most popular British saints, helped by the fact that his corpse refused to decay. The site of Cuthbert's grave is still marked in Durham Cathedral, and his restored coffin can be seen in the Treasury.

🏛 ✝ Cuthbert was Bishop of Lindisfarne, and he left his mark all over the island. It was Cuthbert, according to legend, who discovered the causeway which links Lindisfarne to the mainland; and the socket of the Saint's cross there – known as the **Petting Stone** – is still leaped over by newly weds for luck. Fossil *encrinites* found in Lindisfarne's limestone rocks are known as **Cuthbert's Beads**. He is said to have forged them during his stint there, and his ghost continues to make new beads.

St Cuthbert's Well at Edenhall near Penrith in Cumbria, was the chosen venue for some partying faeries who left behind a glass beaker called *The Luck of Edenhall*. As they departed, the faeries declared:

> *If this cup should break or fall,*
> *Farewell the luck of Edenhall!*

The Musgrave family kept it safe for centuries; but in 1926 they loaned it to the Victoria and Albert Museum. Bad move. Eight years later the hall had been destroyed.

🏛 The 'Luck' is, in reality, a 13th-century Syrian piece brought over during the Crusades. It can still be seen in the V & A in London along with its snug-fit leather pouch. The Edenhall well is still intact.

21st March
Spring Equinox

Metaphysics and Giant Slugs

The **first day of spring** gives druids a chance to practise before the Midsummer madness. One of their modern equinox haunts is at Tower Hill in London, where the head of the god **Bran** was buried. Bran was a sun god, and today for the first time in the year, the days – his territory – begin to outstrip the nights: cause for celebration.

The other key entry in the Pocket Guide to Celtic spring gods is **Angus Mac Og**, another sun deity, the symbol of youthfulness. Angus used the endless interplay of night and day to procure the palace Brugh na Boinn from the god Nuadu. He persuaded Nuadu to lend him the premises for a night and a day, and then refused to leave, claiming that the palace was now his. He backed up his claim with a vast metaphysical argument, saying that night and day were the microcosm which reflected the macrocosm; that they were the pattern, and therefore the embodiment, of eternity. Therefore, Brugh na Boinn was his forever by dint of logic. Staggeringly, he won the case.

That was all very appropriate, as Angus had been conceived and born in the space of one day. His all-powerful father Dagda seduced and impregnated a mortal, then messed about with time so that her husband would not know that nine months had passed. The cuckolded man, wondering why he was so incredibly hungry, arrived home to find Angus born. With such time-warped origins, Angus' later marriage to a swan can perhaps be attributed to a hormone imbalance. Technically it was a were-swan, since it alternated between the forms of a bird and a maiden. The family horse was unusual too, creating Lough Neagh in one huge bladder-movement.

🏛 Brugh na Boinn survives as several wildy carved stones and a large tumulus at Newgrange in County Meath, Ireland. Loch Neagh – the result of the horsey horsey that did not stop – is right in the middle of Northern Ireland. Angus (Mac) Og crops up in various guises in the Gaelic myths of Ireland and Scotland, and there is even an Angus Og cartoon-strip in Scotland's *Daily Record* newspaper.

✝ **Bleaklow Hill** and the Longdendale Valley in north Derbyshire have rich seams of ectoplasm – there are ghostly beams of light, phantom lorries, and a wonderful monster described as a **black slug** the size of a small whale, with large rolling eyes. But at the time of the first full moon after the equinox (which is usually today or tomorrow), Bleaklow's stars are **ghostly Romans**, linked to the old Roman route between the forts at Brough and Glossop. In 1932 a whole legion was seen. The most recent large-scale sighting of roaming Romans was in 1979.

☿ The 21st used to be **St Benedict's Day**. He has since been moved to July 11th for good behaviour. Old Benedict's brings with it a warning about peas. This is your very last chance to sow them, for:

If peas are not sown by Benedick
They had better stay in the rick.

A bit of wind helps too – *A March wind is the salt which seasons the pulse.*

22nd March

Nettle Plus Kettle Equals Fine Fettle

Wilhelmina Dewar, of Whitley Bay, Tyne and Wear, was found today in 1908 by her sister Margaret in the throes of **spontaneous combustion**, that most fashionable piece of turn-of-the-century mythology. At first the judge presiding at the hearing was unimpressed. He suspected that someone must have been carrying a torch for Wilhelmina. Margaret admitted tampering with the human bonfire, but said that her aim had been to remove her frying sister from the bed once she had burst into flame. The judge eventually came round to the idea that Wilhelmina could indeed have spontaneously combusted. He refused to prosecute anyone, and filed the case under 'accidental death by fire'.

Recent perverse experiments have shown that once alight, a person can burn using their own body fat. But despite reports of unexplained human conflagrations during the 1980s, which fanned the flames of public interest in spontaneous combustion, there is still no scientific basis for the unaided ignition of individuals.

During March **nettles** are at their young, tender, juicy peak. Admittedly, an old and incontrovertible saying warns: '*It is ill work plucking nettles with bare hands*'; but with a pair of gloves on, the nettle is one of three great cure-alls:

Drink nettle tea in March and mugwort tea
  in May
And cowslip wine in June to send decline
  away.

The virtue of settling for nettles in March was underlined at Port Glasgow, west of Glasgow in Strathclyde. A mermaid – always a reliable source – is on record as having heckled the funeral procession of a consumptive girl as it passed by. She yelled out this untimely advice to the mourners: '*If they wad drink nettles in March and eat muggons in May, sae mony braw maidens wadna gang to the clay.*'

Fun-loving Romans introduced nettles into Britain in order to whip themselves into a frenzy during the cold winter months. Nicholas Culpeper is probably not recommending the same thing in his 1653 *The English Physician Enlarged* when he says that nettles '*consume the flegmatic superfluities in the body of man that the coldness and moisture of winter hath left behind.*' According to such herbals, nettle is good for the brain, the senses, the appetite and the entire body, as well as curing baldness, insomnia and incontinence. If bored, you can play a toned-down version of the Roman game and paint your chilblains with nettle juice. It has a similar soothing effect on burns and, hair-of-the-dog fashion, on nettle rash. **Dock** makes this latter claim too. When applying dock to nettle stings, chant the following:

Nettle in, dock out; dock in, nettle out,
Nettle in, dock out; dock rub nettle out.

Nettles are also a safeguard against sorcery. In bunches they protect milk from witches. Part of this anti-malevolence ability stems from the benevolent faeries who live in nettle patches. These patches are a supposedly sure-fire indication that there is gold in the earth below, which is why the canny faeries dwell there.

Dyes, rennets, and even cloth can be made from nettles. Scots used them all the time, as recorded by the poet Thomas Campbell (1777–1844): '*Be not nettled . . . at my praise of this useful weed. In Scotland I have eaten nettles, I have slept in nettle sheets and I have dined off a nettle table-cloth.*' None of which explains the plant's folk-names, Devil's Leaf and Naughty-Man's-Plaything.

23rd March

Sink or Swing

Unless taking part in a Gothic horror story, it is customary to die first and get buried later. But on this day in 1660 **Dorothy Mately** of Ashover, Derbyshire, bucked the trend after repeating her pet phrase – '*I would I might sink into the earth if it be so*' – once too often. Dorothy was an ore-washer, sieving through mined rubble for traces of lead, and was renowned for a rich repertoire of blasphemies, lies, curses and theft.

On one occasion the man working beside her removed his pants and continued to sieve in his Y-fronts. When he returned to his trousers he found that his pockets had been picked. Suspicion fell on Dorothy, but she protested her innocence and added her favourite '*I would I might sink into the earth if it be so*'. Legend has it that she then became a human drill and began to twist into the earth complete with her sieve and washing tub, spinning down until she was three feet under. Before anyone could help, a stone popped from the earth and smashed her skull. Dorothy then went under for the last time, and was later found at a depth of four yards.

Geologists have suggested that subsidence due to mining was a possible cause of the incident. Foul play is also likely – Dorothy, who gave as good as she got in a man's world, was probably clubbed to death, buried, discovered, and explained away with the aid of folklore and divine retribution. The coroner swallowed the ludicrous story, and her death entry in the local register uses a novel medical term, saying that Dorothy died because she '*forswore herself*'.

The Great British Public liked nothing better than to watch someone break a neck or choke on a rope at the local **hanging**. With stalls and street entertainment, it was a great day out for all the family, and the cabaret was free. On this day in 1827, a Mr Udale was strung up at Lincoln. A local hack described a capacity crowd '*pressing forward up the hill in one dense unbroken stream*'. The reporter claimed that most of the parents had brought their children along to dissuade them from transgressing: i.e. if you don't eat your greens you will be brutally executed in public.

For the vulture-like opportunist such events did not just provide a great show. They also offered the chance to dab a handkerchief in the hanged man's efficacious sweat – the cloth then had brief powers of healing. At the very least, morbid medical cases could touch the corpse or rub the cloth on an afflicted part of the body. Ghoulish souvenir hunters often took their mementoes too: it was common for flesh to be stripped from the deceased's bones.

A dead man's hand was the chief prize, because of its value among the burgling fraternity. With a candle – ideally made of human fat, or the mixed fats of a bear, a badger and an unbaptised child – burning on a hanged man's mummified hand, a burglar is given an invaluable aid on his rounds – invisibility. This atrocious trophy was called the **hand of glory**. As for the deceased, his last hope was for a spot of posthumous rain, as it was believed that: *Blest is the corpse that the rain raineth on.*

24th March
St Gabriel's Day

Angels, Leviathans and Postmen

March 24th was **New Year's Eve** until 1752, when the Julian Calendar was dropped in favour of the Gregorian one. In England, that is. Scotland had been celebrating on December 31st as early as 1600. The January New Year stems from the fact that this is the traditional date of Christ's circumcision – it was normal Jewish practice to perform this minor operation eight days after a boy's birth. Strictly speaking this should make the Feast of the Circumcision, and the New Year, fall on January 2nd. But the boundary between months was a much more appealing date for the start of the year. When the Gregorian calendar was introduced Old New Year's Eve became April 5th–12 days on from March 24th (only 11 days had been lost, but many dates moved by an extra day). In the world of business and commerce, April 5th still marks the boundary between the old and new financial years.

Today is old **St Gabriel's Day**. The archangel is invoked by those waiting, or looking, for good news. As such he is the patron saint of messengers, the post, and telephones.

Gabriel basks under the grand title 'Prince of Fire', and is in charge of Paradise. His hobbies include playing the trumpet and giving surprising news to virgins. But the big task for which he is psyching himself up, according to Jewish tradition, is a scrap with the Leviathan, who will attempt to destroy the Earth during the Messianic Age. This grudge against all of creation is understandable, as God killed his partner, the only female Leviathan, to prevent these enormous sea-monsters from breeding and taking over the world. As a handy by-product of the slaughter, God made clothes for Adam and Eve from its skin. Come the final showdown, the distressing advance word for the Leviathan is that the pre-determined hero Gabriel will win, helped by his Last Trump card.

🜍 At the foot of southern England's highest cliff, Golden Cap near Bridport in Dorset, are the remains of **St Gabriel's Chapel**. An old story about its founding opens with a storm at sea. All seems lost until young Bertram and his wife offer a prayer, promising to build a church if only Gabriel will intervene. They keep repeating the prayer, and on the third night Gabriel finally pitches in to save the boat. True to his vow, Bertram builds a chapel where the boat lands, and underneath the altar he places his wife – for although Gabriel rescued the boat, by the time he arrived Mrs Bertram had died. Gabriel could easily have intervened sooner – it is said that he takes just two moves to get anywhere. His angelic comrade Michael only takes *one* move. Their chess games must be swift, if predictable.

Vincent Stuckley Lean died today in 1899, and his epic five volume *'Collectanea'* was published at the beginning of the 20th century. As well as recording thousands of folkloric observations, Lean also revels in weird proverbs. The *Collectanea* records such timeless sayings as *'Miss lives upon love and lumps of the cupboard'*; *'A turd's as good as a pancake to a sow'*; *'Where the pig breaks let the shells lie'*; *'You may choke a dog with pudding'*; and, for Latin fans, *'Edo fartum et turdum pistum'*. There are obvious depths of wisdom and large petrol bills in *'He that fetches a wife from Shrewsbury must carry her into Staffordshire or else he shall live in Cumberland'*. And would-be revivalists everywhere would do well to note that *'A bad custom is like a good cake, better broken than kept'*.

25th March
Lady Day

The Giant Hermaphrodite and the Death Dole Crawl

March 25th is the **birthday of Adam**. According to the bits that never made it into the Old Testament, he was created not in the image of God as such, but in the image of Adam Kadmon. Kadmon was a being of light spirited up when God first tried out the creation lark. The Mark II Adam was originally a gigantic but basically good hermaphrodite paired with a female but fundamentally evil creature called Lilith.

This did not work out. So God siphoned off Lilith, made Adam male, and introduced female Eve, Eden, and all the well-documented biblical stuff. But what happened to Lilith? Jewish folklore has it that she now invades men's beds and has her wicked way with the one part of the anatomy which refuses to sleep. This leads to nocturnal emissions, enabling Lilith to conceive and give birth to demon offspring.

Adam's burial place is the Cave of Machpelah, Hebron, near Jerusalem. It contains the bodies of most of the Old Testament heavies, and is used by souls as the entrance to Paradise, according to Jewish tradition.

Robin Hood was in church at Brigstock, near Corby in Northamptonshire, on Lady Day. After his prayers were done he left the church with his men, and was immediately attacked by Sir Ralph de Hanville, who had sat patiently through the service waiting his moment. The arrows began to fly, the priest was wounded, and Ralph was killed. Robin then acted as decoy, leading Ralph's archers towards Rockingham Forest. A mile and a half from Brigstock he threw his bow and arrows into a hollow in the **Bocase Tree** and, passing for a peasant, slunk back to rejoin his men.

🜍 The legend exists to make sense of a long-gone feature, called the **Bocase Tree**. It was probably an ancient moot-point where the local Court Leet met to chat about forestry rights, ferret-legging and gratuitous Robin Hood stories. A nearby field called 'Bowcast' suggests that it may have been something to do with archers and target practice. The tree itself died and was chopped up for timber several centuries ago; but such was its mythical importance that in the 17th century a commemorative stone was erected to mark where it stood, simply inscribed *'In This Plaes Grew Bocase Tree'*.

The stone at least is still there, in woodland on a bridle-path just north of Brigstock. It may not be as exciting as the original hollow home of Robin's bow, but in a world where there is a plaque on Widnes station that says that Paul Simon once sat there and wrote '*Homeward Bound*', surely the Bocase Tree deserves no less.

Lady Day celebrates the Annunciation of the Virgin, a date cleverly fixed nine months before Christmas by a logical early church. Until the 18th century it was New Year's Day (see yesterday for all the calendar calculations) and as such it was one of the four Quarter Days on which rents fell due. But to lighten the gloom, it is also a great day for seeing **faeries**. Dawn and dusk are the best times, and only a cynic would suggest that this is because in the half-light almost anything can take on an otherwordly appearance. This was also a popular fair day: in Devon they were called **Giglet Fairs**, at which women sought domestic work. The Okehampton Giglet Fair also offered a shortcut to love, for men were allowed to dispense with the formalities and ask questions akin to 'How about it then?'. Many marriages kicked off in this disco-floor style.

Old Mother Shipton of Knaresborough in North Yorkshire once declared:

When my Lord falls in my Lady's lap,
England beware of some mishap!

Which means that when Easter coincides with Lady Day, calamity will fall within 12 months. Given that every year tends to have a few 'mishaps', it is an unambitious prediction.

Born Ursula Southeil in 1488, Old Mother Shipton gained a reputation as a fortune-teller. Once, answering witchcraft charges in court, she avoided the usual fate of the accused by uttering the words '*Updraxi, call Stygician Helluei!*' She was then carried to safety by Updraxi, a winged dragon – a truly fabulous way of jumping bail.

Most of these colourful legends were cobbled together in 1871 by a huckster called Hindley, who published her 'prophecies' and took all the royalties. Behind the made-up myths was a deformed woman who, after her husband's death, lived in a cave and staved off starvation by telling fortunes to ruthlessly curious locals. Mother Shipton's Cave in Knaresborough is now a tourist attraction (i.e. you have to pay to peer in), along with its Petrifying Well.

© The **Tichborne Dole** is handed out today to the residents of Tichborne, Cheriton and Lane End, near Winchester in Hampshire. Formerly bread, the dole is now given in self-raising flour at an open-air service at Tichborne Park commemorating Isabella (or Mabella) Tichborne, the founder, to whom there is a monument in the local partly-Saxon church. It is usual for close to two tons of flour to be given out, with each adult applicant given one gallon, and each child half a gallon. The flour is doled out from a wooden trough, and is sprinkled with holy water and incense before the service.

The custom started early in the 12th century when, on her deathbed, Isabella asked her miserly husband Sir Roger to put aside land to feed the poor. Noting her condition, Roger said that she could have as much land as she could crawl round while a faggot from the fire still burned. Isabella crawled around 23 acres before the faggot fizzled out, much to Sir Roger's chagrin. The land is still known as The Crawls, and the grain grown there provides the flour for the dole. In 1948, rationing nearly hit the thing on the head, but public outcry enabled a loophole to appear, and the Dole passed through.

Tichborne Park has been the seat of the Tichborne family for over 800 years, but the last male heir died in the early 1990s. In late 1993, adverts appeared announcing that the Georgian house at Tichborne Park was up for rent (complete with butler and gardener); but it is a condition of the lease that the Tichborne Dole be continued. The owners insist that the custom is not under threat, and today's hand-out remains the oldest and most resilient of all British doles.

26th March

Lost in Her Own Maze

Sir John Vanbrugh, playwright and architect, died of a quinsy (a throat inflammation) today in 1726, and he had an apposite epitaph tucked away for this very occasion. Vanbrugh built many huge edifices, including the Haymarket Theatre, Blenheim Palace and Castle Howard. The man with the golden chisel could not resist the memorial words: '*Lay heavy on him, earth, for he laid many heavy loads on thee.*'

Regrettably, it is seldom possible to build something without destroying whatever was there beforehand. Vanburgh, in building Blenheim, razed the buildings associated with the legend of **Fair Rosamund**.

🗎 Rosamund Clifford was the secret lover of Henry II, and the King eventually had two sons by her. Queen Eleanor, his wife, was not impressed. Henry had protected Rosamund by building a maze around her bower; but Eleanor found her way through by following a length of tell-tale thread which had snagged on the side of the maze. The Minotaur at the end of this particular labyrinth was devout young Rosamund, who was forced by Eleanor to take a large swig from a cup of poison. Henry had her buried in the local nunnery, where her tomb was surrounded by candles and finery. But after the efforts of objecting bishops, the Reformation, and the work of Vanbrugh, only Fair Rosamund's Well – or Everswell – now remains, in Blenheim Park, just outside Woodstock in Oxfordshire.

If visiting Blenheim, also check out its extensive range of follies, including the **Springlock Boulder**, a huge rock dumped in front of a hidden path: it was designed to roll aside when a hidden lever was pulled.

☕ On the **weather** front, all good husbandmen know that '*A peck of March dust is worth a King's ransom*'. Unless orchards are your particular line of business:

March dust on an apple leaf
brings all kinds of fruit to grief.

If in doubt, blame a mild January:

March in Janiveer,
Janiveer in March, I fear.

Rain is bad too, for '*March water is worse than a stain in cloth*'. And there is no winning, as usual, for fair weather is just as bad:

March damp and much warm
Will do farmer much harm.

On the Isle of Man things are much more melodramatic: '*Better slaughter in the country than March should come in mild.*' They are pretty upset about it in Wiltshire too, where the cry '*Better to be bitten by a snake than to feel the sun in March*' is often raised. In practice, March usually delivers all kinds of weather. A warm spell mid-month is known as **False Summer**. Sheep are on their guard during this month too: '*When flies swarm in March sheep come by their death*'; and for fish there is news, but not as we know it:

March whisquer
Was never a good fisher.

Pardon? It all ends happily with the Scots version of '*In like a lion, out like a lamb*', which insists: '*March comes in with adders' heads and goes out with peacocks' tails.*'

27th March

Whistle While You Die

The ominous crying of the **Seven Whistlers** spells disaster. The more that are heard, the more serious the disaster will be. The Whistlers are a nationwide portent of death, and they crop up in everything from folk-songs and legends to the sonnets of Wordsworth. Even well into this century reporters would regularly find fishermen linking the Seven Whistlers with disasters at sea. A Kentish fisherman told one journalist that on a dark night when sailing out of Folkestone, the whole crew had heard the distinctive melancholy cry traditionally associated with the Whistlers. They had immediately tried to turn back, but before they could do so a boat overturned and seven men were drowned.

The fisherman himself knew that what he had heard was not a group of whistling spirits, but the sound of the far from supernatural long-billed **curlew**. But like many others he still believed that the cry of curlew was invariably an omen of gloom and doom. In Scotland – where in some areas the bird is also known as the whaup – they have remythologised the bird by linking it, and the similar whimbrel, with a curve-beaked goblin who snatches away wrongdoers. The anti-curlew lobby maintain that the Whistlers are nothing to do with the birds, and are either the spirits of unbaptised children, or, for sailors, the ghosts of their drowned companions.

The Bromsgrove Messenger of March 27th 1909 tried to sort out the conflicting theories about the Seven Whistlers. In a lengthy article John Cotton reminded his readers of Worcestershire's long-held belief in the Whistlers, whose calls are heard in the county at the onset of disaster. To hear one of them means a death in the family, or a spot of tempest. To hear four means famine and pestilence. Six give a forewarning of earthquakes and annihilation through war. No one has ever heard seven Whistlers curlewing at the same time, but, in Cotton's own words:

Should the Seven Whistlers whoop at once
Then shall earth's fate impend;
Some starry spheres, displaced may be, shall
*   dash*
The world to fragments in a shattering crash,
And all things have an end.

So the Whistlers are a homely version of the Riders of the Apocalypse. No one has ever decided what it means if you hear two, three, five, or more than seven Whistlers, but it cannot be worse than displacement of starry spheres.

♱ The Lickey Hills near Bromsgrove in Hereford and Worcester are the Whistlers' chief haunt. There are supposed to be six of them (war and earthquakes being common in Bromsgrove, presumably) searching the heavens for the fatal seventh. The Lickey Hills are also popular with the Devil and his huntsman Harry-ca-Nab. They hunt boars on their two white bulls with a pack of demon hounds from Halesowen.

A quick Highland cure: cut some **woodbine** during the increase of the moon in March, twist it into a wreath, and pass consumptive or feverish patients through the hoop. This also works for cattle, though you need a heck of a lot of woodbine to make a cow-sized hoop.

28th March
St Alkelda's Day

Bolingbroke Bowling Ball

By AD 800 the Vikings had only been importing to Britain their unique blend of rape, pillage and plunder for seven years. That year they expanded their horizons and sacked Iona and the north. It was also the year in which they bumped off one of their first British saints, **Alkelda**. A Saxon princess and part-time nun, she had been wandering through the hills of North Yorkshire when she was waylaid by a posse of stroppy Viking women. She greeted them in her saintly, beatific way. Not being much good at conversation, they strangled her. St Alkelda was buried at nearby Middleham, south of Leyburn, which made her its patron. ▥ The 13th-century St Alkelda's church is still in use, but Middleham's castle – Richard III's home from home, and a favourite base of Warwick the Kingmaker – is now a picturesque ruin.

♱ The long-gone castle at Old Bolingbroke, midway between Boston and Louth in Lincolnshire, has an appropriate March **ghost in the shape of a hare**. In former days it appeared at the auditors' meetings, ran back and forth, and frightened the dogs. Those in attendance frequently pursued the ghost into the cellar, where it disappeared. Perhaps at the time there was some link between the hare and the spirit of Bolingbroke's great hero, John of Gaunt, or that of his son Henry Bolingbroke, better known as Henry IV, King of England from 1399. Then again, perhaps there wasn't. According to a 17th-century report, the hare-ghost's most common trick – which must have given a phantom frisson to those singled out – was that it '*doeth usually runne betweene theire legs, and sometymes over throws them*'. There are few risks of such hare-line fractures these days: the ghost is seen only rarely and fleetingly, and always at a safe distance.

◉ At the end of March the village of Old Bolingbroke holds a **candle auction** for the use – from April until October – of a grazing meadow called Poor Folks' Close. The sale takes place during the meeting of the council, and is not open to the public, unless they happen to be local councillors. This real estate version of musical chairs ends when a pin-stuck candle burns down far enough for the pin to fall – whoever made the last highest bid has leased the meadow. The proceeds from the land are given to the needy on St Thomas Day, December 21st, linking it with other traditional St Thomas doles.

29th March
St Gwynllyw and
St Gwladys' Day

Separated, But Together in Heaven

Today in 1461 at the **Battle of Towton** near Tadcaster, Edward IV's Yorkists defeated Henry VI's Lancastrians in a snowstorm so severe that the soldiers could hardly see. It has gone down in history as one of the bloodiest battles ever fought in England, and since it fell exactly one week before Easter the day became known as **Sad Palm Sunday**. The hand-to-hand snowball fight went on for six gruelling hours. Some 20,000 Lancastrians died, the blizzard killing off those not finished by the sword. The local stream became a torrent of blood. It was the end of the house of Lancaster, Henry and his Queen Margaret fleeing to Scotland. They raised an army 10 years later, but were defeated at the Battle of Tewkesbury: their son Edward was stabbed, and Henry was murdered after a spell in the Tower of London. Margaret was ransomed in 1476 by Louis XI of France and lived in retirement in Anjou.

Today is the feast day of **St Gwynllyw**, remembered principally for going longer than any other British religious figure without a vowel. Non-Welsh speakers down the years have cheated and called him *Woolos*. Gwynllyw's wife **Gwladys** also became a saint. The couple started out as a pair of 6th-century hellraisers and slaughterers. Their devout Christian son Cadoc – a saint in his own right – tried for ages to convert them. Conversion was eventually achieved via a dream in which Gwynllyw was told to look for a white ox with a black spot on its forehead. It would be chewing the cud on a certain local hill. Next morning, Gwynllyw followed the visionary advice, and found the ox exactly where he was told it would be. There was nothing else for it – he was converted at once, and Gwladys joined him.

After this they lived pious, monk-like lives at Stow Hill in Gwent, until son Cadoc asked them to separate. He was horrified at their extreme athletic asceticism: Gwynllyw and Gwladys liked to strip and pray together in the freezing River Usk. They would then go on nocturnal streaks of a mile or more. The sight of the saintly parts dancing in the moonlight was too much for the offspring of those exposed loins. The couple gave in to their prudish son and parted. Which makes it all the more touching that they are unique in the canon of the canonized, being the only married couple to share a feast day. A small but growing movement is lobbying to have Gwynllyw declared the patron saint of unlucky Scrabble players.

The Cathedral of St Woolos' at Newport in Gwent was built on the site of Gwynllyw and Gwladys' Stow Hill nudist-camp-cum-hermitage. It has survived relatively intact down the centuries, preserved by a **protection curse** which says that anyone who desecrates it will perish. A band of pirates once had a go, but Gwynllyw swept down from heaven and pursued them, riding on the wind. He reclaimed all the stolen church plate, and left the pirates to drown in the storm.

30th March

Frozen Nebs, Hirpling Hoggs and the Large Bigness

1716 was a big year for **optical phenomena** in the Peak District. As already noted, there was a narrowly song-worthy sunset on March 6th at Hartington; and today the residents of Chapel-en-le-Frith in Derbyshire encountered a light '*very terrible to behold*'. In spite of the late hour, locals were able to read by its light – it cannot have been so terrible if people reacted to it by settling down with a good book. It is recorded that the celestial radiation '*streamed up like unto long picks of a large bigness*', a particularly incisive piece of reportage. The illumination was multicoloured, flashed quite a lot, and then gradually faded. In Chapel it was widely perceived as a portent of something or other. Modern meteorologists who have studied the contemporary reports say that it may have been the Northern Lights – unremarkable in the top half of Scotland, unusual this far south, but nothing to enter a monastery over.

The less scientific explanation is that such strange phenomena are something to do with the Peak District itself. There has long been a high incidence of **mysterious lights** there, sometimes emanating from the skies, sometimes coming from uninhabited, inaccessible parts of the hills themselves. Phantom lighthouses, glowing spheres, luminous mists: down the millenia they have been explained away as all manner of natural phenomena, or credited to anything from Will-o'-the-Wisps to Flying Saucers. UFOs are in fact a 20th-century manifestation of faeries. Discuss.

Today is the second of the three **Borrowing Days** which fall at the end of March. They are said to be borrowed, weather-wise, from April. Or, as Sir Walter Scott put it, '*it is feigned that March had borrowed them from April to extend the sphere of his rougher sway*'. The rhyme says it all, and more:

March said to Aperill,
'I see three hoggs upon a hill,
And if you'll lend me dayes three
I'll find a way to make them dee.'
The first o'them wus wind and weet,
The second one wus snaw and sleet,
The third o'them wus sic a freeze
It froze the birds nebs to the trees.
When the three days were past and gane,
The silly hoggs came hirpling hame.

Quite why April agreed to the wanton slaughter of the hoggs (year-old sheep), and why March failed to kill them, are not clear. An alternative, compact version says that April nicks three days back later:

> March borrows of April
> Three days, and they are ill;
> April borrows of March again
> Three days of wind and rain.

Whatever the consequence for the weather, the knock-on effect for mortals is that you must not borrow or lend anything during these three days, for the item may later be used against you in witchcraft.

31st March

The Suicidal Tree

Trees have feelings. Back in 1644 on this day, army deserter Philip Greensmith was strung up on an **elm** at Coton-in-the-Elms, near Burton upon Trent in Staffordshire. The elm was so mortified by this misuse of its branches that it either decided to end it all, or went into terminal shock. From that day, its leaves and branches began to wither, and within a year it was dead.

This is very much in keeping with the traditional personality of the elm. It is said that if you cut one down, a neighbouring elm will die of grief. Such a sentimental species proved an easy target for Dutch elm disease.

It is said that '*the elm and the vine do so naturally entwine*'. Shakespeare alludes to the notion in *The Comedy of Errors*, in which Adriana says to her husband Antipholus of Syracuse:

> *Thou art an elm, my husband, I am a vine*
> *Whose weakness, married to thy stronger state*
> *Makes me with thy strength to communicate.*

The elm not only has deep-rooted emotions: it is also an arbiter of quality. The old maxims '*A good elm never grew on bad land*' and '*Good elm, good barley*' reveal its status as a crop and field guide. And how did the barley-grower cope when there was no handy, leafy, elm around for reference?

> *When the elmen leaf's big as a mouse's ear,*
> *Then to sow barley never fear;*
> *When the elmen leaf's big as an ox's eye,*
> *Then says I, 'Hie, boys, hie!'*

♕ This is the time of the **blackthorn winter**, a spell heralded by chill winds from the north-west. Around now, blackthorn trees have the audacity to produce lots of blossom, not even waiting for their greenery to appear. This fools the perpetually gullible, who equate the arrival of blossom with the end of winter. They rush out and are brassed off when warmth proves elusive. Hence the saying: '*Beware the Blackthorn Winter*'.

♕ Today, March – of which it is said '*March, many weathers*' – has a second and final chance to come up trumps on the weather front:

> *In beginning or in end*
> *March its gifts will send.*

Some were always happy to see the back of the month: an old dairymen's cry runs: '*Good riddance, old March! Now my flock will be full of milk.*'

EASTER

These days **Easter** is generally considered to span four days – Good Friday, Easter Eve, Easter Day, and Easter Monday. The timing of these each year – and of Lent, Whitsun, Hocktide, Rogation and Ascension Day – are determined by the date allocated to Easter Day, which is the Sunday after the first full moon following the Vernal Equinox on March 21st. The date was the subject of hot contention in the early Christian church, and in 525 they opted for this somewhat complex system. The feast is so moveable that it is positively hyper-active – Easter Day can fall anywhere between March 22nd and April 25th. And just to muddy the waters further, the name 'Easter' comes from pagan Spring goddess **Eostre**, a Germanic version of the Scandinavian fertility queen Frigga. Spring and rebirth are invariably the pivotal themes in pagan religions, and the death and resurrection of Christ had all the key ingredients to keep the newly-converted quite happy.

The rebirth inherent in the **Resurrection** was more significant than the sketchy away-in-a-manger physical birth, which is why the tenets of Easter were hammered out years before the established church bothered addressing Christmas in any detail. The Resurrection was a central image which everyone could appreciate and respect. But some clerics are just never satisfied with the straight and narrow. In 1282 at Inverkeithing in Fife a priest called John, captivated by the phalluses of Priapus and Dionysus in the Classical era, decided to celebrate Easter by parading with a larger-than-life model of his genitalia on the end of a pole. And to accompany him he co-opted scantily clad local girls, dancing in circles while John uttered sexual come-ons. There are several ways of losing your job, but this was one of the most efficient.

☀ **Weatherlore** proclaims: '*A fine Easter, a fine Harvest will follow.*' Rain is more of a mixed blessing:

Rain on Good Friday or Easter Day,
A good crop of grass but a bad one of hay.

But weather has no control on the following, which is determined by the vagaries of the calendar: '*Late Easter, long cold Spring.*'

St Ives, now in Cambridgeshire, used to hold its **cloth fair** over Easter. Later it was moved to Whitsun, and later still it stopped moving altogether; but in its heyday it was one of the largest cloth fairs in Europe. At one end of the scale were fine brocades and imported silks – several English kings bought fabrics at the fair, hoping to leave their courtiers gasping. At the opposite end were the stalls in St Audrey's Lane, selling the coarsest hessian and linen. This cheap but often enthusiastically marketed cloth took on the name of the street, St Audrey. This in time became slurred to *tawdry*, and a new word was born. Incidentally, it is St Ives in Cambridgeshire, rather than St Ives in Cornwall, which gave rise to the polygamy-endorsing song and riddle that begins: '*As I was going to St Ives, I met a man with forty wives.*'

It was believed in Dorset that over Easter **calves** were particularly prone to falling into ditches. Once they had plunged in, they could not get out and often died. The farmers' solution to this seasonal problem was to slit the calves' ears. By the time they had healed up, Easter was over and the threat was thought to be past.

GOOD FRIDAY

Reverence offers one of the best excuses for a holiday, which do not come much holier than Good Friday, the day on which Christ died on the Cross. Cambridgeshire farmers, Cornish fisherman and washerwomen everywhere took the day off. Feeling guilty, blacksmiths also did no work today – it was one of the sons of Vulcan, their patron god, who forged the nails that pinned Jesus to the Cross.

The Cross itself was said to have been made from **elder** wood, which is why it is unlucky to burn elder, though this belief predates Christianity. In many areas elders were thought to be transformed witches; but in the north of England the tree was said to harbour good spirits, with benign faeries finding shelter under its boughs. For these various, confused, reasons you have to ask the tree for permission if you want to cut its wood. Lincolnshire woodcutters – firm believers in a Buddhist-like system of reincarnation – used to promise that they would give some wood back in a later life, should they find themselves reborn as trees. As a further bolster to the Christianisation of older beliefs, elder was also said to be the tree upon which Judas hanged himself.

As the man partly responsible for the Crucifixion, **Judas** was subjected to ritual abuse at Easter. On Good Friday in the Dingle area of Liverpool's dockside, Judas was paraded around the streets Guy Fawkes style, escorted by youths attempting to extort cash with the plea: '*Judas is short of a penny for his breakfast.*' After money had been collected, the Judas dummies were burned in the streets. This once-widespread tradition of sanctioned juvenile arson died out in the 1970s. The practice is said to have been learned from the many Spanish seamen docking at Liverpool. At Easter they indulged in the popular Iberian custom of flogging a Judas effigy and slinging it into the sea. But in truth these Judases are latterday versions of a widespread European tradition, the burning of a scapegoat – an effigy representing Winter at Lent or Easter (see Jack-a-Lent in the Lent section).

The Catholic crucifix-bearing processions still found in some European and South American countries today are long gone in Britain. One of the last vestiges of grassroots Christ-effigies took place at Tenby in Dyfed. Reeds were gathered and twisted into human shape before being nailed to a cross in the corner of a field or barn. This probably owed more to pagan dolls than the melodramatic church parades of yesteryear, and it breathed its last in the middle of the 19th century.

© Because of its solemn religious significance, Good Friday was one of the main days for **doles** – the handout of money or food as designated in a will. One of the most curious surviving doles is at St Bartholomew's Church in Smithfield, London. Here money used to be placed on a flat gravestone and collected by needy widows who were made to step over the grave before they were allowed their share of money and bread. It is thought to have been a survival of sin-eating, in which a hired eater 'consumed' the sins of the deceased, leaving them free to enter heaven. The name of the original Smithfield donor is lost, and the hand-out is now called the **Butterworth Dole** after Joshua Butterworth, whose 1887 bequest propped up the tradition. His money yields an annual income of 62p, which, divided among the stipulated 21 widows, would not go far. Hot cross buns are now handed out instead, and even these have become so expensive that a collection is taken to defray costs. They are given to children, as the parish claims to have '*no poor and no widows*'. After the 11.30 am dole there is a full Good Friday service at St Bartholomew's.

Formerly, every Good Friday, seven old women – virgins all – went to the church at Glentham in Lincolnshire to enact an obscure custom known as **Molly Grime**. They washed the 14th-century church effigy of Lady Tournay using water drawn from Newell's Well two miles away near Hemswell. For this deed they were paid a shilling, the money coming from profits made on an associated piece of land. Newell was said to be the name of the otherwise unknown benefactor who had left the land and instructions for the ritual in his will. A local dialect word for a holy image, *malgraen*, is thought to have led to the statue being called 'Molly Grime', and effigy-scrubbing was a popular pre-Reformation Catholic pursuit. But the specific well-water suggests further obscure religious links. Whatever its murky origins, in 1832 the land which financed the custom was sold, and the statue's spring-clean ceased. The only vestige of the tradition is the proverbial 'Molly Grimes', used locally to describe children with dirty faces.

Today was a great day for games-playing, especially at Brighton in East Sussex. Up and down the beach there were various ball games and scores of whirling skipping ropes. It was known as **Long Rope Day** as a result, and this passion for Good Friday skipping was shared by the villages of Linton and Hadstock in Cambridgeshire.

© Having rolled off on Shrove Tuesday, the marble season reaches its climax on Good Friday. The game was chiefly played in the south of England, and still thrives at Tinsley Green, on the outskirts of Crawley in West Sussex, where a bout now known as the **World Marbles Championships** takes place at *The Greyhound Inn*. There have been marbles contests at Tinsley for hundreds of years, and the story goes that the first competition took place in the reign of Elizabeth I. Two men, one from Surrey and one from Sussex, competed for the love of a local lass. They tried all sorts of sports, including falconry and wrestling, but were so evenly matched that neither could gain the upper hand. The issue was only decided by a game of marbles – as an odd number of marbles is used, there is always a winner. Unfortunately, legend fails to record who that winner was.

The version of the game played today is Ring Taw, the object being to knock marbles out of the six-foot ring using a shooting marble called a tolley. The modern championships were established in 1932. What started as a local event soon attracted entrants from across the country: men like Jim Longhurst, nicknamed 'Atomic Thumb', and the Welsh champion Wee Willie Wright who had a concealed hot water bottle sewn into his coat to keep his thumb warm. The championships now have entrants, and winners, from all over the world, and in 1992 the American cable TV station CNN gave the contest extensive coverage.

© Although most playing-with-food takes place either at Shrovetide or on Easter Monday, Bury in Greater Manchester stages its **egg-rolling** on Good Friday morning at Holcome Hill – a chance for dedicated rollers to warm up before the showdown at Preston on Monday.

Good Friday is the first day after Lent, and **hot cross buns** have long been a favourite way to break the fast today. The buns are older than Christianity – pagan celebrants ate wheat cakes at their spring festivals, and the Greeks, Romans and Ancient Egyptians all had buns with a cross etched on the top. The round bun represented the full moon, and the cross divides the bun into the four lunar quarters. Traditional buns have the cross cut into the dough or pricked out with a pin: the brash pastry bands are a more recent thing. Not all Good Friday buns featured a cross, and in some areas they were triangular, like a samosa.

The well-known jingle '*Hot cross buns, one a penny, two a penny*' is a street-seller's cry. The buns were traditionally eaten at breakfast, and the town vendors had to be on the streets before dawn to make the most of their once-a-year wares. The buns have been munched in England today for hundreds of years, but it was only in the last century that the tradition caught on across the rest of Britain.

Hot cross buns bring prosperity to the household, and are especially lucky for sailors. This fact was not unknown to a London pub landlady. In 1788 her son wrote to say that he was due home for Easter after a long voyage, and she put a bun aside for him. Tragically he failed to put in his promised appearance, either that year or any other. Each year his mourning mother added another bun to the pile, hoping that her son would one day walk through the door.

© 🔟 After her death the custom continued, and *The Widow's Son* pub in Devon's Road now has a collection of well over 200 buns. The buns hang in a net suspended from the pub ceiling, though the oldest of the fossil food has crumbled to dust. Each Good Friday a sailor adds a specially baked bun to the centuries of leftovers. Hot cross buns are then handed out to everyone in attendance.

Like the buns, **bread** baked on Good Friday imbues homes with happiness and health. If stored and allowed to dry out, it can be used throughout the coming year as a cure-all tonic, grated into cider or milk. It is an antidote to all manner of digestive disorders, and if marked with a cross it never goes mouldy. The bread can be hung in the kitchen, Widow's Son-style, to offset evil, fire and disaster. Ideally it should be made from the same dough as the day's Sacramental Bread.

To give a slice to ailing **cows** is meant to be equally effective. Another traditional bovine pick-me-up involved mixing psalms or books of the Bible in with their hay. This was said to be a sure-fire cure for any disease.

Easter cakes, also ripe for slicing today, come in all manner of guises, usually along plum-bread or fruit-cake lines. In Lancashire, Good Friday's traditional evening dish was **fig sue**, a mixture of dried fruit, bread, ale and nutmeg, boiled into a thick soup and eaten hot. And today was also the day to eat hoarded **mince pies** saved from Christmas – they may have tasted stale but were believed to have a rich streak of luck running through them.

Today's bonanza extends far beyond food. For anyone who has ever fancied having a go at plate-spinning, this is the perfect day to give it a whirl, as it is lucky to break **crockery** on Good Friday. The shards go straight through the heart of Judas, which gets you an instant gold star on your afterlife wallchart. An egg laid today also brings good fortune, especially if kept about one's person during sessions of cards or dicing. And simply being **born on Good Friday** is to have success stamped on to your genetic code. You will have the lifelong gift of second sight, and can never be drowned, hanged, or even frightened.

Meanwhile, it is unlucky to cut your **finger-nails** today. On the Isle of Portland in Dorset, the manicure results in toothache – which sounds more like a deterrent for *biting* nails. **Washing** is out of the question too. Soapy water turns to blood on Good Friday, and any washing on the line will be spattered with blood. Cleaning clothes will also scrub out the life of someone in the family.

Plants as well as people flourish today, as it is the one day of the year when Satan is unable to tamper with the soil. In garden-lore, any shrubs or seeds planted will burgeon, and flowers will grow double heads. In Dorset **gillyflowers** sown at midnight do especially well. Because it is slow to germinate, **parsley** is associated with the dead. It is said to travel to hell and back three (or sometimes nine) times before growing, but if planted today it will thrive. The Ancient Greeks used to scatter parsley on to family graves; and if thrown into ponds it brings new life to sickly fish.

Potatoes planted today will prosper too, but the best trick of the season is performed by **beans**: in Somerset it is said that if you set them on Good Friday, they will rise with Christ on Easter Sunday. Despite the fat of the land being particularly obese today, ploughmen were discouraged from claiming a share of the bounty:

On Good Friday rest thy plough,
Start nowt, end nowt, that's enough.

Star birds of the day are robins, magpies and pelicans. The **robin** came by its red breast after trying to ease Christ's discomfort by pecking at his crown of thorns. It is very unlucky to kill one as a result; hence the full-scale inquiry after Cock Robin's murder.

The **magpie** traditionally carries a drop of Satan's blood under its tongue. Along with other members of the crow family – the carrion crow, rook, raven and chough – it was in attendance at the Crucifixion. The rest wore black in mourning, but the magpie came partly in white: ever since then the birds have stuck with the same colour schemes.

Pelicans are also associated with blood; but it is all their own. It was believed that the bird fed its young on blood drawn from its own pecked breast, echoing the blood which Christ shed for mankind. A more complex version of this wayward biology, very popular in medieval Britain, says that young pelicans incessantly attack the parent bird until it loses its rag

and kills them all. Instantly remorseful, the pelican then pecks its breast and bleeds on the fledglings, which are magically resurrected by the parental blood. This imagery led to the pelican becoming a Christian symbol of Resurrection.

The cowardly fish family all swam to the bottom of lakes and rivers in awe and fear at the Crucifixion, apart from the bold **pike**, who watched it all. For this reason it is said that the head of a pike bears the visible signs of the cross, the three nails, and a sword.

EASTER EVE AND DAY

✟ On **Easter Eve** – the Saturday before Easter Day – **well-water** throughout Wales was believed to turn into wine between 11 pm and midnight, a miraculous transformation which it also managed on New Year's Eve. Over the border, **Bowmere Lake** near Ellesmere in Shropshire came into existence one Easter Eve as an act of God. The inhabitants of a dissolute town refused to let the sun go down on their pagan pastimes, and so divine retribution drowned them all, saving just one Roman soldier who had been trying to convert his bacchanalian neighbours at the time. He can still be seen in ghost form rowing across the lake, acting out a scene in which he tried to save his true love from the flood. Bells can be heard below the water too.

© At Market Harborough in Leicestershire at 6 pm today choir and congregation sing hymns over the grave of **William Hubbard** in St Mary-in-Arden churchyard. Hubbard died in 1774, and bequeathed the annual sum of a guinea to perpetuate this custom, which in turn has perpetuated his memory.
© Easter Saturday is the big day for the bizarrely clad **Britannia Coconut Dancers** at Bacup, north of Rochdale in Lancashire. Eight men with blackened faces, short white skirts, white plumed hats, black breeches and clogs, perform the Nutters' Dance.

It was a common pagan belief that for magic to be effective, the spell-casters had to be in disguise: this is one possible reason why the luck-bringing dancers of Bacup black-up. They have wooden 'nuts' like castanets on their palms, belts and knees, enabling them to play themselves during regular pauses on their seven-mile dance-cum-trot through and around the streets of Bacup. They are led by a man called the Whipper-In, who symbolically whips away the winter as they go.

The dancers gather at about 9 am in Bacup town centre, and do their eightsome reel around the streets until lunchtime when they invade the local pubs. Then they dance on to the nearby village of Stacksteads, finishing their rounds at approximately 6.30 pm at that most traditional of venues, the Glen service station. The name 'Britannia' may imply loyalty, fealty and patriotism, but more importantly it is the name of a village south of Bacup.

✞ The action starts early on **Easter Sunday**. Under the Downfall, a waterfall near Kinder Reservoir in the Dark Peak area of Derbyshire, is a murky stretch of water called the Mermaid's Pool. As midnight strikes and the day begins, a **mermaid** can be seen swimming through the gloomy depths. This vision will give you one of two things – eternal life, or instant death. She is in fact a Celtic water-goddess: there are similar beings at Blake Mere, also known as Mermaid's Pool, 1,400 feet up on the Morridge Moors north-east of Leek in Staffordshire. Close by, on the old drovers' road between Congleton and Nottingham, is the *Mermaid's Inn*. On its stonework is carved:

> *She calls on you to greet her, combing her*
> *dripping crown,*
> *And if you go to meet her, she ups and drags*
> *you down.*

Cheshire has a mermaid too, at Rostherne Mere, just north of Knutsford. She sings and rings an underwater bell every Easter Sunday. The bell ended up in the lake during the bell-hanging in Rostherne's church. It rolled to the water's edge three times before an exasperated workman declared '*I would the Devil had thee!*' The offended bell jumped up and squashed the blasphemer before rolling into the lake. The Cheshire Plain is said to be home to several other airy water spirits, called the **asrais**. They only appear once every hundred years, just to sit a while and look at the moon. If struck by the rays of the sun, they dissolve.

The most impressive water-spirit in these parts lives in Doxey Pool near the Roaches range of hills just north of Leek in Staffordshire. It was last sighted in 1949, when it rose some 30 feet out of the water covered in weed and slime, with a menacing gesture and baleful eyes, like Swamp Thing after a bad night.

Once the mermaid-spotting is over, sit back and wait the few hours until dawn. When the **sun** appears on the horizon, it dances for joy at the Resurrection. On the Isle of Man the sun

bows three times instead; and in some places a **lamb** can be seen in symbolic silhouette against the jigging orb. Whatever the sunny disposition is in any given area of the country, it is best watched from the highest available hill. But be prepared for disappointment – the Devil is fond of ushering in a skyful of clouds to obscure the view.

After its celestial gambol, lamb also turns up as one of the two traditional meats of the day. The other is duck, as: '*Unless you have duck for dinner on Easter Day, you'll never pay your debts.*' Both should be served with the oddly grey-green coloured **tansey pudding**, which has a pungent taste, a survival of the Jewish Passover tradition of eating bitter herbs. The puddings were often given as prizes in Easter games. An old rhyme celebrates all this:

> *On Easter Sunday let the Pudding be seen*
> *To which the Tansey lends her sober green.*

If put inside shoes, tansey can cure the ague. Some say that it aids conception; others that it promotes miscarriage – an unreliable medicine, to say the least.

Dock pudding was a delicacy today in Cumbria and the north, made from Passion dock – also known as Easter ledger or pink-spiked bistort (see Passion Sunday in the Lent section for the Dock Pudding Championships in the Calder Valley). **Pudding pies** were the favourites in Kent, a pastry filled with currants and a set custard, washed down with cherry beer – a strong ale containing cherry juice.

You cannot go wrong with eggs, today's traditional breakfast dish. Before the advent of cardboard and chocolate versions, Easter eggs – often called **pace eggs**, after the 'Paschal' or Passion Lamb of the season – were simply eggs with decorated shells. Some were hard-boiled, some were not. They were dyed either with dye-resistant wax motifs drawn on beforehand, or with intricate patterns etched on to the coloured shell afterwards. Eggs are a symbol of rebirth, and they appear on menus again today after the long austerities of the Lent diet. Easter eggs used to be blessed in church, with a prayer which began: '*Bless, O Lord, we beseech Thee, this Thy creature of eggs . . .*'

In Scotland as Lent drew to a close, children used to steal eggs, and would then meet today for an orgy of omelette and pancakes. Only stolen eggs were considered kosher ingredients. Welsh youths sought their food and other alms in a more open manner, singing short carols outside houses accompanied by noisy rattles and gentle demands for Easter treats. Children in the Midlands seem to have had the simplest Easter tastes, mixing sugar with well-water – a custom known as **sugar-cupping**.

At Lostwithiel in Cornwall, the day's feasting was presided over by an elected **Mock Prince**, an Easter version of the Misrule Lords and Kings of the old Christmas season. On the Welsh Borders, the main Easter meal was eaten in the middle of a wheatfield. The picnic was known as **corn-showing**, and survived until the end of last century. Traditional food included plum cake, cider, and sometimes '*a yard of toasted cheese*'. But there was a catch: diners had to hold hands and walk through the field saying:

Every step a reap, every reap a sheaf,
And God sent the master a good harvest.

In Hereford and Worcester's Golden Valley, they did not even get to eat the picnic: the cake was buried, and the cider was poured on top. This was a gentle form of the wassailing common to other apple-growing regions.

It must be more than coincidence that many of the traditional British Easter foods are also found at the corresponding and earlier Jewish Spring festival, the **Passover**, which celebrates the liberation from Egypt. Bitter herbs are on the menu to pucker the mouth and so remind the eater of the bitter captivity. Passover eggs are baked in the oven and eaten, along with a sweet cake called Haroseth which resembles some of the Easter Cakes. Passover bread is as central as the Good Friday loaves, though in unleavened form; and lamb is the main dish of the day.

Although all the main Passover items of food can be found on the Easter menu, traditional Passover drinks have not done so well – diluted wine has caught on at some pubs; but there seems to be no demand in Britain for salt water with parsley. This represents the tears of the angels, weeping for the Egyptians who died in the Red Sea after its parted waters were reunited.

Human Easter table manners never stoop as low as those of **ravens**. It is said that '*A raven always dines off a young one on Easter Sunday*'.

© Tall **paschal candles** used to be the centre-pieces in many pre-Reformation churches on Easter Day. They were the exception to the general rule that today was an occasion for the dousing of all fires. Flowers were brought indoors today too: both actions marked a symbolic ending of winter, and were also a reminder to the driving forces of the universe to start edging up the temperature.

For the trip to church, **new clothes** were thought to be essential, which helped make Easter a 'lucky' time of the year for tailors and cobblers. Anyone who could not afford to replace what they were wearing made alterations, perhaps adding a new trim of lace. Neglecting to make some changes could incur lasting bad luck:

At Easter let your clothes be new,
Or else be sure you will it rue.

One immediate consequence of sticking to your old outfit was that unpleasant stuff was likely to stick to it – the wearer became a target for **bird droppings**; but curiously to be '*shat on from a great height*' – to coin an old phrase – was considered a blessing if it happened on Easter Day itself.

Epileptics and others suffering from **fits** could attempt a desperate remedy on Easter Day. First they had to be given nine coppers and nine pieces of silver by nine willing donors. The coppers were used to buy the silver, which was made into a ring. When worn by the afflicted, this ring could supposedly effect a cure.

EASTER MONDAY

During Lent the fees for **getting married** in church were doubled, and so as soon as it had ended there was a lusty rush to the altar. Fees at Manchester Cathedral were particularly small, and the insolvent-but-in-love made a beeline there on Easter Monday. The building was known fondly as Th'owd Church, and the chaplain today conducted mass weddings, averaging a dozen or more at each ceremony. It is said that one year the wrong men were joined to the wrong women; but, unflustered, the chaplain announced: '*Pair as you go out: you're all married; pair as you go out . . .*'

For those already married but doggedly childless, Whitchurch – now part of suburban Cardiff – was the place to go today. Each woman threw 12 white balls and 12 black balls over the church roof. The crowd on the other side scrambled for the balls, and in some inconceivable way this helped the woman to become pregnant. The ceremony became a simple game before it died out altogether.

© Easter Monday is the day for one of the country's most celebrated hand-outs, the **Biddenden Dole**. Biscuits, cheese, bread and packets of tea are given away at 10 am at the Old Workhouse in Biddenden, Kent, which is now a privately occupied home. The biscuits are stamped with a crude image which appears to show two women joined at the hip. It is said to represent Siamese twins Elisa and Mary Chulkhurst, who left the Bread and Cheese lands which pay for the dole when they died at Biddenden in 1134. Both passed away within hours of each other, as the survivor refused to be separated from her sister. It has been argued that the twins were dreamed up to make sense of the image on the dole biscuits; but recent research seems to show that the sisters did exist.

🔟 Today a thousand biscuits are made, stamped with the image of the inseparable sisters, who can also be seen on the village sign on Biddenden green. The bread, cheese and tea go to the village needy, but the biscuits are given to everyone who attends the ceremony, and can be bought for a small sum. Made from flour, water and little else, they are rock-hard, recommended as keepsakes rather than something nice to have with elevenses. The biscuits used to be traded as talismans, as they were believed to have magical properties.

The Easter Bunny, so beloved of Americans and chocolate makers, is actually the **Easter Hare** in modern guise, the hare being a symbol of the Moon goddess, and also of Eostre (see March 9th). At Coleshill in Warwickshire anyone who caught a hare on Easter Monday and gave it to the rector before 10 am could claim a groat (4d), a calf's head, and a hundred eggs.

The hares at Hallaton near Leicester come in a novel form – beef. The **Hare Pie Scramble** used to be performed with real hare-pie, but beefsteak ousted the game many years ago. In spite of its undoubted pagan ancestry, legend does the decent thing by putting forward a more inventive origin. Two women were walking near Hallaton, and before they could do the usual has-it-got-udders check, two bulls were heading towards them at full tilt. Just in time a hare ducked across their path and momentarily confused the charging beasts. The women escaped, and thanked the hare by killing it, baking it in a pie, and throwing it at the locals. This proved such a success that they made it an annual event.

© After a morning service today, the Rector at Hallaton still slices up a giant pie on his lawn and offers it to his audience. Some is then taken to Hare-Pie Bank and scattered for the unhygienic delight of the crowd.

The procession to Hare-Pie Bank, roughly half way between Hallaton and neighbouring Medbourne, also carries three decorated mini-kegs called plough bottles. Two of the kegs contain a gallon of ale, and the other is empty. Once the crowd at the hill has got pie-eyed, the bottles are thrown up and played for in three separate bouts of **Bottle-Kicking**. Locals from Hallaton and Medbourne compete to kick each keg over one or other of their parish boundaries, which are a mile or so apart. Keg-off is at 2.15 pm, and these days any outsider with enough bottle can sign up to play for the Medbourne team. In the 18th century the rector made an effort to stamp out the hare pie and bottle-kicking, as an undesirable, pagan practice. The locals scrawled on his walls the words: '*No pie, no parson, and a job for the glazier.*' The custom has continued ever since.

There were several hare hunts today; and, just as with the Hallaton pie, hare was not an essential ingredient. **Hunting the Buck** used to take place at Stalbridge, near Sherborne in Dorset today. One man played the Buck – a male hare – while others knelt down to block his path. The Buck tried to weave his way through the human obstacle course, and at some point everyone joined hands and danced off down Stalbridge High Street. This ritualised man-hunt belongs to the same family of ever-so-primitive customs as the Horn Dance, which is still enacted at Abbots Bromley.

Wilder and weirder was the **Hunting the Hare** which set off from Black Annis' Bower, a cave in the Dane Hills, now part of suburban Leicester. The corporation turned up on horseback in scarlet robes, and used bloodhounds to track down a dead cat soaked in aniseed which had been dragged up hill, down dale and through the streets of Leicester before the hunt began. The trail always finished at the Mayor's house, and the cat corpse was probably a replacement for what had originally been a real hare hunt. The cave where the chase began was said to be the home of a witch called Black Annis, or Cat Anna, who may be a genuine folk-memory of the pre-Christian, even pre-Celtic blue-faced winter goddess *Anu*. To hunt her representative – the hare or cat – was to drive out the winter.

The **Bald Faced Stag Hunt** at Buckhurst Hill in Essex just managed to outlast the events in Leicester, lingering on into the 1880s. A captured stag was decorated and released, only to be pursued by a crowd of over 500 people. The chief prize of the day was a handful of fur plucked from the slaughtered animal's face. As with Hunting the Hare, this custom is not a leading contender for a revival.

Old Ball did better than his real-animal counterparts, surviving the day's play at Swinton, Worsley, Blackburn, Burnley, and other places across old Lancashire. He was a hobbyhorse, with nails for teeth and eyes made from bottle-bottoms, sometimes with a real horse-skull and calf-skin to make Old Ball look especially macabre. His clumsy antics through the streets were described last century as '*the most ridiculous and boisterous mirth*'. Old Ball snapped his dangerous jaws at unsuspecting passers-by, and on several occasions spectators are said to have fainted or gone hysterical after a close encounter. Old Ball by Old Ball commentary ceased late last century.

Riding the Black Lad at Ashton-under-Lyne, now in Greater Manchester, used to take place today. An effigy in black armour was paraded through the town accompanied by loud music and jeering, and was pelted with stones and rubbish as it went. The bearers then placed it in the pillory, where it was pelted some more, before being shot to oblivion. This violent scene symbolises the end of winter and hunger, which must actively die before summer and fertility can take the reins again.

In the 15th century, the Black Lad became associated with the Lord of Middleton Manor, Sir Rauf de Assheton. Rauf had bizarre **guld-riding** rights, which meant that he could search for *gulds* (corn marigolds) and fine any weedy tenant who had let them grow on his land. Gulds, in former years, had choked the land; but Sir Rauf went about his task with excessive zeal and violence until he was clubbed to death by a man with one weed too many, after which the gulding was discontinued. The Black Lad then had a new lease of life in the guise of Sir Rauf, and he remained the focal hate figure until the custom died out in the 1960s.

© For just over a century the **Cart Horse Parade** has been held at Regent's Park in London on Easter Monday. Upwards of 20,000 people turn up to watch huge horses, laden with brasses and regalia, being put through their heavy paces.

© The **Coal Carrying Championships** at Gawthorpe near Wakefield in West Yorkshire have the feel of a long-established tradition, although the event began only in 1963 following an 'I'm-tougher-than-you-are' argument between two locals at *The Beehive Inn*. Men carry 55 kilograms of coal, women 20 kilograms, up a slight hill for just under a mile. Easter Monday and Tuesday were also the days in some counties for a more ritualised form of lifting – see Hocktide for details.

Handball and skittles were once popular games today, and at Manchester Grammar School pupils went in for an Olde-England style archery contest. But there was only one real sport on Easter Monday – **egg-rolling**. It was a national pastime in Scotland, where the day was known as Egg Monday. Christian rationalisation said that it represented the rolling away of the stone from the tomb where Jesus had been prematurely buried. The chief object of egg-rolling was to see whose egg could go furthest without disintegrating, though sometimes there were goals marked at the bottom of the hills. The eggs were usually hard-boiled; but often they were not – it is surprising how far an unboiled egg can roll before splattering into a rock.

The defeated eggs were eaten, and their shells crushed to prevent **witches** from joyriding in them. Unless you go to work on an egg-shell, a witch can sail out to sea in the unlikely vessel and conjure up storms to drown sailors – who were so perturbed at the prospect that they would not utter the taboo word 'egg' at sea. There is in old saying, '*Break an egg, save a sailor*'. This all stems from the idea that any food you leave can be used to work malign magic against you (as can nail-clippings, hairs, bits of clothing, and other personal detritus).

© Egg-rolling remains a nationwide Easter tradition. The most hard-boiled roll-players head for Fountains Abbey in North Yorkshire today – where rolling was revived in 1958 – or Avenham Park at Preston in Lancashire, which each year attracts in the region of 40,000 people and almost as many eggs. Among the many brightly coloured eggs rolling down the valley slope are some which are noticeably more orange and spherical than the others. They are, indeed, oranges – an innovation thrown in to moisten the palate when it comes to eating the shattered contestants; although no orange is allowed to win the egg-rolling. The game never seems to have been particularly competitive at any of its locations, just a gentle bit of fun symbolising all the things that eggs usually symbolise.

The game of **jauping paste-eggs** was a favourite in the North, particularly around Newcastle-upon-Tyne. Two players grip hard-boiled eggs in their hands, and exchange blows on each other's fists until one of the eggs breaks. A less painful game involved throwing eggs high in the air and catching them. If the egg broke, it was forfeit time. Jauping is a close relative of Shrove Tuesday's egg-shackling.

Pace-egging plays are an Easter version of the mumming plays still seen at Christmas. Miscellaneous outlandish characters parade and recite their lines, sing songs, and make a colourful plea for alms. The plays used to be very common across the north-west of England, particularly in Rochdale, Burnley and the Fylde area around Blackpool. At the villages of Far and Near Sawrey in Cumbria only the children of certain long-established local families were eligible to become Jolly Boys and take part in their pace-egging procession. Many of the pace-egging songs were very similar, the commonest opening verse being:

Here's one or two jolly boys all of one mind,
We've come a-pace-egging, I hope you'll
*   prove kind,*
I hope you'll prove kind with your eggs and
*   strong beer,*
And we'll come no more nigh you until the
*   next year.*

Larger towns sometimes had several gangs of players competing for alms, and at Blackburn rival pace-eggers laid into each other with notorious regularity. Women here circumvented the men-only rule by dressing in male clothing and joining in the fun. Children did the rounds on their own, uttering a minimalist

alms-cry: '*For God's sake! A pace egg!*'

By the early 19th century, Trafalgar heroes Nelson and Collingwood had appeared in the action, ousting the traditional figures in many plays. One character who survived this naval onslaught was **Old Tosspot**, a particular darling of the crowds at Burscough near Ormskirk in Lancashire. Old Tosspot was an intemperate Fool figure with a pin-studded tail, and his antics were invariably fuelled by large amounts of beer.

© The most robust modern survival of the pace-egging play is enacted by boys from West Yorkshire's Calder Valley School in Mytholmroyd. Their version draws heavily on the old play that used to be performed at nearby Midgley. The boys tour from Good Friday, beginning at Heptonstall. They then take in Midgley and the surrounding villages, including Todmorden and Luddenden, and usually put in a final performance at Halifax on the Sunday. The short play features St George defeating various villains, including Bold Slasher, who is resurrected by the Doctor's magic potion. Brighouse, in the same county, has its own revived version of the Midgley play.

Even in the absence of a play, Easter Monday was still able to offer opportunities for simple **alms**-collecting. One shambling chant ran:

Please, good mistress, an Easter Egg, or a
*   flitch of bacon,*
Or a little trundle of cheese of your own
*   making.*

In North Wales the children went **egg-clapping**, making a dreadful noise on wooden clappers before entreating the household for food or money.

HOCKTIDE

The Sunday after Easter marks the beginning of **Hocktide**, a burst of moveable feasts and frolics somewhat eclipsed by the manifold moveable Shrovetide, Lent and Easter celebrations. The origins of Hocktide are obscure. Tradition maintains, somewhat weakly, that it commemorates the massacre of the Danes by King Ethelred in 1002; but that event took place on November 13th. Equally unlikely is the assertion that it is in memory of the death of King Harthacnut on June 8th 1042. The fact is that nobody knows quite what the 'hock' bit means.

Hock Sunday is formally known as Low Sunday, and informally called **Quasimodo Sunday**, after the traditional *Introit* of the day's service, which begins *'Quasi modo geniti infantes'*. Yet another name for the day is **Balaam's Ass Day**, after the story of the talking ass in the Bible, which is traditionally read at the morning's service. It is said that **mackerel** come into season when Balaam's ass speaks in church.

© The weekend including Hock Sunday is the one that Northumberland chooses for its **Morpeth Gathering**, which features sports such as bowling and egg-related games. It runs from Friday to Sunday, and is primarily a celebration of Northumbrian piping and dancing.

© The Saturday of this same weekend is the last of the three dates for the **Uppies and Doonies** football game at Workington in Cumbria: it is also played on Good Friday and the Tuesday after Easter. One of the goals is at the harbour, the other is a mile away at Workington Hall, and rules are virtually non-existent. It is now a titanic struggle between the two halves of the town, but it originated as a bout between rival teams of miners and dockers.

Hocktide was once a time for collecting dues from parishioners, a custom that was turned into a frolic. On Hock Monday men obstructed thoroughfares with rope, demanding a toll from passers-by. On the Tuesday it was the turn of the women. An alternative version of this extortion was known as **lifting** – again with the Monday/Tuesday sex divide. The victim was lured into a chair – which was often decorated with ribbons and flowers – and ceremoniously lifted up three times. In exchange for this sedan-try experience they had to hand over money or gifts, and received a kiss in return. The lifters were usually servants or others in search of donations, while the lifted were their employers or others with cash to spare. Last century the vicar of Barthomley in Cheshire looked forward to his annual lift: *'These little familiarities of the season, coming but once a year, are, I am sure, advantageous to all parties, promoting good humour and kind feeling among classes kept too much apart in England.'* The custom appears to go back a long way. In 1290 King Edward I is said to have been forced to cough up when several maids imprisoned him in his bed and lifted him bodily.

© Without a doubt the most important surviving Hocktide tradition is **Tutti Day** at Hungerford, west of Newbury in Berkshire, on Hock Tuesday. The town discovered the delights of a mayor and council only relatively recently. Its Hocktide merrymaking centres upon the pre-corporation ancient offices of Portreeve, Constable, Bailiff, Water Bailiffs, Overseers of the Port Down, Tithing Men, Ale-Tasters, Blacksmith and Bellman. The various offices are fixed for the year at the Macaroni Supper – a meal of macaroni, cheese and watercress – on the Friday after Easter (i.e. the Friday before Hocktide) at the *John O'Gaunt Inn*.

The choice of pub is no coincidence – the local Hock celebrations are said to commemorate the granting of special grazing and fishing rights by John of Gaunt in 1364, who also donated his hunting horn for the purpose. This fragile original is now locked away; but the replacement Lucas horn – from 1634 – is blown at 8 am on Hock Tuesday, opening Hungerford's Hocktide Court.

Having been elected, the officials are sworn

in on the following Friday. The Court also appoints two **Tutti Men** from the ranks of the Tithing Men. With garlanded poles topped by an impaled orange, the Tutti Men take to the streets on Hock Tuesday in decorated top hats and tails, accompanied by the Orange Scrambler with his feather-adorned hat. This Tutti-fruity ensemble can claim a kiss from any woman it meets, handing over an orange in payment. A one-penny 'fine' is due if the kiss is refused, which it seldom is. Some etymologists say that the Tutti-men derive their name from the word 'tithing', and were originally the town Watchmen, responsible for a prototype neighbourhood-watch scheme and the gathering of the Hocktide penny-tithe. Locals, however, know that the term comes from a West Country word for a nosegay or bunch of flowers – a *tutty*.

The Court's Tuesday lunch venue used to be the *Three Swans Hotel*, but by the 1970s the event had grown so popular that it moved to the larger and grander Corn Exchange. A visiting dignitary gets a free lunch, but suffers the indignity of **Shoeing the Colt**, a ritual which any fresh-face at the function has to undergo. The newcomer is seized by mock-blacksmiths, who nail a horseshoe on to his or her footwear. Take care not to turn up in slippers. Or skirts. The colts are all inverted before the shoeing and the participants admit to a penchant for grabbing women in skirts or dresses so that they can up-end them and reveal their knickers. The nail is hammered into the shoe until the Colt cries 'Punch', indicating that they will put money towards the sizeable drinks bill. After this they are presented with the nail, and everyone adjourns to the *Three Swans* for anchovy toast.

After lunch the Tutti Men and Orange Scrambler are back on the beat, followed by a large crowd of children. They continue to trade fruit for favours until well into the evening, when the last oranges are flung to the crowd to bring the day, and Hocktide, to a close.

APRIL

1st April
All Fool's Day

Huntigowk, the April Fish

The origins of **April Fool's Day** lie in several pagan spring festivals of jollity, such as the Roman end-of-winter orgy, Hilaria – no, that name is not an April Fool's trick. The smirking Celtic god **Lud** had his annual bash at the Old New Year (March 25th), the festival of the Vernal Equinox. April 1st was the *Octave* of this feast: there were eight days of festivities, the first and last being the most important. Japery was first nature to Lud, the god who managed to overcome the **Three Plagues of Ancient Britain**. These bizarre plagues were a tribe of malevolent, all-hearing demons; a Maytime shriek which killed all that heard it; and a curse that spirited away all the royal provisions. The fact that Lud cured the curse of the demons by spraying them with a brew of crushed insects in water attests to his humour.

Other April-Fool-origins candidates include **Perserphine** – she who was snatched away by Pluto from her mother Ceres for a spot of subterranean housework. Ceres followed the trail of Proserpine's indignant shrieks across the land to no avail – the first fool's errand. (See the Harvest section for more on this particular myth.)

Then again, it is said that **Noah** released the dove from the ark on April 1st, and that its fool's errand was to find land when the earth was still apparently covered in water.

Then again, again, All Fools may simply be the foil of Easter, fulfilling a similar letting-off-steam function to the Feast of Fools in January, which parodied Christmas austerities. In this case, the day is thought to commemorate Christ being mocked and tormented before his death. This is the origin of the French All Fools' title, *Poisson d'Avril*, a corruption of 'Passion d'Avril'. A French fool is an 'April Fish', with lots of tasty chocolate fish for sale on streetcorners today. **Mary Queen of Scots** is thought to have brought home to Scotland happy memories of the French fish fun, instigating – or at least rejuvenating – the observation of All Fools in her native country.

As everyone knows, at noon the foolery must cease; except at Christow in Devon where April 1st is Tail-pipe Day, and tricks can only be played in the afternoon. Anyone who perpetrates a practical joke outside the prescribed hours can be admonished in rhyme:

> *April Fool's gone and past*
> *And you're the biggest fool at last.*

Or the more obscure Northumbrian version:

> *The gowk and the titlene sit on the tree,*
> *You're the gowk as well as me.*

A gowk is a cuckoo, and in Scotland the day is known as Gowking or **Huntigowk Day**. The huntigowk is sent on a series of spurious errands, and he is often given a written message to hand to a person at his next destination. Unbeknown to the gullible victim, the message reads '*Hunt the gowk another mile*', and he is sent on his way again. Favourite traditional gowking errands include a trek for a pint of pigeon's milk; some elbow grease; or a new bubble for the spirit-level.

A recurring London prank invites selected fools to come and watch the **washing of the white lions** in either Trafalgar Square or the Tower of London. The most successful con of this kind was in 1860 when a number of gentry turned up at the Tower brandishing their gilt-edged invitation cards.

Weddings are known as April Morns in misogynist circles – a side-splitting reference to the fact that a chap is making a fool of himself by settling down with a woman.

All in all, April 1st was an unfortunate date for **the Diggers** to bring their rebellion to a head and proclaim common ownership of the land.

Their brief 1649 HQ at St George's Hill near Weybridge in Surrey is now deep in the uncommon ownership stockbroker belt. The Diggers were sick and tired of elitism and monopolistic land use. This was in the early days of the Commonwealth – Charles I had been executed just two months earlier – but it was already clear that the wealth would be common to Oliver Cromwell's cronies, not to the peasants in the fields. Hence the Diggers' short-lived communist uprising. A folk song of the time states their ambitions of co-operative equality, using language that could have come straight out of the 1960s:

'*To conquer them with love . . . noe power is like to love.*'

Sadly, it was past noon, and the joke was on them: the movement was ruthlessly crushed, and the Diggers were sent to the gallows.

☾ **Weatherwise**, thunder is a good omen today:

*If it thunders on All Fools' Day
It brings good crops and hay.*

But bad news for brewers, and drinkers, if the month's eponymous showers put in an appearance:

*If April First sees cloud and rain
Then beer will smell like an open drain.*

2nd April

The One-Handed Ghost and the Theoretical Phantom

Lord Edward Stawell had an affair with his young sister-in-law Honoria Stewkeley. This sort of thing always leads to trouble, and Honoria died. Stawell then expired, on April 2nd 1755, of apoplexy. Soon afterwards his bailiff, Isaac Machrel, a man known to have a strange hold on Lord Stawell, also died, crushed when a woodpile collapsed on him. There followed some boisterous, prolonged haunting at Stawell's home. **The Old Manor House**, Hinton Ampner, Hampshire. The leading characters were a man in a plain coat, and a woman in a black dress – thought to be Edward and Honoria. As well as the manifestations of the ghostly couple, there were also

thunderous bangs, groans, terrifying shrieks, heavy objects tumbling invisibly through the ceiling, and strange, tuneless harmonic vibrations in the bedrooms.

Despite hundreds of sightings, and even an investigation by the army, nothing could shift the ghosts. So in desperation the whole manor was torn down in 1793 and rebuilt just a few yards away. After the demolition a tiny human, or monkey, skull was found in a box beneath the floorboards, and an old woman who used to work there came forward claiming to know the dark secret behind the hauntings. About to be interrogated further, she promptly died, adding to the Manor's mysteries.

Lawford Hall near Little Lawford on the outskirts of Rugby in Warwickshire was unique in having a theoretical ghost. Smooth-talking Irishman **Captain Donnellan** had just married into the resident family, the Boughtons. Within a year the Boughton heir, Sir Theodosius, was dead. A post-mortem showed that he had been poisoned with laurel water. A book of poisons was found in Donnellan's room, with the page on laurel water clearly marked. Still protesting his innocence, Donnellan was hanged at Warwick on this day in 1781.

The family tried to prevent Donnellan's young son from finding out about his father's crimes, but the story leaked out, and he killed himself. The house, everyone decided, would doubtless be haunted after this terrible family history, and so it was vacated before anyone could prove the theory, standing empty until its demolition.

✟ At nearby Little Lawford Hall the once hyperactive ghost of **One-handed Broughton** is now confined to one room and sporadic appearances in a coach and six. During the phantom's wilder days, 12 clergymen attempted to oust it, but 11 of their exorcising candles mysteriously blew out. The parson with the still-burning candle struck a deal with the ghost, not laying it, but forcing it to stick to one room.

Just to be different, April 2nd is Orkney's Fools' Day, and tricks here can only be played *after* noon. Known as **Tailing Day**, the chief objective is to pin some embarrassing article or scrawled message, of the *Please Kick Me* type, on the back of the victim. Pigs' tails purloined from the butcher are favourite accoutrements. Elsewhere in Scotland, it was not uncommon for the joke to span the full forty-eight hours, as witnessed in the saying *'The first and second of April, hunt the gowk another mile'*.

☝ Watch out for **fog**, and rejoice in the wonderful homely rhyming of:

*If the first three days of April be foggy,
Rain in June will make the lanes boggy.*

3rd April
St Richard of Chichester's Day

Caraboo and Other Horned Beasts

The **Rev Franke Parker** was no ordinary vicar. In the remote incumbency of Luffin-cott, Devon, he practised the magic arts. He was sometimes seen in dog-posture howling at the moon, and he boasted of his ability to go **shape-shifting**. Toads and lions were high-lights in his diverse portfolio. For over 40 years he put the 'spell' into gospel, until this day in 1883, when he died. He had instructed neigh-bours to bury him deep, otherwise he would return from the dead. The ensuing depth kept him quiet until 1894, when he appeared to his sucessor, Rev Brown. What he said is not known, but Brown fled in panic and refused to return. He would not even allow his belong-ings in the rectory to be forwarded. Shape-shifter Parker was so impressed by this specta-cularly successful haunting that he retired from the ghost business at once.

The first Monday in April is said to be **Cain's birthday**, as well as being the day upon which, years later, he slew his brother Abel. It is therefore a very unlucky day. In Jewish folk-lore Cain was the son of Eve and the Serpent. Adam's first wife was the demon queen Lilith, a charming woman who eats offspring, includ-ing her own (see March 25th). With his own parents setting such a lousy example, angry young rebel-without-a-precedent Cain picked a quarrel with God. He peevishly offered him the worst of his crops as a sacrifice, and had God's favour withdrawn from then on.

When Abel married their sister it was too much for Cain, and he committed the murder-ous deed. Afterwards he was forced to wander the earth with horns, and was eventually killed by his own descendant Lamech, who mistook him for a wild animal.

In 1817 Mary Baker came to Almondsbury near Bristol with a great plan. As a sure-fire way of gaining fame and lodgings she put on a turban and pretended to be **Princess Caraboo** from the made-up land of Javasu. She con-cocted a fake language, met lots of inquisitive people, and ate loads of free lunches as a result. But inevitably suspicions were aroused. On April 3rd 1817, magistrates were alerted to the eccentric 'immigrant', and a prolonged examination revealed that Caraboo was indeed plain old Mary, brought up in poverty at Witheridge, Devon. Around her stamping grounds at Bath and Bristol she was the chief topic of conversation in polite society that year. Several poems about Caraboo appeared in print and in late 1994 she was the subject of the feature film *Princess Caraboo*.

© In the 13th century **St Richard of Chi-chester** made the local **brinepits** at Droitwich, Hereford and Worcester, flow again, much to everyone's delight. Each year thereafter, the salty pits were decorated and danced around on this, his feast-day. The custom lapsed during the Civil War, and the well rapidly dried up again. Only after reviving the old custom did its salty waters reappear. These days the celebra-tions – on or about the 3rd – centre on the statue of St Richard in Vines Park

▥ The Romans knew about the local salt – their settlement here was called *Salinae* – and there are recently restored curative baths in use at Droitwich. The water is slightly radioactive, just the stuff for rheumatism, neuritis (inflam-mation of nerve endings) and other muscular or nervous ailments. The salinity here is 12 times that of the sea – the highest naturally occurring saltwater in the British Isles. But St Richard's part in the proceedings should be taken with a pinch of whatever comes to hand.

4th April

Sailing to Fame on a Cat

On this day in 1810, things began to hot up at **Sampford Peverell**, Devon. John Chave, his wife and maids had just rented a house there, not remotely perturbed by the fact that some-one had once supposedly, fleetingly, glimpsed a ghost there. But by early April they were plagued by phantom footsteps and drum-ming, and six of the maids were beaten up by what they claimed were invisible hands. Curtains danced and ripped, and candlesticks flew across rooms. The Bible and sword of a would-be ghost-watcher were flung across the room, and he was held at ghostly swordpoint. The various phantom tantrums were carried out with an exceptional violence according to eye-witnesses.

It was all pretty spectacular; but the owner of the property, a Mr Talley, mocked the Chaves' claims and said that the noises were made by a local cooper hitting his barrels with a broomstick – one of ghost-lore's more ambitious theories. Chave was accused of mock poltergeisting. The villagers, led by Talley, beat him up and drove him from the area. Later theories claimed that it was all a cover-up for smugglers using the cellar to store their goods. The goings-on at the house continued for three more years, and then suddenly ceased.

'Turn again Whittington, thou worthy citizen, Lord Mayor of London', sang the bells; and back he went. On this day in 1406 Dick and his cat took up the chain and orb of the Lord Mayor's office for a third time. **Dick Whittington** is the archetypal rags-to-riches figure. 'Cat', however, was actually another name for 'ketch', the coal-carrying ship in which Dick made most of his dosh. It is also more correctly a riches-to-more-riches story, as Dick was the son of a wealthy Gloucestershire landowner.

This is the time of year when **adders**, or vipers, begin their courtship rituals. Unlike humans, it is customary for adders to use their tongues on a first date.

🔘 Being the island's only poisonous snakes, adders carry much of the serpent reputation on their zig-zag patterned backs. In legends, snakes are often depicted as well-guardians, vestiges of the serpent-deities who dwelled there before the saints muscled in. The connection between well and snake probably derives simply from the snake's movements, which echo that of rippling water. Ilkley church in West Yorkshire has a carving of Verbeira, Romano-British goddess of the river Wharfe, in which she is clutching what appear to be two snakes, or possibly a couple of French loaves.

In one legend, a man dreams three times that a golden necklace lies under a well. After the third dream he goes to the well and has a feel. He is bitten by an adder and dies – the gold necklace was the pattern on the reptile's back. He should have known that snake bites can traditionally (but not medically) be cured by rubbing the smitten area with an **adder stone.**

These stones can be fossil ammonites, Stone Age artefacts, or stones with holes in – all three fulfil the same requirement. The holey stones are also used to ward adders away from cattle.

Bitten or not, you cannot kill an adder before sundown. Even then you are supposed to chop it into tiny pieces to prevent any of its severed bits reuniting. None of these experiments are recommended, or legal – the adder is now a protected species.

5th April
St Derfel's Day

Puppet Don't Preach

St Derfel was one of King Arthur's knights before he took a turn for the holy. He fought – under the name Cadarn, meaning 'strong' – when Arthur met his nemesis at the battle of Camlann. In reality, Derfel was indeed a successful soldier, and did fight at the historical battle of Camlann in 539, the set-to that eventually got sucked into the various Arthur legends. Derfel later became Abbot at Bardsey. He is the favourite saint at Llandderfel, near Bala in Gwynedd. The church there had a shrine, complete with a wooden, mobile image of Derfel. The head and arms moved mechanically, and like a miraculous ventriloquist's dummy it showered blessings on pilgrims. It was said to cure cows and horses, and to be capable of saving condemned souls from hell. By the early 16th century it was regularly attracting 500 people a day as well as assorted livestock.

But before you could say 'gottle o' geer', the Reformation heavies towed the effigy away in 1538 and burned it at Smithfield, London, along with a passing monk who refused to conform with Henry VIII's reforming mood. This burning fulfilled a prophecy which stated that Derfel would cause an entire forest to perish in flames. The monk's name was John Forest. Prophecies, as Macbeth will tell you, can be very disappointing.

🔘 Derfel's moving effigy may be gone, but you can still see his staff and the remains of the wooden horse upon which his likeness sat, at Llandderfel church.

© The **John Stow** Commemoration centres upon a less outlandish effigy than the Derfel dummy. Stow was the capital's chronicler in the 16th century, his magnum opus being the

Survey of London, a rather stodgy survey of all the city's officials from 1066 onwards. It was not a bread-winning job, however, and he was only saved from penury by King James I, who granted a 'Licence to Beg' two years before Stow's death today in 1605. The licence enabled Stow to receive contributions from appreciative and sympathetic friends and readers.

The **Changing the Quill ceremony** is the central part of the memorial service at St Andrew Undershaft Church in London, on or about April 5th. A top-half-only statue of John Stow writes forever in a stone ledger inside the church, its only non-stone component being a quill. Each year on this date the thoughtful Lord Mayor and his sheriffs issue Stow with a replacement. The quill ceremony is preceded by a service in thanks for Stow's work and example, with an appreciative address from a leading historian.

☻ Today is **Old Lady Day**, 11 days on from March 25th, the current Lady Day. Cold weather is supposed to blow in about now:

On Lady Day the latter,
The cold comes on the water,

which only really works when spoken with a broad Yorkshire accent.

6th April

Booker Pries into the Future

John Booker was a local legend in mystic Manchester during the 17th century. He had a lifelong interest in astrology, eventually graduating to the post of Licenser of Mathematical Publications in London, his speciality being Celestial Sciences. During the Civil War he was in great demand for making predictions; although how he phrased the news 'you're all going to lose and die' is not recorded. Perhaps it was the circumspect nature of his predictions that caused one of his contemporaries to burst on the scene with a pamphlet fulsomely titled '*Mercurio-Coelica Mastyx; or an Anticaveat to all such as have heretofore had the misfortune to be cheated and deluded by the great and treacherous imposter, John Booker*'.

In spite of his critics, Booker had a good reputation as a locator of thieves and a solver of 'love questions'. If alive today he would have been an agony aunt with a metal detector. He predicted the solar eclipse of 1613 and deciphered its prognostications of impending peril for a couple of European kings, who indeed died that year. He was a scrier – using a crystal ball to see into the future – and also 'a great admirer of the **antimonal cup**'. This was a vessel made of antimony, a reactive silvery metal which seeps into the medicinal wine within and makes the drinker throw up – which was often just what the doctor ordered. Booker died of dysentery on April 6th 1667.

The Scots finally sealed their 1314 victory over the English at Bannockburn with the Treaty of Northampton in 1328. This followed the highly regarded **Declaration of Independence**, drafted in Arbroath on April 6th 1320 and sent as a letter to the pro-English Pope John XXII. Chancellor of Scotland Bernard de Lington, who was also Abbot of Arbroath, was the mastermind of the charter, which is also known as the Declaration of Arbroath. It is one of the classic statements of freedom and justice, with such heart-stirring lines as: '*It is not for glory, riches or honour that we fight, it is for liberty alone, the liberty which no good man loses except with his life.*' The Pope was moved by the Declaration's integrity, and urged Edward II to stop being such a rotten bully.

It was all this which inspired the **Arbroath Pageant**, first staged in 1947. Its various plays and processions included a re-enactment of the Declaration, along with the other major events leading up to the country's brief freedom. The pageant was held at irregular intervals until 1981, when the props and costumes were all destroyed in a blaze. An organising committee for the event still exists, and there is speculation that the pageant may yet rise from the ashes.

7th April
St Brynach's Day

Dick Makes Good End

28-year-old **Dick Turpin** threw himself off the gallows ladder in York today, 1739. Such bravura won him the admiration of the crowd, and his legend has never looked back. This was what is known as 'making a good end'. Such was the crowd's appreciation that it retrieved Dick's body from grave-robbers at the local anatomy school and reinterred it in lime.

Turpin had spent his life cattle-rustling, murdering and robbing, though when he was finally apprehended at Welton near Brough in Humberside, it was for the embarrassingly petty crime of killing a gamecock that belonged to the landlord of *The Red Dragon*. Most of Dick's heroic exploits come from folk-ballads, and Harrison Ainsworth's romanticising novel *Rookswood*, which includes the mythical horse Black Bess and the famous ride from London to York. This was done to establish an alibi, as the 200-mile-plus journey was thought to be impossible in one night. Impressive; but it had already been ascribed to 'Swift Nick' Nevison in the previous century, and was a folktale up for grabs by anyone with suitable qualifications. In other words, Turpin did not do it. Neither did he give to the poor. The ending was about the only good exploit in Dick's life.

✟ Meanwhile, in his extremely busy afterlife, Dick haunts the stretch of Watling Street which runs past *The Old Swan Inn*, Woughton on the Green, near Milton Keynes, Buckinghamshire; while he and Black Bess (rare example of ghost of fictional character) also impress the crowds at Woodfield, a house in nearby Aspley Guise, just over the county border in Bedfordshire. Dick and Bess also do their ghostly double-act in the *Spaniards Inn* at Hampstead Heath, London. On the northern edge of the city at Loughton in Epping Forest, Essex, he rides his horse at great speed, with a woman clinging to him. She was one of his many victims, tortured and murdered for her money. Such is the stuff of heroes.

▥ This is St Brynach's Day. On the surprisingly tall and well-preserved 10th-century cross of St Brynach at Nevern, near Newport in Dyfed, the first cuckoo of mid-Wales traditionally alights today and starts singing. The cuckoo is the herald of spring, and it gatecrashes the Christian party here as a result of the cross being on an old pagan site. St Brynach is not alone in claiming the first cuckoo: see April 29th for more candidates.

Brynach himself may be the same figure as Brychan, a mythical Welsh King who sired up to 63 children, according to his biographers. The 16th-century stained glass in the church at St Neot, Cornwall, is said to depict Brychan with 10 of his children. However, after sober reflection, researchers have decided that it is probably a picture of none other than God himself.

8th April

Jurassic Porkies

On this day in 1865, *The Leeds Mercury* reported the findings of a drainage-dig in Durham. Normally even on the most moribund of news-days such events did not make the papers. But the routine retrenching had unexpectedly turned into a palaeontological dig. The workers had split through a rock, 25 feet underground, and out hopped a toad. It had unusually long toes, black eyes and a pale skin, and was dying for a good croak after what scientists quickly estimated had been 6,000 years encased in rock. Hartlepool Museum displayed the toad along with its '*primary habitation*', the limestone rock, in which the creature's impression was clearly visible.

Not alone in fossil folklore, there have been many supposedly ancient amphibians – frogs, toads and newts – similarly exposed in this country, and indeed all over the world. One of the most celebrated examples of the genre occurred in France in 1856 when workers were digging a railway tunnel. They hacked into some Jurassic limestone, and out flopped a pterodactyl. Having waited several million years for this moment, it promptly died.

◉ On the first Tuesday after April 6th the small Stowell Court meets at Tatworth, near Chard in Somerset. It holds a candle-auction for Stowell Mead, a watercress bed, and then enjoys a rather limp repast of bread, cheese . . . and watercress. Bidding lasts until a tallow candle has burnt itself out, which can seem forever when you are getting all excited at the prospect of cress. During the auction the doors are locked, and the only light allowed is that provided by the tyrannical candle. The winner gets the meadow and tries desperately to acquire a taste for aquatic plant-life.

☙ There is a seasonal glut of weather-sayings during April. Classics such as '*From Christmas to May, weak cattle decay*', and '*Never trust an April sunshine*', embody the generally held idea that April will give all the signs of spring and then revert to a bit of late wintering. It is also said that '*In Spring, hair is worth more than meat*', which distresses butchers and winds up bald people, but hints at the same thing – more cold weather ahead, giving animals with thick coats the edge. A touch of apple blossom, however, is a small consolation, as: '*If apples bloom in April, why then they'll be* plentiful.' And whilst sitting in the inevitable rain, remember that 'April showers bring May flowers', a silver lining for the soaked.

If it is pêche-ing down, there is always consolation in fish, as 'An April fish is a dainty dish'. The news, rhyme and grammar are worse for frogs: 'April floods carries off frogs and their broods.' And if you want those little piggies to make it to market, make sure they wrap up well: 'A windy April is death to little pigs'.

Finally, confusing news from the farming fraternity, who insist that 'Snow in April is manure'. Leading to the question, how many of these proverbs are just a pile of April snow?

9th April

Chicken Drumsticks

During March 1661 the Manor House at North Tidworth, Wiltshire, was subject to satanic drumming. John Mompesson, the owner, had instigated the arrest of William Drury, a travelling percussionist, for vagrancy. His drum was placed in a room in Mompesson's house during Drury's incarceration. But, divorced from its owner, this drum became the focus of the poltergeist known as The Drummer of Tedworth.

The invisible drummer began by beating on the roof, and then moved indoors, always ending its drum solo with a tight military tattoo. It then branched out into sheet-pulling, child-beating and furniture juggling, all the usual poltergeist activities.

At one point Mompesson chased the entity under one of the beds, from which hiding place it panted at him like a large dog – one of its favourite noises. On another occasion, one of the servants woke in the night to witness a large dark shape with glowing red eyes. The demon sometimes manifested as glowing blue light too. Large claw-marks were discovered in some scattered ash.

Charles II was intrigued enough to set up a Royal Commission to investigate the events at Tedworth (which, due to a war office printing error earlier this century, is now Tidworth). It failed to drum up any evidence. Having heard all about his drum's new role, William Drury decided to claim that the disturbances were a direct result of his imprisonment, hoping that the authorities might release him. Instead, he was tried as a witch at Salisbury, and was transported. For such a celebrated example of

multi-layered supernatural goings-on, it is odd that events thereafter just petered out. Perhaps even ghosts get bored of drum solos after a while.

On April 9th 1679 a dead orphan at Radcliffe, now in Greater Manchester, was ordered to be 'wound up in woollen only'. Burying ragamuffins in finest woollen shrouds may seem an unusually generous custom. However, it was merely a consequence of an 1678 Act designed to force increased wool sales and fill the royal coffers in the process. The Act was repealed in 1795, but for more than a century fines were slapped on all who failed to place a waif in sheep's clothing.

Francis Bacon is responsible for London's only ghostly chicken – and a semi-frozen, semi-oven-ready one at that. Following a conviction for bribery, former Lord Chancellor Bacon had been banned from high office. A part-time philosopher, he now set his mind to the vexed question of why grass which had been concealed by snow was still green when uncovered. He decided that the snow was a preservative of some sort, and so embarked on some of the first experiments in deep freezing. At Pond Square in Highgate, in April 1626, he stopped his carriage and ordered his coachman to buy and prepare a chicken. This eccentric request was carried out, and Bacon stuffed the bird with snow. He then put it in a sack and surrounded it with more snow. The promising experiment was aborted when Bacon, in the midst of his snow-handling, had a shivering fit and collapsed. He died a few days later, on April 9th.

☥ Bacon himself does not haunt Pond Square, but the chicken does. It is large, white, half-plucked, and runs in frantic circles before disappearing. It was very active in January 1969 and February 1970, and still regularly claims its place near the top of London's ghostly pecking order.

10th April

The Bell of the Ball

Madam Gould was left as a penniless widow at Lewtrenchard, near Launceston in Devon, when her eldest son squandered all the family wealth on ill-advised ventures and gambling. But, indomitable of spirit and elusive of Christian name, Madam Gould struggled on. She gradually bought back all the family land, and went on to manage the estate herself, gaining much local admiration. On April 10th 1795 she was feeling unwell, but tough-minded as ever, she refused to follow advice and go to bed. She eventually compromised by sitting in a chair. And there she swiftly died.

The shutters flew back supernaturally as she breathed her last, and immediately Madam Gould's ghost took up where the woman had left off. She was spied under a walnut tree in the grounds, and was later regularly seen in the moonlight sitting on a plough or wandering about on Galford Down. The house became subject to a gentle haunting, Gould's restless high-heeled footsteps ever-present, her ghostly eye cast protectively on the children of the family. As tales of Gould's ghoul spread, their details became increasingly embroidered, and they soon took on some mythic qualities: flowing hair and white robes, and a radiant white light – very goddess-like attributes.

☥ A carpenter in Lewtrenchard church saw the other side of the ghost's usually mild nature when he made the mistake of peeping into the Gould family vault. The ghost upped and chased him home, her bright glow casting the man's shadow before him. Mrs Gould again seems to have got out on the wrong side of the grave when she cornered a young girl who was out apple-scrumping. The girl found her way blocked at every turn until she dropped all the fruit. The ghost still regularly clip-clops around the house, and sometimes the wheels of a phantom carriage are heard on the gravel of the drive. Anyone checking the source of the noise is greeted by peals of echoing laughter.

© The first records of the **Kate Kennedy Procession**, at St Andrews University in Fife, are from 1848. But by 1874 the event had spilled over into the town, and had become so riotous that the local authorities declared it a *'public scandal'*. It was banned for half a century, and only made a comeback in 1926. Now more of a pageant, it features appearances by many of the greats from Scotland's history – it is not uncommon to see Robert the Bruce sharing a joke with John Napier, the inventor of logarithms. At the head of the parade is Kate Kennedy herself. Or rather himself, as Kate is always played by a first-year male student. She rides in a horse-drawn carriage, accompanied by her 'uncle', Bishop Kennedy.

In 1450 Bishop Kennedy founded the Uni-versity's San Salvator's College. Ten years later he presented the college church with a bell, called Katherine. Legend has it that the bell was named after his niece, but there is no evidence that such a woman existed. An old bell with an unexplained name seems to have been all it took to kickstart the Kate Kennedy Procession, although the festivites may also be linked with a pagan rite called *Cath Cinneachaidh* – the Gaelic for 'rebirth of spring'. There are records of attempts by the University to stamp out the rite in the early 15th century.

11th April
St Guthlac's Day

Chicken in a Pyramid

'Mad Jack' Fuller died on this day in 1834. The 22-stone Jack was MP for East Sussex until, during a debate, he abused the Speaker, got physically ejected, burst back in for some more abuse, and got dragged out again. His political career over, he was able to concentrate on that which has assured his lasting fame – a wonderful series of **follies** around his estate at Brightling near Battle.

🎐 Fuller built a 65-foot high obelisk, the Brightling Needle; a gothic tower; a fully-working observatory; and a Rotunda Temple, the alleged site of orgies. All of these remain very visible around Brightling, as does his **Sugar Loaf** folly, the result of a drunken wager. One night Jack insisted to some visitors that nearby Dallington church spire could be viewed from his dining-room window. This, the guests knew, was twaddle. But when they came back in daylight to settle the bet, they were taken to the dining room where the distinctive spire was clearly visible. They were flabbergasted. What had happened was that Jack, recognising his rash error, had ordered a detached mock-spire to be built between Brightling and Dallington. It was erected in great haste: in 1961 restorers discovered that it was held together with mud, not mortar. It is known as The Sugar Loaf because old loaves of sugar were cone-shaped.

Britain's largest working barrel organ, a gift from Fuller, is inside Brightling church. And outside stands Mad Jack's greatest gift to posterity – his tomb, the 25-foot high **Pyra-mid**, which still dominates both churchyard and church. Completed long before Fuller died, it is said that Jack advertised for a hermit to tomb-sit for him, insisting that the successful applicant must not shave, wash, cut their hair or trim their nails, and must stay silent for seven years. After this time the hermit would be made a gentleman for life. No one applied for the job. When Fuller *did* die, tradition has it that he was buried inside the Pyramid on an iron chair, in full evening dress, sitting at a table laid out with roast chicken and a bottle of claret – in life he sank three bottles of the stuff daily. The floor of the Pyramid was covered in broken glass to prevent the Devil from snatching Mad Jack away.

The 8th-century soldier **Guthlac** quit the army to become a monk at Repton, Derbyshire. He proved too zealous a teetotaller to gain much affection from his fellow monks, and he led the way on the self-deprivation front. But he still found monastic life insufficiently austere, and so he retired to Crowland in the Lincolnshire fens – which, in those days, was only accessible by boat.

During his years at the Crowland hermitage Guthlac was assailed by fenland demons, who ridiculed him in Welsh. All that kept him sane were the regular visits from angels, and the spiritual presence of his patron, 1st-century apostle St Bartholomew. Guthlac used his **scourge** – a gift from Bartholomew – to whip the demons, and it later became his symbol.
🏚 It is said at Fishtoft in Lincolnshire that as long as St Guthlac wields the whip, the village will be free of rats and mice. A window in the church there shows him doing his stuff with the scourge. Such a severe reputation helped elevate Guthlac above the over-crowded ranks of anti-social Saxon hermits; and he became, along with St Cuthbert, one of the most popular pre-Conquest saints.

12th April

I Slay, I Slay, I Slay . . .

In the first two decades of the 18th century, war seemed to be on the way out. Under the Act of Union in 1707, England and Wales had teamed up with Scotland to become Great Britain. Resistance, in the form of the Jacobite Rebellion of 1715, had easily been put down. And victory in the lengthy and costly war with France had left Britain with territory in North America and the West Indies, as well as Gibraltar and Minorca. The 1695 **Window Tax** helped finance these victories, and attempts to avoid this the-more-you-glaze-the-more-you-pays levy led to the bricked-up windows often seen in 18th-century houses.

The tax burden and the lack of interest in a return to war served to make the once invulnerable **recruiting sergeants** – responsible for drumming up 'volunteers' for the King's army – not so much figures of fear as figures of fun. On April 12th 1727, a recruiting sergeant was working the crowd at Hinckley in Leicestershire. Hundreds had gathered to hear his patter, a mixture of grand promises and the more immediate offer of cash upfront – the King's Shilling. He had his eye on a few likely-looking recruits when 20-year-old saddler **Richard Smith** began making fun of the proceedings. Smith's swift wit, jokes and insults soon had the crowd roaring with laughter, and the solider was having a hard time. So the common-sense recruiting sergeant responded by giving his heckler the ultimate put-down – he ran Smith through, with his pike.
✝ Smith's tombstone is in Hinckley churchyard, and every year on this day it is said to **sweat blood** – perhaps a spectacular supernatural attempt by the 17th-century stand-up to have the last laugh.

Ann Howard of Ashford, Derbyshire, died today in 1747, aged 21. Although betrothed at the time, she was still presumed to be virginal, a status that entitled her to the posthumous honour of a **Maiden's Garland**. Before the service the bell-shaped garland was carried into the church by a girl of similar age to Ann, and hung over the pew where Ann's parents regularly sat. It can still be seen in the church, along with three other garlands. They are made of ribbons, paper gloves, handkerchiefs and rosettes, draped around a wire and wood frame shaped like a small bird's cage. Maiden's Garlands were due to any girl who died while betrothed. Other notable examples can be seen at Ilam, near Leek in Staffordshire, and at Abbots Ann in Hampshire – see October 6th.

13th April

The Pebble-Dashed Coffin

Originally from Stratford-upon-Avon in Warwickshire, **Francis Ainge** gained fame back in England when he was visited in 1759 at his adopted home in Somerset County, Maryland,

USA. Newspaper reports of the conversation made much of Francis' appearance – no wrinkles, and just a hint of grey hair at the front and sides. But what the reports led on were his chit-chat about the death of King Charles I and his anecdotes about the activities of Oliver Cromwell. For Ainge these were just reminiscences of youth, but for readers it was ancient history: he was 130 years old at the time of the interview, and had fathered a son at the age of 103. Francis Ainge, born 1629, finally called it a day on April 13th 1766, at the age of 137 years and eight months.

© Younger than Francis Ainge by 104 years, **Ann West** died on this day in 1803. Her tomb can be seen in Pembury Old Church, near Tunbridge Wells in Kent, and it has a small hole in the side. In life, Ann had been terrified by the prospect of premature burial, and had made preventative arrangements. Her will insisted that her body be placed in a lidless coffin with a hole in the surrounding tomb to admit air and enable any post-burial shouts to be heard. Her servant placed bread and water on the tomb every day for a year. Surprisingly for Ann, and disappointingly for fans of Edgar Allen Poe, the doctors got it right and she was actually dead when they interred her.

✝ In spite of all Ann's precautions she still does not rest in peace. Because of her design specifications, a popular local game developed, with children dropping stones through the hole in the tomb to hear them bounce off Ann's skeleton inside. The continual death rattle may be what led Ann's ghost to haunt her former home at Great Bayhall Manor in Pembury. There are footsteps, white floating apparitions and all the usual phantasmagoria, but so far no acts of vengeance on the children who persecute her remains.

© The **Links Market** at Kirkcaldy, Fife, claims to be the largest street fair in Europe. It now takes place in the middle of April, running from Wednesday to Monday, sprawling out from the esplanade and into the streets of the Bethelfield area of the town. Kirkcaldy becomes the Scottish Blackpool for the duration of the market, with many elaborate illuminations. The ruined Ravenscraig Castle, built in 1440, looks down on the proceedings, and can scarcely believe that the fair has been around longer than *it* has. The market began as an Easter feeing (hiring) fair in 1305.

14th April
First Cuckoo Day

Tuesday on Monday and When Cuckoo Clocks Went Back

Recent ups and downs in the world's stock-markets coupled with an imagination-shortfall by some newspapers has led to such a glut of Black Fridays, Wednesdays et cetera, that they have begun to seem almost a fixed point in the calendar. Only one such 'Black-' day is a bona fide annual event. The Monday eight days after Easter Day has, since the late 14th century, been **Black Monday**.

☻ The day's name marks what supposedly happened to Edward III and his troops on Easter Monday, 14th April 1360. They were besieging Paris when the weather turned brutal. It was the meanest, iciest, blackest day in memory. Alarmed accounts of the time described it as '*so full dark of mist and hail and so bitter cold that many men died on their horsebacks with the cold*'. Thousands perished, and Black Monday also marked the start of a prolonged and pronounced bleak spell in England – a fresh dose of bubonic plague arrived in the following year, devastating London and sharply reducing the population. Considering such grim associations, it is surprising that this day of national mourning has stayed on the books for six centuries, even if few shed a tear these days. Even more surprising, no one seems to have noticed until long after Black Monday was established that the 14th of April 1360 was in fact a Tuesday. But the greatest irony of all is that, according to weatherlore, the 14th is supposed to mark the onset of warmth and sunshine.

© ☻ **Today is First Cuckoo Day**, the traditional date for the Cuckoo Fair, also known as Hefful Fair, at Heathfield in East Sussex. According to a local legend, Christ had been feeling peckish and asked one of his disciples to get some bread for him. The disciple had no money, so the baker refused to hand over any of his wares. But the baker's wife got her daughter to sneak a loaf to Jesus behind her husband's back. As a drastic mark of gratitude, Christ turned the woman and her daughter into stars – the constellation **Pleiades**. He also turned the baker into a cuckoo. The bird only appears in Britain when the seven stars of Pleiades are in the sky, which is traditionally between St Tiburtius' Day – today – and St John's Day, June 24th. The bird in turn brings warm weather with it, which spreads upwards from the south coast.

© A supplementary local legend tells of an old woman who, unobserved, used to join the crowds annually at Hefful Fair – 'Hefful' being a local name for Heathfield – and discreetly release the first cuckoo from her basket. On the following day, according to another slice of the same legend, the cuckoo would pay a flying visit to Beaulieu Fair in Hampshire to buy a great-coat. The Beaulieu bash ran out of cuckoos and customers in the 1940s, and the fair at Heathfield – after a 1987 revival – is now a small scale bazaar at the community centre. A man in drag stands in for the mysterious old woman, and a homing pigeon stands in for the not-readily-available cuckoo. At the start of the Fair it is released from a basket while a concealed tape-recorder relays the song of the cuckoo. Guaranteed to fool everyone.

The absence of a cuckoo volunteer can be partly explained by the change from the Old to the New Calendar. By Hefful's old date, April 25th, cuckoos are usually arriving in sufficient numbers to make hearing one a good bet, hence the origins of the fair and the accompanying legends. This first influx of cuckoos is known as a **Gowk Storm**, which is also a proverbial term for any sudden spell of misfortune. But even though today, the new date, is only 11 days earlier, the twitcher's chance of a solitary gowk is a bit slimmer. Birds turning up ahead of the crowds probably need their internal cuckoo clocks adjusting.

◉ If you hear the cuckoo call today you will get a cageful of luck, provided you immediately turn over all the money in your pockets, spit, and do not look at the ground. The luck is only good if you are on soft ground. On hard ground the call indicates misfortune; and if it is heard whilst in bed, it denotes illness, even death.

Alternatively, ignore the don't-look-at-the-ground advice: as soon as you hear the cuckoo call, peek under your shoe. You will find a conspicuous hair, and its colour denotes the hair-hue of your future partner in love. While you are down there, scrape up some dirt from the ground beside your right foot. If subsequently placed on your doorstep, this will keep crawling insects at bay (especially cuckoo flies and cuckoo-spit insects). But on no account adopt a hands-on method and catch the cuckoo itself. It is wildly unlucky to bring the bird indoors.

For more flights of fancy with the cuckoo, see April 29th.

15th April

Bowels of the Earth

In April 1652 young Mary Ellins from Evesham in Hereford and Worcester was out playing with her pals. They stumbled upon Catherine Huxley, aged 40, amusing herself in a ditch. The children pelted her with stones, and shouted 'Witch!' several times before running away. Mary was the slowest in retreat, and was recognised by Catherine, who called out after her: 'Ellins, you shall have enough stones in your stomach!'

Hours later, Ms Ellins was down in the dumps. She felt very constipated, and extremely unwell. Her condition steadily deteriorated, and when she eventually managed a bowel movement out came an avalanche of rocks and pebbles.

The stones kept piling up every time Mary went to the bathroom. She told her parents what had happened at the ditch, and soon Catherine Huxley was on trial, accused of being the **Witch of Worcester**. The damning evidence against her was a pile of gravel found at her bedside, and Catherine was condemned to the gallows.

Mary's rock bottom condition turned out to be a passing phase – ending with Catherine's death – but while it lasted people came from afar to buy the contents of her rectum, hoping that stones from bewitched bowels might bring them good luck.

The island of **Eigg**, west of Mallaig on the west coast of Scotland, has a holy well on its south side. Today the islanders used to gather there and drink the water, before marching sunwise around the well in a ceremony mixing the Christian with the pagan. When the Catholic Father Hugh dedicated the well to St Catherine in the 17th century, he was giving a new name to a site which had long been a centre of worship for other, older, beliefs. The villagers piled stones at the head of the spring as a communal penance, and the priest held a Mass and blessed the well. But rather than attempt to oust completely the old ways, Father Hugh incorporated them into his ceremony. He handed out candles and ordered everyone to 'make a **dressil**' – meaning to walk three times around the well in the direction of the sun (from east to west, anticlockwise). The dressil, or deazil, is a druidical charm, a peculiar option for a Catholic priest. But the water was thought to be sufficiently holy from then on, and no meat was allowed to be boiled in it, as that would offend St Catherine.

🔲 The formal ceremony is no longer held, but today is still considered an auspicious day to visit the well.

Beaulieau has seven vowels, and also used to have a fair today – see yesterday for brief details of its cuckoo clothing.

16th April
St Magnus' Day

Shoulder of Lamentation

🔲 At St Mary's Church, Burwick, at the southern tip of South Ronaldsay in Orkney, there is a flat stone with two footprints in it. They are said to have been made by 12th-century **St Magnus** when he used the stone to sail, or possibly windsurf, across the Pentland Forth. Magnus – whose feast-day is today – was a Norse Earl, and legend says that he had his head split by an axe at the order of his cousin Haakon. In 1919 a skeleton was found hidden in a pillar at Kirkwall Cathedral, Orkney, which is dedicated to the saint. The skull had been cleft almost in two – on the strength of this evidence the bones are now treated as St Magnus' relics.

On this day in 1746, the Duke of Cumberland wiped up the rump of Bonnie Prince Charlie's army of Stuart hopefuls. Charles Edward Stuart was endeavouring to win the British throne for his father James, son of James II; and capitalising on an understrength English army he had made it as far south as Derby. But lack of support forced him to turn round, and when defeat came he was back in the Highlands, at Culloden Moor near Inverness. **The Battle of Culloden** was the last full-scale land battle to be fought in Britain. Subsequently commemorated in numerous songs, it had also been predicted 200 years earlier by the Scots prophet, the Brahan Seer. On visiting Culloden he declared: '*Thy black moor will be stained with the best blood of the Highlands.*'

Culloden is cited as one of the various origins of the **Curse of Scotland**, a tag given to the nine of diamonds (see February 13th for another). Prince Charlie was playing cards just before the battle. During his game the nine fell from the pack and was lost. The Duke of Cumberland, staying in the same house after Culloden, found the missing card. Later, when the Duke was looking for a handy scrap of paper on which to write a death warrant for Charles, the card was the first thing that came to hand. He used it to help authorise Charles' death warrant, writing his fatal signature on the card and sending it to the relevant authorities.

The Scots' defeat at Culloden was foretold by a man gazing through the **shoulder bone of a sheep**. A well-established way of looking into the future, the bone only worked if it had not been touched by iron. This particular prediction took place on the Isle of Skye, in front of many witnesses.

◐ 🔲 A **Culloden Memorial Service** has been held on the Sunday nearest the 16th since the 1920s, on the cairn at the site of the Battle. The only building which survived the battle – the Old Leanach Cottage – now houses a display.

17th April
St Donan and
Companions' Day

Attack of the Big Women

St Donan is one of the few saints to get his entire retinue – 52 of them, say some sources – in on his feast day. **St Donan and his Companions** collectively command the prayers of the devout on April 17th. Irishman Donan was a disciple of Columba's on Iona before he founded the monastery on the island of Eigg, west of Mallaig in the Scottish Highlands. The commune flourished until Easter in 618, when during Mass a gang of armed women burst in. The attack was led by their chieftainess, seeking vengeance because Donan had diddled her out of pasture rights. The Mass was abandoned, and the Amazon army herded the monks into the refectory before setting fire to it. Everyone was killed. As the women celebrated their new status as Britain's first Mass murderers, a strange spectral glow appeared in the sky. The chieftainess and her entire army were hypnotically drawn to it, and walked straight into a loch where they all drowned.

🔲 The loch, in the centre of the island, is now known as Loch nam ban Mora, Gaelic for Loch of the Big Women.

Although **prize-fighting** was illegal, it was still

the most popular national sport in England in the first half of the 19th century, satisfying a timeless taste for gore. On this day in 1860 the last of the 'Great Prize Fights' took place. It was announced by surreptitious messages in newspapers, directing those in the know to an unregulated train, which took coachloads to the secret site of the punch-up. Just outside Farnborough, now in Greater London, the English Champion Tom Sayers met the American J. Heenan – at stake, the Championship of the World.

The two men pulverised each other to the edge of bloody oblivion, driving the crowd wild. As one song later described it:

> Such fibbing and such up and down, Lor, how
>   the swells did shout!
> Their ribs did nicely rattle, their daylight
>   near knocked out.

With the last blow of the bout, Sayers felled Heenan. He hit the canvas just as the police appeared on the scene. Everyone scattered. There was no referee to count Heenan out, and there was nothing for it but to declare the match a draw. Robbed of outright victory, Tom Sayers retired, and became a sporting legend. A popular ballad spread his fame as '*the champion of proud England, and the conqueror of all*'. A life annuity was purchased for him; but he spent most of his cash on drinking with his army of admirers, and died the sad and lonely death of an alcoholic.

The real reason for the official crackdown on prize-fighting was not the main event, but all the violence outside the ring – many contests ended in free-for-all brawls. The 'sport' still survives today as a bloodier semi-legal alternative to boxing, and even shows signs of becoming fashionable. But since the retirement of the immensely well-loved Sayers, it has not packed a fraction of its former punch.

18th April

Rantan and Raving: The Stang in the Tale

Mary Parish died on this day in 1703, one of the great forgotten geniuses of British history. Angels, faeries, powerful spirits and even God himself were at Mary's beck and call. She became pregnant a total of 106 times by the same man, someone she did not meet until she was 53, a little beyond normal child-bearing age. The man was **Goodwin Wharton**, a Whig MP and Lord of the the Admiralty under William III. And it was on his behalf that she communed with other worlds and divine beings.

The 29-year-old Goodwin, like many credulous souls of his time, was fascinated by the pseudo-science of alchemy. He had already been duped by a number of smart operators when he met Mary. At first she offered small-scale magic – charms to help him win at gambling, frog-bone aphrodisiacs, peas that conveyed invisibility. All failed to work, but Mary kept Goodwin hooked by making grander and grander claims. Goodwin was told that a colony of faeries dwelled below Hounslow Heath, and that their Queen wanted him as lover and King. Over a 20-year period, not one of the countless arranged meetings between Goodwin and the faeries came to fruition. Excuses were endlessly inventive, but the main one concerned the Queen's erratic menstrual periods. Mary told Goodwin that the Faerie Queen's lust was nothing special – all women found him irresistible. He believed her – especially when the aged Mary became his mistress – and convinced himself that the queens of James II and William III were under his spell. For almost 20 years he was certain that, should the monarch die, then he was only a swift remarriage away from the English throne. It was not to be. Nor was he any luckier in getting his hands on the vast hoards of treasure which Mary kept finding with the assistance of various spirits. Lost gold from these finds was sometimes mystically transported into Goodwin's chests, but the spirits would never get round to giving him permission to spend or even see the money. And if he impetuously sneaked a peek, the chests were invariably empty – Mary would explain that Goodwin had broken the spell, or offer some other supernatural excuse which the MP accepted without question.

Fortunately Goodwin had divine prophecies and angels to fall back on. Spoken revelations happened only when Mary was in the vicinity; but Goodwin was not one to doubt his '*best of all women*'. God often spoke to him on a daily basis, regularly promising riches and glory. Goodwin came to realise that even omniscient God sometimes gets it wrong.

Meanwhile, Mary conceived children at an alarming rate – if she and Wharton had sex twice in a week, that meant two conceptions, and Mary often claimed to be carrying up to a dozen children. She always gave birth in secret, and Goodwin was never allowed to see any of his offspring. Mary would later report that they had died.

Goodwin had a few fleeting moments of doubt, but kept faith with Mary, faeries, angels and spirits until his own death in 1704. And he also faithfully chronicled his bogus visions and non-existent achievements in a surviving diary which was written for his non-existent son, Peregrine. It provides the basis for the excellent, highly readable, *Goodwin Wharton* by the American literary historian, J. Kent Clark.

During this week in 1879, Market Rasen in Lincolnshire witnessed a late outbreak of **Riding the Stang**. Local wrong-doers – especially wife-beaters and adulterers – lived in fear of the Stang, a ritualised form of vigilantism. The accepted procedure was that if villagers could hold the initial ceremony for three successive nights without being quelled, the law was suspended. They could then dole out their own instant and very rough justice, with no fear of repercussions.

Such ad hoc courts were widespread – known in different parts of the country as randan, rantanning, skimmington, horn-fair, and lewbelling – but quite uniform in their sentence structure. Alleged villains were harrassed with lots of noise; and on the third night an effigy of the miscreant was paraded on a pole or in a chair; though ideally the villain was made to Ride the Stang in person, abused and ridiculed every step of the way. A victim's enemies in the town would often fuel the crowd with food and beer to keep the rantan going, and to ensure that the vigilantes did not lose heart. There were always songs for the occasion. One version sung to husband-beaters has the lines:

> *She struck him so hard and she cut so deep,*
> *Till the blood ran down like a new-stuck*
> *sheep.*

The rantan song was known as the *Nominey*, a mocking reference to the *In Nomine Patris* at church services.

In the Market Rasen example, the accused took his sentence philosophically and survived the horse-play. Unlike an 18th-century Wiltshire cobbler, who was greatly put out. Word got around that he had repeatedly beaten up his apprentice, and one night he came home to find the mob in mid-Stang. On the third day his

effigy was hung from a pole, and the cobbler asked a friend what counter-measures he should take. The 'friend' advised him to follow the will of the crowd. Surprisingly compliant, the man hanged himself

The usual fate of the transgressor was to be *beaned* – a quaint euphemism for being beaten senseless. Women were usually dunked in the ducking stool or *trebucket*. It was a fear of this short, sharp punishment which held together many shaky marriages in the 1800s; although by the end of the century Riding the Stang – in all its forms – had virtually died out.

19th April
St Alphege's Day

John, Paul, George and Alphege

At sunset today in 1824, **Lord Byron**, otherwise known as George Gordon, died of marsh fever in Missolonghi, Greece. He had been summoning troops to help the Greeks fight for independence. His death came as a great blow to the Gordons: Byron would have been the 14th Laird, and was the last of the family line.

The strangely dashing, club-footed poet has drifted from fact to legend, a move spurred chiefly by people's lurid interest in his alleged homosexual and incestuous relationships. His diaries do not survive, and so it is now impossible to sift fact from myth. Hobhouse, his executor, wrote: '*The whole Memoirs were fit only for a brothel, and would damn Lord B. to everlasting infamy if published*'. They were burned.

In Greek legend, Leander drowned while attempting to swim the Hellespont. In a brilliant piece of self-mythologising, Byron gave the supposedly impossible crossing a go, and made it over in one piece. This may explain why Byron's ghost appears regularly near Grantchester, just outside Cambridge, swimming back and forth at the Byron Pool. Someone should tell that to the lonely ghost of one his most devoted fans. Bookseller's daugher Sophia Hyett roams around Byron's ancestral home Newstead Abbey, near Nottingham, crying '*Alas, my Lord Byron!*'.

This was a day noted for wondrous happenings and sudden cures at Canterbury, it being **St Alphege's Day**. Alphege was Archbishop of Canterbury, and is buried in the Cathedral. His miracle-making tomb was a favourite goal for pilgrims for 150 years until he was overshadowed by Thomas Beckett, who arrived on the scene in 1170.

Alphege ended his days in 1012, the captive of some stroppy Vikings. They had carted him off to Greenwich, demanding a huge ransom. He refused to let the sum be paid, and in response the Vikings got drunk and bludgeoned him to death with ox bones. As a final misanthropic gesture they declared that Alphege's body would not be released for burial until a dead stick upon which his blood had spilled sprouted anew. Next day the stick was in full bloom. The Norse men all apologised, and, recognising a good saint when they saw one, began venerating the martyr there and then. Alphege also turned a satanist into the Archbishop of Canterbury – see St Dunstan on May 19th.

On this day in 1985 two brothers in Edinburgh attempted to reject trial by jury in favour of **trial by combat**, the first such challenge since 1603. They argued that since it had never been abolished under Scottish law, it was a perfectly legitimate option. This left the Lord Advocate, Lord Cameron of Lochbroom – the Queen's Champion in Scotland – facing the prospect of wielding a long stave and shield against John Burnside or his brother Paul. Such a trial officially continues until one of the fighters cries '*Craven!*', or until the stars appear in the sky. In the latter case the defendant has won. However, after three days' deliberation, the High Court in Edinburgh decided that trial by combat was no longer a valid option, and the Advocate staved off an embarrassing showdown.

20th April

Man's Best Friend is his Wallet

Having grown fat on the profits of smuggling, the **Hawkhurst Gang** enjoyed a long reign of terror in the mid-18th century. They were based at Hawkhurst in the Weald of Kent, and were the scourge of the south, breeding terror and extorting tribute all the way from the Isle of Sheppey in the Thames Estuary to Poole in Dorset. An unholy marriage between the Wild West and the Mafia, they rode through towns with pistols ablaze, plundering the locals and terminating anyone foolish enough to get in their way.

William Sturt, fresh from the army, was having none of this. He sized up his chances against the gang, and formed an unofficial militia at his hometown of Goudhurst in Kent. He trained and armed the men, and then waited for his chance.

It came soon enough. News that the town was no longer willing to roll over and play dead reached the outlaws, and the leaders of the rabble – the three Kingsmill brothers – announced that on April 20th 1747 they would destroy Goudhurst and its militia. When the day came, Richard Kingsmill, minutes away from death, declared to the townsfolk that he would broil four of their hearts and eat them for supper. But he ate lead instead, dying in the first volley from Sturt's men. Three other gangsters were killed, and many more were injured and taken prisoner. No one in the Goudhurst resistance suffered a scratch. The surviving Kingsmill brothers were hanged; and without its leaders the gang fizzled out.

Skinning dogs was not so much a custom as a messy tax-dodge. A man trading in the outside of labradors was never likely to find a place in the affections of a nation of animal lovers. But skinners started to make economic sense after the introduction of the Dog Tax in 1753. For the first time the happy household hound required a licence, and the licence required money. Paying out a couple of shillings just to keep a dog was a big commitment, and the skinners realised that for just a small cash incentive they could have the raw materials for an entire rack of Afghan coats. This money-for-pets advert appeared on the streets of Derby on April 20th 1773: '*This is to give notice that those persons who will hang their dogs and bring their skins to the* King's Head . . . *shall receive for every skin not less than 2s 6d, and every mastiff or large mongrel 5s. To be clean taken off and without slits. Ready money.*' Five bob for Fido was serious temptation, and locals flocked to the pub for some hair of the dog.

One of the many April cuckoo fairs used to take place today, this time at Tenbury in Hereford and Worcester. See April 14th for the general gist, and April 29th for the in-depth **cuckoo** exposé.

21st April
St Beuno's Day

Cured Meat

King Cadwallon persuaded **St Beuno** to enter the property market. The King offered Beuno a prime site, and the saint agreed to hand over his golden sceptre as payment. But once the deal was done, it transpired that the allotted land had been stolen in the first place from a fatherless child. This was an unsuitable business arrangement for a man of God, and when Beuno found out he cursed the King. Cadwallon was a wise man. Rather than spend the rest of his life with the head of an aubergine and the body odour of a hermit – or whatever the curse was – the King ducked Beuno's wrath by offering him an alternative tract of land on the Gwynedd coast at Clynnog-fawr; and that was where he settled. Once established there, Beuno never looked back, and became second only to St David as top Welsh Saint.

Beuno's most famous cure involved his niece Winefride and her roving head: see November 3rd. But after his death he continued to effect cures through **St Beuno's Well**, opposite the church in Clynnog. Epileptics favoured a two-pronged treatment – they bathed in the water, and then nipped over to the adjoining chapel, where they covered his tomb with rushes, and went to sleep. People with eye problems used to scrape the debris from the chapel walls and sluice it down with a mouthful of the well water. Not such good news for cattle, though. Cows were regularly sacrificed to Beuno at the well, and such ritual slaughter is a sure sign of pagan activities, from a time long before the saint's name had become associated with the site. As recently as the 17th century the sacrificial Beuno meat was held in high esteem as a cure-all.

The bovine-Beuno link still continues. Any local **calf born with misshapen ears** is sold in the churchyard at Clynnog-fawr, and the cash raised is put into an ancient wooden box known as **St Beuno's Chest**. Pragmatism has replaced paganism – the money raised wins hands-down over sacrificing to sub-deities when it comes to giving direct benefit to the church. This chest – hewn from a single piece of oak – has become proverbially permanent, giving rise to a saying: '*You may as well try to break up St Beuno's Chest.*' It can still be seen in the chapel at Clynnog-fawr, near Criccieth in Gwynedd. The saint's shrine is no longer here,

but the church itself is still Beuno's resting place, and is a classic of 16th-century stone and wood work.

There is a second *St Beuno's Well* – Fynnon Beuno, to those in the know – half a mile south of Tremeirchion, near Prestatyn in Clwyd. It is notable for the ugly, crudely carved, worn head which acts as an overflow from the walled pool. It bears an uncanny resemblance to the head of a Teenage Mutant Ninja Turtle.

22nd April

Drowning Sorrows

In 1690 **William Barwick** received a vivid lesson in procreation when his girlfriend Mary announced that she was pregnant. The shot-guns sounded as they made their way to the altar with due haste. After the fuss had died down, William and Mary – appropriate names, considering who was on the throne at the time – were out walking by a pond near Cawood Castle in North Yorkshire in early April. William was deeply unhappy that he had been forced into marriage, and his misery suddenly exploded into murderous action. He grabbed his new wife, forced her head into the water, and held her there until she drowned. He buried the body on the following night, and half-heartedly covered his tracks by telling his brother-in-law Thomas Lofthouse that Mary had gone to stay with her uncle in Selby.

On April 22nd 1690, Lofthouse went to fill a bucket from the pond. He was surprised to see Mary's ghost approach the water and sit by the bank, cradling the unborn child. A few inquiries later and it became clear that Mary had not been anywhere near Selby. Barwick changed his tack, saying that he had in fact sold his wife to another man for five shillings. But when the girl's body was discovered, there were no more excuses to be had. William Barwick went to the gallows, and afterwards his body was left suspended in chains for all to see. Mary's body was properly buried, and the ghost never appeared again.

This used to be the time of year for planting potatoes, on what plain-speaking Sussex folk called **Spud Planting Sunday**. The back-breaking tedium of burying vast numbers of large potato tubers had one consolation – the evening played host to **Tater Beer Night**. Celebrating the health of the spud crop became the flimsy excuse for broaching several barrels of beer and singing songs. In his family saga *A Song For Every Season*, Bob Copper describes the pre-war all-night excesses at *The Black Horse* in Rottingdean near Brighton, East Sussex. Everything earned in the fields went into kittys to pay for barrel upon barrel of ale. Clay pipes were on the house, and the landlord supplemented the drinking by providing a steady supply of beer to the singers of the best songs.

Rottingdean has, since the 18th century, been the stamping ground of the Copper Family, whose tradition of harmony singing stretches back over several generations. One of the county's best kept secrets for a couple of centuries, their family collection of songs became a mainstay of the folk music revival in the 1950s. But Rottingdean has a shadier side too. It is said of any braying **donkey**: '*You're not from Rottingdean.*' The insinuation is that the Rottingdean donkeys spent all night acting as steeds for the local smugglers and were too tired, come daybreak, to make any noise at all.

There is cause to celebrate the **potato** further north too. The residents of Thropton near Rothbury in Northumberland are called 'Tatey-town folks', as it is claimed that the country's first potatoes were grown there.

Still with the spud, there is a case to be made for chips originating in an inspired reading of a line from Shakespeare's *Troilus and Cressida*:

> *How the devil Luxury, with his fat rump and potato-finger, tickles these together! Fry, lechery, fry!*

23rd April
St George's Day

Dragon in Corsets

At Lydda in Palestine, **St George** died on this day sometime in the 4th century. That is all that is known about him with any certainty; though it is also said that he once strode into the shrine of Bacchus in full armour and destroyed the idol of the god: perhaps a template for the dragon-busting stories of later years. As early as AD 494 the exasperated Pope Gelasius declared that George was: '*One of those Saints whose names are justly revered by men, but whose activities are known only to God.*' But all human mythologies have a figure of good/spring triumphing over evil/winter; and George girded

his steed and galloped into the role left vacant by England's banished pagan gods and heroes.

According to the George legend, a dragon in Asia Minor was demanding a sacrifice of two sheep daily, and this was only for starters. After the sheep had begun to pall, the dragon moved on to the main course: humans. Stocks diminished as the lunch-lottery took its toll, and at last the short straw fell to the King's daughter. Fulfilling stereotype, she went to meet her fate dressed in bridal white, a sacrificial virgin.

Enter passing Christian knight George and his trusty lance. He did battle with the dragon and managed to impale it, but refused to finish the creature off. Instead he told the princess to wrap her girdle around the monster's head and neck and lead it into town. She complied, and the bowed and bleeding beast was paraded down the thronged High Street. Cheers turned to confusion when George vowed that he would only kill the dragon if everyone promised to embrace the trendy new religion, Christianity. There and then 15,000 consented and George sliced off the dragon's head.

Years later British legend-mongers tied this dragon fight to the flat-topped **Dragon Hill** near Uffington, south of Farringdon in Oxfordshire. The grassless chalk on the hillside is said to mark the place where the dragon's blood fell; and the nearby White Horse of Uffington, carved into the chalk hillside, is said to be either a psychedelic dragon or a bad picture of George's steed – for more on the White Horse see Whit Sunday. Meanwhile, the village of St George south of Rhyl in Clwyd is also said to be where George filletted the fiend. The footprint of his charger can be seen in one of the stones built into the church wall.

In the early days of Christianity, it was St Michael who had Heaven's exclusive rights to dragon and Satan slaying. But once George's story started to spread there was no stopping him. He appeared to Richard I in mid-crusade, and thereafter became associated with English soldiering, a rallying cry on the battlefield. In the 14th century, Edward III made him patron saint of England, which came as a blow to Edward the Confessor who had previously held the title. George was triumphant, an old god in a new guise. And one with little or no historical basis. But in 1969 the Catholic Church succeeded where the dragon had failed, and gave him the chop. He was scrubbed from the official saints' calendar and demoted to the token status of local saint, optional but not to be encouraged. A hard blow for a universal mythological motif.

The Knights of St George have the garter as their emblem. This dates from a party on this day in 1348. The host, Edward III, intervened when he found that the guests were giggling at Joan, Duchess of Salisbury, whose blue ribbon garter had dropped off. He picked it up, tied it round his own knee and cried the now famous '*Honi Soit Qui Mal Y Pense*' – which, roughly translated, implies shame on anyone who thought ill of the garter-dropping incident – a phrase so eternally resonant that it now adorns many coins, court-rooms and family crests.

◉ Edward III instantly abandoned his plans to form a new Round Table, and instigated instead the **Order of the Garter**. The blue ribbon became its badge of honour, first awarded one year later on St George's Day. The order still exists, and Knight of the Garter is among the highest honours doled out by the monarch each year.

Joan's blue garter is explained by the fact that **blue** was said to be the saint's colour, and it remains customary to wear something blue on St George's Day. This justifies the wearing of bluebells today, as opposed to the otherwise-to-be-expected roses – England's national flower – which are not yet in bloom.

George survives in the mumming plays of Easter and Christmas, often appearing as its central killed-and-resurrected figure. Due to confusions during the Hanoverian era, his character has sometimes mutated into 'King George'.

▥ April 23rd used to be **Mayor's Day** in Norwich, Norfolk. George himself was otherwise engaged, so the Dragon – known as **Snap** – dominated the show. Snap led the mayor to the Cathedral; but being a pagan creature he was not allowed inside for the service, and waited outside on a boulder called The Dragon's Stone, snapping his wooden jaws. As he wound his way through the streets, Snap's greatest ambition was to steal headware: as he lunged at local children they would duck and shout '*Snap, Snap! Steal a boy's cap!*' The pageant and mumming play can be traced back at least as far as 1408, and an elaborate Snap costume still survives which is almost this old. It is now deemed too ancient to leave Norwich's Castle Museum except on very special occasions. But a specially made replica Snap features in Norwich's Lord Mayor's Street Procession, usually held in the early evening of the second Saturday in July. Norwich now marks April 23rd in the same way as many other town and cities, with local scouts teaming up for a parade and service – George is their patron saint.

Today also witnessed the birth in 1564, and the death in 1616, of **William Shakespeare**. Only a few paces in front of St George on the fact front, legend makers have filled in the blank bits with tales of deer-poaching – he is said to have been prosecuted after repeated raids on Charlecote Park – and of excessive beer-swilling. Will was so fond of his pint that he captained the Stratford team against a team from the notoriously beery village of Bidford-on-Avon. They lost, but next day his team-mates were eager for a rematch. A hungover Shakespeare was not interested, improvising a quick rhyme to remind them that he had already had plenty to drink at:

> *Piping Pebworth, dancing Marston,*
> *Haunted Hillborough and hungry Grafton;*
> *Dudging Exhall, papist Wixford,*
> *Beggarly Broom and drunken Bidford.*

This alleged piece of Bardery is the sole reason for these eight places claiming the title 'the **Shakespeare Villages**', and has given them a first-class ticket for the tourism gravy train.

Shakespeare's remains are said to carry a curse. His tomb's inscription ends:

> *Bleste be ye man yt spares thes stones*
> *And curst be he yt moves my bones.*

Despite this, there are stories which claim that Shakespeare's skull spent some 50 years outside his grave. In 1794 Horace Walpole – writer, gothic revivalist and inventor of the word 'serendipity' – blurted out at a party that he would give 300 guineas for Shakespeare's head. One of the other guests, Dr Frank Chambers, was – for professional reasons – already acquainted with a group of grave-robbers led by a Mr Dyer. Deciding that Walpole's offer was serious, the doctor paid the men to break into Shakespeare's tomb.

They succeeded but were puzzled to discover that one of literature's greatest brains had been housed in a surprisingly small skull. Chambers contacted Walpole, offering the Bard's bones to him. Walpole wrote back volunteering to '*give the skulls of all my relatives*' in exchange for it, but made no mention of money. Further negotiations foundered, and an increasingly guilt-ridden Chambers instructed Dyer to put the skull back where he had found it.

Years later, the now respectable Dr Chambers was shocked when Dyer came to see him. The grave-robber had fallen in with forgers, one of whom had taken very ill. Dyer blindfolded the doctor and dragged him miles to the crypt of an old church where the gang was based. While Chambers treated the forger, Dyer revealed that he had never dared to return Shakespeare's skull to its tomb, and that instead he had thrown it into the ossuary of the church in which they were now standing. Dyer let Chambers have a fragment from the forehead, which he had kept in case the skull ever needed identifying.

🎵 Dr Chambers spent the rest of his life trying to find out where he had been taken that night. He failed, but handed down his story, and the chip of bone, among his effects. They came into the possession of someone known to posterity only as 'A Warwickshire Man', who took up the quest. After years of research the church at Beoley, on the edge of Redditch in what is now Hereford and Worcester, emerged as the best candidate, and he bribed the verger to open up its ossuary. Bones were strewn everywhere; but perched on top of the main pile was an undersized skull with a tiny piece missing. The chip fitted it perfectly, and days later the mysterious Warwickshire man made sure that the skeleton of Shakespeare was back in one piece under its slab at Holy Trinity church in Stratford.

© The church is one of the stops on the route of the **Shakespeare Procession** which marches through the streets of Stratford on the Saturday nearest to the 23rd. Flags from numerous nations – especially ones in some way connected with his plays – are furled and unfurled, wreaths are laid, and people dress up as some of the Bard's more easily recognised characters. The pageant starts at 11.00 am at the Knot Garden in New Place, the site of Shakespeare's retirement home. The next day, one of the current leading lights of the Royal Shakespeare Company takes the reading at a service in the Holy Trinity church.

Orleton in Hereford and Worcestershire used to hold a fair today. Like many other April bashes, it was linked with the advent of the **cuckoo**. At Orleton the bird was supposed to buy a horse, which it then rode to Brampton Bryan to sell. See April 29th for the definitive cuckoo guide.

24th April
St Mark's Eve/
The Devil's Harvest

Wraith Against Time

In the 17th century everyone knew that on St **Mark's Eve** it was possible to see the shape of things to come; but few cared to look. Robert Halywell and Edward Vicars, more curious than most, went to the church at Haxey, Humberside to test out the belief. The action was so riveting that Vicars fell asleep. As he snored through the midnight hour, the air became thick with wraiths – 60 in all, parading solemnly round the church. And Halywell noticed that one of them looked uncannily like Vicars. When Vicars awoke, Halywell told him that he had missed seeing his own ghost.

During the year, as the people on Halywell's list keeled over, Vicars lost his nerve and fled in terror. He hid in the marshes hoping that fate would pass him by. But before the year was out he had grown thin and ghostly-pale, and finally died from sheer starvation. It was inevitable. If your wraith appears at the church, or if you fall asleep during your vigil, you are doomed, and Vicars had fallen into both categories.

Radio reception must be lousy tonight, as all the **souls of those who are destined to die** over the next 12 months go walkabout, turning up at the church in which they will be buried. The ghoulishly inclined – the Halywells and Vicars of this world, or the next – must camp out overnight near the church in order to watch the ghostly procession. But the superstition comes with an intimidating rider – nod off, even for a second, and you will not be renewing your Readers' Digest subscription. One sexton in Yorkshire supposedly watched every year, keeping tabs on how much he was to earn from grave-digging over the months ahead.

The specifics of tonight's wraith-watching vary from county to county. Generally, the doomed file into church and stay there, while the ones who re-emerge will merely flirt with dangerous illness and then recover. At Whittlesford in Cambridgeshire, the spirits amble to their future burial plots and dissolve into the earth. Some say that you can only see these things on your third successive annual vigil.

◉ **Divination** devotees should also head for the wraith-stuffed church tonight. Peer through each window in turn, and your future lover will appear through the last window. Alternatively, lay the supper table in silence at midnight, and the spirit of your spouse-to-be will come in to dine. Or for the horticulturally minded, plucking red sage leaves at each stroke of midnight will conjure the form of your next inamorato/a. If dream lovers are more your cup of tea, pluck three blades of grass from a south-facing grave, and sleep with them under your pillow tonight. Alternatively, but probably much less comfortable, substitute a lamb's shoulder blade for the grass.

In Willoughton, Lincolnshire, **Satan** can be spied tonight. Hide in the stable and wait until the horses go down on their knees and begin talking. As they swap tales of things yet to happen, the Devil rides in on a black pig.

But Satan's chief task tonight is to oversee the annual blossoming and seeding of **fern** – the Devil's Harvest is an alternative name for the plant, and for tonight. Fern traditionally manages this entire propagating feat in just 24 hours. Whoever manages to catch the seeds between two pewter plates will become as wise as the Devil: see June 23rd for loads more fern.

With so much paranormal activity tonight, it is appropriate that anyone **born on St Mark's Eve** can see spirits. Not only that, but they are also blessed with a startlingly useful ability: the power to see the stars at midday.

25th April
St Mark's Day

Froggie Went a Courting

When **King John** visited Alnwick, he was appalled at the state of the roads. They were pot-holed, they were badly drained, they were poorly sign-posted. And worst of all, the mud on them had stained his best trousers. He summoned the officials of the town and persuaded them that either the time was right for a massive inward investment in local transport infrastructure, or his swordsmen would introduce a contraflow into their bloodstreams. Within weeks, hasty but comprehensive carriageway repairs were underway across Northumberland; but still John was not happy. His trousers were ruined, and he wanted revenge.

So the King commanded the townsfolk of Alnwick to ride the roads and boundaries of the parish every year on April 25th, taking an undignified route through Freeman's Well, a local pond. The **boundary riders**, dressed in white, with white night-caps and swords, had to canter to the well, paddle through its mud, and remount their steeds on the other side before completing the circuitous and pointless journey. The custom survived long after John and his trousers parted company, but got by-passed sometime in the dim and distant past.

The Mark of today's feast is the famous one from the Bible, having (perhaps) written the eponymous Gospel. There is no evidence that he had any particular vendetta against **frogs** – unless somewhere amongst the Dead Sea Scrolls is St Mark's Letter to the Amphibians – but St Mark marks a traditional turning point in their croaking. For each day in which the frogs *ribbet* before April 25th they must observe a corresponding number of silent days biting their front-hinged tongues.

Frogs are generally lucky. Meet one casually, croaking or silent, and you will soon find gold. And, for the romantically dejected, one powerful charm involves putting a frog in a jar, covering the top with paper, and then sticking pins into the makeshift lid. The next stage is to invert the jar, turning the frog into an amphibious St Sebastian, and to chant:

It's not this frog I wish to stick,
But my lover's heart I wish to stick.

This must be done for nine nights on the trot. But it may be better to stick with celibacy, as, if you kill a frog *'you will have a sin grow on your back'*. One lover equals nine impaled frogs; few backs are broad enough to cultivate such a volume of sin.

Farmhands must limit their activities today. If you **plough** on St Mark's Day, one of the team will die within the year.

⊙ One St Mark's Eve custom which spills over into today will please foot-fetishists everywhere. Scatter ash, chaff or beans on the hearth after the first stroke of midnight, and a sexy **footprint** will have appeared in the mess by breakfast time today. Then invite the entire town to pop round barefoot, match the print with a foot, and you will never be lonely between the sheets again. On the Isle of Man, what is important is the direction of the footprint. If it is facing inwards then rejoice – or panic – for a child is on the way. If pointing towards the door it means death. If it has a broad pad and three forward-facing claws, you will marry a badger.

26th April

Hop Strings Eternal

April 26th was the day on which the Ark came to rest on Mount Ararat after bobbing about on top of the Great Flood for exactly 150 days. Jewish folklore also offers some insights into the Ark's construction. It had a skylight made from a luminous stone which compensated for the darkness outside. And it was divided into three layers: the animals were corralled together on top; while their exotically varied dung accumulated in the bottom deck. The humans occupied an outrageously disproportionate amount of space in the middle, and complained about the noise the neighbours were making. It can get quite lively when the okapis and skinks invite the rest of creation over for a party.

When the zoo finally beached, Noah discovered that there had been a stowaway. The giant **Og, King of Bashan**, had clung to the roof of the Ark for the whole epic journey. Having become the only unsanctioned escapee from the antediluvian era, he turned up again (in *Deuteronomy*) with a bed 16 feet long and six feet wide, and a bone to pick with Moses. Og tried to turn a prophet into a loss by lobbing an entire mountain at the advancing Israelite army, but Moses was able to kill the giant before he had reached his peak.

On a smaller scale, towards the end of April hops reach about six inches in height – this used to be the signal for southern growers to hold hop-stringing contests. The plants grow on wire frames supported by high vertical poles, to which several hundred miles of string are attached. It was the fixing of all this string which formed the basis of the contest. Experienced hoppers worked on stilts for the higher regions. Speed and neatness determined the winner, and the best hop-stringer walked away with a shiny cup and lots of free hops – in the form of beer.

Hops were introduced into British beer in the 16th century, effectively ousting the old unhopped ale which had been drunk since pre-Roman times. There are no reports of a Campaign for Pre-Real Ale resisting the new hoppy beer, and this contemporary critic summed up the reactions of the nation: '*The manifold vertues of Hops do manifestly argue the holsomnesse of Beere . . . the Hops rather make it a Phisicall drinke to keep the body in health, than an ordinarie drinke for the quenching of our thirst.*'

Hops are traditionally supposed to promote good appetite, good sleep, and healthy, copious urine – even if not drunk by the barrel-load. At Doncaster the appearance of the new crop of hops coincided with the song of the first **nightingale** of the year. The two became linked so that the voice of the nightingale became the official start of the hop season. If the bird came late, then so did the beer.

27th April
St Sitha's Day

Walking Between Non-Existent Places

The funeral of **Benjamin Disraeli**, Earl of Beaconsfield, took place today in 1881. On his deathbed the former Prime Minister is said to have turned down a summons from Queen Victoria with the words '*She would only ask me to take a message to Albert*'. After showing such scepticism about the afterlife, it must have come as a surprise to Disraeli when he came back from the dead as a very active phantom. ✝ ⏛ Disraeli is buried at his former home, Hughendon Manor, on the outskirts of High Wycombe in Buckinghamshire. His ghost has been seen there regularly: its favourite haunts are the upper floor, and the foot of the cellar stairs. Also at Hughenden is the lurid 50-foot high pillar of pink granite which Disraeli constructed in memory of his father.

⏛ The last Sunday in April is the traditional time for **Tyburn Walk**, which honours London's Catholic martyrs. In the 16th century Protestantism was a new sect: zealotry abounded, and many other Christians were killed simply for belonging to the 'rival' denomination. Tyburn Tree was the epicentre of these and other London executions, and its long-gone gallows are now marked by a plaque near Marble Arch. The tree was finally felled in the late 18th century and the executions moved to Newgate Prison, which was itself demolished in 1902. Tyburn Walk follows the route of the condemned men from Newgate – where the Old Bailey now stands – to the site of Tyburn, via several churches which fortunately do still survive.

⏛ At the start of the Walk is **St Sepulchre without Newgate**. As the name implies, it stood just outside Newgate Prison. Inside the church in a glass case is a handbell. Thanks to a £50 payment from Robert Dowe in 1605, its death-knell sounded at midnight on the eve of every execution, as the bellman intoned these morbid lines:

All you that in the condemned hole do lie,
Prepare you, for tomorrow you shall die.
Examine well yourselves, in time repent,
That you may not to eternal flames be sent.
And when St Sepulchre's Bell in the morning tolls,
The Lord have mercy on your souls.

Come the morning, St Sepulchre's great bell was rung; and in compensation for having the peace of their last night on earth shattered, the condemned men were given a nosegay as they passed the church en route to Tyburn.

⛪ Also on the route, the Catholic church of St Etheldreda in Ely Place contains statues of four of the Catholic martyrs executed at Tyburn, and a splendid, gory window showing four victims hanging on Tyburn tree. The church is all that survives of the sprawling 13th-century Ely Palace, former home of John of Gaunt.

👁 If you happen to have lost your keys, then a prayer to St Sitha – also known as Zita – is the answer, and today is her feast day. As well as helping lost fobs find their way home, she is also a short-distance version of St Christopher, protecting her votaries from the many hazards inherent in crossing rivers or bridges.

28th April
Floralia/St Vitalis Day

The High Queen

As Elizabeth I entered Westminster Abbey on this day in 1603, she was not looking her best. Not only was she dead, but she had died more than a month beforehand on March 24th. With coffin wisely nailed tight, she was brought into the Abbey and buried, amidst much pomp and pong.

✟ Elizabeth's ghost occasionally short-cuts through the library at Windsor Castle in Berkshire with hurried footsteps. She was also indirectly responsible for another ghost, over at Richmond Palace in Richmond, Greater London. While the Queen was on her deathbed there, Sir Robert Carey was on horseback outside the Gatehouse, waiting for a signal. As soon as the Queen died her ring was

slipped from her finger and thrown out of the window to Sir Robert. This was the signal, and he rode almost non-stop to the Royal Court in Edinburgh – covering the 400 miles in 62 hours – to break the news that James VI of Scotland had just become James I of England. The sound of Carey's horse galloping is still sometimes heard in Old Palace Yard at Richmond; and Elizabeth has occasionally been spied at the nearby site of the Gatehouse.

Elizabeth had done all she could to cling to life for as long as possible. Around her neck she always wore a piece of gold inscribed with mystic longevity-boosting characters; and she kept the Queen of Hearts under her favourite chair, held there by an iron nail punched neatly and deliberately through the forehead of the Queen on the card. Such actions are scarcely more superstitious than current blind faith in healing crystals or arthritis-inducing jogging. And they did Queen Elizabeth no harm – she died at the then ripe old age of 70.

May 1st has since time immemorial been a day of springtime celebration in Britain. But the Romans were too impatient, and kicked off their festival on April 28th instead. Floralia honoured their fruit & veg goddess, Flora. Our May Day concepts of mischief and lawlessness sprang from under the shady togas of the past. The custom of fetching chariot-loads of greenery into the house was a Floralian fetish too. Some folklorists have even tried to establish Floralia as the direct historical and etymological root of the Furry, or Floral, Dance at Helston in Cornwall (see May 9th). Roman scholars like to claim that every last shred of festive vegetation – on May Day and at other times of year – stems from Flora and her festival. But the truth is that all the religions that once graced these islands had a Maying festival, and Flora's offshoots may be a little less lush and verdant than some classicists would claim.

Coincidentally, Flora is not the only widespread polyunsaturated slice of divinity sandwiched into this day. This is also the feast day of 3rd-century female saint Vitalis, which sounds vaguely like 'Vitalite'.

29th April
St Endellion's Day

Gotham's Batty-Men

This is St Endellion's Day. She spent her time at Tregony in 6th-century Cornwall with a live-in cow. The holy heifer was her sole source of sustenance; until, one day, the beast strayed on to land owned by the Lord of Tregony, who killed it. Endellion's godfather was enraged, and he redressed the balance by killing the Lord. But Endellion, saintly to the last, brought him back from the dead. Oddly, she did not do the same for her cow.

⛪ Part of Endellion's shrine survives at the hilltop church of St Endellion, near Wadebridge in Cornwall. The village also boasts two wells named after the saint.

The Sunday nearest the 28th used to be **Towednack Cuckoo Feast**, at Towednack in Cornwall. The feast is supposed to have come about in prehistory when a farmer invited some friends indoors for food one freezing April morning. He threw a log on to the fire, and the first cuckoo of spring flew from the hearth.

There are many other tales about the first **cuckoo** of the year, usually linked to fairs. Also common are stories in which locals build a wall or hedge around the roosting cuckoo in order to pen it and thus keep eternal spring. Illustrating the folly of trying to fight nature, the bird simply flies over the top of the hedge, and winter returns. This is said to have happened at Lorbottle in Northumberland; at Wing in Leicestershire; at Zennor in Cornwall; and at the Wittenham Clumps near the appropriately named Little Wittenham in Oxfordshire, where the ring of trees on the hilltop is known as The Cuckoo Pen.

⛪ Close to Gotham, just south of Nottingham, is Cuckoo Bush Hill, and the village has a pub called *The Cuckoo Bush*. Both are reminders that cuckoo-penning was one of the bird-brained exploits of the **Wise Men of Gotham**. Either a hamlet of half-wits, or – say some – a village feigning insanity to ward off King John's plans to build a hunting lodge there, its other antics include punishing an eel by throwing it into a pond to drown, and chopping a horse in two to see if it had swallowed the moon.

Across the country the return of the cuckoo was greeted with outbursts of what is probably the oldest British song that is still widely sung – the early 13th-century *'Sumer is icumen in, Loud sing cuckoo'* – and special cuckoo ale was brewed. At Mere in Wiltshire, this was drunk at a beery feast called the Church Ale, presided over by an autonomous mock-Lord/Master of Ceremonies figure called the **Cuckowe King**. In Shropshire, when the first cuckoo arrived miners downed their tools for an instant 24-hour holiday known as **Gaudy Day**.

After their job as embodiment-of-spring is over, cuckoos bung their eggs into other birds' nests – the origin of 'cuckold' – and then spend the winter months either transformed into hawks, or hiding in faerie hills. This piece of ornimythology is based on observation: the bird *does* disappear during winter – migrating to Africa rather than faerieland – and seen at a distance the cuckoo resembles the sparrowhawk, which is present all year round. The cuckoos' disappearance – adults start leaving in July, while the last of their offspring linger until the end of September – traditionally marked the end of summer. See April 14th for more cuckoo superstitions and tales.

30th April
May Eve/Beltane

Rood Stones,
Complimentary Flowers

This is as old as it gets: pre-Celt, perhaps pre-Ice Age. Today, May Eve, witnesses the annual death of the blue-skinned **Cailleach Bheur** (pronounced something like *Calyach Ver*), an ancient British goddess. This is the Highland version of her name. In Ulster she is called *Cally Berry*; and Manxmen know her as *Caillagh ny Groamagh*, the Old Woman of Gloominess. She is the icy-nosed daughter of the winter sun, Grianon, who reigns from Hallowe'en to May Day. On the last day of April, Cailleach throws her staff under a holly or gorse bush, and turns to stone.

⛪ Representing a goddess as a block of unhewn rock did not pose many problems for Stone Age sculptors and their descendants, which may explain many of the country's enigmatic standing stones. A key example of such a stone, thought to have been linked with May festivities, is the **Rudston monolith** at Rudston, near Bridlington in Humberside. At 25 feet high (and with a reputed further 25 feet underground), it is the tallest standing stone in the country, and was too heavy for the Christian church to remove. Instead they tried to tame it by building a church next door and plonking a cross – or rood – on top of the stone. Hence the village name, *Rood-stone*. Local legend says that the monolith was a typically poorly-aimed missile from Satan, who threw it at the church; or that it fell from the skies to kill a party of pagans dancing below; or even that it grew overnight from a pebble in the soil.

▥ As late as the early 20th century it was believed in some areas, notably East Anglia, that rocks were organic. Removing pebbles from stony ground was seen as a fool's errand as the rocks would simply grow back. The **Blaxhall Stone** is said still to be growing. The size of a loaf of bread when it first came to attention a century ago at Stone Farm near Blaxhall, midway between Southwold and Ipswich in Suffolk, it now weighs in at around five tons, and is getting bigger every year.

Back with Cailleach Bheur, in spite of being the harsh goddess of winter, she is also the guardian of wild creatures, deer being her especial favourites, along with wild pigs, goats, cattle and wolves. In some legends she does not turn into stone on May Eve, but becomes a beautiful woman, the goddess of summer.

▥ Cailleach was so powerful that she was able to make mountains. She once tripped and landed in a crevice before the rocks had set properly: the imprint of the goddess' left heel can still be seen in the crevice between her former home at Cronk yn Irree Lhaa and the neighbouring peak of Barrule, on the Isle of Man.

There are lots of **faeries** around today, many of them malevolent, so it is just as well to have a rowan cross handy to ward them off. Elder leaves gathered today protect houses from the faeries too, and also have the power to heal wounds.

If **birth** was imminent, then it was often artificially induced on May Eve, for if a baby emerged on May 1st it would be the unluckiest child alive – assuming that it had not been swapped for a faerie changeling in the first place. If birth was not possible, a mother was sometimes zonked out to prevent her from giving birth on May Day.

◉ For those not quite at the child-bearing stage, take a **snail** today and put it on a pewter plate. It will form the initials of future lovers in the patterns of its slime.

In the Highlands **Beltane Bannocks** were baked on April 30th. Etched on one side was a cross, the symbol of life; and on the reverse, a symbol of death. The bannocks were then rolled down a hillside three times. If at the end of the rolling the life-sign was uppermost more times than death, then the year ahead would be healthy and prosperous. If not, it was time to order the coffin. At Kingussie the rolling took place on May Day, and rather than go in for decorating the bannocks, it was said that the first loaf to break belonged to the man who was to die first in the coming year.

Another traditional Highlands feature originally went even further. The innocuous-sounding **May Day cakes**, served either today or tomorrow, did not just predict who would die, but actually marked someone for death. Seated around a newly-cut turf table, men would bake oat-cakes, mark one with soot, and bung the lot into a bag. The man who drew the blackened piece became the scapegoat *Cailleach Bealtine*, representing – once again – Cailleach Bheur. He had to leap through bonfire flames, receive insults, become a temporary outcast, and count himself lucky: in earlier times the one who picked the sooty cake became that year's sacrifice to the Beltane god Baal. In Wales, such cakes were split fifty-fifty, with half the revellers forced to run the gamut of fire and jibes.

© In the late 1980s Edinburgh revived the **Beltane Fire** which used to burn in the city each May Eve until the early 19th century. Now an excuse for a bonfire-illuminated outdoor party, the festivities start at 10 pm next to the mock Acropolis on Calton Hill.

This was also the day for **May birching** across much of the Midlands and the northwest of England. At dead of night May birchers crept round their village, hanging sprigs on their neighbours' houses. Different plants and trees were used to convey different sentiments. In rhyme. Complimentary vegetation to find on your eaves included lime (rhymes with *prime*) and pear (*fair*). Conversely, you might wake up to a sprig of thorn (*scorn*), holly (*folly*) or briar (*liar*). Even worse were nut (*slut*) and gorse (*whore-s*). Wicken – rowan, or mountain ash – was used because it rhymes with *chicken*, which was a compliment to a loved one.

Rowan is put to a different use on the Isle of Man today, and made into a protective cross known as a **Crosh Keirn**. The twigs must be broken off from the tree, not cut with an iron blade, and are bound together with sheep's wool. The Crosh is hung on front doors to keep witches and evil spirits at bay.

May Eve is the night on which two fighting **dragons** shriek, blighting the landscape: see September 25th for the full story.

ROGATIONTIDE

ROGATION WEEK

Rogation Sunday is the fifth after Easter, and the start of Rogation Week which effectively climaxes on the Thursday, Ascension Day. Rogation comes from the Latin *rogare*, meaning to beseech. It is the traditional time for beseeching on behalf of crops, fisheries, buildings – any place or object where a well-received prayer or plea might make the season ahead a little easier. Although Christian in tone, Rogation's origins lie in Roman ceremonies: during the May feast of *Ambervailia* crops were blessed, and at *Terminalia* there was an orgy of sacrifices and bounds-beating.

© Most surviving **Beating the Bounds** tend to take place on Ascension Day, but the one at Oddington, on the edge of Ot Moor in Oxfordshire, is still flexible, and is held on a convenient date in Rogation Week. A scaled-down version of the event was revived in 1993 after a gap of some 20 years. In the 1970s a merging of parish boundaries meant that circumnavigating Oddington's boundary had become a taxing 12-mile hike. After experimenting with an annual patrol of the borders by car, the revived version has now opted for a symbolic beating of the bounds. The procession makes a token circuit within the village, halting for prayers at selected spots including the site of the old well.

The moor itself became common land in medieval times. The tale told locally is that the owner had more acres than they knew what to do with, and agreed to hand over a portion of their land for use by everyone. The amount was to be determined by however many acres a woman could encircle in the time it took for an oat sheaf to burn. The woman turned out to be the Liz McColgan of her day, and got round the entire circumference of what is now Ot Moor. But it was a mixed blessing – the moor is said to be a place of witchery and ill luck, and grazing cattle often used to contract a type of marsh fever, known locally as the 'Moor Evil'. The damp, peaty water of the well at Oddington was said to cure the cows, and to be good for humans with skin or eye diseases.

🔔 St Clement Danes in London used to beat its bounds in Rogation week, and was still doing so early this century. It is now the church of the RAF, rather than a parish church, and so it no longer has any bounds to beat. Many of the plaques defining the boundary points survive, each marked with the anvil emblem of St Clement. The ancient boundary goes through shops and into vaults – a highlight of the old ceremony came when a choir boy was dangled by the heels to enable him to beat a subterranean marker.

Leicester used to mark out its territory only once every three years, but even that has now proved too much for the city, and the custom is currently mothballed. Traditionally, any new parish officer taking part in their grand procession had his head stuck in a hole at Redhill, and was then beaten with a shovel.

© A few words of thanksgiving feature in most Beating the Bounds ceremonies, but at Cannington near Bridgwater in Somerset the boundary element has gone, leaving a two-and-a-half hour walking and blessing procession. On the afternoon of Rogation Sunday, celebrants armed with banners and flower-adorned staffs, hymns and prayers visit and bless surrounding fields, crops, animals and all who work with the land.

Many other rural areas also directed Rogation blessings towards the crops and the bountiful earth; and it was equally logical for many coastal areas to hold a **Blessing the Sea** ceremony at this time of year. Some of these still survive, and a few new ones have recently been either revived or drastically overhauled to make them more appealing to tourists. In addition to blessing the briny deep, these celebrations also serve to bless local boats and local fish. Sometimes they also commemorate those lost at sea, and one or two even incorporate an element of nautical beating the bounds. © Mudeford, now almost swallowed up by Christchurch in Hampshire, still holds its **Blessing of the Waters** on Rogation Sunday. In the 1930s, All Saints' Church was strewn with lobster pots and fishing nets for the service, but the custom lapsed. When revived in the 1950s the decision was made not to go overboard on the fish imagery. After a short service at All Saints' at 3.20 pm, the choir and a silver band lead a procession down to the quay. After hymns and prayers the resident priest clambers into a rowing boat with one of the local fishermen and is taken out into the middle of 'The Run' – a narrow channel seperating Christchurch harbour from the open sea. There he asks God to bless the harvest of the waters, and lobs a small cross into the sea. One year the priest forgot the cross and had to go back – a special folding cross has since been designed so that he can keep it in his pocket until the crucial moment.

© The Rogation Week ceremony at North Shields in Tyne and Wear has now moved to the Late Spring Bank Holiday. It starts with an open-air service on the quay. Clergy and choir then set off in a launch down the Tyne, blessing the boats of Shields and Cullercoats, and travelling along the North Shields-South Shields boundary.

© There are similar fishy frolics at Hastings in Sussex. Their service used to be held strictly in Rogation Week, but in 1992 it was revamped and is now held on a Sunday afternoon in May as determined by *'Rogation-tide, the tides, and the tide of tourists'* – to quote the current vicar in charge of the service. Large processions from the main denominational churches in Hastings meet up at the harbour-side church of St Mary's Star of the Sea. After a few open-air sea-faring hymns, the lifeboat is launched with an Anglican and Roman Catholic priest on board. As the onshore congregation say the Blessing of the Sea, the priests throw a cross of flowers into the water.

© Great Wishford in Wiltshire has its **Midsummer Tithes** on Rogation Monday; though, impressively, there are no tithes involved, and it is not Midsummer. The event is an auction, and locals bid for the lease, from November 1st until August 12th, of two parcels of land bequeathed by an unknown benefactor. At 8 pm all interested parties gather at the church gates and the auction is conducted using the church door key as the gavel. Money raised goes towards church repairs. There are no deeds relating to the ceremony but in 1833 the Charities Commission described it as *'very ancient'*. A clue to its age may come from the names of the two chunks of land – Bonham's Mead and Abbey Mead. The Bonham's had a manor at Wishford

from 1287–1597, and there was an abbey near the village until the Dissolution of the Monasteries in 1536. Until recently, bidding started at sunset with the land going to the last person to bid before the last glimmer of sun slipped over the horizon.

ROGATION WEDNESDAY

In 1159 Ralph de Percy, William de Bruce and their friend Allatson were in hot pursuit of a boar. They chased it all over Eskdale Forest until it ducked into a hermitage and would not come out. The friendly hermit locked out the dogs and let the pig die quietly of exhaustion in the corner. When the three men caught up with their hounds they were infuriated with this prototype hunt saboteur, and beat the hermit to within an inch of his life. Then they beat him some more.

By the time the Abbot of Whitby arrived, nothing could be done. Just before the hermit died from his wounds, he begged the Abbot to show Christian forgiveness and go easy on the men. The Abbot spared the huntsmen's lives, but imposed a humbling penance. All their lands became the property of the Abbot, but were immediately loaned back to the men for all time on one annual condition. Each Rogation Wednesday they, or their descendants, had to take knives worth one penny and cut wood to erect a fence in Whitby harbour, strong enough to survive three high tides. If the tide got the better of the fence all their lands were forfeit. The custom's only get-out clause applied if the high-tide ever got so high as to make the erecting of a fence impossible, in which case the custom would be abandoned and the lands restored to the men, or their successors.

© Against the odds the custom has survived, even if the story of its origins contains only trace elements of truth. **Planting the Penny Hedge** – or *Horngarth* – probably originated in Saxon times as a means of making tenants maintain an important fence, in the same way as landowners are obliged to maintain footpaths which cut through their land. Late last century a Whitby canon described the tradition as *'A farcical, objectless ceremony'*, which must make it the longest running farce this side of the West End.

After the dissolution of Whitby Abbey the land came into the hands of the Hutton family, and the onus now falls on them to ensure that the fence goes up each year. The Penny Hedge – *penny* is simply a contraction of *penance*, and nothing to do with cut-price knives – is made of stakes called *stowers*, and interweaving osiers called *yethers*. It still has to withstand three tides, and is wonderfully unglamorous, standing in the mud of the Esk estuary in Whitby's Upper Harbour. It must be in position by 9 am each Rogation Wednesday (also known as Ascension Eve). There is no longer a town crier to read out the original 'crime' while the hedge is being erected, but the manor bailiff still watches over things, and shouts the traditional '*Out on ye!*' when the task is complete.

After at least 800 and more probably 1300 years of unbroken tradition and unbroken fences, in 1981 the unthinkable happened. There was a 'Full Sea' – the water was so high that the fence could not be built by 9 am. This fulfilled the penance and effectively activated the custom's auto-destruct mechanism. Instead of being all over, a Save the Hedge appeal was set up, with locals campaigning to keep the ceremony afloat. After considering the possibilities of involving schoolchildren, pageantry or other commercialism, Whitby, to its quite possibly everlasting credit, did the decent thing. It changed nothing, and the town continues to erect a very dull, wonderful hedge every Rogation Wednesday.

ASCENSION DAY

Ascension Day, or Holy Thursday, is the traditional day on which Jesus ascended into Heaven. It is also the single most important day of the year for customs related to water-worship, and the main day for a physical reminder of the extent and importance of the parish by the ritual **Beating the Bounds** – a tradition that has its roots in *Terminalia*, a May-time Roman festival full of beatings and sacrifices to honour their boundary god Terminus.

In the north of England this period of bounds-beating was known as the **Gang Days** or Ganging Days, as in the dialect *gang/gan*, meaning 'go'. According to 17th-century poet and clergyman George Herbert, ganging along the boundaries fulfilled many functions. He called the custom a genuine thanksgiving which invoked God's blessing on the land, adding that it also had an imporant social role, enabling locals to get together in peace and love; that it offered an opportunity to collect money for the poor; and that it imprinted the boundaries in the memories of the parishioners. It also offered a chance for participants to let off steam by hitting things with big sticks.

Children were originally the chief boundary-beaters, thrashing away with their sticks on the relevant stone, tree or other landmark which marked the edge of a town or parish. And the children were, in turn, beaten themselves, receiving a coin for their pains. Boys were pummelled with the sticks, ducked in way-marking ponds, dragged through intruding hedges, and even had to climb over buildings that straddled the boundary. This instilled in them a sense of place, with a wound for every landmark.

The traditional bloom for the day was **milkwort**, known as Rogation or Gang Flower. There were prayers or hymns along the way, with a major sermon at the chief boundary marker – very often a tree with the grand title of Gospel Oak.

Beating the Bounds seems to suit the mood of the late 20th century, and there have been a whole series of recent revivals and one-offs. A few have now been going long enough to stand alongside the handful of genuine survivors as established traditions.

© At **Oxford** the bounds are beaten today after a 9 am service at St Michael's in Northgate. A procession of clergy and choirboys sets out at 10 am, rambling through shops and college grounds, ducking into the market cellars at Broad Street and clambering over a wall at St Peter's college which now blocks the boundary path. At each boundary stone there is a short sermon and the stones are chalked and beaten with bamboo canes. One of the stones is now in Marks and Spencer's. Oxford's is a long boundary to beat, and en route Lincoln College provides a snack, and much needed refreshment in the traditional form of ground-ivy ale.

© On Ascension Day the Chief Yeoman Warder of the **Tower of London**, accompanied by the Tower chaplain and choirboys, parades round the 31 stones which mark the edge of the Tower Liberty – the land upon which the Tower of London stands. He is accompanied by a choir, the tower chaplain, and the pike-carrying Yeomen in their full state dress of red and gold. Following just behind is a mass of snap-happy spectators. At each mark the chaplain shouts '*Cursed be he who removeth his neighbour's landmark!*', and the Chief Warder commands '*Whack it boys, whack it!*' The choirboys then brutalise the stones with their willow wands. This tradition is triennial, next due in 1996, and it takes place after Evensong at 6.30 pm.

⌂ © The **Manor of Savoy** is a little corner of London that is forever part of Lancaster. It is an ill-defined area between the Strand and the Embankment and at its borders are 12 surviving cast iron boundary marks, showing three lions and a crown and bearing the words 'Duchy of Lancaster'. The manor gets its name from the 13th-century Peter, Count of Savoy in France, who was given the land by Henry III. The area was responsible for its own local government and appointed its own officers, and these rights continued when the land later passed into the hands of the Earls of Lancaster. It was not until 1863 that the Constables, Aleconners and Flesh-tasters of the Manor of Savoy were laid off and their duties assumed by central government. The only remaining role for Savoy's ruling body, the Court Leet, is the Beating of its Bounds, which now takes place at approximate five-year intervals. After a meeting of the Leet a Jury is appointed to go round the remaining marks accompanied by the choir of the Queen's Chapel – a private Royal chapel over which even the Archbishop of Canterbury has no jurisdiction. At several of the boundary marks the choirboys are inverted and bumped repeatedly on a cushion.

© The bounds-beating around Cathedral Close at **Lichfield** in Staffordshire today has many splendidly idiosyncratic details, one of which is that it is not known locally as Beating the Bounds. The cathedral is in what was once a fortified close, complete with moat and portcullis, and on Ascension Day morning leafy lime branches are stuffed through the letter-boxes of all the houses in the close. The procession starts at 10.15 am, with the clergy and choir laden with boughs of elm and other greenery, and a crowd of children in tow all carrying fronds. At six different points around the cathedral everyone halts to say prayers. Some of the stops correspond to where towers of the close's old fortifications once stood; others mark the sites of old wells – the ceremony is probably just as rooted in water-god worship as it is in perambulating the cathedral's boundaries. Backing up this theory, the service ends inside the cathedral with the children all dipping their fronds of greenery into the font; although the choristers have evolved their own custom – they throw their boughs and branches at the Dean.

The ceremony at Lichfield combines the two great themes of Ascension Day – beating the bounds, and **water-worship**. When Christianity first established a foothold, and later a stranglehold, on the body of pagan beliefs in

Britain, it was water-worship that proved the most tenacious of the old ways. As late as the 16th century Henry VIII was forced to issue a decree attempting to ban well worship. Long before this the Church had realised that rather than trying to dam up these beliefs, it was better to divert them so that they flowed right through the heartlands of the Christian credo. Pagan wells became linked with saints, and believers were encouraged to give thanks in prayer for the gift of water. Ascension Day became the chief festival for water, and many wells up and down the country were decorated with flowers – as they had often been in pre-Christian ceremonies. The custom became known as **well-dressing**.

© The tradition still thrives in the Peak District, and the showpiece of all well-dressings takes place on Ascension Day at **Tissington** near Ashbourne in Derbyshire. With only slight variations, the formula for making the flower-pictures at Tissington today is identical to the method employed by all the other well-dressing villages. First, the frames on which the pictures are later mounted are soaked in water – at Tissington they are dunked in the village pond. Next comes the **clay-puddling**, which is like grape-treading except that the stuff underfoot is an undrinkable mixture of local clay, water and salt. Once at uniform consistency this mixture helps keep the flowers fresh and is much less prone to cracking than untreated clay would be.

The puddled clay is splodged on to the nail-studded frames, and the making of the picture begins. The outline is first picked out in tiny alder cones, in a process known as **black-knobbing**, though berries or even haricot beans are sometimes used instead. It is then time for the fiddly business of adding the flowers, leaves, mosses, seeds and bits of bark which bring depth and colour to the picture. Most well-dressing villages only allow materials of vegetable origin; though a few bits of hair or wool are occasionally sneaked in.

When completed, the petal pictures are taken to the local well or wells, sometimes amid much fanfare, sometimes with none. There are six wells at Tissington, and for the purposes of this custom a well can be anything from a hole in the ground, to a tap, to a place where there is no obvious water source at all. The designs favour biblical scenes, with a few opting for topical tableaux and one or two developing a running theme, such as the series of representations of great cathedrals still progressing year by year at Tideswell in Derbyshire. Wirksworth in the same county has nine wells, and in 1982 the dressers calculated that making that year's pictures had involved 80 people and a list of ingredients including 10,000 petals, 80 yards of cones, 3,800 bits of corn, and three buckets of spurge.

Once erected on site, the well-dressing lasts a week or so before deterioration sets in. Even with its special additives the clay soon dries, and insinuating cracks and fissures swiftly turn scenes of biblical bliss into something reminiscent of Armageddon.

© It remains unclear quite why this vibrant custom should be the almost exclusive preserve of Derbyshire and the Peak District – the limestone that defines much of the area is found in many other parts of Britain – but there is only one long-established well-dressing outside this area. It takes place today at **Bisley** east of Stroud in Gloucestershire. The tradition was instigated in 1863 by the Rev Thomas Keble when he restored the village wells. Just to be different, Nantwich in Cheshire used to decorate its brine-pit today, but the salt-water cannot have suited the flowers and the custom has withered away.

In the absence of a handy healing well, Ascension Day **rain** is good for curing eye complaints, and if added to bread dough it will make the loaf light and delicious. Rain or shine, today's **weather** is also supposed to give an advance taste of what it will be like in autumn, and to be the exact opposite of the conditions on Whit Monday.

Drinking, bathing, raining, healing, worshipping – the one thing you must not do with water on Ascension Day is **wash clothes**, as to leave anything drying today means that someone in the family will die.

Slate miners at the Penrhyn quarries near Bangor in Gwynedd used to take Ascension Day off, convinced that to work then was to risk a dreadful accident. Whenever their bosses did succeed in getting them to clock on today, the superstition proved true, with at the very least a mishap, and at the worst a full blown catastrophe. Eventually the management grew to accept that Ascension Day was best treated as an unofficial quarry holiday.

© In general, accidents can be averted by bringing *hawthorn* indoors today. But make sure that there are no blooms on it:

Hawthorn bloom and elder flowers
Fill the house with evil powers.

Alternatively, look to your chickens. An egg laid today will protect the house over the coming months.

© Wicken in Northamptonshire was originally two rival settlements, Wyke Dyve and Wyke Hamon. In 1587, locals got fed up with all the scrapping and teamed up to become Wicken. They marked the unification with food, drink and a burst of the 100th Psalm at the elm tree in the centre of Wicken. The **Celebration of the Gospel Elm** continued to be held each Ascension Day, with a short service followed by a trip to the village hotel where specially made old-recipe cakes and extra-strong ale were laid on. In 1993 the hotel became a swish Japanese restaurant, which was the end of the hotel-made cakes and ale, and the start of extended jokes about the celebration climaxing with sushi and saki. But after a period of uncertainty, all is now well, and the 400-year-old celebration looks set to continue until Wyke Hamon and Wyke Dyve split up.

According to history, the rebel Earl of Tyrone, Hugh O'Neill, fled England in 1607 and died peacefully in Rome in 1616. He never went anywhere near Devon. But according to legend O'Neill was shipwrecked off Ilfracombe on his way to the continent. He managed to make it ashore, and went to ground in Lady's Wood near Combe Martin, living on the ships' biscuits which he had salvaged from the wreck. Rumours about the renegade hermit leaked out, and after some weeks O'Neill was tracked down and captured by a contingent of grenadiers.

This fact-free fable became the basis of the Ascension Day custom of **Hunting the Earl of Rone** at Combe Martin. A group of men dressed as grenadiers, with beribboned hats and masks, marched to Lady's Wood, followed at an indiscreet distance by a crowd of spectators. There they searched high and low for the errant Earl before finding him in hiding – in the same place as he was hidden every other year. O'Neill, aka Rone, was represented by a man with a straw-stuffed jacket and a necklace of 12 ships' biscuits. With him in the wood were his faithful friends: the Fool, and The Mapper – a fast-moving, jaw-snapping Hobby Horse. Once the Earl had been discovered, the grenadiers sat him back-to-front on a donkey, which also sported a string of sea-biscuits as a fashion accessory.

The procession then headed for the sea. Every now and then the Grenadiers fired their guns, and the Earl was 'dead' until the Fool and

Mapper revived him. The crowd were solicited for money along the way: non-payment incurred an on-the-spot fine of a dousing with dirty water and a savaging by the Mapper. Nine pubs were visited on the way; and in 1837 pub number three proved the downfall for one reveller. He fell down the step and broke his neck. Not even the Fool and Mapper could cure a genuine death. It was this tragic accident that gave the custom's opponents the excuse they had been looking for in order to kill off this unique blurring of mock-hunt, mumming play, and apocryphal local legend.

Generous Edward Richardson of Ince, now in Greater Manchester, stipulated in his will of 1784 that on each Ascension Day five 240lb sacks of oatmeal were to be dished out at his expense to the local needy. However, Richardson was not *that* generous. After 50 years the **Oatmeal Charity** was to cease. And it did.

MAY

1st May
May Day

Moggie May

Today **faeries** are at their busiest, putting changelings in place of mortal babies. They also kidnap any foolish humans who stray too close – on May Day the barriers between the Other World and our own are at their most permeable.

It was on May Day that Queen Heurodis, wife of **King Orfeo**, dozed off beneath a grafted apple tree – in Celtic mythology a tree to which faeries are particularly attached. As she slept she was whisked away for a guided tour of the land within the hollow hills, and in her dream the King of the Faeries promised that during the next night he would enter her realm and take Heurodis into his world forever.

The Queen told her husband about her strange experience. Next evening Orfeo posted soldiers everywhere, but it was to no avail: the King of the Faeries appeared and vanished with Heurodis before a sword could be unsheathed. Orfeo was tormented by his queen's disappearance. He left his kingdom in the care of a regent, took his harp, and went into the wilderness. For 10 years he wandered, looking everywhere but finding nothing. Finally, hairy and sickly and close to starvation, he collapsed on a riverbank. As Orfeo lay there, a group of a thousand faerie knights passed by. Travelling with them, still clearly spell-bound, was Heurodis. Spurred by the sight of his queen, Orfeo summoned the strength to follow, and he was able to pursue the knights as they rode through a cleft in a nearby rockface.

Orfeo found himself in the faerie kingdom. He managed to get an audience with the King, and stunned the entire court with his exquisite harp-playing. The King was so impressed that he granted Orfeo anything he desired. Orfeo chose Heurodis; but the Faerie King faltered, saying that it would be a shame to give a beautiful woman to a hideous harpist. Orfeo pointed out that it was a greater crime for a king to renege on his word. So Orfeo took Heurodis back home, had a shave, relieved the regent; and they ruled happily ever after. The tale comes from the Middle English poem, *Sir Orfeo*, a 14th-century adaptation – with happy ending – of the Greek myth of Orpheus and Eurydice.

One of the biggest **faerie kingdoms** is said to lie within Schiehallion, a mountain near Loch Rannoch in Tayside. Locals visited Schiehallion Well on May Day with offerings for the faerie occupants. Near Crickhowell in Powys lies Puck's Dale. Today a door opens in the Dale, giving access to the faerie lands. Enter and you will see magnificent gardens and tables laden with food. Obliging faeries will tell your fortune; but you must not take anything from that world back into this one, as to do so results in insanity. The chief problem facing the day-tripper is that even when open, the door remains hidden.

♔ At dawn on May Day, at Loch Ashie just south of Inverness in the Highlands, two silent **phantom armies** get their swords out and hack each other to pieces. It is said that they are ghosts of the slain in a battle fought and won by the legendary Irish warrior Finn MacCool. Finn led by rule of thumb – he had touched the Salmon of Knowledge and whenever he sucked his thumb he could see into the future. He also had two nephews in the shape of hunting dogs, and – like Arthur – is not dead but merely asleep.

♔ There are further ghosts in the Cambridgeshire fens. Fishermen keep their boats moored on May Day as anyone who sets afloat will see the ghosts of all the **dead fenmen** who ever lived – not a particularly pleasant prospect.

The fishing was also at risk on Lewis in the Western Isles. If a woman was the first person to cross the Barvas river at Barvas today, all the salmon would high-tail it and never be hooked again. Just after midnight men used to cross the river to ensure that an early-rising woman did not render their river barren.

In other parts of the country this is a fine day for fish. **Mackerel** are generally a good omen; but in Sussex the first catch on May Day is almost magical in its luck-bringing. All year round, a dream of mackerel means that glad tidings are imminent, unless the fish are rotten – in which case your current affections will be unreciprocated. Formerly, to soak up all the good luck, Sussex mackerel-fishermen held the **Bendin' In** today, a May Day feast on Brighton beach.

It is not just its inhabitants but the water itself which is on good form on May Day. Many individual **wells** have special days when they reach their personal peak; but this, more than any other day of the year, is when wells everywhere are generally at their most potent and magical, able to grant the wildest wishes and heal the strangest ailments. At Wooler in Northumberland, the Pin Well was visited on May Day by aspiring lovers. Bent pins were thrown in, and wishes of a sexual-fulfilment nature were muttered. And at Culloden near Inverness in Highland Region, St Mary's Well goes for one of the classic miracles this morning – it turns its water into wine.

© The power of water extends to **dew** gathered this morning. In Somerset, May Day dew could wipe away all freckles, and across most of the country it was believed that such dew cures sore eyes and improves the complexion. Just before sunrise is the best time, which could cause more sore-eye problems than it cures. Blankets left to soak in the May dew can cure sick children if rubbed into their loins. At Arthur's Seat in Edinburgh, it is still customary to wash in the dew today and make a wish; but across Scotland, for the magic to be really effective, the dew had to be gathered from lavender. In Cornwall the best dawn-dew comes from the graves of the recently deceased. A third contender for supplying the dew with most juice is that favourite pagan tree, the **hawthorn**, also known as the May bush:

The fair maid who on the First of May
Goes to the fields at break of day
And washes in dew from the hawthorn tree
Will ever after handsome be.

Hawthorn was sacred to the spring goddess Persephone (see Harvest), and in some areas the time of its blossoming, rather than a fixed date, determined when Beltane began each year (see yesterday). In Suffolk the maid who handed her mistress the first sprig of hawthorn today was awarded a bowl of cream; and yet in most of Britain to bring hawthorn indoors on May Day was an open invitation to misfortune and death.

It was important to choose all plants and flowers carefully on May Day. A beribboned birch bough in a stable will turn away faeries and witches, and willow also provides protection, especially if it is a gift. The pungent smell of a bunch of rosemary, rue, blackthorn and hemlock, burnt indoors today, drives out evil. The same goes for **rowan**. In Scotland rowan was also used to make giant hoops through which farm animals were driven to innoculate them against all diseases. Marsh marigolds were worn on May Day as personal protection, and this was the ideal day for making dandelion wine. There were many other local favoured and shunned May Day plants; but the one nationwide golden greenery rule today was not to turn wood of any kind into a **broom** today – such an act is almost inconceivably unlucky.

In most regions the plant gathering was discretionary, with many less superstitious households opting to ignore the vegetation and just vegetate. But on the Sunday after May Day at Newport on the Isle of Wight, locals were compelled to rise at dawn and collect hawthorn and other plants. On the way back everyone sang and danced in a slow procession. All those who failed to take part in the ritual were fined a gallon of wine and a goose.

Beltane-related festivities were in full flow today, and the main cause of deforestation across the country was the making of celebratory **garlands**. These came in various guises – some like crosses, some like bird-cages, others on poles, and others laid out on silver platters. Any flower was acceptable, except cuckoo flower, which the faeries will not allow mortals to tamper with today. Only Oxford dared to thwart the faeries, using cuckoo flower in great profusion.

In the south of England, notably at Edlesborough in Buckinghamshire and Bishopsteignton in Devon, it was common for wreaths to have **May Dolls** secreted inside – a broad hint that garlanding originated as a way of venerating old floral goddesses. The wreath at Edlesborough used to contain two dolls, a mother and child – evidence of Mary and Jesus muscling in on the pagan ways. In *Lark Rise to Candleford* Flora Thompson describes the garlands and dolls in her part of Oxfordshire just over a century ago. She says that May Day was then the most exciting day of the year for children, who spent all morning constructing a *Bowery*, a garland home for their May doll. Dolls still crop up in some of the May time parades in the south, usually on the weekend and Bank Holiday following the 1st.

Once you had got your garland, you needed a crowd to form a **May Day parade**. A high percentage of women was particularly desirable, and in Newcastle upon Tyne the male garlanders arrived early to sing them from their beds:

Rise up, maidens, fy for shame!
For I've been four lang miles from hame,
I've been gathering my garlands gay;
Rise up, fair maids, and take in your May!

Milkmaids brought a bit of extra colour to many parades. On their head was a decorated bucket stuffed with greenery, and at their side wandered a garlanded cow, looking a little embarrassed in the midst of the throng. In North Wales the **Cadi**, a man dressed as a woman – greatcoat, petticoats and painted face – led a parade of people carrying pewter and silver, which represented the rays of the sun.

Horncastle in Lincolnshire made its garlands, known as **may-gads**, from willow sticks twined with cowslip. May-gads were beaten together to scatter the flowers and make as much mess as possible. The garlands in Wiltshire left even more carnage in their wake. Their **May-blobs** were bunches of flowers on the end of a length of string. They were whirled overhead, scattering petals everywhere, and scattering the crowd if they got in the way.

© One of the most notable garland towns is Charlton-on-Otmoor in Oxfordshire. Unlike many ceremonies which have drifted to the nearest weekend or the Bank Holiday Monday, their **garlanding** is still strictly fixed on May 1st. The garland itself is enormous – a 10-yard-long rope of greenery, with seven lampshade-like wire wheels woven in and scores of small bunches of flowers dotted along its length.

Just before 10 am, the seven oldest children in the village carry the garland for half a mile to the local church, accompanied by all the other children, who carry small crosses decorated with flowers. May-carols are sung along the route, and once at the church the garland is sprinkled with holy water, and draped on the rood screen. After a service there is dancing round a netball post disguised as a Maypole. As part of the garland service, a fresh cross made of highly pagan box-wood is placed in the church. The same things happen before the church's annual Thanksgiving service – for the significance of this box-wood cross see September 19th.

© The king of all the garlanders was and is the **Jack-in-the-Green**, a man dressed as a hedge. He represents the greenery – a version of the original Green Man – and is a symbol of fertility and rebirth to mark the return of summer. Jacks are still regularly seen at some modern May festivities, and in 1993 he turned up at Westminster to complain about the threatened axing of the May Day holiday – a proposed right-wing reaction against the day's secondary status as a socialist holiday. Jack told the press: '*I've been doing this for thousands of years. I may be old but I'm not withered, and I'm not letting the government wipe me out.*' The government climbed down, and the May Day Bank Holiday survives intact for the time being.

© There is a **Jack-in-the-Green Festival** at Hastings in Sussex over May Bank Holiday weekend. Their Jack, a revival based on old designs, is a 10-foot conical bush with a floral crown on top – if Marvel Comics ever devise a half-human, half-Christmas tree super-hero, he will look much like this. After several days of intense morris-dancing, Jack is ceremonially slain at Hastings Castle at 3.15 pm on the holiday Monday, when his head (the crown) is sliced off. Everyone then grabs the flowers and foliage for luck.

© Jack-in-the-Green puts in a more surprising appearance at the **Rochester Sweeps Festival** in Kent. 'Sweeps' was originally a name given to black-faced dancers taking part in the town's Beltane-derived May Day celebrations. Later, real chimney sweeps got involved; partly because with the lean summer months ahead it was a chance to get dressed up and beg for cash, and partly because someone who makes their living by thrusting a great long weapon up a dark orifice is ideal company at a fertility festival. More importantly, May Day was the official Climbing Boys Holiday, until the 1868 Climbing Boys Act banned the use of children as chimney sweeps. Today the sweeps and Jack-in-the-Green are surrounded by throngs of Morris dancers – as at Hastings there is a Jack-awakening dance on a local hilltop at dawn – and among the many odd figures are numerous animal guisers: men dressed as horses, cows and other creatures.

Animal guisering derives from Beltane animal sacrifices – it was deemed an honour to wear the head and hide of one of the slaughtered animals. Amidst all the revivals and make-it-up-as-we-go-along 'ancient' rituals that crowd May Day, are two ceremonies in the West Country that are the genuine, guisering article: hobby horsing. Both, happily, stick to the traditional date of May 1st.

© Minehead in Somerset boasts two eight-foot long, canvas and ribbon **hobby horses**, each shaped like a boat, keel uppermost, with a masked head in the middle and a rope and cow-tail appendage at one end. The Sailor's Horse – once cared for by the local fishing community – is stabled at the quay, and has gyrated through the streets since before the streets were there to be gyrated through. Legend insists, very lamely, that on April 30th 1722 a ship sank offshore, and that the only booty washed up was a dead cow. Which is where the date and the tail element of the creature come from. And still ignoring the animal's likely Beltane-sacrifice origins, the rest of the horse is supposed to be a commemoration of a boat disguised as a sea monster which was used to rout a company of violent Vikings a millenium or so ago.

The hobby horses are out and a boat from April 30th – Warning Eve – to May 3rd, at Minehead and nearby Dunster, dancing to drums and melodeons. As well as the Sailors' Horse, there is the more recent Town Horse. It emerges from its stable in *The Old Ship Afloat* pub in Minehead at 5 am on May Day, accompanied by attendants called Gullivers. Anyone who refused their demand for money used to be beaten on the buttocks with an old boot. Last century the Gullivers once took their duties too seriously. A man refused to pay up, and was beaten to death. That was the end of the Gullivers until quite recently, when, forgiven but not forgotten, they returned to the streets of Minehead.

Any woman keen on ritual humiliation should volunteer for the **booting**: especially on May 3rd, known as Booting Day. This involves being held down and touched 10 times with the hobby horse's head, and then forced to dance in public with the creature. Sadly this dancing no longer weaves in and out of local houses as it did for centuries.

© Even Minehead's abandon seems staid compared with the revelry surrounding the **'Obby 'Oss** at Padstow, near Wadebridge in Cornwall. In the very small hours of May 1st the locals sing the traditional Padstow May Song, collect acres of greenery, and then hit the streets to rouse the inhabitants. At 10 am the Blue Ribbon or Temperance 'Oss steps out from the Institute; and at 11 am the Old, or Red Ribbon, 'Obby 'Oss emerges from his stable at the *Golden Lion Inn*. As at Minehead, the resemblance to a real horse is minimal – each 'Oss consists of a six-foot diameter circular frame covered by black material, with a masked head in the middle, and a second vestigial snapping horse's head on the rim. The Blue Ribbon 'Oss entered the fray at the turn of the century; but it is the much older Red Ribbon 'Oss which hogs the limelight. The music plays incessantly, and the 'Oss bows and twirls and leaps through the village, goaded by an official 'teaser' with a decorated stick. Any woman caught under the frame will become pregnant in the the coming year; and to dance and sing with the 'Oss brings as much luck as you can carry without stooping. Every now and then on its circuit of the village, the 'Oss 'dies', and a sadder section of the traditional song is sung, with particularly obscure lyrics:

> Oh where is St George, oh where is he oh?
> He's out in his longboat all on the salt sea-oh;
> Up flies the kite, down falls the lark-oh,
> Aunt Ursula Birdhood she had an old yowe,
> And it died in her own park-oh.

The 'Oss then decides that being dead is not all it is cracked up to be, and leaps into life once more to the merrier strains of:

> Unite and unite and let us all unite,
> For summer is a-coming today,
> And whither we are going we all will unite
> In the merry morning of May.

For that is the whole point – summer is here, in spite of all the rain, parking problems and modern cynicism. Padstow is one of the joys of the year.

If horses can become boats and two-headed discs today, then there is no reason why birds cannot become vampires. In England the yellowhammer is fondly known for its staccato song, transcribed ambitiously as '*a-little-bit-of-bread-and-no-cheese*'. But north of the border it is a bird out of Hell, crying *'Wheitil te, wheitil te, whae, harry my nest and the de'il tak' ye'*, followed by a satanic shriek. Its colours, yellow and black, are the Devil's livery, and on May Day it drinks a drop of Satan's blood. Some stories even say that the vampire-bird sucks blood all year round. Such beliefs led to yellowhammer persecution on a grand scale.

The blood of the Devil is only one of the strange foods, and strange uses of food, on today's menu. Egg-custards were popular at Beltane/May Day fireside parties, as were **nipple cakes**. These had nine or so nipples on the top, which were pulled off one at a time and thrown over the shoulder with a prayer, for the safety of house and livestock, along the lines of: *'This I give thee, o hooded crow! Spare thou my lambs!'* Traditional sites for these May Day fire-and-food bashes include Arthur's Seat in Edinburgh, Dechmont Hill at Cambuslang in Glasgow, Tullybelton (meaning 'Beltane Hill') north of Perth in Tayside, and Tarbolton ('Beltane Hillock') near Mauchline in Strathclyde. At Tullybelton the path to boundless prosperity on May Day is open to anyone who takes a hillside drink, walks nine times round the hill sunwise, and then goes nine times round the nearby standing stones in the same anti-clockwise direction.

Holne Ram Feast in Devon died out last century, a sacrificial rave without any Christian concessions. A ram was chased over Dartmoor, captured, and decorated with roses and other flowers. It was then carried to a standing stone, over which its throat was cut. It was roasted whole and unskinned, and there was a scramble for the best cuts at midday. A revival seems unlikely. As well as a May Day feast, there was also often a second sacrifice at Old Midsummer, July 6th.

This ritual slaughter continued well into the last century, as did the less gory but equally paganism-rooted custom of having sex all night and all morning on May Day. It was at Portland in Dorset that these mass marathons – or perhaps fun runs is a better expression – lingered longest, and it became customary for a Portland woman to marry only if she was pregnant beforehand. Thomas Hardy describes this in his novel *The Well Beloved*.

There is thought to be just one area of Britain where paganism still lingers. Not as a jolly revival or as the basis of some custom or tradition, but as a genuine belief. The main A628 Manchester to Sheffield road goes right through Longdendale in Derbyshire. Beyond the road stretches a sprawling and often bleak area of High Peak moorland, and it is far from difficult to imagine how some of its more remote hamlets could have been by-passed by invading hordes and Christian proselytisers. In one such corner of the valley lie a few scattered farmhouses, the occupants of which have little interest in the outside world, and profess a continued reverence for 'the Old Ways'. On May Day they continue to garland their wells, light fires and worship images in the shape of the human head. Improbable as all this seems, it was the subject of a 1986 BBC documentary, and all the evidence suggests that these people are not farcical romantics like the Druids, but genuine relics, privately and harmlessly persevering in their own sincere beliefs.

© Many Christian traditions have infiltrated the former pagan preserve of May Day, and one of the most moving is the singing of the *Te Deum Patrem Colimus* at Magdalen College in Oxford on May Day morning. This fine hymn is sung from the top of the tower at 6 am. Bells then ring out, and Morris Men leap into the fray, along with all sorts of street music and entertainment. As usual not everyone is happy with the idea that the roots of such a spiritually uplifting tradition could be grounded in the appeasing of an ancient sun-god. Alternative theories suggest that it commemorates the completion of the tower in 1509, or that the hymn has replaced the May 1st Requiem which used to be sung for Henry VII.

© Hymns are also sung at 6 am on May Day from the Bargate in Southampton. May songs in general have been around for as long as May. It used to be yet another occasion for going from door to door in the hope of food and money. The May carols that accompanied this trip were more reflective than is usual when providing entertainment in the hope of gaining payment:

The life of a man it is but a span
He flourishes like a flower,
Today he is here and tomorrow he is gone,
And he's dead all in one hour.

And when you're dead and you're in your
  grave
And covered in clay so cold,
The worms shall eat your flesh, good man,
And your bones turn to good mould.

Wherever there was singing, there was dancing,

and wherever there was dancing there were **maypoles**. Compared to many other traditions, **maypoles** have survived well; though in former years every town and village in England, and many elsewhere in Britain, had a pole erected on May Day. These ranged from the 134-footer to be seen in the Strand in London soon after the Restoration; to the humblest of stripped tree-boughs dragged in from the nearest copse. Hawthorn was the preferred wood.

As a symbol of unbounded joy, the Puritans were quick to dismiss maypoles as a malign social influence. Philip Stubbes declared that '*this stinking idol*' should be banned. In 1644 they were, and the poet Randolph lamented:

> *And harmless maypoles are rail'd upon*
> *As if they were the Tow'rs of Babylon.*

The purge on poles was not new. On 'Evil May Day' in 1517 the pole in Leadenhall Street, London, was chopped down to put an end to the fun. Rival tradesmen had fought a pitched battle that year, and the pole became the law's scapegoat. It had stood higher than the steeple at the neighbouring St Andrew's church – which became known as St Andrew's Undershaft.

🜨 The most famous ex-pole was the one which until last century stood on The Trendle, an earthwork above the head of Dorset's chalk hill figure, the **Cerne Abbas Giant**. He is 180-feet long, with a 120-foot club and a 20-foot erect penis. If the May Pole is a phallic symbol, then it can have found no happier home than in the environs of the Giant. Until well into last century an engagement or marriage was sealed with a visit to Cerne Abbas, and it was long customary for couples – especially childless couples – to have sex there on May Day, as the Giant's copious fertility guaranteed conception.

In 1958 the Marquis of Bath and his wife Virginia visited the site. For five years they had tried without success to have children together, and then someone told them about the Giant. They 'sat on him', and 10 months later their daughter Silvy was born. The Marquis was aware that he was in the Giant's debt: '*It worked for us and in gratitude we gave Cerne as Silvy's middle name, and made G. Cerne godfather at the christening – the vicar never noticed.*' Until he became too old to continue his visits, the Marquis made an annual spring pilgrimage to the Giant with Silvy – now Lady Silvy Cerne McQuiston – tagging along so that she could tell her godfather what she had been up to since last they met.

🜨 Locally the Giant is known as Helith, a cousin of Hercules. It is said that a Danish giant was waylaid on the hill and beheaded, and his outline was traced in the chalk. An even more fanciful theory says that the Giant is real and can reanimate at will. He sometimes strolls down the hill to drink at the stream and pick up his favourite snack – a woman. The traces of these legends are underlined by the presence of giants carved in the church at Cerne Abbas.

© Maypoles are both a fertility symbol and a representation of the sacred tree and its attendant spirits. These spirits bring the village good luck, and that is the origin of **maypole raiding**, with covetous adjoining settlements trying to steal their neighbour's luck. At Lanreath, near Fowey in Cornwall, the maypole – a simple stripped young tree – is still sought by neighbouring villages. There are tales of raiders getting the Lanreath guards drunk, or letting down car tyres to avoid pursuit after the theft. Lanreath's pole is renewed every year. After the festivities it is chopped up and made into skittles. Similar rivalry existed between Burnsall and Thorpe, near Skipton in North Yorkshire. Thorpe has a history of raiding, and in 1991 its for-old-time's-sake efforts made the national press: Burnsall's £350 pole was spirited away, and it later appeared cemented down at a new location in Thorpe. Police had a quiet word, and the pole was returned in time for Burnsall's Maying.

© The beribboned short poles and ribbon dances were a 19th-century innovation. The tallest survivors are the 90-foot pole at Barwick in Elmet, near Leeds in West Yorkshire (see Whitsun); and the 70-footer at Welford-on-Avon, near Stratford in Warwickshire. Morris dancers have a hop round the Welford pole at dawn today; but the main village May Day festivities have moved to July when it is more convenient for the schools. **Permanent maypoles** are now rare. The one at Belton, near Oakham in Leicestershire, is now the axis of village activities on the second Saturday after Whitsun. The pole at Wellow, just outside Ollerton in Nottinghamshire, is danced around on the Late Spring Bank Holiday, and is always renewed with wood from Sherwood Forest. Gawthorpe, near Wakefield in West Yorkshire, also has a permanent pole, and its festivities take place on the first weekend in May. The dancing at Gawthorpe is the highlight of a gala funded chiefly by profits from the

Coal-Carrying Championships enacted on Easter Monday.

© Another all-year-round maypole stands on the enormous four-section village green at Ickwell Green, south-east of Bedford, as it has done for at least 400 years. Again there is a May Day dawn raid on the pole by local Morris men, but the main celebrations now start at 1 pm on the Bank Holiday Monday. A May Queen is elected, and Morris dancers in 19th-century costume cavort around the maypole led by two **Moggies** – men with wild clothing and blacked-up faces, carrying money-boxes and brooms (not made on May Day, of course).

© The **Royal May Day Festival** at Knutsford in Cheshire, held on the first Saturday in May, has maypole dancing and other parades and ceremonies common to celebrations across the land. But it has one feature that in the words of a young Queen Victoria, who once came to have a look, is *'peculiar to this town'* – the **Sanding Ceremony**. Coloured sand is trickled through funnels to make decorative patterns, and no one is entirely sure why. The local legend is that after King Cnut had forded the river here, he stopped to tip the sand from his shoes. The sand-tipping used to be performed at every Knutsford wedding, and is still the central strand of the Royal May Day celebrations. Elizabeth Gaskell lived in Knutsford for years, and her more down-to-earth hypothesis was that the readily available sand had taken the place of strewing flowers, which were not always easy to find. Curiously, a very similar custom to the Sanding Ceremony takes place on the island of Teneriffe on the feast of Corpus Christi. In the last few years Knutsford has also started a separate Sanding Festival in late June.

The Knutsford festivities also include one of the grandest **May Queen** crowning ceremonies. The May Queens are the precursors of all the other pageant Queens of the 1990s, now a guaranteed feature in any parade, anywhere in the country, at any time of year. It was not always an honour that every young girl craved – it was said that the chosen girl brought luck to the whole village; but that she would probably die within a year.

2nd May
Rood Een

The Ruttin' and Nozzlin' Lottery

Beltane is still in full swing: in some areas the Beltane fires lit on April 30th had to burn for three days before the old gods would let it lie. Cattle were driven through the fires for ritual purification and protection; and in Scotland a man was chosen to leap through the conflagration too. He was the **Beltane Carle**, chosen by lottery. He made three leaps through the flames to bring good fortune to the whole company. Originally he was a sacrifice to the sun god. Death by lottery was a favourite party game with the Celts, and their May gods had a predilection for roasted flesh. As recently as last century rams were being sacrificed, their blood gushing over a sacred stone and the surrounding earth to ensure a plentiful harvest at the other end of the summer.

This notion of sacrifice was known to a canny member of the morbid crowd which gathered in 1555 to watch the star turn of the afternoon – Protestant Bishops **Hugh Latimer** and **Nicholas Ridley** getting burned alive, a consequence of Queen Mary's brief revival of zealous Catholicism. The execution happened just outside Oxford, and someone complained that if the bonfires had been built just a few days earlier at the start of Beltane there would have been a couple of great sacrifices to see the crops well on their way.

In the folk song *Bell Tune* (a corruption of *Beltane*), a cheery gloss is put on dark Beltane goings-on. A woman and her lover go to the woods, where the standing stones and trees are strangely restless. The couple then stumble upon the rest of the girl's family, caught mid-ritual carrying out some intriguingly named practices: her father is *'nozzlin'*, and her brother is *'ruttin'*. Her mother is only dancing, but all three are decked out in grotesque animal-head masks. This is all alarmingly pagan – such ceremonies were usually the preliminaries to human or animal sacrifices. Having discovered their secret rites, the family decide to kill the girl but relent when the man offers to marry her. Not so much losing a daughter, as gaining a son.

May 2nd is **Rood Een**. Highland cow sheds used to be draped with honeysuckle and rowan to protect the animals from the malign influence of witches.

Honeysuckle is powerful stuff. Brought

indoors it ensures a fruitful, imminent marriage; but it must be kept away from children. The scent of the plant inspires erotic dreams in young girls. So it may be safer to stick with less X-rated anti-witch plants such as primroses, and marigolds – also known as the Herb of Britain. In fact anything yellow is effective, a case of superstition showing a practical inclination, as yellow flowers predominate at this time of year.

May Week – the one surrounding May Day – was once jam-packed with **hiring fairs**, offering the chance for farm-hands to move on, and for seasonal workers to get hired where they were needed most. One such fair took place at Brigg. The lead character in the old song *Brigg Fair* claims '. . . *unto Brigg Fair I did repair, for love I was inclined*'; but most were there for labour rather than love. At Brigg's May Hiring the first to arrive for selection were given free beer, an added incentive which guaranteed an early turn-out. Some came before dawn, just to be sure of their pint.

3rd May
Rood Day/Avoiding Day

Bullocks' Bollocks and Buttocks

The scene is **King Arthur's** court in Carlisle. On May 3rd a richly-clad lad strides in and displays a golden cloak. He explains that the garment will look good only on a faithful woman. Guinevere then tries it on, but it looks terrible. Sir Kay's wife has a go, but it fits so badly that – according to the song *The Boy and the Mantle* – 'she was bare all above the buttocks'. Step forward Lady Briefbras, the only woman in folklore to be named after two separate undergarments. The mantle fits her snugly, though the hemline is a tad messy. She admits to having kissed her husband Caradoc before they were married. Having confessed this colossal sin, the mantle looks perfect.

But Guinevere is having none of this. She accuses Lady Briefbras of sleeping around and taking up to 15 men at once. The boy with the mantle, not one to mince his words, even with mythological queens, declares that Guinevere '*is a bitch and a witch and a whore bold! King, in thine own court, thou art a cuckhold!*'

To prove his point he briefly exits, returning with the head of a freshly-killed wild boar. The boy declares that only a man with a faithful wife

can cut it. Most of the knights present pretend to have no knives, but Caradoc pulls out his dagger and proves himself a deft bacon-slicer. Finally the boy hands round a cup, saying that cuckolded men will spill the drink. The rest was all red faces and stained shirts:

> *Some shed on their shoulder and some on*
> *their knee;*
> *He that could not hit his mouth put it in his*
> *eye.*

Caradoc as usual had no problems. His wife won the mantle; and the whole point of the exercise seems to have been to expose Guinevere.

Today is **Rood Day**, also known as Crossmas or The Finding of the Cross, celebrating St Helen's finding of Christ's cross in AD 335 (even though Helen in fact died five years earlier). She is said to have actually found several old crosses, all good candidates. So a dead body was stretched out on each. The corpse that revived was deemed to have been lying on the one true Cross. Such a story began to reek of myth by the 20th century, and in 1969 Rood Day was crossed off the saintly calendar.

Rood Day is the traditional time to put **bulls** to cows. The bull can be aided in the cause of fertility by smearing its genitals with a mixture of burned hart's tail and wine. Bizarrely, tying up the left testicle encourages the siring of a bullock; doing the same to the right means a cow. Do not try this at home.

At **Bovey Tracey** in Devon the Monday after Rood Day used to witness a procession around the village boundaries, led by officials carrying flower-crowned staves. The houses were all profusely decorated with greenery for the occasion.

In Scotland this is **Avoiding Day**, with malevolent faeries out to make trouble. It is a bad day for marriage, travel, new undertakings, and the counting of livestock. A cross of tarred wood, or woodbine and rowan, if hung over the byre protects animals. Farmers can also placate the faeries by taking a few drops of milk from every cow on the farm, and allowing the cupful to soak into the earth.

With the arrival of Christianity the superstitions remained but the explanation changed. Avoiding Day became the date upon which Satan and his hordes were kicked out of heaven, and these displaced devils inherited the blame for today's mischief.

4th May

Fast Race Runs

When **Ann Moore** of Tutbury, Staffordshire, heard about a 17th-century woman who had made a small fortune by fasting for 16 months, she rose to the challenge. Announcing a long-term loss of appetite, she sat in her bedroom and waited for the cash to flow in. Sure enough, a report of her fasting was published, and paying sightseers came to have a look. Ann's scheme was simple, if a little uncomfortable. She would fast for several days, and then request to be left alone with her daughter. The girl would come in with food stuffed down her bodice, and Ann would surreptitiously pig out.

Ann Moore had collected several hundred pounds before an investigating team decided to keep vigil with her. She was trapped. After nine days it became clear that she was dying, and the hoax was revealed. On May 4th 1813 she signed a confession admitting to evil deceit and the taking of occasional sustenance during her so-called fast, and acknowledging the offence that she had given to God during this time. The 46-year-old Ann was then imprisoned for fraud, and sent off to try a prison diet for a few years. This was not so much a punishment as a peevish revenge from people who were embarrassed at having been hoodwinked.

© The first **Derby at Epsom** was run today in 1780 following a dinner party at which Sir Charles Bunbury and the Earl of Derby tossed a coin. They had decided to instigate a new flat race for three-year-old horses (originally over a distance of one mile, but extended by another half mile in 1784) on the Epsom downs in Surrey. The winner of the toff's toss would have the honour of naming the new event. Derby won, and so sadly we do not get an annual Epsom Bunbury. The short distance and high stakes made this a popular event from the onset. Legend hints that the race may in fact still take place, usually on the first Wednesday in June.

Epsom's other claim to fame is its salts. **Epsom salts** were discovered in 1618 by local farmer Henry Whicker. He found that his cattle would not drink at a local pool, in spite of their evident thirst. With the age-old belief that distasteful substances must be good for you, Henry set up the first spa in Epsom. By sheer coincidence the nasty-tasting magnesium sulphate has desirable effects on recalcitrant bowels, and Pepys and Nell Gwynn were soon among the spa's many customers. An alleged epitaph sings the praises of the waters at the expense of a rival spa town:

> *Here lie I and my three daughters,*
> *Killed by drinking the Cheltenham waters;*
> *If we had stuck to Epsom salts*
> *We shouldn't be lying in these here vaults.*

May 4th, along with the other days between April 30th and May 8th, is **Between the Beltanes**. Anyone born during this brief spell has power and influence over all living things. The key to this power is a mix of brains and brawn, as borne out by the Scottish saying:

> *You have the skill of man and beast,*
> *If you are born between the Beltanes.*

5th May

Automatic for the People

Tyburn Tree was the main gallows in London. On 5th May 1760 Earl Ferrers had some small consolation, as he was about to go down in history as the first man to try out the new Hangman's Drop. The new automated hanging worked perfectly. A trapdoor opened beneath Ferrers, who plummeted through, dying instantly.

▥ Nine people at a time could be hung on the triangular wooden structure which stood at Tyburn until 1783 – the site, near Marble Arch, is marked with a plaque. In 1678 the old gallows fell down, purportedly uprooted by the ghosts of its victims. Many outlaws opted to 'Preach on Tyburn Cross', delivering their own resounding eulogy or elegy and get the crowd on their side. Sam Hall's 'Goodnight' mix of venom and bravado did well in 1707. It secured him an immediate folk song, which was widely sung in music halls this century, and is still current in folk circles.

After the downfall of the gallows, the name Tyburn – from 'two burns', it being the junction of two now culverted streams – survived in the term **Tyburn Ticket**. This highly saleable item was awarded to anyone who secured a conviction that sent a felon to the gallows. The ticket was desirable because it exempted the possessor from all duties in the parish where the original offence had been committed. Prices went as high as £300 – a phenomenal amount of money in the 1800s. As late as 1856 a Tyburn Ticket was successfully used to get someone off jury service at the Old Bailey in London. It is unclear whether this incentive to convict actually affected the verdicts.

The stretched-neck-of-the-woods around the old gallows site – which roughly corresponds with what is now Marylebone and Paddington – was known as Tyburnia. A.J.C. Hare, writing in 1876, was not impressed: '*Tyburn still gives a name to the white streets and squares of Tyburnia, which are wholly devoid of interest or beauty.*'

Criminals always stuck their necks out at **Paddington Fair** – the name given to the carnival-like atmosphere at a Tyburn hanging. There were stalls, shows, and lots of beer. After all, everyone likes a drop at Tyburn. For details of the Tyburn Walk, which commemorates Catholic martyrs executed at Tyburn, see April 27th.

On the first Sunday in May, Barrowford in Lancashire used to celebrate **Nick o' Thungs Day**. The men climbed Pendle Hill and cooked **Nettle Pudding** in three large pans on the hilltop. Legend says that Nick Driver, in 1670, was mugged at Pendle. Samaritans from nearby Downham came to his rescue, and once he had recovered he vowed to give any traveller the sustenance of meat and drink. The custom was revived in the late 1860s by an American Civil War veteran. The men were proud of their robust efforts, combining nettles with various meats, sausages, oatmeal, duck eggs and dripping, which was washed down with beer, and accompanied by conventional foodstuffs. Women were tolerated, but patronised. This was all organised by the Lamb Club, and the Nick o'Thung's recipe was kept secret. Initiates could only learn the-way-of-the-nettle after successfully repeating a tongue-twister which began: '*Thimble Rig Thistlethwaite thievishly thought to thrive through thick and thin . . .*'

Thungs are not what they once were – the Nickers lost the knack in 1939.

6th May

Punch Sober

Early in May the farmers and livestock of Alderney in the Channel Islands used to take part in **Milk-a-Punch Sunday**. A procession of men and cows trooped down to a local spring. The men then sat down, milked the cattle, and drank the fresh, warm, frothy liquid. They toasted the spring – both the water and the season – and then went to the local pub for a pint of . . . more fresh milk. This was the milk-a-punch, and it was free of charge. But with the passing of time the tradition degenerated: the ritual became condensed, and the milking of the animals was enacted with the merest of symbolic tweaks on the udder. More and more alcohol worked its way into the festivities, and eventually the event lost its milky way altogether, and died out.

But cry not over spoilt traditions, for the spirit if not the ceremony of Milk-a-Punch Sunday lives on. On the first or second Sunday in May, many on Alderney still raid the fridge and raise a milky toast to the spring.

◎ The first Sunday of the month is **Spaw Sunday** around Calderdale in West Yorkshire, and involves much sipping of the sulphurous local waters. The celebrations were revived briefly in 1987, and the well at Cragg Vale near Hebden Bridge was decorated with flowers and branches. Several Morris teams turned up, everyone took a gulp of the licorice-infused water, and a great time was had by all. In 1988, however, the first Sunday in May suffered appalling weather: the booked Morris teams cried off, and the tradition was dead before the morning was out. It has remained dormant ever since.

'Spaw' is from 'Spa', which comes from a town in Belgium, the first place in Europe to which people came as tourists for the sole purpose of taking the waters.

◎ On the first Sunday in May, part one of an old Hocktide custom, **Randwick Wap**, takes place at Randwick, near Stroud in Gloucestershire. At 11.15 am there is an outdoor service at St John the Baptist's church in Randwick, during which two sizeable **cheeses** are blessed. They tend to be Double Gloucesters, and in 1993 they were donated by Dairy Crest. In a suspiciously pagan manner, they are then rolled three times round the church, anticlockwise. One is then eaten on the spot, and the other cheese goes forward to the next and final heat of the Wap, which is on the second Saturday in May – ie usually, but not always, the following Saturday. For details of what happens then, see May 10th.

At last it can be revealed – the elusive link between *nightingales* and **eels**. In Worcestershire they say, without the benefit of rhyme:

> *When the eels be in the nightingale comes,*
> *To be ready to sing in May.*

Other denizens of the deep are stirring this month too:

> *Cockles and ray*
> *Come in in May.*

This is not a forecast of shellfish showers with added mantas, but a reminder that these exotic seafoods are now in season.

7th May
St John of Beverley's Day

The Beverley Brothers

William the Conqueror had reached Yorkshire during his Wasting of the North tour. At Beverley he delegated one of his most brutal henchmen, Toustain, to ransack the Minster where several locals were hiding. But when Toustain entered the church there was a burst of blinding light. He fell; all his limbs became bulbous lumps of meat; and his head span through 360 degrees, just like in *The Exorcist*. But this was not Satan at work, it was St John of Beverley who had interceded to protect the area of Sanctuary around the town's *Frith Stool*. William got the message and allowed the Minster, and its rights, to go untouched.
King Æthelstan instigated Sanctuary at Beverley in 938 after successfully invoking St John to help him slaughter the Scots; and it survived as a legal right until the 1530s, when Henry VIII abolished it as part of his Reformation package. For a mile and a half in every direction from the Frith Stool, transgressors could claim immunity from the law. Violating this holy asylum met with harsh penalties. At the limit of the safety zone there was a then-stiff £8 fine for messing with a fugitive. But tamper with an alleged offender at the altar and you forfeited your life.
Sanctuary lasted a maximum of 30 days. If after this time there was no sign of a pardon, the accused had three options. He could face the music, do a runner, or become one of the band of brothers known as the **Frithmen of Beverley**. This involved swearing an oath to become a servant of the church, handing over all property to the crown, and living forever in the Humberside town. The 1,000-year-old Frith stool can still be seen inside the Minister.
St John was born in the 7th century at Harpham, near Bridlington in Humberside. Beverley Minster – which still contains his tomb – and the **St John's well** in Harpham were both said to work animal magic, taming the wildest of creatures. Beverley Minster is the only church in the land to have made such a claim: frothing cattle and mad dogs were once a regular sight in its aisles. On the Tuesday nearest the 7th there is a special St John service at the well in Harpham. Following a procession the flower-decorated well is blessed. Its water are supposedly still an effective cure-all for humans as well as animals.

The unusual variety of apples known as **apple-johns** gets its name from the fact that the fruit is supposedly ripe enough to eat today, on the feast of St John of Beverley. But they are supposed to taste even better if kept for a further two years, when they will be shrivelled but delicious. Their appearance is proverbial. One of the Drawers in *King Henry IV, Part Two* says of (Sir John) Falstaff:

> *The prince once set a dish of apple-johns*
> *before him, and told him there were five Sir*
> *Johns; and, putting off his hat, said 'I will*
> *now take my leave of these six dry, round,*
> *old, withered knights'.*

Chances are that the John referred to is actually St John the Baptist, whose main feast day falls on June 24th – when the apples were more likely to have been munchable – but someone, somewhere seems to have got their wires crossed and given the apple-john a free transfer to St John of Beverley.

8th May
Furry Day/St Indract's Day/
Feast of the Apparition
of St Michael

Furry Ball

In the year 700 **St Indract** and 10 companions were in Somerset on a famine relief mission. They were en route to Ireland, their purses stuffed with grain to offset the poor Irish harvest. However, believing that the purses contained gold, covetous Saxon thugs attacked and killed everyone. Indract and Co. were thrown into a hastily excavated corpse-pit at Shapwick. But the communal grave revealed itself to the world by giving forth great beams of light, and the bodies were swiftly exhumed. During the reinterment ceremony at Shepton Mallet the watching murderers were so overcome with grief that they became frenzied and tore each other to pieces. Meanwhile the companions became as fertile as their grain. By the 19th century their number had grown from 10 to 100, just to make the story more exciting; though if there had been that many, they might have put up more of a fight.

© In Helston, Cornwall, May 8th is Furry Day unless it falls on a Sunday or Monday, in which case the festivities are held on the preceding Saturday. Furry Dancing is not a revival, but a genuine uninterrupted tradition, and is all the more robust and joyous for that. Flowers and branches adorn every building, and many of the people too. Dressing up for the main dance is compulsory: top hats and buttonholes for the men, long frocks and summer hats for the women. 'Furry' may be linked with the Roman goddess of greenery, Flora, or with the Latin feria, meaning a holy day.

It all kicks off at 7 am with the Early Morning Dance, instigated by the Mayor. The Furry Tune rings out, trying to ignore the fact that under the title Floral Dance it accompanied Terry Wogan into the charts in the 1970s. Morning is also the stamping ground of the Hal-an-Tow. Part parade, part mumming play, it is a crop-fertility ritual which is probably even older than the dance. It has its own song:

> Hal-an-Tow, jolly rum-be-low,
> And we were up as soon as any day-o,
> And for to fetch the summer home, the
>   summer and the May-o,
> For summer is a-come-o, and winter is a-
>   gone-o.

The song also mentions many of the characters who take part in the play and procession – St George and his pet dragon, St Michael, Robin Hood, Little John, Friar Tuck, and the local stand-in for Maid Marian, Aunt Mary Moses.

The children begin their dance at about 10 am; and the principal Furry Dance steps out from the Guildhall at noon. Hundreds of dancing couples try to weave in and out of all the houses, ideally entering and leaving through different doors as this brings extra luck. At 5 pm a free-for-all ball begins, and visitors to the town can at last put on their own dancing shoes – formal dress not required – and get Furry with the locals.

⬚ The local version of why all this happens today revolves around the fact that it is one of the feast days of Helston's patron saint, St Michael. The town's name comes from the Hell's Stone. Satan was brawling with Michael for possession of the town when in desperation he plucked the stone from the mouth of Hell and threw it at the saint. His missile missed and plunged into the yard of the Angel Hotel, where it can still be seen, incorporated into a wall. Satan then gave up the battle. The townsfolk danced for joy, and had such a good time that they decided to make it an annual event.

9th May
Lemuralia

You may not kiss the Bride

The Classical writer Ovid was the first to note that 'the common people consider it unlucky to marry in the month of May'. The same belief was widespread in Britain, and especially in Scotland: in 1567 the 'common people' could have told Mary Queen of Scots that marrying James, Earl of Bothwell, in May was a bad move. The fact that he was suspected of involvement in the probable murder of Mary's previous husband Darnley, as well as sitting on charges of rape and adultery made for a particularly bad start.

The parish minister would not proclaim the banns until he had a writ from Mary. The Bishop of Orkney, conducting the ceremony, went out of his way to state that Bothwell had renounced his evil life: a salve to the Bishop's conscience rather than a statement of the truth. To add some extra bad luck, Mary wore a black gown at the wedding.

No couple could shoulder such a weight of superstition. In June of the same year they parted: Mary was imprisoned in England, and was forced to step down from the Scottish throne. Bothwell fled, and died in Denmark in 1578. His son, the 5th Earl, became a notorious warlock whose sorcery created a tempest that almost led to Mary's successor, James I and VI, drowning at sea.

'*Marry in May and you'll rue the day*', is a British version of Ovid's observations. There is also the quirkier:

> *The people say*
> *That only wantons marry in the month of*
> *May,*

which has an anti-Mary ring to it. But the real reason seems to be:

> *O' the marriages in May,*
> *A' the bairns die o' decay.*

In other words, children of a May-union are doomed.

A report in an 1818 edition of *Edinburgh Magazine* describes a **May bride** who added to her bad luck by putting on her petticoats the wrong way round: the first of several mishaps. Her gloves turned out to be both for the left hand. She went on to break her stays four times, and when she got to church her apron fell off, and she tripped over the threshold on the way in. In the ceremony, arms and hands all got tangled. Finally, her garter fell down as she left the church.

All this May-marriage paranoia stems, as Ovid knew well, from the Roman festival of the dead, **Lemuralia**, which began today. *Lemures* were the Roman spirits of the dead: the cuddly, round-eyed primates of Madagascar derive their name from these spirits as a result of their ghoulish cry and appearance. Marriage, with its symbolism of life and new beginnings, is the antithesis of the Lemuralia. It seems that the church in Britain wished to reinforce the taboo, to dissociate marriage from the pagan overtones of May and the ongoing goings-on between amorous Maying lads and lasses in the greenwood.

The Roman festival was in some ways similar to our Hallowe'en. Ghosts walked the earth, and houses could only be rendered spirit-free via animal sacrifices. In Britain, despite the Roman occupation, most souls stick to October 31st for their excursions.

10th May
Dotterel Day

Dotterel, Wap and Shuttlefeathers

Dotterel Day was the height of the bird-netting season, which may explain why there are so few of them about these days – less than a hundred pairs of these plovers survive, mostly in the north of Britain. In folk-tale terms, though, the bird has only itself to blame. Dotterels supposedly imitate men, and so make themselves easy to catch. One hunter would lead the bird in a series of Marcel Marceau routines while the other sneaked up and bagged it. This led to the use of the word 'dotterel' as a tag for a gullible person: 'to dor the dotterel' means to trick the fool.

☻ Comprehensively clueless, dotterels are somehow weather-wise:

> *When dotterel do first appear*
> *It shows that frost is very near;*
> *But when the dotterel do go*
> *Then you may look for heavy snow.*

© The main course of **Runnick Wap** takes place on **Wap Saturday**, the second Saturday in May (for the starter, see May 6th). A sprawling fair fills the streets of Randwick, near Stroud in Gloucestershire. At 1 pm the parade participants, all dressed in 18th- or 19th-century clothes, gather at the War Memorial. To the rousing strains of *The Runnick Weavers' Song* a Wap Mayor and a young Wap Queen are carried shoulder high to the village pond, accompanied by other elected figures, including a Sword-Bearer, a High-Sheriff and a Mop Man – whose job it is to spray the crowd with water. At the pond, the Mayor is dumped in, and a local ditty called *Mayor's Song* is sung. He is fished out in time for the day's main event on the school playing field, which was the old village green. The Queen and Mayor each have three goes at rolling a real cheese and several wooden ones down a steep bank, competing for the longest and straightest roll. Afterwards the wooden cheeses are put away for next year, and the real one is divided and devoured.

◉ In the old West Riding of Yorkshire the second Sunday in May was the traditional day for playing **battledore and shuttlefeathers**, a rudimentary form of badminton. Curiously, the sport began as a means of divination, played solo. You hit the shuttlefeather up and down on a racket, whilst muttering a few choice rhymes and counting the number of hits achieved before the shuttle falls. The sum total is the answer to your queries. For example, to see how long you will live:

> *Shuttlecock, shuttlecock, tell me true,*

How many years have I to go through? One,
two, three, four . . . etc.

Drop the shuttlefeather on the first count, and
expect to expire before tea. Similar insights can
be had from the following:

Grandmother, grandmother, tell me no lie,
How many children before I die? One, two,
three, four . . . etc.

Hopefully the 'etc.' will not be too large. The
game can be played using letters instead of
numbers, to denote the initial of a prospective
partner:

Blackcurrant, redcurrant, raspberry tart,
Tell me the name of my sweetheart; A, B, C,
D . . . etc.

11th May
Old May Eve

Cut Down in his Prime

John Williams of Redruth, Cornwall, woke up
from a troubled sleep on May 3rd 1812. He had
just had the third in a series of identical dreams.
In the night he had seen **Spencer Perceval**,
Tory Prime Minister since 1809, being assas-
sinated in the lobby of the House of Commons.
Williams could recall people and place in vivid
detail, in spite of the fact that he had never set
foot near Parliament.

John Williams was eager to travel to London
and warn Perceval; but his family advised
against it, and suggested that medication
might be a better course of action. Eight days
later on May 11th, Perceval was shot and killed
in the Commons lobby by John Bellingham, a
bankrupt merchant. It was all exactly as Williams had forecast, and when he later visited the
Commons eyewitnesses to the killing could
only nod in agreement as he correctly pin-
pointed what had happened where on the
fateful day. At the time of going to press,
Perceval remains the only British Prime Minister to have been shot dead in office, though
several others have been stabbed in the back.

Today gives another opportunity to visit healing wells or bring greenery indoors – the things
that should have been done on May Eve and
May Day. But May 11th is a bad day for
choosing to pluck **blackthorn**. A moody fa-

erie tribe called the **Lunantishee** guard this
particular tree, and are especially vigilant today
– Old May Eve – and on Old Hallowe'en,
November 11th. They will foul up plans to
reach the tree, and bring misfortune or sloe
death to anyone who makes off with a branch.

The second Tuesday in May used to herald
Ashendon Feast in Lancashire, and the date
became the customary one for planting **beans**
in that part of the country. There are alternative
indicators for the cautious bean-planter too:

When elum leaves are as big as a farden,
'Tis time to plant kidney beans in the garden.

That is 'farden' as in *farthing*. Tradition also
says that, to ensure a good crop, beans must be
planted in a north-south line – which makes
sense in terms of sunlight.

On the Isle of Man this was the day for torching
furze – which is also known as gorse or whin.
This was done to scare away witches, and all
other furze dwellers. The burning puts paid to
any chance of a crafty kiss too:

When furze is out of bloom,
Kissing's out of tune,

And anyone planning marriage should get in
there before the fires are lit, as custom insists
that a bride should wear 'Something old,
something new, something borrowed, something blue, and a sprig of furze' – a fifth line
which is usually forgotten these days. Do not
under any circumstances choose a sprig in full
bloom though:

Sprig of gorse in full bloom,
A whore at noon.

12th May
Old May Day/St Pancras' Day

A Brain Infested With Mythological
Invertebrates

To most people **St Pancras** is either the
guardian of misspelt internal organs, or the
patron saint of trains going to Sheffield. The
magnificent redbrick Victorian St Pancras
Station in London took its name from a nearby
church dedicated to the saint.

But in superstition terms Pancras is one of
the main men when it comes to headaches. A

prayer to the saint should be enough to restore harmony in your head. But if it persists, the praying can be backed up with a seasonal remedy. Stuff your ears with the marrow of a cow killed in May. The pseudo-scientific theory here is that the brain-worms that cause the headache will forsake the skull for the much tastier cow marrow. Always a drastic and disgusting treatment, the advent of mad cow disease makes this a precipitate prescription, more likely to do harm than good.

Old May Day is the traditional time for putting cattle out to pasture. It also heralds the start of the cheese-making season, and was once a widespread holiday. The reason for the holiday was that it gave an opportunity for **flitting** – moving to a new job. It was called Leaving Day in Yorkshire. An alternative moving-on date at this time of the month was Pag Rag Day – see May 14th.

Animals born in May are troublesome, particularly horses, sows and cats. May horses are said to be so mean that only rodeo owners should have any dealings with them; and colts born this month like nothing better than to lie down when crossing water. May-farrowing sows are said to have the disagreeable habit of devouring their own litters. In Cheshire, to offset this risk, farmers used to give the postnatal sows a placatory dinner of bread and butter. This apparently took the pig's mind off cannibalism.

   May cats will not kill mice and rats, but will bring adders, slow worms and toads into the house, which is a skill few seek in a household pet. This belief led to most kittens born in May being unceremoniously drowned – before they had a chance to prove the superstition wrong.

   Such treatment is humane in comparison to that meted out to two cats at Hastings in East Sussex. During 19th-century restoration a pair of **mummified cats** were found in the chimney of the Elizabethan *Stag Inn*. Chances are that they were stuffed up there as a sacrifice to keep malign forces at bay. A more elaborate version of the story says that the cats belonged to Hastings witch Hannah Clarke. One of the friendlier members of the weird sisterhood, Hannah helped to keep the Spanish Armada away from Hastings and generally used her magic for the town's protection. Eventually she moved on, leaving her two familiars in her stead. They got on fine until the plague hit Hastings. It was commonly believed that cats (rather than the rats they ate) were plague-

carriers, and the cats of a witch seemed particularly culpable. So they were mummified and walled in at the pub.

▥ After being rediscovered the poor creatures did not receive a decent burial. A decision was made to display them. The cats can still be seen in a glass case on the wall of *The Stag Inn*, which has the added attraction of being an excellent pub.

13th May

Old Tetty Gives a Toss

At Bishop Norton in Lincolnshire last century, local worthy Old Tetty celebrated every May 13th in a strange fashion. Year in, year out, she walked two miles to a particular field and gathered a bagful of **cowslips**. Back at her cottage she made the cowslips into balls and threw them over her roof to the accompaniment of strange – but alas unrecorded – rhymes and chants. The person who recounted this to a historian did so after the demise of Old Tetty, and had no idea why the old woman had thought the ritual to be so important. For all we know it could have held the key to saving the universe.

   Tetty's cowslip observance was probably linked with Old May Day: it was quite common in Lincolnshire to hold the celebrations today (whereas Old May is more properly May 12th). She may have been half-remembering a divination ceremony known as **tissty-tossty**, or tissy ball. The cowslip ball is tossed in the air until it is dropped, while the player recites a list of partners, numbers, horses in the 3.15, etc. The dropped ball halts the game, and the number (or whatever) reached indicates the relevant name/age/winner. It is essentially the same game as shuttlefeather, mentioned on May 10th.

   Cowslip-balls themselves are among the traditional May Day garlanding accoutrements. They were often hung up, and objects were thrown over them in a rudimentary game of handball. If made into hoops, the garlands offered a more challenging game, as the balls had to be thrown through the hole in the middle.

In Humberside, the village of Barnoldby le Beck had its **May holiday** today. It was a time for changing jobs, linked to Old May Day (see May 14th for more moving-on, on Pag Rag

Day). A reporter last century summed up the merrymaking as a time of '*much fighting, drinking and dancing*', just like any bad disco. The villages in the Lincolnshire Marsh area had revelries today which were described as '*a constant whirl of amusement, which too often degenerates into debauchery*'.

© The port of Abbotsbury, near Weymouth in Dorset, still holds its **Garland Day** today, in spite of the demise of the fishing industry. A garland was made for each boat in the fleet, and was paraded through the streets before being blessed and taken to the vessels. The fishermen then set sail and dumped the blooms into the briny, a donation to the local sea god. This marked the opening of the fishing season, and there were dances and games on the beach to celebrate. But in spite of this annual appease-ment of the sea, the mackerel stocks eventually dried up, and the last boat carried the last fishing garland out many years ago. The custom as it survives is something of a ghost, but with none of the sombre mood of a wake. Large garlands on wire frames are still taken through the streets, and are then left on the town's war memorial, or placed on graves at the church. In recent years a garland of wild flowers has sometimes been thrown into the sea at the end of the day – a revival of the old custom.

14th May
Pag Rag Day

Pag Up Your Troubles and Leave Your Old Kit Back

Two centuries before hypochondriacs added mad cow disease to their daily check-list, the nation was gripped by the fear that many people might suddenly become bovine. It was on this day in 1796 that Edward Jenner first used the milder **cowpox** as a vaccine against the killer disease smallpox. Sceptics and oppo-nents spread stories that everyone inoculated would turn into cows, and newspaper reports appeared claiming that several of Jenner's vaccinated patients had begun running around on all fours and mooing. The tales were pure fantasy: Jenner's treatment revolutionised medicine, and went a long way towards eradi-cating the previously incurable smallpox.

Today was **Pag Rag Day**, the time to 'pag' belongings onto back or cart and move on to the next job, once a routine annual procedure for many unattached agricultural labourers. But one Lancashire couple were forced to flit due to the attentions of their resident **boggart**. The boggart – a mischievous spirit – had become increasingly noxious, turning the milk sour, undoing all the day's work, making their lives a misery. So, in spite of being old and settled, the couple pagged their rags on to the cart. They were leaving by the back road when one of their neighbours shouted: '*You're flitting then?*' '*Aye, we're flitting*', came the reply; but not from the old couple. The words had issued from one of the milk-churns on the back of the cart, where the boggart had settled down for the journey. The couple turned the cart round, deciding that if they could not be rid of their tormentor, they might as well suffer on home ground.

A family get-together usually followed a pag-ragging as workers were able to snatch a few days' holiday in between residences. But a flitter would usually leave his or her cat behind, as it is very **unlucky to flit a cat**. If the oversentimental could not possibly forsake Tiddles, then superstition did offer one drastic alternative. The poor animal could be bundled into the new home and left in an oven over-night, its feet covered in butter. This reliable method shed much of the bad luck, and stopped the cat from running away in the morning.

Several **folk songs** are set on May 14th. The uncertificated action of *The Bonny Black Hare* takes place on this date. Superficially about a hunt for hares, anyone with a cortex will soon realise that it is more about rabbit-like beha-viour than anything to do with hares. The hunter soon closes on the burrow of his quarry and gets out his double-barrelled euphemisms:

> *I laid this girl down with her face to the sky,*
> *I took out my ramrod and bullets likewise,*
> *I said 'lock your legs round me, dig in with*
>   *your heels,*
> *For the closer we get, love, the better it feels.*

The bout comes to an end when the man declares '*my ramrod is limp and I cannot fire on*'; but they promise to do it all over again on the following day.

May 14th is also the date in the song *Cod Banging*. But delete images of a guilty-looking Captain Birdseye being led from dock to dock: this is no fishy version of *The Bonny Black*

Hare. Cod-banging simply means sailing on the type of trawler known as a cod-banger.

15th May
St Dympna's Day

Cock Tales

St Dympna was the daughter of a 6th-century Celtic king who tragically lost his wife. Even more tragically, he decided that Dympna looked just like her mother, and would therefore make a perfect substitute. Dympna had to flee from his lusty advances, and accompanied by her chaplain St Gerebernus she ended up in Antwerp. The King pursued the pair, and managed to trace them by keeping tabs on the flow of spent British coins which they left in their wake. When confronted, Dympna and Gerebernus refused to return home. The King killed them both. A shrine later appeared at Gheel in Belgium, dedicated to the martyrs. Many incidents of epilepsy and mental disorders being miraculously cured were credited to St Dympna, and she became patron saint of the insane. This in turn led to Gheel becoming a world centre for treating the mentally ill, a role that it has maintained from medieval times to the present day.

On this day in 1805 advertising paid off and a large crowd turned 'out for a **cockfight** '*Between the Gentlemen of Lincolnshire and Gentlemen of Yorkshire*' at Thorganby in Lincolnshire. It was not the gentlemen who vied for eminence, though, but their aggressive chickens. Champion birds achieved fame on a par with successful racehorses today. The commonly staged fight to the death between several birds is the origin of the phrase **battle royal**.

Cock-fighting was outlawed in 1835; but that just drove the contests underground, and there are still regular, illegal cockfights to this day. In 1841 *The Stamford Mercury* was lamenting: '*We regret to learn that, notwithstanding the progress of knowledge and refinement, and all which poets and moralists have written, this barbarous and inhuman practice is patronised by names in other respect reputable . . . How can well-disposed parents allow their youth to be seduced to witness scenes which must blunt their moral sensibilities?*'

One of the most voiciferous supporters of cock-fighting was a 19th-century **vicar of Wednesbury** north of Birmingham. He fol-

lowed the contests assiduously. He even encouraged fights to take place in his own churchyard so that he could watch them through the church window during services. His fanaticism extended to installing a chicken-shaped lectern in Wednesbury church, in place of the commoner eagle. It can still be seen there. For more on cock-fighting see Shrove Tuesday.

John Smale came to regret having **sold his wife**, a horse, and some 'chattels' to Edward Salter in October 1810 for the sum of four pounds and 10 shillings. On May 15th the next year, Smale applied to Plymouth magistrates to get his wife back, and Salter was reluctantly forced to part with the much-coveted Mrs Smale.

In 1476 Edward IV granted Stow-on-the-Wold in Gloucestershire a charter allowing it to hold two annual **fairs**, one on May 12th, one on October 24th. Half a millenium later, both still take place – with the May gatherings being by far the biggest – although they are now held 'sometime around' these dates. What started as sheep fairs are now get-togethers for gypsies and travellers, making them less than popular with some residents of Stow. But the florid spectacle of the horse-trading and sheer scale of the fairs still attract onlookers from across the county, and country.

16th May

Luck be a French Lady Tonight

Today in 1568 Mary Queen of Scots arrived at Workington Hall in Cumbria. It was her first day of exile in England, and the only one spent as a free woman – on the next day she was arrested, and for the next 19 years she effectively lived as a prisoner of the English crown. In gratitude for the brief burst of hospitality bestowed by the Hall, Mary gave its owner, Sir Henry 'Galloping Harry' Curwen, a glass bowl. This gift became known as the **Luck of Workington**, as it was believed that if it was ever broken or stolen, the Hall would be destroyed.

Galloping Harry, having kept the Luck and the Hall safe from harm, was waylaid on his deathbed. As he lay dying, he was savagely set upon by a visiting French lady and her young maid. They dragged him from between the sheets, bounced him downstairs, and hid him in one of the rooms while they filled their bags with the family's treasure. Their sacks a-jingle with spoons and jewels, the thieves set sail from Workington Harbour.

☦ Half a century passed before anything more was heard about the robbery. But a haggard old woman arrived at Workington Hall one day. It was the maid, gnawed away by guilt and full of apologies. She revealed that the French lady had drowned just weeks after the theft when their boat was wrecked off the Scilly Isles. For the next 49 years and 11 months, the maid had lived with her shame over the crime that she had helped to commit. But now she was close to death, and had come back to beg forgiveness. Having unburdened her conscience, the maid then swiftly expired. But Galloping Harry was not assuaged by these apologies, and he haunts the Hall to this day. His head can sometimes be heard as it bumps downstairs, echoing the GBH committed on the night of the robbery. Many visitors have claimed to 'feel' the presence of the ghost.

🏚 The Hall is now derelict, having lost the last of its luck in 1923. In the 1960s the council tried to smarten it up a bit, but unfortunately they ran out of money. The Luck can still be seen though, on Belle Isle, Windermere, Cumbria. For another example of the 'Luck' tradition of north-west England, see the Luck of Edenhall on March 20th.

In May 'the changing of the moon' – when the sky is empty just before the new moon begins waxing – was a traditional time for self-proclaimed wizards to hold a **Toad Fair**. These were unorthodox alfresco surgeries for the afflicted. The patient would have a freshly decapitated toad dropped down the inside of their vest. If they were in any way nauseated or adversely affected by its death throes, they were doomed. A stiff upper lip meant survival and speedy recovery. Stalbridge in Dorset still held its annual Toad Fair as late as last century. One of their resident wizard's favourite remedies was to pluck the legs from toads and sell them as a cure for scrofula and the evil eye.

17th May
St Madron's Day

Mayor or Less

In 14th-century Sussex the **Earl de Warrenne** was saved from death by a timely prayer. He had lost a duel and was about to be run through by Lord Pevensey; but the Earl's wife invoked St Nicholas, and the merciful saint deflected the death blow. The miracle had its smallprint, however. As a sign of gratitude, the de Warrennes had to send their first-born son to distant Byzantium to lay the Belt of St Nicholas on the tomb of the Blessed Virgin there. The son could only wed after this pilgrimage.

Decades passed and the family forgot their promises. Their oldest son, **Lord Manfred**, fell in love with Lady Edona and was married on May 17th, exactly 21 years after divine intervention had saved his father. Half-way through the wedding feast an uninvited wind swept icily through the hall, blowing out the fire and candles. In a manner not dissimilar to the biblical Belshazzar's Feast, the assembled guests were treated to a slide-show vision depicting the de Warrenne-Pevensey bout, the saint's intervention, and the neglected Belt-and-Virgin pilgrimage. Lord Manfred was moved: abandoning his new wife, he called for his ship and immediately set off in the vague direction of Byzantium.

One year later, on May 17th, Lord Manfred's returning ship was spied off Worthing Point, and the wedding party took to the clifftops to welcome the hero home. But as they watched, a huge rock materialised in the water: the ship struck it and capsized. Edona collapsed and died on the spot, and Earl de Warrenne was said never to have smiled again. He devoted his remaining energies to a belated gesture of remorse, building a church to St Nicholas near the spot where Edona died, in what is now central Brighton, East Sussex.

☦ 🏚 Lord Manfred re-enacts his shipwreck every year at midnight on May 17th, off the coast near the church. The site of Edona's grave is marked by a stone slab. The slab is also said to mark the grave of a knight, who was buried along with his horse, both in full armour. Whenever the moon is full, the horse leaves the tomb for a quick trot around the graveyard.

© This is St **Madron's Day**, and all through May his well at Madron near Penzance in Cornwall offers insights into the future. Ask the longevity question, and it will undergo a series of bubblings to reveal your remaining number of years amongst the living. It can also cure lunatics and sickly children, who are supposed to pray in the now-ruined large chapel, and sleep all night on the grassy area called St Madron's Bed. Alternatively, there is a hawthorn nearby, upon which rags from the patient's clothing can be tied. The reputation of the well rests on the fact that it cured John Trelille in 1640. He had been crippled in a farming accident 16 years previously. After taking the waters he was fit enough to join the army. Ironically, he was soon killed in service.

© At High Wycombe in Buckinghamshire on the third Thursday in May, it is time for **weighing the dignitaries**. The mayor and his cronies suffer the ignominy of being paraded through the town, and ceremonially weighed in front of a crowd. The town-crier calls out the weights. If an official has shed a few pounds during his or her year of office, it is taken as a sign that he or she has toiled hard, and everyone cheers. Should they have gained weight, there are jeers and a loss of dignitary dignity.

18th May

Red Barn at Night – Hangman's Delight

It became the most celebrated murder of its time. Today in 1827 **Maria Marten** and her lover William Corder headed to what was to be their last tryst, at the **Red Barn** at Polstead in Suffolk. Corder was the son of a rich farmer, and had told Maria that he would marry her in Ipswich. But at the barn either they had some sort of fight, or Corder carried out a brutal, premeditated killing. He shot Maria and buried the body on the spot. The rendezvous had been kept in secret, as both sets of parents disapproved of the match. Consequently no one knew where the girl had gone, and Corder parried everyone's enquiries by saying that he had married Maria, and that she was living with him in London.

It was not so improbable that if she had married against her parents' wishes, Maria would choose to sever contacts with them, and so Corder's story survived unchallenged for over 11 months. But then Maria's stepmother began to dream that the girl was dead, murdered by Corder and buried in the Red Barn. She had the dream three times; and realising that all was not well, she sent her husband to investigate. As the subsequent bestselling ballad put it:

She sent her father to the spot, and he the ground did thrust,
And there he found his daughter a-mingling with the dust.

Once the body was recovered, Corder's story collapsed. He was found guilty of murder, and was hanged. The trial had dominated the headlines, and Red Barn mania gripped the country. A simple folk song was not enough to satisfy the passion for Corder memorabilia: the floor of the barn was ripped up and the pieces were taken away as souvenirs; and Corder's hanging-rope was sold by the inch after the event. The man had pleased the crowd by putting on a gruesome show: the rope was badly knotted, and he found it hard to die, writhing and swinging for several seconds before the hangman pulled on his legs to hurry things along.

⬜ William Corder's skin was used to bind a copy of the court proceedings – a grisly relic which can still be seen in Moyses Hall Museum, Bury St Edmunds, Suffolk.

© On the Wednesday nearest the 18th, Newbiggin-by-the-Sea, near Morpeth in Northumberland, **Beats the Bounds**. It is claimed that the ceremony originated in 1235, and its modern form features a walk around the old common on Newbiggin Moor. There is also a special treat in store for any new freeholder in the town. They are taken to the moor's **Dunting Stone**, where they are well and truly *dunted*. Birthday-victims in many a playground down the years will know all about this. Dunting is the same as the bumps. The freeholder is bounced upon the stone three times.

© On the Sunday nearest the 16th there is a blessing ceremony and small fair at the Church of St Mary and St Walstan in **Bawburgh**, Norfolk, the modern form of an ancient observance – see May 30th for more on Walstan and his well.

19th May
St Dunstan's Day

Old Nick's Nicked Nose

Before he was converted by St Alphege, **St Dunstan**, destined to become Archbishop of Canterbury, was said to have been a nasty piece of work, dabbling in black magic and devil-worship (see tomorrow for a possible example). Alternatively, he was a travelling minstrel. Either way, after embracing Christianity he traded songs for tongs, or evil for anvil, to become a holy blacksmith in 10th-century Mayfield, East Sussex.

He was so succeessful as a preacher that his alleged former associate, Satan, paid him a visit. Disguised as a beautiful woman, the Devil flirted while Dunstan worked away at his forge. Satan did not succeed in fanning the saint's own flames – Dunstan spotted a tell-tale hoof beneath the skirts of his visitor. In one smooth action, he picked up his red-hot tongs and grabbed Satan by the nose. Screaming with pain, the Devil flew north to Tunbridge Wells to douse his smouldering nose in its waters; which is why, to this day, they are tinged red and smell of sulphur. The tongs became Dunstan's symbol, and the convent of the Holy Child Jesus at Mayfield claims to have the pair which put Satan's nose out of joint.

Eternal, infernal mug as he is, Satan later revisited Dunstan to have his hooves shod. Dunstan complied, but drove a nail deep into the satanic foot. The Devil was released from his agonies only after promising never to tamper wherever a horseshoe was nailed up. Horseshoes have been symbols of good luck ever since.

When hanging up lucky **horse-shoes**, they must be pinned with the ends upwards, otherwise the luck drains away and Satan can be a house guest again. The shoes' association with good luck actually predates the Dunstan legend. They are potent on two accounts: being shaped like the crescent moon, and being made of iron, which averts the evil influence of faeries and witches.

✝ **Anne Boleyn** was executed on this day in 1536, and she appears as a **ghost** at many venues. She haunts Marwell Hall in Owslebury, near Eastleigh in Hampshire, supposedly to annoy her fellow ghost and rival-in-love, Jane Seymour, who lived at the Hall. The Tower of London boasts regular year-round wanderings – in 1933 a sentry fled after attempting to bayonet Anne and seeing his blade pass harmlessly through her body. On May 19th every year at her alleged birth place – Blickling Hall, near Cromer in Norfolk – Anne appears in classic head-in-lap pose, accompanied by a coach with headless driver and horses. Hever Castle, near Tonbridge in Kent, also has a ghostly Anne, backing up its counter-claim to be her birthplace.

In life, the thousand-day Queen had many detractors. Charges of being aloof gave way to accusations of witchcraft and an 'unnatural' interest in women. Henry VIII instigated the entire Reformation in 1533 while putting the latter theory to the test. Their first child was a girl – later to become Elizabeth I – and their second was still-born. Henry became convinced that their marriage was damned, and trumped-up charges of incest, rather than lesbianism, led Anne to the executioner's block.

✝ The **ghost of Sir Thomas Boleyn**, Anne's father, also makes its annual appearance tonight. Cursed by Henry VIII for landing him with Anne, Sir Thomas must race on horseback around Caister Castle, near Great Yarmouth in Norfolk, crossing 40 bridges between midnight and cock-crow, pursued by a shrieking pack of demon dogs.

20th May
Frankinmas/
St Ethelbert's Day

The Quality of Mercia is Strange

Plucky King of East Anglia and saint-in-waiting Ethelbert rode to see his intended bride in 794. The lucky girl was Ælfrith, daughter of King Offa of Mercia. Ethelbert was not a superstitious man, and on his way to Offa's Sutton Walls palace, at Marden near Hereford, he ignored several omens which would have made other, wiser, men turn back. The earth shook, the sun went black, and he had a vision in which his bridal bed was destroyed while his mother wept tears of blood. But Ethelbert rode on to his doom. On the eve of the wedding his head was lopped off at the instigation of Offa and his wife Cynefrith, not because they disapproved of Ethelbert, but because they were jealous of the joy which the marriage would bring to their daughter.

🔲 Ethelbert's body was quickly dumped in an unmarked grave; but phantom lights appeared, hovering above it. So the corpse was dug up and reinterred at another secret site. More heavenly luminescence marked the spot. Offa recognised that he was out of his league, and went to Rome to beg the Pope for forgiveness. It was decided that Offa should again exhume Ethelbert and build a shrine for him at Hereford. This time when the saint's body was unearthed, a well appeared – it is now one of the few wells to be found inside a church, at Marden. On its way to Hereford, the body touched the ground briefly, and up sprang what became known as St Ethelbert's Well, the site of which is still visible at Castle Green in Hereford. The shrine that Offa erected to Ethelbert in 795 became the site of Hereford Cathedral, which is dedicated to the saint. Fragments of the shrine survive in the Cathedral, which also has a chained library containing a 1290 map of the known, flat, world.

☕ The 19th to the 21st of May are **Frankinmas**, a period in which furtive frost descends and ruins apple blossoms. Unlike other people who have been granted the coveted '-mas' suffix, Frankan was no saint. He may even have been quite the reverse. Frankan ran a brewery, and to help business boom he entered into a pact with the Devil. He exchanged his soul for a three-day frost which wrecked that year's apples, ruining the rival cider industry. It seems likely that cider-makers' anti-brewer propaganda is the source of one twist in this tale – their version has the Devil agreeing to the bargain only on condition that the brewer waters down his beer thenceforth.

There are other variants – in one, Frankan is not a brewer of beer, but a cider and perry maker who appeals to Satan to give him an extra fine crop. God overhears the blasphemous request and blights all the apple and pear trees. In another, Frankan – or Frankum – is the Devil himself, and so needed no pact. In the most outlandish version of them all, it is St Dunstan who sells his soul to the Devil in order to blight the apple crop with frost on these three days, and so allow his own beer-making interests to prosper. For a more sanctified biography of Dunstan, see yesterday, his feast day.

© **Throwing the Kitchels** takes place at Harwich in Essex on the third Thursday in May. After the new mayor has been installed, he goes to the Guildhall at noon and throws small buns to the crowd. 'Kechel' is an old word for cakes, and they are said to have been thrown at Harwich since the early 17th century. During wartime bread-rationing, the mayor handed out apples, telling the recipients to think of them as cakes.

21st May
St Collen's Day

Collen Occupants of Under-Planet Faerie Craft

St Collen lived in a cell at the foot of Glastonbury Tor in the 7th century. His nearest neighbours were the faeries who lived inside the hollow hill. Gwyn ap Nudd, the **King of the Faeries**, invited Collen to visit his kingdom, but the saint declined, aware that most visitors never made it back. So the King sent another invite, and again the saint politely turned it down. The King then showed his true colours by accompanying the third invite with threats of physical violence in the event of further refusals. So Collen had no choice but to go, and like all good guests he took a bottle – in this case a small phial of holy water.

Collen entered the faerie kingdom through a gateway on top of the Tor, and the King received him courteously, inviting him to try some of the food. Collen knew about faeries and their illusions, and denounced the glorious spread as nothing but withered leaves transformed by magic. He uncorked his phial, and doused the feasting hall with holy water. It all vanished in a flash, and Collen was alone on the Tor.

Flushed with success, St Collen went on to slay a female giant at Llangollen in Clwyd, founding a church there afterwards – the name means 'church of Collen'. He is also remembered in the town of Colan in Cornwall. The Glastonbury legend casts him as an important pagan-bashing saint, but it is a reworking of older, Celtic myths, in which the Tor was identified as a gateway to Annwn, the Celtic land of the dead. Its ruler, the Lord of the Dead, was Gwyn, son of the mighty Nudd. Nudd, also known as Nodons, was a Celtic god, analagous to the Roman Neptune. More recently, some wild-eyed new-agers have claimed that the Tor's domed shape derives from the giant UFO parked underneath it.

◉ **Henry VI** was only eight months old at the time of his accession. He was imprisoned, deposed twice, and he suffered from a mental disorder, remaining a political pawn throughout his life. His only consolations are the trilogy of plays written by Shakespeare, and the private **Lilies and Roses Ceremony**, still held today at the Oratory in Wakefields Tower at the Tower of London, where the King was probably murdered on this day in 1471, aged

50. Euphemistic contemporary reports say that he passed away out of '*pure displeasure and melancholy*'.

Henry founded Eton College in Berkshire, and King's College, Cambridge. Both send representatives to the ceremony, which includes one of Henry's self-penned prayers. Flowers are laid at a marble slab, the traditional site of Henry's death. Eton brings bunches of lilies bound with pale blue silk, and King's provides the roses, bound with purple ribbon. The flowers are left there for 24 hours and then burned.

▥ The service itself is not open to the public, but during the rest of the year visitors to the Tower can see the marble slab, which marks where Henry was at prayer when the killers burst in. For more on Henry VI see, by coincidence, tomorrow.

Culmstock in Devon used to hold its **May fair** today. It was all very touch and go on the **apple** front in this cider-making part of the world:

Till Culmstock Fair be come and gone,
There mid be apples and there mid be none.

There were also the dangers of Frankinmas and its frosts, as dealt with yesterday.

22nd May

Well Done Satan

✟ Today in 1455 the **Battle of St Albans** marked the start of 30 years of war in England. The Yorkists marched in and abducted the hapless Lancastrian king, **Henry VI**. The struggle for the English crown that followed took several centuries to be given a catchy title, but Sir Walter Scott came up with one that stuck – The Wars of the Roses. Some 120 soldiers were killed in the fighting at St Albans, and each May 22nd the old buildings there ring out with the clamour of war.

Henry VI's mental instability and disastrous military record (he was like his father Henry V, only in reverse – losing most of France by the end of his reign) did not prevent him from becoming a cult figure after his death. He was reputed to have been responsible for 150 miracles, and his corpse bled twice – sure signs of a saint-designate. The campaign to have him canonised was well on course when

Henry VIII scuppered everything by breaking away from the Church of Rome.

✟ St Albans has several other slices of supernature. Medieval monks from the Abbey can be heard chanting at Battlefield House in Chequers Street. This building is also haunted by notorious witch, **Mother Haggy**. At first a helpful healer, in old age she became malevolent, zipping through the daytime streets on her broomstick, and using a kettle to sail across the river.

It was widely reported that early in the 17th century **the Devil** came to sample St Albans' ales. He showed up in the cellar of a local pub, and was promptly killed by the innkeeper. A practical man, the publican made a meal of his achievement, and amid much publicity served up Satan as the main course on that night's menu.

▥ At Perranarworthal near Falmouth in Cornwall, there is a large stone called the **Cornish Pebble**, balanced on two other rocks. In May if you crawl round the stone and then under it, your sciatica and rheumatism will be cured.

☙ May is rich in proverbial advice. It is by far the best time to see **bees**:

A swarm of bees in May is worth a load of hay;
A swarm of bees in June is worth a silver spoon;
A swarm of bees in July is not worth a fly.

Moving from bees to **fish**:

The haddocks are good
When dipped in May flood.

But too much rain makes the farmers behave in peculiar way:

Many thunderstorms in May
And the farmer sings 'hey hey!'

There is an alternative to the well-known '*cast not a clout 'til May be out*':

Keep buttoned to the chin till May be out.

And finally, a great trick with disappearing sheep:

Shear your sheep in May
And shear them all away.

23rd May

The Importance of Banning Earnest

© **Hiring Fairs** such as the one at **Knighton** in Powys – which in its modern stock-and-pleasure-fair guise takes place in the third week of May – came under concerted attack last century. Knighton followed the common Hiring Fair and Mop Fair format. People lined up with symbols of their trade, and would-be employers took them for free drinks in the local pub in the hope of employing them at a reduced rate afterwards. They would then hand over a couple of shillings '**earnest money**' to seal the deal.

Some took the advance and did a runner. That was the downside for the farmer. Those who took the work had a rougher deal as a rule. The farmer effectively owned the hirelings for the season: he could feed them in whatever manner he saw fit and dismiss them without notice. There are tales of bountiful households offering slap-up meals to the men and women of the farm; but more often than not the food was meagre, and sometimes downright beggarly in its size and quality.

But it was not the plight of the worker that most moralists attacked; although in the 18th century Thomas Paine did bring the slave-like nature of such mass employment to national attention. What raised the majority of hackles was the fact that the combination of fair, something to celebrate, and upfront earnest money, was a formula that reliably produced scenes of excessive drinking. Last century, even at top price, two shillings could buy a gallon of beer. One commentator noted: '*Liberty without salutary restraints will almost certainly degenerate into licentiousness.*' There was a call for proper registration of workers, with contracts of employment to eliminate the need for earnest money. This lobby was successful, and the hiring fair was steadily denuded of importance and finally phased out in favour of the folklorically barren Job Centre.

© **May 23rd** was **Mayoring Day** at Rye in East Sussex: the festival now takes place on a convenient date chosen by the mayor, usually the early or late May Bank Holiday. After electing a new mayor, there is a short public service at St Mary's church, and at 11.00 am the mayor throws £20 in hot pennies from the upper floor of the town hall. Only the first few pounds-worth are heated in an oven, and these days it is no longer fishermen who scramble for the coins, but children.

Mayors used to be the nucleus of many rumbustious town feasts. But they were responsible for taming the **Mould Washing** at Grimsby in Humberside. The moulds were the ones used to make bricks, and they were – metaphorically – washed when the brick-makers gathered for their annual drinking marathon, in the third week of May. The colourful celebrations were once neatly summed up as '*a disorderly carouse of strong beer . . . ending in quarrels and bloodshed*'. But in 1840 Grimsby's mayor decided to tone down the festivities and sober up the participants. From then on, beer was off the agenda, and the bricklayers were given flour as a curious substitute.

A report on that year's event exalted an evening '*spent in joy and harmony, and in social conversation instead of quarrelling, and of those who were not already teetotallers, fifteen signed the pledge*'. Such zeal in the face of custom leaves one hoping that some of the men managed to sneak away for a few pints before closing time. Reduced to an alcohol-free tea-party, the once vibrant tradition of mould washing stood no chance of survival, and passed away peacefully late last century.

24th May

Bye-Bye Byzant

Today in 1757 at Arlingham near Gloucester, the occupants of **Court House** had their social gathering interrupted by an approaching funeral party. They rushed out to meet the sombre procession, but there was no one there. Exactly 12 months later the last heir to the Court House estate, John Yate, died; as prophesied by the ghostly cortege.

♱ The **ghost** at Hazel Cottage – at Weare Giffard, near Great Torrington in Devon – was, in life, the girlfriend of William Dillon. He murdered her there, late in May, 1887. Attempting suicide afterwards, Dillon botched the job. His slit throat festered for 15 days before the guilt-ridden lunatic died, and it is surprising that with such a demise he has not qualified for his own phantom. But there are other local ghosts to keep wraith-watchers happy. At Weare Giffard Hall Sir Walter Giffard, who died in 1243, still wanders abroad. And there is also a rather alarming spirit at the Hall which challenges all comers with the words '*Get you gone!*'

Prior to 1830, at an agreed date in May – usually the Monday before Ascension Day – Shaftesbury in Dorset held its **Byzant Ceremony**. Shaftesbury has always been extremely picturesque, but for centuries it had one huge problem: no water supply to call its own. The best way around this dilemma was to siphon off some of that supplied by the Enmore Green wells at nearby Motcombe. The deal which Shaftesbury struck with Motcombe was formally renewed every year, by means of the Byzant (also known as Bezant) ceremony.

A procession descended from Shaftesbury headed by an official carrying a decorated calf's head with a purse of money in its mouth. Next in line came a man carrying the Prize Byzant itself – a bulbous, rococo mace, resplendent in gold, jewels and peacocks' feathers. The mayor and his team were next, with the townsfolk bringing up the rear. They danced and sang their way to Enmore Green, where they gave Motcombe's bailiff the head and purse, the Byzant, some bread, some beer, and a pair of laced gloves. The bailiff then handed back the Byzant, its function in the ceremony being purely symbolic, and the visitors trudged up-hill back to Shaftesbury, leaving Motcombe's merrymakers to carry on with the singing and dancing.

⚅ Without this annual ritual Motcombe could, theoretically, refuse to give up its water. The enemy of the piece is the artesian well sunk at Shaftesbury in 1830, killing the ceremony dead. The last Prize Byzant can still be seen in Shaftesbury's Local History Museum.

The word 'byzant' seems to derive from the old coin of the same name – not from *Byzantine* as in 'fiendishly complicated', which might seem more appropriate. Kings would present a bezant at religious festivals or when taking Mass, and the coins were often replaced with a symbolic gift, still retaining the name 'byzant'.

25th May
St Aldhelm's Day

Ash-Shrew! – Bless You

Founder of Malmesbury Abbey, and Bishop of Sherbourne in Dorset, **St Aldhelm** was the first great scholar to write in English as well as Latin. Aldhelm's capacity for generating the written word was limitless, and his outpourings often had nothing to do with religion – he loved puns, riddles and word-games. He often wrote vast tracts which were so involved that no-one else could decipher his meanings. He was also a prolific singer/songwriter: he composed songs and then sang them in public, his vision – or even Eurovision – being to '*win men's ears, and then their souls*'. Aldhelm was said to be the first Englishman to champion the cause of poetry, and he lured his congregations into church with evocative harp ditties.

Sadly, Aldhelm's writings, songs, hymns and word-play, are all lost, apart from a Latin poem in praise of maidens and a treatise on virginity which he wrote for some nuns. He died at Doulting near Shepton Mallet in Somerset in 709, and between there and his burial place at Malmesbury in Wiltshire, crosses were erected at seven mile intervals on the funeral journey. His estates included the Dorset coastal area called St Alban's Head: the name is, in fact, a corruption of *St Aldhelm's Head*.

Aldhelm was a legendarily tidy man. Once during Mass, his servant casually slung his cloak to the ground. Aldhelm calmly picked it up and hung it from a sunbeam. He also performed a Joseph of Arimathea-style miracle at Bishopstrow in Wiltshire. He thrust his ash staff into the ground, where it took root and bloomed; and ever since then ash has also been known as **bishop's tree.**

With or without Saint Aldhelm, **ash** was held to be a great curative for rickets or hernias, although each tree can only effect one cure in its lifetime. Children suffering from either ailment should be passed through a large slit freshly carved in the trunk of a sapling. The child must be naked, and has to go through from east to west, three times, manhandled by a boy and a girl while the dew is still lying on the grass. The cleft should then be sealed with clay, and as the tree's wound heals, so will the ills of the child.

To cure animals using the ash requires the services of a **shrew**. Once captured – no mean feat in itself – the shrew must be sealed into a hole in the tree; and as the poor rodent dies and the hole heals over, the afflicted animal will be cured. Illness in livestock was often attributable to shrews in the first place: they were thought to blight animals by running over their backs while they were resting. So their involvement in this treatment is from the hair-of-the-dog school of medicine. The wood from such a **shrew ash** then has a beneficial power. It can be used to protect house and home from malign magic, and to cure a shrewed beast, without having to repeat the shrew-sealing ritual all over again. For a less powerful but kinder-to-shrews remedy, bury a horseshoe under the ash instead, and this will offset illness. To cure toothache, simply sit under an ash and cut your toenails.

In 1606 at Brampton in Lincolnshire, an ash became renowned for its moaning and muttering. It was clear to all who listened that it was a **talking tree**; but exactly what it was trying to say remained unclear. Locals decided that if the ash would only speak up, or if they could get closer to the sound, then they would be able to catch its drift. So a hole was drilled into its trunk; but even though the tree continued to babble on incomprehensibly, would-be translators were still foxed.

26th May
St Augustine's Day

Warring Gods and Wearing Cod

St Augustine came to England in 596, a monk on a mission. Pope Gregory had sent him here with the formidable task of converting the country to Christianity. After winning round King Ethelbert of Kent (see February 25th), the first English cathedral was erected at Canterbury in 601, and Augustine became its first Archbishop. He realised from the onset that rivalling the sacred haunts of the natives was likely to be less effective than incorporating their ancient shrines and customs into Christian buildings and beliefs. So Augustine's chief policy was to reconsecrate pagan sites and transform their old altars into Christian ones, often with little more structural alteration than a splash of holy water and a swift blessing. God ousted Woden, backed up by an army of saints – each with their own stories and attributes, making them every bit the equal of the pagan deities that they had to displace.

St Augustine took his mission far beyond Kent. He is said to have preached at Long Compton, near Chipping Norton in Warwickshire, in 604. During the service he warned that no excommunicated man could attend Mass. This news was more pulse-quickening than even Augustine could have realised – as he reached his conclusion, a recently buried man rose from the dead and vacated the churchyard. An ancient effigy in the church at Long Compton is said to represent St Augustine.

At either Strood or Rochester in Kent,

unrepentent pagans were amused by this new religion which made so much of fish – marketing men had yet to latch on to the salespotential of the crucifix, and were still relying on fish-imagery. During an evangelical visit from Augustine, the townsfolk hurled fish offal at him and pinned fish-tails to their shirts. Rather than turn the other cheek, Augustine cursed the town, saying that for evermore their children would be born with tails. There is another version of this yarn from Cerne Abbas in Dorset, where ox-tails are used instead. The legend is common, not just limited to Augustine. But it is curious among stories involving senior Christian saints in that the curse clearly had no physical effect, although in Kent 'fish-tailed' remains a term of abuse.

When Augustine came to preach to the parched population of Elham Valley, north of Folkestone in Kent, he arrived during a local crisis. A severe drought had dragged on despite numerous supplications to the pagan deities. It appeared that the old gods heard these pleas, but were too lazy to do anything. Augustine promised that *his* God was more understanding, and he instantly caused a spring to bubble forth. The impressionable locals were converted at once, much to the chagrin of the old gods. They belatedly roused themselves to action, and conjured a storm which blocked the stream at its source. Again it was their former flock who suffered. Augustine intervened for a second time, and commanded the Nailbourne stream to unblock and flow once every seven years so that the locals would not take it – and therefore God – for granted. Ever since, the **Nailbourne stream** at Elham Valley has flowed only one year in every seven.

27th May
St Bede's Day

The Veneer-able Bede

The **Venerable Bede** scarcely put a foot wrong. Both devout and clever, he churned out learned tomes until his death in 735, which came with the textbook last words '*Glory be to the Father, the Son and the Holy Ghost*'. After his passing, his friends all agreed that the candle of the church had been extinguished. The first English historian, his *Ecclesiastical History* was a record of the early British holy men and women's lives, an exhaustive set of biographies. It is, however, a little skimpy on its natural history. His description of the island's wildlife sums up without the burden of detail: *'There are many land and sea birds of various species, and it is famous for its plentiful springs and rivers abounding in fish.'*

For such a holy man, Bede's legendary residue is oddly pagan. His oaken chair at St Paul's in Jarrow, Tyne and Wear, has strong fertility links. Unmarried girls used to put a splinter of the wood under their pillows in order to dream of future husbands. Once the partner had coalesced from dream to wedded reality, the self-same Bede-chips steeped in water gave relief from labour pangs when swallowed. And the newly-married would not leave the church without sitting on the chair, as this ensured fertile loins. The chair is still there for all to see at St Paul's, but taking chippings is now actively discouraged. Bede's venerated relics are in the Galilee Chapel at Durham Cathedral.

© On the Saturday nearest Oak Apple Day, May 29th, the Hearts of Oak Friendly Society at Fownhope, near Hereford, has its annual club walk, with members carrying staffs which are decorated with oak-apples. On the same day there is similar club-footing at Langport and Huish Episcopi, near Taunton in Somerset. For more on club walks and the accompanying club feasts, see Whit Friday and Saturday.

Using various roads, fields and river boundaries, people with maps and time on their hands have managed to trace the outline of a dog on to the landscape around Langport, calling it The Great Dog of Langport. This 'explains' a line in an old local wassailers' rhyme: *'The Black Dog of Langport have a-burned off his tail.'* However obscurely, this is also thought to refer to the routing of the Vikings on this spot by King Alfred in 878. As well as the Great Dog, an entire join-the-dots zodiac, 30 miles in circumference, has been 'discovered' in the features around nearby Glastonbury. At the site of the dog's tail is the village of Wagg, which has been taken as irrefutable evidence that these grand designs are the work of old gods or aliens; though they are obviously lousy at free-hand drawing. Even more desperately, since the outline which dimly resembles Aries the ram passes through Ivythorn Hill, the old rhyme/song with the line *'little lambs eat ivy'* has been dragged in as evidence that the shape is not just the results of an overactive imagina-

tion. What is more, it doubles as the sacrificial lamb of Christian imagery; and the entire zodiac is said to represent King Arthur's court and table. Wow! All myths, legends and religions starring together on one stage for the first time.

28th May

Not Throwing the Baby Out with the Bathwater

On this day in 1881 Worcester underwent a three-pronged heavenly assault. First came the hail, ripping all the leaves from the trees. Rain was next, flooding fields around the town. Finally the clouds delivered bucketful after bucketful of periwinkles – not the plants, but the sea-snail variety – which were either buried on impact, or bounced like ricocheting bullets from the ground. A few pebbles joined them in this torrent, and a lone hermit crab also fell on the town – which is 70 miles from the nearest seashore.

© The last weekend of the month hosts the Ancient Scorton Silver Arrow tournament, at a moveable location in Yorkshire. It is organised by the oldest sports club in Britain, with the first shoot-out taking place in 1673 at Scorton, North Yorkshire. Would-be Robin Hoods compete for prizes including the Silver Arrow, a silver spoon, and a bowl. Over the years, the bows have become more sophisticated, though there is still a nostalgic contingent of old long-bows to be seen: they compete for a separate prize or two. Old Scorton contestants take a dim view of the many participants who merely fire an arrow from their fancy modern bows and then retire to the pub until the next shoot. The winner of the main event – the one who first hits a 2-inch disc placed over the gold bull's-eye – becomes the Captain and has the onus of organising next year's tournament. Any swearing on the field incurs an on-the-spot fine of one shilling (5p). Swearing is thus encouraged, as all the cash raised in this way goes to charity. The coveted Silver Arrow itself probably dates from the original 1673 Scorton meet. In the past this priceless relic has been stolen, pawned, left on a park bench, and lost after one of the winning captains had a fit of madness.

© The Atholl Gathering and Parade at Blair Atholl, near Pitlochry in Tayside, starts on the last Sunday in May. It is headed by the Atholl Highlanders, the last private army in Europe. They are a relic of the days when Scottish kings, who had no army of their own as such, had to call on the clans for military assistance. The Atholls, though, do not date from the mists of time, but from 1777, when they were formed to fight for Britain in the American War of Independence. The gathering, with its Highland games, is a celebration of national identity. The traditional tune *The Atholl Highlanders* is an almost compulsory ingredient of the event's heavily bagpipe-dominated musical accompaniment.

May is a month packed with superstitions. May **babies** are thought to be unlucky, mainly because they are so attractive that faeries will attempt to steal them and leave a changeling, one of their own kind, in its place. Constant vigilance is the only sure way for parents of newborn May babes to prevent such a swap taking place. With or without infants, May is also the month for smelly **bedclothes**:

> *You must not wash your blankets in May*
> *Or else you'll wash your soul away.*

This is also the month for avoiding the bath, and for eating ramsons (wild garlic) – a potentially formidable combination. **Washing**, and cleaning in general, is thought to wash life or luck away this month.

29th May
Oak Apple Day/Arbor Tree Day/Shit-Shack Day/ Pinch-Bum Day etc.

Stuart's Inquiry at the oaks

After the Battle of Worcester, Charles Stuart – the future **Charles II** – shinned up an oak tree in the grounds of Boscobel Hall at Boscobel, Staffordshire on 6th September 1651. The Parliamentarians did not bother to search the tree, as birds were still sitting undisturbed in its branches. When Charles finally sat on the post-Commonwealth throne, on 29th May 1660, it was the Boscobel incident with its Royal Oak and colluding birdlife which captured the public imagination. It was very convenient that many of the old May celebrations snuffed out under Cromwell's Commonwealth had

made much of oak and other greenery. Celebrating the 29th became an excuse to bring these festivities back; a shift from Puritan austerity to royalist merriment.

© There are not enough hours in the day for the customs-and-traditions junkie on the 29th. For starters, at **Castleton Garland** in Derbyshire the silver band plays the insistent *Garland Tune* – very similar to the *Furry Tune* mentioned on May 8th, but without the Radio Two airplay – while girls in white dance and the Garland King leads the parade through Castleton with his Lady consort, both of them dressed in Stuart costume. However, for the entire journey the King's decorative upper-half is hidden under a six-stone bell-shaped frame covered with garlands and crowned with a bouquet of flowers called the Queen.

It all kicks off at 6 pm, stopping at each of Castleton's six pubs for refreshments; and at about 9 pm the procession reaches the church, where the King is relieved of his vegetation. It is hoisted up on to the church tower (where it remains for a week), surrounded by sprays of oak. The girls then dance at the maypole in the Market Place, and the Queen bouquet is placed, by the King, on the War Memorial while the Last Post is played. The Stuart dress is a thin disguise for pagan May Day practice, the King being an incarnation of Jack-in-the-Green.

© Stuart paraphernalia is absent on **Arbor Tree Day** at Aston on Clun, near Ludlow in Shropshire. A large black poplar in the village is decorated with flags, which stay in the tree until their replacements arrive, same time, same place, next year. Always game for a bit of modern tree-worship, Morris teams dance through the carnival-atmosphere of the streets. The local non-pagan, non-Stuart explanation for the event says that it stems from the wedding of Mary Carter to the local Lord of the Manor in 1786. Flags were hoisted into the poplar as part of the marital celebrations, and the sight so impressed Mary she decreed that the tree should be decorated in the same manner every year. Each year local children act out a pageant version of the wedding as part of the Arbor Tree Day celebrations.

It is a touching story, but has very little to do with the truth. The original 'bride' may have been the fertility-goddess Bride: the flags are still used as pregnancy aids. They used to be worn for at least a month by childless women before being hung on the tree. **Fertility twigs** from the poplar can still, supposedly, make women pregnant. In 1959 the event was banned, largely in response to a surge in demand for the twigs from women across the country who had heard about the tree's powers. The chairman of the council was a Reverend, and he was not amused; he told reporters: *'These poor women seemed to believe that even if they merely stood in the shade of the tree they would have babies. The Church scotched all this nonsense centuries ago.'* How wrong could he be? The ban did not last long.

© The Royal Hospital for old and wounded soldiers, at Chelsea in London, was founded in 1682, reputedly at the suggestion of Charles II's mistress Nell Gwyn. The Chelsea Pensioners celebrate their Founder's Day today with a parade, which includes the covering of Charles II's statue with oak. The ceremony has continued without interruption since 1692. Similar goings-on can also be seen today at Lord Leycester's Hospital in Warwick and the Guildhall in Worcester.

© At All Saints Church in Northampton a leafy **garland of oak-apples** is laid on the statue of Charles II at noon. He reinforced local oak-fetishism here by giving the town a thousand tons of wood from Whittlewood Forest after the entire settlement burnt down in 1675.

● © Oak is at the forefront at Wishford Magna (Great Wishford) in Wiltshire today, although Charles is not. The celebrations reassert ancient wood-cutting rights in the forest of **Grovely**, a mile or so from the village. In the small hours local insomniacs repeatedly blast on their horns and shout '*Grovely!* '. Then, at dawn, they hike off to the forest to bring back branches of oak. It must all be done without the aid of horse or engine power – no sneaking round the back way in the family saloon and filling the boot with wood. There are prizes for the most decorative oak boughs, and a special award for the bough with most shit-shacks – oak-apples – attached. So far, so private; but spectators are welcome at part two, a procession through the streets at noon led by a banner bearing the slogan '*Grovely! Grovely! Grovely! And all Grovely! Unity is Strength.*' As at Castleton, an oak bough is placed on the church tower. It is called the Marriage Bough, and it brings luck – as well as Aston-like fertility – to all the couplings of the coming year. Later in the day there is a fair, with processions, more '*Grovely*' yelling, and other jollities.

Prior to the fair, four women lead a band of representatives to Salisbury Cathedral, six miles away, and at 10 am they present armfuls of green oak and firewood to the Dean before the High Altar. Again '*Grovely*' is bellowed several times, this time with the curious coda '*Unity is Strength*'. They then dance briefly outside the Cathedral, and head for home. Until recently the custom was more demanding – those taking part had to dance the entire 12-mile round trip, lugging the wood as they jigged.

Failure to wear a **sprig of oak** today indicated a lack of support for the restored monarchy, or acute absent-mindedness, and in some areas ritualised punishments for this offence were enacted. The unsprigged were whipped with nettles, kicked and pinched in the upper-trouser region, or pelted with eggs. This has led to assorted alternative names for the day, including **Pinch Bum Day**, and **Oak and Nettle Day**. In Wiltshire and Berkshire the colloquial term for oak-apples led to the 29th becoming **Shit-shack Day** or **Shitsack Day**.

🗍 The real hero of the day, the original **Royal Oak** at Boscobel, has gone the way of all bark, but it has left its shit-shack seeds for future generations: the oak at Boscobel House in Staffordshire was allegedly grown from an acorn dropped by the tree in which Charles evaded the Roundheads. The secret room in which he hid during the previous night can also be seen at the house.

© Durham Cathedral has anthems commemorating the **Battle of Neville's Cross** on the Saturday nearest the 29th – see October 17th, the date of the Battle.

30th May
St Walstan of Bawburgh's
Day/St Hubert's Day

Werewolves of Maastricht

The 11th-century **Walstan** was the son of a prince but laboured as a humble farmboy on the road to canonisation. His boundless energy and gentle way with animals so impressed the farmer that, when Walstan was ready to leave, he invited him to become his heir. The saint refused, but asked if he could take a certain cow with him which was about to give birth. The farmer granted the request, and Walstan became the proud father of twin calves. They were his chief companions from then on.

Before Walstan died, with a prayer on behalf of all sick men and kine, he persuaded his neighbours to shackle him to his cattle, and to let them go wherever they saw fit. The two animals wandered over the fields, and then walked over the water at a river near Costessey in Norfolk, leaving tracks as if there had been a ford. They continued through the walls of the church at nearby Bawburgh, without harming either themselves or the wall. And there they came to a halt. Walstan was buried at Bawburgh church, which soon became a place of pilgrimage. Thousands identified with Walstan's lowly labouring life, and the offerings at his tomb made him the top saint in Norfolk – even though his biography is apocryphal, and his very existence remains unproven.

Today, farm workers used to visit Walstan's shrine in Bawburgh church, and the nearby **St Walstan's Well**, to bless both themselves and their cattle. There is a pagan element at the bottom of all this, for the well on the hill near the church predates the Walstan legend, and a simple explanation for the saint's shaky story is that he was invented merely to Christianise its curative waters.

The official line is that the well sprang up when his cattle stopped for a breather on their way to his final resting place. The waters can heal any ailing organ – in 1913 a large group of pilgrims rolled up to give thanks. One of them was suffering from a chronic eye-disorder, and was cured with water and moss from the well. But the well's chief magic is of a trouser-filling nature. Applied and consumed, its water can restore lost genitals in both man and beast. The water used to be bottled and sold for a tidy profit in Norwich. Those lacking that certain something still visit the well, hoping against hope that its healing properties are not a phallusy.

The Bawburgh celebrations have survived; although the cattle-aspect has been removed: see May 18th.

This is also **St Hubert's Day**. It was believed that the only way to stop a **werewolf** was by shooting it with a bullet that had been blessed in a chapel dedicated to Hubert. Making the bullet from silver was optional. Hubert was the bishop of an obscure town called Maastricht, and is the patron of huntsmen. None of which entirely explains the werewolf link.

31st May

One Bride for Seven Brothers

✠ At midnight tonight on the site of 16th-century Hill Hall at Theydon Bois, just on the London side of the M25 in Essex, out rides the **Duke de Morrow**. The eccentric who lived in the Hall at the turn of the century invented this daft title for himself and is now stuck with it for eternity. He haunts in a mustard-coloured coach, probably because neither Heaven nor Hell would let him in with such an awful colour sense.

The Hall has had its share of weirdness over the years. One of the first residents was a young woman lusted after by seven brothers. They all fought for her affections, and succeeded only in slaughtering each other. Their blood was a feature of the Hall's walls for several centuries, as it could not be washed away. There have been ghosts too: a grey-haired woman – perhaps the girl at the wrong end of the family affair – wanders through the site of the Hall; and a black dog used to be seen lying on one of the beds. The Hall partly burned down in the 1960s, and is now used as a prison; not the most uplifting of days out.

This was the day when, in 1669, **Samuel Pepys** closed his Diary. He thought that it was making him lose his sight. This was not the case – although what he wrote indicates Pepys' propensity to another favourite traditional cause of blindness. He was only 36 when he quit, but lived until he was 70.

✠ On this day in 1742 the fabulously beautiful **Lady Carew of Potter Heigham**, Norfolk, got married. She had sold her soul to the Devil to gain her exquisite appearance, and on her wedding night he rolled up to claim his side of the bargain. A black coach-and-four driven by two skeletons pulled up at the honeymoon suite. Lady Carew fought and yelled, but the cadaverous coachmen dragged her into the carriage and set off at full pelt. They took the most direct route to Hell, careering off a bridge over the River Thurne and plunging into the water amid clouds of steam. At midnight every May 31st, there is a ghostly action replay.

'King of the Clowns' Joseph Grimaldi died on May 31st 1837. He provided the vital link between the harlequins and jesters of yesteryear and the red-nosed, white-faced circus clowns of today. Crippling illness forced 'Joey' to retire early, and led to his premature death, but Grimaldi is remembered each year at the **Clowns Service**. It takes place at Holy Trinity Church, at Dalston in east London: the day is almost always a Sunday, but the actual date is highly variable, February and March being the favourite months.

© At the start of the service several small cars are driven up the nave. They stop at the altar, and dozens of clowns pour out of each vehicle. The clowns begin hitting each other and throwing pretend buckets of water, while at the same time the cars fall apart piece by piece as the congregation sings *All People that on Earth do Dwell*. Well, not quite. But the service is attended by clowns from all over the world, with everyone in full make-up and costumes, including the vicar. Afterwards there is a free clown show in the church hall.

WHITSUNTIDE

Whit Sunday is the seventh Sunday after Easter, the equivalent of the Jewish Pentecost and the traditional day on which the Apostles were filled with knowledge by the Holy Ghost. One dubious derivation of Whit is from 'wit', as in the wit and wisdom which miraculously infused the Apostles. More plausibly, the name comes from *Hwitan Sunnandæy*, White Sunday, so called because of the white baptismal robes worn at Pentecostal services. Whitsuntide is the week starting with Whit Sunday. The holiday element of the week has now evaporated, and in recent years many Whit customs and fairs have made the short leap to its modern replacement – the Late Spring Bank Holiday at the end of May, still often called the Whit Bank Holiday.

For **Ellen 'Nell Cook' Bean**, Whitsun brought more revelry than she bargained for. In the early 16th century she earned herself a reputation as the finest cook in Kent, keeping her employer, a friar at the Priory of St Saviour in Canterbury, fat and happy. One Whitsun a young woman turned up claiming to be the friar's niece. The friar seemed over-overjoyed to see her, and Nell smelled a rat. She began laying traps for the woman, leaving tongs and bedpans in her bed. Her suspicions were confirmed when, days later, the items were still undisturbed. Something was awry, and its exact nature became clear when Nell caught 'uncle' and 'niece' engaged in some vigorous family planning. Nell was appalled and sought solace in food. She prepared her speciality, Warden Pie, with an added dollop of poison. The friar and his mistress were later discovered dead, and were buried quietly together in a grave to avoid scandal. Nell disappeared, and it later transpired that the Priory's suspicious Brothers had sealed her under the floor with a portion of pie, giving her the option of poison or slow starvation. Either way, she was a has-Bean.

☦ When the body was disinterred by a later generation, the ghost of Nell flew out in a rage. She decided to go a-haunting every Friday, and anyone who sees her is doomed. The three

masons who uncovered the bones were the first victims: two of them were hanged for murdering the third. Nell is one of Kent's best-known ghosts, and her main haunt is Canterbury Cathedral's Dark Entry.

© One of the best examples of **well-dressing** outside Derbyshire takes place at Endon in Staffordshire. It has now moved from the first few days of Whitsun to the Spring Bank Holiday weekend. Water from the well is believed to have tonic powers, and after the dressing a May Queen takes the first swig. The crowning of the Queen is so popular that it takes place four times over the weekend, alongside various services, blessings, maypole dances, tug-of-wars, ye olde jazz band parades, and bouts of the traditional sport **Tossing the Sheaf**. Men heave sacks of straw over a bar, which is raised after every round until only one person is left in the contest, and that's the last straw. For buckets more on well-dressing, see Ascension Day.

© Out riding near Corby in Northamptonshire in 1585, Queen Elizabeth I slipped from the saddle and landed in a bog. Locals rushed to her rescue, and she was so grateful that she issued a charter which exempted the town from various tolls, jury and militia service. It did not give them licence to hold a fair; but Corby was in the mood to celebrate, and so it instigated one anyway. The **Pole Fair** is still held at Whitsuntide every 20 years, and is next due in 2002. Beforehand the roads are barricaded and travellers are felt for cash. Any man who refuses is hoisted on to a pole and carried to one of three sets of stocks. Women travel there in the comfort of a chair. Corby claims that these are the only stocks still in active use in England.

Elephants, hurling and wrestling were among the many attractions of the **Whitsuntide Fair at Truro** in Cornwall. It died out within living memory, a pale shadow of the event which once attracted thousands every year. The surviving song *Truro Whitsun Fair* recalls the experience of four Cornishmen who came to regret their visit:

The end came at last, 'tis sad to relate,
'Twas not what they drank, not what they
ate;
Three picked up black eyes and one a bruised
pate,
That fateful Whitsun morning.
Their watches were pinched, their money all
spent,
Money all spent, no use to lament,
They looked at each other with great
discontent,
That awful Whitsun morning.

The centrepiece of the long deceased Whit fair at Manningtree in Essex was the roasting of a whole ox. The carvery was so famous that the animal became proverbial. In *Henry IV, Part One*, Shakespeare's Prince Hal likens Falstaff to *'a roasted Manningtree ox, with the pudding in his belly'*.

At fairs or beyond, this was a great week for sports, climaxing with the Olimpick Games in the Cotswolds – see Whit Friday. At Bury St Edmunds in Suffolk, 12 old women used to play **Trap, Bat and Ball** at Whitsuntide, a variation of Knur and Spell. Another great seasonal pastime was **Lying for the Whetstone**, a widespread contest in which competitors would concoct wonderful porky-pies, hoping to receive the first prize – a whetstone, to metaphorically sharpen the winner's Whit wits.

Not everyone was in favour of the holiday spirit of Whitsun, of course. The inimitable **Philip Stubbes**, foaming Puritan, wrote in the 17th century: *'Why should they abstaine from bodely labor, peradventure the whole week, spending it in drunkennesse, whordome, gluttonie, and other filthie Sodomiticall exercyses?'* It was the complete lack of such excesses in the modern version of the holiday that led Laurence Whistler in his 1947 book *The English Festivals* to describe Whitsun as: *'. . . a formless Bank Holiday . . . the car, the crowd on the bypass, the fire on the common, the sandwich paper in the wood.'*

© The holy healing wells at the shrine of Our Lady of **Walsingham** in Norfolk attract vast numbers of visitors all year round, but Whitsun is one of the chief periods of pilgrimage. See 15th August for more on 'England's Nazareth'.

WHIT SUNDAY

Children **born on Whit Sunday** have little to look forward to – they will die prematurely in unfortunate circumstances. So there is only one thing to do with a Whit baby: wait a day or two and put it in a shallow grave, sprinkle it with clay, and cover it with twigs. When extracted from this extraordinary premature burial a few seconds later, the baby is 'born again', and the new date becomes the child's replacement birthday, thus avoiding the traditional fate of Whit children.

In Cleveland it was customary to wear **new clothes** today. Those who failed to observe this custom were liable to be spattered by passing birds. As for the clothes themselves, white was the only acceptable colour – at the very least a white flower or ribbon was worn.

© Churches were often decked out too, but their colour scheme favoured green. Birch, yew and assorted blooms were brought inside for today's **Flower Sermon**. At St Mary Redcliffe in Bristol the Lord Mayor still turns up for the morning service on Whit Sunday in the midst of fanfares, to a church strewn with rushes and flowers. This flower power has been going on since the mid-15th century, and gives the day the local name of **Rush Sunday**. Medieval clerics, to liven up the decor, dramatised the Coming of the Holy Spirit by installing mobile wooden doves on pieces of wire, and sending fireballs down from the roof.

Open-air acts of worship were also encouraged on Whit Sunday: it was said that if you offered a prayer at sunrise, God would grant your wish. But there were times when the behaviour of the **sun** today could distract even the most devout. A mid-17th-century diarist described how he saw the Whit sun *'rise, skip, play, dance, and turn about like a wheel'*. This dawn-chorus-line has since been identified as recurring meteorological phenomena. Last century, Richard Inwards' *Weatherlore* observed that: *'Under certain atmospheric conditions . . . the sun's disk at rising and setting appears to undergo strange transformations; it may assume the shape of a loaf of bread, a mushroom or a fish, or even divide into two more parts.'* They just don't make weather reports like that any more.

☼ If the sun has got his hat and tap-shoes on, then all is well on the farm:

Whitsunday bright and clear
Will bring a fertile year.

Conversely and perversely, if it is damp then prospects are also good:

Whitsuntide rain, blessing for wine.
Whitsunday wet, Christmas fat.

It was also maintained that rain at Whitsun will cause meat in every larder to be mildewed. There is only one appropriate reponse if asked how often such **weatherlore** is reliable: '*At Whitsuntide Poke-Monday, where people shear Kogs*' – a long-winded way of saying 'never'.

© After the evening service today at St Briavels, near Coleford in Gloucestershire, a local forester stands on the high wall in the churchyard and throws small pieces of **bread and cheese** at the baying crowd. Forgetting that it is bad manners to chant with your mouth full, the grateful villagers respond:

St Briavels water and Whyrl's Wheat
Are the best bread and water King John ever
ate.

Despite the King John reference, this one-off dole is said to have started in the 17th century when the Earl of Hereford unexpectedly axed the villagers' wood-gathering rights. The Earl's wife thought this treatment heavy-handed, and tried to persuade her husband to reconsider. He agreed to a compromise: the villagers could have back the rights to whatever area of the wood she was prepared to ride round naked. Even though it meant humiliation, she rose to the challenge. The wood which the Earl's wife encircled is known as the Hudnalls; and to this day locals can get out their choppers here with impunity. So far the story is conspicuous for its lack of cheese; but tacked uncomfortably on to the end of the tale is the coda that in gratitude the villagers instigated an annual penny-a-head whip-round on behalf of the needy, and this hand-out later became the cheese hurl-out. The gouda-neighbour ceremony used to be held in the church but was moved outside as a result of 19th-century rowdiness. During the last war locals pooled their cheese rations to keep the custom going.

© Making a Double Gloucester Gloucester double, there is a second heat of cheese athletics at Cooper's Hill in Brockworth, where they go in for an early evening session of **cheese-rolling**. From 6 pm, hardy competitors go scrambling after wood-encased cheeses down the one-in-two gradient; and there are often multiple injuries in the fromage-fray. The winners of the four separate races get to keep what they catch, and anyone can join in the pursuit as long as they register in advance. The rolling at Brockworth has remained unbroken since the Middle Ages, and during wartime rationing wooden effigy cheeses did the trick. This is another custom which has moved from Whitsun: it now takes place on Spring Bank Holiday Monday at the end of May.

🗍 Cheeses no longer roll today at the spectacular location of the **Uffington White Horse** in Oxfordshire. The roll came at the climax of the Whitsuntide Scouring of the Horse, a massed weeding which took place every seven years. The White Horse is a couple of lengths short of 400 feet, and is thought to have been etched into the chalk hillside at Uffington at least 1,000 years ago. It is probably twice that age, a pre-Roman representation of the horse-goddess Epona; though local legend has two ripostes. It is said to be either the horse of St George, or else the dragon which he slew on nearby Dragon Hill. The figure, after all, is heavily surreal, with disjointed limbs and a strange beak – an image available in all good record stores courtesy of the cover of XTC's album *English Settlement*. Theory number two says that it was carved by King Alfred to celebrate victory at the Battle of Ashdown in 871. Whatever, the septennial chalk and cheese scouring was scrubbed from the calendar in 1857, and National Trust volunteers now give the Horse an informal grooming every few months.

Cheesecakes have always been a traditional Whit food, though not in the form found in the freezer section at the local supermarket. They were curd-tarts, like the ones still found in many northern bakers' shops, made of egg, sugar, fruit, rum, and that extra something, **beastlings**. Beastlings are the first offerings of a newly-calved cow, a fatty substance known even less appetisingly as colostrom.

WHIT MONDAY

Whereas many of the traditions associated with Whit Sunday had a religious tone, Whit Monday was all-out fairs, dancing and strangeness. Although many of these events survive, all but a handful have now moved to the Spring Bank Holiday Monday.

© Whit Monday used to be the biggest day of the year for Morris dancing. The **Headington Quarry Morris** Team, from near Oxford, are almost the only group who still turn out today, with a performance outside the local pub in Headington; but in response to the change in the calendar they now put in a second evening appearance on Spring Bank Holiday Monday. This is also now the day for the **Bampton Morris**, at Bampton west of Oxford, to go on their rounds. They appear at the village outskirts at 8.30 am, and spend the day dancing in and around pubs, large houses, and an old people's home, before being joined by other Morris teams at 5.30 pm. This is the only day of the year when Bampton Morris dance in their own village. Their speciality is a Swordbearer, whose garlanded weapon has a cake-box attached to it. The cake, which bestows luck, is handed out to the crowd. One of the main flowers in the garlands is peony, which – whether the Morris realises it or not – is a traditional cure for those common dancers' complaints, breathlessness and epilepsy.

© The Whitsun Morris celebrations at Charing, near Ashford in Kent, have also succumbed to the pressure and moved to the Holiday Monday. The 11 am service at Charing church stars the East Kent Morris and their **Hooden Horse**, a snapping-jawed hobby horse for which the Thanet area of Kent is renowned. The horse is no longer allowed into the church, but chases the vicar and engages in general horseplay outside. There is then a Morris display outside the church, before the dancers move on to nearby Westwell and perform there. For the straight-from-the-horse's-mouth details of hoodening plays over Christmas, see December 18th.

© The **Dunmow Flitch** of Great Dunmow in Essex is a side of bacon awarded to a husband and wife who have '*not repented of their marriage for a year and a day*'. The custom is thought to date from the 13th century, and to get their hands on the bacon contending contented couples have to undergo a series of trials and quizzings designed to demonstrate their worthiness and fidelity, a sort of old-world *Mr and Mrs*. Before the trials comes the swearing in, which begins:

*You shall swear by custom of confession
If ever you made nuptial transgression . . .*

and ends with:

*For this is our custom at Dunmow well
  knowne,
Though the pleasure be ours, the bacon's your
  own.*

The mock court making these joint decisions used to meet on Whit Monday, but has now moved into an eccentric orbit, usually returning every Leap Year on a Saturday in late June which does not clash with Wimbledon or the Essex show. All this piggery-pokery led to the proverbial term for a blissful marriage: *To eat Dunmow Bacon*.

🔲 A similar Flitch ceremony existed at Wychnor, near Burton upon Trent in Staffordshire. Here a layman had to prove his conjugal bliss, or a priest had to prove his religious worth. However, unique in the annals of tradition, the Flitch appears never to have been awarded. The fact that it hung all year on a hook in the manorial hall may have had something to do with the lack of contestants. A wooden flitch still hangs at the manor as a reminder of the unclaimed prize.

© The **Court of Arraye** at Lichfield – formerly on Whit Monday, now on the Spring Bank Holiday – harks back to a statute of 1176, which decreed that everyone must turn out with homemade armour and weapons for inspection. In the 15th century Lichfield had to produce, in addition, 12 suits of chain mail and two sets of full knights' armour. The military dues have been defunct since the reign of James I, but the court has continued albeit in a more frivolous mode – it was described in 1806 as '*an idle and useless ceremony, adapted for the amusement of children*'. Now held at the Guildhall at 10 am on the Holiday Monday, the mayor and his cohorts inspect a platoon of men in medieval armour, and then join up with a separate strand of Lichfield tradition, the **Greenhill Bower**. Said to have been started by 7th-century King Oswy, its copious garlands and flower-wrapped poles reek of an earlier, pagan ancestry. There are processions, sports and a Bower Queen crowning ceremony.

© Formerly held in Rogation week, Blessing the Sea is now part of the North Shields Fish Quay Festival, and takes place over the Late Spring Bank Holiday weekend at North Shields near Newcastle upon Tyne – see Rogation Week for details.

In 1399 **John of Gaunt**, Duke of Lancaster, was riding through Ratby near Leicester when he saw a bunch of locals frolicking in the field. They were celebrating Lammas Day, the end of their hay-mowing chores, and after joining in the fun John was so delighted by their unconstrained exuberance that he vowed: '*I'll give you something to marry your Lamb*', and instructed them to meet him in Leicester. Not sure what he meant by this Lamb-Lammas pun, 14 of the men turned up on the appointed day to find that the Duke had a generous and complex way of showing his gratitude.

Each man was given a ewe, a wether (a castrated ram) and a parcel of land in the neighbouring parish of Enderby. As well as their own bits of land, called the Ewes, there were two other pieces, the Boots and the Wether, which were to be rented out at Whitsun each year, with the money raised financing a huge feast on the night of the auction. This, so the story goes, is the origin of the long-running **Selling of the Keep of the Wether** at Enderby on Whit Monday. At the auction a coin was passed round the table: bidding was only allowed if you were holding the coin, and the sale closed when the coin had managed three circuits without anyone upping their bid.

After the land had been rented out for another year, the men went down to the Wether, took a sod of earth and some grass, and tied it to their hats with a silken lace. They then rode to Leicester and threw laces, sods, and grass into the crowd at High Cross, to indicate that the sale had been completed. After that it was back to a pub in Enderby, usually *The Nags Head*, for a toast to good old John of Gaunt, and a feast including the Duke's favourite delicacy, calf's head.

This wonderfully convoluted piece of weirdness was still going strong in 1975 when it was killed stone-dead by the council, who declared the Wether common land. This meant that it could no longer be sold. Whether the Wether can ever be revived remains to be seen.

WHIT TUESDAY

© **Fairwater Spring** at Kingsteignton near Newton Abbot in Devon never ran dry; until, one day, it did. The locals resorted to primitive remedies: they took a ram to the dry bed of the spring, and slit open its throat. The water-god was impressed by the offering, and the Fairwater has flowed ever since. As a perpetual reminder to the god to keep up the good work, the people annually sacrificed a ram on Whit Tuesday, with the god getting the blood, and the poor of the parish getting the meat. Prior to the butchery the beast was blessed at the church and paraded through the streets with ribbons and garlands. These days the animal is humanely clubbed over the head and dressed before the parade. The vicar no longer goes in for sheep-blessing, and the roasted meat goes not to the needy, but to the lucky revellers

whose programme numbers are read out over the tannoy. Whoever gets to eat the ram is said to be swathed in good fortune. During meat rationing in the last war, deer used to deputise for the ram; and on one occasion a luckless reindeer went to Devon on a one-way trip from London. The **Ram Roasting Fair** is now on Spring Bank Holiday Monday.

© Barwick in Elmet near Leeds in West Yorkshire has what is regularly claimed to be the tallest **maypole** in England. Every three years it was taken down down at Easter and re-erected on Whit Tuesday as the hub of an all-drinking, all-dancing, all-garlanding extravaganza. Virtually unchanged, the fair has now moved to the Tuesday after Late Spring Bank Holiday, and the grand finale still involves a local man shinning up the 86-foot pole and spinning its silver fox weathervane. Barwick celebrated its last erection in 1993, and will have another in 1996.

Until last century, each Whit Tuesday the villagers of Churt near Frensham in Surrey used to dance and drink and dance some more at the easternmost and highest of three conical hills known as **The Devil's Jumps**. Their partying seems to have been a celebration of how the hills, and four others nearby, traditionally came into being, a tale which casts Satan as a sneak-thief.

▥ **Mother Ludlum**, a benevolent witch, owned a huge magical cauldron. One day Satan popped by to borrow it in order to make some lentil and brimstone soup, but Mother Ludlum spotted his cloven feet and kicked him out. The Devil snatched the cauldron and bolted, making seven great leaps in his seven-league boots, scuffing up the ground into a hillock with each hop. Mother Ludlum flew after him, and he panicked, dropping the pot on Kettlebury Hill near Elstead, the highest of the seven demonic divots. Deciding that it was too valuable to be left lying around at home, Mother Ludlum put her cauldron in the church at Frensham, where it can be seen to this day. Mother Ludlum's Cave is in Moor Park near Waverley Abbey, in that most traditional of locations – a lane beside the Adult Education Centre.

© One of the oddest sports of the season takes place on the evening of Whit Tuesday at St Ives in Cambridgeshire. Six boys and six girls go **Dicing for Bibles** at the local church. The edifying prizes obviously excuse the gambling.

The money for the books comes from the Bible Orchard, purchased with £50 bequeathed by the will of Puritan Dr Robert Wilde in 1675. The dicers must be literate children 'of good report'. The dice now roll on a table in the church, not on the altar as instructed by Wilde.

WHIT FRIDAY AND SATURDAY

© There were no great customs associated with Whit Wednesday and Whit Thursday, but at the end of the week Chipping Campden in Gloucestershire came into its own with a brace of surviving traditional events, both now transferred to the corresponding days after the Late Spring Bank Holiday. **Robert Dover's Olimpick Games** go back at the very least to the early 16th century, when they were either started or updated by Robert Dover. They are the oldest athletics meeting of any kind in Britain, including all the 'ancient' Highland games, and when the ancient Greek Olympics were revived in their modern format in 1896, they knew where to go for advice – the organisers of Dover's Games. The Olimpicks used to include '*men playing at cudgels, wrestling, leaping, pitching the bar, throwing the iron hammer, handling the pyke, leaping over the heads of men kneeling, standing upon their hands, etc.*' The current incarnation, a revival from 1951, has added assorted costumed characters and amusements, but has also kept many of the old sports alive, notably **shin-kicking**, a form of wrestling with added brutality. The Olimpicks now take place at Dover's Hill near Chipping Camden at 7.30 pm on the Friday after Late Spring Bank Holiday.

© On the next day Chipping Camden holds the **Scuttlebrook Wake**, formerly one of the rowdiest bouts of hell-raising in the country. These days the event has been tamed and so has the brook in the Wake's title: it now scuttles discreetly through the culverts under the village's High Street. At 2.30 pm a May Queen, attendants and page ride through the streets on a cart pulled by Morris men, who took over the lugging duties when the last shire horse disappeared from the area. In the town square the old Queen formally enthrones the new Queen; there is dancing around a maypole; and the Morris team perform a display dance – having hopefully recovered from their horsing around.

© On Whit Friday, Saddleworth in Yorkshire has its **Whit Walk**, which is now combined with an evening brass band contest. These walks came in many forms, and were just a step or two removed from the Beating the Bounds ceremonies of Rogationtide – perambulation without flagellation. The Whit Walk tradition was taken up by the pre-Welfare State **Friendly Societies**, and is the forerunner of modern parades and galas. The biggest were held at Salford and Manchester; and of surviving Whit Walks, notable treading boldly occurs at **Bradford** in West Yorkshire on Spring Bank Holiday Monday. Organisers claim that it is the oldest continually held athletic event in Britain. Its current form is a 50-kilometre walking race from Bradford to Bradford again, via Ilkley and Otley. Almost as strenuous, at **Laugharne** near Carmarthen in Dyfed, participants walk round the village's 20-mile boundary. The event is so taxing that it only happens once every seven years. It is next due in 1996.

Whitsun Walking was associated with the **Club Feast**. The Sick Clubs received everyone's pennies during the year, paid out money to those who fell ill, and put the surplus towards the Whitsun nosh-up. Club Feasts were teetotal total tea-and-cake affairs which ousted the older and wilder **Whitsun Ale** festivities. Again, many modern gala elements stem from the Ales – shooting ranges, stalls, prizes, dances. They were a mixture of May Day mummery and an afternoon at Skegness. There were often Miracle Plays (see Corpus Christi), and hunting bouts. Wychwood Forest in Oxfordshire centred its Ale around a stag-hunt. Human participants came from the forest settlements of Witney, Crawley and Hailey.

TRINITY

Trinity – the eighth Sunday after Easter, and first after Whitsun – used to be the start of some intensive feasting and fair-going, celebrating the three-in-oneness of God as Father, Son and Holy Ghost. Almost all of the Trinity events have now jumped ship, or sunk without trace; and even though Southwold in Suffolk still has a hale and hearty **Trinity Fair**, it has moved to the first Monday in June – see June 2nd.

© One survivor, albeit in a watered down form, is the Trinity Monday fair at Kirtlington near Oxford. Since 1958 it has been a well-behaved dinner, cricket match and village fete, but until the revamp it was the last of the traditional **Oxfordshire Lamb Ales**. Kirtlington, Eynsham and Kidlington all went in for this ram-a-lamb-a-ding-dong, and all featured a strange Trinity structure called the Bower or Bowery, a bucolic beer-tent constructed of branches and greenery.

At Kirtlington a lamb was carted round the village from Monday until Wednesday. It was usually not eaten at all, as it had to be the finest lamb in the village, and a canny shepherd knew that the best lamb would fetch the best price at market. Mutton pies were still made for the occasion; and if the paraded lamb *was* actually killed, its head went into the Head Pie, with wool intact. A portion of this brought loads of luck, and acted as a prototype dental floss.

At nearby **Kidlington** the main attraction of the Lamb Ale belonged in one of the kinkier video nasties. Young girls had their thumbs tied behind their backs, and had to chase a sacrificial lamb, catching it with their teeth. For agreeing to this, they were awarded the title Lady of the Lamb. The badly nipped beast was then killed, dressed, and paraded through the village on a pole with its fleece re-attached. This happened on Trinity Monday, and the lamb was finally eaten on the Tuesday. By the end of last century, the Kidlington Lamb Ale had lost its flavour, and local girls and sheep can now get through the day unmolested.

The Trinity celebrations at Shenington in Oxfordshire ignored the sheep and messed up the church instead. Hay was poured over the pews on Trinity Sunday – a once widespread custom, not just limited to Trinity. And Trinity was also the time to hit the hay at Clee in Grimsby, Humberside. Last century the day's decor was described thus: '*The Church is gaily strewed with fresh mown grass, the fragrance of which is extremely grateful.*' The strewing was a tenure custom here, in gratitude for several hay-making acres that had been left for the use of the villagers.

The drinking and dancing of **Kirkham Bird Fair** in North Yorkshire lasted from midnight on Trinity Sunday to midnight the following day. The excuse for the merriment was nothing if not flimsy. It is said that lovers used to meet on the bridge over the Derwent at Kirkham to exchange pet birds, and from these mynah beginnings sprang the field-Fair.

CORPUS CHRISTI

Corpus Christi ('the body of Christ') celebrates the presence of Christ in the bread and wine of the Eucharist. The feast takes place on the Thursday after Trinity Sunday, which is one week on from Whit Sunday.

Coventry Fair was one of the major feasts of Corpus Christi. Amongst its parading revellers each year was an over-exposed woman representing **Lady Godiva**, her blushes spared by a combination of body stocking, long wig and ridiculously large feather hat. She was accompanied by a Fool-figure, who made rude gestures and outdid Frankie Howerd in the oo-er stakes.

The Godiva legend is built on a solid framework of truth. In the 11th century Godiva – or, more correctly, Godgifu – was married to the all-powerful, all-nasty Earl Leofric, right-hand man to King Cnut. Leofric taxed and tyrannised Coventry so close to the edge of oblivion that Godgifu interceded, begging her husband to ease off and show the people some respect. In a fit of whimsy, Leofric said that he would only swap groat-winning for vote-winning if his wife rode naked through Coventry on market day. Godgifu held her husband to his word, and next market day went bareback riding through the town's streets.

In the first version of the story Godiva's long hair keeps everything under wraps, apart from her face and legs. Leofric decides that only prudish divine intervention could have preserved his wife's modesty, and therefore his own reputation; and so he immediately repents, slashing taxes and founding a Benedictine monastery in Coventry.

In version two, which took another 500 years to get script-approval, Leofric still turns over a new leaf; but in the key scene everyone agrees to hide indoors behind shuttered windows, enabling the good Lady Godiva to ride through without voyeurs. Only Tom the tailor breaks his word and sneaks a peek. But the white flesh is followed by a white flash and he is blinded by a Heaven-hurled bolt of lightning. This **Peeping Tom** story seems to have been invented to account for a strange wooden effigy

of a man, which used to stand in the lobby of the Hotel Leofric in Coventry. Some of the paint on the figure had peeled, leaving the eyes blank and blinded. Peeping Tom has now been rehoused in the city's Herbert Art Gallery.

Coventry Fair, with its Godiva gawping, took over from the more biblically-inspired **Miracle Plays** which were held at Corpus Christi until the Reformation. Everything has now come full circle, for although the fair became defunct in 1962, the Miracle Plays have now been revived; and there are also periodic attempts to establish a separate annual Lady Godiva parade in the city.

Miracle Plays were popular around the Whitsun-Corpus Christi period. The town guilds performed them, each cycle of plays telling the Judaeo-Christian story of the Earth from Creation to Doomsday. They were also known as Mystery Plays – not because the action defied comprehension, but because *mystery* is an old word for a trade. Each trade was responsible for one play in the cycle, and tended to emphasise elements of its own work: the Carpenters' Guild would knock up a robust and ornate Ark; whereas the Bakers' rejigged the Last Supper to give pride of place to their loaves.

The plays were usually in rhyming couplets, full of slapstick and gags. Mobile stages trundled through the streets all day – stay long enough at any one spot and the entire past, present and future of the world would roll by. Some churches made people watch the whole cycle as a penance, which says little for its entertainment value.

© The chief centres for the plays were Coventry, Chester, York and Wakefield. Proving that miracles never cease, all four continue to stage the plays; but not on annual basis, and not at Corpus Christi. The Coventry Miracle Plays are held once every three years, and are next due in 1996. They are performed in promenade at the ruins of the old cathedral, usually towards the end of July. York's Mystery Plays are also next scheduled for 1996, taking place every four years as part of the city's arts festival, which is normally held in June. The cycle of plays at Chester is staged once every five years, and will next be enacted there in 1997. At Wakefield there is no exact formula, with a five- to ten-year gap between performances. 1998 is the most likely date for the cycle's next appeerance. Each place sticks to its own, old, text, with each new production sprinkling a few topical refences amid the ancient themes. In the 1980s the Mystery Plays became a rapturously received, long-running hit for the National Theatre when the poet Tony Harrison adapted them as a trio of promenade productions.

Corpus Christi is still a major festival in Catholic countries, and was once important enough in Britain to merit its own *Corpus Christi Carol*, which is now often appropriated by Christmas carollers. The song is downright weird, presenting a picture of the dead Christ in a medieval mystical style. One early 16th-century version has the riddling chorus:

> *Lully, lulley, lully, lulley,*
> *The falcon hath borne my mak away.*

Nothing to do with waterproofs, *mak* here means 'mate'. The rest of the hypnotic song unfolds like a slow cinematic tracking shot, moving in from the edge of the orchard to the dog lapping at the bleeding knight:

> *He bare him up, he bare him down, he bare*
> *him into an orchard brown.*
> *In that orchard there was a hall that was*
> *hanged with purple and pall.*
> *And in that hall there was a bed: it was*
> *hanged with gold so red.*
> *And in that bed there lieth a knight, his*
> *wounds bleeding day and night.*
> *And by that bedside sits a hound that licks*
> *the blood as it daily runs down.*
> *And by that bedside there kneeleth a may and*
> *she weepeth both night and day.*
> *And by that bedside there standeth a stone,*
> *'Corpus Christi' written thereon.*

The words have been interpreted in several different ways. Some think that they are simply a description of the Eucharist on the altar, while others have interpreted the orchard and knight in the song as veiled references to Avalon and the wounded King Arthur with the Holy Grail. When composer and song collector Ralph Vaughan Williams learned a version of the Corpus Christi carol from an old man in Derbyshire, the singer insisted that the song was '*as old as Jesus Christ*'.

JUNE

1st June
St Wite's Day/St Wistan's Day

Skull-Splitting Hairs

Saxon prince St Wistan died in AD 850, the victim of an outbreak of incest. His cousin was making eyes at Wistan's widowed mother, the Queen of Mercia, and the saint was not amused. He said that the Church could not possibly sanction such a relationship, and so the cousin cut Wistan's head in half and buried the corpse in secret. It did not stay secret for long, however. A spotlight from Heaven shone down on the grave, and where Wistan's blood had fallen, human hair sprouted. Seeing mud grow a beard drove the transgressing cousin insane, and he lived the rest of his life as a deranged outcast.

Fans of saintly geo-follicles must dash to Leicestershire today. For one hour only, you will see hair sprout from the earth somewhere between Arnesby and Great Glen; though no one knows exactly where. You must have abundant faith, watch carefully, and not be misled by the five o'clock shadows.

If St Wistan is unshaveable, his stable-mate St Wite is inscrutable. Nothing is known about her. Ironically, hers is one of only two Anglo-Saxon saints' tombs to have survived intact. It is at Whitchurch Canonicorum church in Dorset. Diseased limbs can be placed in one of its three apertures for curative purposes. It used to be customary to bring cake and cheese to the tomb on June 1st in offering to St Wite.

© Charlton in Wiltshire has its **Duck Feast** today, or if the date is at a weekend on the following Monday. Stephen Duck was a thresher-cum-poet of the 18th century who became Keeper of the Queen's Library after George II's wife, Queen Caroline, took a shine to him. Duck later took holy orders, and tried learning Latin and the complex byways of theology. It all proved too much, and he jumped into the Thames in 1756. Unlike other ducks, this one could not swim.

Lord Palmerston gave land called Duck's Acre to raise money so that his friend's life could in some way be commemorated. The feast was born, and Duck's health was – and is – drunk, along with that of Palmerston himself. Seems like a reasonable explanation. However, the whole event was thriving well before Duck's death, and appears to have been linked with him through the coincidence of name.

© There are 13 men who attend, which has led to the claim that it is all down to ancient witchery – covens have 13 members. Whatever the explanation, the content is as follows. The Duck Men have a Chief Duck in their midst, and drink from a vessel called the Duck Goblet, which holds five eighths of a pint. The chief's tall hat is decorated with duck feathers and a picture of a thresher. The venue is *The Charlton Cat*. Although some of Duck's poems are displayed in the pub, feasting is by invitation only. Saying 'Yes Mallard' to the Chief Duck ceased to be funny during the early years of the custom.

© Kilbarchan, near Paisley in Strathclyde, has its **Lilias Day** on the first Saturday in early June, a pageant commemorating local piper Habbie Simpson. During his lifetime – from 1550 to 1620 – he played at every fête, wedding and party in the area, bringing joy and dance wherever he went. But the name Lilias has nothing to do with him, coming from the daughter of an 18th-century nobleman who started the annual feast. Lilias is represented each year by a young girl.

2nd June
St Elmo's Day

Friendly Fire

St Elmo has a choice of two deaths in legend, both unpleasant. In one he is covered in pitch and set alight, only to be rescued by an intervening angel, recaptured, tortured some more, transported by a second angel, and finally killed. In the alternative version, Elmo's bowels are wound from his body with a windlass. For this reason the windlass is the saint's emblem, and Elmo is the patron saint of stomach disorders – especially those afflicting children, for some reason. The tarring and burning version of the legend links in with St Elmo's Fire – the flickering electrical flashes seen on ships' masts around the time of a storm. In Spain St Elmo is the sailors' patron, and they named the lights after him, believing that they represent his manifest blessing.

Beyond Spain, St Elmo's Fire is not viewed so positively. It is said to lead to suicide by drowning, and is associated with violent storms. Appropriately, Shakespeare's *The Tempest* features St Elmo's Fire, although Ariel claims the credit:

> Sometime I'd divide and burn in many
>   places: on the topmast,
> The yards and bowsprit, would I flame
>   distinctly,
> Then meet and join.

The confusion of curse/blessing is partly clarified by the fact that in Classical times the single flame was said to be Helena, who brought bad luck, whereas a multi-flame was Castor and Pollux, which meant good luck. If the fire came from the topmast, bowsprit or foreship and moved downwards, it was tempest time. A pig's squeal can offset the malevolent version of the fire; but as pigs bring colossally bad luck to ships, their presence on board would be something of a mixed blessing.

Faversham in Kent used to have an altar to Elmo in its church, covered in perpetually burning candles; but it has long been snuffed out. The film *St Elmo's Fire* has nothing to do with meteorological phenomena, and little to do with good cinema.

© Politics is not all swings and roundabouts: now and again it is dodgems. After the mayor of Southwold in Suffolk opens the town's **Trinity** Fair on the first Monday in June, a tape of the national anthem is played, and he goes for a ride on the dodgems decked out in full mayoral regalia. In the rival dodgems are the mace-bearer with his mace, the bellman with his bell, and the town-clerk carrying the fair's proclamation. There are multiple head-on crashes and hat-losses, and leading dignitaries have been known to be so ill that they were unable to attend the Trinity lunch held afterwards. The three-day fair goes back to 1489 and used to be started from the merry-go-round; but it failed to show up one year and after an unsatisfactory dalliance with the big wheel, the dodgems are now firmly established in the ritual. Earlier in the day the mayor visits the children of Southwold Primary School and hands them all 50p Trinity Money, which nowadays is not quite enough for a fairground ride.

Southwold's Trinity Fair used to be held on **Trinity Sunday**, the Sunday after Whitsun, but moved due to the problem of booking showmen for what is a highly moveable date – see the Trinity section for more on the day's old fairs and feasts.

3rd June

Quackery Comes into Circulation

William Harvey died today in 1657. One of myth and superstition's arch-enemies, his studies in anatomy scotched innocent beliefs which had viewed the body as a mysterious vessel at the mercy of external forces. Once he had explained the basics of blood circulation, it was only a matter of time before people ceased to believe that dried toads could stop nose-bleeds, or that diseases could be cured by chanting prayers over a blood-stained rag.

Harvey also unscrambled the fundamentals of reproduction, in his *De Generatione Animalium* of 1653. It was all to do with healthy sperm, egg and womb. Hares did not cause hare-lips in children, and being frightened by a mouse could not result in birth-marks. There seemed little hope for superstition once science and logic had flattened out all the kinks of the universe.

In truth the interaction between old ways and the dimly understood breakthroughs of Harvey and others bred whole legions of wild new beliefs. The following century saw the rise of quack medicine – a pseudo-science, or pretend science, to cure 'quaking' patients.

© The festivities of the **West Linton Whipman Play**, at West Linton near Edinburgh, start on the first Friday in June and last more than a week; but there is no play as such. It all started around 1803. The Whipman used to ride to all the local landowners, after which there was sport and feasting, featuring displays of horsemanship, ploughing and horse-decorating, and a drama called the Whipman Play. These elements died out after the Second World War, but the event was revived in 1949 as a variant of the many Common Ridings which take place over the summer months – see June 13th for the bareback essentials.

© On the first Saturday in June, Chawleigh Friendly Society, at Chawleigh near South Molton in Devon, has its annual **Club Walk**, followed by a feast. The day begins with a roll call at the *Royal Oak Inn* at 11.30 am. Founded in 1869, it is one of the last of these local insurance schemes still in existence. For more on Friendly Societies, see Whit Friday and Saturday.

☙ **Weather**wise, June likes a bit of rain . . . at least we assume that is what is being referred to in:

A good leak in June
Sets all in tune.

If you fancy your lore a bit more geographically precise, try:

A misty and a dropping June
Brings the bonny land of Moray aboon.

All this rain makes good medicine, as June water cures eye ailments. It must be collected straight from the cloud: drippings from trees or eaves will not do. It can be bottled and used throughout the year, and is cheaper than going to the optician.

Being the month of the Roman goddess Juno, June is prime time for all women, over whom she watches. It is also said to be '*Good to the man and happy to the maid*' if they marry this month.

4th June
St Petroc's Day

A Giant Among Lawyers

The 6th century **St Petroc** founded the two monasteries at Padstow and Little Petherick in Cornwall; rescued a stag from marauding huntsmen; led a generally saintly life; and died. Over a thousand years later, he got his big shot at legend after being caught up in one of the great supernatural courtroom battles, and one of the toughest sentences.

Two 17th-century Cornish families were disputing the ownership of some land. Adding to the confusion, the lawyer for one side had fiddled the whole deal in his own favour before dying. That lawyer was the notorious **Jan Tregeagle**, who had sold his soul to the Devil. To resolve the mess, one of the defendants called a special witness – Tregeagle's phantom. Under cross-examination Tregeagle admitted to the swindle; but having been summoned from Hell, he was not too keen to go back.

It was decided that as long as Tregeagle was kept busy, he would be free from the Devil's clutches. Petroc's spirit was invoked as a special warden, and Tregeagle was given a leaky limpet shell and told to empty the bottomless Dozmary Pool. All around him on Bodmin Moor lurked headless hounds, ready to attack if he shirked.

One stormy night Tregeagle did a runner. He made it across the moor to Roche Rock Chapel and got his head inside. But the demon dogs caught up and did unspeakable things to the rest of him. After the mauling, Petroc bound Tregeagle in chains and set him a fresh batch of endless, pointless tasks. He still labours at them to this day, with Petroc moving him on each time his howls of frustration upset the locals.

At Padstow beach Tregeagle has to weave ropes out of sand. At Berepper he must carry bags of sand across Loe estuary to Porthleven until Berepper beach has gone – on one occasion there a demon tripped him up, and the sand which he had been carrying formed Loe Bar, blocking the harbour. At Lands End Jan has to sweep all the sand of Porthcurno Cove into Mill Bay. At each location the sea destroys all the work, suggesting that Hercules had an easy time of it after all. '*To roar like Tregeagle*' is a Cornish proverb.

Jan Tregeagle was a real man, an unpopular magistrate in the early 1600s. But in his mythical form his roots lie in Celtic tales of a giant who lived on the site of Dozmary Pool until it was flooded. The pool is one of the entrances into the Celtic Otherworld. The giant's labours are elemental, causing the various storms and winds of Bodmin Moor and the Cornish coast, and even restructuring the shape of the land.

Tregeagle's howls are still heard in the places which he visits during his task-phase; and on Bodmin Moor he races at the head of demon dogs during storms. Bottomless Dozmary Pool – unsuccessfully drained with the limpet – is one of the many resting places of Arthur's sword Excalibur. It is so bottomless that it often dries out.

🕮 St Petroc's Sicilian-Islamic head-reliquary is one of the finest to have survived the Reformation, and it can still be seen in the parish church at Bodmin.

© Eton College in Berkshire has its **Speeches Day** on the Thursday nearest June 4th, marking the birthday of founder George III. Senior boys in breeches and buckles read from literary works. This private part of the ceremony is followed by the more public Thames regatta in 18th-century costumes, with flowers, salutes and fireworks. The eight nine-oared boats are led by a ten-oared one, *The Monarch*.

5th June
St Boniface's Day

Sheep-Ho!

When heroes pass away the rumour is always the same, be it Arthur or Elvis – they'll be back. On this day in 1916 **Lord Kitchener** (he of the excessive moustache and pointy finger who insisted '*Your Country Needs You*' on the posters) sank with his ship. It was widely believed that he was not dead, and would return to win the First World War just when he was needed. Like his predecessors, he failed to fulfil expectations.

St Boniface – plain Winfrith to his parents – was born at Crediton in Devon in 675. He wrote England's first Latin Grammar and went on to become an influential missionary, not only converting the German and Frankish tribes but forming lasting European alliances. In one celebrated incident he chopped down an oak tree sacred to pagan deities. There was no divine retribution, and the locals agreed that their gods must be either apathetic or nonexistent. Conversion was the only possible outcome. Some less-impressed pagans lynched Boniface, the lumberjack of God, in 754.

🕮 In Britain, Boniface is associated with the **Cloutie Well**, aka St Boniface's Well, near Munlochy, north of Inverness in the Highlands. It is a Rag Well, where offerings of cloth are still left on the surrounding foliage to effect cures on their owners. This works by primitive sympathetic magic: the cloth takes on the disease, and when it is left behind, so is the ailment. Sufferers sprinkle Cloutie Well water three times on the ground, tie their rags, make the sign of the cross, and drink some of the well's contents. If anyone removes a rag they will contract the affliction of its erstwhile owner. For this reason there are an estimated 50,000 shreds of cloth on the surrounding bushes at the St Boniface Well, with more added all the time. The spectacular shrubbery-shrine is superstition's most unmissable rubbish-tip.

June is the chief month for **sheep-shearing** in England and Wales. In Sussex, they formerly kicked off with White Ram Night, when the captain of the contract shearing gangs gathered his men and outlined the itinerary. When the woolly work was done several sweaty days later, it was time for payment and merrymaking at the **Black Ram Night**. Black Ram was the name for a strong Sussex ale. The festivities were always on the Saturday following the final post-shearing cry of '*Sheep-ho!*', when the last beast had been left naked and confused.

Black Ram was financed by a system of shearing fines for such offences as abuse, letting your sheep escape, leaving some wool on the animal, nicking it with the blade, et cetera. Song and drink were the only goal of Black Ram, with a few games such as **Turn the Cap Over**. A glass of beer was balanced on the captain's felt hat, and holding it by the brim the participant drained the ale while the others sang encouragement. After imbibing he had to flip the empty glass into the upturned hat. If he failed, he tried again. After several goes he had no chance, and was as good as comatose. As the Sussex *Sheep-Shearing Song* says:

And yet before the night is through I'll bet you half a crown,
That if you haven't a special care that Ram will knock you down.

Which seems appropriate, considering the old saying: '*A black sheep is a biting beast.*'

6th June

Appleby the Day

🔟 ♱ When law-reformer, philosopher and economist **Jeremy Bentham** died in 1832 at the age of 84, his last wishes were dutifully carried out. He was dissected in front of his many friends. The skeleton was then reassembled, padded, and dressed in Bentham's best clothes. A wax head was placed on top. He was exhibited in a glass case with his own mummified head at his feet, at University College, London. And his body is not the only thing still on show. Bentham's ghost, as he should have guessed, mumbles and roams around the college still.

© **Appleby Horse Fair** begins on the Thursday before the second Wednesday of the month, at Appleby-in-Westmorland – which these days is Appleby-in-Cumbria. This is the St Leger, Derby and Grand National (1993 excluded) of horse fairs, the biggest event of its kind in the world. Thousands of travelling folk descend on Appleby for a week of bargaining, bragging and booze. With attitudes to travellers and gypsies being what they are, some locals and store-keepers abandon the town, while other stay to make the most of the fistfuls of cash flying about.

Unlike many surviving old fairs, which may have kept the title but are now nothing more than rides and amusements, Appleby is still all about horses and trading. The traditional sites for the event are the lane leading to Long Marton, where the fairgoers camp; Fair Hill, where the bartering takes place; and Holme Fair Meadow where the pre-sales horse-race has punters gambling their pocket money. In 1992 the highest side-bet was estimated at £17,000. Prior to the haggling, the horses are washed in the River Eden, an event guaranteed to be one of the most memorable parts of the fair for spectators. It all started in 1685 when James II handed over a licence '*for the purchase and sale of all manner of goods, cattle, horses mares and geldings*'.

When selling a nag at the fair, or elsewhere, bear in mind that '*In selling your horse praise the bad points and leave the good ones to take care of themselves.*' Or, better still, sell posthumously,

for '*A dead man's sock always smells well*'. Sorry, that should have read: '*A dead man's stock always sells well*'. There are also a few traditional 'petitions' on behalf of the horses. One from north-east Scotland runs: '*Up the hill trot me not; doon the hill gallop me not; in the fair road spare me not; in the stable forget me not.*'

© The first Thursday on or after June 6th is the official start of **Lanimers Week** at Lanark in Strathclyde, with the main Riding held on the previous day. There is a strong case for Lanark's horseback version of Beating the Bounds being the oldest surviving Borders' Riding, and because of this it is led not by a common or garden Cornet, but a Lord Cornet. A bell dating from the year 1100 is rung while the riding takes place. It only has the one note, but no one seems to mind. On the Thursday a procession called The Birks (after the birch twigs which the participants carry) lays wreaths at the statue of Scotland's great rebel hero, William Wallace, and a Lanimer Queen is crowned. To become saddled with more details about the Ridings, see June 13th.

7th June
St Meriasek's Day/
St Colman's Day

Ghost in High Heels

♱ **Sarah Fletcher** thwarted her husband's bigamous marriage. She made a surprise appearance at the altar, with good cause to chip in on the '*any just impediment*' clause. But after breaking up the ceremony she hanged herself with a pocket handkerchief, on this day in 1799. A verdict of lunacy was passed, enabling her to be buried on church grounds. That did not stop her from haunting her old home at Clifton Hampden, near Abingdon in Oxfordshire. Rooms and corridors echo with footsteps rhythmically stepping out in high heels, and cold gusts of wind.

The Rev Edward Crake first saw Sarah's ghost when he was a pupil in the 1860s – the house was a school in those days, and is now a private house. She was dressed in black, with a purple ribbon in curly red hair. She smiled, and disappeared. Crake saw her a few more times after this, including during a visit on June 7th 1864, the anniversary of her death; but the ghost became increasingly noisy. In the 1890s

Crake tried to exorcise it, but it became even noisier than before. He died in 1915, and Sarah Fletcher haunted on, usually with a look of anguish in place of the smile which Crake had first seen. She seems quiet enough now though, and only rarely deigns to put on her ghostly stilettos.

The 6th-century **St Meriasek** of Camborne, Cornwall, was a patron saint of tin-miners. Even at the turn of the century it was common to find a clay-image of the saint in place at the entrance to each level of the workings. At the start of each shift the miners would say '*Saint Meriasek, we pray thee*', to invoke his protection via the dolls. Tin-miners were very superstitious, just like their coal-carrying counterparts. If they met a snail while they were going to work they would give it some lantern wax 'for luck'. Whether the snails also found such an encounter lucky is unclear.

This is also **St Colman of Dromore**'s Day. His well is on top form today, and throughout June and May. It is by the ruined Cranfield church on the shore of Lough Neagh, near Churchtown in County Antrim. The well offers the usual general cures; and if you are lucky enough to find a **Cranfield Pebble** in the water, all the better. These are gypsum crystals resembling amber, and to own one ensures trouble-free childbirth for women, and prevents men from drowning. In the 1970s a car park was built nearby, and the well was cleaned. There were lots of coins in the bottom, and in spite of the fact that to remove such offerings brings bad luck, one workman allegedly took the money and went on a spree. He was killed by a car on the way home.

🔟 Early in June, Belton used to hold its **Horse Fair**, founded in the 13th century by Lady Roesia de Verdon, who also set up the now ruined Gracedieu Nunnery a couple of miles south of Belton, near Coalville in Leicestershire. Her tomb can be seen in Belton church.

8th June
St William of York's Day

Prince of Darkness

William of York was the city's favourite saint. The nephew of King Stephen, he was Arch-

bishop there in 1141. Deposed at the instigation of his enemies, in 1154 he was reinstated, re-entering York as a hero. Great crowds turned out, but proved too much for the wooden bridge over the Ouse. It collapsed, sending hundreds into the water. Cool customer as he was, William prayed, and the waters rose to form a new bridge, enabling his drowning followers to escape. This is just one of the 36 miracles attributed to the saint, most of which were credited to him long after he had died. His spirit-form regularly appeared out of nowhere to restore someone's sight, cure leprosy or – in one case – make a student fall out of love and return to his studies.
🔟 Each of William's miracles is illustrated in stained-glass in the gorgeous St William's window at York Minster.

Edward the Black Prince died on this day in 1376 after his syphilis flared up in Spain, despite swigging his favourite Kentish cure-all. A well in the village of Harbledown in Kent was so dear to the Prince that it became known as **Black Prince's Well**. He drank a flask of its water every day, at home or abroad, and claimed that it kept him fighting fit. Many Canterbury pilgrims tried out the waters on their way to the city, Harbledown being the last stopping-off point on the Pilgrims' Way.
♱ 🔟 By wearing black armour and gaining great honours early – he helped win the Battle of Crécy in 1346 at the age of 16 – Edward secured his place in the popular imagination. His ghost haunts Hall Place at Bexley in Greater London, where he stayed en route to war with France. In armour and sometimes with medieval music backing, he is seen at dusk during times of national crisis – three times during the First World War his appearance preceded military defeats. Edward's effigy can be seen in recline at Canterbury Cathedral, Kent.

Drinking whilst standing upright is supposed to lead to inflammation and possible death. Just ask King **Harthacnut**. *The Anglo-Saxon Chronicle* states that on this day in 1042, Harthacnut was in upright drinking mode and '*he suddenly fell to the ground with a horrible convulsion; and those who were near thereto took hold of him, but he never spoke again.*' He had reigned for a massive 10 days.

© The Thursday of the first full week in June is the established start-date of the three-day **Hawick Common Riding** in the Borders. Records of the festivities go back to 1703, but it is claimed that the event is a commemoration of young men – callants – from Hawick who routed the English in 1514 and absconded with their flag. To be elected as the leading figure, the Cornet, is a singular honour – married men cannot apply, and locals have been known to postpone a walk down the aisle in the hope of being selected. Those who complete the 30-mile round-trip to Mosspaul Hotel on the Friday are made members of the all-male Ancient Order of Mosstroopers, and can tuck into the traditional dish of curds and cream. For more on the Borders' Ridings, see June 13th.

☕ Brace yourself for the bad **weather** rhyme:

If on the 8th of June it rain,
It foretells a wet harvest, men sayn.

9th June
St Columba's Day

Wolf in Dove's Clothing Tackles Monster, Demon and Fish

As men of peace go, **St Columba** was abnormally violent and competitive. His mission to Scotland started after he lost a copyright fight back home in Ireland, known as The Battle of the Books. He had pirated a psalter belonging to the Magh Bile monastery, which told him to hand the copy over at once. He refused, and following a battle at Cooldrebhne, Columba's superiors confiscated his sword and sent him out into the wilds to do some converting and so make amends. Landing on Iona with 12 companions in 565, Columcille, as he was to be known – meaning Dove of the Church – buried his previous nickname, The Wolf.

But the wolf was still evident in the saint's robust personality. Slipping on a **flounder** one day, he cursed the unfortunate fish forever, which is said to be why the flounder's face is lopsided. And he tackled a lecherous Scottish royal, Broichan, by *'smiting him with an angel'*. Needless to say, the blow floored poor Broichan. Always a hands-on saint, Columba physically kicked a demon out of a loch on Skye in the Inner Hebrides. His most famous exploit was the tackling of the **Loch Ness Monster**. Making its debut appearance in myth and legend, it loomed up over one of Columba's monks who was swimming across the loch. The

Saint shouted *'Go no further, nor touch the man! Go back!'* Since then the monster has harmed no one, still shrinking from the holy admonishments.

Legend says that Loch Ness was once a fertile plain containing a magic well. The plain would thrive as long as well-users replaced the lid. One day a woman trekked over the plain for water, but heard her child screaming back at home. She ran back to the child, neglecting to close the well. Its water overflowed, and the next thing she knew, neighbours were saying *'Tha loch nis ann'*, meaning 'There is a lake now', thus giving Loch Ness its name.

📖 Before he died, Columba predicted that Iona would be visited by great kings. Sure enough, there are 48 of them buried here, and some of their tombs can still be viewed. Columba himself converted at least one monarch, the Pictish King Brude; and he went on to crown King Aidan. He also found time to write several slivers of poetry, some of which have survived. His followers thought him no less than an embodiment of Christ himself, and they often saw him chatting with angels, who clearly bore no grudge against Columba for having used one of their race as a cudgel. The old monastery, church, cemetery of the Kings, and Street of the Dead can all be visited on Iona in the Inner Hebrides – travel via Mull.

👁 If you wear the flower **St John's Wort** in your armpit, like St Columba did, it will ward off evil. Independently of this, June 9th is very lucky, especially when it falls on a Thursday.

10th June

Snail Creep Winds up the Bush Faggot

Today in 1829 the first **Oxford and Cambridge Boat Race** took to the Thames. The scene was set for a closely-contested, exemplary demonstration of skill, strength and buoyancy. But fate was having none of that. The two teams collided and sank. When they started again there was no contest, for Oxford won by miles. Miraculously, someone still thought that this was worth repeating every year. But it was decided that it would be even more fun in cold weather: the race now takes place on a Saturday in March or April, and Oxford still almost invariably win.

June 10th is **White Rose Day**. This is when

Scotland traditionally remembers the Jacobites and their doomed cause, being the birthday of James Edward Stuart, the Old Pretender. He was the son of the exiled Catholic King James II, and was unofficially crowned in France as a rival to the Protestant replacement King William of Orange. It was the Old Pretender's son, Bonnie Prince Charlie, who first plucked and wore the rose, at Fassfern by Loch Eil, in the Highlands. He and his men sported it at their defeat at Culloden in 1746, and since then the White Cockade, as it is known, has been a symbol of hope/lost hope/national pride, you name it.

In the second week of June the people of Roche and the surrounding district in Cornwall used to hold a feast. The unique attraction was a dance called the **Snail Creep**. While the band played, the dancers wound themselves in ever-decreasing circles, forming a coil of hot dancing bodies, before unwinding again. The shape they formed resembles the spiral of a snail's shell.

Other traditional games echo this. One is the resonant **Wind Up The Bush Faggot**. This time the head of the line stays put, and the others coil in round the nucleus while singing an old song that only has two notes. Once fully coiled, tune and words change and everyone jumps up and down, until the coil disintegrates. This all harks back to tree or stone worship, say folklorists, with the faithful dancing around their favourite lump of wood or rock; although the serpent-worship school of thought has quite a full class too.

In **Troy Walls** a maze is drawn on paper or a slate, and competitors have to work their way through with finger or pencil. The original versions took place in sacred mazes: the grooves on Glastonbury Tor are said by some to be remnants of a winding maze-like path to the top.

In **Green Grass** a lone figure stands before a line of chums and sings the first verse of the game, after which a partner steps forward. The two then continue the game, co-opting a third, and so on until everyone has been drafted in. Here is the first stanza from a version sung at Lanark in Strathelyde:

> *A-diss, a-diss a green grass, a-diss, a-diss, a-dass,*
> *Come my pretty fair maid and walk along with us,*
> *For you shall have a dik-ma-day, you shall have a dragon,*

> *You shall have a nice young man with princes for his thegan.*

In many versions someone dies in the last stanza. There are several theories as to the meaning of the game, but the favourite is that it echoes an old burial rite in which a dish of herbs (*a diss of green griss*) was left by a fire and danced around.

11th June
St Barnabas' Day

Barnaby Grudge

St Barnabas was a 1st-century colleague of the Apostles, and he takes no nonsense on this, his day. Near Darlington in County Durham a reckless carter was once getting his hay-cart ready on June 11th, a day when the devout were not meant to be working. As he rode by the pools known as **Hell's Kettles**, he pushed his luck by shouting:

> *Barnaby yea, Barnaby nay,*
> *I'll hae me hay whether God will or nay.*

No sooner had he rhymed 'nay' with 'nay' than Hell's Kettles sucked him in and swallowed him up for the sacrilege. When the water is clear, he can still be seen – horse, cart, damp hay and all – adrift in the Kettles' depths.

A pseudo-historical 12th-century yarn claims that Hell's Kettles were formed by an earthquake. The ground rose to the height of the church tops, and then at sunset it plunged down into a pit, forming the three pools. Several people died of fright during the earth's unexpected excursions. Besides carter and horse, Hell's Kettles are said to moan and seethe with other restless spirits. And there is certainly room for plenty of these, for '*As bottomless as Hell's Kettles*' is a proverbial utterance. Sadly, myth-busting surveyors have measured the three pits, and they average 17 feet in depth. They are now in suburban Darlington, a mile from the town centre.

☙ Barnabas' Day is the traditional start of **haysel**, or hay-making. There is an old memory-jogging saying: '*By St Barnabas, put scythe to grass*'; and the saint is often depicted in old drawings carrying a hay-rake. On this day churchgoers – even priests – would often wear small bouquets of wild flowers and grasses.

Flower-fans could easily be misled by the old rhyme:

When Barnaby bright shines night and day,
Poor Ragged Robin blooms in the hay,

as 'hay' means 'hedge' in this context. Whilst dealing with hay-sayings, here is a fog-warning: '*A good hay year, a bad fog year.*'

There is not much old lore at haysel, just hard work and – formerly, before whacking great machines did the job – lots of beer and cider. A traditional joke involved sending a naive haysel boy to fetch some 'rick mould'. The unfortunate lad tramped a mile or two to the allotted destination, where a colluding bloke would put the rick mould – a heavy rock, dead yak or similar weighty item – into a sack. The errand boy then had to carry it back in the blazing sun, with strict orders not to drop it. Hilarious. Similar jolly japes abound. Youths often found their errand for 'strap-oil' ending with stripey buttocks oiled by the joker's leather belt.

Snowshill in Gloucestershire used to stage a **mumming play** today, a good six months before most other mummers strutted their stuff. A very hot, unseasonal Father Christmas acted as compere, with the stars of the drama being King George and *Bold Slasher*. For more mumming see December 18th and 26th.

12th June

Needles and Pins

Today in 1785 Kitty '**The Human Pin-Cushion**' Hudson emerged from hospital in Nottingham, a cured woman. Since childhood she had been a pin-fetishist, sleeping with a mouthful of the things. It had all started when she was given a toffee for every mouthful of pins collected in her local church during the cleaning. For some reason the church appears to have been plagued by pins.

The doctors noted that the metal had worn down the girl's teeth, and they removed several pins and needles from various parts of her body. But there were still hundreds more inside, and although she never ate another, she continued to sprout pins for the rest of her life. While in hospital she met an old admirer: John Goddard, from Kitty's birth-

place at Arnold near Nottingham, who was having an eye out. Not much fun in those pre-anaesthetic days, but he managed to woo Kitty during his stay, and they got married. None of their 19 children made it past the age of 19.

The spirit of Kitty Hudson lived on in an appropriately modern form, if we can believe a *Daily Mail* report from 1921. A girl from Harrogate was reported to have had two strips of tin, a pen nib, and 200 gramophone needles removed from her stomach, with no ill effects afterwards. The paper reported, inscrutably: '*She is reticent about the swallowing of the needles.*'

Martha Taylor of Over Haddon, Derbyshire, did not eat pins. She did not eat anything. Following a blow on the back by a passing neighbour in 1669, Martha became paralysed, and completely lost her will to eat. For nine months she subsisted on just an occasional raisin, and a drop of milk or wine. She was skeletal, and suffered from temporary deaf and dumbness, convulsions, vomiting fits and tears of blood. She refused to have any flowers in her room, claiming that they were too strong for her brain. She became famous for this F-all-plan diet, pamphlets were published about the case, and she was declared '*one of the great wonders of the world*'. Her appetite eventually returned, and Martha died 25 years later on June 12th 1684.

© The second week of June is time for **Guid Nychburris Day** (Good Neighbours Day) in Dumfries, combining a Riding the Marches with sports, processions and entertainment. Their Riding is led by a Cornet, accompanied by a Pursuivant and four Lynors, who have the job of marking the boundaries with flags and posts. Despite being a 'Day', the events are a week-long festival of fraternity and merriment, and an old song about the event runs:

Frae faur an' near
We gaither here,
A Loreburne's loyal blude,
To keep wi' mirth an graun' array
Oor ain Dumfries Guid Nychburris Day
Wi' richt guid nychburhude.

© Biggar in Strathclyde usually has its Gala Day on the second Saturday in June. There are floats, festivities and feasts, with a **Fleming Queen** elected for good measure. The next day, Biggar has its **Riding of the Marches**. For the full Ridings itinerary, see June 13th.

13th June
St Antony of Padua's Day

Thunderbolt and Lightfoot

In 1364 crusader Edward Estur went to the Holy Land, got a severe blow to the head, and was dispatched home to Gatcombe, near Newport on the Isle of Wight. Under the circumstances it is almost forgiveable that he forgot to bring back his true-love, **Lucy Lightfoot**, who was in Cyprus awaiting his return from the wars. He died, and Lucy was never seen again. As a war-hero Estur was given an elaborate tomb in Gatcombe church, capped with his effigy in oak.

Fast-forward 500 years, to another Lucy Lightfoot. She lived in Bowcombe, near Gatcombe, and became obsessed with Edward's effigy. When quizzed by concerned relatives, she admitted '*I love to be with him in my thoughts and dreams*'. Unaware of her name-link with Edward's mistress, she visited his tomb every day until the morning of June 13th 1831. As soon as she entered the church that day, a tempest blew up, attended by an eclipse of the sun. When the thunder and lightning abated, the church was empty. Just like the original Lightfoot, the Mark II Lucy was never seen again.

🏛 Edward Estur's lust-inspiring effigy is still at Gatcombe church.

This is the feast-day of **St Antony of Padua**. He should have been called in to locate the missing pair of Lightfeet, as he can be invoked to find any lost object. This notion originated when a novice borrowed the saint's psalter and was told by a no-nonsense apparition to give it back.

Antony died in 1231; but as recently as October 1991 he was back in the headlines when thieves stole his relics in Rome. Black market demand for old bones, however blessed, is limited. What caught the thieves' eye was probably the gold, jewel-encrusted reliquary which contained the fragments. In life Antony had been a lay preacher, famed for his eloquence. After the rest of his body had turned to dust, his lower jaw and tongue were found fleshy and intact. That tongue's most spectacular achievement came when it shamed a lakeful of irreligious fish into repenting their sins.

Antony shares fish-conversations and lost-and-found skills with the Celtic god **Nodons**, who was still popular up to the 5th century AD.

It may well be that Antony's talents were embroidered as a way of bringing followers of Nodons into the Christian fold. The shrine built for Nodons at Lydney in the Forest of Dean around AD 365 was very sophisticated, with an annex to house the foot-weary worshipper. In his Irish guise, Nodons communed not just with finned sinners, but with the top-fish, the **Salmon of Knowledge**. This fish-deity knew all the secrets of the universe, and gained its knowledge by eating hazelnuts which had been left as offerings in wells. The combination of the sacred well water and the mystical nature of the hazelnuts themselves were what enabled the salmon to answer questions on any Topic.

🏛 The remains of Nodon's temple can be tripped over in the grounds of Lydney Park, at Lydney which is near Coleford in Gloucestershire.

The area on either side of the Scotland-England border was known as the Marches, and it was only in the 16th century that the border was officially fixed in law. Until then this had been 'the Debatable Land', liable to be stolen from under the noses of settlers as raiders from both countries did their best to encroach. It was the duty of sheriffs from both sides to send men regularly into this war zone to re-establish territorial rights.

This is the spirit behind the Borders' numerous **Riding the Marches** celebrations of June, July and August – the need repeatedly to re-emphasise local boundaries; and the need to assert the common rights of wood-and-peat cutting. The Ridings in their present form were a 19th-century invention, taking nostalgic notions planted in the previous century and turning them into full scale instant traditions. The Riders, in their hundreds, follow an elected leader – usually known as the Whipman, or Standard Bearer, or Callant, or Cornet – around the boundaries, or further afield. In some cases they stop at allotted spots for traditional words or a song, and the symbolic cutting of peat and bracken to reaffirm rights. During the various parades the burgh's flag is usually bussed – decorated with multi-coloured ribbons – and there are accompanying sports, games and feasts.

© The timing of the 400-year-old **Selkirk Common Riding** traditionally set the date for all the others, though many of the events have now gone their own way. Selkirk's runners and riders usually get under starter's orders on the Friday after the second Monday in June.

On the eve of the Ridings, a fife and drum band parades through the streets 'crying the burley', summoning the participants for the next day's events. On the big day the Standard Bearer leads the other horsemen on a four-hour up-hill and down-dale ride, finishing with a gallop back into Selkirk. There he 'casts the colours', to commemorate the Scots near-annihilation at Flodden in 1513, at which 80 men from Selkirk took part in the battle; only one survived. A captured English flag which that survivor brought with him was the supposed impetus for the Selkirk Riding – its leader is, for this reason, known as the Standard Bearer. © The much smaller, recently revived, Riding the Marches at **Linlithgow** in Lothian are also held in mid-June, and the second Saturday in June is the traditional date for the Cornet and his cronies to gallop out at **Lockerbie** near Dumfries. During the Ride, the Cornet reasserts the burgh's turf-digging rights at the area's common peat bogs.

14th June

Marling – A Dear Trick

Charles I's Royalist army suffered a crushing defeat at the **Battle of Naseby**, Northamptonshire, on this day in 1645, which effectively ended the Civil War. Charles could have kicked himself. Before the battle, whilst staying in nearby Daventry, he had been visited in his dreams, two nights on the trot, by one of his generals, Stafford, who warned him that he could not win a battle at this location, and should march north to a more advantageous site. But Prince Rupert – a war-hero despite having a dog running at his horse's heels whenever he rode into battle – persuaded Charles to stay put.

On 14th June 1949 – 304 years later – two cyclists stopped for a breather near Naseby. As they lay there, they saw several leather-jerkined men pushing dusty carts along the old drovers' road. Both cyclists began to feel very uncomfortable and uneasy, and without exchanging a word they got on their bikes and pedalled away. Only later did they discover that they had rested at the site of the battle, on the same day as it had been fought, and that what they had encountered were ghosts of the Civil War dead.

This was the time of year when **marling** took place. Marl was dug from pits by gangs and spread over the land like geological dung. Clay soil with a heavy lime content, it is more useful on some types of land than others, as revealed in the rhyme:

He that marls sand may buy the land,
He that marls moss shall suffer no loss;
But he that marls clay flings all away.

The marlers had a foreman called the Lord of the Pit or Soil, responsible for the workload. He also spent much of the day ritually extracting money from passers-by. Everyone was assailed, and when anyone coughed up loose change, the Lord of the Pit would formally declare: '*Oyez! Oyez! Oyez! This is to give notice that X has given us marlers part of a hundred pound, and to whomsoever will do the same we will give thanks and shout!*' If the gift was more than 6d, the words '*a part of a thousand pounds*' were substituted, and all the men bawled '*Largesse! Largesse!*'

At the end of the marling, the pit was garlanded, and the men descended on the inn or the landowner's house for beer, fun and feasting. As marl lasted 20 years or so, the owner could afford to splash out. All that remains of marling now are a few local Marlpit road or field names, and a Cheshire saying, '*Marling a man*', meaning to cheer him as vociferously as the marlers used to cry '*Largesse!*'.

One tale from a Warwickshire marl-pit gives a twist to a familiar ghost story. A man claimed to have been visited by the spirit of a widow's murdered husband. The phantom revealed the identity of his murderer, and said that the killer had thrown the body into the pit to moulder with the marl. The named man was duly arrested, but the evidence against him proved too tenuous. In desperation the ghost was summoned to court to testify, but it failed to appear and the accused was acquitted. Meanwhile, the man to whom the ghost had supposedly made its visit was investigated and found to be less than squeaky clean in the matter. The ghost-ruse had proved to be his undoing. Eventually he confessed that *he* had murdered the man in the marl-pit, and was hanged.

15th June
St Vitus and
Companions' Day

Demons in Vitus to Dance

Wyom and Evra Hendon stood to inherit a fortune from their father, a silver miner in Nevada. He sent them to England to be schooled, leaving them in the care of his partner, Herbert Dingwall. On this day in 1815, Dingwall took them to Salford Hall convent (now a private house) at Abbots Salford, west of Stratford-upon-Avon in Warwickshire. The Abbess was given money for their upkeep, along with instructions to put a coded advert in the newspaper for nine days commencing June 15th 1820. All a bit strange. Five years later, the instructions were duly carried out. The advert brought a response, requesting that Wyom, by now 18, should travel to Buckinghamshire.

Perplexed, Wyom bade her sister farewell, and set out for the mystery address. Nothing was heard for months, and meanwhile Evra became feverish. She began sleep-walking, and had strange visions every night in which her sister spoke to her. She heard men threatening Wyom, trying to force her to sign something. Distraught, Evra feared that her sister really was in trouble, and dearly wished to help in some way.

She did not realise it during her lifetime, but she was helping. Wyom was being held against her will by Dingwall, who wanted her either to marry his son, or sign away her rights to her inheritance. Each time Evra heard her sister, Wyom and Dingwall saw a fearful apparition of Evra, floating in through the window. Dingwall and his son slowly became unhinged by the ghost, and in their madness one of them stabbed Wyom. A doctor was called, and he suspected foul-play. The whole matter eventually wound up in court. Wyom recovered, and married the doctor who had rescued her. Dingwall was sentenced to transportation. But the nightly astral exertions proved too much for Evra, who died. Her only consolation is that she is remembered as the only ghost to haunt while still alive and stop once dead.

☙ St Swithin does not have exclusive rights on lengthy spells of rain:

If St Vitus' day be rainy weather,
It will rain for thirty days together.

St Vitus is the patron saint of nervous disorders. In the past such conditions were thought to be caused by demonic possession, and Vitus is especially good at casting out squatting devils. He was regularly invoked on this day for such purposes. The ailment called St Vitus' Dance – Sydenham's chorea, more properly – was his speciality. And by a leap of black humour he is also patron of dancers. This is due to the quaking which is one of the disease's symptoms; but it is also explained by the activities of an angel which danced for the saint while he was in prison before his death in AD 303: a pre-execution angelic cabaret.

There is more black humour and a certain resigned tone in the following cure for St Vitus' Dance, from Devon. It should be written on parchment to gain full effect:

Shake her, good Devil, shake her once well;
Then shake her no more till you shake her in
*   hell.*

St Vitus also helps sluggards get out of bed, apparently. And the Companions, in case you wondered, are Modestus and Crescentia, both martyred on the same day as Vitus.

16th June

Skeleton Key and
Amphibious Landings

After defeat at the Battle of Stoke, south of East Stoke in Nottinghamshire, on June 16th 1487, the last **Lord Lovell** scrambled home to Minster Lovell to take refuge in the family Hall. He had ill-advisedly supported the cause of the Pretender Lambert Simnel against Henry VII. At home he concealed himself in a secret room, and gave his servant the only key, plus enough money to keep himself and the rest of the household fed and watered until Henry VII's pique peaked. But the servant was either fatally absent-minded or grotesquely opportunist. Lovell was not seen again until 1708 when workmen knocked down the wall of the secret room to find a skeleton looking as neglected as a skeleton can, complete with pen and paper at hand. Even the bones did not last, as the inrush of fresh air caused Lovell to crumble to dust.

▥ Time has taken a similar if less drastic toll on Minster Lovell Hall, near Witney in Oxfordshire, which is now a picturesque ruin.

✝ Lyme Hall in Macclesfield, Cheshire, has a **bell-ringing ghost**, the phantom of a man who became trapped in a cavity beneath the building. No one heard his cries for help in life, and so he annoys everyone with bells now.

Lyme Hall has a stronger link with today in the form of Sir Peter Legh's incorporeal cortege. Legh died in Paris on June 16th 1422, but was buried at Lyme Hall. His **ghostly funeral procession** can still be seen in the surrounding park, and ascending the nearby hill Knight's Low. At the rear of the phantom mourners is a woman in white called Blanche. She was Legh's lover – his Legh-over – and died of grief when she heard of his demise. Her body was found beside the local River Bollin, on a spot since known as Lady's Grave.

Freak storms produce all manner of surprising precipitation. Today in 1939 a downpour of tiny frogs fell on Trowbridge in Wiltshire. And in June 1892, a shower of white – either albino or terrified – frogs gatecrashed the delights of Moseley near Dudley in the West Midlands. In June 1982 at Doncaster, a team of Morris men were slaughtered by a shower of small bison. One, but only one, of the above is a lie.

© Sometime in June, at Pewsey near Marlborough in Wiltshire, **the Towncriers' Competition** is held, and bombasters from all over the country compete. Judges look for impressive voices, baroque robe-and-hat costumes, and an ability to shout while impersonating a school dinner bell. Although Pewsey's is an ancient competition, the tourist appeal of town-crier show-downs means that there are usually several other challenge matches over the summer months, often at seaside resorts.

.

17th June
St Nectan/St Botolph's Day

Square-Deal Serf

The **Peasants' Revolt** of 1381 ended on this day when the leader of the uprising, Wat Tyler, was killed. The rebellion had started when a taxman tried to examine Tyler's daughter in Dartford. If she had visibly passed puberty, she was liable to pay the newly-introduced, ever-popular Poll Tax. The enraged Tyler killed the taxman and found himself stepping out of his bit-part as a serf into a lead role as a revolutionary. He was aware of the mass discontent which every decent citizen felt on the subject of the tax, and led the first batch of anti-Poll Taxers through Rochester and Maidstone in Kent, freeing prisoners from the local jails and gaining unhindered access to London.

Once Wat Tyler's men had congregated in the capital, a petition was read to the teenage King Richard II. Richard agreed to make the malcontents free men, and to improve their lot during his reign. But this was just the usual con. A few over-enthusiastic revellers were used as an excuse to crush the rebels at their next meeting with the King in Smithfield. William Walworth, Mayor of London, stabbed Tyler. The treaties were torn up and several other prime-movers were murdered. Another great day for justice.

Hartland Point near Stoke, north of Bude in Cornwall, is also known as the **Headland Of Hercules**. On some sort of hero-exchange scheme Hercules is said to have landed there, beaten up the local giants, and gone on to govern Britain until he got bored and returned to his rightful place in Graeco-Roman mythology.

● Mass is traditionally held today at **St Nectan's Well**, Hartland Point, and is followed by a procession of children carrying **foxgloves**. When 6th-century Nectan was killed, he carried his head half a mile in order to hurl it into the well. Wherever his blood fell along the way, foxgloves sprang up. The ceremony is now staged intermittently on or around St Nectan's Day, in years when enough interested people can be assembled.

St Nectan has been allotted more than one death; and the alternative demise, which took place in St Nectan's Glen at Trethevy in Cornwall, is even more fantastical. With his last gasp, Nectan threw his silver chapel bell into the waterfall there and declared that it would only reappear when religion had removed the taint of paganism, and ironed out its corruption. Ironically, well-worshipping – which lingers behind the foxglove ceremony in Devon – is just the sort of pagan hang-over to which Nectan was referring. The saint was buried in the Glen with a modest store of treasure. Well over a millenium later Cornish miners tried to blast their way in; but repeated dynamiting had no effect. Then they heard a bell ring, accompanied by Nectan's sonorous voice: '*The child is not yet born who shall recover this treasure*', he announced. Work ceased at once, and has never recommenced. Saved by the concealed bell.

Today's other saint is Botolph, the man after whom Boston – ie *Botolph's town* – in Lincolnshire is named. The main church in the town has an exposed tower, known as Boston Stump. The wintry winds which whistle round it are said to result from a no-blows-barred contest between **St Botolph and the Devil**. The ceaseless gales are made by Satan, who is still trying to get his breath back after being roundly trounced by the wily saint.

18th June
Waterloo Day

Waterloo Moonset

On June 18th 1178 a group of men were watching the skies. To their surprise the **moon split** in two. From the fissure, according to chronicler Gervase of Canterbury, '*a flaming torch sprang up, spewing out, over a considerable distance, fire, hot coals, and sparks. Meanwhile the body of the moon which was below writhed, as it were, in anxiety.*' After a while the moon turned black and calmed down. Posterity was all set to laugh the whole thing off when, this century, a theory was advanced saying that Gervase had recorded the meteor collision which created *Giordano Bruno*, a 12-mile radius crater on the surface of the moon.

© At Appleton Thorn, near Warrington in Cheshire, **Bawming the Thorn** takes place at 2.15 pm on the Saturday before the longest day. The longest day is usually the 21st, which means that the Bawming nearly always occurs on the third Saturday in June. Originally it was a Midsummer festival celebrated on July 5th, Old Midsummer Day. There have been various lapses due to rowdiness over the years, and in its present form it is very genteel. Children dance around the Appleton Thorn, a hawthorn tree, and decorate it with ribbons and garlands. There is then a procession and gala. The original Appleton tree can be traced back to the Glastonbury Thorn – which supposedly grew from Joseph of Arimathea's staff. Unfortunately, whatever its ancestry, in 1967 the Appleton Thorn fell down and died. In earlier times this might have killed off the custom; but the villagers simply acquired a new Thorn – which is now protected by railings – and carried on. The word *bawming* means 'anointing' or 'decorating'. Even in its present heavily pruned

guise, this is a form of living tree worship, one of the most ancient of all religions.

● 🗓 The **Duke of Wellington's** manor at Stratfield Saye, near Basingstoke in Hampshire, is held on condition that a Quit Rent is paid. This particular Quit Rent comes to the princely sum of one small silk tricolour flag per annum. The flag – a replica of one captured at Waterloo in Belgium – is presented to the monarch today, before noon, and is then fastened above the Duke of Wellington's bust in the Guard Room at Windsor Castle, Berkshire. When the 'Iron Duke' won the day at Waterloo in 1815, he was in his military colours of blue and yellow, and these colours decorate Windsor Castle's Waterloo Chamber during the private feast which takes place there this evening. Stratfield Saye house is open to the public.

In 1815, the poets **Wordsworth and Southey** celebrated the victory in fine style: they held a party on the top of Skiddaw in the Lake District and threw lighted tar-barrels down the hillside.

🗓 At Llanfairpwllgwyngyllgogerychwyrndrobwllantysiliogogogoch on the isle of Anglesey, there is a monument to the **Marquess of Anglesey**, who was second in command at Waterloo. The monument consists of a 91-foot-high column, ascended by an internal spiral staircase, with a statue on top. The Marquess found fame when his pained cry on the battlefield – '*By God sir, I've lost me leg!*' – prompted Wellington's reply: '*By God sir, so you have!*'

19th June

King of the Faeries

At the age of nought years, nought days and one second, **King James VI** of Scotland – later James I of England – entered the realms of folklore. He was born on this day in 1566 with a caul – part of the placental membrane – on his head. A caul brings untold good fortune (see August 23rd for total re: caul). Its chief attribute is to prevent its owner from drowning; and when James VI escaped such a fate following an accident on the Leith/Kirkcaldy ferry in 1600, it came as no surprise to those who knew about his caul.

When in 1800 a child's bones were found at Edinburgh Castle, James' birthplace, a new rumour sprang up saying that the man we know as James VI/I was a changeling, and that the bones belonged to the rightful heir. Some went for the faerie-changeling tack; others said that the changeling boy was in fact the offspring of the Earl of Mar.

© On the Saturday on or before June 20th, Abingdon in Oxfordshire elects the **Mayor of Ock Street**. This is done by ballot, but escapes Gallup polls, *Newsnight* specials and the like, as all the candidates must be local Morris men. All residents of Ock Street are entitled to vote, and the results are announced at 4 pm. The winner receives the 'Mayor' title, and becomes the Squire of the Morris team for a year. There is much dancing. This is all said to have originated at the village's annual fair in 1700, when the traditional roast ox became the centre of a squabble. Everyone fought for the horns, and the Squire of the Morris men won the punch-up. The horns have been carried by the Abingdon team ever since, on a flat wooden mock Ock oxhead with '*1700*' painted on its forehead.

Plausible, but not necessarily true. The totem horns and mock mayors suggest that it may be yet another event putting a modern – albeit 300-year-old – slant on its ancient origins. Traditionally, the mock-mayor is a symbol of anarchy, and also a sacrificial figure; and the horns have connotations of animal worship.

© **Mela** is an Asian word for a fair or bizarre, and in 1988 the Mela mêlée became the centrepiece of the new multi-cultural Bradford Festival, in West Yorkshire. Each June there are processions and shows of all kinds, and in 1992 a quarter of a million people turned up, making it the biggest Asian fair in Europe. In that year the Mayor of Bradford earned his Mela ticket by opening the event from a glittering throne on the back of a huge carved elephant. And not a Morris man in sight.

© ⛫ At **Melrose**, near Galashiels in the Borders, in the third week of June, it is **Festival Week**, with various sports and processions, the latter led by an official called the Melrosian. His exploits are part of the Scottish tradition of Common Ridings – see June 13th. On the Thursday of Festival Week the Melrosian is officially installed in a ceremony at the beautifully preserved 12th-century Melrose Abbey, at which a Festival Queen is also crowned.

20th June
St Govan's Day/
St Alban's Day

Rose from the Dead

The Diocletian Persecutions, around AD 305, gave a pre-English England its first Christian martyr, **St Alban**. He had recently been converted by a fugitive priest to whom he had given shelter, and was so taken with the new religion that, when pressed, he refused to recant and offer sacrifices to the Roman gods. He was imprisoned and carted off from Verulamium – later to become the city of St Albans in Hertfordshire – to nearby Holmeshurst Hill for execution. Alban wanted to get the messy business over with, and at the foot of the hill a stream which he needed to cross dried up so as not to hinder his progress. But after the ascent Alban needed a drink, and so the spring helpfully gushed forth again on the hilltop. Witnessing these miracles the executioner threw down his axe, and he too converted to the faith. A second mercenary was called for to dispose of them both. He successfully removed Alban's head; but in divine retribution his eyes immediately sprang out.

⛫ Alban's relics were placed in a shrine around which the new town of St Albans grew. These relics went missing a few hundred years later, until King Offa of Mercia was told by an angel where to disinter them. He was instructed to build a new monastery to house them, and erected a spanking new shrine. Most of this second relic-repository was stolen during the Reformation. But not to worry – Ely in Cambridgeshire had a second set of Alban relics on standby, even though St Albans Cathedral insisted they were fakes. In 1993, to celebrate the 1,200th anniversary of Offa's supposed foundation of the monastery, St Alban's shrine was restored.

That 12th-century fount of much British saintly knowledge Geoffrey of Monmouth named the priest sheltered by Alban as **St Amphibalus**. He accumulated several legends and a cult following, aided by the discovery in 1178 of his remains at St Albans. Unfortunately, he is a figment of Geoffrey's Latin-English dictionary: the name Amphibalus comes from a mistranslation of 'cloak'.

© On the Sunday of or after St Alban's Day, the Cathedral at St Albans has a **Rose Service**. Children parade with roses to the saint's shrine, which still retains a few of its holes, built into the structure to receive votive offerings from Alban pilgrims. The roses are blessed, and tossed on to the floor to make a herbaceous carpet, which stays on show in the Cathedral for a week or so. This links in not only with the city's being the headquarters of the National Rose Society, but with another pre-execution saint legend, which claims that all the roses on Holmeshurst Hill burst into bloom just before St Alban's death.

🛆 June 20th's second saint, **Govan**, lived in a tiny chapel at St Govan's Head, near Bosherston, south of Pembroke in Dyfed. Govan has been identified with Gawain, King Arthur's noble knight. He is said to have come to the chapel after the Round Table had rolled into oblivion, to live the life of a hermit. To escape from pursuing enemies he hid in a magic cleft in the rock wall of the chapel. This fissure can still be seen. If you stand inside it, your wishes and hopes will all come true within the year, as long as you are firm and decisive as you formulate the wishes, and as long as you turn round each time a wish is made. The steps leading to and from the chapel are weird too: their number is different, so they say, depending on whether you are ascending or descending.

21st June
Summer Solstice

Stoned Circles

Druids, golden sickles, dawn rituals at stone circles, pagan ceremonies stretching back to the Dawn of Time. These are the stuff of the **Summer Solstice**. But with cops and convoys due to battle it out at Stonehenge and other ancient sites across the land today, it seems churlish to point out that all this mysticism is a major outbreak of tosh.

There are those who claim that Druidry goes back to time immemorial. They tend to be Druids. Their ceremonies, cobbled together from various religious and occult left-overs, date mostly from the Victorian rather than the Pre-Cambrian era. This does not prevent practising Druids, sincere in their beliefs, from being thrust reluctantly into the headlines each Summer Solstice as they form a nucleus for crowds seeking anything from spiritual elevation to a good chuckle. The usual running order

is: arrival at stone circle; dancing; fire-building; dancing round fire; audience participation in mystic rites involving flowing white nightshirts and pretend-sacrifice; surprise concert by Hawkwind; more dancing. Dawn and drugs are both optional. As is the stone circle itself, for police intervention often makes access impossible.

Even though the ceremonies have transparently dodgy origins, these summer solstice gatherings are no dafter than many other rituals covered in this book. The only difference here is that this is a new tradition, with many of those taking part still quite convinced that they are at the dawning of the Age of Aquarius. Or whatever.

The ceremonies themselves may be dubious, but the reason for picking the shortest night of the year is not. This period of the year is rich in genuinely ancient customs. Centuries ago the Celtic and Romano-British peoples used to doff their hats to the sun god, reach for the sunblock cream and celebrate the marriage of that immortal Sunny and Cher, Jupiter and Juno (or local equivalents). But soon after the coming of Christianity, anything with vestigial meaning shifted to St John's Eve and Day (23rd and 24th).

© Predictable trouble at Stonehenge and its sacred fence, car park and visitors' centre will be witnessed today. Of the genuine surviving solstice ceremonies, the **Peebles Beltane Festival** at Peebles, Borders, seems relatively untroubled by the passing of time and the rusting of golden sickles. (Okay, so gold doesn't rust.) The week of Ridings, concerts, discos and parades starts on the penultimate Saturday in June. For more on the Ridings aspect, see June 13th. There are horse races on the local golf course. The chief racing prize of the day is a bell. Throughout the day the rousing tones of *The Cornet Reel* ring out. *Beltane* is a misnomer, however, being the festival of early May. The fact that it has the word 'Bell' in it was probably more important than any attempt at historical accuracy.

🛆 Every summer solstice – usually the 21st, sometimes the 20th or 22nd – crowds gather at the Parish Church of Edward the Confessor in Leek, Staffordshire to witness the strange **double sunset**. From the north-east corner of the churchyard – known as Doctor's Corner due to the eight doctors buried there – the sun sinks behind Cloud End hill, only to reappear further north a few minutes later and set for a second time. Even better, there is sometimes an additional optical illusion, with a mirror-image of the sun following hot on the heels of the real sun below the brow of the hill.

22nd June
Old St Barnabas' Day/
St Thomas More's Day

Tyron Ashore As Wrecks

On 22nd June 1893 **Sir George Tyron** was on HMS *Victoria* off the coast of Syria. Hence the considerable surprise of the house-guests who saw him walk across the room at Lady Tyron's party in Eaton Square, London, on that very day. It was, of course, a ghost. George had just died, and in retrospect the cause of his circumnavigational restlessness was not hard to pin down. He had ordered his vessel *Victoria* and its sister ship HMS *Camperdown* to alter course and sail towards each other, in spite of his officers' observation – straight from page one of *The Ladybird Book of Sailing* – that this would cause a collision. Eventually George commanded the steersmen to resume their original course, but it was too late. The two ships collided, hundreds of men drowned, and the *Victoria* blew up when water hit the engines. The Admiral's understated last words were, allegedly, '*It is all my fault*'.

Old Barnabas' Day is the traditional date for **Boroughbridge Horse Fair** in North Yorkshire. Known as Barnaby Fair, it used to take place the Tuesday after the 22nd, until the axe finally fell in the late 1980s. Horses were always the stars of this particular show, though in the 1980s it had become a shadow of its former self, and local pressure succeeded in making it a horse fair with no horse traders.

Special Barnaby Boats brought outsiders down the rivers for the festivities, and top of the day's menu was the Barnaby Tart – a kind of lemon curd pastry. The tarts were accompanied by a mug of beer. The 1622 charter sanctioning the fair allowed locals to brew their own ale for the occasion, which laid the roots of its rowdiness.

© The village of Steetley, just west of Worksop in Nottinghamshire, was almost wiped out by the Black Death. Its exquisite

52-feet by 15-feet 12th-century private chapel fell into disuse, and took on an extended lease of life as a cowshed. In 1880 it was restored to a close approximation of its former glory, and ever since on the Sunday nearest June 20th there has been an open-air service at the former chapel (now All Saints' Church), which now stands in splendid isolation. The 3.15 pm hymn-prayer-sermon sandwich celebrates the life of the community. A new waymarked footpath goes from All Saints' to the church at Whitwell, via the ancient **Shire Oak** which marks the traditional three-way boundary of Yorkshire, Derbyshire and Nottinghamshire.

✝ **Thomas More** was executed in 1535, a martyr to the Catholic faith, refusing to recognise big fat Henry VIII as head of the big fat church. After execution, More's head was impaled on Tower Bridge until his daughter, Margaret Roper, bribed the executioner to hand it over to her. She took the head back to Bayards Park at Cranleigh in Surrey, and More chose that spot to do his share of haunting. He is still spied there occasionally. It was not until 1935 that Sir Thomas became St Thomas.

At the back-end of June the **Tanbark Festival** at Cricklade in Wiltshire used to mark the end of the season in the tanneries, during which bark was stripped off trees for tanning. The village had its own out-of-season mumming play to mark the occasion, as well as a big feast.

23rd June
Midsummer Eve

Centaurs, Selkies
and the Voice of Cod

In 1626 on **Midsummer Eve** a Cambridge fishwife found a book inside a large cod. The event was witnessed by a crowd that included a Mr Mead of Christ's Church College, who took charge of the find. Wrapped in sailcloth and distinctly slimy, the book was still legible. It was a treatise on theology written by John Frith, a supposed heretic who had been imprisoned one hundred years earlier in a fish cellar. With God clearly taking an interest in the distribution, the book was immediately reprinted under the title *Vox Piscis* – '**The Voice of the Fish**'.

William Lancaster ran Blake Farm near Souther Fell in Cumbria. On Midsummer Eve 1735 one of his servants reported a ghostly encounter. Not for him a solitary spook – he claimed to have seen several thousand, an entire **afterlife army** marching over the top of the fell. General ridiculing ensued. But two years to the day later, Lancaster himself saw the same phenomenon on the east side of the fell – a column half a mile long and five men wide, led not by officers on horseback, but by centaurs. Wishing to avoid the mockery meted out to his servant, Lancaster summoned his family who watched the half-man, half-horse army march on until the light faded.

All quiet on the east fell front for another eight years, when – again on Midsummer Eve – Lancaster and dozens of friends witnessed the spirit soldiers. Several people hunted in vain for hoof-prints, convinced that the vision was real. The events attracted enormous nationwide coverage, including a poem by Wordsworth (not one of his better efforts). Pseudo-scientists explained it all away as the effects of *'an undulating lambient meteor'*, while others said it was a supernatural sneak preview of the 1745 Scottish Rebellion which began days later. Or it may just have been an even more freakish foretaste of Lake District crowds 250 years on.

📖 Another Midsummer Eve, another time, another place, a fiddler was hired to play at an outdoor wedding feast. He kept everyone bopping until midnight; but it was then the Sabbath, when dancing was forbidden. In spite of loud protests he broke off and left. The slave-to-the-rhythm bride demanded more music even if she *'had to go to Hell for it'*. Such a remark in an old tale usually means an unhappy end is imminent, and in this case an old man appeared (horns and cloven feet optional) and volunteered to play on. As the devout fiddler watched from a handy nearby bush, the old man's music got faster and faster, but no one could stop dancing. Daybreak came, the cock crowed, the old man smiled and vanished; and – blisters and all – the exhausted dancers were turned to stone. Only the fiddler survived to report the events of that night at Stanton Drew, south of Bristol in Avon. The three stone circles there are still known locally as **The Devil's Wedding**.

The Rollright Stones in Oxfordshire are another piece of Midsummer Eve reverse anthropomorphosis. A local king and his knights sought dominion over the entire country. On a hill near the village of Long Compton they met a witch. She persuaded them that if their leader took seven long strides and then looked down on the village, he would become King of all England. Piece of cake, thought the king, and bit into the challenge with a burst of impro-poetry: *'Stick, stock, stone, as King of England I shall be known'*. But on his last stride a long barrow suddenly sprang from the ground, blocking his view. Forfeits were tough in those days, and the witch turned the entire company to stone. For no apparent reason, the witch herself became an elder tree.

📖 There are about 70 Rollright Stones near Little Rollright, north of Chipping Norton, but it is supposedly impossible to count the exact number. They include the King Stone; a circle known as the King's Men; and an isolated group, the Whispering Knights. For several hundred years pilgrims surrounded the King Stone each Midsummer Eve to commemorate Rollright's legend of royalty turned to rock. A branch was cut off the elder tree, which then bled, while the King Stone 'moved its head'. At the same time the **Whispering Knights** shared gossip, with eavesdropping crowds straining to hear any noise emanating from the stones, as it was believed that the Knights would reveal the low-down on your future love-life, if only you could make out their geological whisperings.

🜨 Making this one of myth's few three-ringed circuses, faeries also pop out of a hole near the King Stone tonight and jig around the stone circle.

🜨 Tonight is the Netherworld heat of Come Dancing. As well as their bottom-of-the-bill appearance at the Rollright Rock festival, **faeries** can also be seen dancing all over the South Downs – notably at Cissbury Hill, Torberry Hill and Harrow Hill near Patching, north of Worthing in West Sussex. It is no coincidence that faeries feature prominently in *'A Midsummer Night's Dream'*.

🜨 Still in Sussex, at Broadwater Green, **skeletons** emerge from the roots of an old oak and dance around it until dawn. The green is now part of a road junction in suburban Worthing, so this should prove interesting. And throughout the county at midnight **cows** go down on their knees for some low lowing.

Far to the north in the Shetlands, the dance goes on. The contestants here are grey seals.

Called **selkies** locally, they are actually bewitched human beings. On this one short night they find an isolated beach, shed their skins, and dance until dawn. Then it is back to their seal-form, and back to the sea.

Not all the night's creatures confine themselves to dancing. Second only to Hallowe'en, tonight's the night when otherworldly forces are likeliest to make a frontal assault on your hearth and home. Apart from checking the very small print of insurance policies, the best safeguard is a **protective herb garland**. The herbs must be gathered at dawn while they are still dewy. It is worth keeping some of the dew itself, as, made into a cake, this can cure colds and other infections. The key garland ingredient is **St John's Wort** – a golden flower which was the emblem of the sun-god. Still a part-time pagan, St John's Wort is said to uproot and wander about to avoid having its flowers picked. Once tracked down, add to it a few of the following: yarrow, corn marigold, mugwort, plantain, ivy, dwarf elder, vervain and orpine. Twist them into a pungent garland; and once nailed to the door this will guarantee a faerie-free night. Better still, throw the herbs into a bonfire as the sun sets.

Having risen early to scour the fields for herbs, there was little hope of returning to bed for the next 24 hours. This being the traditional shortest night of the year, everyone gathered together to dance until the following dawn. The all-night hilltop fireside rave was a UK-wide custom. Couples jumped through the flames holding flowers for extra luck, and cattle were driven through the embers as protection against disease – diluted versions of ancient human and animal sacrifices. The older ways survived in isolated areas well into the 19th century, with animals ritually burned alive to honour the sun god. On Orkney and Shetland, the cows get to share in the luck. Got those bovine sterility blues? No problem – a blazing brand from the bonfire carried round the cow in its stall ensures an instant return to fertility.

© Like other fire customs, most bonfires have now moved to November 5th. But thanks to a 1920s revival, a chain of fires link hilltops and tors from Chapel Carn Brae near Land's End in Cornwall to the Tamar in Devon tonight, mostly organised by the Federation of Old Cornwall Societies. The other chief sites in Cornwall are on St Agnes' Beacon, Four Burrows, and the Carn Brae near Redruth, all within striking distance of Truro; Castle An Dynas near St Columb, east of Newquay; St Breok Downs just outside Wadebridge; Bodmin Beacon near Bodmin; and Kit Hill near Callington, west of Tavistock. There is usually a short ceremony offering thanks to God. Flowers are thrown into the flames, with accompanying words along the same lines as the ones used at St Columb:

In one bunch together bound
Flowers for burning here are found,
Both good and ill.
Thousandfold let good seed spring,
Wicked weeds fast withering,
Let this fire kill.

Young couples still often leap the bonfire in an athletic imitation of a Burger King Whopper. To add to their power to ward off evil spirits and witches, some of the fires are topped with a broomstick, and an oak-handled sickle is added to guarantee the fertility of crops and men.

Go clockwise round the church seven times at midnight tonight, and over your left shoulder you will see the form of your future lover, carrying – of all things – a scythe. There is a catch: during this kirkumnavigation you have to scatter hempseed and say:

Hempseed I sow, hempseed I hoe,
Let him that is my true love come after me
and mow.

In some versions it is **fern-seed** which you have to scatter. Fern-seed bestows the supernatural property of invisibility on its user, a myth that was apparently inspired by the fact that the seeds are so tiny as to be scarcely visible. As Gadshill says in *Henry IV, Part One*: '*We have the receipt of fern-seed, we walk invisible.*' The magic works only if you catch the seed on a pewter plate at midnight, without touching the fern. Making matters trickier, the seed will pass through not just one, but 10 such plates, landing safely only on the eleventh, which may be stretching your pewter reserves a little. The Devil will try his best to thwart the harvesting, so if the process does not work, you conveniently have someone to blame.

✝ For more than 500 years Cadbury Castle, near Wincanton in Somerset, and wondrous Camelot have been deemed one and the same place. Highly unreliable evidence backs up this claim by saying that the hill upon which Cadbury Castle stands is hollow. Every seven years on Midsummer Eve a door in the hillside opens and out ride **Arthur** and several rusty knights, complete with flaming lances. After watering their horses at nearby Sutton Montis church – the sole reason for the excursion – it's back to the hill until England's time of greatest need, or until another seven years have passed.

🎵 Several Arthur stories invoke the King as something beyond a mere human being. In some Celtic tales he turns up as a dwarf, riding a goat. But more usually he is a giant. At Carmarthen in Dyfed, on the way to the Battle of Camlann in AD 39, Arthur removed a pebble from his shoe and threw it over his shoulder. The 25-ton **Arthur's Stone** landed 20 miles away near the coast at Reynoldston in West Glamorgan's Gower Peninsula. At full moon women can magically attract lovers by placing milk-dipped honey cakes on the stone and crawling round it three times on all fours. Desperation is the word that springs to mind. Tonight and on Hallowe'en this same stone and all the neighbouring rocks go for a walk down to the sea where they have a nice long, salty drink.

There are more magical Welsh rocks near St Nicholas, just west of Cardiff in South Glamorgan. Thanks to a Druid's curse, if you sleep among the standing stones there tonight you will become mad, dead, or – worst of all – a poet.

Midsummer Eve is also óne of two nights for visions of the soon-to-be-dead – for details see St Mark's Eve, April 24th.

24th June
Midsummer Day/St John the Baptist's Day

Landowner Stung by Bee

Irish **St Bega** was out boating back in the 7th century, and got herself shipwrecked off the Cumbrian coast. Wet and miserable she asked the Lord of Egremont for shelter, and he invited Bega and her friends to step in and dry off. By the time Bega had recovered from her ordeal, she realised that she had stumbled upon the ideal location for an abbey. Always one to push her luck, Bega asked her host to give them the necessary land. The put-upon Egremont said that they could have as much

land as was covered in snow the following day, Midsummer – not renowned for its ice-blizzards.

However, next morning three miles of land were all white and glistening, and Bega had her Abbey, at modern St Bees – a corruption of the saint's name. Sadly for Bega/Bee and her legend, her name comes from the *beag* – an Anglo-Saxon bracelet – once kept at her defunct shrine. Nothing at all was known about the woman in the shrine, and so her entire life story was improvised from a piece of jewellery.

In 1381 **Sir Robert Knollys** of Seething Lane, London, closed his front door, crossed the street, and opened his other front door. It was a very tedious way of passing from kitchen to living room, and he resolved to link his two residences with an overhead footbridge-cum-gallery. When the work was completed Sir Robert had a visit from some local officials. Even in the 14th century, such a construction needed planning permission, and he had failed to get any. Because Knollys was a hero of the city and the army, they imposed a crushing fine of one red rose, to be delivered to the Lord Mayor every Midsummer Day. Knollys paid the fee annually for the rest of his life.

◉ The **Knollys Rose Ceremony** continued after Sir Robert's death, dying out only after it had become pointless – the building in question had long been torn down. But it was not so pointless that the custom could not be revived. In 1924 the rose appeared once more, and now makes its way to the Lord Mayor at the Mansion House every Midsummer Day, delivered on a cushion by the churchwardens of All-Hallows-by-the-Tower, which stands on the site of Knolly's former home.

◉ A related rent system applies to the **Crown and Thistle** pub in Leicester. Their landlord is the Lord Mayor, and on Midsummer Day they ceremonially hand him their annual stipend – 4d in old money, and a damask rose. Making the rent even more of a bargain, the Mayor hands the money straight back.

© Magdalen College in Cambridge has an **open-air sermon** today from a pulpit built into the stone wall in the quadrangle. The quad used to be surrounded by greenery for the occasion, harking back to a pagan past. The Christian excuse for all this was that it represented the wilderness through which John the Baptist wandered. A hospital dedicated to the saint used to stand on the site. Cambridge also has a Midsummer Fair, which dates from at least the 13th century.

© On the Sunday nearest June 24th there is a **fair at Flookburgh**, near Grange-over-Sands in Cumbria. The village grew around the fluke-fishing industry, and the fish are still a local favourite.

© **Bilston Carnival** takes place on the last weekend of the month at Hickman Park in Bilston near Wolverhampton, West Midlands. An old November Wakes, it was moved to June when it was revived in 1930, and still – within the limits of the law – tries to keep the old Wakes spirit. As they do at **Winster**, near Matlock in Derbyshire. The week around the 24th is Wakes Week there. Celebrants include Winster Morris, the last surviving ancient Morris team in the county.

© And on the same weekend two of the best of Derbyshire's well-dressings take place today, at Youlgreave near Bakewell and Tideswell near Buxton. See Ascension Day for more on well-dressing.

At Barrule on the Isle of Man, well into the 19th century, bundles of grass were laid down today for **Manninan-beg-mac-y-Lear**, the Celtic god with special reponsibility for the Blessed Isles of Man and Arran. Usually known as Mannannan, he often appears as a heron, and is not averse to wooing mortal women. Beware Midsummer one-night-stands that have long legs and French-kiss like a wet chisel.

🏚 **Callanish** is a weird cruciform collection of ancient stones on the beach near Callanish on Lewis in the Western Isles, every bit the equal of the more easily accessible Stonehenge. St Ciaran built a church here, and tried to enlist the local giants in his work. They refused, and so Ciaran turned them to stone and called them *Fir Chreig*, the False Men. On Midsummer Day at least one of them reanimates. The cuckoo – an emissary from Tir-nan-Og, the Celtic land of Youth – heralds the sunrise, at which point the chief stone, The Shining One, takes a stroll down the main avenue of stones. It is still customary to visit the stones today, though not everyone is watching for signs of movement in The Shining One: any couple who have sex in the circle unchain all sorts of fertile magic, and ensure that their relationship will last forever.

Today was one of the big days for **dancing trees**. Usually oaks or elms, they were found in villages scattered all over the country, but especially in the Dartmoor area of Devon. Places such as Moretonhampstead, Dunsford and Meavy had mature trees within which a platform used to be erected at Midsummer and other local feast days. Dancing then took place in the tree tops to the strains of an arboreal band. There are records of up to 30 seated couples, an orchestra, and six dancing couples, all swaying to the music on top of Moreton-hampstead's dancing elm. In 1903 this elm, one of the last surviving dancing trees, tragically blew down in a storm.

Tin Miners had a paid holiday today, for to work on Midsummer was deemed very un-lucky. One of their most exuberant ways of celebrating the day off was to stuff gunpowder into boulders and blow them up.

To dream of a future lover tonight, go in search of a lump of coal under a plantain plant, and then sleep with it under your pillow. To turn the dream into reality, take a red rose – also plucked today – and wrap it in paper. Wear it to church on Christmas Day, and the person of your dreams will claim the rose, and you. This was originally a women-only superstition, but there is no evidence of it being any less effective for men.

The Devil can be summoned on Midsummer Day at the Chanctonbury Ring earthwork, just west of Steyning in West Sussex. Run round the ring backwards seven times either at mid-night or at 7 am, and Satan will appear with his most terrible and potent weapon – a bowl of porridge. He will offer the porridge to whoever has summoned him; but as long as they do not sup with the Devil, they will be safe, and he will briefly be at their bidding.

Gooseberries officially ripen today in Somer-set. But do not go weeding thistles in excite-ment, as:

> *Cut off thistles before St John,*
> *You will have two instead of one.*

👄 Pooling the advice of several different bits of **weatherlore**, rain today indicates a wet harvest, a lousy time on the nut-gathering front, and a bumper crop of apples and pears.

25th June
St Non's Day

Witney – I Will Always Love Ewes

In the Middle Ages Witney in Oxfordshire became world-famous for its **wool-making**. The place was renowned for the 'Four Bs of Witney': beauty, bread, beer and blankets. Over the years Witney and Newbury in Berkshire have competed for new sheep-to-shop record times. For over a century Newbury had all the prestige because on 25th June 1811 townsfolk managed to take wool from a sheep's back at sunrise, and produce a finished coat by sunset the same day. Sir John Throckmorton had wagered a thousand guineas on their success, and that night he dined at the *Pelican Inn*, Speenhamland, in his new coat. The achievement generated such publicity that the coat was displayed at the Great Exhibition of 1851. In 1906 Witney fought back by smashing Newbury's record with a shearing, spinning and blanketing time of 10½ hours. The last Witney attempt, in 1969, got their time down to eight hours 11 minutes. One of the record-breaking blankets was flown to New York and was in a shop window that same night, along with the notice: '*The wool of which this blanket is made was shorn from sheep at Witney, England, early this morning.*'

▥ This is **St Non's Day** at Altarnum in Cornwall. St Non's Well is beside the 14th-century church at Altarnun, Cornwall. It was a good place for people with a lunatic to cure; but a terrible place for the lunatic. The suspected madman had to stand on the well wall, from which he was knocked into the water. An accomplice then tossed him up and down until his strength was sapped, in a ceremony known as **Bowsenning**. The unfortunate was then carried to the church for Mass. If the sufferer was not cured, they were bowsenned again. Lunatics left Altarnun either dead or cured. If cured, Non got all the credit.

© The Galashiels Gathering, led by the **Braw Lad and Lass**, starts on the last weekend in June. One of the many summer Borders' Ridings – for more details see June 13th – it features a mounted parade to the Raid Stane, where in 1337 Gala lads surprised and slaughtered English raiders in a field of wild plums. The stream ran red with blood, and 'sour plums' became the Burgh's Emblem. The Gathering was first held in 1930.

26th June

How to Handle a Legend

On this day in 1471 King Arthur's unofficial biographer **Sir Thomas Malory** died. Malory had himself been an active knight, and his nostalgia-trip book, *Le Morte D'Arthur*, had the thickness and single-mindedness of a door stop. It was an instant classic, drawing on the Frenchified Arthurian legends of chivalry and courtly manners which had spilled into Britain via Geoffrey of Monmouth's 1135 epic *History of the Kings of Britain*, much of which came straight from Geoff's fertile mind.

Arthur appears in ancient tales as an otherworldly giant poised to bring down on Britain a pagan judgement day; but it is now the Malory-moulded 'once and future king' that dominates depictions of Arthur. The image has been further warped by Richard Harris crooning, and Graham Chapman 'riding' to Terry Gilliam's coconuts.

One of many similar tales from various corners of the island, a Scottish yarn tells of Canonbie Dick and his discovery of **Arthur's resting place**. Dick was invited to a cave in the Eildon Hills near Melrose, Borders, by a stranger who had bought several of his horses. Once inside, Dick saw the sleeping King with his knights, a horn, and a sword. Going for the horn, he tried to waken Arthur. This was the wrong choice. A voice told him that the sword must be drawn to assert bravery before the horn can be blown to summon help. Dick did not get a second chance. A wind whipped up and carried him away. He told his tale to some shepherds, then died.

▥ *The Castle* in Cowcross Street, London, is Britain's only **pawnbroking pub**. Legend says this is down to George IV (1762–1830). He had lost his money at the Clerkenwell cockfighting, and went into *The Castle* in disguise to pawn his watch and get some more money to squander on chickens. The landlord accepted the King's watch; and the following morning he returned it to one of the King's messengers. George was thrilled at the landlord's sense of honest enterprise, and he granted *The Castle* a licence to pawn for as long as the building was standing. The pub still maintains its rights, but these days almost all items offered for pawning are, politely, refused.

This used to be the date for old Worcestershire's **Pershore Fair**:

*The cuckoo comes in April, and sings his song
  in May,
He buys a horse at Pershore Fair and then he
  rides away.*

If the cherry harvest was good, the fair was called the God-bless-me Fair. If cherries had failed, it was the God-help-me Fair. The village had a cherry-based economy.

☦ Boughton, just outside Northampton, held a huge **Horse Fair** from June 24th to 26th. Its most infamous regular was anti-hero **Captain Slash**, who terrorised stall holders until he was arrested in 1826. His extortions of toll and tribute ended at Northampton: on the scaffold there he thwarted his mother's prediction that he would die with his boots on by kicking them off just before he swung. Slash now haunts Boughton Church, especially at Christmas. He also plays guitar with Guns'n'Roses.

Close to Boughton is the **Marvel Sike**, a spring that flows only at times of national or local disaster. It is said to have bubbled in 1916 when the Horse Fair was held for the final time. No one now seems sure of its precise location, although in the 17th century it was identified as being '*two bow-shots from Brampton Bridge*', in Boughton Field, mid-way between Boughton and Chapel Brampton.

27th June

Sheep-Shaped Kate

Between the 23rd and 29th **faeries** are hyper-active. One of their favourite occupations is dancing; but if they choose you as their partner, you could end up jigging into an early grave. Unless you have a pal like **Kate Crackernuts** . . .

Kate's step-sister – another Kate, confusingly – looked into the mirror each morning with understandable dismay. Following a well-aimed curse, she had the head of a sheep. Problem number two was the local prince, who woke up every morning knackered. The cause of this remained a mystery until one evening Kate Crackernuts kept watch and saw some faeries whisk the prince away for a night at the faerie-land ballroom. Kate followed the party-goers, taking her secret weapon – a bag of hazelnuts. At the height of the dance, the concealed Kate removed her nuts and started to roll them across the doorway of the ballroom.

Sure enough, a nut-fixated faerie came to pick them up, enabling Kate to pounce and nick his handy all-purpose magic wand. She ran back to sheep-head sister Kate, and one blow in the mutton-chops restored the ugly ungulate to human form.

Next night Kate pursued the prince again, and repeated her nut trick. The hazels lured the same faerie from the dance floor, and this time Kate grabbed a dead blackbird which he was carrying. She knew, from eavesdropping, that this bird could rid the prince of his nocturnal dancing shoes. The next morning's breakfast table had an exciting new dish on offer. After his third mouthful of blackbird the prince was cured of enchantment. Cue the inevitable marriage and all-night nut-cracking.

For would-be **faerie**-watchers, just a few species to look out for until the 29th: eyes peeled for Bogan, Boggle-boo, Bullbeggar, Scar-bug, Shag-foal, Hobthrust and Mum-poker; as well as Jenny Greenteeth, Churn-milk Peg, Melsh-dick, Spunky, Gringe, Nicker, Trash, Cuthbert, Dibble and Grub.

Paying a visit to your chums is hardly an exciting custom; but if the visitor happens to be dead, it becomes a little more interesting. On this day in 1728 at Beaminster, Dorset, John Daniel, **schoolboy from beyond the grave**, appeared to his pals in the local church. An enquiry was set up on the strength of the friends' colourful evidence, and John was disinterred. The original verdict of death by fits was immediately in doubt, as John's body bore the hallmarks of a strangling. But justice lost interest; and that was that.

© The last Saturday in June is the date of the **Glastonbury Pilgrimage** in Somerset. It began in 1924, and is now the biggest event of its kind, attracting up to 8,000 pilgrims and large numbers of spectators, for a procession and series of services in and around the ruined Glastonbury Abbey. In 1994 there was a drop in attendance after a decision not to allow women priests to officiate at any Pilgrimage services until at least the next millenium. Just in case anyone takes the day too frivolously, a note in the official programme reminds pilgrims: '*Do not start your picnic until Mass has ended.*'

© There is more **well dressing** in Derbyshire on the last Saturday in June, this time at Hope and Bakewell: see Ascension Day for details.

28th June

Unpleasant Pheasant Peasant Fate

Littleport and Ely in Cambridgeshire were the chief centres of unrest during the 1816 riots. The Napoleonic wars were just over, and the country was suffering an economic depression, which the arrival of 400,000 demobilised ex-soldiers did nothing to alleviate. Thousands lost their jobs. Penalties were harsh for the army of impoverished **poachers** that descended on the estates of the land-owners. But they were determined men, and many charged with protecting the land feared for their lives. Several gamekeepers were clubbed to death by rabbit-bagging desperadoes. Dozens of poachers were hanged, banged up or transported in return.

On June 28th 1816 five men from Mill Pond in Ely were hanged for poaching pheasants. Soon after their deaths, the butcher who owned the gallows cart was found suffocated, thrust head-first into his own cess-pit. The coffin-maker was discovered dead in a large pipe that transported water to Ely's brewery. Desperate times. As the 19th-century ballad *The Poachers' Fate* has it:

> *Me and five more a poaching went, to kill*
> *some game was our intent,*
> *Our money being gone and spent, we'd*
> *nothing left to try.*

🔟 The Mill Pond Five are commemorated with a plaque on the south side of St Mary's Church in Ely.

© Do-gooder Jankyn Smith, of Bury St Edmunds in Suffolk, died on June 28th 1481. He left money in his will for a Mass to be held on the anniversary of his death. As an incentive for the clergy at St Mary's church not to forget, he provided money for cakes and ale. This sort of thing was all a bit High Church to be swallowed by the Protestant Reformation of the next century. But the custom did not die out: it was simply toned down. The Mass became a sermon, and was moved to a quieter date in mid-January. **Jankyn Smyth's Charity** still continues, and the ceremony has now moved back, and takes place on the Thursday nearest to June 28th. Smyth helped to fund the local almshouses, and each of the residents who attend the service are given a shilling. Afterwards the cakes are still served, and there is now a choice of ale or sherry.

© On the last Saturday in June the ancient **Ceres Festival and Games** shake off their dust at Ceres in Fife. The games started life as a celebration of the Ceres soldiers who walked back home after their victory at the Battle of Bannockburn near Stirling on June 24th 1314. Robert the Bruce granted the town a charter for a market and games, which for centuries took place on the village green called Bow Butts, claiming to be the oldest Highland Games in Scotland. The soldiers' walk between Bannockburn and Ceres is still sporadically re-enacted to coincide with the games.

One of the many legends about the Scots victory over Edward II at Bannockburn – a real morale booster after a string of defeats – is that it was down to Scots optimism, and English myopia. The Scots baggage-carriers and cart-drivers had been left behind on a large hill while the soldiers did their business. When the servants prematurely thought the day was won, they ran down the hill to share the plunder. The English thought it was a whole new army descending on them, and fled.

29th June
St Peter and St Paul's Day

Don't All Rush at Once

From 1067 until 1071 **Hereward the Wake** held the newly-invaded forces of William the Conqueror at bay in the Fens. In 1070 the sympathetic Abbot of Peterborough was replaced by a Norman lackey, and this was the cue for Hereward's men to attack both town and monastery, running off with anything they could get their hands on, including the Abbot. But **St Peter** came to Hereward in a dream, telling him to restore the treasure, as well as the Abbot. He complied, and the saint was so impressed that when Hereward and his gang later got lost in Rockingham Forest, he sent a wolf to lead them to safety. Backing up this eccentric guide, St Peter also put candles on all the trees and on top of the men's shields, and the rebel army were soon back on course.

Hereward and his followers holed up at Ely in Cambridgeshire, which was then an outcrop of firm land in a sea of treacherous swamps. To attack, William had to build a causeway. But when he finished it and sent his troops across, Hereward set fire to the surrounding reeds. Soon the causeway was burning, and in the chaos William's army was routed.

Hereward eventually reconciled himself to William as king, and returned to his restored lands at Bourne in Lincolnshire. But a jealous Norman mob waylaid him, and although he managed to slay 15 men with his trusty sword Brainbiter, he was killed, never to Wake again. Later, Hereward grew in heroic stature. In one tale he kills an unruly Cornish giant; and in an even weirder set-to he grapples with a bear that has strayed over from the faerie kingdom.

A thief can be exposed, or a lost object located, by taking a wooden sieve and a pair of old-fashioned sheep shears and invoking the help of Sts Peter and Paul. First attack the sieve with the shears, so that they become embedded in the sieve's handle. Then balance the combined sieve-shear on your hand and name the likely places or suspects. When the correct location/ culprit has been named, the whole thing will overbalance, and that will be the answer to your question.

According to a slanderous old adage, fishermen change their mates and repaint their boats on St Peter's Day. East coast Scottish fishermen used to light small fires outside their houses in honour of Peter today. And St Peter's Bell at Heighington Church, near Darlington in County Durham, has a peal that drives away storm and tempest. It should have its work cut out if the Greenhouse Effect kicks in.

At Fareham in Hampshire, the millpond used to be drained today, leaving the eels and other fish floundering in the mud. This was a roundabout tribute to St Peter having been a fisherman. The unfortunate inhabitants of the pond were collected and ceremonially eaten. Perhaps the diminishing stock is why this custom died out.

Rushbearing and hay-strewing originated in the days when church floors lacked floorboards and needed a few rushes or armfuls of hay to dry, soften and sweeten them. Brightening up the otherwise tedious task of repeatedly dragging in the rushes, ceremonies and processions evolved which made it all a bit more fun. It is a practice that was particularly popular in churches dedicated to St Peter, and so many of the bearings and hay-strewings were on or about today.
© Many of the old rushbearings have fallen into disuse. **Warcop Rushbearing**, near Brough in Cumbria, has not. The girls carry a flower-decorated wicker frame in the shape of a crown. Boys carry a cross made of rushes and tied with red ribbons. The parade starts in the village centre at 2 pm, and if the 29th is a Sunday, the event takes place on the preceding day. During the 3 pm service the vegetation is not used as carpeting, but is reverently propped up next to the communion table. A rush-bearing hymn unique to Warcop is sung at the service.

Braunstone, on the outskirts of Leicester, held its celebrations on the Sunday nearest the 29th – **Hay Sunday**. Legend here maintains that a woman who had wandered off the path in Leicester Forest was pursued by a gang of ne'er-do-wells. The clerk of Braunstone's St Peter's Church, Tarzan-like, whisked her to safety, and as a thankyou she bequeathed to his church an acre of meadow land. This was used to provide the vegetation for the day's service. A gasworks now stands on the site of the meadow, and the gas board has for years paid the church £1.50 annual compensation, to enable it to buy hay elsewhere. But although the money is still coming in, the service stopped in the 1970s, after complaints from hayfever-sufferers.
◉ **Wingrave**, near Aylesbury in Buckinghamshire, still strews hay over the church floor on the Sunday after June 29th, although it now does so with the minimum of ceremony. Once again, legend toes the common line about the uncommon lino and tells of a woman who became lost on her way home. In the freezing night air Elizabeth Seed became convinced that she was a goner. But just then the bells of St Peter and St Paul's Church in Wingrave rang out – she followed the sound, and fell head-first down a quarry. No she didn't: she got home safely. As a mark of her gratitude, she gave two roods of land to the church in her will of 1786: money from the field still finances the hay-strewing, even though a house now stands on the site.

Haworth's rushbearing in West Yorkshire used to take place on the Sunday after June 18th, or on the handiest weekend at this end of the month. It was a great social occasion, and the locals did almost anything apart from touching rushes or hay. The name was simply a hangover from previous times, when rushes were scattered throughout the pewless church – the old one which the Brontës attended, not the new edifice, which dates from 1879. A local hymn at Haworth runs:

Our Fathers to the House of God,
As yet a building rude,
Bore offerings from the flowery sod,
And fragrant rushes strewed.

© **Bromsgrove Court Leet** in Hereford and Worcester starts on the penultimate or, more usually, the last Saturday in June. The Bailiff and his Court – vestiges of an ancient medieval institution – parade in full regalia, with a team of ale-tasters, bread-weighers and other arcane officers.

The boar's head on Bromsgrove's coat of arms represents the legendary deeds of **Sir Ryalas the Jovial Hunter**. Ryalas once met a wild woman who told him of a ravaging boar. Sir Ryalas soon found the boar, and after a tough fight he managed to kill it and bring it home for dinner. He then went back to tell the wild woman. '*You wicked man, you have slain my pretty pig!*' she cried, for the swine had been her son. Sir Ryalas now realised that he was meant to have been the pig's breakfast. The enchantress unsheathed her claws and layed into Ryalas; but to no avail. The Jovial Hunter cleaved her head in two.

30th June

The Sinister Staircase

There are plentiful examples of gallows humour, but few instances of the pithy post-execution comment. **Everard Digby** died today in 1606. He was one of the Gunpowder Plotters – the handsome one, according to reports of the time. Sentenced to be hung, drawn and quartered, he lay in a position of considerable discomfort upon the executioner's slab on this grim day. The man with the messy job split open Digby's chest, plucked out what he found and declared: '*Here is the heart of a traitor*.' Digby, crowd-pleaser to the last, allegedly replied: '*Thou liest*.'

What finer way to spend a family day out than to take a gentle stroll to the village green and pelt some incapacitated felon with whatever rocks and rubbish come to hand? That gentle and charming custom, torturing people in the **pillory**, came to an end on this day in 1837 when Queen Victoria gave approval to an Abolition Bill. By this time the pillory was only in use for the crime of perjury.

© **Jedburgh Callants Festival**, with its Riding and sports, starts on the last Saturday in June and goes on until the second Saturday in July. The highlight of the festivities is a ride to Redeswire on the Friday. As with most other Borders' Ridings (see June 13th) this commemorates a battle against the English. Scots bows and arrows were used in combat for the last time during the battle, in 1575, when the Jedburgh 'cavalry' came to the aid of outnumbered locals and routed the English. A mounted cavalcade also visits the 16th-century Ferniehirst Castle, just south of Jedburgh, and halts for a ceremony at the **Capon Tree**, a lone survivor of the ancient Jed Forest.

🏛 **Ferniehirst Castle** is the family home of the Kerrs, whose head is the Marquess of Lothian. 'Kerr' is pronounced 'car' in the Jedburgh area, and is an old word for left-handed. The family had many sinister scions, and the spiral staircase at Ferniehirst was built the wrong way round so that it could be defended by left-handed swordsmen. The equally imposing Jedburgh Castle, which looks as if it might have witnessed several centuries of border warfare, was in fact built in 1823 as a model prison, and now serves as the local museum.

© On the last Monday of June, Hepworth, near Holmfirth in West Yorkshire has its **feast**, which started in 1665 to commemorate the end of the plague. The Beever family had ordered a batch of cloth from London, and when it arrived at their home in Foster Place, one of the maids had a sneak-preview. She tried on one of the expensive garments, little realising that the whole consignment was contaminated by bubonic plague fleas. She caught the disease, which rapidly spread through the immediate neighbourhood. All prospective victims were cordoned off in a section of the town and threatened with death if they left the area. It was a no-win situation. The feast – a series of processions and brass-band accompanied songs – starts at 2 pm and is a thanksgiving for clean water, and a commemoration of the plague victims.

JULY

1st July
St Serf's Day

All Hail Grim Cherry Reaper

At South Wingfield in Derbyshire on this day in 1826, local diarist Abraham James recorded a 'mournful visitation' of **hail the size of pigeon and goose eggs**. The meteor-like shower destroyed crops and killed birds. In spite of subsequent sun, the whale-of-a-hail hung around for another four days before melting. James estimated the property damage at several thousand pounds, which in today's money is still several thousand pounds.

The people of South Wingfield were thankful that the following **weather** rhyme only applies to ordinary rain:

If the 1st of July be rainy weather,
It will rain more or less for four weeks
* together.*

If a Friday, the rain becomes inevitable, for '*The first Friday in July is always wet*'. It might dampen the picnics, but lore has it that all this July precipitation is good news:

A shower of rain in July when the corn begins
* to fill*
Is worth a plough of oxen, and all belongs
* theretill.*

And yet the rain must not be particularly violent, or you will harvest novelty corn:

No tempest, good July,
Lest the corn come off bluely.

But do not use any of the rain for brewing: it has a bad effect on vocabulary:

Bow-wow, dandy fly,
Brew no beer in July.

Cherry fairs were once a byword for harmless hedonism. '*Alle is but a cherye fayre*', said Chaucer. Of only slightly later vintage is this 15th-century lip-quiverer, *Farewell to this World*:

This life, I see, is but a cherry-fair.
All things pass, and so must I, algate,
Today I sat full royal in a chair,
Till subtle death knockéd at my gate.

One of the biggest cherry-fairs was at Odiham in Hampshire. Held each July 1st, it was an anything-goes celebration marking the end of the cherry harvest. As with other cherry fairs, over time the 'anything' became centred around booze and brawls. Similar problems in the main centres where such events blossomed – Hertfordshire, Hereford and Worcester, Warwickshire and Hampshire – led to these counties all losing their cherry fairs by the early part of this century.

Carrying 11 green branches, the local burgesses at Culross in Fife used to go marching today in honour of their favourite saint, **Serf**, the tutor of Glasgow's St Mungo (Kentigern). Serf's legend has been described as a '*farrago of wild impossibilities*', which hardly makes him a rarity amongst saints. But Serf suffered more than many others in the canon of the canonised – his name is now nowhere to be found in religious calendars and the standard hagiographies, and his Culross procession ground to a halt in the 1860s.

2nd July

Lots of Men Went to Mow, Went to Mow a Meadow

18th-century Doctor Daniel Day owned much land around Hainault Forest in Essex. He was a zealous collector of rents, but a man with a sense of occasion. On the first Friday in July he used to ride to Fairlop Oak in the forest, an agreed meeting place where his tenants handed over their rents. There were many of them, and he allowed them to pitch stalls around the oak so that they could milk a bit of custom while they waited. To further encourage the mood of practical fraternity, Day provided the stall-holders with a meal of beans and bacon. The rents and tents gathering grew into **Fairlop Fair** which was still going strong until the Fairlop Oak blew down in 1820. Its wood was used to make the pews for St Pancras' Church in north London – now the site of a well-known station. In 1853 the fair at Fairlop was abolished. What is left of Hainault Forest is now at the far eastern end of the Central Line, and the wind-felled tree itself is remembered in the fine pub, the *New Fairlop Oak*, at nearby Barkingside.

☙ On July 2nd 1644 the Parliamentarian victory at **Marston Moor** near York was the first decisive one of the Civil War: 4,000 Cavaliers were killed, and 1,500 were captured. The Roundheads failed to consolidate their position at first: certain sections of the army were squeamish about inflicting out-and-out defeat on Charles, while the King's men won a few notable battles in the south during that year, notably at Alresford in Essex and Cropredy in Oxfordshire. But the victories were a false dawn for the Cavaliers; they had already effectively lost the Civil War. In a symbolic act of disgruntlement, the ghosts of Cavaliers killed at Marston Moor still wander the roads around Long Marston.

▥ Until recently Yarnton in Oxfordshire held its **Lot Meadow Mowing** on the first Monday in July, a tradition that arose soon after the Norman Conquest. Certain Thameside meadows were leased by lottery using 13 ancient holly-wood balls, each inscribed with the name of the 11th-century lot-holders. There was a fair, a plum-pudding feast, and a race for 'The Garland', which the winner hung in the church. In 1817 a man died in a mêlée at the mowing; but the event survived another 170 years until numbers interested in bidding for the hay drastically dwindled. The ceremony was suspended in 1978, and the land is now a conservation area, mown in the good old way, but not requiring the aid of 13 lucky leasees. A footpath now runs through the meadows, which in July are teeming with wild flowers. The ceremony's officials were called Meads-

men – a hereditary title which they are still allowed to use today. One Meadsman, Pat Shurmur, guards Yarnton's holly balls – just in case of a revival.

© The week starting on the first Monday of July is **Reivers Week** at Duns, Borders – an old custom revived and repackaged in 1949. Carrying the Burgh flag, the Reiver leads Rides all week – see June 13th for more on Ridings. On the Wednesday 'The Wynsome Mayde o' Dunse' is crowned, with a symbolic cutting of turf at Duns Castle in the evening. On Friday there is a grudge-match **Ba' Game** between single and married men of the town. The *Common Riding Song* celebrates the doings of Duns:

> *Whae hasna read in Border lore, that Duns*
> *o'ferlies hauds a store,*
> *Her castle, Hen Poo', Bogs and Law – whae*
> *disna ken that Duns dings a'?*

The last line is the town motto, meaning 'Duns beats them all'.

3rd July

Some Brownie Points

▥ On July 3rd 1609 stable boy Roger Skelton was asleep with the horses, a short nap which preceded a much longer one. His boss, Richard Hilton of Hylton Castle in Sunderland, Tyne and Wear, had called for a horse some time ago, and he was not amused by Skelton's lack of alacrity. He descended on the stables and impaled Roger on a pitchfork. The trial came to court, and Hilton was found guilty; but he was pardoned regardless – a light doze clearly being seen as sufficient grounds for justified manslaughter. Roger's ghost returned to haunt Hylton Castle; but in an unconventional manner. He became the **Cauld Lad of Hilton**, a brownie, or household spirit. Servants called him the Cauld Lad due to his naked – and therefore cold – goblin-like appearance.

The Cauld Lad undid any tasks finished during the day; but he also completed any jobs left partly done – a work pattern which could be manipulated so that the creature proved a boon rather than a bane. And being a brownie, all the Cauld Lad asked in return was a bit of bread and milk. In spite of conforming to brownie type, Roger Skelton was not happy in his new guise. The servants heard him singing:

> Woe is me, woe is me,
> The acorn's not yet fallen from the tree
> That's to grow the wood that's to make the cradle
> That's to rock the bairn that's to grow to the man
> That's to lay me.

The servants were not wild about the prospect of the Cauld Lad staying on indefinitely; and, besides, they had taken pity on him after hearing his plaintive song. They knew that the classic way to get rid of a brownie was to procure clothes or other extravagances and leave them out – an action known as *laying*. The brownie, after donning the clothes, is released from its spell of servitude. So one night the servants left some garments for Skelton, and this did the trick. The Cauld Lad dressed up, warmed up, danced around, and took his leave, singing:

> Here's a cloak, here's a hood –
> The Cauld Lad of Hilton will do no more good.

Writing about a **fire-storm** in Grimsby, Humberside today in 1610, Reverend Abraham de la Pryme suspected that it was divine retribution, brought on by the town's reputation for vice and corruption. Even its Abbey was not spared: '*There was plainly seen to come a great sheet of fire from out of Holderness, over the Humber, and to light upon Abbey House, as they called it, which burnt it all down to the bare ground, with the men in it.*'

© **Rush-bearing** season is still in full swing: on the first Saturday of July Great Musgrave, near Brough in Cumbria, rushes to church. Twelve young maidens used to carry a rush crown to the service, but now anyone under 15 can get involved, waving their own rush crown or cross. The procession from the Village Institute to St Theobald's church starts at 2.15 pm. For more on rush-bearing, see June 29th.

© **St Monans Sea Queen Festival** at St Monans, Fife, takes place on the first Saturday in July. Sometime in the afternoon – depending on tides – the Queen and juvenile entourage go to Anstruther Harbour and board a flag-strewn 19th-century fifie, a type of trawler. Having taken their sea-sickness pills, they embark on the three-mile voyage to St Monan's Harbour. On arrival they are met by a guard of honour composed of scouts and cubs, and the new Queen is crowned by the previous year's Queen at the Town Hall. On the following day she attends church, on a rock overlooking the sea, for the *Kirkin' o' the Queen* ceremony.

© On the first Saturday in July **Annan**, near Gretna Green, stages one of the few Ridings not in the Borders region – it is in Dumfries and Galloway. For more extensive Riding writings, see June 13th.

© On the Sunday after June 29th (St Peter's Day) there is a **Blessing-of-the-Sea** service at the mariners' church of St Peter's at Folkestone in Kent. After a procession from the church to Folkestone's harbour-side fishmarket, there is an open-air ecumenical service at 3 pm. Bands, choirs and a crowd of several hundred give thanks for fish, crabs and safe voyages. A guest bishop blesses the fishermen's boats, sprinkling both the vessels and the sea with holy water. Until early this century, the bishop and a rowboat full of clerics used to bob in the water, blessing everything in sight.

At Congresbury in Somerset on the Saturday before July 5th, an area of land used to be divided into acres, and each acre was marked with a hieroglyph. Apples were then given corresponding hieroglyphs, and were doled out at random to prospective land-users. All except four acres, which were auctioned to raise money for the ceremony and party. It was a **candle-auction**, the action lasting until an inserted pin had fallen from a lighted candle. Sadly, the ceremony is now no more.

4th July
Old Midsummer Eve/
St Martin o' Ballymus' Day

The Dissent of the Peak

📕 The Second Marquis of Rockingham died on this day in 1782, and was buried in a ludicrously ostentatious three-storey mausoleum at Nether Haugh, near Rotherham in South Yorkshire. In 1780 he made an even more outrageous contribution to the local landscape in the shape of the **Needle's Eye** at nearby Wentworth Woodhouse. Under the influence of drink the Marquis had wagered that he could drive a coach-and-four through the eye of a needle, and the thin pyramid-folly was built to prove him right – it has an arch through which he was able to drive his carriage.

After a religious purge later known as **Black Bartholomew Day** in 1662, 46 clergymen were cast from office for refusing to accept the religious dogmas of the day. Hounded out as '*psalm-singing rascals*', some of the Dissenters went to ground in one of the most isolated parts of the Peak District – Alport Castles in Derbyshire. It had a remote barn which became a refuge for the wayward worshippers. They met here to hold services and receive alms, posting sentries on the highest points of the moor to warn of approaching church-police. This all evolved into the Love Feast, revived in the 18th century by the Methodists under John Wesley.
© **Alport Castles Love Feast**, pre-empting hippies by 300 years, takes place at 1.30 pm on the first Sunday of July, (up a track from Hayridge Farm, one mile along the minor road running west from the A57 Snake Pass near Woodlands Chapel). The Alport barn has straw on the floor, some makeshift wooden benches, and little else. Hymns are sung unaccompanied; and because the communion bread and wine of a normal church service are not allowed, water and fruit cake have been substituted. The water is passed round in a two-handled loving-cup.

© This is Old Midsummer Eve, and at Whalton, near Morpeth in Northumberland, it is the day of **The Bale**, or Baal Fire. 'Bale' is a Saxon word meaning a bonfire, and derives from the name of the sun-god Bel, or Baal. At 7.45 pm fiddlers and pipers play, and children dance around a great bonfire which blazes on its traditional site in front of the public lavatories on the village green. There is Morris and sword dancing too, all echoing the event's sun/fire worship origins, when locals used to leap through the flames for luck. Many other communities refused to adjust the date of their Midsummer fires when the calendar changed; all but Whalton have now let the custom move or ex-pyre. If the event falls on a weekend, it becomes a full-scale carnival.

☻ This is also **St Martin o' Ballymus' Day**. St Martin is a classic weather-predicting saint,

his name deriving ultimately from the Latin *calidi*, meaning 'hot'. The word entered Old French as *Bouillant*, was corrupted in Scotland *Bullion*, and on Shetland as *Billimas* or *Bally-mus*, from 'Bullion-mass'. He is Scotland's version of St Swithin:

> *Bullion's Day, gif ye bring rain,*
> *For forty days it will remain.*
> *Bullion's day, gif ye be fair,*
> *For forty days 'twill rain nae mair.*

5th July
Old Midsummer Day/
St Modwenna's Day

Do that Viking Thing

▥ The now-ruined castle at Deganwy, near Conwy in Gwynedd, was built by the Normans, the limit of their incursion against the Welsh princes. In July 1088 the owner, **Robert of Rhuddlan**, was wakened from his sleep with news of Welsh resistance fighters, who were waiting for the tide to turn and carry them away. Heroic to a fault, Robert rushed, armourless, from the castle. Confronting Cymru in his night-shirt he turned and found, to his dismay, that only one alert Norman retainer had followed him. He was, needless to say, slaughtered.

The 7th-century **St Modwenna** and her friend St Ffraidd (one of the many pseudonyms of Bride – see February 1st) were exploring the coast of Ireland, when the chunk of land under their feet broke away from the rest of the island and put to sea. Unperturbed, Modwenna and Ffraidd sat quietly while their rocky raft ploughed eastwards. A day later it hit Wales at the mouth of the River Conwy, forming the peninsular of Deganwy in Gwynedd. St Modwenna rebuffed the advances of Welsh ferry companies and settled instead in England, living as a hermit near Burton upon Trent in Staffordshire.

St Modwenna will answer your prayers if you **sacrifice a pig** to her. The porcine slaughter reached almost epidemic proportions in 16th-century London as it was widely believed that such an appeal was the best route towards a childless couple being granted offspring.

© On Tynwald Hill at St John's on the Isle of Man today, a precis of all the year's new laws is read at the **Tynwald Ceremony**, in English and Manx. Only then are those laws officially in place. Everything used to be read in full in both languages, but the edited-highlights approach was adopted 130 years ago to fend off mass catatonia. The hill is a 12-foot-high man-made mound of Viking origin, built from earth taken from all 17 of the island's parishes. The ceremony dates from the Viking occupation of the island, and takes place on Old Midsummer Day. 'Tyn' is the Norse word *Thing*, meaning a meeting. At the Thing, disputes were settled and laws were passed, all very democratically, which conflicts somewhat with common perceptions of the Vikings. But they managed to guard this democracy in a more typically Viking way – a local law said that anyone creating a disturbance at Tynwald was to be hung and drawn. The Ceremony today is still very ritualistic, with lots of pomp and pageantry to please the large crowds which it always attracts.

© Cornwall's **Bodmin Riding** takes place on the first Saturday in July, at the climax of **Heritage Day**. Horse-riders carry garlanded poles in a procession through the town, a custom that originated as an annual tribute to the priory of St Benet's at nearby Lanivet. On the preceding Friday, ale-tasters go from door to door, with various householders invited to sample the specially-made brew. Traditionally the beer is brewed in the previous October. It used to be paraded with pride of place, and the Town Crier greeted each residence with the words: '*To the people of this house, a prosperous morning, long life, health and merry riding!*' Anyone taking a sip was expected to make a small financial contribution.

6th July

Hanging Ham

July 6th 1685 saw the defeat of the Duke of Monmouth's uprising. Monmouth was the illegitimate son of Charles II, and had been unofficially crowned at Taunton in Somerset, hoping to oust James II. But at the **Battle of Sedgemoor** a thousand pro-Monmouth rebels died, and another thousand were subsequently executed or transported. Monmouth was beheaded nine days later, after infamous executioner Jack Ketch took five blows of the axe to complete the messy job.

✟ After the battle, rebel Sir John Plumley scarpered back home to Locking Hall, at Locking near Weston-super-Mare in Avon, where he hid from the King's men. He locked himself in a concealed room; but his dog still expected its daily ration of walkies. When the officers burst in, they found the enthusiastic pet barking and wagging its tail outside the hidden room, and they rapidly deduced what was going on. Plumley was dragged out of the room and hanged from a tree in his garden. Inconsolable, his wife grabbed the dog and jumped down Locking Well, a tragic end to the farce. Her leap and doggie-paddle are regularly re-enacted in wraith-form, complete with phantom hound and occasional guest ghost appearances from Sir John.

✟ Another of the rebels was offered mercy if he could justify his reputation as the best runner in the West Country by keeping pace with a galloping horse. He more than matched the stallion for pace; but having had their sport the King's men killed him anyway. His girlfriend was so distressed that she drowned herself in Sedgemoor Levels. Her ghost is sometimes spotted, accompanied by the galloping of hooves and the panting breath of her racey lover, at Westonzoyland, near Bridgwater in Somerset.

✟ Monmouth was widely vilified as an impetuous fool and coward; but the real villain of the 1685 uprising is **'Hanging' Judge George Jeffreys**. His 'bloody assizes' after the rebellion sent over 300 to the gallows, and sentenced hundreds more to be flogged, jailed or transported. *The Coach and Horses* at Buckland Brewer, near Bideford in Devon, is on a site where many of his victims were hanged – several are still regulars in ghostly form. Jeffreys himself died in the Tower of London, captured while fleeing the country after the Glorious Revolution of 1688. He haunts a house in Broad Street, Lyme Regis, Dorset, gnawing a gory bone. Jeffreys also turns up at the *White Hart Hotel* in Exeter, Devon; and, in the same county, he hams it up in the castle at Lydford, near Tavistock, appearing in the form of a large **black pig**.

✟ **Monmouth** himself appears annually at the battlefield with ghostly lights overhead. Other phantom soldiers prowl these fields too; and by the River Carey the rebels' last cry of '*Come over and fight!*' can still be heard. They shouted it as the enemy mowed them down with cannon fire.

This was formerly **Scotter Shaw Day** at the village of that name in Lincolnshire. Horses were the key currency here, and all the dead horse-dealers of bygone years attended in the form of gadflies. The flies were said to descend on the fair to goad the horses, as the dealers had done in their previous incarnations.

7th July

The Last of the Phoenicians

William Turner, father of modern botany, died on this day in 1568. His *Herbal* of 1551 moved away from the folklore of the genre, and he was sceptical of beliefs such as the one that maintained that cowslips steeped in white wine can cure wrinkles. But Turner did manage to record that parsley restores sick fish and that a piece of bearfoot inserted into a freshly cut hole in a sick cow's ear makes the ear drop off, but cures the rest of the cow. Turner also recommends '*stynkyng thynges*' for curing opium addicts. Onions are not included in this category: they result, he said, in headaches, or even amnesia.

✞ The **ghost of Elizabeth Shepherd** manifests whenever anyone tampers with her memorial stone, near the A60-B6020 junction at Harlow Woods, north of Nottingham. She was murdered on this day in 1817 by a scissors-grinder. He attacked her with a sharp fence-stake, and was later caught trying to sell her shoes and umbrella. He was executed for his brolly folly at Gallows Hill in Nottingham.
✞ **Mary Tudor** haunts **Sawston Hall**, south of Cambridge. She came here as a fugitive on this day in 1553, hiding from the Duke of Northumberland's men, who favoured Lady Jane Grey as the successor to Edward VI. The next day at dawn the Duke's men surrounded the house, but Mary managed to flee, disguised as a milkmaid. Northumberland set fire to the building in frustration – it was rebuilt by Mary after she came to the throne later in 1553. Her ghost flits all over the new house, but its favourite location is known as Mary's Room – it is said to be impossible to spend a night here without being disturbed by the ex-Queen's ghostly entourage. There are other Sawston ghosts too, including the disembodied music of a spinet; and the Grey Lady, who knocks three times before entering the Tapestry Room.

When bells are rung today at Langford Budville, near Wellington in Somerset, it is said that the Devil is driven back from Thorne St Margaret, where he is banished annually with a **bell-peal** on Midsummer Day. It has never occurred to anyone just to leave him there.

On this day in 1846 the last court on Isle of Portland, Dorset, was closed, and the last **Reeve-staff** was locked away. It had formerly been used by the annually-elected Reeve-man, who collected all the rents of the island and made a notch on the eight-foot staff for each payment received.

This was a relatively uneccentric tradition for Portland, whose inhabitants set themselves apart from the rest of England, claiming to be descended from Phoenicians. Portlanders also had a custom called **the Jump** for newly-wed quarrymen. On his wedding day the groom's neck was gripped in iron tongs until he shouted the magic release-word '*Beer!*', after which everyone drank, at his expense, the 'randy-quart'. Day-one back at work after the wedding was marked by a feast, during which the groom had to leap a plank of wood while stick-wielding men aimed blows at him.

8th July

Hung for a Sheep

At this time of year the calendar was speckled with sheep fairs, each attracting a small criminal element, hell-bent on **sheep-stealing**. Near Kirton in Lindsey, Lincolnshire – or, alternatively, at Catton in Northumberland – some time last century, one such thief crept out in the middle of the night, trussed up the creature of his choice with a rope, and headed for home. At one high wall he balanced the sheep on the top and began the ascent himself. But flock wallpaper is one thing, flock wall-balancing quite another – the animal fell down the other side, the rope caught the man by the neck, and he was found the next morning hanged by his own sheep.

Brothertoft in Lincolnshire used to stage **Toft Drift Feast** today, to which fen-reeves drove thousands of sheep from the south of the county for buyers in Boston and the surrounding villages. The chief hazard at the fair was *comassing*: the transmigration of one's personal effects to the swag-bag of the local pickpockets.

Lapford in Devon had its **Revel** on the Sunday after the 7th. Pestle Pies were dish of the day: ham, tongue and whole game in huge crusty pies, whose towering pastry needed iron hoops for support. On the same day at **Crockerton**, Wiltshire, St Thomas Beckett was said to have appeared at the local **Revel** in all his finery, only to depart in the garments of a beggar, having lost cash and clothes during the riotous festivities. July 7th is one of the saint's feast days.

◉ The four-day **Kilburn Feast**, near Thirsk in North Yorkshire starts on the Sunday after the 7th. Tourism is discouraged, as this is very much a local celebration. It begins with an open-air sermon, and includes a foot-race to Kilburn White Horse, which was scoured from the rocky hillside in 1857. The final day of the feast sees the procession of a Mock Mayor and Mayoress, the latter being a man in drag, with almost his own bodyweight in clothes and make-up. For him to be recognised would forfeit the luck that these transvestite characters traditionally bring. The couple demand fines from the local people, for such dread offences as not opening the windows, owning a dog, wearing socks – major crimes all.

© ⛊ **Swearing on the Horns** is still staged twice a year in the Highgate area of London, following a revival on this day in 1960. *The Old Wrestlers Tavern* in North Road is a favourite venue, and a plaque in the pub details the 200-year-old custom's origins. These days the Horns are usually brought out in March and August, but no-one is willing to swear to precise dates. Participants in fancy dress choose whether to kiss a pair of horns, or a woman. It originated as a protection racket: you paid money, swore a long-winded but largely meaningless oath, and this kept the horn bearers off your back indefinitely. The swearers vow never to drink small beer if they can find strong, unless small is their favourite tipple; never to eat brown bread if they can get white, unless they happen to like brown; and never to kiss the maid in preference to the mistress, unless they find the maid preferable. This is sworn in front of a pair of horns mounted on a pole. Each swearer is then declared a 'Freeman of Highgate', a title that brings with it just two privileges: the right to kick a pig out of a ditch and sleep in its place; and the right to displace the middle one of three pigs and nestle in between the other two.

9th July
St Everild's Day

Every Dog Has Its Days

Canonisation was relatively easy back in AD 700. A good deal of patience and modest ambition are the only features breaking up the otherwise almost fact-free landscape that is the life of virgin **St Everild**. She travelled from Wessex northwards, eventually founding a nunnery with her companions at Bishops Farm, somewhere near Ripon in North Yorkshire.

It was once thought, erroneously, that Everild gave her name to the town of Everingham in Humberside. Such place-name confusion was common. Everingham, in fact, comes from Anglo-Saxon, meaning 'the Ham of Eofor'. *Ham* means 'settlement' and *Eofor* is Saxon for 'wild boar'. York derives from this same word, being a trimmed down version of *Eoforwic*, 'the camp of the wild boar'. When the Vikings took over the city the word was slurred into 'Jorvik'. *Vik* is the Viking word for a bay; a little odd given York's distance from the sea. The Saxons had come up with their name after misreading the city's Roman title, *Eboracum*, which derives from the Celtic name 'Eburos', designating a man who had an estate full of yew trees. *The Bay of the Camp of the Wild Pig with lots of Yews*: it was quite an achievement, cramming all this information into the four letters of 'York'.

'*Like pois'nous vermin in a dog-day sun,*' said Edward Young in his 1719 play *Busiris*. By the 9th of July the **Dog Days** have begun (they last until early August). They mark the period when Sirius, the Dog-star, rises with the sun. The Romans knew the period as *caniculares dies*, and their risible rising theory was that the heat from the bright Sirius, coupled with the normal daily dose from the sun, accounted for these being the hottest weeks of the year. So great was this influence that dogs were thought to go temporarily mad, and overheated humans were liable to commit dastardly deeds or behave very oddly (which is loosely the premise of the Sidney Lumet/Al Pacino film, *Dog Day Afternoon*). There appears to be an element of common sense behind all these beliefs. Recent statistics have shown that the greater the temperature, the greater the number of crimes committed.

👄 Old cynics, aware of the brevity of British summers, used to say that '*As the Dog Days commence, so they end.'* The days also indicate the weather to come:

Dog Days bright and clear
Indicate a happy year;
But when accompanied by rain
For better times our hopes are vain.

The July **Gala** at **Moira** in Leicestershire is, sadly, defunct. The colliery band used to parade and salute a beribboned pig at the height of the excitement. This all began when a pig climbed a wall to watch the musicians go past; and the band realised that they were face to snout with the perfect mascot.

10th July

Shot-Gun Wedding Whiddon

✝ **Mary Whiddon** could make one man happy only by incensing another. In 1641 she stood at the marriage altar in Chagford church, with the successful suitor, while the unsuccessful one loaded his gun behind the pews. Forever holding his piece, the thwarted lover took aim and shot Mary dead. As her tombstone in the churchyard puts it: *'Behold, a Matron yet a Maid.'* But Mary was not one to disappear from the limelight. She has since intermittently manifested in full bridal rig at her former home, Whiddon Park, which is just outside Chagford, near Bovey Tracey in Devon. On this day in 1971 Mary, wearing the dress in which she had been shot, appeared to a wedding guest. She smiled and disappeared. The bride, a member of the Whiddon family, placed her bouquet on Mary's grave in sympathy.

© **Rushbearing** takes place at St Mary's church at Ambleside in Cumbria on the first or second Saturday of July. Cross, harp and orb-shaped frames are covered with sphagnum moss and bedecked with flowers and rushes from Windermere. From 2.30 pm, hundreds of schoolchildren and adults carry the greenery around Ambleside, stopping at the marketplace to sing a rush-bearing hymn. After a stuffed-to-the-rafters service at the now rush-strewn church there is tea and Ambleside gingerbread for all, followed by games and sports on the school playing field. For more on rush-bearing, see June 29th.

🏛 The 1994 celebrations also marked the 50th anniversary of the Royal College of Art's evacuation to the area during the Second World War. Artist Gordon Ransome did not confine himself to knocking off Lakeland landscapes: he was so impressed by the Ambleside festivities that he designed the still-impressive 20-foot wide, 10-foot high rushbearing mural at St Mary's, immortalising the faces of many locals.

© The **well-dressing** at Dore in South Yorkshire begins on the second Saturday of the month. Instigated in 1959, it has become a symbol of the village's Derbyshire origins since it was swallowed whole by Sheffield in 1974. See Ascension Day for more details on well-dressing.

© When he died in 1554 John Huntingdon of Sawston in Cambridgeshire left money and lands to his wife on condition that she planted two acres of it with white peas, which were to be given annually to the poor, forever. There has been the odd hiatus down the years, but his **pea-picking charity** is still going, and is now in the relatively safe hands of the parish council. The town peas – as they are known – are harvested each July, and anyone from Sawston, rich or poor, is entitled to a share. A Queen of the Gleaners used to be chosen to oversee the dawn-to-dusk picking.

☂ Today's **weatherlore** is less familiar than that of St Swithin's Day in five days' time, but is even more grandiose in its claims: *'If it rains on 10th July, it will rain for seven weeks.'*

11th July
St Benedict's Day

A different kettle of fish

St Benedict (480–550) set the template for countless Benedictine monks with his detailed *Rule*. All the orders of monasticism – Gilbertines, Franciscans, etc. – were based upon a Rule set down by their founders. Benedict's flexible approach to monasticism was centred around a strict timetable of prayer and reading, giving plenty of time for dabbling at length in medicine, agriculture, and librarianship. This put the monasteries at the forefront of advancement and learning, increasing the in-house efficiency, and ensuring that lots more money poured into the monastery coffers. Henry VIII's motive in dissolving the monasteries was first and foremost a financial one – he wanted their loot.

Benedict's main tenets were obedience, authority, stability and community life, details of which he set down explicitly in the *Rule*. On that ageless dilemma, to bathe or not to bathe, he made the following observations: '*Let baths be granted to the sick as often as it shall be expedient; but to those in health, and especially to the young, baths shall be seldom permitted.*' Soap-dodging children have been keen to invoke Benedict's modest bathing rules ever since.

At Grantham in Lincolnshire the Sunday after July 10th was called, tantalisingly, **Forty Feast Sunday**. This was meant to be self-explanatory, as 40 feasts were said to fall on that day. Regrettably, no one ever jotted down just what those 40 feasts were.

🛏 A contemporary curiosity in Grantham is the sign on the pub *The Beehive*, which is renowned for its realism. You can almost hear the bees buzzing, and almost see the insects flying in and out. In fact, it *is* a real hive. It is only when the sign of *The Blue Pig* just down the road starts grunting that you are in big trouble.

© The **Tweedmouth Feast**, at Berwick-upon-Tweed in Northumberland, is alive and well, starting on a Thursday in mid-month, and presided over by a Salmon Queen. The traditional food here is Salmon Kettles, a meal of tea, local salmon, and gooseberry tarts. The event begins with the crowning of the Queen, in a lorry-park just outside the town, and continues with a fair, concerts, parades and a rose-show.

◉ July was until recently the month for the Peel Viking Festival on the Isle of Man. The festival is no longer a going concern, but during July Peel still stages several **Viking Longboat Races**, which take place in authentic mock-longboats, as and when the summer tides permit.

♱ Among Peel's other claims to fame is the hell-hound **Moddey Dhoo**, a distant ancestor of Scooby Doo. It kept watch over a secret treasure at Peel Castle until an intemperate soldier lured it away and was turned insane for his troubles. The Dhoo – also known as Mauthe Doog – has occasionally appeared since, though it is always a death-omen. Walter Scott mentions the mad-dog-soldier tale in his *Lay of the Last Minstrel:*

> *For he was speechless, ghastly, wan*
> *Like him of whom the story ran,*
> *Who spoke the spectre-hound of Man.*

12th July

Circular Arguments

Bampfylde-Moore Carew was born on this day in 1690, respectable son of a rector in Bickleigh, Devon. At school he was sidetracked by a love of hunting: he had the loudest hound-rallying cry in the county, and dogs seemed to obey his every command. His youthful downfall came after his pack pursued a tame deer over new corn, ruining the crop. To avoid retribution, he hid out with some gipsies at Brickhouse near Bampton, Devon. His life then became one of adventure and con-tricks. He disguised himself as a variety of worthy causes, from ailing sailors and sick soldiers to poor peasants and washer-women. Carew extracted alms from friends and family without once being recognised. He was later elected **King of the Gipsies** by his tribe, and had that title chiselled on his grave-stone when he died, at Bickleigh, in 1758.

◉ Custom reaches the heights of tension today in Ulster, and in many parts of Scotland, when the Orange Men march in an attempt to re-evoke memories of the **Battle of the Boyne** in 1690, at which William of Orange defeated the ousted Catholic King of England James II. The Orange Order was founded in 1795, by which time William had become a nationalist emblem for the Protestants.

◉ Not the biggest Battle of the Boyne commemoration, but the one where the symbolism is most direct, the **Sham Fight** takes place at Scarva, near Portadown in County Down. Scarva was where William camped before the battle, and each year after a parade the set-to is restaged as a one-on-one fight between two horsemen – one dressed as James, the other as William. This is one contest with no side-betting: William always wins. As most of the participants and spectators are otherwise engaged on the 12th, the fight usually takes place on the 13th or 14th.

It was on July 12th 1992 that the myth of **Crop Circles** was largely debunked. A competition masterminded by the *Guardian* newspaper was staged in a large Buckinghamshire field, challenging crop-circle hoaxers to do their best, with a £5,000 prize carrot beckoning the most impressive efforts. Expert 'Cereologists' invoked freak winds, rutting stags and Martian job-creation schemes as possible causes, but the one thing on which they all agreed was that human hands could not possibly reproduce the beauty and perfection of the 'true' circles. Entrants were given complex designs a few hours beforehand, and then had to reproduce them accurately, that night.

The best efforts, revealed in the morning light, were indistinguishable from the finest of the 'genuine' circles previously trumpeted by the experts. The hoaxers had worked in darkness without fuss and noise, severely dinting the reputation of the 1980s' greatest contribution to national folklore. By the summer of 1993 the alien convoys seemed to find an alternative route and crop circle stories had virtually disappeared.

☙ **Weatherlore** today gloats about the abundant summer daylight:

To the 12th of July from the 12th of May,
All is day.

13th July
St Mildred's Day

Grizzel and Bones

🎞 In 1685 Sir John Cochrane of Ochiltree, Strathclyde attempted to oust King James II. He failed. And so in July that year he found himself in prison in Edinburgh. Before his friends had time to mount any kind of defence, an execution warrant was on its way northwards. But near Buckton in Northumberland the mail coach was waylaid by a crafty cross-dressing highwayperson – Cochrane's daughter, Grizzel. At a spot now known as **Grizzy's Clump**, she snatched the mail-bag and sped away. This gave Cochrane's colleagues time to appeal on his behalf, and they succeeded in winning a royal pardon for their man.

🎞 A Hollywood-style imprint on a stone near the river at Ebbsfleet, north of Sandwich in Kent, marks the place where **St Mildred** is said to have stamped her foot with undue emphasis while in a state of post-trance euphoria (though counter-claims say that it was St Augustine who left the good impression, when he landed at this same spot). For centuries it was a sacred place, and it was believed that if the stone was moved, it would always return to its original location.

Mildred – daughter of Thanet princess St Ermenburga – died in 700; and her body survived the Vikings' razing of the nunnery at Minster, on the Isle of Thanet in Kent, in 1011. Her remains proved to be as stubborn as the homing-stone when in 1035 Canterbury monks attempted to take them from the nunnery. The body refused to budge, until the Abbot of St Augustine's in Canterbury asked God to intervene personally. The corpse then became mobile enough to be dragged to a boat; though the body-snatching monks still had to fight off Minster locals who attacked them with swords and cudgels – their way of saying that they wanted Mildred to stay put.

By the middle of the century two rival sets of her bones were doing the rounds in Canterbury; while a miscellany of Mildred body parts had turned up in Holland.

☙ Ever since the Sybil first said *sooth*, a degree of ambiguity has been a key element in prophetic statements. They can usually mean all things to all comers, with a wording which prevents people from refuting them outright. But an all-time champion for multiple-interpretations must be the Lincolnshire lore which insists: '*When bracken is down in July it means a hard winter.*' Does 'down' here refer to being down on the ground – as in noticeable and widespread? Or is it 'down' in terms of volume – meaning there is less of it about? Or perhaps it simply means down in terms of directions – indicating that the plant is growing further down the hillside? All this leaves the intending diviner feeling down – as in depressed.

There are more straightforward July plant-sayings. Now is the time for fanatical weeders and those with a grudge against **thistles** to launch the final assault:

Cut thistles in May, they grow in a day;
Cut them in June, that is too soon;
Cut them in July, then they will die.

St John's Wort, powdered and worn in a bag around the neck during July, will bring success in love. It will also cure mental illness, and 'the vapours'.

The Cornish have a great three word saying: '*Heat and pilchards.*' A succinct reminder that a July hot spell is traditionally the best time to catch shoals of the tin-bound fish.

14th July

Rust in Peace

John 'Iron Mad' Wilkinson of Lindale, near Grange-over-Sands in Cumbria, was heavily involved in the iron trade, and he loved his work. He died at Bilston, West Midlands, today in 1808, and his will called on the special skills of some of his friends in the industry. First of all, he wanted to be transported back to his home, Castle Head, in an iron coffin. The cargo nearly went under when crossing the treacherous sands at Morecambe. Having made it safely to Castle Head, it was discovered that the lead and wood coffin lining, constructed according to the stipulations of Iron Mad's will, was too bulky to fit the coffin in which the body had been carried thus far. So a second iron overcoat was soldered together. This bulkier new structure was too big to fit into the grave, and several extra feet of earth had to be hacked out there and then, before Wilkinson's body could finally be laid to rest in accordance with his iron will. The will had also decreed that a massive 20-ton iron pyramid should be placed over Wilkinson's burial place. The structure was duly built; but a few years later the new owners of the estate complained that the monument to Iron Mad had ruined the otherwise glorious view. In a final iron irony his remains were disinterred and laid in Lindale churchyard. The pyramid was moved aside, behind the lodge at Castle Head.

The mid-19th-century folk song *I'Anson's Racehorse* is set on July 14th. The I'Ansons are a Yorkshire family closely linked with horse racing, and the song is the nags-to-riches story of how their horse Little Dunnee wins at Newmarket, recovering impressively after being ridiculed pre-race for having cropped ears. It is a straight racing song, in spite of the red herring lines:

The jockeys were weighed, likewise the whips,
And then the bold riders began for to strip.

© The Tuesday before the third Wednesday of July – which at the earliest is the 14th – is the traditional date for Exeter in Devon to proclaim its **Lammas Fair**. There are several anomalies here. Lammas falls on August 1st; the fair no longer sticks to its own formula (it is now incorporated into the early-July Exeter Festival); and even though there is a procession, followed by the mayor reading the Lammas Fair proclamation and the raising of a symbolic stuffed glove on a pole, there is no fair. The ceremony dates back over 900 years – when the fair ran out of steam, the annual proclamation kept going.

In 1669 a **winged dragon** descended and uncoiled its three-yard-long body on mortal soil. This was not the sun-baked banks of the Styx, but a cowfield at Henham in Essex, where it lazed around in the sun and then flew away. A pamphlet of the time captured the incident for posterity, and every year at July's **Henham Fair** model dragons were sold, along with a local beer called snakebite – nothing to do with attempts to liven up fizzy chemical lager by adding fizzy chemical cider. Sadly, fair, dragons and beer have long since died out.

15th July
St Swithun's Day

Poor with Rain

St Swithun (or Swithin) died in AD 862, a champion of the poor and a builder of churches and almshouses around Winchester in Hampshire. He once came to the assistance of a woman whose box of eggs had been knocked messily to the floor by a hasty monk. He simply magicked the eggs back into their shells – this is why his shrine and the cathedral altar screen at Winchester both feature an eggshell motif. In accordance with his wishes, after his death Swithun was buried outdoors so that humbling rain could fall on his tomb. However, when Winchester's Minster got an extension it was decided that the Saint ought to have a comfy corner inside. The digging began, and Swithun sent his famous 40-days-worth of rain to deter the disinterrers. The soaked monks got the message; but they still managed to bring Swithun indoors to dry, on this day in 971. Swithun's shrine, wrecked during the 16th century Reformation, was reinstated in 1962.

☙ Few realise that today predicts dry spells just as much as heavy rain:

St Swithin's Day, if ye do rain,
For forty days it will remain;
St Swithin's Day, an ye be fair,
For forty days 'twill rain nae mair.

In myth and legend, 40 is a magical but woolly number meaning simply 'a long time'. It was the duration of the biblical Flood and the length of Jesus' stint in the wilderness. Fines and rights of Sanctuary often had a 40-day limit too. It is usually the case that on each of the 40 days after the 15th it will be wet somewhere in Britain – but there are no records of any one spot staying damp over the whole period. 1993 got off to a good start, but only managed 14 out of the 40 in the environs of the Met Office. In 1887 a drought was interrupted by rain on St Swithun's . . . but then the drought returned.

The incongruity between the yearly prediction and what actually happens did not escape our forebears. In Ben Jonson's 17th-century play *Every Man Out of His Humour*, one of the characters contemplates after the 15th: '*why it should rain 40 days after, now more or less; it was a rule held afore I was able to hold a plough, and yet here are two days no rain: ha! It makes me muse.*'

Swithun also **blesses the apple crop** today, making the fruit fit to eat:

Till Swithun's Day be past,
The apples be not fit to taste

© St Swithun's stamping ground of Winchester has a daily **Wayfarers' Dole**, available every day of the year – very much in the spirit of champion-of-the-needy Swithun. It was established in 1136 by Henry de Blois, Bishop of Winchester and grandson of William the Conqueror. Up to a hundred people daily can claim a small piece of bread and one-sixth of a pint of ale from the Porter's Lodge of the Hospital of St Cross, one mile south of the cathedral in Winchester. It is never offered, only given to those who ask for it. One of the needy recently making the request was the Queen Mother, who in 1986 helped mark the Dole's 850th anniversary.

© At Seamer, near Scarborough in North Yorkshire, proclamations are read today for **Seamer Fair**. Then everyone goes to the pub, as the day now lacks the fair itself, which fizzled out in the 1930s. The horse-traders want it back; the residents do not.

16th July

Osmund's Crazy Horses

William Wood had successfully sold his bundles of cloth in Manchester, filling his pockets with profit. He was on his way home to Eyam in Derbyshire on this day in 1823, and stopped for a drink at a roadside pub. His cash-heavy jacket came to the attention of three villains, Taylor, Dale and Platt, who followed Wood to the eastern slopes of Black Hill in the north-western corner of the Peak District. There they attacked, and when Wood refused to hand over his money, they clubbed him to the ground and pummelled his head into the earth with a large rock.

⛧ Taylor was arrested, 48 hours later. He attempted suicide but only half succeeded, dying a few days later having confessed all on his death-bed. Dale was executed at Chester in the following April; but Platt escaped. A monument detailing Wood's untimely demise still stands at the roadside where he was killed, just on the Derbyshire side of the minor road between Disley in Cheshire and Whaley Bridge in Derbyshire. The hole that had been made by Wood's head became barren. By the mid-19th century it was more than two feet long and four inches deep, and no grass would grow there. When anyone tried to fill it with stones or turf, the infill was later found scattered by the road. It was a fine way of exerting posthumous influence, without spending tiring man-ghost-hours haunting.

Today, the eve of St Kenelm's Day, was the start of the Clent Wake in Hereford and Worcester. The chief amusement was **Crabbing the Parson**. Visitors and locals alike gathered baskets of crab-apples, and engaged in fruitful warfare, pelting each other and the unfortunate incumbent parson with crabs. A tragic loss, this fine tradition died out in the middle of last century.

© Traditionally held on the third Sunday in July, the first **Mapplewell and Staincross Sing** took place in South Yorkshire in 1887. An almost unique survivor of the many organised mass sing-songs which used to take place until well into this century, the event is still in good voice. The choral singalong is now held at the local Junior School in Staincross, near Barnsley. The funds go to the Barnsley Beckett Hospital, having formerly been claimed by the defunct Old Peoples' Tree Fund. There is an accompanying fair too.

🎠 Salisbury in Wiltshire used to wheel out its garish hobby horse today, commemorating St Osmund with a parade and various theatricals. Unfortunately the custom was put out to pasture long ago; though the old hobby horse can still be seen in Salisbury Museum.

Today is the date when, in 1457, St Osmund's relics are thought to have been moved to a new shrine at Salisbury. Movement of a saint's bones from one place to another was and is a big deal, and such **translations** remain an alternative day for celebrating a saint. Especially if the saint's main feast day is at a time of year when parades and street-theatre seem a distinctly dodgy prospect. For more on a certain 11th-century Bishop of Salisbury, see St Osmund's Day – December 5th.

17th July
St Kenelm's Day

The Eyes have it

Ruthless Quendreda wanted to be Queen of Mercia. In her way stood her seven-year old brother **Kenelm** who had just been crowned King. Quendreda bribed her lover Askbert, who was also Kenelm's tutor, to kill the boy on a hunting trip between Winchcombe in Gloucestershire and Clent (formerly Kenelmstowe), Hereford and Worcester. Alone in the wilds, Askbert tried to murder the boy, but Kenelm simply said: '*This is not the place ordained for you to kill me.*' As proof, he planted his staff in the ground, and up sprang a thorn tree. This deterred Askbert; but later, at what must have been the 'ordained place', he succeeded in slicing off his pupil's head.

The murder did not remain secret for long. Kenelm's skull burst open, and out flapped a dove with a parchment in its beak. It flew straight to Rome and dropped its load into the Pope's lap; who, dusting down his Anglo-Saxon, read the strained verse:

In Clent cow-pasture under a thorn;
Of head bereft lies Kenelm, king-born.

🎠 The Pope contacted all the kings in England, who organised a manhunt for the missing boy. The searchers were led to the grave by a white cow. Bright light shone from the ground when the corpse was retrieved, and at the same instant a healing well began to flow: it can still be seen in a valley in the Clent Hills behind the church at Romsley, Hereford and Worcester. An alternative site for Kenelm's grave is marked by an 18th-century grotto in the garden of Bleby House in Winchcombe.

🎠 As the funeral procession made its way to Winchcombe Abbey, Quendreda tried to bewitch Kenelm's body by reading the Cursing Psalm – 108 (or possibly 107) – backwards. But her eyes fell out and spattered the psalter: the bloody book can still be seen in St Pancras' Church, Winchcombe, along with St Kenelm's coffin.

The legend is not even on nodding terms with the facts. The duller truth is that Kenelm died before his father, King Kenulf – also buried in the Winchcombe church – during a war in 821, and Quendreda was an innocent Abbess of Minster in Kent.

The most famous regular at the annual July **Wroot Feast** at Wroot in Humberside was local giant, Tommy Lindrum. A large stone in a Wroot field is said to have been thrown there by Tommy all the way from his house several miles away. It feeds on moss, which is why none ever grows on it; and should anyone move the stone, the ground will be covered in blood.

One year Tommy's father left him birdscaring while he went to enjoy all the fun of the fair. Tommy, anxious not to miss out on the festivities, rounded-up all the marauding sparrows, locked them into a barn, and went off to Wroot Feast. Next morning when Tommy released them, the sparrows had all turned white. Which explains why, to this day, white and white-flecked sparrows are common in the area.

The figure of Tommy was probably based on the hermit William of Lindholme, which makes it all the odder that he is also said to have sold his soul to the Devil. In exchange, Satan helped him with various enterprises, including building an unfinished causeway near Wroot – the remains of which could still be seen until late last century. Near to death, Tommy dug his own grave, climbed in, and covered himself with a huge stone slab. Perhaps the giant was trying to hide from Satan.

18th July

Foxe Gone to Ground

In July 1874 as a forester was passing by a huge tree near the Castle of Dalhousie in Lothian a large branch fell off. His dog was startled; but even more so when the forester said '*The Laird's deid noo!*' The forester knew that the state of the **Edgewell Tree**, an ancient yew, had long been linked with the fate of the Earls of Dalhousie. When a piece fell off it was a sure sign that death was about to come calling, and sure enough, Foxe Maule, the oddly-named seventh Earl, passed away soon afterwards. The 14th-century castle is now a hotel. The yew is said to be just as old, and if it ever falls down in its entirety, it is believed that the castle's walls will crumble.

Horsham Pleasure Fair in West Sussex used to kick off today. The first 24 hours were given over to sheep-trading and other business transactions: a concession to seriousness. The rest of the week was devoted to having fun. A writer reminiscing about the fair at the turn of the century described threading his way through a maze of wonderfully tawdry attractions, including '*fat women and living skeleton shows, drinking booths, pickled salmon tents, whelk and fruit stalls*'. Beer tents and private residences selling liquor used to hang bushes over their entrances, Roman style, and were known as Bough Houses.

Not everyone could hold their drink, unfortunately. 1835 was a particularly bad year. Outsiders ran amok against defending police and locals, and the Riot Act was read from the Town Hall before order was resumed.

© St Swithin's church at Old Weston, near Huntingdon in Cambridgeshire, has a charitable field, the profits from which are ploughed back into worthy local causes. The field no longer provides the hay for the church's annual **hay-strewing**, although the custom has continued using specially bought-in hay. On what is known locally as Feast Sunday – the Sunday nearest to St Swithin's Day – hay is carried into the church and strewn on the floor. Legend has it that the field itself was donated by a local woman who could not abide the clattering of noisy boots on the church floor when farm labourers made their special visit to the church for its Feast Day.

© **Aikey Brae Fair** at Old Deer, Grampian, is held on the weekend nearest the 17th. It began as a Sunday fair – a rarity in an area of strong Sabbath observance. An old yarn describes how a pedlar tripped up and dropped his wares into the river. Drying them on the bank, he was accosted by nick-nack hungry shoppers on their way home from church. Good business sense prevailed and he returned annually to plug the gap in the local market.

© Usually in the third week of July, depending on the tides, London stages the **Watermen's Race for Doggett's Coat and Badge**. Actor-manager Thomas Doggett founded it in 1715, partly in gratitude for a waterman who had given him a late-night lift home over the Thames to Chelsea; and partly as a lasting tribute to the House of Hanover – the first race was on the anniversary of George I's accession, August 1. Doggett left money, coat, badge and responsibility with the Fishmongers' Guild. It is the world's oldest sculling race, with teams rowing between London Bridge and Chelsea.

19th July

Woollies from Heaven

The **Spanish Armada** was first sighted off Lizard Point, Cornwall, today in 1588. Several ballads rolled off the presses in the following months, including '*A Joyfull New Ballad*' which ducked the involvement of Francis Drake, attributing victory not to the vice-admiral's tactical skills, nor even his oft-alleged sorcery, but to '*the mightie providence of God, being a speciall token of his gracious and fatherly goodnes towards us*'.

The weather and a lack of navigational know-how were also important factors, with many hapless Spanish ships foundering off the northern coastlands. Herdwick sheep are said to have swum ashore from one sinking vessel, landing close to the present site of Sellafield nuclear power station at Seascale in Cumbria: they were the ancestors of the present Cumbrian flocks. Similarly, dark-skinned northerners for years afterwards were said to be the descendants of Spanish soldiers rescued from the sea. On Orkney, dark-haired men were nicknamed Don in memory of the Spaniards who had been washed up on the islands.

Another shipwreck is said to account for the

origin of **Fair Isle sweaters**. When the crew came ashore after their vessel *El Gran Grifon* ran aground off Fair Isle (between Orkney and Shetland), the locals at first thought the new arrivals were heralds of the heavenly army itelf. On that particular point they proved to be mistaken; but local knitters took a shine to the patterns and colours of the Spaniards' clothes, incorporating them into the design of their now famous, crew-necked, sweaters.

© An event that gives the Devil his due, the St **Ronan Games** are held at Innerleithen, near Peebles in the Borders, on the Friday and Saturday of the third week of July. Sir Walter Scott brought the area to national attention in his novel *St Ronan's Well* (1823). The games were instigated in the first half of last century, with the 'Ettrick Shepherd', poet James Hogg, as the first captain of the event. The sport starts with a ride to the town's well and a swig of its magical waters. Robert Burns knew it as the Dow or Dubh (black) Well. Its dark, peaty, sulphurous waters were famous for curing all manner of eye and skin complaints, and made Innerleithen a busy spa-town. Scott rechristened it St Ronan's Well to romanticise the connection with St Ronan, who is supposed to have been partial to the waters, and was said to have fought the Devil nearby, banishing him forever.

On the evening of the Friday the games restage this fight as the Cleikum Ceremony, popularly known as **Cleiking the Deil**. A schoolboy is chosen to represent the saint. Accompanied by 'monks' with staffs, he carries a crozier, with which he symbolically *cleiks*, or hooks, the Devil, cowing and driving him out anew. The ceremony dates from 1901, and the accompanying pageant includes the verse:

Rouse ye, men of old St Ronan's, gather in
*   from hills and commons,*
Ready aye to hear the summons, on St
*   Ronan's, on!*

At the end of the festival the devil is ceremonially torched on a bonfire.

© **Corby** is not in Scotland, it is in Northamptonshire, but it still has a **Highland Games** each year, starting on the third Saturday in July. Decades ago, vast numbers of Scots migrated to Corby, providing the backbone of its steel industry. The town is still known as Little Scotland, and the games feature all the caber-tossing, bagpipe-playing and tartan excess usually associated with events north of the border.

20th July
St Margaret's Day/
St Uncumber's Day

Puff Goes the Magic Dragon

St Margaret sought an antidote to Antioch's excesses. The pagan lifestyle in ancient Syria did not suit her, even though her father was a chieftain. She retired to a life of shepherdessing, but Antioch's crazed-with-lust governor Olybrius came after Margaret, and dragged her off to his pagan palace. Olybrius tried charm, bribery, assault and even torture in an attempt to persuade Margaret to part with her virginity. Nothing worked, and the governor decided to bring the whole non-affair to a close by feeding her to a dragon. It swallowed Margaret whole, but she made the sign of the cross from inside, the dragon exploded and Margaret walked away unscathed.

On her deathbed Margaret declared that anyone reading or writing her history would be guaranteed an unfading crown in Heaven. She also said that if the dying prayed to her she would guarantee them protected passage to Heaven – an apparently sure-fire way to salvation, regardless of previous transgressions.

The downside to all this is that Margaret never existed. As early as 494 she had been declared apocryphal, and her cult was officially suppressed by the Holy See in 1969. Symbolising virtue is easier if you are a complete stranger to flesh and blood.

Women in labour can pray to Margaret for safe passage. The same prayer will also protect the unborn child.

☙ Margaret is good for fruit and flowers. For a start she traditionally brings rain every July 20th – it is known as **Margaret's Flood**. Dodging the deluge, it is an ideal day on which to harvest the first pears:

If St Margaret brings the first pear,
Pears will abound for the rest of the year.

Today Nympsfield Feast, Gloucestershire, used to serve **Heg-Peg Dumps**, a dish of plain dumplings, in honour of the saint – Peg being a pet form of Margaret. And an old flower calendar links the redness of **poppies** with Margaret's inside-job on the dragon:

Poppies a sanguine mantle spread
For the blood of the Dragon St Margaret
shed.

Something to consider on Remembrance Day.

Second Holy Virgin off the blocks today is **Uncumber**, alias Wilgefortis. If offered a peck of oats at an altar or statue, she will un(en)cumber women of troublesome husbands by sending a horse on which the accused man must ride straight to Hell.

Uncumber's dates are as elusive as Margaret's; but it is said that she was forcibly engaged to the King of Sicily. The problem was that she had taken Christian vows of chastity. She prayed that her suitor might find her unsuitable, and by the next morning she had sprouted a beard. The Sicilian took one look and decided that he must dash; but Uncumber's father was so shamed by his daughter's sudden circussideshow appearance that he crucified her. On the cross Uncumber promised that all who remembered her passion would be relieved of their burdens.

It has been suggested that this legend was inspired by paintings that depicted Christ on the Cross complete with flowing robes. But it takes O-level obtuse to conclude that they must be representations of a bearded lady. The only surviving statue of Uncumber is in the Henry VII chapel at Westminster Abbey. Bring oats and saddle.

21st July

Ding-Dong at Shrewsbury

Tyne and Wear and Northumberland commemorate the great medieval family the Percys, Earls of Northumberland, with several 'Percy' and 'Hotspur' street and pub names. Today in 1403 was the family's darkest hour – they met their nemesis Henry IV in battle at Shrewsbury in Shropshire, and lost. The reason for the enmity was primarily financial – Henry had reneged on a promise to give the Percy's £20,000 – a lot of money now, and the equivalent of several millions then.

The Earl of Northumberland's impetuous son Henry 'Hotspur' Percy led the rebel nobles and the armies, backed up by large numbers of men from Cheshire, where word had spread that the deposed king Richard II was alive and well and in Sandiway ready to join the rebellion. Richard had in fact been killed three years earlier, and this rumour helped consign many of his supporters to their deaths. At Shrewsbury Percy's forces also teamed up with the Welsh leader Owain Glyndwr. In Shakespeare's version of the events, this is something of a forced marriage. Hotspur finds the formal, mystical Glyndwr tedious, declaring that he would '*rather live with cheese and garlic in a windmill*' than talk with him.

Prince Hal – soon to be Henry V – never fought his hot-spurred namesake at Shrewsbury, nor were they even of the same generation: in 1403 the prince was 16, whereas Hotspur was 39. But in *Henry IV, Part One* it is the climax of the play when the two youths clash. '*Two stars cannot keep their motion in one sphere*', explains Prince Henry, and promptly kills Hotspur, against the odds. The play and the memorable nickname ensured Percy a place in legend, and on newsagent's shelves where his nickname appeared as the title of a oncepopular children's comic.

Customs Battlefield Church, just north of Shrewsbury, was erected in commemoration of the mêlée. According to a compilation of last century called *Shropshire Bell Jingles* when its bells chime, they offer some belated tactical advice: '*Hold up your shields, say the bells of Battlefield.*'

The Shropshire bells' messages include wise ones: '*You're too fond of beer, say the bells of Ellesmere*'; unhelpful ones: '*A lump of old wood, say the bells of Leebotwood*'; ornithological ones: '*An owl in the tree say the bells of Norbury*'; depressing ones: '*We must all die, say the bells of Lydbury*'; medical ones: '*Itchy and scabby, say the bells of the Abbey*'; rude ones: '*Up the ridge and down the butt, say the bells of Smethycote.*' And some are just plain obscure: '*Axes and brummocks say the bells of Clungunnus*' (now Clungunford).

© On the first Tuesday after St Margaret's Eve, which is on the 19th, **Honiton Fair** in Devon opens with the proclamation: '*Oyez! Oyez! The glove is up! The Fair is begun! No man shall be arrested until the glove is taken down!*' But even while the gilded leather glove remains on the end of the town-crier's garlanded pole, do not bank on immunity from subsequent prosecution. Hot pennies are then thrown in the air, and children risk burns and bruises to scramble for the small change.

22nd July
St Mary Magdelene's Day

Disintarred

Madam Beswick was buried today in 1868, a century after her death. For the previous hundred years she had lain above ground embalmed in tar. This posthumous period had been spent first at Sale Priory, and then in the vaults of the Manchester Natural History Society, who arranged the burial after re-evaluating their specimen as officially 'undesirable'. Beswick brought this strange fate on herself because of her morbid fear of premature burial. She had never been quite the same after her brother had woken up just as his coffin lid was being nailed down. In her will Madam Beswick promised a certain Doctor White all her possessions if he would keep her from burial. The tarring had been his solution.

These precautions did not lead to an undisturbed afterlife. Last century, Madam Beswick, in rustling black silk, was regularly spotted wandering around her former home at Birchen Bower near Manchester. In the 1890s she was seen in an aggressive pose by the well in the grounds, her eyes emitting a blue light. At the time her family were involved in a court case attempting to reclaim the Birchen Bower property. It was assumed that only when that was restored to their ancestral home would Madam's restless spirit find peace. Years earlier Beswick had been in the habit of manifesting inside the house, and then disappearing above a certain flagstone. Eventually someone took a look at the spot, and her personal treasure was found buried underneath. She had hidden it there in 1745 so that the invading Bonnie Prince Charlie could not get his paws on it.

🎣 ✝ The **Loch Ness Monster** is now a major tourist industry. Fruitlessly aiming binoculars over the deep icy waters here in the middle of the Highland region has become an international custom. But this was not always the case. In spite of a handful of medieval sightings (see St Columba's Day, June 9th), it was not until July 22nd 1933 that modern media attention fixed on the site, and every bobbing twig or paddling vole began to be positively identified as a mysterious denizen of the deep. On that day a six-foot-long slimy grey monster was spotted dashing across a road near the Loch. Two years later Nessie was being described as a 20-foot-long cross between a seal and a pleisiosaur.

By the 1950s photographs of the beast or beasts started appearing. In the 1970s high-profile naturalist Sir Peter Scott put his seal of approval on the believers' cause, basing his faith on some spectacular close-ups and giving the monster a scientific name, *Nessiteras rhombopteryx*, 'the Ness monster with the diamond-shaped fins'. A short while later crossword-crackers pointed out that the name was an anagram of 'monster hoax by Sir Peter S.'

👄 One week into St Swithin's 40-day downpour the rain gets some extra help from **Mary Magdelene**. It is traditionally, and imaginatively, said that on her feast day – today – it will rain, as Mary is washing her handkerchief prior to visiting St James Fair on the 25th. Red roses are said to be blushing today, on behalf of the penitent Mary, a prostitute out of whose body Jesus cast seven demons. At Calvary she stood by his Cross, and later anointed his dead body. Mary was also the first person to see him after his Resurrection.

23rd July

Godstone and God's stones

Today in 1885 a street in Davidson's Mains, Edinburgh, was visited by a sight-seeing **luminous cloud**. It lurked in the road briefly, and then rushed forwards towards some apprehensive spectators. As it engulfed them they felt an electric tingling all over their bodies, and sparks flew from their extremities. The glowing mass moved onwards and upwards, and a few minutes later thunder was heard. In another time and place it would have been seen as a visitation by an irate god. In 1880s' Auld Reekie it was ascribed to unusual electrical phenomena, much less exciting.

The years following the Reformation in the 16th century were troublesome for anyone of devout beliefs. First of all Henry VIII had dissolved the monasteries and superimposed Anglican practices on a thousand years of Catholicism; and then in 1553 there was an about-turn in prejudice as new Catholic Queen 'Bloody' Mary I reversed the bigotry. Completing the cycle, her Protestant sister Elizabeth came to the throne in 1558 and turned everything on its head once again.

It was during the back-to-Catholicism Mary-phase that on this day in 1555 Protestant John Launder was burned at the stake in Steyning, West Sussex, for failing to recant. He and his friend Thomas Iveson, executed around the same time in nearby Chichester, became known as the **Godstone Martyrs**, as both came from Godstone in Surrey. They had languished in prison for seven months after being caught attending illicit Anglican services in Brighton. During the course of the trial, Iveson declared '*I would not recant and forsake my opinion for all the goods of London*'.

🔲 Perhaps it was a perceived wish to get back to religious basics which on this day in 1928 prompted Mr Whitley of Buckland, Devon, to begin work on carving the **Ten Commandments** which can still be seen on two rocks at Buckland Beacon Tor, near Kingsbridge.

© **Swan-Upping** takes place on the Thames at the back end of July. All mute swans belong to the Crown, apart from those allocated in the 15th century to the Vintners' and Dyers' Livery Companies. The Queen's Swanherd and his men meet the Swan Wardens of the two Companies, and they go swanning up the river in striped jerseys, catching all the birds between Sunbury in Surrey and Pangbourne in Berkshire. Dyers' swans have a single nick on their beaks, while Vintners' have two nicks – the old pub sign *The Swan with Two Necks* is a slightly distorted tribute to the Vintners' birds.

The offspring of the existing marked birds are given the relevant marks (half and half if the swans have inter-bred). The Queen's Swanherd merely notes the number of his own, unmarked birds, grateful that the excessive former practise of putting five nicks on royal swans has now ceased. As the boats pass Windsor Castle, everyone salutes, saying '*Her Majesty the Queen, Seigneur of Swans*'. The Upping lasts for several days, and is rounded off with a feast, at which the centre-piece is a traditional roast cygnet.

24th July

Casting Straws in the Wind

Today in 1827 the farmers of Denbigh in Clwyd made hay while the wind blew. The air was thick with the stuff as a storm of **flying hay** swept through the area. It left stray straws in its wake, giving locals something to chew over for weeks to come.

The Julys of last century were a great time for UFOs (Unusual and Farcical Objects). In 1821 a shower of herring fell near Melfort in the Lorn district of old Argyllshire, now Strathclyde. In 1842 a girl from Cupar in Fife had her load of laundry whisked from under her feet by a freak wind and sent in a Red Arrows-style display across the hillside. In 1841 Derby was the lucky target for a storm of sticklebacks and bean-sized frogs. A frozen block, 20 feet in circumference and consisting of inch to three-inch long crystals of transparent ice, made a lonely, heavy descent on to a farmhouse near Ord on the Isle of Skye in 1849. Toads tumbled from the clouds by the River Waveney near Aldeby in Norfolk one balmy July day in 1860. Black angular pebbles clattered down on Wolverhampton in the same year. But Bath in 1871 made the best claim of the lot: a shower of tubular, locust-headed larvae encased in jelly.

The shower of explanatory theories has been equally curious. Ghostly or deific influence has been invoked. So have time-warps. It has been claimed that the unorthodox downpours are the flotsam and jetsam of inquisitive aliens passing overhead. Whatever the explanation, the hay is still up there. On July 20th 1993 the BBC's evening weather bulletin reported clouds of hay once again taking to the air, this time over the Midlands.

© **Kelso's Yetholm Ride** and Civic Week takes place in mid-July, the main Ride – headed by the Kelso Laddie and his Left and Right Hand Men – being on the Saturday. The accompanying sports include raft-racing on the River Tweed. Kelso, in the Borders, was one of the main centres for the old Whipman's society of ploughmen, and for this reason the Laddie is also known as the Kelso Whipman, and he leads a mounted procession to the ploughmen's traditional meeting place, the Trysting Tree.

© **Lauder Common Riding**, near Galashiels in the Borders, has records of the event taking place in the mid-18th century, although the modern proceedings stem from a 1910 revival. On the last Saturday in July the Cornet receives the Burgh Flag, and leads a procession, which takes in the only surviving boundary stone in the area: the Burgess Cairn. The celebrations last until the first Saturday in August.

© **Langholm** in Dumfries and Galloway has warm-up rideouts on the two Saturdays before the main event, which is on the last Friday in the month. It begins at 5.30 am, with a procession led by the Langholm Flute Band; followed by hound-trailing in the surrounding hills later in the morning. At 8.30 am the Cornet leads the Riding, carrying, bizarrely, the colours of that year's Epsom Derby winner. Other chief features in the parade include a giant thistle made of, er, thistles; a large crown woven from roses; a heather-covered spade; and a salt-herring nailed to a large bannock. The event continues into the afternoon, with dancing, sports and horse-racing. For all the riding tidings, see June 13th.

25th July
St James' Day/Grotto Day/ St Christopher's Day
Chicory Tips

It was at Lancashire's Whalley Rushbearing feast on this day in 1688 that Richard Dugdale decided to sell his soul to the Devil. All he wanted in exchange was to be a terrific dancer. Satan accepted the bargain; and amidst fits, talking in tongues, and vomiting stones, Dugdale performed his amazing dance routines at his home in Surey, part of Whalley. As he gyrated, the amazed crowd watched a large boil travel from its original position on his leg, up to his chest, where it began to mumble and suppurate.

The men who exorcised Dugdale were unimpressed by all this devilry. They decided to tackle Satan with a novel weapon: ridicule. Documents of the time record them as heckling: *'Canst thou dance no better, Satan? Pump thine intervention dry! Cannot that universal seed-plot of subtle wile and stratagems spring up one new method of cutting capers? Is this the top of skill and pride, to shuffle feet and brandish knees thus, and to trip like a doe, and skip like a squirrel? And wherein differs thy leapings from the hoppings of a frog, or bounces of a goat, or friskings of a dog, or gesticulations of a monkey? Dost thou not twirl like a calf that has the turn, and twitch up thy houghs like a spring-haught tit?'*

The abuse produced results. Richard eventually recovered, and the Devil abandoned choreography to devote more time to writing good tunes.

St James' badge is the scallop, a bivalve mollusc. After his death in 1st-century Jerusalem, his relics underwent a miraculous journey in a marble boat headed for Compostella in Spain. As it passed Portugal, a man riding along the coast was so astounded at the sight of floating marble that he plunged off the road and into the sea. St James, although dead, intervened. The man was raised from the depths, all covered in scallops. Ever since, pilgrims have come to offer prayers at Compostella and take home a scallop: to own one means favourable treatment on Judgement Day.

Anyone unable or unwilling to make the journey to Spain used to visit a shell-grotto, many of which were constructed today. Hence the alternative name Grotto Day. By last century it had become mainly a child's activity, an excuse for demanding pennies from passers-by, Guy Fawkes-style. A traditional plea ran:

Please to remember the grotto,
It's only once a yĕar; Father's gone to sea,
Mother's gone to fetch him back, so please
*   remember me.*

Grottoes – or Grotters – appeared today in some parts of south London as recently as the early 1960s. The Museum of London has a grotto in its collection, but it is not always on display.

There is a risk of a one-night July 25th crime-wave, led by superstitious burglars. On St James' Day chicory not only renders its wearer invisible – which is why explorers and invaders often carried a lucky chicory emblem – it also helps a thief gain access to locked rooms, safes, jars of beetroot, and other maximum security areas. Hold the chicory to the lock at midnight tonight, and release the mechanism with a golden knife. This must be done in complete silence, otherwise there is instant death.

Today is also St Christopher's Day. A legendary giant, he once bore the terrific load of the young Christ and all the weight of the mortal world across a flood, the River of Death. Since those metaphorical days he has been patron saint of wayfarers, motorists, and those close to the edge: to gaze upon his image is supposed to prevent sudden death. Originally Christopher – whose name means 'Christ-bearer' – had decided to serve the Devil; but he lost his respect for Old Nick when the latter admitted to being afraid of Christ and his Cross. Christopher was demoted to the status of local cult in 1969, but that caused discontent in the grassroots of the Catholic church: he may only be a metaphor, but he is a symbol that seems to have lasting resonance.

⛫ Salisbury Museum, Wiltshire, has a 12-foot tall, dark effigy of a black-bearded giant. Since time immemorial it has been known as St Christopher. Wheeled out at times of national celebration, he used to be linked with the Tailors' Guild and their Midsummer feast. He is probably some old god, still hanging in there.

© **Ebernoe Horn Fair** takes place today in West Sussex – or 24 hours earlier if the 25th is a Sunday. Its only surviving feature is a funfair, and an 11 am cricket match, during which a whole black ram is roasted in a pit. The sheep is provided by Lord Egremont, and during the mutton supper which follows the man with the highest score during the game is given the ram's head and horns as a prize. The fair was a remnant of a fertility festival; the horned head is a potent, if monstrous, phallic symbol. This old song is still sung at the fair:

> *If you would see the Horn Fair you must*
> *   walk on your way,*
> *I will not let you ride my grey mare today:*
> *You'd rumple all my muslin and uncurl my*
> *   hair,*
> *And leave me all distressed to be seen at*
> *   Horn Fair.*

© **John Knill** instigated the **Knillian** at Knill's Monument on Worvas Hill just south of St Ives, Cornwall. Every five years at just after 10.30 am on St James' Day, a fiddler and 10 dancing young girls, all daughters of seamen or tinners, lead a procession of townsfolk from the Guildhall to the bus station. There they hop on the next bus up to the monument – a large, granite steeple – where they rendevous with the mayor of St Ives and a handful of local widows, then sing the Hundredth Psalm.

Knill's will also provided for several doles to be issued on the same occasion – the dancing girls, the widows, and the fiddler all get a pound or two; with the mayor and a customs man each getting £10. There are also cash prizes for such splendid feats as the best fish-net stitcher and the best pilchard-curer. The next Knillian is in 1996.

⛫ It is said that Knill – bachelor, one-time mayor and alleged king of the local smugglers –

built the monument to help his illegal shipping activities, since it acted, and still acts, as a useful navigation mark. He had intended that on his death the monument would become his mausoleum, but consecration of the site proved elusive, and when Knill died in 1782 he was buried instead in St Andrew's Church, at Holborn in London. Knill could not have foreseen the change of venue, and the Knillian and accompanying doles were just his ill-fated attempts to ensure that his grave was kept clean.

Pre-RSPB, July 25th was the first day of **wheatear-shooting** on the Sussex Downs. The summer migrant is now protected from the blazing firearms. It was an easy target thanks to its 'white arse' – the Old English origin of the name 'wheatear'.

26th July
St Anne's Day

Faint-Hearted

John Wilmot, young **Earl of Rochester**, died today at Woodstock, Oxfordshire, in 1680. A notorious womaniser, shortly before the end he attempted to make amends by embracing God. When, in his prime, he had met Elizabeth Mallet at the court of Charles II, Wilmot's amorous exploits had nearly been his undoing. He was smitten, but so was half the court. Rather than wait for an opportune moment to press his suit, he kidnapped her, subsequently spending several months in jail for the abduction. A commoner might have been hanged for the offence; but Wilmot was pardoned after serving a stint in the King's navy. In 1667 he was allowed to marry Elizabeth – who strangely seems to have agreed to their union – and they set up home in Adderbury.

Wilmot was not cut out for the settled life: he continued to sow his insatiable oats, until he was riddled with disease and had grown old before his time. Of his later escapades, the most celebrated occurred when he entered a woman's house while her puritanical husband was away. Dressed as another woman and faking a swoon, Wilmot was taken in. So was she: the seduction was evidently irresistible, for she eloped with the cross-dressing dastardly Earl, taking her husband's gold with her.

🗓 **St Anne's curative well** at Buxton in Derbyshire appears to have been in use for as long as there have been people in that part of the country to use it. In the Romano-British period Buxton was called *Aquae Arnemetiae*, Arnemetia being the local water goddess. Along came Christianity, and the pagan deity became St Anne, fulfilling the same functions under a different guise. The spa-boom of the 19th century rejuvenated the water-cult, with drinking and immersions drawing several thousand people a year to the well and spa-baths. The source still produces 200,000 gallons of water a day, at a constant temperature of 82 degrees Fahrenheit.

As for St Anne herself, she was the apocryphal mother of the Virgin Mary. This made her a natural replacement for the powerful Earth Mother goddesses of pagan religions – especially life-giving Anu (or Danu), whose name was so similar it seems likely that Anne was tailor-made as a Christian rationalisation of the goddess. In typical life-giving – if anatomically confused – style, the carving of Anne at St Anne's Well in Llanfihangel, South Glamorgan, used to have the water flowing from between her breasts.

🗓 Apart from Buxton, there is a very impressive St Anne's Well with 19th-century spa buildings at Malvern Wells, south of Great Malvern in Hereford and Worcester. Her well at Trellech, Gwent, can bestow good luck – or bad. If you drop a stone in the water and lots of bubbles rise, your wish will come true. If there are just a few bubbles, dark days lie ahead.

27th July

The Cures of the Mummy

Graham of Claverhouse, **Viscount 'Bonnie' Dundee**, was on the receiving end of a stray musket ball and died at the moment of his victory today in 1689 at the Battle of Killiecrankie. He had led the Highlanders against William III's men, captained by Hugh Mackay, at the Pass of Killiecrankie in Tayside. Blood flowed through the pass in a wave, and a thousand spades were later needed to level the graves of the dead. The musket shot must have been an all-important secret weapon, for Dundee's enemies said that he was a warlock who could only be killed with a silver bullet. The Soldier's Leap in the pass marks where one defeated man made a prodigious leap over the torrential river to escape death.

The **herbals** of the 16th century were in a direct line of descent from the Anglo-Saxon herbals of the pre-Conquest era: collections of folk belief and DIY pharmacology. Some of this was wild superstition, but there were also potent remedies with which modern medicine is only just catching up. **Peter Treveris'** *Grete Herball* was published today in 1526, describing '*grene herbes of the gardyn and wedys of ye feldys as well as costly receptes of the potycarys prepayred*'. It warns against cold bathing: death will surely follow. And there is an unlikely winner of the evil-liquid prize: water. Too much of the stuff in youth leads to a waterlogged early grave.

The book is written with a certain economy. Take Treveris' recipe for Oil of Violets: '*Oyle of vyolettes is made thus. Sethe vyolettes in oyle and strayne it. It will be oyle of vyolettes.*' He is a great advocate of the sprinkling method. To make people merry, for example, sprinkle water of bugloss around the house; or, to liven up a dull dinner party, spray the guests with a shower of vervain in wine.

Not all his ingredients are pleasant. He extols **mummy**, a stinking substance found in old tombs, the remnants of decay and anointing oils from the corpses. It is, he says, found mainly in the brain and ridge of the back, and helps '*restrayn and staunche*'. This was in the age before the sticking-plaster.

© Amongst the many July well-dressings in Derbyshire are ones at Cutthorpe, Heath, Ault Hucknall, Glapwell (all near Chesterfield) and Pilsey (near Bakewell) in mid-month. Buxton's dressing is in the second week of the month; and Stoney Middleton (near Bakewell) and Bonsall (near Matlock) have theirs on the last Saturday. June and August are the other two months associated with well-dressing. See Ascension Day for a complete dressing down.

© Around noon on the last Saturday in July, at Tenby in Dyfed, the mayor leads a procession around the town's walls, a sort of pub-crawl without the pubs. This is a signal for **St Margaret's Fair** to burst into action, once he has completed his circuit.

28th July
St Botvid's Day

Blanket Ban

St Botvid was renowned for his missionary work. A Swede by birth, he was converted in England and preached all over Europe. He once freed a Finnish slave; but the slave finished him – he stabbed Botvid to death as they were rowing across the Baltic Sea. Monks searching for his body were guided by a bird which sang on their prow until their boat was over Botvid's watery grave, a motif which links in with the notion that seabirds are the souls of drowned sailors. The story adds a colourful bit of myth to a saint who, in spite of his name, is not the patron of dirty videos.

☼ Marie Lairre, celebrated nun and ghost, manifests at one of Britain's prime haunted sites: the old Rectory, near the church in Borley, Essex. July 28th is the day upon which she most often appears, and it has been speculated that this may have been the date of her death. She materialises with a woebegone expression, sometimes gliding a foot above the ground. In 1943 during excavations the jaw-bone of a young woman was found, deformed by a bad abscess. It gives a prosaic clue as to the possible source of Maire's distressed expression: a mixture of pain and physical disfigurement.

Most of the ghost activity in Borley now centres on the church, where a sighing ghost has been heard opening a now blocked-in door and throwing things around. It was the subject of investigation – resulting in an impressively scary tape-recording of the groans and creaks – used on a 1975 BBC programme, *The Ghost Watchers*. The tape frightened fresh audiences in 1993 when it was played at the end of the Hallowe'en edition of the BBC chat-show, *Danny Baker: After All*. For more on the hauntings at Borley, see February 27th.

© When covenanting preachers travelled the length and breadth of Scotland in the early days of Presbyterianism, the religious oppression of Charles I meant that they were often barred from their services in church. Many preachers and their congregations were forced to meet on the hillsides, huddling together under the shelter of blankets. The **Blanket Preaching**, held on the last Sunday in July in the Yarrow Valley of the Scottish Borders, is said to date back to these times, and commemorates the proselytising achievements of the 17th-century Covenanters. It is now a large scale open-air service, next to St Mary's Kirk of the Lowes, at Yarrow near Selkirk.

On the Friday before Lammas (August 1st), the **Struell Wells** near Downpatrick in County Down, Northern Ireland, were visited for general cures. There are four wells, each with their own small building: a Drinking Well, an Eye Well, and two bath-houses – one for each sex. They are equally potent on Midsummer Eve, and are said to have been blessed by St Patrick personally.

29th July
St Olaf's Day

Football Fens

King Offa of Mercia died on this day in AD 796. His palace was on the 30-acre site at Sutton Walls on the hill above Sutton St Nicholas, Hereford and Worcester. This hill and the one at Kentchurch, south of Hereford, were said to be the most fertile, and valuable, land in England. A local claim ran:

Sutton Wall and Kentchester Hill,
Are able to buy London, were it to sell.

▯ Offa's main mark on posterity is Offa's Dyke, a 70-mile earthwork from Prestatyn in Clwyd to Chepstow in Gwent, boldly marking the English-Welsh boundary. He may have got his name on it, but there is no proof that the dyke was built by Offa.

Mary Carpenter and family were cruising off the coast of Norfolk on this day in 1938. After a lull in the conversation her husband looked up to ascertain the cause of Mary's silence. There was a simple explanation. She had burst into flames – another unexplained case of **spontaneous combustion**. See February 19th for more on this phenomenon.

St Olaf (995–1030) was King of Norway, and such a champion of Christianity that he often used extreme force to convert his countrymen. The King of England, the Danish Cnut, used evidence of this repression to overthrow Olaf, who died trying to regain his lost throne. It was sweet revenge for Cnut – Olaf had sided with

Ethelred the Unready in an attempt to kick Cnut's forces out of England in 1013; but now Cnut ruled over an empire which included England and Norway.

After his death Olaf rapidly became associated with various miracles and cures, and was very popular in the Viking-settled areas of Britain, from Orkney and Shetland right down the North Sea coast to East Anglia. St Olaf's Well at Cruden Bay, Grampian, was a powerful source of healing and good fortune for the fishing community. A local rhyme describes this:

St Olaf's Well, low by the sea,
Where pest nor plague shall ever be.

In the late 18th century, Holland Fen was being enclosed, much to the dismay of locals in south Lincolnshire who saw their common land being blatantly stolen. Discussing the best way to manifest their protest, they came up with a 200-a-side **anti-enclosure football match**. The first July fixture ended in a pitched battle – police, dragoons and heavies from Boston moved in to round up the ringleaders, who found themselves going over the match reports in Spalding jail. But by the time of the game on July 29th the authorities realised that they would do better to ignore it, and leave discipline to the referee – though it is hard to imagine a team of 200 being worried by a few sendings-off. So the protests were ignored; the land was enclosed; and the games died out.

30th July

Kingston or Commonston?

The **Earl of Kingston** could not make his mind up: Should he back the King or the Commons during the Civil War? Stalling, he once announced: '*When I take up arms with the King against Parliament, or with Parliament against the King, let a cannon-bullet divide me between them.*' It was a prophetic utterance. Kingston was taken prisoner by the Roundheads in the Humber near Kingston upon Hull. Whilst being held captive he waved to an oncoming King's ship to show that it was he, the vacillating Earl, quite definitely on the King's side . . . for the time being. The King's ship fired, and Kingston was, indeed, divided down the middle by a cannon-ball, on this day in 1643.

© On October 14th 1881, 129 fishermen from 23 boats were lost from Eyemouth in the Borders. Some of the vessels' names added to the poignancy – *Good Intent, Guiding Star*, and *Forget me not*. The dead of that dreadful night, which was known afterwards as Black Friday, are remembered each year amid the festivities of the **Eyemouth Herring Queen Festival**. Held since 1939 on a Saturday in July – quite which Saturday depends on the tides – the festival has evolved from the much older local holiday and celebration, the Fishermen's Picnic. The schoolgirls of the town elect a Herring Queen, and the skippers of the fishing boats – which catch white fish rather than herring these days – nominate a girl who becomes a member of her court. Wearing all manner of fish-related costumes, they sail from St Abbs to Eyemouth harbour accompanied by the remains of the town's fishing fleet, bunting dripping from every mast. After a crowning ceremony there is a short service and a parade with the Queen at the head. She carries fruit, corn and fish, a symbolic offering to the local sea-god, who struck so mercilessly on that October night.

🏛 In 1981 – the centenary of the disaster – a museum opened in Eyemouth. The history of local fishing is its main theme, centring upon Black Friday itself. It also details the nomadic women who used to 'travel the herring', following the fleets up and down the coast of Scotland and England, gutting and barrelling the catch.

© Church-clipping is a survival from an ancient, pre-Christian era when people's idea of a good time was to hold hands and dance around a sacred tree or standing stone. The **Burbage Clypping**, just outside Buxton in Derbyshire, spoils this continuity theory as it only started in 1851 when the church was dedicated. On the Sunday nearest the dedication date of August 2nd – often the last Sunday in July – there is a morning service, during which the church is surrounded by a ring of people with linked hands. This is followed by a hymn and a blessing.

31st July
St Neot's Day

British Summer Time Begins, and Ends

St Neot was 15 inches high, but that did nothing to hinder the tall stories. An angel called round one day, and presented him with three fish, revealing that if the saint ate just one a day, their number would never diminish. St Neot kept the fish in his well, and several contented years of fish suppers followed. When he fell ill his female retainer, as a special treat, cooked two of the fish for him. Neot was aghast and began frantically praying. He knew that there were plenty more in the sea, but not like these. The fish were returned to their well, where they miraculously shook off the batter and swam away, none the worse for their close encounter with the frying pan.

Neot was a great improviser. After his oxen were stolen, he used two wild deer to pull his plough. He relied on a pike-tooth-studded comb to keep himself groomed; and – because of his height – he stood on a stool so that he could see over the altar during Mass. His reputation as a holy man was sufficient for King Alfred to pay him a visit. Ignoring host's etiquette, Neot told Alfred that he was an evil sinner – an outrageous slur on the great and pious man. But the saint made amends a year after his death by appearing to Alfred before the vital battle of Edington in 878.

⑪ The saint's now fishless well is just outside the village of St Neot in Cornwall, which also had the diminutive saint's relics until St Neots in Cambridgeshire swiped the lot, apart from one arm.

© The last Saturday in July is the date of the **World Flounder Tramping Championships** in the Solway Firth mud flats near Palnackie, just south of Dalbeattie in Dumfries and Galloway. This began in 1972, but is based firmly on ancient fishing techniques. Using heavy camouflage and minimal movements, men stalk the flounder by walking barefoot in the water. As the fish tend to lie flat on the river bed, the idea is to tread on one, then reach down to pull it from the water. The use of the traditional spear, the *liester*, is frowned upon by modern participants, and the only risk is from crabs and sharp cockles. These days, backed by a distillery, the prize for the heaviest catch is £150 and three litres of whisky. The winner on July 31st 1993 had trampled on a two-pound two-ounce specimen.

Epitaphs have stretched rhyme and brain-cell down the centuries. When John Hewet and Sarah Drew of Stanton Harcourt, near Witney in Oxfordshire, died in a thunderstorm on July 31st 1711, the poet Alexander Pope, who was staying in the village, was moved to write:

> *Virtue unmov'd can hear the call*
> *And face the flash that melts the Ball.*

⑪ This impenetrable metaphor can be seen in the church at Stanton Harcourt, which is also cluttered with the Harcourt family's unrivalled group of 14th- to 19th-century monuments. The poet stayed at the 15th-century building now know as Pope's Tower.

☕ It is said that the **English summer** starts on July 31st, only to end on August 1st. To extend the strained jest even further, it is also said that winter ends on July 31st, and recommences . . . yes, you guessed it.

AUGUST

1st August
Lughnasad/Lammastide/
Feast of St Peter in Chains/
Minden Day

Races, Roses and Dances at Lughnasa

Lugh, pronounced *Loo*, was of mixed god and demon stock, arriving on the mythological scene as a self-proclaimed master of absolutely everything. With his formidable weapon the Sword of Light, Lugh was the embodiment of the autumn sun which brings on the harvest – a crucial presence at this time of year. But to bring on the autumn sun, Lugh first had to kill his grandfather Balar – the same god as Bel or Baal, remembered in the May festival of Beltane. Balar personified the bright summer sun, and Lugh killed him by knocking his one huge glaring eye through the back of his head with a sling. This uncompromising god was honoured with the festival of **Lughnasad**, or Lunasdal, 'the assembly of Lugh', at which fairs and feasts were held – as recently popularised in Brian Friel's hit play *Dancing at Lughnasa*.

Ulster had special cause to honour Lugh, as he was the half-father (it's a long story) of **Cuchulainn**, who single-handedly fought off the rest of Ireland while the warriors of Ulster were crippled with the pains of labour (another long story), as recounted in the epic *Tain bo Cuilange*. Only once did Lugh himself have to intervene to assist his precocious son. Cuchulainn's performance on the battlefield was aided by his secret weapon the *gae bolga*, a spear with special barbs for pulling out a victim's guts; and by his dread-inducing *warp-spasm*: when in the throes of this fighting frenzy, his bottom half turned back to front, one eye was sucked to the back of his head, the other eye dangled out on his cheek, and a jet of hot black blood spurted up through the top of his skull. When faced with this, most enemies either ran off or threw up.

Lammas means 'loaf-mass', a Christian name plonked on top of the old Lughnasad festivities. It was the day when harvesting officially got under way. Loaves made with the first of the year's ripened corn were taken to church for a blessing. Lammas was also one of the Celtic Quarter days, when rents fell due and contracts were renewed or terminated.

The **Lammas Fair** at Kirkwall in Orkney was one of the biggest of its kind. All the islanders converged on the town, sleeping among strangers on straw-lined floors in a fraternal open-house atmosphere. Taking a sexual partner for the 11-day duration of the fair was common practice. The couples were known as Lammas brothers and sisters, in lugh of the real thing. And for couples thinking more in the long-term, Lammas was a good day for **handfasting**: joining hands through a hole in an ancient stone to plight troths to each other for a trial period of a year and a day. If they were still on good terms 366 days later, the couple became man and wife. The Stone of Odin at Stenness on the Mainland of Orkney was often used for handfasting.

© Fife in Scotland has two surviving medieval **Lammas Fairs**. The one at St Andrews received its charter from James VI (James I of England), and still manages to block the streets with its fairground attractions on the first weekend in August. One of the privileges granted to the fair gave it a monopoly on sales of ironmongery in the surrounding district, an entitlement that ceased in 1800. Also in the first week of August, Inverkeithing stages its Lammas Fair. The chief event is the **Hat and Ribbon Race**, a foot-race originally devised for herdsmen in the 1500s. The beribboned prize hat is paraded through the streets prior to the sport. A 17th-century writer summed up the fair as '*fun, frolic, fit races, ale and drunken fools*' – a general description that few modern fair-goers would dispute.

Faeries were regular visitors to fairs, their sole aim often being to replace human babies with changelings. Lammas was a night when mortals could attempt to reverse a faerie-snatch, by placing a suspected changeling child in a hole overnight. In the morning either the original snatched baby was restored, or the same child was still there accompanied by an angry social worker. This drastic transaction was only attempted if the potent anti-changeling charms had failed. One such charm required putting the new-born baby into a basket filled with bread and cheese, walking round a fire three times, and then eating the basket's contents . . . excluding the baby.

Witches can be a pain in the neck at Lammas too. Tiree in the Inner Hebrides offers the following deterrent: put a ball of hair in a pail of milk today, and witches will leave your cows alone.

The old Scottish school-yard game of Lammas commemorates the hiring fair custom of cowhands offering their labour with a straw in the mouth to denote their line of work. In the game you grip a straw between chin and bottom lip. The winner is the one who can say the following rhyme the most times without dropping the straw:

> *I bought a beard at Lammas Fair,*
> *It's a' awa' but ae hair – wag, beardie, wag!*

Until early this century, **St Patrick's Well and Chair**, in Favour Royal Forest near Altadaven in County Tyrone, were the scene of wild Lammas celebrations. It was at this spot that St Patrick – St Brigid in some legends – drove a herd of devils off the cliff. The stone chair is thought to have been an inauguration throne, and the site remained practically untouched by Christian practices, the link with the saints' names being no more than a thin veneer on the pagan partying.

◉ Minden Day commemorates an against-the-odds victory over the French at the Battle of Minden in Germany in 1759 – the year became known as the *Annus Mirabilis*, the year of victories, following a run of British military triumphs across the world. Minden Heath was covered with wild roses during the fight, and by the end so were many of the British troops. As a reminder the regiments involved wear roses in their hats on this day. The Lancashire Fusiliers – now part of the Royal Regiment of Fusiliers – also hold a slap-up meal at which newcomers undergo the **Eating a Rose** ceremony. The rose is pre-sented in a champagne-filled finger-bowl, and is consumed by the initiate.

One of the heroes of the battle was John Manners, the Marquis of Granby – the man responsible for the many pubs of that name. His party-piece was to lose his wig at the height of battle – this is the origin of the phrase 'to go at it/someone bald-headed'.

✟ ⌗ Queen Anne, whose reign began on 1703, died on this day in 1714. At Queen Anne's Gate in Westminster, London, her statue climbs down from its plinth tonight and goes for a stroll through town. Before a clean-up in the 1930s, which revealed the statue's true identity, many believed that it represented Queen Mary Tudor – Bloody Mary – and it was a popular target for abuse and stone-throwing.

2nd August
St Sidwell's Day

Bowing to Public Pressure

Today in 1100 **William Rufus** – aka William II of England – was hunting with friends in the New Forest. Out came the deer, twang went the bows, down went Rufus. Blame was pinned on a deflected arrow, and the panicking hunters ran away. Suspicion then fell on the oh-look-I-seem-to-be-king-now Henry I. But Rufus was hated by church and people alike, and it probably came as no great shock that his death might have been other than accidental. The most colourful of the murder-theories suggests that Rufus was a sacrificial victim dispatched to the old gods at Lughnasad, a bloodthirsty Celtic harvest festival (see yesterday).

The evidence used to back up this hypothesis is the fact that as Rufus' body was being carried to Winchester, his royal blood was allowed to spill on to the earth – one of the basic requirements of a blood sacrifice. It is true that the King was buried unceremoniously and without last rites; although history maintains that, rather than being a cover-up, these were Rufus' own last wishes. The notion of killing a king as the ultimate sacrifice to the gods is as old as religion itself. J.G. Frazer grounded his weighty tome *The Golden Bough* on this idea, taking as his starting point the assassination of the King of the Wood who guarded Diana's sacred lake at Nemi, Italy.

⌗ ✟ The Rufus Stone in the New Forest at

Upper Canterton near Lyndhurst, Hampshire marks the supposed site of William II's death, and on this day he goes haunting in its immediate vicinity. The nearby Ocknell Pond is said to turn red today, linking in with the tale that Rufus washed the blood from his hands here.

Rufus is said to have given Newcastle-upon-Tyne its name, with his proverbial utterance: '*If we cannot win the old castle we must build a new castle.*'

◉ At Meriden, near Coventry in the West Midlands, the **Woodmen of Arden** stage their **Grand Wardmote** from Wednesday to Saturday, the Saturday falling in the first weekend of August. Several smaller summer meetings precede it, but this is the big one – four days of exotic bows, arrows and targets. The origins of the competitions are lost in time, although the Woodmen only formally assembled in 1785. There are 80 of them, all men, many inter-related, with royalty and the aristocracy traditionally well represented in their ranks. Actor and longbow-expert Robert Hardy is currently among their number. The Woodmen shoot with old yew longbows, over distances measured in roods, at old targets. A favourite is the *clout*, which is about the size of dustbin-lid and derives from the medieval practice of shooting at coats – this is a clout as in the kind not supposed to be cast 'til May is out. The star prize on the last day is an old bugle, and women guests are each given the number of an archer – if their man wins, they get to be his 'lassie', and also get to keep a small golden bugle. The event is low-profile but the organisers are 'not coy' about spectators.

🎦 Beyond Exeter's east wall is the chapel of St Sidwell, an heiress who had a wicked stepmother. The jealous woman coveted Sidwell's land so much that she hired killers, who scythed off Sidwell's head. A spring gushed forth – the ensuing healing well, no longer visible, used to be near the chapel. The fact that the name *Sidwell* derives from the words *scythe* and *well* implies that she post-dates the story, and may have been invented to Christianise a popular pagan harvest-sacrifice legend.

3rd August

Ripon Yarns

Lady Anne Harvey had a coachman. According to a journal of the time, on this day in 1719 he was taken to bed with an illness. He had held his coaching job for 16 years, but his career was about to take a drastic turn. The illness turned out to be a pregnancy, and the coachman gave birth, leading his employers to the inescapable conclusion that he was a woman. Although the 18th-century journalist thought that the discovery of a pregnant transvestite on the payroll was worth noting, it was not considered important enough to merit jotting down the coachman's name.

© On the first Saturday in August, Ripon in North Yorkshire has its **Wilfrid Feast Procession**. St Wilfrid came to Ripon from exile in Rome in 686. Just outside the town he fell ill, and was diagnosed as a goner. But after five days hovering on the brink he recovered, and said that during his fever he had had a vision of a big parade – reason enough for Ripon to instigate its annual procession.

A man in white representing Wilfrid rides at its head – an effigy was used until the Reformation gave the thumbs-down to such idolatrous activities. Wilfrid and his entourage take a long hike to the church through the crowded streets. Delicacy of the day is Wilfrid Pie, a dish containing apples, sugar and cheese.

The story about Wilfrid recovering from illness is remembered in an old cure for cattle. If they are suffering from the murrain, an infectious bovine disease, they can be marked with the cross of the saint, and they will supposedly recover.

© 🎦 Ripon's other leading custom takes place at 9 pm every night of the year, as the **City Hornblower** sounds the huge semi-circular Wakeman's Horn at the four corners of the Obelisk and outside the mayor's residence. Until 1604 this task was performed by the Wakeman, a cross between a mayor and a constable of the law. The Town Hall here still bears the legend '*Except ye Lord keep ye cittie ye wakeman waketh in vain*'. This all began in 886, when King Alfred gave the town a charter and a horn. The original Charter Horn is still wheeled out on the special Horn Days – Wilfrid Sunday (the one after August 1st), Candlemas, Boxing Day, Easter Monday and Rogation Wednesday. At other times it is on show at the mayor's parlour in the town.

One of the key props at the **Congleton Wakes** in Cheshire was a set of very old leather belts with bells on. Once a year in early August monks attempted to whip up some worshipping by putting them on and running through the streets at midnight, the tinkling of the bells representing the clanking of the town's patron, St Peter in Chains, whose Feast Day is on August 1st. At some point the bells passed into the hands of a local family of sweeps. Their jangling soon became a cue for excess and the whole drunken event became known as **Bell-Belt Day**. Congleton's adherence to the pleasure principle was such that when the town's bear died in 1601, the inhabitants diverted money from the church to buy a new one; or as a rhyme of the time put it:

Congleton rare, Congleton rare,
Sold the Bible to pay for a bear.

© By the mid-19th century the festivities were so out of control that the Corporation stepped in. They reclaimed the belt-bells, and still have three sets; while what is left of the Wakes now starts in the last week of July or the first week of August.

4th August

Shuck that Door

On August 4th 1577, Suffolk was invaded by **Black Shuck the Demon Dog**. At Blythburgh, near Southwold in Suffolk, he killed three church-goers by sending the steeple crashing through the roof; and then he bounded out leaving still-visible claw-marks on the door. Across at Bungay he killed another three people before whirling away at the heart of a storm. A less melodramatic era would have put all this down to a hurricane.

Black Shuck is a portent of death throughout East Anglia, related to the nationwide superstitions surrounding phantom black dogs. He is most likely to pounce in churchyards or at crossroads. Sometimes Shuck is subtle and makes his presence known by brushing softly past your knees. At other times he goes for broke, a black slavering monster howling at the moon with flaming saucer-sized eyes. He even does an impressive impression of the Egyptian god Anubis, appearing with the head of a hound and the body of a monk to guard the lost treasure of Clopton Hall at Stowmarket in Suffolk.

In St Mary's churchyard at Black Shuck's pawing ground in Bungay, near Beccles in Suffolk, stands the **Druid's Stone**. If you dance round it three times, you will not meet Black Shuck, but will encounter the next best thing: Satan. Black Shuck himself, riding a lightning bolt, can be seen on a 1933 lamppost's weathervane in the town, near the Butter Cross.

© The Reformation got rid of every abbot in Britain bar one. The Lord Bishop of Norwich was at that time also the Abbot of St Benet's in Norfolk, and he was allowed to keep the title. On the first Sunday in August in his capacity as Abbot, the Lord Bishop sails from nearby Horning to St Benet's on a Norfolk wherry, for the 3.30 pm **St Benet's Abbey Service** during which he blesses the Norfolk broads.

August is the month for cures at St Fillan's Well near St Fillans, west of Crieff in Tayside. The well used to be on the hill, near the rocky outcrop of St Fillan's Chair, but is said to have got bored with the view and upped and moved to its present location. To gain the curative benefits of the water, walk (or get carried) three times round the well before drinking some of its contents and bathing in it. The finishing touch is to place a pebble or rag on Fillan's Chair, which has a reputation for curing rheumatism, though in a very undignified way. The sufferer must sit in it for a moment, before being dragged down the hill by the feet. To be further filled in about Fillan, see his feast day – January 9th.

© The first Monday of August is the date of the **well-dressing** at Bradwell, near Castleton in Derbyshire. Hydrangeas are a local favourite: box-loads of the blooms are shipped across from the National Trust's Trelissick Garden in Cornwall. But local gardeners in Bradwell must also beware, as the saying '*no garden is sacred*' reverberates when the flower-pictures are being assembled. See Ascension Day for more on well-dressing.

5th August
Old St James' Day/
St Oswald's Day/Oyster Day

You Are Now Entering 'Oink'

Tom Hickathrift was an 11th-century Cambridgeshire giant who conformed to all the usual giant clichés – he ate impossibly large amounts, lifted ridiculously heavy objects, and was educationally subnormal – before becoming a hero on Old St James' Day. Tom had a new job delivering beer from King's Lynn to Wisbech, and he came to resent the huge detour that he had to take to avoid the territory of the notoriously nasty Wisbech giant. One day – August 5th by modern reckoning – emboldened by what he was meant to be transporting, Tom cut straight across the no-go area. Enter the Wisbech giant. He pointed out his collection of severed heads, and went to his cave to fetch a weapon. Tom ripped the wheel off the brewers'-cart to use as a shield, and took one of its axles as a club. Battle commenced, and after many hours Tom's youth and vigour won the day. The Wisbech giant begged for quarter; but Tom whacked his head off with the axle. The dead monster's cave was brimming with gold and silver, enough to last Tom a lifetime. The bumbling giant Tom became the respected 'Mr Thomas' Hickathrift, a hero across East Anglia.

🕮 There are many other stories detailing Tom's gigantic achievements; and there are several memorials linked to him, five of which are close to King's Lynn in Norfolk. An elongated effigy at Walpole St Peter's church is said to be Tom. Three old stone crosses are known as **Hickathrift's Candlesticks** – one is in the vicarage garden at Terrington St John's, and two others are at Tilney All Saints, which also has an eight-foot-long stone said to be Tom's grave. And beyond East Anglia the gables of the *Sun Inn* at Saffron Walden, Essex, are decorated with a 17th-century pargeted picture of Tom's victory over the Wisbech giant.

🕮 The extraordinarily pious **St Oswald**, King of Northumbria, was renowned for his handouts to beggars, and his hands-on approach to Christian charity. When the much-impressed St Aidan blessed Oswald, he knew what to concentrate on, declaring *'May this hand never wither with age.'* Years later at the Battle of Maserfield in Shropshire in 642, Oswald was dismembered by the Woden-worshipping King Penda of Mercia. One of the slain King's arms was recovered and for almost a thousand years it remained uncorrupted with that 'just-severed' look; but it finally disappeared during the Reformation. A wooden hand in St Oswald's church at Lower Peover, near Knutsford in Cheshire, is said to represent Oswald's miraculous limb, but is more likely to be a medieval

'glove' of the sort used to indicate that a free-trading fair was underway.

🕮 A second site claims to be the one at which Oswald died – the village now known as Winwick, near Warrington in Cheshire. A pig is said to have carried stones to where Oswald fell, repeatedly squealing *win-wick!* – so giving the village its name. A representation of this improbable pig can be seen in stone above the west door of the church at Winwick.

The dust and earth at the place where Oswald was killed gained a reputation for bringing about great cures, as did a **cross** that he erected at Heavenfield near Hexham in Northumberland prior to defeating the Northumbrian king Cadwalla in 634. The Cross marked the beginning of Christianity in the area, and its wood and moss became valued cure-alls – the new faith, as ever, relying on some pagan finishing touches.

After his death, what was left of Oswald is said to have been taken to **Bardney Abbey** in Lincolnshire. In spite of his holy reputation, the body received a cool welcome – the monks were reluctant to waste their time on the corpse of an enemy king. Oswald's corpse was dumped in a field; but bright light shone from the site right up to the Heavens. The monks realised that they had erred and brought in the remains, vowing never to close their doors again. Since then it has been proverbial in Lincolnshire to say of a person who habitually leaves doors open, *'You must have been born in Bardney'*.

© Guiseley, near Otley in West Yorkshire, has a church dedicated to Saint Oswald. On the Sunday of or nearest the 5th, after the morning service the town engages in a bout of **church-clipping** – walking round the church hand in hand, and asking God to bless the edifice.

© In the Old Calendar, August the 5th was St James' Day, the formal start of London's oyster season – hence today's other name, **Oyster Day**. On this opening day the shellfish were at a premium, and could only be afforded by the very rich. This led to the self-fulfilling prophecy: *'He who eats oysters on St James' Day will never want.'*

© It is almost end of term for the Borders' **Common Ridings**. Coldstream's festivities begin to flow freely from the first full week of August. They start with the investiture of the Coldstreamer, who leads the Ridings. There are parades and sports all week, with a total of four Ridings, including a Thursday trip to Flodden Field, scene of the disastrous Scots defeat in 1513. Wreaths are laid on the memorial there, and there is a short service. The Friday has a parade and firework dislay. For the inside track on the Ridings, see June 13th.

⊙ The Old Green at Lower Canal Walk in Southampton was laid down in the 13th century, which makes it a leading contender for the much-coveted title of 'oldest bowling green in the world'. On the first Wednesday of August, 'gentlemen commoners' – members of the Old Green Bowling Club – traditionally battle it out for the title **Knight of the Old Green**. This is the oldest bowls tournament in Britain – players competed for a Knighthood in 1776. The officials are all past winners, and so must be addressed as 'Sir'. They wear top hats and tails for the occasion, and round each Knight's neck is a silver champion's medal inscribed '*Win it and wear it*'. Playing under the original rules, it usually takes three days for one of the gentlemen commoners to get the seven points needed to earn their Knighthood.

In the last few years the busy bowls season in August has sometimes resulted in the tournament moving to the end of the month, or even into the first week of September, but the organisers hope eventually to reestablish it on its traditional early August date.

6th August

Touch and go

At 5 am today in 1762, the all-gambling, all-nibbling John Montagu, **Earl of Sandwich** was running out of steam at an all-night card session, and called for something that he could eat without having to stop play. The choice of food was minimal, so Sandwich opted to have some ham between two slices of bread, and in so doing invented the snack known forever afterwards as the Montagu. Or so legend has it. In reality he merely popularised a dish that went back at least as far as Roman times, where it had the unappetising name *Offula*.

Until well into last century it was believed that on the first Sunday in August a **faerie woman** appeared at the Welsh mountain lake Llyn y Fan Fach, six miles south of Myddfai in Dyfed. According to legend she lived in the lake, but fell in love with a mortal farmer from Myddfai after being wooed with loaves of bread. Her faerie father said that he would only assent to

their marriage if the farmer could differentiate his bride-to-be from her identical twin sister. He succeeded by noting the idiosyncratic way in which she laced her sandals – a sign of true love and foot fetishism in equal doses. Her father was so impressed with this that he threw in a farmful of faerie livestock as a dowry.

There was one strange condition appended to their wedding vows. If the farmer struck the woman three times, she would have to return to live with the faeries. This was not as draconian as it seems – the couple had a long and happy marriage, and she bore the farmer three sons. But the definition of 'strike' was extremely woolly – if he tapped her on the shoulder or patted her on the arm, he had struck her. The farmer took enormous care, but every few years he slipped up. On the third occasion his wife wept and had to bid him farewell. She dived back into Llyn y Fan Fach along with all the faerie livestock. The farmer never saw her again, but she sometimes appeared to her sons to teach them the arts of herblore; and, armed with this other-worldly knowledge, the family became renowned as great physicians.

© **Egton Bridge Old Gooseberry Show**, near Whitby in North Yorkshire is held on the first Tuesday of August, at the Village School in Egton Bridge. It is the oldest gooseberry show in the county – one of only nine such competitions surviving in the country – founded in 1800, when an estimated 722 varieties of gooseberry were being grown in Britain. Red, yellow and white specimens compete along with the commoner green variety, with prizes going to the heaviest fruit in each category. Egton Bridge Gooseberry Society organises the event, and two ounces is usually a winning weight – which makes a champion gooseberry roughly the size of a golf-ball, only much tastier.

Tan Hill Fair used to be the biggest sheep, livestock and general funfair in Wiltshire. Some etymologists say that Tan Hill, near All Cannings, takes its name from the Celtic fire god *Tana*; though others claim that it comes from 'St Anne', this being Old St Anne's Day. Salt beef and beans were the traditional dish of the fair.

7th August

Half-Foal, Half-Kow

On this day in 1729 Thomas Stevenson was riding to Hedley on the Hill in Northumberland when he saw something very peculiar coming towards him. Sometimes it had the form of a man, sometimes a foal – the only thing that was constant about the creature was its impish expression. Stevenson braced himself. The shape-shifter grabbed his bridle and beat him with it, dragging him three miles to Coalburns before running away amidst peals of laughter.

The man had been waylaid by a notorious boggle, the **Hedley Kow**. Confusion and cruel pranks were its calling cards, but it usually drew the line at anything that caused lasting injury or death. The boggle's favourite tricks included upsetting cooking pots, undoing all the day's knitting and, at its most malicious, routing the horses of men riding to summon midwives. The Kow had several favourite shapes, including a donkey, and a horse; and it was quite happy to transmogrify into a pile of straw. It was also able to appear as any number of people at one time, and always ended its annoying stint with frenzied laughter.

The Hedley Kow was last spotted in the 19th century. There used to be a whole genus of similar shape-shifting practical-jokers in Britain: some were also known as Kows, while others went under such names as Brag, Shagfoal and Dunnie. On one occasion a Kow even appeared as a cow.

© On the Saturday nearest August 5th – the feast-day of St Oswald – **Grasmere** in Cumbria has its **rushbearing**, the most famous of such ceremonies. Children assemble at 3 pm on the flat-topped churchyard wall, all carrying home-made bearings woven from rushes and wild-flowers. Traditional designs include herbaceous harps, crowns, St Oswald's miraculous hand (see the 5th), a serpent-on-a-pole, and a Moses-in-a-basket. They parade round the village accompanied by a band, and half-way round there is an open-air service, after which they make their way back to St Oswald's church accompanied by the clanging of its bells. At 4.15 there is a service inside the church, which is resplendent with rush-decorations on its walls and shelves. Each of the children is given a shiny new 20p piece and some special Grasmere rushbearing gingerbread stamped with the words 'St Oswald'.

The recipe for this delicacy is supposedly so secret that it is kept in a bank vault, although the finished product can now be bought from Grasmere's gingerbread shop. It is tasty, but a poor substitute for the rushbearers' original 'payment' – beer. On the Monday after the ceremony there is a Rushbearing Sports Day at the local school; and the fruits of the bearing stay in the church until Wednesday.

The rushbearing has been going without a break since long before the church floor was first boarded in 1841 – the point at which the festivities lost their functional element and became purely ceremonial – and William Wordsworth, famous ex-resident of Grasmere's Dove Cottage, is known to have attended. At this time of year Grasmere lives on a diet of Wordsworth, beer, and gingerbread; though the former is not recommended for those prone to indigestion. For more on the origins of rush-bearing see June 29th.

8th August
St Lide's Day

Jailhouse Ruck

The 11th-century **St Lide** lived as a hermit on the Isles of Scilly, giving his name to the tiny island now known as St Helens. Lide's own name – also written as Elid or Elidius – apparently lacked the staying power. At one time his chapel was a popular place of pilgrimage, and pirates were warned that if they raided his shrine they would be instantly excommunicated. Tantalisingly vague, the writer Leland recorded that '*Saynct Lide's Isle, . . . in times past at her sepulchre was gret supersition.*' The 'her' in the quote may mark the beginning of the end for manly Lide's eponymous isle.

The Isles are said to have once been the mountainous regions of **Lyonesse**, which was ruled by King Arthur and has long since sunk into the sea between the Scillies and Land's End.

© There is a tradition which says that the stone that was used to make the Norman church of St Lawrence's at **Whitwell** in Derbyshire was hewn out of the nearby open crag at High Hill. Which is why on the Sunday nearest the 10th – St Laurence's Day – there was, until the 1980s, an **open-air thanksgiving service** with the parishioners at the top of the crag and the clergy and choir 20 feet down at the bottom. Public-safety worries have now put a stop to the craggy complexion of the service, but it is still held in the open air close to the church in an area of cleared graveyard known as the Precinct. Many locals now living outside the area return to the village for the ceremony, which starts at 2.30 pm and includes the unique turn-of-the-century hymm *The Ballad of St Lawrence*. The current vicar, the Reverend Chris Rogers, is a rock-climber and gently points out that the stone of the church and the stone of the crag are not actually related.

Shropshire's 'Poet Laureate of Ellesmere', David Studley, committed to verse a bout of the traditional game **Prison-Bars** played on August 8th 1764. Also known as Prison Base, two sides face each other, hands linked, and when a player attempts to dash to the other end of the pitch, one – but only one – of his opponents must give chase and try to stop him. With players from each team simultaneously racing in different directions, each with a personal marker in hot pursuit, ordered chaos ensues. A point is scored for completing the escape run, or for apprehending an opponent before they make it to the end of the pitch.

☕ **Weatherlore** maintains that what crops need in August is sunshine:

> *Dry August and warm*
> *Doth harvest no harm.*

Whereas a few late summer showers are not so welcome:

> *A rainy August*
> *Makes a hard bread crust.*

The number of fogs in August is said to equate exactly with the number of mists in store during the coming winter; and if August is particularly foggy, the season ahead will be unusually harsh and snowy. A thunderstorm early in August paves the way for an entire month of storms. Heavy dew early in the month, though, means that a calm, warm few weeks will follow.

9th August

Dandy Lined With Burdock

Elizabeth I visited **Tilbury Fort**, Kent, today in 1588 to rally the troops for their fight against the Spanish Armada. Tilbury was expecting the Duke of Parma's men from Flanders at any moment, and to show solidarity Good Queen Bess made her famous tally-ho speech about having '*the body of a weak, feeble woman but the heart and stomach of a King*'. Presumably she was not referring to the colossal gut of her father, Henry VIII.

Surprisingly the song-makers churned out some rather prosaic, matter-of-fact recounts of Elizabeth's morale-boosting visit. Withing 24 hours the less than epic *The Queene's visiting of the campe at Tilsbury with her entertaining there* stumbled off the presses. The Queen gate-crashes in her barge, instructs the soldiers not to grovel, chivvies them on a bit, has a slap-up meal, tells everyone that she will be with them in the battle, and then confuses the statement by clearing off.

© On the second Friday in August the **Queensferry Burryman** does the rounds of South Queensferry in Lothian Region. With arms outstretched and legs unbending, he carries two staves covered in flowers, wears a garlanded head-dress, and is covered from top to toe with inch-wide burrs from the burdock plant. Lurching unsteadily like Boris Karloff on an off night, the Burryman is – even within the weird world of customs – a strange and impressive sight.

After two hours spent putting on his costume – no adhesive is used, as the thousands of burrs stick to the material, and each other – the Burryman appears on Queensferry High street at 9 am, propped up by two assistants and ready to begin alms-collecting. No-one wants to miss out on the luck which the Burryman brings, and so his nine-mile tour of the town takes close to nine hours. The role is not for the weak, either of will or bladder. As the town has expanded, so has the Burryman's route, and his itinerary now takes in Queensferry's newest housing estates as well as its oldest pubs. The Burryman is one of the few primeval folklore figures who can be caught having a crafty fag during the regular stops at the town's pubs. The man inside the burrs is a native of Queensferry, elected by the Ferry Fair committee. Each year at around 6 pm, close to exhaustion having survived the day on little more than water sucked through a straw, his final function is to officially open the Ferry Fair by mounting a platform next to the *Hawes Inn*.

The Burryman's origins are obscure. He is explicitly a symbol of greenery – you cannot cover yourself in foliage and claim to be otherwise. It has been argued that he is derived from the once-commonplace scapegoat figure – a man wheeled through a town to siphon off local sins, before being dumped in the sea or otherwise abused. Similar traditions in Europe – i.e. covering people in greenery and parading them – use a green man, often known as Green George, to invoke rainfall. Another theory is that the Burryman came into existence to propitiate the gods responsible for the richness of the local fisheries. Support for this notion comes from the fact that the ports of Buckie and Fraserburgh in north-east Scotland also once had figures very like the Burryman.

The one possible threat to this ancient custom is environmental – the large-scale destruction of the habitat of burdock plants and the increased use of modern herbicides has made it increasingly difficult to find enough burrs for the Burryman's costume.

10th August
St Laurence's Day/
St Bertram of Ilam's Day

Tortured, Broiled, Roasted and Eaten by Wolves

St Laurence was broiled in a gridiron in the 3rd century. With that odd mixture of reverence and black humour that was prevalent in the early Church, he became patron saint of cooks, bakers and confectioners. His spectacularly unlikely last words were:

This side is toasted, so turn me, tyrant, eat, and see whether raw or roasted I make the better meat.

In 1442 Chorley in Lancashire came by four of his thigh bones and a skull authenticated by the Vicar of Croston (also in Lancashire). Hang on. *Four* thigh bones? Perhaps a more dignified memory lies in St Laurence's Fiery Tears – meteors to you and me – which are at their most apparent around August 10th.

'St Laurence bids wages.' Not a very impressive saying, it's true. The implication, appar-

ently, is that it is a day of laziness, due to the heat.

🔲 **St Bertram's Chapel** is in the church at Ilam in Staffordshire, just over the border from Ashbourne in Derbyshire. With Ilam being Anglican, the presence of the miraculous saint is not advertised very much. But you cannot help noticing the piles of postcards on top of his stone tomb, each carrying a request for healing, written with the pencils provided. Pop a note of your medicinal requirements on the tomb, and who knows?

As for the man himself, legend states that Bertram was a Mercian prince who eloped with an Irish princess. Nine months later, he had to leave her in a forest when the woman went into labour. Arriving back with an emergency midwife, Bertram was just in time to see his beloved being eaten by wolves. So he decided to shun worldly things, and set up camp in the wilds of Staffordshire some time in the 8th century.

Not even a prayer to St Bertram could save the **Reverend Richard Godwin** of Gateacre, Derbyshire, in 1787. He died on this day, and a novel diagnosis recorded that his life had been pruned away after eating too many plums.

The second Monday of the month is traditionally the day on which **Sodom and Gomorrah** were destroyed, and is supposed to be very unlucky. Sodom's favourite pastime was the sexual abuse of all strangers. They also liked dipping girls in honey and feeding them to bees, and either stretching or hacking down their enemies until they reached a standard required size. Only Lot and his family (most of them, at least) managed to escape the destruction of the city, after harbouring an angel; but you can take that story with a pillar of salt.

11th August
Old Lammas Eve

On Ewe Marks

The second Monday in August was the date of the old **Horncastle Fair** in Lincolnshire, an event that inspired the racy song overheard by avid folk-song collector Frank Kidson late last century. In the song, a man ducks out of the biting wind to visit a woman friend, and she invites him in for an afternoon of wild and abandoned sex. And that's just the first verse. Unfortunately, it was the only verse which the singer could remember, so Kidson handed the fragment over to his wife Ethel for embellishment. With the deft hand of a Victorian bowdleriser, Ethel cleaned up the storyline, and scrapped the only bona fide verse. So, in the surviving version of *Horncastle Fair* the man meets a girl, promises not to harm her as he escorts her to the fair, then suddenly marries her in the last verse. This is a typical and unusually well documented example of the fate that befell many folk songs. It should be remembered that this was an era when *King Lear* was still often performed with a happy ending and thought all the better for it.

Old Lammas was when some of the biggest **sheep fairs** were held, chiefly on the grassy downs of the south. Warminster in Wiltshire had its fair today; while in the same county Britford and Highworth staged their sheep-bashes on the 12th and 13th respectively. These were massive affairs, with several thousand sheep to be spied filling the byways, sometimes with just a few yards between flocks. At Bretton in Derbyshire **sheep-races** were held, the skittish nature of the beasts making the events about as organised as the 1993 Grand National, even though only one sheep took part at a time. The stroppiest ram in the herd was captured, covered in soap, and released on to the track. The race was between men who endeavoured to catch and keep hold of the animal. The last ram ran at Bretton late last century.

Tonight is **Old Lammas Eve**, and in Scotland the farmers plundered that ever-useful tree, the **rowan** – also known as mountain ash or wicken. Branches were suspended over doors today after being wound into a cross. Rowan was also braided into cows' tails with red and blue thread. For the magic to be effective, the wood had to be collected in silence and in secret.

© The three-day **Cranham Feast** – at Cranham, near Painswick in Gloucestershire – always finishes on the second Monday of August. It all started when locals asserted their common rights by roasting a poached deer (or poaching a roasted deer) in front of the land-owning gentry. Records of the feast go back to 1703, although it seems to have been well into its stride by then. The event is now known as the Cranham Feast and Ox Roast, although venison is still regularly top of the menu at the Saturday Banquet – such whole-animal barbeques seem to be an increasingly popular fixture at modern fairs. Cranham also has a small funfair and various sports and parades, though it no longer indulges one of its formerly favourite pursuits, bowling for pigs.

12th August

Some You Gwynwynwyn, Some You Lose

The Welsh hero Gwynwynwyn had two reasons for hating the English. He was trying to avenge his brother who had been dragged through the streets and then beheaded; and he was striving to unite Wales as a nation. After a series of victories, his campaign was stopped in its tracks on this day in 1198 when he fought the armies of William de Breos, the **Ogre of Abergavenny**. During the battle near Painscastle in Powys, de Breos and his troops slew 3,000 Welshmen, and the rivers ran red for weeks afterwards.

It was a brutal take-no-prisoners victory, and William de Breos became such a focus of hatred in Wales that his wife Maud was invoked as a witch to frighten children into good behaviour. The Ogre enjoyed a few years of power, but died in poverty after offending King John. Maud and her son died in prison. They had been slung into Corfe Castle, Dorset, with a sheaf of wheat and a lump of bacon. On the 11th day the cell door was opened for the first time. Both were dead, and Maud had eaten her son's cheeks in desperation.

✞ For almost 200 years after her death in 1794, **Mary Gibson's tomb** was examined carefully each August 12th. The tomb-inspectors unlocked the crypt door in her mausoleum at Sutton in Greater London and took a good look round. Mary was said to have had a fear of premature burial, and to have made arrangements for the annual check in her will as a safety measure. But it appears that Mary never actually specified any of this, and that it was a procedure which grew spontaneously – probably originating as a precaution against graverobbers. So despite it having become a local tradition, the vicar called a halt to the annual inspection in 1990. Fortunately it does not quite end there, as Mary still appears at the tomb in ghostly form, occasionally emerging from the urn at the top of the mausoleum.

✤ 🏛 Knebworth House, near Stevenage in Hertfordshire, is open to the public, it has occasional big rock festivals, and it is home to the ominous ghost known as the **Radiant Boy**. He appears when death is in the air at the house. The Radiant Boy was seen on this day in 1822 shortly before Lord Castlereagh cut his own throat at Knebworth. The boy crawled from the dying embers of a bedroom fireplace in the form of a naked child, growing bigger in stature as he approached, until he was a huge, pale monster with a livid wound on the forehead. He then retreated, glowing as he went, back to the grate. Such an apparition, meant merely to foretell death, seems enough to drive anyone over the edge. On his death Castlereagh himself made a one-off appearance in ghostly form – several people swore that they saw him on the volcanic island of Stromboli, north of Sicily, at the exact moment of his suicide.

© It is last orders time for the Scottish Ridings: see June 13th for a stable-full of details of the many such events over the summer months. The week-long **Ridings Festival** at Sanquhar in Dumfries and Galloway brings the season to a close, and usually starts on the Friday of the second week in August.

13th August
St Hippolytus' Day

Dee Dead Deed

On this day in 1560 alchemist **Dr John Dee** visited the churchyard at Walton-le-Dale, Lancashire, to bring back to life the corpse of a man who had died without revealing the whereabouts of his treasure. Reanimated, the zombie had no choice but to divulge the details, throwing in a few prophecies for good measure.

John Dee served in the courts of Mary I, Edward VI and Elizabeth I. His CV detailed work as a wizard, astrologer, alchemist, inventor and secret agent. He was famous, but surprisingly gullible. His colleague Edward Kelley was a conman who claimed to see spirits, one of whom – Dee was told – insisted that Kelley should sleep with Dee's wife. Dee went along with this arrangement and, funnily enough, so did Kelley and Mrs Dee.

The *Black Horse Inn* at Cirencester, Gloucestershire, had a brief **haunting** fit in 1933. A woman awoke at midnight on August 13th to find her room bathed in ghostly light. A hideous, rustling silk-clad woman glided across the floor and out through the wall. The only mark left behind was the scratching of the name *James* on one of the pub's windows. A local ghost huntress revealed that a long-dead woman had done some unpleasant deed in one of the rooms, and it was suggested that James might have been the name of her victim. Ghost-busters of the inter-war years had simpler methods than their cinematic successors. Three white flowers were placed in the room, behind a locked door. This belated floral tribute worked, and the ghost was laid to rest.
✤ Today is one of the favourite haunting days for the **ghostly Roman** who appears alongside the broad at Wroxham in Norfolk between March and October. If you see the ghost, he will order you away. But ignore his command, or else you will miss the star attractions, for the ghost is clearing the way for a procession of even more fabulous phantoms – centurions and chariots, horses and lions, gladiators and prisoners – all trekking from Brancaster on the north coast of Norfolk to the arena which stood close to Wroxham.

The first Sunday after Old Lammas, August 12th, was **Lhuany's Day** on the Isle of Man, a festival named after the god Lugh (see August 1st). Manxmen hiked up Snaefell and behaved, as one 19th-century writer vaguely but tantalisingly put it, *'very rudely and indecently'*. The custom is said to have been ended by a minister who was canny enough to start taking a collection on the hilltop.
🏛 The wells on Man are on top healing form today. The St Maughold Well near Ramsey, for example, is said to cure sterility: either dip your sterile bits into the waters, or throw a pin down the well. The latter habit was still very popular at the turn of the century.

St Ippollitts in Hertfordshire gets its name from St **Hippolytus**, whose relics are said to be buried at the local church, and are said to have featured in the ceremony held there annually. Today – the saint's feast day – **sickly horses** were led up to the altar and touched with one of his bones. Hippolytus was a 3rd-century horse-doctor who had a particularly messy martyrdom: he was torn apart by a couple of his prospective patients.

14th August

The Welsh Play

This was the day when, in 1040, **Macbeth** killed King Duncan I at Glamis Castle in Tayside. The King's blood – which indelibly stains the hand of Lady Macbeth in Shakespeare's play – stained the floorboards at the castle, and could not be wiped away. In the end the gory patch was boarded over. Macbeth and Duncan had a grandfather in common – King Malcolm II. Macbeth's claim to the throne was therefore not as tenuous as certain dramatists would have us believe.

The 6th-century **St Morwenna** founded Marhamchurch in Cornwall. To get the building under way she went to the foot of a cliff, put a large rock on her head, and started back for the site which she had chosen for her church. Stopping to rest, she dropped the rock, and a well sprang forth. She then finished the journey and placed the boulder at the church's foundations.

🕮 Undermining this story, Morwenna is also said to have founded the church at Morwenstow, near Bude in the same county. She chose a huge rock for its font, and balanced it on her head. On her way back, she stopped to rest, dropped the boulder . . . etc. Whatever its origins, the ancient font can still be seen at the church.

© Marhamchurch, also near Bude, has celebrated Morwenna's founding of the village ever since, not on her feast day (July 5th), but on the Monday after August 12th at a Lammas-linked affair called **Marhamchurch Revel**. At the site of Morwenna's cell in front of the church a Queen of the Revel, elected by local children, is crowned by a figure representing Father Time, whose identity is always kept secret.

© August is the time for the **Royal National Eisteddfod**, a gathering of music-makers, poets and craftspeople. The word *Eisteddfod* means 'the sitting down place', and each year its seat moves to a different venue in Wales. The first took place in AD 12 or, more reliably AD 1176; but even that was a one-off, and it is only since the 15th century that it has been a regular fixture. Most of the modern trappings of the event were added by opium-fiend Edward Williams in 1792, when a Gorsedd of Bards made its debut at Primrose Hill in London. The proceedings are all in Welsh, and the event remains popular – the 1993 bash

in Llanelwedd attracted more than 150,000 people. And, theoretically, not one of them managed to swill a single drop of beer – the event is officially an alcohol-free zone. At the Thieves' Eisteddfod in 1858 at Llangollen, Clwyd, the organisers gave themselves a bad name by awarding each other the best prizes and then eloping with the profits.

© Today is the last of **Mitcham Fair's** three days in London. In spite of a four-foot-long gilded Charter Key which symbolically '*unlocks the joys of the fair*', and a story that claims that Sir Walter Raleigh obtained a charter for the event from Elizabeth I, no such charter was ever granted. And so the fair is, in theory, illegal. Perhaps that is why it has outlived so many of the licit fairs.

15th August
Feast of the Assumption/ Marymass

Making an Assumption

In 1061 the Virgin Mary appeared in a vision to Lady Richeldis de Faverches of **Walsingham**, and gave her a guided tour of her home in Nazareth. After this divine planning permission, Lady Richeldis built a shrine at Little Walsingham in Norfolk, containing what she claimed to be an exact replica of Mary's house. The village also acquired a magical well and a phial of Mary's milk. (Now how on earth did they get that?) Even the sky at night provided sign-posts to the shrine – the Milky Way was renamed the **Walsingham Way** as it was said to point pilgrims in the right direction for what became known as England's Nazareth.

The Feast of the Assumption of the Virgin Mary was the chief Marian feast, the day upon which, in AD 45, Mary's physical body rose up into heaven. The coy Anglicans often refer to it as The Falling Asleep of the Blessed Virgin.

🕮 In the 12th century, theological treatises established Mary as the great intercessor in human affairs, and the Marian cult never looked back. On the strength of its Mary-connections, Walsingham in Norfolk had already become one of Europe's leading places of pilgrimage. Even though the Reformation turned most of Walsingham to rubble, and the Feast of the Assumption was expunged from the English calendar in 1549, the village remains a prime pilgrim site. Reconstruction of the shrine began in 1931, and it is now firmly re-established, with tens of thousands of visitors each year sampling the waters of its two pristine wells. Whitsun is one of the chief pilgrimage days now, and some 100,000 people turn up annually to see what all the fuss is about. The waters are still reputed to have miraculous healing powers – especially good for head or stomach disorders – and are traditionally slurped from a long silver spoon.

In the Highlands the Assumption was a first-fruits festival. Corn was hand-picked, dried in the sun, ground in a quern, kneaded in a sheepskin, and made into a bannock called the *Moilean Moire*, 'Mary's fatling'. The fatling was baked over a fire of rowan wood, and the new-baked loaf was handed out by the father of the household. The family sang songs in praise of Mary, and danced sunwise around the flames. The homestead was then blessed by the family's circling it carrying the embers of the fire.

© There are two extant **Marymass** – also known as Murmuss – Fairs in Scotland. The one held at **Inverness** in Highland Region on the Saturday nearest the 15th is a 1986 revival of an event first staged in 1591. There are various stalls, shows and processions throughout the day. The fair at **Irvine**, near Kilmarnock in Strathclyde starts on the Thursday nearest the 15th and lasts for 12 days. It centres on a live music festival, and still holds traditional horse-races – horses have always been a feature at Murmuss, either in the form of races or dray parades.

Irvine's fair was started in the 12th century as a celebration of the Assumption, and from its earliest days featured a parade with a Marymass Queen. But as a result of a visit by Mary Queen of Scots to Irvine in 1563, an elected young girl of the town now dresses to embody Mary Stuart rather than Mary the Virgin. A similar substitution happened at Inverness after Mary Queen of Scots came calling there in 1562.

16th August
St Roch's Day

Plague of Giant Albatrosses

Wheeling over the spire of the cathedral, the portentous **White Birds of Salisbury Plain**

in Wiltshire appear only when the Bishop of Salisbury is about to cease to be incumbent. The bishop's daughter spotted them just before her father died in 1885. And on August 16th 1911 as Miss Edith Oliver was riding through Hurdcott on her way home from an outing with the choir boys, she saw two huge, radiant white birds like albatrosses sailing overhead without moving their wings. When she returned to the cathedral, the bishop had unexpectedly passed away. Oliver later maintained that she knew nothing of the ominous white birds of local folklore; but her descriptions tied in uncannily with the portrayal of the birds in legend.

© Barlow has the oldest **well-dressing** tradition in the non-limestone part of Derbyshire. The ceremony has taken place without a break since the village's well was given a pump and round stone basin in 1840. It is now held on the Wednesday after the Sunday following the 10th, and inhabitants are very fussy about the flower-pictures used to decorate the well: only whole blooms can be used. The completed design is invariably impressive, and is usually in the form of a triptych. See the main well-dressing entry on Ascension Day.

© Forest Chapel, near Macclesfield in Cheshire, has its **rushbearing** on a convenient Sunday around August 12th. 'Convenient' here means a date which fits in with the diary of local landowner the Earl of Derby, who returns to the area for a post-'Glorious Twelfth' shooting expedition, and likes to see a bit of rushbearing while he is up. Bunches of rushes with flowers stuck on the top are placed in the church porch, and around the pews. At 2.30 pm there is an open-air service, with the congregation sitting on the tombs. Macclesfield's rush utilisation used to extend far beyond floor-strewing – chairs made in the area traditionally featured rush-seats.

© Mid-August is the time of the **Battle of the Flowers** on the Channel Islands. This is not *Gardener's Question Time* with light artillery, but a tourist-friendly series of floral floats and parades, with the islanders competing to see who can make the best flower-pictures. It originated in the 19th century, though the tradition of making pictures and patterns from flowers had existed long before that.

St Roch (or Roque) is the saint to turn to if you are afflicted with the plague. In his lifetime he managed to cure many sufferers even though he was himself infected. In religious pictures St Roch is often shown lifting his habit to reveal the mark of plague on his thigh. Sometimes a dog is also shown, as for months the saint is said to have survived on a daily diet of loaves brought to him by the generous hound. Roch was reinvoked last century during an outbreak of cholera.

Most saints associated with ancient festivals are themselves ancient. Roch is unusual in that he dates only from the 14th century – relatively late by saintly standards – and yet his feast became the key day for English end-of-harvest celebrations.

17th August

Harrison Fraud

On August 17th 1659 the search began for **William Harrison**, steward of Campden House, Chipping Campden, Gloucestershire. He had been out collecting rents, and failed to reappear. Suspicion fell on house servant John Perry, along with Perry's brother and his mother Joan. John said that the other two had killed Harrison in order to purloin the rent monies, and that they had buried him in the house cesspit. A search failed to come up with his body, but all three Perrys were hanged anyway.

Justice appeared to have been done; but three years later William Harrison reappeared at Chipping Campden. His story was that three horsemen had wounded and abducted him, carrying him to Deal in Kent. There they had shoved cash into his pockets and sent him on a six-week sea-voyage. Harrison had then been sold by Turkish slave-traders, and ended up working for an 80-year-old medicine man in Smyrna (now Izmir in Turkey). After 18 months his owner had died, and Harrison, bribing a sea-captain with a silver bowl, had been ferried back to England.

The case aroused a great deal of interest, with numerous competing theories as to why John Perry should confess to a murder that never happened. Some investigators have since claimed that Harrison was an Engish spy, and that his story was an elaborate cover-up. Others have suggested that he wanted the ambitious Perrys out of the way, and so feigned his own death and concocted the rest of the story later. Another possibility is that Harrison was ab-ducted, with the brains behind the plot being his own wife, a woman described in one contemporary report as '*a snotty, covetous presbyterian*'. She hanged herself soon after Harrison's return. The most ambitious theory of all is put forward in a ballad of the time, which said that Harrison had been bewitched by Joan Perry and magically transported to a rock near Turkey.

© **Grasmere Sports** in Cumbria take place on the Thursday nearest the 20th. There are hound trails – a form of fox-hunting without horses – fell races, and various track and field events. But the reason for many to visit is that the sports offer a now rare chance to see the ancient art of **Cumberland and Westmorland wrestling**, a ritualised form of the man-to-man combat common in the bad old days in the Borders. Only amateurs can take part, and the Grasmere grapplers dress fetchingly in silky long-johns and embroidered trunks, worn Superman-style. Contests are open-air, and one fall is all it takes to decide the winner.

The great 19th-century Cumberland wrestling champion was George Steadman, whose 51½-inch chest helped him to win the Grasmere title 14 times. But the real key to Steadman throwing his opponents off-balance is said to have been his resemblance to a benign old vicar. This also seems to have been an advantage in the 1700s, when many of the wrestling champions were Lakeland clergymen.

18th August
St Helen's Day

Cole Minor Mistake

Theophilus Brome of Chilton Cantelo, Somerset, died today in 1670. His last request was that his head be removed before burial and kept at Higher Chilton farm. This wish was carried out, and the **skull** became so attached to its home that it put down roots. When later tenants tried to bury it, the mournful skull let out a prolonged wail, and the interrers were deterred. On another occasion a sexton broke his spade whilst trying to dig a suitably head-shaped grave.

Theophilus' skull was then left in peace. When the farm buildings were being rebuilt in 1826 the skull was briefly used as a drinking vessel, but no one suffered any physical or paranormal ill-effects. These sort of skull stories are linked to the old Celtic idea that the severed head has powers which transcend death. Knowledge and power could be gained by using a skull as a drinking vessel. One way to guarantee that beer had a good head.

St Helen was born around AD 250 at Drepanum in Asia Minor. The mother of the mighty Constantine, first Christian Emperor of Rome, Helen came from humble stock. English historians claimed that she was a British princess, the daughter of Old King Cole, of merry-old-soul fame. Helen was the woman who found the True Cross (see May 3rd), which makes it all the more paradoxical that she is associated with several pagan wells in Britain. This was simply because her name sounded like that of the old water-goddess, Elen.

St Helen's Well at Walton, near Wetherby in West Yorkshire, was used as a rag well. People with afflictions could rub their diseased bits – mainly the eyes at this particular site – with a rag, which was then pinned near the well. The idea behind this sort of sympathetic magic is that a person can be influenced by an item which has previously touched them or been a part of them, a concept at the very heart of witchcraft. In this case, as the rag rotted so would the ailment diminish.

The Walton well's other claim to fame came when the 17th-century highwayman 'Swift Nick' Nevison fell asleep next to it, and was ambushed by local lawmen. Nevison managed to escape after convincing them that the stick he was brandishing was a heavily disguised gun. As a consequence of this shambling rout locals have ever since been known as 'Walton Calves'.
🏠 St Helen's Well at Rushton Spencer, near Congleton, is said to dry up in times of calamity. It happened during the Civil War, and again when Charles I lost his head. It disappeared during a corn famine in 1670; when Edward VII died in 1910; and during the First World War. Conversely, it is said that large pool of St Helen's Well at Great Asby, south of Appleby in Cumbria, has never been known to fail.

19th August

Chevy Chase is not Funny

The **Battle of Otterburn** took place by moonlight tonight in 1388. The Scots army, led by James, 2nd Earl of Douglas, had been ransacking Northumberland unopposed until they ran into Henry 'Hotspur' Percy and his troops at Chevy Chase near Otterburn. Before the battle Douglas slept fitfully, and prophetically:

> But I hae dreamed a dreary dream, beyond
>   the Isle of Skye;
> I saw a dead man win a fight, and I think
>   that man was I.

During the skirmish Douglas was fatally wounded, and with his dying breath instructed that his body should be left concealed beneath a nearby bush until the battle was over. The Scots won the day, and Hotspur was captured, dragged in front of the bush and forced to yield – a dead man had thus won the fight, as the dream predicted.
🏠 Two classic Border ballads jostle for attention here. The English version of events came out under the title *The Battle of Otterburn*, which is also the name of a popular Northumbrian pipe tune. The legend of Douglas and his deadly dream is one of the details included in the alternative, epically dour 60-verse Scots account, *Chevy Chase*. The scene of Douglas' fall at Otterburn is marked by a monument called, somewhat unfairly, Percy's Cross. The river here is the Rede, so named after the red blood of the men which flowed into it after the battle.

⚓ Loch Morar, near Mallaig in Highland Region, has a monster called **Morag**. Morag turned up today in 1969 after a fallow period of a hundred years or so. Her appearance put the wind up a couple of sailors who promptly shot her. For a while it seemed that it was all over for Nessie's little-known sister; but Morag has been sighted since, and the sailors have been forced to conclude that they had only winged – or flippered – the creature.

© The **Festival of Boys and Horses Ploughing Match** usually takes place on the third Saturday in August at St Margaret's Hope on South Ronaldsay, the southernmost island of Orkney. A survival of an old Viking gathering, the festival begins with costume-judging. There are two categories: Ploughboys and Horses. The Horses are girls, wearing elaborate head-dresses and horse collars, as well as jackets covered with ribbons and shiny objects which make them resemble Orcadian Pearly Queens. Afterwards, the beach is cleared, and the ploughing match begins. Only the boys take part: each has his own plough –

many are very old – and the winner is the one who can turn the truest furrow in the sand. Dances and games then take over.

Beaches were first ploughed to get on the right side of the sea gods, symbolically preparing the ground for the sea-harvest to come. Urine used to be dribbled on to the plough to add to its fertility-inducing powers.

20th August
St Philibert's Day

Every Witch Way But Truth

Ten women from Pendle Forest, near Clitheroe in Lancashire, were hanged at Lancaster today in 1612. King James I had set the scene for witch-hysteria with his factually wayward book *Dæmonologie*, and scapegoats for local ills were cropping up all over the country. The Pendle women ultimately brought about their own downfall. The two key characters, Mother Demdike and Old Chattox, had a mutual hatred and may have accused each other out of misplaced malice. In all probability their only crimes were the guiltless ones of credulity, decrepitude, poverty and ugliness.

Demdike's grand-daughter Alizon attracted the authorities' attention when a pedlar had a stroke minutes after meeting her. He blamed Alizon, saying that she had cursed him. Alizon was questioned by magistrate Roger Nowell – a man with a remarkable gift for securing confessions – and admitted to the 'crime', adding that it was no big deal as she was a fully fledged witch, as were most of her family and friends.

After that, a trial was inevitable. The pedlar testified, and the court – with the help of several more colourful confessions obtained by Nowell – produced a multitude of trumped-up charges, including the murder of at least 16 people, and an alleged attempt to blow up Lancaster Castle using magic. The women were also accused of turning beer sour, and of making butter from skimmed milk – both of which suddenly became capital offences in that part of Lancashire. Alizon's mother Bessie was strip-searched and 'shown' to have an extra nipple, used for suckling Satan. In summing up the judge said that the women should be thankful, considering their poor backgrounds, for receiving a fair trial. The official line which condemned the 10 women to the gallows was *'bewitching to death by devilish practices and hellish means'*.

🔲 The tower at St Mary's Church at nearby Newchurch was built during the time of the witch-trials. On its stonework is a carving known as the Eye of God, supposedly put there as a talisman to offset the mischief of Demdike, Chattox and company. The Pendle witch-myth has generated a lively tourism industry in the area, with tours around the key sites, often stopping at St Mary's to admire a grave which is said to be that of one of the executed women. It is, in fact, the last resting place of someone with a similar name to one of the accused – as convicted witches, the Pendle 10 were all buried in unconsecrated ground.

At the annual meeting of the **Grinders' Misfortune Society**, which was founded on this day in 1804, it was customary to sing the traditional *Grinders' Song*. The Grinders were the men employed in Sheffield's steel industry. The song speaks of the dreadful dangers of the job, each verse ending with the lines: '*There's few who brave such hardships as we poor grinders do.*'

The 7th-century **St Philibert** gave his name to the filbert nut, said to ripen around the saint's feast day, which some areas celebrated today, others – notably Kent – on August 22nd. The filbert is the nut of the cultivated hazel, a relative of the slightly more popular cobnut – though both are a long way short of bar-snack status. To offset this, Kentish Cobnuts launched a campaign in the summer of 1991, their aim being to reintroduce it into the national diet. Even if this fails, Philibert can console himself by having also given the name to Filbert Street, home of Leicester City F.C.

21st August

A Salty Dog-Fight

On this day in 1702 **Admiral John Benbow** was in pursuit of French ships in the West Indies. The scrappy mêlée had lasted days, and was not going well. Benbow had been mortally wounded, but he fought on doggedly. His captains were fed up with the battle and were getting downright mutinous. All but one refused to help the valorous Admiral continue the chase; and ignoring his orders and patriotic bluster they turned the ships round and headed back to port:

Brave Benbow lost his legs,
And all on his stumps he begs,
'Fight on my English lads,
'Tis our lot'.

The event became the stuff of legend and several songs. Fight-to-his-own-death Benbow was seen to typify British pluck, and he became a folk-hero; whereas the rebellious captains were seen as rank cowards, and were all either shot or suspended.

John Benbow had risen from lowly stock. Having fled a dead-end apprenticeship in his home town of Shrewsbury in Shropshire, he eventually got to own a ship, and patrolled the seas. His first notable confrontation came when he defeated some Moorish pirates, and threw 13 of their severed heads into a barrel of pork-pickle. The heads – labelled *Salt provisions for the Captain's use'* – were then transferred to a sack, and shown to Carlos II of Spain. Carlos was so impressed that he recommended Benbow to James II of England, who made him a captain in his navy.

🏛 A monument to Admiral Benbow stands in St Mary's Church in Shrewsbury, next to the vicarage in which he was born, and there are still a good number of pubs up and down the country named after him.

© The **Saddleworth Rushbearing Festival**, in the villages on the western edge of Saddleworth Moor, near Manchester, died out just after the First World War, its demise accelerated after a runaway rush-cart killed a little girl. In 1975 it was revived, virtually unchanged and thankfully devoid of the gentrification that has marred some born-again customs. Now held on the second weekend after August 12th, it is organised by local Morris men – dancing and drinking are therefore very much on the agenda. Two tons of rushes are piled to a height of around 15 feet on a two-wheeled cart, and perched on top of all this is a jockey with a large copper kettle. The rush-cart and rider are dragged all over Saddleworth Parish. At every pub the kettle is lowered and filled with beer, which the jockey must drink – hence the local term for advanced drunkeness, *'getting kettled'.*

This form of rushbearing – a distant cousin of the many covering-the-church-floor rush-bearing services – derives from ancient fertility rites, and it used to be said that any woman touching the rush-cart would become pregnant within 12 months. To mock this paganism, a few years ago the landlady of the *Cross Keys* in Uppermill made great show of touching the cart. The next year she gave it a wide berth, having herself just given birth to a girl – belief in the tradition is now as strong as ever.

The cart sets off from the *Commercial Inn*, Uppermill, at 9.30 on the Saturday morning, and carries on via the villages of Greenfield, Dobcross and Delph over the course of the day. There is drinking and dancing at all stops, with displays from invited Morris Dance teams – in 1993 there were 24 visiting groups to choose from. On the Sunday the rush-cart is heaved up the steep hill at Uppermill to St Chad's for a 10.30 am service during which the top rushes are strewn on the church floor. In the afternoon there are games outside the church, including wrestling, gurning, clog-stepping, and a contest to find the worst singer.

Priddy Fair used to be held today in Somerset. A local saying makes the premature prediction: *'The first rain after Priddy Fair is the first rain of Winter.'*

© On the Saturday after August 19th, Cilgerran, near Cardigan in Dyfed, has its **coracle races**, the climax of the village's Festive Week. Coracles are small, circular fishing boats of prehistoric origin, made by stretching tarred animal hide over a frame of wood. They are still used by salmon fishermen from the area, but are not ideally suited to racing. Which makes the series of events a great deal of fun, as coraclers try to out-manoeuvre each other on the fast-flowing River Teifi, without smashing into any of its many rocks, or being sucked into one of its vicious whirlpools.

🏛 The **Head Stone**, or Stump John, on Hallam Moor, near Sheffield in South Yorkshire, does strange things in late August. At this time of year a 'face' is said to appear on the west side of the 20-foot-high stone at sunrise. Even more vaguely and intriguingly, local custom has it that at cock-crow 'on a certain day' the stone turns its massive head.

© The British Open **Crabbing Championship** at Walberswick, near Southwold in Suffolk, is as old as time itself. Alternatively, it started in 1981. Sources differ, but the key detail is that it takes place on whichever Sunday in August offers tides most conducive to the catching of crabs. Anyone who falls in the water and scares off the crustaceans is fined £10, and killing or taunting the crabs is a definite no-no. The person who catches the heaviest crab is allowed on to the winner's rostrum to collect a prize only if he or she is under 17 – the structure is so dilapidated that the weight of an extra adult poses too great a risk. Everyone who survives the competition is given a memento – a pot of crab paste.

22nd August

That Condemned Moment

The epoch-making events of August 22nd 1485, ending the Wars of the Roses and bringing the Tudors to the throne, came as no shock to a woman in Warminster, Wiltshire. As the Battle of Bosworth raged several counties away, she picked up two sheaves of wheat, shouting 'Now for Richard, now for Henry!' She then dropped exhibit A, crying 'Now for King Henry, Richard is slain!' Ignored at the time as an insane old woman, she had correctly relayed what had happened at Bosworth Field in Warwickshire: Richard III was dead, and Henry Tudor was about to become Henry VII.

Richard's crown was retrieved from the hawthorn bush beneath which it had tumbled – which is why the Tudors chose a crown and bush as their device. This incident is also the origin of the ultra-loyalist saying: 'Cleave to the crown though it hang on a bush.'

With the Tudor shrubbery came the Plantagenet character assassination. Almost overnight Richard III – an ordinary jobbing, battling king in the war-arena – became a murderous, physically and emotionally twisted hunchback. When Shakespeare got his Tudor-friendly hands on the character, the distorted image was sealed. No contemporary portrait gives Richard a deformity, and the awkward shoulder in the famous painting in the National Portrait Gallery in London was added during the reign of the Tudors.

Eighty-year-old Catholic priest **John Kemble** had spent 54 years as a religious rebel. He was celebrating Mass at Pembridge Castle, Hereford and Worcester, when the faith police of Charles II appeared and arrested him. Strapped to a horse and taken to London for questioning, Kemble was convicted for his convictions. He was sentenced to be hung, drawn and quartered after refusing to confess to a non-existent papist plot. He prepared to meet his fate on this day in 1679. He asked for

and was given time enough to say his prayers, to have a drink of wine and to smoke a last pipeful of tobacco with the sheriff. The old county of Herefordshire was thus handed a new proverb: a **Kemble Pipe** means to have one last smoke: usually at the end of a day rather than the end of a life. *A Kemble Pipe* is also used as the name for the last person sitting at a dinner-party or other gathering.

🏛 The hangman was so impressed by Kemble's dignified courage that he killed him during the hanging, to spare him the horrors of the rest of the procedure. And as a final solace Kemble was made a saint by the Catholic church in 1970. His feast day is October 22nd, and his gravestone is in the churchyard at Welsh Newton, near Ross-on-Wye, Hereford and Worcester. His room can be viewed at nearby Pembridge Castle, and his altar and missal are kept at the Roman Catholic church in Monmouth, Gwent.

♰ **Sir John Gates** was executed on this day in 1553, a luckless supporter of the seven-day 'Queen' Lady Jane Grey. His headless ghost mopes around Beeleigh Abbey, near Chelmsford in Essex, on the anniversary of his death.

23rd August

Caul of Supernature

Sir William Wallace was executed in London on this day in 1305. The murder of his wife by Lanark's English sheriff Hazelrig had prompted Wallace's change from grumbling malcontent to active rebel. He avenged the death by killing Hazelrig, and then tried to rally an already disgruntled Scotland into kicking the occupying armies of Edward I out of the country. But when his tired troops were clobbered by the English at Falkirk in 1298, Wallace, the Guardian of Scotland, became a fugitive.

Sir William's end was ignominious: he was betrayed and captured in his sleep at Glasgow, given a show trial and executed in London. Death by hanging, drawing and quartering had been introduced only in 1284, and Wallace was its first celebrity victim: the first such man to have his guts burned before his dying gaze. As a reminder of the likely reward for all rebels, different chunks of his remains went on show in Stirling, Perth, Berwick and Newcastle.

Legend-makers cast Wallace as a dashing, death-dealing hero. He symbolised – in spite of being a knight – the common man fighting the English aristocracy. Ostensibly of Norman small-time-knight stock, his family was probably Celtic: the name *Wallace* is from the same derogatory root as the word *Welsh*, meaning 'foreigner' – the Saxon's term for the Britons. ✠ © A plaque at West Smithfield in London – just round the corner from the famous market – marks the site of Wallace's execution; and there is an annual commemoration for the ill-fated hero at his birthplace in Elderslie near Paisley, Strathclyde, on or about this day.

Of all the customs observed after a birth, the most important involved salvaging any **caul** that was present. Also known as a silly-hood (from the Saxon *selig*, meaning 'happy') or mother's-smock, the caul appears infrequently, a piece of placental membrane on the baby's head. It is a potent charm, and can protect the owner during travel, especially at sea. A person born with a caul can never drown, and ships with one on board are unlikely to sink. This made these placental placebos very popular with sea-faring folk. As recently as 1904, on this very day, a caul was advertised for sale at the port of Lymington in Hampshire. Cauls were not unknown in the navy kitbag of sailors during the Second World War. On the opening page of Charles Dickens' *David Copperfield* the newborn David's caul ends up being won in a raffle by a woman who '*never drowned, but died triumphantly in bed at 92 . . . her proudest boast that she had never been on water in her life, except upon a bridge*'.

Cauls were usually stretched out on the pages of a book, which was then closed to dry and press them. There they stayed; for provided a caul remains firm and crisp, its owner's health will remain sound. Cauls also aid healing, although each time someone draws on this curing power they sap their own life energy. If a caul-owner falls ill, the caul sweats for the duration of the illness; and if they die it shrivels up – there are no second-hand cauls. Anyone losing a caul is liable to become an inveterate wanderer, and runs the risk of developing webbed feet. The other bad news is that although they prevent drowning, cauls may make a trip to the gallows more likely – it was said that: '*he that is born to be hanged will never be drowned*'.

24th August
St Bartholomew's Day

Beating Bounds, Boys, Prostitutes and Frenchmen

Today in 1736, a butcher was reunited with his prize pig. It had spent the previous five months in the sewers, and re-emerged at the mouth of Fleet Street Ditch by the side of the Thames in London. As with the giant alligators in the apocryphal stories/silly American horror films, the pig had grown in stature as a result of its biodegraded diet. It went into the sewer priced at 10 shillings, and came out valued at two guineas.

On August 24th 1217, the men of Sandwich prayed to **St Bartholomew** to assist them in battle: if he came to the aid of Sandwich and the other Cinque Ports, they would build him a chapel. The enemy was, as is so often the case, the French, who had already managed to burn much of Sandwich to the ground. The approaching French fleet was commanded by an English traitor, **Eustace the Monk**. Eustace was a particularly dangerous opponent as he was a wizard, and had magically made his own vessel invisible.

Stephen Crabbe, an ex-pupil of this mad monk, rescued the Kent town from the jaws of defeat. Crabbe used his skills in the black arts to locate the cloaked boat, sailed across, and cut off Eustace's head. The vessel, without its master, was revealed for all to see. Emboldened, the English threw quicklime into the wind, which blew into the faces of the French and blinded them. The men of Kent were then able to board several of the invading ships, while the rest were routed by the direct intervention of St Bartholomew himself. He appeared in red and summoned a storm which washed many of the French sailors overboard. Kent celebrated its sudden victory by parading the head of Eustace the Monk through the streets of Dover and Canterbury. Sadly one of the few casualties on the English side was Stephen Crabbe – having decapitated Eustace he was hacked to pieces by the French before he could make good his own escape.

The chapel to St Bartholomew was built in Sandwich, as promised, along with some almshouses. The hospital in which the wounded of the battle were treated changed its name from Sandwich Hospital to St Bartholomew's, and is still standing on the town's outskirts.

© This was one of the chief days for **Autumn fairs**. The one held at Smithfield in London started in the 12th century, and each year attracted hundreds of traders, showmen, gamblers, hypocrites, con-men and con-victims – all characters immortalised in Ben Jonson's 1614 comedy set in the midst of the Smithfield shindig, *Bartholomew Fair*. The notoriously rowdy fair died out in 1855 but was recently brought back, in a drastically cleaned up form, as a fundraising event for St Bartholomew's Hospital in the City.

© The **Keaw Yed Wakes** (or Cow Head Wakes) at Westhoughton, near Wigan in Greater Manchester, had as its main dish Desperate-Dan-style whole cow's head pies – known as 'keaw yed pies'. The fair and the food allegedly originated when a cow got its head stuck between the bars of a gate. The enterprising farmer freed his prize beast by sawing off its head. In remembrance of this, the town's *Victoria* pub has a stuffed cow's head, gate and saw display. The chief sport of the fair was a rugby-type game of football played with a cow's head. This suggests that the true origins of the event might lie in the shady world of pagan bull-sacrifice games. An even more drastic form of offering is hinted at by a former delicacy of the day: pork pies with human clay dolls inside. The Wakes are still alive and kicking (but not cow's heads) and take place on the Sunday of or nearest the 24th.

© The 800-year-old **Lee Gap Fair** in West Yorkshire is also extant, but has survived only by shunning its beery, brawling past and banning alcohol altogether. A drastic measure. Its first leg takes place today at West Ardsley, near Wakefield, and horses are the chief currency, with few concessions to would-be pleasure-fair-goers. It used to last right through until September 19th, but now all but the beginning and end of this span have gone, with today's fair known as the Former Lee, and the one on September 19th the Latter Lee.

Of the many vanished St Bartholomew's celebrations, the most important to have disappeared is **Stourbridge Fair**, held at Chesterton near Cambridge. The writer Daniel Defoe claimed that it was the greatest fair in the world, and it was certainly for a long time the biggest in Britain. All manner of trading, sports and sideshows were here, as well as a veritable army of prostitutes, whom the town-crier was licensed to beat with his whip.

St Bartholomew, being a patron saint of **bee-keepers**, used to be invoked by the mead-making monks of Gulval in Cornwall, until their meadery closed in the mid-1950s. The invocation was spoken by The Almoner of the Fraternity of St Bartholomew of the Craft or Mystery of Free Meadmakers of Great Britain and Ireland. A.F.S.B.C.M.F.M.G.B.I., for short.

☀ Remember the one about raining for 40 days and nights after St Swithun's Day? Today is 40 days on from that prediction, so stand by for a change in the **weather**:

St Bartlemy's mantle wipes dry
All the tears St Swithin can cry.

Rousay in the Orkney Islands had a strange tradition which said that if you worked the land today, the **furrows would bleed**. An out of left field excuse for not working.

Printers, chiefly in London, had a holiday today, called the **Wayzgoose**. The 24th marked the point when they officially recognised the shortening days and began working by candlelight. As compensation their employers gave them a small one-off payment today, which was used to finance a goose feast or, by the 19th century, a seaside outing.

This was the old day for **beating the bounds in Grimsby**, Humberside. And while the inhabitants were at it, they used to beat the boys as well: by scourging the boys at the boundaries, the limits of the parish would be indelibly spanked on to their memories.

The tie-breaker when electing **Grimsby's Mayors** was equally unforgettable. If no clear candidate emerged, the contesting Aldermen, accompanied by a baying crowd, trekked to Scartho in the south of the town. Here they had straw trusses tied to their hind-quarters, and the election was determined by a hungry calf. It was released among the Aldermen, and the one to get his truss nibbled first became mayor.

25th August

Bartle of the Giants

Strapped for cash on this day in 1836, a man from Spring Gardens in Gainsborough, Lincolnshire, resorted to desperate measures. He sold his daughter to a man bound for America. Pocketing the 10 shillings, his hopes of hushing up his callous act were shattered when a man appeared at his house bearing his effigy. A crowd gathered beneath his window and he was thoroughly rantanned with derisive song and noise. The crowd then decided to rantan their message home, smashing the windows and invading the house. They made off with whatever booty they could find, and the man was left far more than 10 shillings worse off (see April 18th for more on rantanning).

© More effigies, this time at West Witton, near Leyburn in North Yorkshire. **Burning Bartle** takes place on the Saturday nearest the 24th. For starters there is a procession at 9 pm featuring a fierce looking straw man – Bartle – who usually comes complete with lightbulb eyes, like something straight off the ghost-train. Drinks are handed out at pubs and houses; and Bartle, in return, brings prosperity wherever he goes. The accompanying chant explains:

> *At Penhill Crags he tore his rags,*
> *At Hunter's Thorn he blew his horn,*
> *At Capplebank Stee he brak his knee*
> *At Grassgill Beck he brak his neck,*
> *At Waddam's End he couldn't fend*
> *At Grassgill End he made his end;*
> *Shout, lads, shout!*

At Grassgill End, Bartle is thrown on to a bonfire to burn.

The tradition of Burning Bartle probably originated as a sacrificial harvest ceremony. But the name *Bartle* is from 'Bartholomew', whose feast-day is on the 24th; and Bartle may long ago have been St Bartholomew. When the 16th-century Reformation looters came to remove treasures and statues from the parish churches of the land, the West Witton folk are said to have absconded with their effigy of St Bartholomew, leading the officers on the chase described in the verse, finally losing the Bartle/Bartholomew statue at Grassgill End.

An alternative story says that Bartle represents local Abbot Adam Sedburgh of Jervaulx Abbey, who tried to avoid the Pilgrimage of Grace – a mass march to London by ordinary people to fight against the Protestant Reformation and its desecration of the churches. Sedburgh hid from the men at first, but they manhandled him at Waddam's End, and he joined their march. All to no avail: his mon-astery was ransacked, and he was hanged at Tyburn in 1537.

But the best Bartle legend involves pigs. A giant, the son of the Norse god Thor, had a pig-farm near West Witton. He was enraged to discover one day that his prize boar had been stolen. He commanded all the men of West Witton to appear before him with their youngest sons, and promised to kill their children at regular intervals until someone spilled the beans on the pig-napping. Local holy man the Seer of Carperby warned the giant that he would be destroyed if he pursued this line of enquiry. Next morning Thor's son found every one of his pigs dead in rows of nine; worse still, his castle was ablaze. And worst of all, ghosts of his past victims then advanced on him, and he was driven over a precipice – presumably the one at Grassgill End.

26th August
St Ninian's Day

The Beast with Ten Fingers

St Ninian, a British missionary, knocked himself into shape by training in Rome. When his stint on the papal bullworker was done, the Pope sent him out to fight the good fight against some tough opponents – Pictish Scotland. In 397 Ninian set up his first Christian church at Whithorn near Burrow Head in Dumfries and Galloway – a good contender for the earliest church anywhere in Scotland. It was the first stone building the Picts had seen, and they called it the White House, impressed by the bright stone-work. There is a priory on the site now. The jury is still out as to just how far the saint's influence actually spread; but St Ninian's Isle – just off Mainland, Shetland – claims to be the limit of his old domain, though it was probably his followers who established base here late in the 5th century. A ruined medieval structure marks the site of the original chapel erected on this site: the first Christian foothold on the northern islands. Both this and the nearby St Ninian's Well were held in high holy esteem.

The profile of this part of the world was upped in 1958 when the St Ninian's Isle Hoard was discovered, a collection of 8th-century Celtic silver probably buried to keep it out of the hands of invading Vikings. It is now on permanent display at Edinburgh's Museum of Antiquities. St Ninian's cave can be seen on the shore near Whithorn.

☞ The **Hairy Hands** are a mutually dependent phenomenon which haunt a section of the B3212 Dartmoor road between Post Bridge and Two Bridges in Devon. On August 26th 1921 an army officer claimed that two strong, hairy hands had closed over his own as he rode a motorcycle, sending his machine out of control. He escaped with cuts and bruises, the third person that year to have a mysterious accident at the same spot. In March a prison doctor had been killed when his motorbike went out of control there. The children in the adjoining side-car reported that his last words were: '*There is something wrong, jump!*' And in June a woman passenger had suffered injuries when a coach went out of control on the same stretch of road.

There were earlier stories of cyclists being manually compromised and of pony traps finding an uninvited hand on the reins, and there was a solitary sighting in 1924 when the hands were seen clawing outside a caravan window. In 1921 the hairy hands, and the media interest, were most active. Heavy but fruitless press speculation as to their origin led one 'expert' to go on the record with his hairy-brained theory that the answer lay in '*prehistoric races long since vanished from the earth . . . a thought-form originally generated by hatred, revenge or lust has survived those far distant days and is still roaming about the astral world . . .*' Sounds uncannily like the '*Monsters from the Id*' of the 1950s sci-fi film *Forbidden Planet*. The expert even explained how prehistoric hands were able to sabotage motorbikes and coaches: '*Such an entity, if it came into contact with appropriate psychic conditions such as the presence of a "sensitive" would be able to gain an appropriate vehicle for its malevolence.*' Indeed.

27th August
St Maelrubba's Day/
Little St Hugh's Day

You're Once, Twice, Three Times a Loony

Kett's Rebellion ended on this day in 1549 at Norwich, when 3,000 men were slain. Robert Kett was a tanner, and the rebellion began life as a protest against enclosures – the fencing-off of common land, in this case for the use of landowners' sheep. Some 16,000 commoners backed his cause; and when evil landowners fell into Kett's hands, they were tried at mass meetings held under the Oak of Reformation near Wymondham in Norfolk. Edward VI offered a pardon; but Kett declared '*Kings are wont to pardon wicked persons, not innocent men. We have done nothing to deserve such a pardon. We have been guilty of no crime.*' While they were passing through Norwich, a few misguided rioters in the rebel ranks gave the authorities the excuse they had been looking for to rout the men. Kett and his brother William were hanged; and their goal of common ownership remains as elusive as ever.

▥ The **Reformation Oak** still survives, just north-east of Wymondham. Harder to see – it is on private land – is **Kett's Oak** at nearby Ryston Hall, long the home of the Pratt family. The oak's gnarled and twisted bough has a plaque, on which is the message left by Kett's rebels after rustling up their dinner: '*Mister Pratt your Shepe are very fat . . . We have left you the skynns to buy your Lady pinnes . . .*'

Truth to tell, folk-tales and racism are not always mutually exclusive. The legend of **Little Sir Hugh** – or St Hugh, this being his feast day – is a good, bad example. Hugh was found with his throat cut, at the bottom of a well in Lincoln. Prejudice rather than evidence, led to the local Jewish population being blamed. The ballad *Hugh of Lincoln* describes how young Hugh and accidentally kicked a ball over the wall of the Jews' garden. In goes Hugh, in go the knives, up comes the lid of the well, and down goes a familiar dose of xenophobia. His mother later encounters Hugh's ghost, the body is discovered, all the bells ring at once while all the books read themselves aloud. The Jews are rounded up and 19 are sent to their deaths. The End.

Today's other saint is Maelrubba, or Malrubius, an Irish missionary who lived from 642 to 722. Because his name sounded like that of the pagan god Mourie, saint and god became blurred. At the saint's chapel on Eilean Maree – an island in Loch Maree, in the north-west Highlands – he became known to locals as **God Mourie**. Bulls were sacrificed to him, a practice that continued into the 1700s. Shocked churchmen in the area reported that other less brutal but equally pagan God Mourie observances had survived right into the 19th century. These included tree-worshipping, prayers directed at St Mourie's Well, and the pouring of milk into the ground to help protect local cattle from disease.

Lunatics could be cured at the well. They drank its water at an altar, and were taken on a sunwise (anticlockwise) trip around the small island, during which they were dipped into the loch three times. This procedure continued for several days until the lunatic was either cured or dead. But the real St Maelrubba's final vengeance seems to have descended on all this paganism, for the well has now dried up; although the island's reputation as a sacred place still survives.

28th August

Swing and Hand Jive

1829 delivered a particularly harsh winter, the breaking point for many hard-up, Kentish labourers. High taxes and church tithes had resulted in farmers paying their workers less and less, and the advent of automation meant that many risked losing their jobs. With no money, no food, and every sign that things were about to get worse, the men ceased grumbling in private and began to rebel en masse, in what became known as the **Captain Swing Riots**. On this day in 1830 the first of the true villains of the piece, the steam threshing machines, was ripped apart at Lower Hardres near Canterbury. Land-owners ran scared as they began receiving letters from a mythical figurehead called Captain Swing. The initial activists came from Elham and the surrounding villages, and their just cause swiftly gained momentum and popular support.

At the height of the riots, the Swingers got through something in the region of a hundred man-displacing pieces of steam-driven machinery in just three weeks, with some hay-rick and barn arson thrown in for good measure. For two years the landed gentry lived in fear of Captain Swing, whose fame was such that several versions of his life story were published, even though he did not exist. In 1832 the authorities got tough; 102 men were arrested and variously transported, imprisoned, or executed. Only 25 of the prisoners were not convicted, and although those who had been transported were pardoned two years later, few were able to rustle up enough cash for the passage home. Poverty continued unabated, and it was once again full steam ahead on the track to factory farming.

Father Arrowsmith, a Lancashire Catholic, was executed today in 1628 for practising his illicit faith. He was hung, drawn and quartered. Or, rather, fifthed, as his right hand was also chopped off. This relic, called **The Dead Man's Hand**, once kept at Garswood in what is now Merseyside, became an object of veneration and pilgrimage. There were many claims relating to its intercessory powers; though it does not seem to have handed out miracles to everyone. Last century a mad woman, supposedly possessed, was dragged screaming by her parents from the train to receive the macabre golden handshake. A short while later the police had to assist as she was hauled back to the train, demon intact. Decades later, the hand was still being sought out for its healing touch, but it has now disappeared.

© The **Aunt Sally** World Championships are held in Oxford in late August or early September. Depending on sponsor support, they can be anything from a glittering sport-cum-showbiz extravaganza with dozens of teams, to a tense but largely covert showdown between the champions of the two main Aunt Sally leagues – one from Oxford, one from Abingdon. The game itself is an ancient one, a form of skittles in which wooden batons are thrown at a stationary 'doll' on a swivelling plinth, with the object of knocking it off cleanly. In some versions the doll is on a pole, and the object is to hit its nose or break a clay pipe stuck in its mouth. Teams of eight each throw six batons, making the maximum score 48 in any given round. The game originated in less enlightened times as a chicken sport – throwing sticks at tethered birds was once thought to be the height of fun. The *Folly* and the *Tandem* are two of Oxford's better known Aunt Sally-playing pubs.

29th August
The Feast of the Beheading of St John the Baptist

Has the Tongue Got Your Cat?

In 1770 a young man in Cambridge made a bid for fame by eating far too much food. Trying for the local **Glutton** title, he munched his way through eight pounds of mutton with trimmings to match. But such stuffings were old hat, and the crowd pressured him to whet their appetite with something more exciting. So the next day, August 29th, the man ate a cat covered in onions. The audience had to concede that this was something new, but the man was encouraged not to repeat his revolting party trick.

◉ Every even-numbered year, on or about today's Feast of the Beheading of St John, the **Kirby Hill Rates** are staged at Kirby Hill, near Richmond in North Yorkshire. Runners, riders, cyclists and Nigel Mansell need not apply: the races are an election ceremony for wardens of the John Dakyn Trust. Dakyn established the trust in his will of 1556, to maintain an almshouse – now six self-contained flats known as John Dakyn House – which he had built in his life-time for '*the support and relief of poor and diligent people*'. The lucky residents have to be pensioners who have lived in the parish for at least 10 years. The accommodation is still rent-free; though the original stipulation that every day each occupant must pray for the deliverance of John Dakyn has now been eased.

In the unique, private, election procedure, the vicar and churchwardens choose the six '*gravest and most honest*' candidates for the job. Their names are sealed in wax and floated in a tub of water. Two are then plucked out '*as chance shall offer them*', and the winning names become the wardens. The other four wax balls are kept in the tub, just in case one of the incumbents dies during the two-year stint.

Seven veils, a dance routine, and a big knife were all it took for Salome to separate St John the Baptist from his head. Tradition has it that the plant **St John's Wort** covers itself in red spots today in memory of this bloody occasion. With or without the spots, the herb is a powerful charm, warding off evil and supposedly able to ward off flower-collectors too by moving around to avoid being picked. It was the vital ingredient in herb garlands made on St John's Eve – see June 23rd.

Similarly in medieval Scotland **gowans** (daisies) were displayed in churches today as the red at the edge of their petals – especially notable when the flower is closed – also symbolises the blood of St John.

Being beheaded is one of the reasons for St John's premiere-league status in the British saintly calendar. When Christianity arrived, it was grafted on to a body of belief suffused with several thousand years of Celtic head-cults. As recently as the 15th century there was a thriving industry around Nottingham, churning out by the hundred albaster models of John's decapitated head.

Whittingham Fair in Northumberland has just cause to feel overlooked and underlistened to. It was formerly held on August 29th, and got great turn-outs. But most important for posterity, it had a song named after it. The hugely popular tune also did the rounds with one word changed – out went 'Whittingham', in came 'Scarborough'. This alternative version became the one that everybody knows, thanks largely to British folk singer supreme Martin Carthy who taught it to a Mr Paul Simon.

30th August

Village of the Damned

August 30th, 1879. A storm was rattling the roofs at Falkland in the Lomond Hills, Fife. Anyone caught in the downpour returned with a wig of slime, kelp and bladderwrack. It was a squally **shower of seaweed**, which left trees and bushes in the area looking as if they had been caught in a massive lime jelly explosion.

© ▥ The last weekend in August is the time for Eyam to dress its wells and, on **Plague Sunday**, hold its Commemoration Service for William Mompesson. He was rector at Eyam – near Bakewell in Derbyshire – in 1665 when a contaminated batch of cloth from London brought the killer disease to the village. Mompesson immediately sealed off the area to contain the plague, a move which saved the rest of the county but condemned many in Eyam to a slow and isolated death. The outside world left food on the village outskirts, collecting as payment coins which were left in water disinfected with vinegar. Out of a population of 350, 259 died, including Mompesson's wife Catherine; but the disease was contained. For the 14 months in which the epidemic raged, services were held in nearby Cucklett Delf, and it is here that the commemoration takes place every year, after a procession from the church. Several of the original 'plague cottages' survive in Eyam, as does the well – now known as Mompesson's well – where the villagers' disinfected money was left.

© August bank holiday weekend – the last in the month – is the time of the **Notting Hill**

Carnival in London, which in terms of scale and popularity blows away every other custom in this book. It is a celebration of life, West Indian style, with endless processions of outrageous floats and costumes, accompanied by the throb of steel drums, calypso rhythms, reggae, ragga, rap and other music forms too hip for us to recognise. Organisers estimate that around a million people join in over the two days; but police sources like to quote less than half this number. And with around 10,000 of them on the Notting Hill beat, at a cost of nearly £4 million, it could be argued that there are plenty of them there to do the sums. The carnival is the biggest outdoor festival in Europe, and the biggest in the world outside Brazil. It was first staged in 1965; though embryonic festivities were cropping up in the 1950s, notably after some anti-black riots at Notting Hill in 1959.

Steel drums have featured in West Indian music since the 1940s. Colonial law had banned African drums, and so the ingenious locals made use of discarded American oil drums. (A parallel action was taken in the Yemen area of the Arabian peninsula, when ingenious indigenous Jews got round Muslim bans on musical instruments by making percussive use of old petrol cans: still a feature in Yemenite Jewish music).

The carnival in the 1990s has been peaceful, the last major reveller-police clashes being in 1989. The violence peaked in 1976 with 408 police and 200 members of the public injured. But as other quoted examples of fairs through the year reveal, the biggest events seldom evolve without a crisis of violence at some stage. Notting Hill has not exceeded some of the blood-bath-bashes of last century; but it has bettered most of them by surviving. Its cosmopolitan stake in the next century puts it at the forefront of national customs.

August 31st
St Aidan's Day

Through the Pearly Floodgates

St Aidan started life in Ireland, then made the short hop to Iona, before eventually settling in Lindisfarne. An immediate hit with Northumbrian King Oswald, he received a royal gift of horse and trappings, the best that the court could offer. But to the king's dismay Aidan handed over these riches to a passing beggar. When accused of showing contempt for the king's largesse, the saint retorted: '*Is this child of a mare more valuable to you than this child of God?*' That was enough to humble Oswald (whose own feast day is August 5th).

Aidan, who died in AD 641, was the first Bishop of Lindisfarne, in Northumberland, and was noted for his miracles. Once, his oxen and cart tripped and fell over a cliff. But as they plummeted Aidan made the sign of the Cross, and the animals landed unscathed, if a little bemused, on the beach below. On another occasion the saint provided some magic oil for the boat that was ferrying new King Oswy's wife-to-be from Kent. Sprinkled on raging waters, the oil was capable of calming the torrent. Aidan was on the Farne islands when King 'Psycho' Penda of Mercia came to the area for a burn and pillage. When he saw flames leaping from Bamburgh on the mainland, Aidan wept and cried out '*Lord! See what evil Penda does!*' God doused the flames in a trice.

St Aidan's Well at Tamlaghtard, near Coleraine in County Derry, is a thriving ragwell. Anyone with an illness can seek a cure here through sympathetic magic: make a wish and tie a piece of your clothing to a bush near the well.

At Beacon Hill in Penrith, Cumbria, the body of murderer Thomas Nicholson was hanged from a gibbet today in 1767, and it remained a feature of the landscape for ages. His skeletal ghost still haunts the site.

The Last Trump sounded prematurely today in 1754 for the corpses of Hayfield in Derbyshire. An entire communal grave of flood victims in the village's churchyard reanimated, and – in full view of several eyewitnesses – their decayed flesh and bones ascended straight up to Heaven in their hundreds. They sang a heavenly chorus, and left behind a pleasant odour.

© Preston Guild in Lancashire takes place every 20 years in the week following August 29th. The right of local traders to hold a Guild Merchant was granted in 1179, though the first evidence of a Guild taking place was in 1328. It remained intermittent until 1542, when the 20-year rule was introduced. This was adhered to until 1942, when the war postponed the event for 10 years.

Preston has long been an important cotton

town, so in 1822 when the Journeymen Tailors' Guild was placed seventh in a parade of 13 trades, the Tailors boycotted the event in protest, issuing an over-the-top statement demanding the Number One title, '*which has always been assigned to them from the creation of the world to the present time*'. Poor conditions in the cotton industry meant that the Guilds were sometimes preceded by riots – in 1862 five were killed and several injured when soldiers fired on the crowds. There were nearly riots again in 1974 when local government reorganisation left Preston without the rights to stage the Guild. But the Queen stepped in and restored them later that year in a special charter. The next Preston Guild is due in 2012.

HARVEST

August and September are the main times for harvesting and all its related ceremonies. The precise timing varies from year to year and region to region (in Scotland it often stretches deep into October), and alongside the many localised traditions were more widespread customs such as Crying the Neck, corn dollies and the Harvest Home feast. Harvesting is also a time rich in tales of humans and faeries going back and forth between each other's worlds.

The crops were all gathered, and William Noy set off to order Harvest Home drink from the inn, which lay on the far side of **Selena Moor** in Cornwall. Rather than take the safe round-the-houses route, William nipped across the moor even though twilight was rapidly giving way to darkness. He was soon hopelessly lost. Eventually he saw lights and heard voices, and sighed with relief to think that his ordeal was over. Wrong. He had stumbled upon the faeries' own grand and yet passionless version of Harvest Home celebrations, the most lavish banquet that William had ever beheld.

Just as he was about to gate-crash the party, a woman stepped from the throng and pushed him back into the gloom. To his surprise, it was none other than Grace Allen, a former love of his who had mysteriously disappeared years earlier. Grace explained how she had been on her way to meet William one day when she got lost on the moor, found herself in an orchard, and consoled herself by eating a plum. One mouthful was all it took to bind Grace to the will of the faeries. She had been their dogsbody ever since.

William was ill-equipped to play the role of damsel-saving hero. All he had in his pockets was a pair of thick hedging gloves. But he knew that turning clothes inside out could confuse faeries, and so he took them out, reversed them, and threw them on to the faeries' dining table. The lights went out, he was clubbed over the head, and woke up on the moor three days later. Grace was not with him. He was distraught, and from that day onwards he abandoned his sociable ways for the life of a near-recluse. William did get to see Grace Allen again –

his rescue mission had not freed her from her other-worldly slavery, but she was able to hover around him occasionally in the shape of a small bird. Not quite the result he was hoping for.

Sometimes the world-hopping occurs the other way round. During the 12th century at Woolpit in Suffolk, a boy and girl appeared one harvest at the side of one of the old wolf-pits, after which the village is named. Their strange clothes and inability to speak English made them a novelty. Even more startling was their bright green skin. The **Green Children** were hustled into the household of local noble Sir Richard de Calne, and they refused to eat anything except green beans.

The boy soon died; but the girl thrived. She moved on to a more varied diet, learned to speak English, and married a man from King's Lynn in Norfolk – surely a first for the faerie world. She reached a ripe old age in King's Lynn, but not a ripe green one – she gradually lost her strange pigmentation, and became indistinguishable from the locals. She regularly recounted the story of her former life in a Christian country called St Martin's Land, separated from this world by a wide river. The sun never shone there, and everyone had the complexion of the Incredible Hulk. She and her brother had stumbled into a cave during a routine sheep-herding operation, and had emerged at the wolf-pit in the alien world of pale pink people.

Harvest also attracted interest from other supernatural entities. A farmer at Little Comberton in Hereford and Worcester watched in awe as one particular mower scythed and carted and threshed like a squad of combine harvesters. The farmer became suspicious of the worker's superhuman achievements, and went to the local Cunning Man for advice. He was told to set the harvester ridiculously impractical tasks, and was assured that whoever the stranger was, if he failed to complete any of the chores, his power over the farmer would be broken and he would be forced to leave. The farmer made the man count all the ears of wheat taken in; made him fill a barrel with water using nothing but a sieve; and asked him to scythe down a field set with iron spikes. The harvester succeeded in all tasks. But in doing so the occasional glint of horns and flash of cloven hooves revealed to the farmer just why his employee was so good at wielding a scythe.

Even though **Satan** had saved the farmer a fortune in labour costs, he was an unwelcome addition to the payroll. The farmer came up with the ultimate impossible task – he took some of his wife's wiry, curly hair and asked the Devil to straighten it on an anvil. The Prince of Darkness called on all his powers but failed miserably. With a snort of disgust Satan threw down the hammer and stomped off, leaving the farmer thankful for his hair's-breadth escape.

What is possibly the oldest British harvest legend is fleshed out in the widespread folksong *John Barleycorn*. Three men have a vendetta against the eponymous hero and swear that he must die. They bury John Barleycorn alive, and are then amazed to see his head resurface. After a while it grows a beard, a sign of adulthood. But just as he reaches full height, the men cut him down, bind him to a cart, strip off his flesh, and grind him between two stones. The final verses celebrate the second resurrection/triumph, with John Barleycorn reappearing as wonderful beer. In this form JB gets a measure of revenge and proves '*the stronger man at last*' by sentencing drinkers to an eternity of empty pockets and hangovers.

The gods and the god-like have cropped up in harvest tales from all ages and cultures. In Greek myth **Persephone**, daughter of the corn-spirit Ceres, was whisked away by god of the Underworld Pluto. She had to spend half of every year with him, during which time the earth was barren: a myth which accounts for the seasons of the year.

Both Ancient Greece and Ancient Egypt had harvesting ceremonies involving corn dollies and Last Sheaf rites, almost exactly the same as those being practised before the mechanisation of the harvest in Britain early this century. The increased reliance on machinery did what the coming and going of creeds and races could not: it diminished the number of farmers and farm-workers and undermined their need to give ritual thanks for the bounty of the land.

Before automation cut a swathe through the season's traditions, each harvesting day was usually heralded by a bell-peal from the local church. In Cheshire it was said that bells should be rung three times over the crop before it could be taken in. The days usually ran from 5 am to 7 pm, the work and rest-periods being dictated by a foreman called the **Lord of the Harvest**, or King of the Mowers. His badge of office was a straw hat bedecked with poppies and bindweed. The Lord upended any newcomer to the team and struck the soles of his boots with a stone. The novice was released from the mock-shoeing only once he put a shilling towards the mowers' beer. The long days of reaping usually lasted two or three weeks, concluding with the celebrations of Harvest Home. On most farms, everyone had to muck in: hence the Scottish saying, '*In Harvest time lairds are labourers*'.

Some areas dragged in the local clergy to kick off the harvest. The priest would bless the crop; and sometimes the first sheaf was used to make sacramental bread – a Christian/pagan cross-over which still excites impressionable theologians. Elsewhere, the clergy were not so welcome. It was common for the church to demand a **tithe** of one tenth of the crop; and it was equally common for the harvesters to try and thwart the tithe. One harvest chant runs:

We've cheated the Parson, we'll cheat him again,
Why should the Vicar have one in ten?

The **harvest-spirit** lived in the field, and as the mowers progressed, the spirit was thought to be forced into the corn which remained, retreating further and further until there was nowhere left to run. This led to the various **Last Sheaf** rites. Rather than have one mower risk divine persecution by committing deicide single-handed, the onus of scything the last corn was dispersed amongst everyone, firing-squad fashion. The men threw their sickles, with their eyes closed or with their backs to the sheaf. This cowardly courtesy often degenerated into a simple sickle-lobbing game: the first to successfully cut the so-called Luck Sheaf won the prize.

In northern Scotland, after the final sheaf was cut, the young men raced home – to win the race meant that they would be the **first to marry**. Where the Last Sheaf was not equated quite so closely with a god or spirit, the very act of cutting it ensured early nuptial bliss. The desperate and devious often tried to increase their chances of wedlock by concealing an uncut sheaf under a blanket. Then, when someone else had made a big show of scything what was in fact only the penultimate sheaf, they would creep back and cut the Last Sheaf themselves. But not after sunset: that would mean spectacularly bad luck.

The Last Sheaf had many names, the Neck of the Mare being the commonest. Localised favourites included Plaiky or Old Sow in Lincolnshire; Cripple Goat on Skye; and the Hare in Galloway. Where it was given an animal name, before the sickle contests the last straws were often plaited into four 'legs'; or, in the case of the Hare, two 'ears'. In Skye the first team to complete their work made the **Cripple Goat** and threw it into a neighbouring field where mowing was still in progress. As each farm finished their mowing the beastly sheaf was hurled on. The last farm to finish was stuck with the Goat, and was destined to have the blackest of luck all year.

This 'curse of the corn' idea was common to other parts of Scotland and northern England. Elsewhere in the Highlands, the final sheaf was called the **Maiden** if the harvest was taken before Hallowe'en; and the **Cailleach** if taken afterwards. The Cailleach was a symbol of bad luck, whereas the Maiden was benevolent. So only the Cailleach was thrown from field to field. It is said that a crofter would rather see his best cow die than receive the last Cailleach of the year – it was known as the Famine of the Farm. Where it occurred in England and the Lowlands of Scotland, the corn-throwing was less intimidatory. Galloway's Hare was catapulted over the hedge with the sarcastic speech: '*Oyez! Oyez! Oyez! This is to give notice that our master has given the old sack a turn, and sent the Old Hare to Mr X's standing corn!*' The jokers then joined hands, bowed down low, and howled like dogs.

It seems that only the East Riding of Yorkshire went in for setting the Last Sheaf ablaze in the field. The ceremony was known as **Burning the Old Witch**. It got rid of the spirit quickly and cleanly in preparation for a trouble-free resurrection. Peas were cooked in the ashes of the Witch, and there were songs and games round the embers of the blaze.

When the last sheaf is cut, the harvest spirit lurking in the corn dies, its throat symbolically slit by the scythe. Within a few minutes of this act cultures all over the world used to engage in variants of a custom known in Britain as **Crying the Neck**. In Cornwall and Devon the final sheaf was made into a Corn Dolly, and lowered to the ground. The men then rose

slowly, drawing out the words '*A Neck!*' until they were upright with their hats aloft. They then leaped into the air, whooping. The ensuing chant went:

> *We ha' neck! We ha' neck!*
> *Well a-ploughed! Well a-sowed!*
> *We've a-reaped and we've a-mowed!*
> *Hurrah! Hurrah! Hurrah!*
> *Well a-cut, well a-bound!*
> *Well a-zot upon the ground!*
> *We ha' neck! We ha' neck!*
> *Hurrah! Hurrah! Hurrah!*

As the last sheaf is cut, the mowers called '*We have it!*' The response came back: '*What have 'ee?*', to which the reply was '*A neck! A neck!*' The sheaf was made into a dolly, and was usually carried to the farmhouse, where it reigned over the fireplace until ploughing time. © Crying the Neck (sometimes called the Gander's Neck) has been revived at a few locations in Cornwall. At **Helston** it takes place in a nearby field at 7.30 pm on the last Friday in August. St Ives' Crying is held at a time convenient for the local farmers, usually early in September. Unfortunately in 1992 and 1993, none of the local farmers planted corn, so the event was temporarily cried off. The ceremony at **Madron** near Penzance – at 6.30 pm on the first Friday in September – has an element of make-believe to it. Rather than interrupt harvesting, the Crying is acted out in a field next to the village church, using a sheaf of freshly-scythed corn. A dolly made from the sheaf hangs in Madron church – or, on alternate years, its chapel – until the next harvest. Each of the Crying the Necks is usually followed by a short service and a supper of Cornish pasties, saffron buns and heavy-cake.

Even in areas where Crying the Neck or its equivalent had long been forgotten, making the last sheaf into a **corn dolly** or kern baby was still widespread well into this century. The figure was known as the Carlin in Scotland, the Wrach in Wales, and the Ivy Queen in Kent. Over the years various styles have arisen; and this century the deft fingers of countless Women's Institutes have made corn dollies into an intricate art-form. The type of corn used for dolly making is markedly different from the high-yield hybrids that end up sliced and toasted, and a single field of specially-grown wheat, near Milton Keynes, now supplies most of Britain's dolly-makers.

The original purpose of the corn dolly was to

preserve the spirit of the corn through the winter. Come January, the dolly would be ploughed back into the soil, or given to a plough-horses to eat. Until then she presided over the kitchen or parlour. In places where the importance of recycling the dolly-spirit was forgotten, the Last Sheaf was bound and hung over the fireplace until Christmas. The farmer's youngest girl then received an apple which had been secreted inside the sheaf, and a cow would be given the corn-goddess to chew on.

📗 © Occasionally the dolly was hung in the **church**. This practice survives at St Faith's in Overbury, near Evesham in Hereford and Worcester; though the present vicar is not keen on the tradition, and says that if a mouse gets at the dolly, there will be no replacement. The dolly at Whalton near Morpeth in Northumberland is also current, thanks to a revival of the tradition in the 1980s. It is replaced every Harvest Sunday; though in 1993 it was omitted through an oversight. The vicar has promised not to be so absent-minded again.

Several books still insist that St Michael's in Little Waltham, Essex has a corn dolly. When a reporter from a local radio station recently visited the church to do a story on it, it was explained that the dolly had been removed decades ago, and that the books were wrong. The reporter left, deprived of his scoop; but was soon back at the church clutching a fresh dolly. If they would instantly reinstate the old custom, he explained, then he would be able to go ahead with the story as originally planned. St Michael's politely declined.

Even in the age of combines, the last sheaf was often left so that a dolly could be made in the old fashion. It would be fun to imagine that there are still farms out there – not just in Cornwall – switching off the engines and reaching for an old scythe.

At Balquhidder, near Callander in Central Region, the youngest girl in the field would be asked to cut the last sheaf for the dolly-making. This automatically gave her the title **Queen of the Harvest**. Across the Highlands the leftovers not used in the dolly went into making **corn-brooches**. They carried with them a tiny bit of the goddess' fertility, and were tokens of good luck.

Left on a rick, a corn-dolly prevents witches from landing on the bales. In the Lincolnshire Marsh in 1899 an old woman told an inquirer how corn-dollies kept lightning at bay, revealing at the same time how old pagan beliefs manage to linger centuries after their official demise: '. . . *she be thear to fey away t'thoon'er an' lightnin' an' sich-loike. Prayers be good enuff ez fur as they goas, but t' Awmoighty mun be strange an' throng* [distracted and busy] *wi' soa much corn to look efter, an' in these here bad toimes we moan't fergit owd Providence. Happen, it's best to keep in wi' both parties.*'

Once the last individual sheaf and dolly were disposed of, the next episode in the cereal was to bring home the last cart-load of corn from the fields. This was known as the Horkey or **Hockey Load**, and both cart and horse were dressed with ribbons and garlands. Sometimes the men followed the cart in drag, with the boys decked out in their best clothes. Often a single woman sat on top of the load and threw apples at the children below as the procession advanced. At Royston in Hertfordshire all this was accompanied by the Hockey Watering: women and children queued up to throw buckets of water over the men. This was probably welcome after a hard hot day in the field.

The cart and procession wound its way to the farm, where it was greeted with food and drink. In Hertfordshire the feast was called the Hockey Supper, and was followed by a holiday known, unsubtly, as **Drinking Day**. At Rottingdean in East Sussex there was no feast, but the last sheaf went round the village with the men on a pub crawl known as the Hollerin' Pot.

Rottingdean was unusual in not having a grand meal to mark the end of this intense period of work. Until the middle of last century, most harvesters could expect the **Harvest Home** to follow the taking-in of the last load. As a Dorset chant succinctly puts it:

> *When the Harvest is over to our master we will steer*
> *And wet a good supper with a drink of strong beer.*

The Harvest Home was a feast with the farmer footing the bill, somewhere between a show of thanks by the generous employer and a stomach-ripping annual blow-out to take the men's minds off how little they had been paid for their labours. The usual fare was a roast, along with hare or rabbit pie (often made from the animals caught during the harvesting), plum pudding, and an endless supply of beer or cider. The face-feeding was followed by a round of toasts to master and mistress. These were sing-song toasts, inviting the company to imbibe, and promising that anyone who spilled one drink would have to swallow two as punishment. Thomas Hardy paints a fine Harvest Home picture in *Far From the Madding Crowd*; and the Dorset poet William Barnes summed up the atmosphere last century in his dialect piece *Harvest Hwome*:

An'zoo they munch'd their hearty cheer
An' dipp'd their beards in frothy beer,
An' laugh'd, an' jok'd – they couldden hear
What woone another zaid.
An' all o'm drink'd, wi' woone accword,
The wold vo'ks' health: and beat the bwoard,
An' swung their earms about, an'roar'd,
Enough to crack woone's head.

The most popular Harvest Home game was **forfeits**: each person sang cumulative or tongue-twisting verses, taking a drink for every mistake. The more ale consumed, the more chance of further slip-ups, and the less chance the victim had of surviving the night.

© It is now impossible to recapture the spirit which must have pervaded tens of thousands of annual Harvest Homes and the hundreds of thousands of celebrating farm-workers. But at Putley, near Ledbury in Hereford and Worcester, they are giving the impossible a shot, having revived their Harvest Home festivities in the late 1960s. The rowdy jollities there are undertaken in the main by people who have never been anywhere near a scythe or Last Sheaf. There is a mass meal with harvest songs belted out from round the table, followed by a ceilidh. Curiously, this all now takes place on the first Saturday in November.

At Harvest Homes or simply at home over harvest, other favoured foods included **geese**, presented to men who had not dropped any of their loads. Here they used to sing:

For all this good feasting, yet thou art not loose
Till ploughman thou givest his Harvest Home goose,
Though goose go in stubble I pass not for that,
Let goose have a goose, be she lean, be she fat.

On Orkney a **harvest bannock** was given to the man who managed to climb the highest of the ricks while his companions did everything they could short of putting a match to the entire stack in an effort to prevent him. The man who brought in the last cartload was given a bannock too; but only after his trousers had been ripped off and his bottom scrubbed with the sharp end of a wheatsheaf. Even then he could only keep his prize if he outran his persecutors, who endeavoured to do him even more damage. An Orkney man could also claim a bottle of whisky from the farmer after harvesting; but only if he managed to stick a straw into the toe of the farmer's boot without him realising.

Harvest **drinks**, if they were not plain old beer or cider, were made from hops and ginger; or else from newly threshed wheat, cooked in the oven with water and then mixed with all sorts of sweets and spices to become a slack version of frumenty.

A direct consequence of harvest is lots of new bread, and getting a mouthful of the first batch to leave the ovens guaranteed a larder laden with food in the coming year. Then again, the first loaves were sometimes made from corn which had been harvested too early. Such bread tasted and felt so much like rope that it gave rise to the word 'ropy' as a general term of abuse. To prevent the next batch being the same, a ropy loaf should be impaled on a stick and hung in a cupboard, a procedure known dramatically as **gibbeting the bread**.

Harvest Homes were under threat by the middle of the 19th century. Flora Thompson talks of the old style parties in the 1880s in *Lark Rise to Candleford*; but the end was already nigh. Such gatherings had begun to turn inexorably into church feasts after the first **Harvest Thanksgiving** was held in 1843 at Morwenstow in Cornwall. The noble new idea was to meet at the church for prayers and a blessing of the crop, before retiring for a decorous meal, after giving a sackful of produce to the needy. This is the tradition which survives today, with an endless display of spaghetti hoops and packets of jelly filling schools and churches up and down the country.

After the fuss and fun following the end of Harvest, it was time for the **gleaners** to take centre stage. The gleaners were women who knew that the end of the Harvest was not really the *end* of the harvest. In all the fields stalks of stray corn were scattered about, and it was the gleaners' job to tidy up, as shown in Millet's painting *The Gleaners*, which is in the Musée D'Orsay in Paris and so does not really qualify for a 🔟. Like the harvesters before them, the women had a bell to summon them to work. There was a **Gleaning Queen** to mirror the Lord of the Harvest, and the task usually lasted a full three weeks. A good gleaner with a couple of her children might hope to take in an entire comb of corn – 18 stones of grain. Gleaning was an essential, unwritten law in almost every parish. The collected corn was ground by the miller, who kept a percentage, and the flour-sack of gleanings helped many households stave off starvation over the winter months. The miller suffered an unenviable reputation, as the portion that he took in payment was said to be over-large:

> Miller, O miller, O dusty poll!
> How many sacks of flower hast thou stole?
> In goes a bushel, out comes a peck;
> Hang old Miller-dee up by the neck!

There is an old **crop-grower's adage**, which should also be the rallying cry of the vegetarian movement: '*It is a shame to see beasts' meat growing where men's meat should grow.*' It is also said that '*To break a pasture will make a man; to make a pasture will break a man.*'

Harvest is the optimum time of year to take advantage of **toads**. Their mythical 'venom' is neutralised at Harvest, and sprains can be cured by rubbing the afflicted part with a small warty amphibian.

At the end of harvest, it is possible to use a **sickle** to get a handle on fickle fate and gaze into the future. The tool is thrown into the air: if it lands with its blade in the ground, you will be married during the year ahead; if it lies flat the blade points in the direction of your next place of employment; but if the sickle breaks, you will die.

In Kent, and Hereford and Worcester, an alternative crop celebration used to take place at the hop-harvest in August and September. **Hops** were essential to the local economy, and until very recently the chief hopping workforce came from the relevant urban areas: London for the Kent hopyards, and the Black Country further north. Originally this was a form of slave labour, with outrageously bad living conditions for the labourers, and very poor wages. 🏠 Towards the end of the 19th century the conditions were brought to the attention of Father Richard Wilson of Five Oak Green, just outside Tonbridge in Kent. He was spurred into action by his first-hand observation of illness, damp bedding straw, and a sanitation system which used as a toilet the same stream which fed the drinking-water pond. In 1896 he built the **Little Hoppers'**

Hospital in the village. It was later known as the Richard Wilson Memorial Hospital, and the building (mark two) can still be seen.

Even when conditions improved it was all work and no play. The traditional song *Hopping Down In Kent* sums that up in its final verse:

> Now hopping is all over, all the money spent,
> And don't I wish I'd never gone hopping
> down in Kent.

Mechanisation had seen off most of the migrant labour by the 1960s, with a few stragglers making it into the 1970s. Prior to this, one of the most difficult jobs was that of **stilt man**: a lone dare-devil on 18-foot stilts, who tied the vines to the top of the poles during the growing season.

In the Hereford and Worcester yards, the foreman – known as the **Busheller** – underwent symbolic burial with his chosen lady after the harvest. He was thrown into the **Crib** (a large hop-container) and buried under the crop, only to be tipped out a few seconds later. This resurrection ensured a good crop in the following year, and heralded the Hop Feast. In a variant on the theme, unmarried girls were **Cribbed** – that is, stuffed unceremoniously into the crib with no regard for dignity or poor underwear.

© Most of the smaller hop celebrations have disappeared; but two large-scale ones have developed as some form of compensation. Faversham in Kent stages the **English Hop Festival** over the first weekend in September. Multitudinous Morris teams weave in and out of assorted street entertainers. There are hop vines on stands; countless chances to have a go at picking your own hops; and a Saturday night hopper's ball. Not calling the dance a hop seems like a missed opportunity. On the Sunday at 3 pm there is a hop procession through the town, featuring all the Morris men and a hop-picking stilt man.

© On the first Saturday in September Canterbury Cathedral has one of Britain's few remaining church services featuring a horse, the **Hop Hoodening**. Before the service several Morris teams take part in a parade led by snapping-jawed hooden horses and the less blatantly pagan hobby horse Invicta, which represents the white horse of Kent. The procession includes a bower of freshly-harvested hops, and secreted within is a newly-elected Hop Queen. They arrive at the Cathedral at 10.30 am – the hooden horses, being pagan, have to stay outside, but Invicta is allowed in along with all the Morris men, who play their own music, ring their handbells, and are allowed to dance in front of the hop-covered altar during a break in this very odd service. Hop hoodening only dates from the 1950s, by which time the hop industry was already in decline; but otherwise it has all the makings of genuine strange tradition. For more on hooden horses and hoodening plays, see December 26th.

Hops are a profitable but fickle crop. There is truth in the concise adage: *Hops make or break*. Dried, hops can be strung up for good luck; and in a pillowcase they can cure insomnia. They can also be used to great effect in something known as 'beer'.

SEPTEMBER

1st September
St Giles' Day

Pro-clam-ation

St Giles died in AD 710. For most of his life he had suffered after having been maimed by the French King, Wamba. The King had been trying to shoot down Giles' pet hind, but the saint had thrown himself in the way. The arrow penetrated deep into Giles' knee, crippling him for life. The hind's milk helped sustain Giles during convalescence in his hermitage at the mouth of the Rhone. Cripples and beggars adopted Giles as their patron saint, and the slums around the outside of European town walls became known as St Giles' Parish.

St Giles' Day was a popular date for **feasts and fairs**. The one at Great Coxwell in Oxfordshire was renowned for its music and dancing. It was said that you could wear away the soles of your shoes in the ceaseless jigging there. To keep up the energy levels of the dancers, Coxwell specialised in feasts of ham and plum pudding. For details of St Giles' Fair in Oxford, see September 6th.

At Berkhamsted in Berkshire, today was the beginning of the **gorse and bracken cutting season**: the former for oven-fuel, the latter for bedding. Claims could not be staked out on the local common until it was St Giles' Day. So at the first stroke of midnight there was a race from the church to the common to mark out the richest patches.

© At Colchester, Essex, on the first Friday in September or the last one in August, the new **oyster season** gets underway. The Mayor of Colchester and supporting dignitaries sail from Brightlingsea up Pyfleet Creek, where a clerk reads the 1256 Proclamation asserting Colchester's rights to fish in the River Colne. This, says the charter, has been a local monopoly *'from the time beyond which memory runneth not to the contrary'*. The Monarch is then toasted in gin and gingerbread, a vestige of the food and drink offerings formerly given to the friendly neighbourhood seagod. The mayor then drops the first trawl, and the oysters commence their panic. Having opened the entire season, the attention then turns to opening the oysters themselves at an invitation-only celebratory banquet. See October 26th for Colchester's Oyster Feast, the culmination of the season.

☀ It is said that a fine 1st September signifies a fine spell of **weather** in the month ahead.

2nd September

Pudding and Pie Cook for Six Days

Today in 1666 the **Great Fire of London** began in Pudding Lane. Six days later over 13,000 houses had gone up in flames, along with 89 churches and St Paul's Cathedral. Medieval London, in its seedy wooden splendour, was razed – or, according to a hotter-than-usual-off-the-press ballad of the time, *'burn'd and drown'd in tears'*. One man who had very little time for weeping was Sir Christopher Wren, who suddenly found himself with an extremely full diary.

▥ Conflagration conspiracy theories spread like wildfire: alleged arsonists included the Dutch, the French and the Catholics – evidence for the latter theory was that a Catholic chapel in the Strand was mysteriously untouched by the blaze. The Catholics said that this was just some divine favouritism. Others blamed Satan – 1666 was one millenium on from the number of the beast. Most Londoners, though, realised that the fire was the work of God, venting his wrath on the sinful. Opinions differed as to which particular sin He had in mind. Many singled out Gluttony – after all, it had begun in Pudding Lane and was finally doused at Pie Corner, which is now the junction of Cock Lane and Giltspur Street. On the corner there, tucked in a niche, is **The Golden Boy of Pye Corner**: a gilt, and guilt, image of a fat child. Engraved underneath are the words '*In memmory put up for the late fire of London, occasion'd by the sin of Gluttony*'. Better known is the Great Fire memorial at Pudding Lane, the Monument, complete with its own Underground station. Atop the 202-foot column (it is the same height as it is distant from the start of the fire) are symbolic flames which uncannily resemble an irate hedgehog.

After the Fire of London, a Portuguese man was accused of spreading the blaze. Witnesses claimed to have seem him toss a fireball into a house in one of the streets that burned down. In court the man insisted that what he had thrown was a small **loaf of bread**. And, by a slice of luck, when investigators went to the relevant spot the house was still standing, and they found a loaf propped on a shelf inside the door. The man was guilty only of observing an old custom which maintains that if you see bread on the floor, you must put it on a shelf to offset bad luck.

◉ Early September sees the opening of the **Whitebait season** at Southend-on-Sea in Essex. Whitebait are very young fish, usually herring or mackerel, doomed to end their days crisp-fried. The first catch of the day is blessed by the Archdeacon, and the lucky mayor and dignitaries get to feed their fishy faces behind closed doors.
© Fish are also in the limelight at Musselburgh, Lothian. Even though little is left of the local fishing industry, **The Fishermen's Walk** is still held the first Saturday in September. A couple called the Fish Callant and the Fishwife lead a colourful parade through the town which has been decorated with nets, lobsters and all things piscine. The various sports of the day include a shawl race, and rope-throwing for a silver log trophy, while the ladies get to 'load a needle'.

The fish thrive, but September's dogs have said chow. Wool **Dog Fair** in Dorset was a straightforward, swings and roundabouts affair, apart from the fact that visitors were incited to chase and beat any dog which they could find – demonstrating that fairs and violence have always gone hand in hound.

3rd September

Cromwell's A-round head

Mythologised to Hell and back, it is fortunate that **Oliver Cromwell** understood the value of tradition. Early in the Civil War, his troops had Charles I cornered in the Littleport Fens in Cambridgeshire. Charles escaped through the brilliant strategy of showing a **split goosefeather** to the Roundhead sentries, who reluctantly let him pass. Ancient custom dictated that no Fenman could refuse to help someone in trouble if they were carrying such a feather. The guards expected to be punished for allowing Public Enemy No. 1 to slip though the net, but Cromwell applauded the men's inaction, saying that it was better to let the King go free than to go against tradition. That said, when Cromwell got into power, he banned every tradition going – even Christmas.

Cromwell died today in 1658. A harbinger of his death supposedly came in the shape of large whale, sighted in the Thames at Greenwich – not the most clear-cut of omens. As the Lord Protector slipped away a violent tempest blew up, ripping trees out of the ground. It was said that Cromwell had sold his soul to the Devil to win the Civil War, and that now he was kicking up a storm as the Devil dragged him to Hell.

Posterity had a habit of blaming all breakages on Oliver's army. The 18th-century traveller John Byng noted: '*Whenever I enquire about ruins, I always get the same answer, that it was some Popish place destroyed by Oliver Cromwell.*' It is true that his New Model Army did their share of shattering stained-glass and smashing idols; but sheer limitations of time make the truth-to-myth ratio very low among the scores of churches and cathedrals which still maintain that Cromwell oversaw the devastation in person. Many claim that he stabled his horses in their naves.
⛪ Ely Cathedral has a gun alleged to have been used by Cromwell's men when they wrecked its tower. The damage to the tower dates from 200 years before Cromwell, and the gun from 200 years after his death – but the tale still gets told. An even bigger whopper is the story that **Swansdown** – a town larger than neighbouring London and vehemently pro-Royalist – was utterly obliterated by Cromwell's troops when it refused to surrender. No such place ever existed.

From the Civil War onwards, this sort of propaganda served to demonise the Puritans. But after the Restoration, damaging Cromwell's reputation was not enough. Three years after his £60,000 funeral and burial in Westminster Abbey, his body was dug up, hung from the gallows at Tyburn, and then decapitated. **Cromwell's head** was stuck on a pike lashed to the roof at Westminster Hall, and left to rot. There it remained, a potent symbol of pointless vengeance, until dislodged 20 years later in a storm. The head rolled down the roof of the Hall, landing at the feet of a sentry who took it home and stuffed it up his chimney. Only on his deathbed, years later, did he admit to having it. This pattern of disappearances and reappearances was repeated over the next 250 years. The head was sold, resold, and exhibited several times; and the artist Sir Joshua Reynolds was among the many whose hands it passed through.

By the 1940s Canon Horace Wilkinson of Woodbridge, Suffolk had become the headkeeper. It was suggested to him that he give it back to Westminster Abbey so that it could be reburied. '*Not likely. The last time they had it they stuck it on a pole*', was his response. The Canon died in 1957 and soon afterwards his son gave the head to Cromwell's old college, Sidney Sussex in Cambridge. Dark brown, with tufts of hair but lacking the famous warts, Cromwell's head was buried in the college grounds in 1960. Its belated last (?) resting place is marked by a plaque in their chapel.

The head may have been pinned down to one location, but no less than five sites purport to be the burial place of the rest of his remains; and all come complete with **Cromwell's ghost**. He appears at Naseby in Northamptonshire; at the Old Hall Inn at Long Marsden, North Yorkshire; and at three haunts in London: Chiswick Church, Red Lion Square, and Number I Connaught Place. Cromwell's deathbed struggle with Satan took place at Brampton Bryan in Hereford and Worcester. The felled trees there have long been replanted, but they are said to shake tonight as Cromwell's ghost re-enacts the stormy tug-of-war with Satan.

In 1788 on September 3rd the first **Denby Dale Pie** was baked in West Yorkshire. The giant pie fed hundreds, and was made to commemorate George III's return to rude health. Unfortunately the King was soon back fighting bouts of madness, setting the tone for a tradition which, though durable, has been ill-starred.

In 1846 five sheep and more than 50 birds went into the pie baked to mark the repeal of the Corn Laws. On its way to the official slicing ceremony, the 13-horse-drawn cart in which it was being transported was overturned by the hungry hordes. When it finally arrived, in several pieces, the man making the pre-cutting speech was so long-winded that the crowd tipped him into the pie's remains.

When the 1887 Jubilee Pie was cut open, it had decayed inside to such a degree that the crowd stampeded away to escape the stench. The baker fled Denby Dale, and mock funeral cards were printed *in memoriam* for the pie, which was buried in quicklime as an emergency measure. Much the same happened in 1924 when a pack of salivating dogs chased the semi-rotten pie down the street.

1964's effort was successfully edible; but it was too big to get out of the barn where it had been baked. It appeared on the streets only after half the building had been torn down. 1988's 50,000-portion Bicentenary Pie was remarkably farce-free, and contained 3,000 kilos of beef, 3,000 kilos of potatotes, and 700 kilos of onions.

An 18-foot long Denby Dale Pie-dish can be seen in its new guise as a flower bed outside the Pie Hall community centre in the village. The Hall was purchased with cash generated by the 1964 festivities, which celebrated the birth of four royal babies that year. The bakers of Denby Dale await news of a royal wedding, coronation or other suitable national celebration as an excuse to once again get out their pie dishes.

4th September

Cat Flap

On September 4th 1894 a hiker rested near Ivinghoe Beacon in Buckinghamshire. It was a classic English scene: clear dawn sky, verdant hills and trees, a distant cock crowing, and a huge black animal howling demonically. The hiker took swift note of its girth – four feet high, six feet long – and, even more swiftly, ran back down the hill.

Sightings of mysterious **giant cats and dogs** have occurred all through history. The 1960s' Surrey Puma brought the long-running story back into the headlines, and after a spate of Peak Panthers and Fen Tigers, in 1983 the focus moved to Exmoor in Devon, where a hideous dog-cat-thing kept newspapers happy for weeks, stalking the moor and killing more than 80 sheep. A witness described the creature's '*bulging green eyes*', but then spoilt it by adding '. . . *just like a lion*'. The Royal Marines, stuck for something better to do, tracked the beast and said that it was simply a large, cunning wild dog. This did not hinder that year's rash of 'Beast of Exmoor' T-shirts.

In 1993 the beast was back, this time as a huge cat stalking Bodmin, Cornwall. Some of the tabloids even managed photographs of the creature. But by then rational theory had taken over. The Dangerous Animals Act of 1976 had meant that many unregistered large animals were surreptitiously unleashed into the wilds. In 1980 a puma was caught, and later stuffed, after stalking the area around Loch Ness, and there are several verified incidents of drivers running over what turned out to be big cats. The keeping of exotic cats as pets is nothing new – Henry VIII had a pet puma, as did the actor David Garrick. Pumas and black leopards (panthers) probably account for the bulk of the sightings. The animals have been spotted all over the British Isles, including at such less obvious sites as Port Talbot in West Glamorgan, Oswestry in Shropshire, East Grinstead in West Sussex, West Hampstead in London, and St Mary's in the Isles of Scilly. In County Durham – another place were the cat-nip grows high – an hotelier recently offered discount prices for any guest who discovered big-cat droppings. Guests should take a careful look before eating the 'black pudding' at breakfast.

© June or July are the main months for such festivities; but the Sowerby Bridge area, near Halifax in West Yorkshire, avoids the rush by holding its **rushbearing** on the first Saturday and Sunday of September. The rushes are piled high on a cart at Warley on the Saturday, which is blessed at 11 am at Warley church. Over the weekend the rush-cart trundles around Sowerby, Ripponden, Triangle and Cotton Stones, loaded down with a pyramid of greenery, and pulled by 60 locals wearing clogs and Panama hats. Precariously perched on top of this heap is a well-balanced local with nothing to cling on to except a large wooden triangle. There are all sorts of processions and entertainments at the festival, including performances en route by the Bradshaw Mummers, a duck race, and an inordinate amount of Morris-dancing.

The original rushbearing died out in the 19th century; but after a one-off in 1906 and a second revival for the Queen's Silver Jubilee in 1977, it is now in full swing again and has become one of the most spectacular of the many rushbearing events. For the origins of rushbearing see July 13th.

© **Arbroath Pageant**, staged for the first time in 1947, lapsed in 1955, but still occasionally rises from the ashes in early September. It was last held in 1980. It features re-enactments of the events surrounding the Declaration of Independence (see April 6th), as well as other relevant plays and pageantry.

5th September

Eccles-iastic Edict

Today in 1538 Thomas Cromwell, Henry VIII's influential henchman, issued the **Injunctions of the Clergy**. From then on every church had to keep official records of all births, deaths and marriages. Family tree lumberjacks no longer had an axe to grind; and claiming to be descended from mythical creatures, royalty, or deities became harder to sustain. Such extravagant assertions were far from uncommon, the glint of a fabulous past adding lustre to a humdrum present. Even the usually dependable head-screwed-on King Alfred the Great insisted that his bloodline could be traced back to the leader of the Saxon gods, Woden.

© **Barnet Fair**, at the northern edge of London, was the chief livestock mart in the area. It took place from the 4th to the 6th of September. Famous for its range of stalls and shows, and its fixed traditional seafood menu, one 19th-century visitor summed it all up as '*roundabouts and palmists, pickpockets and pretty girls*'. The fair now takes place on the first weekend in September at Greengate Farm, Mays Lane in Barnet. It is mostly a standard funfair, but even in 1990 several hundred horses were sold and the trading was subjected to close scrutiny by the RSPCA.

Eccles Wake, banned in 1877, took place on the first weekend of September. One of its chief attractions was a full timetable of sporting events, including '*That most ancient, loyal, rational, constitutional, and lawful diversion, bull-baiting, in all its primitive excellence*'. There were also more human/humane events, and prizes for victory included such enviable goods as a pound of tobacco, a 'stuff-hat', a pair of panniers, a mysterious 'leathern prize', and a dog chain. Cakes and ale were the traditional fare, with Eccles-cake and Banbury-cake sellers vying with each other for the best turnover. An

Eccles ballad pulled together the disparate elements of the fair, and threw in a smidgeon of local bias, by telling how a baited bull tossed the Banbury seller into the air along with the bulldogs. The event's popularity led to a Lancashire saying: *As thrang* (thronged) *as Eccles Wakes*.

☻ Another fair formerly held today was at Crewkerne in Somerset. It is chiefly remembered for providing this sliver of **weather-lore**:

The first rain after Crewkerne Fair,
Is the first rain of winter.

6th September

Fingered by a Glove

On September 6th, sometime during the reign of Henry VII, the church at Holbeach in Lincolnshire was looted. Everything valuable was taken, including the church's famous collection of silver spoons. The only clue left behind by the crooks was a pair of leather gloves. Local **soothsayer** John Lamkyn took matters and gloves into his own hands and consulted Edmund Nasche, an even more notable diviner. Examining the gloves, Nasche declared that the robber was one John Patriche of Holbeach. Patriche was astonished. So were his friends. They started to give Patriche collective cold shoulders, threats, and broken windows, so he sought the aid of the Star Chamber to clear his name.

Patriche declared that he was '*Brought into infamy slander and oute of credens*' thanks to the accusation, '*to his utter undoying in this world for ever*'. He pointed out that the soothsayers, as witches, were the obvious villains of the piece. The recriminations bounced back and forth and the gloves came in handy as various parties challenged each other to duels. From the somewhat jumbled local records it appears that everyone got off the hook in the end, and the silver spoons of Holbeach were never recovered.

© The first Monday and Tuesday after September 2nd are the days for the massive **St Giles Fair in Oxford**. The fair never actually had a legal charter, but it has nonetheless survived the five Oxford fairs that did.

It grew from the medieval Walton Wakes, and although most of the trade stands are now no more, it is still one of the chief pleasure fairs of the south.

Even bigger than the Oxford fair was the one at **Winchester** in Hampshire. It was described as a self-contained city of hastily erected stalls and resultant inter-connecting streets. It became the compulsory nucleus of all trade for the 16 days around September 12th: nowhere else, within seven leagues of the central fair hill, were any business transactions allowed. Tolls from the stalls went to swell the piggy-bank of the Bishop of Winchester.

🏛 All this had been going on since William II granted the Fair its charter in the 11th century. Winchester was then the capital of all England, and Castle Hall in Westgate is all that remains of the castle that William the Conqueror built there. It contains what is claimed to be **King Arthur's Round Table**. There are several rivals for this top table title, even though it does not feature in either the historical evidence about Arthur nor in the version romanticised in the early 12th century by Geoffrey of Monmouth, whose highly imaginative part-historical, part-hysterical *History of the Kings of Britain* has provided most of the details which make up the Arthur legend. It was not until 1155 and Robert Wace's *Roman de Brut* that the Round Table first appeared. These various strands were knitted together in Thomas Malory's 15th-century *Le Morte D'Arthur*. It is probable that the circular table at Winchester was actually put there by Henry de Blois who also instituted the still-surviving Wayfarer's Dole – see July 15th. And for more on Arthur, see June 26th.

7th September

Grace and Danger

'*Shout, ye waves! Send forth a song of triumph . . . Ye screaming Sea-mews in the concert join!*', as Wordsworth said in commemoration of the watery deeds of **Grace Darling**. On this day in 1838 at her father's lighthouse on Longstone, one of Northumberland's Farne Islands, Grace spotted a vessel on the losing end of a tussle with the waves. It was *The Forfarshire*, and Grace led the way as she and her dad William took the lifeboat to rescue nine drowning men.

Wordsworth was not alone in waxing lyrical. A heroic ballad about the deed was in the top 10 back in the mid-19th century, and is still well known to this day.

✝ Whatever the identity of the **ghost at Old Oak Cottage** in Minster, Kent, this is his favourite month. The cottage was once part of St Mildred's Abbey and was used to house its visitors. It is speculated that the ghost might be the monk who was in charge of the rations at this medieval guest-house. He appears indoors during September, both day and night. First comes the sound of shuffling, sandalled feet, then a wavering outline appears surrounded by an ethereal glow – very much the kind of back-lighting effect which is Steven Spielberg's stock-in-trade.

© The **Braemar Highland Gathering** and Games open on the first Saturday in September. Although officially established in the early 19th century, the inspiration for the games is said to have come from Malcolm Canmore, an 11th-century Scottish King who liked to watch kilted Celts manhandling large pieces of wood. Stones, hammers, cabers and almost anything else throwable get tossed round the Princess Royal and Duke of Fife Memorial Park. There are also assorted permutations of running and jumping, a tug-of-war, Highland Dancing and a competition for pibroch-playing. The pipes, the pipes are calling from 9.30 a.m.

© Also in early September is the 1974-revived **Blairgowrie Highland Games**. Smaller than the get-together at Braemar, its chief event involves 300 men pulling on opposite ends of a 736-foot long rope.

8th September

Deadly Dudley – The Leicester Molester

Today in 1705 Mrs Veal paid a surprise visit to Mrs Bargrave in Canterbury, Kent. She explained that she needed a gravestone for her mother, and asked her friend to order one, making sure that it had a space left on it for Mrs Veal's name, to be inserted after her own death. Mrs Bargrave was a little perplexed – why could Mrs Veal not get the stone herself? – but she agreed nevertheless, and waved her friend off. Mrs Bargave soon found out why: her friend had died in Dover on the day before

the visit. It had been **Mrs Veal's ghost** which had given the beyond-the-grave, about-the-grave instructions. The orders were obeyed, and the phantom never returned. The story so enthralled Daniel Defoe, of *Robinson Crusoe* fame, that he published a pamphlet outlining the weird tale.

The **ghost of Amy Robsart** was less chatty than Mrs Veal's. Amy died on September 8th, 1560 at Cumnor Place, Oxfordshire. The house's servants had all gone to Abingdon Fair, and Amy – wife of Robert Dudley, one of Queen Elizabeth I's favourites – was discovered later at the foot of the stairs with a broken neck. Suspicion passed to Dudley, who perhaps fancied his chances with the Queen. Whatever the truth, he was found not guilty at the inquiry: he remained 'just good friends' with Elizabeth and was later made Earl of Leicester.

▥ In 1588 Amy's ghost met Dudley at Cornbury Park, Oxfordshire. She told him that he had just 10 days to live. No histrionics, no shrieking and rattling of chains; but perhaps the most unsettling form of revenge: calm delivery of bad news. Sure enough, Dudley died 10 days later. But Amy was not at peace after his death. She haunted both the Park and Cumnor Place, even after 1810 when the hall there was pulled down to provide stone for the rebuilt church – the fireplace of the old hall can still be seen, forming part of a grassy bank in Cumnor churchyard.

✝ Some time after 1810, following many reports of the Elizabethan ghost by distressed Cumnor folk, nine jobbing exorcists came to deal with Amy, banishing her to the churchyard's pool, which has since been known as Lady Dudley's Pond. Despite these supernatural shackles Amy still roams through Cornbury Park, and to spot her there is a sure portent of imminent death.

© The **Sheriff's Ride** at Lichfield, Staffordshire, takes place on the Saturday nearest September 8th, getting under starter's orders in the Market Square at 10.30 am. The Sheriff is elected by the Brethren of Lichfield. If he turns down the job he can – according to the charter instigated in the mid-16th century – be fined, imprisoned, and stripped of civil liberties. So he usually comes quietly. A posse of around 100 horsemen, Land Rovers and other vehicles go on a long-winded 16-mile canter around the town boundaries, pausing for food and races.

© St Mary's at Wirksworth in Derbyshire goes **church-clipping** on the Sunday following the 8th. Parishioners stomp around the church with hands held. Whiffs of pagan ancestry are doused afterwards in a church service. For a less clipped version of the tradition, see September 19th.

9th September

Antediluvian Antler Antics

In 1513 the Scots were in alliance with the French. Against his better judgement James IV led his troops south on September 9th to meet the English at **Flodden** near Branxton in Northumberland. Under the command of Thomas Howard, the English annihilated the invaders, killing the King and some 10,000 more besides. A monument to James IV and the battle can be seen in Branxton church.

The shock of this huge defeat reverberated in Scotland for decades. The original air *The Flowers of the Forest* was made into a lengthy song in the 19th century. Its author was melancholy poet, Jane Elliot:

> *The Flowers of the Forest, that fought aye the foremost,*
> *The pride of our land, lie cold in the clay.*

The body of James – or what was assumed to be his body – was retrieved from the battlefield by the English, and entered into a strange post-humous adventure. It was disembowelled and embalmed, and sent in a lead casket to London, and later to a monastery which, after the Dissolution, became the lodgings of the Duke of Suffolk. The Duke threw the body into a lumber room with lots of old wood, and it was later mutilated by workmen who used the severed head as a ball. Elizabeth I's master glazier Lancelot Young became fascinated with this head – still sporting its long red hair and beard – which he described as strangely sweet-smelling. This was all somewhat unhealthy, and in the end the body was handed over to the sexton at St Michael's church in Wood Street, London, where, at last, it was buried in an unmarked communal grave along with a pile of bones from the crypt.

Meanwhile many Scots maintained that the English had got the wrong body and that James – a popular, scholarly, womanising hero of the Burns school – was not dead at all. He is said to be biding his time under a faerie hill until Scotland needs him. The national football team are drawing up a contract right now.

© On the Monday after September 4th, Abbots Bromley in Staffordshire has its **Horn Dance**. If the 4th is a Sunday, the dance is a week later, on the 12th. It is thought to be the oldest extant dance in Europe, dating back to the Stone Age. Six Deer-men carry heavy reindeer antlers set in wooden 'heads', and perform dignified dances and mock-battles over a 20-mile all-day luck-bringing hike. It starts at the vicarage at 8 am and goes on into the late evening. En route they dance at Blithfield Hall – the only day of the year on which it is open to the public. The Deermen are accompanied by music, as well as a hobby-horse, a man dressed as a woman, and two boys – one with a triangle, one with a crossbow. At certain junctures the bowman pretends to fire at the Deer-men. Such rituals were well-established 20,000 years ago judging by evidence in the cave paintings at Lascaux in France. Miming a hunt gives power through imitative magic. A duller, alternative story is that the Horn Dance originated in the reign of Henry I (1100–35) as an assertion of local forestry rights.

The horns used these days are estimated to be about a thousand years old. During the rest of the year they can be seen in a side-chapel at St Nicholas' church. The dance was originally performed during the Christmas season. And just before anti-pagans get worried, the cash raised from the event all goes to the church.

10th September

Look at the Assize of that Herring

Near the staircase at Wardley Hall in Worsley west of Manchester is the 300-year-old **Wardley skull**. Down the centuries there have been several attempts at putting the skull six feet under, but each triggered off an outbreak of supernatural chaos – unexplained deaths, cacodemonic noises, grotesque visions, and other associated horrors. So the Hall went to the lengths of acquiring a special charter forbidding the skull's burial or even its concealment. Legend says that the skull is that of Roger Downe, who was killed during a violent brawl in 1676. Roger and his friends had been heckling some pub fiddlers, trying to get them to play a favourite tune. The musicians refused to bow to their pressure. So Roger and his gang seized them and tossed them up and down in a blanket. Fists flew, fiddles were smashed and the law soon intervened, but not soon enough to save Roger's life.

The only flaw in this myth is that a later autopsy – long after the Wardley skull was doing its thing – showed that Roger's remains still came complete with head. In fact the skull's former owner is Alexander Barlow, a Benedictine Catholic missionary, who met his fate on September 10th 1641, condemned to death for belonging to the wrong limb of the Christian church. The Lancaster Assize sentenced him to be hanged and pulled apart. His head ended up at Wardley Hall, where – since it is still deeply unlucky to bury or even move it – it will presumably stay for all time.

Assizes such as the one which condemned Alexander Barlow were a cross between a visit to the dentist and Judgement Day. About four times a year judges visited the shires to dole out meagre wisdom and generous sentences. Many unfortunates met their end at the Assize. At the Dorchester Summer Assize in Dorset on this day in 1660, the judge had a barrelful of Sherbourne witches to grapple with. Despite the handed-down image of pre-determined guilty verdicts on such occasions, many witch trials relied so heavily on dodgy evidence – lots of imaginative eyewitness testimonies of supernatural goings-on, but very little in the way of proof – that they ended in farce, and the accused walked free. The Sherbourne batch were not so lucky.

Doubtless they would have preferred the old policy of Henry II (1216–72), who abolished the Assizes in favour of trial by battle. The two sides slugged it out, duel-like; and it was perhaps no more a mockery of justice than many ineptly handled or rigged courtroom trials.

The other alternative assize was the Scottish Assize-Herring. This did not, sadly, involve clubbing offenders down with a wet fish: it was a tax of a thousand herring which each fishing boat had to deliver annually to the King.

♱ In the 18th century the building which is now the Grenadier pub in Wilton Row, near Hyde Park Corner in London, was an army-officers' mess. After one session of cards a soldier accused of cheating was stripped and flogged to death. He died of his wounds afterwards; and ever since has regularly manifested

in the pub – usually in September – as a cold, intangible, unpleasant presence. There are scores of pubs which have this kind of atmosphere, but lack this kind of excuse.

11th September

Badgers Set the Price

William Wallace's finest hour, the **Battle of Stirling Bridge**, took place on this day in 1297, at Abbey Craig near Stirling. After defeating the English troops of Edward I, rebel leader Wallace led his makeshift army south to trash Carlisle in Cumbria. It was a short-lived heyday, however, and the army was later crushed at Falkirk – see August 23rd. Legend tells how Wallace, in the guise of dashing knight once met the English Queen – who had a soft spot for him – at St Albans in Hertfordshire. Unfortunately for legend, Edward had no Queen at the time; and, apart from a later visit to London for his execution, Wallace never travelled as far south as St·Albans.

🎞 The towering, rocket-like, 19th-century Wallace monument can be seen at Stirling in Central Region, on the site of the battle. An earlier statue at Dryburgh in the Borders commemorates the '*Great patriot hero, Ill-requited Chief*' and depicts him in Roman attire.

© Richmond in North Yorkshire has its Festival of First Fruits during September on a convenient Saturday after the harvest has been taken in. A prayer of thanksgiving is offered under the town clock in the market place, and a sack of corn is given a cursory but symbolic examination and declared to be '*a goodly sample*'. The supplier of the corn gets a bottle of wine for his trouble, and villagers and assorted dignitaries drink a sherry toast to the farmers of the district. This custom is thought to have begun in Norman times as a competition between the farmers. Each raced to have their corn ripe, reaped and sacked. The first harvest was rewarded with food and drink. Not everyone played fair: favourite cheats included nicking sacks from neighbouring farms, and attempting to pass off last year's corn as a fresh batch.

Richmond was once the largest corn market in the country. During the season, **badgers** descended on the town in search of the corn. They bought it all up, then sold it on elsewhere at a substantial profit. Apart from the corn-badger, there was also the cheese-badger, butter-badger and fish-badger. An Act of Edward VI in 1552 declared that a licence from the Justices was required for *'the buying of any corn, fish, butter or cheese by any such badger'*. These badgers are not mammalian plantigrade quadrupeds, but middle-men traders – defined in 1862 as men who traverse the country *'with ass and panniers'*.

© **Widecombe Fair** is held on the second Tuesday of the month. Its only real claim to fame is Old Uncle Tom Cobbley and All. Their ride to the fair in the famous song, and the subsequent death of the poor mare and its haunting of the Dartmoor roads, are probably the best-known chunk of Devonshire folklore. Tom and the mare are represented at the fair, and indeed it is impossible to avoid the man and the song in this neck of the woods during the tourist season. The fact that the song was originally just a template rather than a historical record, with gaps for the names of any locals you cared to bung in, coupled with the fact that the present fair was probably founded after the historical Tom Cobbley's death, may be viewed as a small annoyance rather than an all-out party pooper. Widecombe Fair is now rich in rides and jugglers, but is still in part an agricultural event, and a small amount of livestock continues to be sold there. See March 6th for the life, death and afterlife of the real Tom Cobbley.

12th September

Braining Cats and Dogs

Each September 12th the Salisbury Plain shepherds left their flocks and made tracks for the **Wilton Great Fair** in Wiltshire. The highlight of the bash was an all-day brutal, beerful battle royal for the title **King of the Shepherds**: red sky at night, shepherds fight; red sky in the morning, shepherds brawling. Rules were few and far between – they fought each other by right hook and by crook, and used cudgels to stun, gouge and maim. The last man standing was crowned King, and the rest slept off their combat fatigue in the Wilton barn. The slumbering shepherds formed a giant circle, each with his legs pointing outwards, and his head resting on his faithful dog. This ritual abuse of beast and man led to the fair being quashed late last century.

'For fun and cakes, the best of Wakes' was an 1842 ballad's eight-word summary of the **Newcastle Wakes** in Staffordshire. Games – not the kind with crooks and cudgels – were its principal attraction. These included foot races, and gurning through a horse-collar, with a prize for the ugliest face pulled. And then there was **Tip Cat**. In a favourite version of this popular game, a length of wood is set up like a small see-saw, with an object – usually a lump of wood, known as the Cat – balanced on one end. The opposite end of the plank is struck with a bat – normally a stout stick – sending the object spinning into the air. It has to be whacked as far as possible with the bat, before it hits the ground. Points are scored not just for big hits, but for correct guesses as to how far the Cat has gone. This form of Tip Cat is a close relative of the Yorkshire game Knur and Spell (see Shrove Tuesday). In the 1970s a revived version of Tip Cat was filmed by the BBC but for some reason was referred to as 'Biss Cat' in the programme's opening credits.

On top of cat-tipping, the Wakes also offered various types of music, including Italian Balladeers, and a feast culminating in a slop of congealed stickiness called Stir-pudding. Newcastle Wakes were unusual in being actively encouraged by the local authorities. But for the worst of motives. It was thought that by keeping the working classes absorbed in their Tip Cat, they could be kept clear of rational thinking and politics, and so do nothing about poor working conditions and low wages. The Wakes eventually died out with the coming of the First World War.

© On the second weekend in September, Ryedale Folk Museum at Hutton-le-Hole in North Yorkshire holds the **Word Merrills Championships**. Merrills is the local name for Nine Men's Morris, a complex version of noughts and crosses which was so popular at the time of Shakespeare that he sneaked a mention into *A Midsummer Night's Dream*, using it as a symbol of the lost spirit of frivolous games-playing:

> *The Nine Men's Morris is filled up with mud*
> *And the quaint mazes in the wanton green*
> *For lack of tread are indistinguishable.*

Shepherds often marked out a board in the ground and played using sticks; and a wooden Merrills board was a common feature in many North Yorkshire farmhouses. The earliest dateable board was discovered on the Gokstad

Viking burial ship of AD 870, and a Merrills board was found carved on the top of a barrel on Henry VIII's recently-salvaged ship, the *Mary Rose*.

13th September

The Boy Who Died Wolfe

At the moment of victory on this day in 1759, General James Wolfe was breathing his last. The English and French had been knocking each other about in Canada, and this was to be a decisive victory at the Plains of Abraham in Quebec. Wolfe, who had received his first army commission at 14, was the common soldier's hero. He became the subject of several songs and ballads after his death, immortalised as the Bold Youth in spite of the fact that he was 32 when he died.

The French commanded the high ground, but before the fight the British troops dragged themselves up the hillside using trees for support on the single-file track, surprising the French camp: 150 were killed in the first British volley. One of the commemorative songs describes the scene poetically:

I see them falling like moths in the sun,
Thro' smoke and fire, thro' smoke and
fire . . .

A favourite apocryphal scene in some of the Wolfe songs has the hero chatting amiably with the enemy commander Montcalm before the battle. But one thing on which the songs and the history books all agree is the fact that a few hours – or verses – later, Wolfe was dying, after receiving his third wound of the day. He asks '*How goes the battle?*', and when given the news that '*Quebec is all our own, none can contend it*', he expires with the words '*I die contented*'. His fellow commander on the field, Sanders, survived the day; but Montcalm died on the following day. By September 18th, Canada was officially British.

🏛 James Wolfe was born at the vicarage in Westerham, Kent. Relics and historical paraphernalia relating to the man can be seen at the National Trust's Quebec House, and at Squerryes Court, both in the village. There is also a statue of Wolfe by the village green, in suitably heroic pose. For those who like their history complete with cable cars, the Heights of Abraham at Matlock Bath in Derbyshire, were named after the site of the battle by a man who said the steep spot reminded him of his days by Wolfe's side in Canada.

🏛 On a more bizarre commemorative note, the area called Quebec near Studley Roger just outside Ripon in North Yorkshire has a bridge and pond, and a Wolfe Monument, along with a grotto in the hillside and a Temple of Fame built in Wolfe's memory – true Follies all.

🐾 There have been sightings, occasionally, of a ghostly wolf running about at Woolpit, Suffolk, a village named after the old wolf-pits there. Sadly, the ghost does not rally its troops to famous victory and then fall from its horse with a wound in the right breast. Otherwise it would have linked in nicely.

14th September
Rood Day/Holy Cross Day/
Hally Loo Day

Lord Rockingham – There's a Zouch Loose Aboot this Hoose

It was like some thinly-plotted sci-fi movie. When the population of Britain rose from their slumbers after the night of 2nd September 1752, everything had changed. They were not suddenly blind and at the mercy of rampaging triffids, but it seemed almost as alien – it was suddenly 14th September. The 3rd, 4th, 5th, 6th, 7th, 8th, 9th, 10th, 11th, 12th and 13th had been sucked into a void of logic by the introduction of the continental-style Gregorian calendar. There were Calendar Riots, with clock-watching mobs taking to the streets to demand their eleven days back.

For more on the demise of the Julian Calendar and the resulting chaos, see 29th February.

The 12th-century Lord Zouch of Rockingham learned from Lord Neville that his wife was cheating on him with a young squire. When Zouch galloped home to his castle and found the squire there, he ran him through without stopping to check for corroborating evidence. Too late he discovered that he had killed no squire – he had slain his wife's sister. An ex-nun, she had disguised herself as a man to flee secretly from the convent and meet with her true love.

🏛 Zouch realised that the treacherous Neville

had set him up. But en route to wreak his revenge, he met the ghost of an old monk. It told him that all was lost; and indeed it was – mad, jealous Neville had sneaked back to the castle and killed Zouch's wife and son, and was now dead himself, face down in the River Welland. Zouch died within the week, from grief. For seven years afterwards he haunted Rockingham Castle on Holy Rood Day, striding in with noisy footsteps to warn the living of his arrival, and re-enacting the unfortunate stabbing of his sister-in-law. After the seven year ghostly itch, he dematerialised. The present impressive Rockingham Castle near Corby in Northamptonshire is Zouchless, having been built in 1544.

The cross of Christ's crucifixion used to qualify for its own feast-day with accompanying **Holy Cross** or **Rood Day Fairs**. These died out with the Reformation in the 16th century – the Anglicans decided there and then that giving a saint's day to a piece of wood was not really on.

☀ It is still an important day for odd goings-on in the **weather** world:

If dry be the buck's horn on Holyrood morn,
  'tis worth a kist of gold;
But if wet it be seen ere Holyrood E'en, bad
  harvest is foretold.

And the rood rain meets the rude rut in the following Scottish rhyme:

If the hart and the hind meet dry and part
  dry on Rood Day fair,
For sax weeks, of rain there'll be nae mair.

Passion Flowers supposedly bloom on Rood Day. Their flowers are alleged to resemble the instruments of Christ's Passion – the cross, the nails, and the crown of thorns. Parts of the flower also symbolise his wounds, the apostles, and Heaven.

In Lincolnshire it was thought that those who went nutting today – known locally as **Hally Loo Day** – would come to grief in some horrible but unspecified way. Perhaps because the **Devil** goes nutting today, say some; although his main outing is on the 21st, Devil's Nutting Day.

15th September

The Look of the Devil

Today in 1613 **Sir Thomas Overbury** died, having been poisoned with arsenic and mercury. The verdict? Natural causes. Overbury's tale begins at his birthplace, Compton Scorpion south of Stratford in Warwickshire. He teamed up there with Viscount Rochester, under whose light he then rose to prominence in the court of James I. But their friendship soured when Rochester fell in love with scheming sex goddess Frances Howard, Countess of Essex. At first Overbury provided Cyrano-like help, and composed love poems for the not-particularly-bright Rochester to send to the Countess. But when the couple planned to marry, Overbury thought it was going too far. He warned Rochester that the Countess would swallow him alive. It was an image which no man could resist: the pair were betrothed, and Overbury was ostracised. He ended up in the Tower of London without charges or trial, and the Countess oversaw the administration of his poison over a six-month period.

After Overbury died, rumours leaked out that Howard and Rochester had accelerated his demise. They went on trial for murder. But Overbury was not to be avenged. The Countess tugged on some her many influential connections, and James I – ignoring the weight of evidence against the couple – found them not guilty.

The saying '*He looks on him as* **The Devil** *looks over Lincoln*' implies a gaze full of contempt. It is thought to have originated not in Lincolnshire, but in Oxford. One of the many gargoyles in Oxford was a carved stone devil which used to stare malevolently across at Lincoln College until it was taken down today in 1731.

📖 But the city of Lincoln was not going to give up an eponymous phrase without a fight. One local explanation claims that having been kicked from on high to the depths of Hell, Satan was jealous of Lincoln Cathedral, which had the highest towers in England – formerly topped with sky-scraping spires – and that his envious gaze is still perpetually fixed on the building. Alternatively, the Devil in the expression is said to be the **Lincoln Imp**, a grotesque figure carved in the Cathedral's Angel Choir. Certainly, this figure remains an object of controversy. In 1990 a handful of extremists campaigned to have the Imp torn down, blaming it for the rise in local evil and Satanism. Perhaps this is what happened to the Devil at Lincoln College 250 years ago.

In legend the cross-legged Imp was one of the spirits which fell from Heaven after Lucifer's unsuccessful celestial palace coup. He flitted into the cathedral and wreaked havoc, before an angel manifested in the Angel Choir (so called because it is full of carved angels) and turned him to stone.

Satan is also responsible for a lingering Lincoln wind. Outside the south-west corner of the Cathedral there is a constantly chafing gust, said to be a small tempest which once accompanied the Devil on a day-trip to Lincoln. Satan nipped into the Cathedral, and left it outside. The tempest is still waiting for the absent-minded Prince of Darkness to return.

In 1993, after years studying astronomical and biblical evidence, a group of scientists declared that they believed the exact date of **Jesus's** birth to be September 15th, 8BC.

☼ There is traditionally an 86% chance of good weather today. It is said that September 15th *'will be fine six years out of seven'*.

16th September
St Edith of Wilton's Day

Thumbs Up for the Invisible Prince

On 16th September 1400, **Owain Glyndwr** began a Welsh rebellion against the English at Glyndyfrdwy in Gwynedd. Glyndwr – Glendower to his enemies – was proclaimed Prince of Wales, and for 10 years the country scented the sweet whiff of independence. Glyndwr was a respected soldier with a few unorthodox tricks up his sleeve. He owned a stone which made him invisible when he touched it, and he could summon tempests. Shakespeare mocks Glyndwr's reputation as a wizard in *Henry IV, Part One*, in which the Prince sides with Harry Hotspur's rebels against the King. When Glendower claims *'I can call spirits from the vasty deep'*, Hotspur snaps back *'Why, so can I, or so can any man; but will they come when you do call for them?'* Glyndwr was a learned man though, not a village witch-doctor. He was a friend of the poet Geoffrey Chaucer, and intended setting up Welsh universities for a Celtic renaissance.

⌂ But in 1400 the English crushed his rebellion, and Glyndwr disappeared – probably one of the foundation stones of his invisible-rock legend. There are tales of him dying quietly in Herefordshire in 1416, having escaped his pursuers at Glendower's Chimney on Moel Hebog, a mountain west of Beddgelert in Gwynedd. Now a favourite with climbers, the Chimney is a sheer slope, and Owain was reputedly its first conqueror. In the absence of Glyndwr's body many Welsh followed standard 'lost leader' procedure and claimed that he had not died, or escaped, but was asleep – Arthur-like – in Castle Cave in the Vale of Gwent. He is to slumber until England has decayed in its own decadence. Another branch of this belief says that his return has already been and gone: by 1485 his relatives the Tudors ruled over England and Wales, and it was said that they embodied Glyndwr's spirit. If so, they showed little sign of it – during more than a century in power the Tudors did Wales no great favours; and, disregarding their genuine Welsh lineage, preferred to spread the story that they were descended from the mythical King Arthur.

Glyndwr's rallying point at Glyndyfrdwy was an appropriate spot at which to begin a Welsh renaissance. The **goddess Aerfen** lived here in the River Dee, presiding over battles between the Welsh and English. Her fee to ensure a favourable outcome was three human sacrifices a year. Glyndwr's defeat suggests that the goddess had not received her dues.

© ⌂ At Kemsing in Kent on or near the 16th, there is a procession to St **Edith's** Well, this being her day. The well is good for curing eye complaints, as so many of these saintly watering-holes are. Another St Edith's Well at Church Eaton, near Stafford, claims the same powers, and also works wonders with scrofula. A third Edith Well is at Stoke Edith, Hereford and Worcester. It appeared when the 10th-century saint prayed for a water supply when founding the local church, and is still flowing very obediently.

St Edith of Wilton turned down several solo offers in the Abbess job market, opting to stay with her mother at Wilton Priory, Wiltshire. She also turned down the throne itself, when her brother Edward the Martyr died. And when Edith herself passed away she left behind a small but beautifully formed relic – an incorruptible thumb. She ought to be – but is not – the patron saint of hitch-hikers.

17th September

Sow in Boar's Clothing

John Smith was the last in a large Derbyshire family of boys and grew up as one of the lads. But despite this upbringing there was something that John was reluctant to bring up. He was in fact a she. Once, during a public brawl, John's shirt was ripped, revealing all. But s/he buttoned up, and so did the witnesses. John later accepted £5 to save the reputation of a pregnant serving girl. They were married in Winster, and having acquired a ready-made family, John had no obvious reason to come clean about gender-bending.

Seven years – and several mistresses – later, John abandoned marriage and family to move in with a new common-law wife and her 11 children at New Mills. Fourteen years into this relationship, illness struck, and John took to his bed, on this day in 1848, never to rise again. The examining doctor commented on John's womanly features, but cannot have carried out his examination *that* thoroughly, for he failed to realise the full extent of John's feminine side. Only when the patient died did the coy doctor discover that John was a woman.

John Smith, revealed the posthumously spilled beans, was really Sophia Locke. She had been dressed in boys' clothes as a child, and had never grown out of the habit. But rather than make a big fuss, John's common-law wife discreetly sewed up her beloved in a winding sheet, and burial took place before the story became common currency.

◉ On the Sunday after the 14th, Avening near Stroud in Gloucestershire has the **Pig's Face Feast**, held on what is known in these parts as Pig Face Day. It was first staged in 1080, instigated by Matilda, repenting Queen of William I. She had been in love with Byrhtric, Lord of Gloucester, whose lands were usurped after the Conquest in 1066. For the crime of not returning Matilda's affections, he was executed. Matilda then realised what an absolute swine she had been, and to make amends built a church in Byrhtric's honour. A boar's-head feast and a Mass were held to celebrate the completion of the building. Pot-bellied locals thought the pig-out was terrific, and the feast is re-enacted every second year (even numbers) with a mock 11th century banquet and a concert. Pig's Face sandwiches are available on the day from the pubs of Avening, and are also dished out in church, after Evensong.

© The three-day **Barnstaple Fair**, first held in the 12th century, starts on the Wednesday before September 20th. Spiced Elizabethan Ale is brewed for the event, and the brewers refuse to divulge their secret recipe. At the opening ceremony outside the Guildhall the attending officials drink the Bess bitter from silver cups. A white glove is then hoisted on the building, an ancient symbol of free-for-all trading.

Barnstable Fair was the subject of a 19th-century song, a particularly obscure, 72-lined, jolly piece, which often leaves you too puzzled to sing along:

> *If pigeon's wings are plucked, and peacocks*
>   *tails refuse to grow, friend!*
> *In Spring; you may depend upon't in*
>   *Autumn they will shew, friend!*
> *If feathers hang about your fowls in drooping*
>   *style and spare, friend!*
> *Both cocks and hens will get their pens to*
>   *Barnstaple Fair, friend!*
> *Then friend, leave off your wig, and Barum's*
>   *privileges share, too*
> *Where everything grows once a year, wings,*
>   *feathers, tails, and hair, too!*

18th September

Sinning in the Rain

Samuel Johnson was too eager for greatness to help out on his father's lowly bookstall in Uttoxeter, Staffordshire. He intended studying and writing books, not selling them. But after his father's death, Dr Johnson looked up 'remorse' and 'guilt' in his own 1755 *Dictionary* – the first book of its kind – and realised that a penance was in order. He returned to the site of the now defunct stall, and stood bareheaded in the rain, contemplating his vanity and folly. His consolation is that since his own death in 1784 this scene has become a morality tale, the stuff of sermonising.

© The story of the great man's humbling is retold annually to a group of Uttoxeter children in the **Johnson Sermon**. It takes place at 11 am in Uttoxeter Market Place on the Monday nearest to the 18th, his birthday. There is usually a distinguished speaker, and wreaths are laid on Dr Johnson's statue. If it rains the children do not themselves nobly stand bareheaded in the downpour, but duck into the nearby St Mary's church.

© 🔲 Another Johnson commemoration takes place on the Saturday nearest the 18th in the same county at Lichfield, where Johnson was a schoolmaster. Wreaths are again laid on his statue, and the choir sing their greatest hits. In the evening there is a feast for a select few. The menu at the **Johnson Supper** is predictable, consisting of all the Doctor's favourite dishes: steak and kidney pudding, saddle of lamb, apple pie with cream, washed down with ale and punch and rounded off with church-warden pipes (to give the saturated fat a bit of crunch and roughage). Johnson's childhood home in Lichfield Market Square is now a museum, as is his house in Gough Square, London.

Woodbury Hill Fair used to commence today, a massive sheep-do held on the site of an Iron Age hill fort near Bere Regis, Dorset. And this venue seems to indicate the event's pedigree, making it a truly ancient beast market. Over to local correspondent Thomas Hardy, writing about Woodbury – which he called 'Greenhill' in his Wessex books – in *Far From The Madding Crowd*:

> *Multitude after multitude, horned and hornless, blue flocks and red flocks, buff flocks and brown flocks, even green and salmon-tinted flocks, according to the fancy of the colourist and custom of the farmer. Men were shouting, dogs were barking with great animation, but the thronging travellers in so long a journey had grown nearly indifferent to such terrors, though they still bleated piteously at the unwontedness of their experiences, a tall shepherd rising here and there in the midst of them like a gigantic idol amid a crowd of prostrate devotees.*

Equally colourfully, Hardy also describes the Fair as '*the Nijni Novgorod of South Wessex*'. This was the old name for Gorky in Russia, famous for its mammoth (as in large, not as in exotic local livestock) fairs.

© The third Sunday in September is known as **Horseman's Sunday** at St John's church in Hyde Park Crescent, London. The priest leads this steeple-chase on horseback at 11.30 am, blessing a congregation of horses, who pray to their patron St Leger.

19th September

Braffin-Gurning with Hissing Crabs

Eighty-three-year-old Sarah Smith of Cold Harbour, Dorset, was out picking potatoes today in 1884 when her neighbour Tamar Humphries appeared with a darning needle. Sarah put down her muddy spuds hoping for a neighbourly chat. But Tamar stabbed her repeatedly. From her accompanying tirades Sarah realised that Tamar believed her rheumatic daughter to be bewitched, and for some reason she thought that Sarah was to blame. **Drawing blood from a witch** saps its power. A couple of generations later and Tamar would have been jailed for assault; a couple of generations earlier and Sarah would probably have burned at the stake. But in 1884 this sort of nonsense was thrown out of court.

© **Egremont Crab Fair** is held on the third Saturday of September. Crustacean fans will be disappointed, as the crabs in question are crab-apples, which were traditionally given out at the fair. And even crab-apples fans will feel let down – these days it is a cartful of ordinary apples which is driven around Egremont, Cumbria, and distributed to the crowd. In less genteel days there used to be pitched crab fights, with fruit missiles flying back and forth; and roasted crabs – which '*hiss in the bowl*' according to Shakespeare – were the delicacies of the day. The modern scarcity of crab-apples is the simple reason for the substitution of Cox's and Granny Smiths.

The fair's non-livestock-trading attractions include racing, hound trailing, and a climb up a 30-foot greasy pole, on top of which used to be an entire sheep. This has now been scaled down to a more portable leg of lamb. Most famous of the events, though, is the **Gurning through a Braffin** competition – grinning through a horse-collar – which takes place in the evening. The winner is the one who can produce the most hideous, contorted face, and the event claims to be The World Gurning Championship. Egremont has been doing all this since its fair charter of 1267.

© **Charlton-on-Otmoor** in Oxfordshire used to go **garlanding** today, and a vestigial form of the ceremony still survives. Before the Reformation the church here had statues of Mary and St John. Mary was interpolated into a Roman greenery goddess Flora-type celebration, and was garlanded prior to a parade.

When the statues were destroyed in the 16th century, crosses of evergreen box and yew were put in their place, and the 'Mary' cross continued to be garlanded on May Day, and again on September 19th. It was even carted over the moor for a blessing at the local Benedictine monastery just as the original statue had been. Morris dancers later accompanied it on its moor jaunt. The May Day festivities are still in full swing (see Mayday), but although the box cross is redressed around the 19th – in anticipation of the church's Thanksgiving Service – it is done with little ceremony. It is taken from the church today, covered with fresh flowers and greenery, and then put back. All this is a vestige of a custom still widely popular in Catholic countries: the carting of a saintly statue around the town on the local feast day.

© **Worcester Great Fair**, held today, has come full circle, losing its funfair and going back to its roots: trade stalls. Hops, cheese, and livestock are the chief items on offer.

20th September

Clipping the Love-Goat

The Glover brothers of Mancetter, Warwickshire, were passionate Protestants at a time when such sentiments were not in vogue. Catholic Queen Mary was on the throne, and was after their blood – many other hard-liners had already been imprisoned or burned. John and William fled after being tipped off by their friend the Sheriff, but their brother Robert was too ill to escape, and was taken in for questioning. Failing a religious dogma test, Robert was condemned as a heretic and burned at the stake on September 20th 1555. He seemed to die quite contentedly, crying out 'He is come!' minutes before his death. That's faith for you; or perhaps it was more down to starvation and maltreatment in a diseased cell over a period of weeks.

John Glover died on the run and was buried in Mancetter, only to be dug up two months later and flung over the churchyard wall for passers-by to trample on. William was the last to go, at Wem in Shropshire. His body lay above ground until the local bishop ordered it to be taken by dung-cart to a hole on the parish boundary and thrown in.

These three Glovers became known as the **Mancetter Martyrs**. Such inhumanity was too much for Joyce Lewis, another Mancetter resident and soon to be the fourth of its martyrs. She lost her Catholic faith in the aftermath of all this barbarity. But she made the mistake of publicising her religious dilemma, and it was soon an early bonfire night for Lewis.

Ballad sellers had a bad time back in the 1640s. Most of the Civil War ballads had been pro-Royalist, which in retrospect was a bad move. After an Act passed on this day in 1649, balladeers were to have their song-sheets confiscated, followed by a sound whipping in the House of Correction. Singer-sellers could not relax again until the Restoration in 1660, when the Act was revoked.

© At **Painswick** in Gloucestershire on the Sunday nearest the 19th, **church clipping** takes place. After a procession the villagers encircle St Mary's church and dance round it three times singing The Clipping Hymn. Afterwards a Clipping Sermon is held. Years ago the children used to race away shouting 'Highgates!', a mysterious cry which one vicar ingeniously linked back to the Greek aig-aitis, meaning 'Goat of Love'. He explained that the clipping is a survival of an ancient Greek-via-Roman custom, at which people danced around a sacred altar and sacrificed goats and dogs. To the Romans this feast was known as Lupercalia (usually associated with St Valentine's Day), one of whose sports involved whipping each other with goat thongs.

The dog element of this theory is backed up by the fact that the delicacy of the day in Painswick is something called **Puppy-dog Pie**, a round cake with a china dog inside. Formerly it was made of real puppies (and collie flour). The local explanation is that the custom started when two travellers rolled up at a Painswick Inn demanding food. The eager-to-please landlord had nothing in the larder, and so he killed his own dog, serving Rover to the rovers.

Painswick's clipped churchyard has 99 ancient yews, a tree which symbolises eternity and lives to a prodigious age. It is said that if a hundredth is planted, it will always die.

In the 1960s a local man was convicted for giving the superstition an illegal helping hand. Every time the churchyard trunk-count threatened to go into three figures he had sneakily killed off a tree or two by pouring acid on its roots.

21st September
Devil's Nutting Day/
St Matthew's Day

A Nutter Disgrace

Once upon a time the Devil was out gathering nuts in Warwickshire, this being **Devil's Nutting Day**. He had gathered a sackful when he ran smack bang into the Virgin Mary, who commanded him to stand and deliver. The Devil dropped his load and fled. The resulting nut-mound soon became a grassy hill, and the story explains why it is known as **The Devil's Nut Bag**; but not why it is also known as the Devil's Night-Cap, a name which suggests an alternative legend out there somewhere.

The same schizophrenic mound, off the A422 near the Haselor-Temple Grafton crossroads in Warwickshire, is also known as **Alcock's Arbour**. Local legend has it that Alcock was a robber who buried his swag here in an iron-bound, thrice-locked chest. He left a **giant cockerel** on site to guard the booty. Only one man ever made it past the first lock on the treasure-chest; but the chicken then pounced and ripped him apart before he could get any further. The only way to placate this formidable fowl is to show it one of Alcock's bones. But since no one knows where to find the robber's remains, the loot remains within the hill, safely under cock and lee.

On **Devil's Nutting Day** no one should go gathering nuts unless they happen to be Old Nick or an immediate relative. Those ignoring the warnings will be driven insane, or else gathered by Satan and taken straight to Hell.

Nuts are notorious for inducing fertility. Girls who go nutting are in danger of premature pregnancy; and it is said that a good nut harvest means a crop of bastards in a few months' time. This danger is inherent in a folksong called *The Nutting Girl*, with its *'And what few nuts that poor girl had she threw them all away'* refrain.

☕ Today is also St Matthew's Day, and **weatherwise**, it is said that:

Matthew's Day bright and clear
Brings good wine in next year.

At **Baunton** in Gloucestershire a table chose this day in 1646 to start bleeding. Contemporaries were baffled and amazed in equal measure. Modern spoilsports suggest that it was simply an outbreak of the red microbe *Serratia marescens*.

Science falters on the subject of **Angel Hair**. In his *Natural History of Selbourne* the normally down-to-earth Gilbert White recorded finding several acres of angel hair on this day in 1741. Some say that the phenomenon is made from tangled masses of spiders' webs. Others claim that it is a deposit from passing UFOs. The idea of Gabriel, Michael and company cleaning their combs seems no less plausible.

✝ **Edward II** was murdered on this day in 1327 at Berkeley Castle in Gloucestershire. In a horrific parody of a homosexual act, a hot poker was inserted into the King from behind, a murder which left no obvious signs on the outside of the body, and which inspired hundred years of tasteless jokes and the moderately successful accordion-crossover band Edward II and the Red Hot Polkas. Edward's shrieks can still be heard in the vicinity.

This is the **Autumn Equinox**, so spare a few seconds – no more – for modern Druids braving old gods and traffic pollution on Primrose Hill at Hampstead Heath, London.

22nd September

Inter-Galactic Joy-Riders

UFOs and ghosts are this century's chief sources of folklore. Today in 1956 a whole townful of promenaders at Cleethorpes in Humberside saw an object described as a 'glass disc' hovering in the sky. It was estimated to be 25 metres long and over 10 miles above ground, according to RAF Manby in Lincolnshire. Jets were sent in to investigate, but the UFO was long gone by the time they arrived. Another page in the ever-swelling UFO annals – a catalogue that goes back three and half thousand years at the very least: a papyrus from the reign of Pharaoh Thutmose III describes how several fiery round objects brighter than the sun whizzed through the Ancient Egyptian sky.

Various British sites, including Cradle Hill near Warminster in Wiltshire, are alleged to be places of constant UFO sojourns. Given these frequent alien day-trips to Earth, the only real mystery is why they are so camera-shy once they get here. Perhaps terrifying the puny Earthlings is their main aim. It certainly worked back in 12th-century North Yorkshire at Byland's Abbey. A spaceship flew over the monks and 'caused the utmost terror' according to a chronicler of the time. Angels had wings of course, but the monks were concerned that Satan might have developed something more sophisticated.

© Ashby-de-la-Zouch was famous for its fairs. Much of Leicestershire once flocked to its annual Hiring Fair to seek employment or, failing that, entertainment. The event has survived, if only in name. **Ashby Statute Fair** is still a big gathering – four days of fun ending on the Tuesday nearest September 20th. The main street of the town is blocked off; but instead of offering opportunities to work closely with mud and animals, it is now an all-entertainment jamboree of rides-and-stalls.

☁ The **weather** on the 20th, 21st and 22nd supposedly indicates the weather outlook for the next three months respectively – today's the day for checking whether or not it will be a white Christmas, with the possibility of a quick dash to the betting shop before the odds start to shorten.

Still with weatherlore, thunder in September points to a good harvest; and any accompanying downpour is also good news for some: '*September rain is much liked by the farmer.*'

23rd September
St Tegla's Day

Bird of Pray

The early life of **St Tegla** – or Thecla – reads like a 1st-century *Perils of Pauline*. A follower of St Paul, she baptised herself in a ditch, and vowed to live and die a virgin. As punishment, the Romans made her the centrepiece of a bonfire. When all seemed lost a storm blew up and blew out the flames. Tegla was then sent to the amphitheatre to face hungry beasts: they prowled and growled long enough to whet the crowd's appetite, but none of the animals were willing to tuck in to her saintly flesh.

After her early adventures, she spent over 70 years being quietly miraculous in a cave, until some pursuers forced her to reprise her role as an action heroine. She said some powerful prayers, and was sucked into the rock, never to be seen again. The Tegla of these tales and

the one associated with Llandegley in Powys and Llandegla in Clwyd may well be entirely different people, but this has not dampened local enthusiasm for the saint.

St Tegla's Well at Llandegla (which means 'the place of Tegla') near Ruthin in Clwyd offered radical therapy to epilepsy sufferers. The afflicted approached the well at sunset, the men carrying a cockerel, and the women brandishing a hen. Hands and feet were washed in the water, the poultry was pricked with a pin, the pin was thrown down the well, and fourpence (a groat) was handed to the clerk of the well. Three renditions of the Lord's Prayer followed, while the sufferer walked three times around the church, clutching the bird. They then retired to spend the night under the altar, using the church carpet as a blanket, the Bible as a pillow, and the chicken as a substitute teddy bear.

Next morning the patient blew down the chicken's beak, and this transferred the ailment to the bird, which was left in the church clucking in confusion while the hopeful man or woman did a final three circuits of the well, having left another groat in the Poor Box. The sufferer was said to be cured only if the bird then died in the church. Hastening its demise with an axe was not permitted, and consequently in bad years the death-wish poultry outnumbered the congregation.

Incidentally, the rectory at Llandegla used to be haunted. The ghost was terminated by show-off exorcists who turned it into a blue-bottle and buried it at the bottom of a stream. Almost exactly the same tale is told about the church of St Andrew at Presteigne in Powys. In the 17th century, 13 priests exorcised the malevolent spirit of **Black Vaughan** by converting him into a fly and banishing him to a nearby pond.

Baron Digby of Sherborne, the Earl of Bristol, died on this day in 1698. He left cash for the church at Sherborne in Dorset in his will, and requested an annual ringing of bells in his memory. On September 23rd the town used to celebrate with **Tolling Day**, six hours of peals, meals, beer and cheer. Local ear-plug sales soared, and Digby's original solicitation for six hours on the bells was reduced to a mere two hours of noise-making. The two hours have since been reduced to zero.

24th September
St Robert of
Knaresborough's Day

Moonstruck

The **Fairy Gump**, a hill at St Just in Cornwall, had a reputation as a great party venue. And not one of the guests was over six inches in height. A local miser, refusing to pick on someone his own size, decided to gatecrash the fun and make off with a few faerie trinkets. The moment he chose was the night of the Harvest Moon – lighting up the skies round about now – when, as he knew, the faeries would be holding one of their main revels, and collecting moonbeams.

The miser watched a courtly procession of faeries emerge from the Gump, with piles of food and treasure, and an army of Spriggans – fierce wiry creatures who acted as security guards. Choosing his moment, the miser leaped into the open and tried to scoop up the gems and gold with his hat. But the Spriggans were on to him. All the lights went out and the glow of the Harvest Moon was doused. The miser felt himself being beaten and pierced all over, trapped in hundreds of tiny, strong ropes.

In the morning the man awoke, dazed and bruised, to find himself lying on the hillside covered in cobwebs. A chastened man, he never crossed the faeries again.

The **Harvest Moon** is the first full moon after the 21st. It is the moon at its most potent. It symbolises the fertile earth and an abundant harvest. Women are in danger of becoming pregnant under the light of this moon, and newly-weds taking advantage of this fact and sleeping with the Harvest Moon shining on them are the luckiest people in the cosmos. But they must bed down indoors – the moon's harvest magic is so powerful that anyone sleeping outside will become blind and/or disfigured. A child born under the Harvest Moon will be a moon-calf, a monstrous child of the moon. 'Moon-calf' is the tag given to the semi-human Caliban by his drunken companions in Shakespeare's *The Tempest*.

The **Man in the Moon** is said to be Cain, or Endymion who was transported there by Diana. But the traditional British explanation is that it was a wood-cutter put there because he went stick-collecting on a Sunday. He was reprimanded, but insisted, very reasonably,

that a woodcutter needs wood. For his cold logic he was banished to the moon, with the bundle of twigs, a lantern and a dog, features often alluded to in literature. In *A Midsummer Night's Dream* one of the bit-players in the mechanicals' play is decked out as Moonshine, complete with '*lantern, dog, and bush of thorn*' – details which after hard gazing can still be made out on the moon's surface. And if that all seems a bit surreal, what about the aftermath? Here it comes:

> *The Man in the Moon came down too soon*
> *and asked his way to Norwich,*
> *He went to the south, and burnt his mouth,*
> *by eating cold plum porridge.*

This is a children's rhyme, ancient and obscure in equal measure.

🛏 Today is **St Robert of Knaresborough's Day**. He lived from 1160 to 1218, spending most of his time in caves, with a stint living under a church wall at Spofforth, and a short sojourn in North Yorkshire at Knaresborough hermitage. His reward for being a pauper was sainthood; though in life he made several enemies by giving refuge to outlaws. His tomb at Knaresborough was a popular place of pilgrimage in the Middle Ages, as healing oil flowed from it. The site of the Knaresborough hermitage can still be seen.

25th September
Old Holy Rood Day

The Order of the Bath

In 1066 the downfall of England was brought about not by William, Duke of Normandy, but by Earl Tostig, who was responsible for sapping the strength of the English army before the grand finale on the south coast. Tostig had been Earl of Northumbria but had been kicked into exile after a popular uprising. He returned from his enforced foreign holiday with an army led by Harold Hardrada, King of Norway. And on this day in 1066 he took on his brother, the King of England Harold Godwinson, at the **Battle of Stamford Bridge** in North Yorkshire. Tostig was killed and the Viking-Rebel alliance defeated; but the English troops then had to rush back south to meet William the soon-to-be Conqueror the following month. Not surprisingly, the army was knackered, and that is why it lost to the Normans. Well, it's *one* of the reasons, anyway.

The outcome of the Stamford Bridge battle pivoted on an unorthodox tactic. The Tostig-Hardrada army had the upper hand, having sent a Viking of monstrous proportions on to the bridge, which he proceeded to defend single-handedly. But Harold sent a spearman down the river Derwent in a wash-tub. He was somehow able to drift under the bridge unseen, and harpooned the giant where it counts – his way of pointing out that it was a toll bridge.

This incident used to be commemorated at Stamford Bridge on this day, but disappeared at the turn of the century. Tub-shaped pies, called **Spear Pies** were baked and handed out in memory of the unnamed soldier who spear-headed the English victory. No one in the village can now remember the pies, but they are thought to have been made with upright pears, their stalks poking from the crust in a spear-like fashion. Then again, it is possible that the 'spear' part is a contraction of 'sparrow', and that the pies were originally a meagre repast for the poor. The entire 1066 incident may have been invented to explain the pies' name.

Today is **Old Holy Rood Day**. In parts of Scotland it is the night when the Devil poisons **brambles**. According to a traditional rhyme:

This nicht the Deil gangs ower them a'
To touch them with his pooshioned paw.

They shrivel up, and you can no longer harbour thoughts of bramble jam, for to eat any of the *pooshioned* fruit will cause worms to gnaw away your insides. The story is a way of formalising the end of the so-called **Blackberry Summer**, the period in which the fruits are ripe. In England, the Devil does this bramble trick at Michaelmas.

© On the last Wednesday in September, **Frome** in Somerset has its **Cheese Show**, presided over by the Frome District Agricultural Society. Setting it apart from other such gatherings, the competing cheeses are ceremonially rolled down to the river and given a good ducking. The event began only in 1877, but is a descendant of the old Frome Fair, which dates from the 13th century. At the peak of farmhouse cheese-making, the show attracted almost 500 different types of cheese; these days there are fewer than 100 entries, and most come from factories.

26th September

Inter the Dragon

Today in 1449 a black dragon from Keddington Hill, Suffolk, and a red dragon from Ballingdon Hill in Essex fought tooth, claw and fiery breath near Little Cornard in Suffolk. The monsters fought for an hour in Sharpfight Meadow (now called Shalford Meadow), until the Essex dragon got the upper hand, and both contestants retreated to their corners to lick their scales. The Essex dragon won on points.

The meadow in which they fought was the place where Boadicea and her Iceni army defeated the Roman Ninth Legion from Colchester. The **dragons' fight** may be a symbolic echo of this battle, or some other local skirmish. Then again, it has close parallels with an old British myth of two battling dragons – a red one representing the indigenous Celts (the Welsh) and a white one usually identified with the invading Saxons.

According to the myth, the arrival of the two dragons, coincided with an outbreak of plague across the country. King Llud sought counsel and acted on the bizarrest advice available. He calculated the exact centre of his kingdom, near Oxford, and dug a hole there, into which he placed a bowl of mead underneath a silk sheet. The brawling dragons then manifested in mid-air, locked in battle. But after a while they grew tired, and to conserve energy they changed into small pigs. They fell into the silk sheet, which in turn sank into the bowl. The pigs drank the mead, fell into a drunken sleep, and were tied up in the silk. Sheet and dragons were buried in a chest at the hill fort Dinas Emrys near Beddgelert in Gwynedd. And the plague vanished.

Many years later, 5th-century King Vortigern tried to build a castle at Dinas Emrys, but the building kept falling down. He sought the advice of the boy-magician **Ambrosius Aurelianus** (also known as Emrys Gweldig, and often claimed to be one of Merlin's many alter-egos), who revealed that the dragons were still alive and well, battling in a lake beneath Dinas Emrys. The white one seemed to be winning, and that meant a time of hardship for the Britons; but eventually it was driven back by the red dragon, suggesting ultimate Celtic victory over the Saxons. This convoluted and ambiguous parable was interpreted as a prediction of events a thousand years later, when the Welsh Tudors took to the throne.

🎲 Ambrosius managed to calm down the feuding pig-dragons, and he also interred his treasure on the same spot at Dinas Emrys for safe keeping. He prophesied that the bounty would be revealed to a blond person with blue eyes, but he neglected to say which one. For those with Aryan looks the mountain and the hill-fort may be worth a visit: if a bell suddenly rings out and a door appears in the rock, then your luck is in.

© **Masham Sheep Fair** was revived in 1986 after several decades in the wilderness. It now takes place on a Saturday and Sunday in September, usually towards the end of the month. At its height last century it attracted over 750,000 sheep to this corner of North Yorkshire. The scene was so crowded that several of the animals sought refuge on the low-lying roofs of Masham village, presenting a bizarre two-tier landscape of woolly ruminants. These days the animals are on show in much smaller numbers, along with demonstrations of everything sheep-related, from knitting their wool to eating their chops

27th September
St Barry's Day

Burying Barry

Attempting to invade England is a custom in which many have dabbled over the years. The last successful contestant was **William of Normandy**. William and his troops disembarked at Pevensey Bay, Kent today in 1066; while poor Harold and his men, weary from the Battle of Stamford Bridge, rode south to meet them.

Racial stereotypes are happily confused by the fact that William was legitimately related to the previous King, Edward the Confessor (William being the illegitimate son of Robert Duke of Normandy, one of Edward's cousins), who had promised him the succession in 1051. William also gained the fair-weather dynastic support of Harold in 1061. Only on his deathbed did Edward renege and tell Harold that the throne was his. Harold, meanwhile, was a Godwinson, a Viking family related to Edward in theory rather than by genetics: their respective fathers had a wife, Emma, in common. And the Normans were, literally, the North Men, more Vikings, who had colonised that bit of France a few generations back.

🎲 Kentish folk say that they alone remained unconquered in 1066, hence the county's motto *Invicta*. The horse on Kent's coat-of-arms is also known as *Invicta*, as is the hobby horse used by some Morris-teams from the county. A stone at Swanscombe marks the spot where locals – disguised as trees – sneaked up on William, forcing him to give the county several concessions in exchange for his safe passage. Most durable of these concessions was the law of **gavelkind**, by which land was distributed to all the children of the deceased – under normal Norman law only the eldest male inherited.

© The **Statute Fair at Dunstable** is yet another event which was once an economic necessity, but is now all candyfloss and ghost trains. Its once important role in matching employers with employees long over, it is now an afternoon and evening funfair held on the last Monday in September at the Queensway Hall car park in Dunstable, Bedfordshire.

🎲 **St Barry** lived most of his life and died on Glamorgan Island in South Glamorgan. He was buried there, and his chapel became such a popular place of pilgrimage that the island was renamed Barry Island. He was also buried at Fowey in Cornwall. Saints are like that. These days Barry Island is best known as the home of a sprawling, permanent funfair boasting the latest rides and attracting its own more progressive pilgrims.

28th September
Michaelmas Eve/
Nut Crack Day

Peril Bainbridge

Virosidum was a **Roman fort** near present day Bainbridge in North Yorkshire. The Romans manned the outpost here from AD 80 until the beginning of the 5th century. The settlement was on the edge of the then massive forest of Wensleydale. In case of disorientation, or attack by a huge marauding cheese, the Roman soldiers carried large horns with them on their travels. Any hint that they were not on course for Virosidum after all, and they would give a blast on the horn.

Thus was born the local **horn tradition** of Bainbridge. In the Middle Ages the loud retort acted as a curfew call, warning anyone still wandering in the forest after dusk that the wolves were about to put their bibs on. The blast also served as a signal to douse all fires. In the 1500s the Metcalfe family, local squires, got a firm grip on the horns, and the tradition has continued in the safe hands of that family ever since.

©   Bainbridge gives three resonant blasts on the **Curfew horn** (of 19th-century buffalo origin), at 9 pm every day from September 28th to Shrove Tuesday. Each lasts up to seven seconds, and is pitched at top C. The Metcalfes still blow hot and cold, and these days they are popular at local weddings too, providing a festive, luck-bringing trump. The older cow horn is seldom used, having lost its mouthpiece, and being capable only of unpredictable farting noises. When not in service, the two horns can be seen in the town's 1445 *Rose and Crown* pub. The site of Virosidum is east of the town, and the old Roman road still runs southwest from here to Lancaster.

This is **Michaelmas Eve**, which had its own set of customs honouring the all-important Saint Michael. In the Hebrides, Michael was patron saint of the sea, taking on many of the attributes of the old sea gods. **Struan Micheil** was baked for him today – a cake made from samples of all the locally grown cereals, mixed with butter, eggs and sheep's milk and cooked in a lamb's skin over a fire of bramble, rowan and oak. The cakes were marked with a cross, and a piece was thrown on the fire afterwards to pacify the Devil. There were then special Michaelmas Eve dances, and sometimes a mumming play in which the principal, killed-and-resurrected character was, unusually, a woman.

A **lamb** used to be killed and roasted in Scotland on this night in Michael's name. The animal had to be an unblemished young ram to satisfy the all-powerful angel-saint – he was known as the God Michael in parts of the Highlands and Islands.

In Lincolnshire Michaelmas Eve **bonfires** were lit today, and seed was scattered on the land for the birds to forage. This brought luck to the farm.

In Surrey tonight was also called **Nut Crack Night**. Nuts were opened and eaten during the church services, with no objections from the pulpit.

♱ Tonight the ghost of **Sir Walter Raleigh** perambulates around Sherborne Castle in Dorset. For Walter-wall information, see Raleigh's death-day, October 29th.

29th September
Michaelmas

The Goose with Ten Toes and the Cormorant of Death

The good folk of Boston, Lincolnshire, were horrified to see a **portentous cormorant** settle on the tower of St Botolph's church on this day in 1860. Compared to this, a colony of albatrosses would have been considered a welcome sight. The cormorant was in no hurry to leave Boston Stump – as the tower is called locally – staying there all day and into the next morning. At first the locals did nothing, knowing that to interfere with such an ominous bird was only likely to make things worse. But eventually its presence became too much to bear, and the church caretaker shot it.

The news of anticipated tragedy soon reached Boston. *The Lady Elgin* had sunk, taking with it 300 lives, including that of the local MP and his son. The knowledge that they had killed the harbinger of this disaster was small consolation for the town.

Michael does not fit the usual saints' profiles. For a start he is not a mortal, but an angel – the prince of all angels, in fact. And he is hedging his bets by being protector of both Christian and Jewish places of worship. It was Michael who personally evicted Lucifer and threw him bodily from Heaven. With this ultimate anti-Devil act, he has always been a reliable character to invoke for keeping demons at bay. Many pagan sites were reconsecrated to Michael after the coming of Christianity. Michael's Mount on Glastonbury Tor was evidently built there to counteract a strong pagan site with the best that Heaven could offer.

It is said that after Michael had sent Lucifer, rapidly turning into **Satan**, arcing out of heaven, he did not go straight to Hell. He landed first on Earth, smack dab in the middle of a bramble bush. For this reason Satan comes back every year on the feast of his tormentor and **blights the brambles** by spitting, breathing, and trampling on them. So, no brambling (aka *mooching*) after the 29th. In Scotland he brings the picking season to a close a little earlier, on Holy Rood Day.

Michaelmas was the end of Harvest, often the end of the farming year itself. And that meant that there were dozens of fairs, trading in people and livestock. Workers, in between farm jobs, had a relatively large amount of cash to spend at these fairs – hence the reference in a Norfolk folk song *The Jolly Waggoners*:

Now Michaelmas is coming, boys, what
*   pleasure we shall find,*
We'll make the gold and silver fly like chaff
*   before the wind.*

At Kidderminster, Hereford and Worcester, the now defunct fair had a Lawless Hour, called **Kellums**. It started at 3 pm when the old bailiff stepped down, and finished at 4 pm when his replacement was elected. During Kellums there were pitched fruit and veg fights, the bailiff-designate receiving much pre-emptive abuse with hurled apples, while the villagers bombarded each other with cabbage stalks.

Other Michaelmas Lawless pursuits included **bumping**: pouncing on a passer-by, hoisting him up, and throwing him at the next passer-by. There were many other local quirks at the Michaelmas celebrations. At Clixby in Lincolnshire, for example, **land tenure** was fixed by an eccentric annual gift to the King of a nightcap and a falcon.

On several Hebridean islands, **beach-racing** was the sport of the day. The horses were ridden bare-back, and the harnesses were made of straw. This was a survival of a sea-god festival. Michael, as mentioned yesterday, took on board many pagan aquatic attributes, and was the patron of horsemen and fishermen.

Up to the beginning of this century, there was a national set menu on St Michael's Day, and the only thing on it was **goose**. As an incentive not to buck the trend, it was said: '*If you eat goose on Michaelmas Day you will never want money all the year round.*' Once again, this is 'want' as in 'lack'. The French had an equivalent country-wide goose feast on St Martin's Day (November 11th), though the only bird that currently has a set day devoted to its mass slaughter is the turkey.

Geese became a temporary form of currency. They were given as a payment by the labourers to the farmer, and tenants to their landlords: a bribe to ensure continued good business relations. Lancashire called this gift-bird the **Goose Intentos**. Strictly speaking, a Goose Intentos fell due on the twelfth Sunday after

Pentecost, but was usually transmuted into a Michaelmas Goose. The origin of the name comes from the traditional reading given in church on the aforementioned Sunday. It ends with the words '*as bonis operibus jugiter praestet esse intentos*'. Somehow '*esse intentos*' became '*goose intentos*', and among those with even poorer Latin it was sometimes further corrupted to a '*goose with ten toes*'.

The notion of eating a goose today supposedly began when **Queen Elizabeth I** heard news of the Spanish Armada's destruction at sea. She was enjoying a goose supper at the time, on September 29th 1588, and ate one every year on this date in commemoration and celebration, urging others to do the same. Although once widely believed this is actually a wild goose tale. The Armada had been polished off by the weather in July, and even in 16th-century England, news did not take two months to reach the Queen.

In the West Country girls used to collect **crabapples** today. Not to make a sauce to accompany the goose, but to arrange the fruit into the initials of the men they loved, as a less than subtle clue that the named man should do the decent thing.

Michaelmas was once one of the calendar's big set-pieces; but apart from its continued use as the name of some colleges' autumn terms, it is really only thanks to **Michaelmas daisies** that the word survives in popular usage. An early rhyme assures us:

The Michaelmas Daisies, among dede weeds
Bloom for St Michael's valourous deeds.

◉ The daises can also be used petal-by-petal for the favourite 'he or she loves me/loves me not' routine.
♨ A clear, sunny show on the Michaelmas **weather** front means a fine but cold winter ahead. This notion is slightly contradicted by the Berkshire line: '*A dark Michaelmas, a light Christmas.*'

30th September

Banshee in Eden

On this day in 1399 Henry Bolingbroke became both parts of **Henry IV**. It was the day of his coronation, and he rode to the throne through driving rain. A contemporary account of his progress is enough to make a Barbour green – well, greener – with envy. It was said that he 'arrived dry, as God had preserved him from the elements'. He became the first of the Lancastrian kings.

Henry had deposed and displaced his cousin Richard II, partly because when Richard was on the throne, he had confiscated the family lands at Bolingbroke, Lincolnshire, which had belonged to Henry's father, John of Gaunt. Richard died as Henry's prisoner in Pontefract, West Yorkshire. In Shakespeare's Richard II he is murdered, but there is no firm historical evidence to back this up; though it is more than feasible that he was left to starve. His diehard supporters, however, maintained that Richard was still alive. The belief was particularly strong in Cheshire: many of the rebellions of Henry IV's reign, notably the Battle of Shrewsbury in 1403, were spurred by the conviction that the old King might be restored.

Banshees do the bulk of their shrieking when someone is about to die. They are the original kindred spirits, preferring to confine their ominous cries to their immediate relatives. The banshee at Crackenthorpe Hall in Appleby, Cumbria, had in life been Elizabeth Sleddall. In the mid-17th century she had been married to Lancelot, the head of the Machell family. Her husband's will was not to her taste, and she never let anyone forget it. Her ghost howled whenever the head of the family was about to die. In this banshee guise Elizabeth became known as **Peg Sneddle**.

In an attempt to dismantle this unwanted early warning system, the body of Elizabeth 'Peg Sneddle' Sleddall was eventually disin-

terred and buried in the River Eden with a huge granite boulder to hold her down. A priest then read the exorcism over her, and she was banished to the river for 999 years.

The boulder can still be seen in the river; but there were evidently get-out clauses. Peg Sneddle began appearing under a tree called the Sleddall Oak – now long gone – whenever misfortune was about to befall the Machells. The last Machell died in the First World War, but by then Peg had branched out into all-purpose haunting. Whenever the Helm Wind blew from the Cumbrian Fells she rode through the neighbourhood in a black coach – complete with six red-eyed, fiery-nostrilled long-tailed black horses, and accompanied by other black riders all uttering unholy shrieks. Indeed, Peg was personally linked to the elements. The Helm Wind is still said to be her bad moods manifest, while days of calm indicate that she has temporarily forgotten her grievances. And every year in September Peg Sneddle rises from the River Eden and enters the Hall through a blocked-up window.

Peg's origins may be a rationalisation of a more ancient spirit, probably a water deity, or a spirit of the elements. 'Pech' is lowland Scots for faerie – and much of north-west England used to be part of the Kingdom of Strathclyde. There are other watery Peg-spirits in the country: Peg O'Nell in the Ribble, and Peg Powler in the Tees. **Peg O'Nell** has a well at Bungerley Bridge near Clitheroe, Lancashire, and takes a life there once every seven years. A cat or dog is enough to slake her bloodlust, but in the absence of an animal sacrifice, Peg claims a human victim.

OCTOBER

1st October
St Mylor's Day

Heart of Gold, Foot of Bronze

St Mylor is the patron of Amesbury Abbey in Wiltshire. This is because the Abbey owned his relics but found it hard explaining exactly what he had done to get commemorated and canonised. Cue some gory but particularly inventive legend-making.

Mylor, said the rallying monks, was a disinherited prince. Evil uncle Rivoldus had murdered his father and now wanted to dispatch young Mylor. Fortunately some all-powerful bishops intervened and came up with a down-to-earth compromise. Rivoldus would not get to kill the Prince: instead, Mylor's right hand would be chopped off and replaced with one of silver. His left foot was also to be forcibly removed, and a bronze one put in its place. Unaware that he might well have grounds to lodge an appeal, Mylor accepted the bishops' verdict – along with the subsequent surgery plus metalwork – and hobbled off to a do-gooding life at an obscure monastery.

Here Mylor's precious extremities miraculously began working as well as their fleshy predecessors. Rivoldus decided that another even more drastic operation was in order, and decapitated Mylor. But as soon as Rivoldus touched Mylor's saintly head, he fell sick, and three days later he was dead. Mylor's head was taken to Amesbury where it remained for centuries, protected by a curse which warned that anyone who touched the relic would meet the same fate as Rivoldus.

🏛 It is claimed that the Norman abbey-church at Amesbury was founded by **Guinevere**. She retired there after her fling with Lancelot and her body is allegedly buried under the building. A medieval stained-glass window at the abbey is said to depict the once and former queen.

Until a hundred years ago, Rochford in Essex held its **Great Lawless Court** on the Wednesday after Michaelmas (September 29th). Legend says that it was a penance for plotters who conspired against the Lord of the Manor. Everyone involved had to gather in absolute silence, with only a single burning torch to light them. All business was done by mime, and all writing in coal. It might seem that there is a finite limit to what you can do silently with coal, but the Great Lawless Court somehow lasted from midnight right through until cockcrow. Like some protracted game of charades, noise gradually crept in, and in its latter stages late last century the Court had degenerated into a rowdy party. The real origin of the Lawless Court probably lies in the ancient folk-moots of the Anglo-Saxons. Villagers used to gather near an ancient tree to sort out local business and laws, and to make moot points.

The Sunday before October 2nd was **Tap-Up Sunday** on St Catherine's Hill near Guildford in Surrey. It was the one day of the year when you could broach a barrel and legally sell your own homebrew.

2nd October

Lust for a Goose

Sixteenth-century Matthew Wall was in a coffin and heading gravewards at Braughing in Hertfordshire. But in the churchyard the coffin was dropped, and Matthew was jolted back from death. He was understandably pleased about this rude awakening, and in his will he left £1 to keep the memory of the occasion alive. He is thus the only charitable zombie in British folklore.

© Matthew Wall's money was used to finance **Old Man's Day** in Braughing, near Bishop's Stortford. It still takes place at 4 pm today, unless the date falls at a weekend in which case it moves to 10 am. Local schoolchildren sweep Fleece Lane with brooms, and then congregate in the churchyard around Matthew Wall's grave. After some hymns and prayers, the church bells are tolled funereally, and are then speeded up in a joyous peal, symbolising Wall's ungainly resurrection. Originally 20 worthy children and 10 pensioners were given a share of the £1 to say prayers for Old Man Wall, but no one knows what has happened to the money from the bequest and the rector now funds Old Man's Day from his own pocket. Holes permitting, the ceremony will be celebrating its 400th anniversary in 1995.

© The first Thursday in October is the start of **Nottingham Goose Fair**. At its height some 20,000 birds were driven to the town, mainly from the Fens. These days the few remaining goose arrivals are overshadowed by a large three-day funfair at the Forest Recreation Ground.

According to a wildly improbable local legend, the name 'Goose Fair' does not derive from geese. The story goes that a farmer's beloved wife died while she was giving birth to their only son. The farmer brought up the child in isolation, hoping to instil knowledge and sound judgement in him away from society's many distractions. When the lad was 21, his father took him to Nottingham Fair for his first taste of the real world. The son was entranced by the fair's many women, finding these strange creatures remarkably alluring, even though his father said that they were 'nothing but silly geese'. At the end of the day the farmer offered his boy anything he wanted. Back came the predictable reply, 'Buy me a goose'. According to the tale the event was called Nottingham Goose Fair from then on. The radical alternative theory is that it is called Nottingham Goose Fair because there are lots of geese and it is held in Nottingham. You are the jury.

The fair featured a **Pie Powder Court** dispensing instant justice for on-the-spot offenders. The name comes from the French *pied-poudre* – dusty-feet – referring to the state of the many travellers who arrived.

There is a whole gaggle of Goose Fair songs, and a few rhymes. One of them sums up the noisy, cosmopolitan atmosphere:

'Twas Goose Fair cracked the merriest wheeze
Where Babel's babble filled the breeze.

3rd October

Dried Frog and Two Veg

At Penrhos Bradwn Farm on Anglesey today in 1872, workers accidentally unearthed a black pot sealed with a piece of slate. On the slate were the words 'Nanney Roberts'. Inside the pot they found a dried frog with 40 piercing pins. What they had stumbled upon was an **anti-witching device**, designed to stop Ms Roberts from doing some nasty deed or other. Debilitating the local witch was once a popular pastime. Pin-stuck hearts were a favourite charm, along with frogs and toads. More drastic self-defence included pulling the insides from a living dove and hanging them over the door. Since the witchery of Nanney Roberts has not passed into posterity, it may be assumed that the pot and frog worked like a charm.

© At 3 pm on the first Sunday in October at St Martin-in-the-Fields Church in London, small girls dressed like dainty Daleks appear with handfuls of vegetables. The parade is part of the annual **Harvest Festival of Costermongers**, when the **Pearly Kings and Queens** (or Donahs, as they call themselves) fish their button-bedecked whistles and flutes from the mothballs and do their Eastenders-meets-Come-Dancing routine.

The costermongers – fruit and veg sellers – enthroned their kings to protect their local patches, until licences were granted last century. The titles are hereditary, and the first Pearly King appeared following a huge shipment of then-trendy Japanese pearl buttons in the 1880s. The suits are sown in mystic patterns, with symbolic eyes, trees, animals, asteroids, anglepoise lamps, et cetera. St Martin's is filled with the costermongers' produce, and one of the Pearly Kings reads a Lesson. The Pearlies' previous church was St Mary Magdalene in the Old Kent Road, which was destroyed during an air-raid in the Second World War.

These Costermonger cavortings were meant to be one of hundreds of events taking place on this same day – the **Act of Convocation** in 1536 declared that henceforth all village Wakes and Feasts would be held on the first Sunday in October. Like many of the best Parliamentary rulings, it was completely ignored.

© St Mary at Hill in Lovat Lane, used to be the parish church of Billingsgate, London's ancient fishmarket. Even though the market has now moved to the Docklands, the merchants return to the church on the first Sunday in October for their **Harvest of the Sea Thanksgiving**. The church is filled with fish, a variety of species in a variety of colourful and complex patterns. The designs are the work of the men of Billingsgate, who also strew the church with nets which add to the salty atmosphere. Everyone is welcome, not just holy fishmongers and monk-fish; and afterwards all of the edible decorations are given to the needy.

Fish have inspired many fine old sayings, such as '*A fresh fish and a poor friend soon grow ill-faured*'; the enigmatic '*No herring, no wedding*' from the Isle of Man; and that Great Yarmouth warning for tea-makers: '*Big fish spring out of the kettle.*'

4th October
St Francis' Day

Low-Flying Saint

Just like Dr Doolittle, **St Francis** is remembered for talking to the animals. It was all part of the hermit-like state of innocent grace which he found after receiving the stigmata – the wounds of Christ – in 1224. His grace was so extreme that a monk once watched Francis levitate high into the sky, causing a hazard to medieval air traffic. More commonly Francis would float along just a few feet from the ground – a height designed to allow standing monks to kiss his toes as they bobbed past.

Swallows traditionally start their annual migration on St Francis' Day. They congregate on telephone wires, discussing the best way back to South Africa given the prevailing wind and political climate. Before migration was understood, the swallows' disappearance each winter was explained away by the theory that they hibernated in the mud at the bottom of ponds.

During their nesting season here, swallows bestow good luck wherever they settle. To shoot one in a barn means misfortune, and brings blood into the cows' milk. But some marksmen may have been tempted into killing the bird anyway. It was believed that each swallow contains two precious stones: one black, one red. The black one brings prosperity – but presumably not enough to offset the bad luck caused by shooting the swallow. The red stone cures insanity – which is handy, as you would have to be crazy to go prospecting for a swallow in the first place.

© If sheep are your preferred tipple, there is always the **Corby Glen Sheep Fair** near Grantham in Lincolnshire. A straightforward fair-with-sheep, it has been held for more than 750 years. At its late 19th-century peak George Bird described it as '*the largest shew of sheep, beasts and horses that has ever been seen on the ground before.*' Close to 100 carriages of animals came to the fair by train alone. Corby Glen's station closed in 1959, and the sheep-day returns have ceased, but the sheep now arrive by lorry and the fair continues to thrive. Its usual date is the first Monday after the 4th.

© Southampton in Hampshire has what is believed to be the oldest unbroken **Court Leet** anywhere in Britain. It appears to have been well established by 1549 when it first shows up in the records. It was a collection of freemen, getting together to hear complaints and try petty offenders. These days it has no legal powers, but exists as a free forum, an annual chance for locals to air their grievances – known as 'presentments' – and attempt to change things through force of public opinion.

The Leet meets at Southampton civic centre on the first Tuesday of October, and is preceded by a **Beating the Bounds**, with the sheriff and miscellaneous dignitaries parading round the city boundaries.

5th October
St Faith's Eve

Suburban Rodeo

Early this century, the *Ye Olde Cheshire Cheese* in Fleet Steet, London, had a parrot called **Polly**, who made such a good impression that she was invited to all the best parties. Polly joined in the 1918 Armistice celebrations by mimicking the sound of a popping champagne cork. She performed this feat 400 times during the festivities, and then keeled over. The fit did not prove fatal, and Polly lived to the ripe old age of 40, making national headlines when she went the way of all feathers in 1926.

On the first Monday in October, even after Polly's demise, *Ye Olde Cheshire Cheese* used to open its **Pudding Season** with a gigantic pie. The recommended cooking time was 26 hours, and in 1775 the pie consisted of beef steak, larks, mushrooms, spice and gravy under pastry. Larks were sometimes ousted by a vague ingredient called 'plover birds'; but during its latter stages, following a brief revival in 1954, the larks were back, in a mammoth concotion featuring kidneys and oysters. Only the manager knew the recipe, and he omitted to commit it to posterity.

© The first Monday in October is also now the date of the **Wibsey Horse Fair**, held just off Fair Road in the former village of Wibsey in West Yorkshire:

> *I'm collier Jack, through Wibsey Slack, I'm allus praad to tell*
> *That few fairs in old England can Wibsey Slack excel;*
> *There's plenty raam for cattle, and other sports we share,*
> *I'm allus praad t' go wi' my mates to t'seets at Wibsey Fair.*

There is not so much 'raam' for cattle these days as Wibsey is now part of suburban Bradford. The fair used to start on St Faith's Eve and last a week, but now the horse-trading is very limited, and the event is mostly a funfair. Wibsey used to be the spiritual home of horse-dealers across the land – '*a fine, jolly, plump, fat body of men, with their ruddy cheeks, smart appearance and jovial countenances*', according to a turn-of-the-century account. Their chief delights were cited as being good company, money, feasting and whisky. The fair was always as much a social as a business gathering.

Odder, but sadly no longer with us, the **Audlem Wakes** were held today in Cheshire. The first man to get drunk at the event was proclaimed Mayor of Audlem for a year. The Wakes' contestants embraced feats of sado-masochism – they drank scalding tea, smoked plantations of strong tobacco, then raced to finish a dish of hot porridge and treacle whilst sitting on the church steps. For abusing their insides in this manner they received a prize.

◉ This being St Faith's Eve, it is the night to see a vision of future love by baking **Faith Cakes**. Three women must turn the cake twice during baking. It is then cut in three, and each third is divided into nine morsels. These must

then be crammed through the wedding ring of someone married for at least seven years. The resulting mess is then eaten whilst saying:

> *Oh good St Faith be kind tonight, and bring to me my heart's delight*
> *Let me my future husband view, and be my vision chaste and true.*

Hang the ring near your bed, and you will dream of Mr Right. Or Mr Kipling.

6th October
St Faith's Day

All the King's Horses, Some of the King's Men

Sir Ingram Hopwood could not wait to get home after the Battle of Wincey, Lincolnshire, on October 6th 1643 in the Civil War. It was a tough tussle, but afterwards his horse did him proud, galloping all the way back to Horncastle. But there was to be no warm welcome for their master from the Hopwood household. Sir Ingram had been decapitated during the battle, and his family were made all too aware of this when the horse arrived with his headless body still in the saddle. Oliver Cromwell had great respect for the man, and had (most of) him buried with all honours, in spite of the fact that Sir Ingram had fought for the King. Whereas Sir Ingram's body remained active after he had lost his head, Cromwell didn't lose his head until long after he had ceased to be active – in 1660 Restoration-fever led to his peacefully-buried body being exhumed and posthumously beheaded.

🛏 There is a monument to Sir Ingram Hopwood in St Mary's church at Horncastle in Lincolnshire. An inscription says that he '*paid his debt to nature . . . in the attempt of seizing the arch-rebel in the bloody skirmish near Winceby*'.

If all went well with the Faith Cakes yesterday, women should have awoken today knowing what their future husbands will look like. The cake is St Faith's symbol as a result of her being a 3rd-century grilled virgin, martyred over a slow flame until golden brown. Devotion and charred-black humour are close bed-fellows in these cases.

🛏 The **Virgins' Crowns** at St Mary's church at Abbots Ann, just outside Andover in Hampshire, used to be blessed during the St Faith's Day service. The ceremony has long ceased, but Abbots Ann remains the one place in Britain where such crowns are still awarded. The Virgins' Crowns commemorate unmarried women and men '*of unblemished reputation*', who were born, baptised, confirmed and buried in the parish. After the death of a local 'virgin', a hazel-wood garland is decorated with paper gloves, a symbolic throwing-down of the gauntlet to any who would disparage the character of the deceased. Each crown is suspended from the church gallery for three Sundays, and if there are no challenges, it is hung from the roof of the church until such time as it falls apart. St Mary's has about 25 crowns attached to its roof, dating from 1716 to 1978, when the latest one was awarded. To date, the vast majority of crowns have been awarded to women, but men can qualify if they fulfil all the criteria.

7th October
St Osyth's Day

Not Tonight, Deer

William Davis, riding home through Hampshire, lost all his sense of direction. It was dark and he was galloping at full stretch when he heard the distinctive sound of Twyford church bells, but coming from an unexpected direction. He pulled sharply on his reins, just in time to prevent horse and rider from plunging into a quarry. Saved by the bells, he made his way home safely. So grateful was Davis that in his will of 1754 he left a massive £1 to fund an annual bell-ringers' peal-and-meal.

© Given the limited clout of £1 in the nation's supermarkets, Twyford's feast is now somewhat scaled down. But the **Lost in the Dark Bells** are still rung today in memory of William Davis.

☉ Tonight by invoking **St Osyth**, hearth and homes can be kept free of calamity in the year ahead. Last thing before bed, rake the ashes in the grate and mark them with a cross. A prayer should then be offered to the saint to protect the house from 'fire, water and all other calamities'. You can then drift into a peaceful and protected sleep. The custom originates at Aylesbury and Quarrendon in Buckinghamshire.

St Osyth was a royal Essex-woman, the wife of the 7th-century King Sighere. Despite having a son by Sighere, Osyth is legendarily chaste – determined to quit courtly life for a nunnery, she repeatedly fended off the King's amorous advances. Osyth did not battle lusty Sighere single-handed. Every time the King got the horn, he got the horns – a ferocious giant white stag appeared to ward off his heartfelt, hart-fought assaults.

🗓 All this belated purity did not help Osyth in the end. She was captured and beheaded by pirates, but did not die until she had carried her head to the spot at which she wished to be buried, a full three miles away. Her place of murder, Chich, is now called St Osyth (in Essex), and has a ruined priory which contains Osyth's shrine. Head not included.

So what does this hart-over-head chaste mother have to do with the Osyth who can be evoked for home-insurance tonight? Nothing – scholars reckon that two completely different saints got muddled centuries ago, and ended up sharing the same name and several of their best stories. But as long as she protects the house from everything, who cares?

8th October
St Keyne's Day

Keyne-Stone Cobras

St Keyne was one of the 15 offspring of 6th-century King Brychan of Wales. The family was collectively responsible for christianising South Wales and Cornwall. When Keyne turned up at what is now Keynsham in Avon, she was given a cool reception by a local Lord of the Manor, who did not want an outbreak of religious fanaticism in his neighbourhood – and certainly not a crazy new meek-shall-inherit-the-earth cult like Christianity. So when Keyne asked for some land as her preaching HQ, he granted her a scabby acre plagued by enough venomous snakes to keep all would-be followers at bay. Keyne was not deterred. She dashed off a couple of prayers, and the snakes turned to stone. The large number of fossil ammonites around Keynsham are said to be serpent proof of Keyne's petrifying powers.

🗓 St Keyne's Well at St Keyne in Cornwall offers an interesting prize to newly-weds. The first of the couple to drink the water after marriage will be the boss in that particular union. The 19th-century Poet Laureate Robert Southey's ballad *The Well of St Keyne* tells of a groom being outsmarted by his bride:

I hastened as soon as the wedding was o'er
And left my good wife in the porch,
But i'faith she had been wiser than I
For she took a bottle to church.

Similar marital mastery can be gained from the stone seat in the castle at St Michael's Mount. The mere presence of the great St Keyne is said to have given both sources their powers.

Sadly for the saint, none of these tales appear to be anything other than apocrypha. The one certain fact is that she had nothing to do with Keynsham, which is derived from 'Caega's hamlet'.

Watch out this month for low-flying **weather**. There are few finer weather rhymes than:

A good October and a good blast
To blow the hog acorn and mast.

More straightforwardly, a harsh October means a mild January and February. In Kent they say that there are at least 19 fine days this month, which is handy for beer-fans because:

Dry your barley in October
Or you will perforce be sober.

And above all, don't forget the dung:

In October dung your field
And your land its wealth shall yield.

9th October

Stubbling Geese with Prong and Flibberts

Walton Hall in Stratford upon Avon has the best **ghosts** in the town. A lady of the house once had a fling with a stray member of the royal family. The couple, limbs akimbo, were caught by the irate, armed husband. The Lord of the Hall discharged his weapon at the fleeing princeling, but only succeeded in killing the royal white horse (what it was doing in the bedroom is unclear). Nine months later the now disgraced lady gave birth to a son. Deranged and prone to fits, the child was locked in the west wing of the building and died in his youth.

✞ Every five years on October 9th a ghostly white horse gallops across the lawns of what is now Walton Hall Hotel. And as a more permanent feature, the spirit of the deranged son roams the bar and library, in a calm and sometimes playful mood. His tantrums only occur in room 117 – said to have been the site of his imprisonment – where he sometimes scatters the contents of the wardrobe across the floor, giving the occupants an unexpected early morning call.

© The second Wednesday in the month is the chief day of the week-long **Tavistock Goosey Fair** in Devon. The event gets by without geese these days, apart from on the Wednesday, when the birds turn up at the cattle market. Formerly the geese arrived by the thousand. They were in prime condition for their trip to the fair, having gone 'a-stubbling' after harvest, feeding on all the dropped grain in the fields. Geese travelling from afar were 'shod' before the journey, walking through warm tar to reinforce their feet. On arrival there was much competition for the most prominent pens, to show off the geese to the bidders.

The pubs of Tavistock habitually removed their doors for the fair, enabling barmen to eject the many drunks with greater ease and less damage. The song *Tavistock Goosey Fair*, written early this century, concentrates on two men who arrive following a grey mare, Widecombe Fair style; and in fact Jan Stewer, moonlighting from Widecombe, puts in a brief appearance. Unlike the Widecombe song's unhappy ending, with the mare dying of exhaustion, the Tavistock ballad finishes off with: '*'Er kicked the tap to flibberts and 'er trotted off alone.*' The song has the rousing but slightly more comprehensible chorus:

And it's oh, and where you be a-gwain, and
what be a-doin' of there?
'Aive down your prong and stap along to
Tavistock Goosey Fair.

'Aive' means 'heave', and a prong is the stick used to chastise the geese.

10th October
Old Michaelmas/
St Paulinus of York's Day

Horning Has Broken

St Paulinus was riding on an ass at Fonaby near Caistor in Lincolnshire, and from the rumblings and gurglings beneath him he realised that his ass was hungry. He then spotted a smug farmer with a very full sack on his back. St Paulinus cantered across and asked if he could have a handful of grain from the sack. 'Sack?', said the farmer. 'This isn't a sack, it's a stone'. 'Then stone it shall be', responded the saint; and, in one of the more petty and pointless miracles on record, divinely transmogrified the sack of grain into a stone, known locally afterwards as The Sack Stone. A lesson in manners for the farmer, but not much help to the hungry ass.

The Sack Stone stood, rather awkwardly, in the middle of a field. There are many local tales of attempts to move it, all of which end in death or disaster. When nearby Pelham's Pillar was being erected in the 19th century, a mason took a piece of the Sack Stone to make a model of the pillar. He fell from the real thing and broke his neck. In 1914 the Sack Stone ominously split into three pieces. Days later the First World War started. The prediction of global conflict, and the split, seemed to have drained the Stone's power, and it has now been shoved to the edge of the field.

Old Michaelmas' **Weyhill Fair** in Hampshire was a huge sheep market, also specialising in horses, cheese, hops, and – in literature – women. As 'Weydon-Priors' Fair it is the place in Thomas Hardy's *The Mayor of Casterbridge* where Michael Henchard sells his wife. The fair's origins lie in early Norman times; but despite having survived both World Wars – the death of many customs and old events – it finally petered out in the 1950s. At the *Weyhill Fair* pub – formerly the *Star Inn* – there is now talk of reviving the fair and its central event, the **Horning the Colt** ceremony. Shepherds used to gather at the *Star Inn* for a Horn Supper. Initiates, known as Colts, had to wear a headpiece consisting of two horns and a filled ale-cup, while the other shepherds sang, with slight variants:

Swift is the hare, cunning is the fox;
Why shouldn't this little calf grow up to be
an ox?

To get his own living among the briars and
thorns,
And die like his daddy, with a great pair of
horns!

The Colt then drank the ale and had to buy half a gallon for the others.
🏛 The pub used to have a set of these horns; but the only known pair are now in Andover Museum, and a wondrous strange sight they are.

11th October
St Canice's Day

Bans, Bands and Bandits

The 6th-century **St Canice** was an Irish abbot who spent much time on the remote islands of Scotland. His chief base was at Inchkenneth on Mull. A pal to all animals, he none the less tried to clamp down on their bad habits. He once formally admonished local seabirds for chattering on Sundays, and he banished all mice after they were caught nibbling his sandals.

In the 16th century, the area around Dinas Mawddwy in Gwynedd was terrorised by outlaws – **the Red Bandits**. Local sherriff, Baron Lewis Owen, finally captured most of the gang and, despite pleas from the mother of one of the condemned men, they were executed. The mother cursed Lewis, baring her breasts and saying that others who had suckled there would bathe in his blood. They did. The sherriff was horribly murdered on this day in 1555, ambushed by the woman's other son – one of the few Red Bandits who had managed to elude capture.
🏛 A mound where several Red Bandits were buried can be seen on Rhos Goch, a hill two miles from Mallwyd in Gwynedd.

It was today in 1216 that **King John lost his crown and jewels** whilst crossing the Wash. There have been numerous supposed sightings of treasure down the centuries, and some optimists continue to dredge the waters looking for them, but so far nothing definite has surfaced.

© In 1490 the extensive restoration of fire-damaged Sherborne Abbey of St Mary in Dorset was completed when masons' foreman Teddy Rowe finished the fan vaulting. There was only one way to celebrate – Teddy formed a cow's-horn band and embarked on an epic, tuneless, all-night concert. And for more than 500 years **Teddy Rowe's Band** have continued to create annual calamitous cacophony; marching about the town augmented by bugles, dustbin lids, pans, rattles and kettles.

Sherborne's **Michaelmas Fair** is held on the Monday after October 10th, and the night before is when Teddy Rowe's Band play. None too popular with the law – especially as there are impromptu 'warm-ups' on Sherborne's streets for a month beforehand – there was even a Band ban in 1963. But they still go on shattering the Sunday night peace, preparing locals for the fun of the fair to come, redefining the boundaries of thrash metal music. The Band's performance is preceded by a hint of the oddness to come – at midnight the Abbey bells strike 13. And a 15-minute 4 am peal to revive anyone who *did* manage to nod off used to bring things to a rousing climax, until it was deemed too noisy even for Sherborne.

Also called Pack Monday Fair, supposedly after the packing away of the masons' gear in 1490, it is now mostly a funfair, but an 1826 list of its delights includes: '*the learned pig, the giantess and dwarf, the menagerie of wild beasts ... Mr Merry Andrew cracking his jokes ... Rebecca Swain with her black and red cock ... pricking in the garter ... raffling for gingerbread ... the Sheffield hardwareman, sporting a worn-out wig and large pair of spectacles.*'

12th October
St Wilfrid's Day

Rights Said Frid

Hexham's **Frid Stool** (also known as the Frith Stool) has chilled the buttocks of bishop, king and vagabond alike. St Wilfrid's were the first pair, in the 7th century. He persuaded Rome to give Hexham the rights of sanctuary in about 675. From then on, anyone within a one mile radius of the Frid Stool was immune from persecution and prosecution. The boundary was marked with crosses, and anybody manhandling anyone within this area was fined. Yanking someone off the Frid Stool itself was even more serious – it meant instant excommunication. Fair enough for those seeking to avoid unjust oppression or unfair laws; but the sanctuary tended to have most appeal to out-and-out criminals, and Hexham became a neutral zone for wrong-doers. Its powers were set in stone almost a thousand years before James I put an end to the silly state of affairs by bringing the Frid Stool back within his jurisdiction in the 17th century. Frid, by the way, means *peace*; and the stool can still be seen at Hexham Abbey in Northumberland.

© **Redruth Goose Fair** used to take place today. Charitably, the poor of the town were served a hot meal of goose or other meat. Less charitably, they – along with many other labourers up and down the land – had to present a goose to their master around this time of year, at Michaelmas. So what they ate was a portion of what they had to give up.

Stratford-upon-Avon holds its **Mop Fair** today, unless it is a Sunday in which case the festivities are held a day early. At the opening, the fair's charter from 1216 is read, stating that the event was founded at a time '*when the mind of man runneth not to the contrary*'. Slices of roast ox are sold to the public: the beast is cooked whole in a specially constructed open-air brick oven. The mop part – the hiring bit of the fair – came to the fore after the Black Deaths of the 14th century had decimated the workforce. The event is now a funfair, but a big one, with many Stratford streets closed and much of the town centre engulfed by stalls and rides. In case Mop Fair hirings did not work out, there was often a **Runaway Mop** held shortly afterwards to give the disgruntled new employees a second chance. The one at Stratford is a rare survivor. It has also transmuted into a funfair, and now takes place a week after the Friday following the much bigger Mop Fair.

🕯 **Jane Seymour** goes walkabout at Hampton Court today, the birthday of her son Edward VI. Dressed in white, with unflickering candle and glowing face, she has been the cause of one or two premature resignations amongst the Court staff, allegedly. For more about Jane Seymour, see 24th October.

☕ One of the most straightforward, not to say dull, pieces of **weatherlore** is attached to today. A west wind on October 12th indicates a spell of fine weather ahead.

13th October
St Edward
the Confessor's Day

Rufford Deal

In 1850 the Rufford Abbey estate near Mansfield in Nottinghamshire was besieged by poachers. These poachers were not interested in catching any game – the traps they laid on October 13th were purely symbolic. **Rufford Park** had been common land, part of Sherwood Forest. The newly-passed Enclosures Act had transformed it into private land surrounded by fences and *Keep Out* notices, and the locals were robbed of their hunting rights. As the subsequent song *The Rufford Park Poachers* put it:

A buck or doe, believe it so, a pheasant or a hare
Were put on earth for everyone quite equally to share.

The poachers' demonstration on that day was not a peaceful one: 10 gamekeepers tried to keep them out, and a pitched flail-and-rock battle ensued. One of the keepers, William Roberts, died of a fractured skull. Four of the poachers were put on trial and transported for 14 years. The one accused of causing the death wound had alibis which proved that he was elsewhere, but the court refused to call witnesses. Rufford Abbey Park is still closed to the public – a somewhat poignant postscript.

What remains most memorable about **Edward the Confessor**'s life (1003–1066) is his death. For starters, it was prophesied. At Havering in Essex the devout Edward met a man seeking alms, and the king offered him a ring. The same man was later spotted in the Holy Land. He gave the ring to some passing pilgrims saying that he was John the Evangelist and that they should return the ring to Edward as the king only had six months to live.

Six months later in January 1066, as Edward lay on his deathbed – with the ring presumably nearby – he made a decision that was destined to up tapestry production in northern France and lead to several major skirmishes (see tomorrow). He reneged on his controversial naming of distant relative William of Normandy as heir, switching to his own brother-in-law Harold. When William gained the throne he might have been expected to bear a grudge

against Edward for this change of sides. Instead William I helped build his predecessor's reputation as a holy man, and Edward the Confessor eventually became Patron Saint of England – a title which he held until ousted by the mythical George in the 15th century.

From the time of Edward the Confessor until the reign of Queen Anne in the early 1700s, it was believed that monarchs could cure scrofula, **'The King's Evil'**. The ceremony involved the laying on of hands, and the gift of a gold necklace which the scrofula sufferer kept in order to ward off further outbreaks. Feigning scrofula was a risky but popular way of getting a solid gold medieval tax rebate.

🛏 St Edward's resting place is in Westminster Abbey, which he helped to found and fund. The tale of the ring can be seen in stained glass at Ludlow church in Shropshire.

14th October
St Selevan's Day

And All That

October 14th was the date of the **Battle of Hastings**. 1066 was an eventful year. The ailing King Edward (see, by coincidence, yesterday) belatedly opted for Harold Godwinson as his successor, and the freshly crowned Harold was soon at war. Vikings and rebels in the north forced his Saxon army to march to battle at Stamford Bridge in Yorkshire. Harold's men won, but by now the main event was under way – William and a lot of Normans had landed at Pevensey Bay in Sussex.

Harold raced back to see off the invasion, but made multiple tactical boobs. His men were exhausted after the march from Yorkshire to Sussex. They desperately needed reinforcements. And their one advantage – they had encamped on easily defended high ground – was abandoned by Harold when he chose to rush into battle.

William's army was not huge: adverse weather had kept his reinforcements at bay. But still he managed to clobber the Saxons. Harold was killed; but the arrow-in-the-eye legend may be down to a bit of dodgy perspective in the Bayeux tapestry. After Harold's death there was a swift *Witan* (a meeting of the High Council) which placed Edgar Atheling on the English throne. Technically, no king of England has had a shorter reign, as Edgar's cowardly first act as monarch was to offer the crown to William. On Christmas Day in 1066, amid much burning and looting, William was crowned in London. It was the biggest social/ cultural/linguistic course-change in English history. No longer was it hip to be an Æthelstan or Byrhtric.

Helping to focus resistance against the Normans, a rumour persisted that Harold was still alive. He had been to Rome on a pilgrimage and was living as a hermit at Cheswardine in Shropshire while attempting to rally allies in Europe. The rumour lived on for a couple of hundred years.

The Norman Conquest was predicted by the eccentric Oliver the Monk of Malmesbury Abbey in Wiltshire. Gazing at the then-unnamed Halley's Comet, which manifested in 1066, he declared: '*I see thee most dreadfully, threatening the destruction of England.*' Oliver said this from his wheel-chair, for in 1010 he had made himself a pair of wings and leaped from a high-tower. One of the earliest English flying accidents, he plummeted to the ground and was crippled for life.

St Selevan was seemingly invented merely to explain the occurrence of two carved fish on a bench-end at the chapel of St Levan near Land's End in Cornwall. The story says that while fishing there, Selevan hooked two bream on one line. Odd; but Selevan just chucked the fish back. A few minutes later it happened again – two bream, one line. They were released a second time. The whole sequence happened a third time before Selevan gave up and went home. On the doorstep were visitors – his sister and her two sons. That, apparently, was what the fish had been getting at.

15th October

Cor Baby, That's Really Freaky

John Otway Wynyard appeared before his brother and one Captain Sherbroke in Canada on this day in 1785. John was looking a little peaky, and tottered towards the bedroom as if to lie down. Sherbroke and the brother followed him into the room, but he was nowhere to be found. This was – with hindsight – hardly surprising, as John was still in England at the time, on his deathbed. The phantom came calling at 4 pm, the precise hour at which John died several thousand miles away.

At this time of year **ploughing matches** used to keep the husbandry industry busy. The ones in Lincolnshire started around the third Wednesday in October. The matches were simply feats of mastery with horse and plough. The complicated bit was beforehand, getting the animal ready for its ordeal.

Horsemen had, and continue to have, clandestine societies with codes of Masonic complexity. And whereas Masons are now beginning to lower their guard slightly, **horsemen** continue to deny the existence of their own mysterious societies (see November 11th for the Horsemen's Word Ceremony). Among the most jealously defended secrets were the conditioning recipes, designed to lighten up even the heaviest heavy horse before the ploughing contests got under way. A month beforehand the animals would find strange things such as sulphuric acid and steel filings creeping into their feed amongst the oats and mangolds. The chief aim of these partly magical medicines was to keep the horses' appetites regular and healthy, while some ingredients were for flatulence or had laxative qualities.

One recipe to have escaped the shroud of secrecy includes Castille soap, tobacco, sulphur, and turps. Never look a gift horse in the mouth in Lincolnshire. Such concoctions were often made into balls, administered by grabbing the horse's tongue and ramming the ball to the back of its throat. It is not unknown for an overdose of such tonics to prove fatal.

© Now timed to catch the Monday of the school half-term holiday in October, the **Titchfield Carnival** attracts thousands to Hampshire for an event which used to climax with the burning of an effigy of the Earl of Southampton. The Earl incurred the wrath of Titchfield in 1610 when he began to charge boatmen for the rights to use the newly-built tidal canal which connected the village to the sea. The canal wrecked the local economy, and what began as a protest evolved over time into the ritual burning of a hate figure, and over even more time into an excuse for a party and bonfire. The Earl now escapes unscathed, but there is still a 7 pm torchlit procession which goes via the village bypass to the bonfire site, where the crowds are treated to some early fireworks. Titchfield closes its borders for the day, and all traders shut up shop – even the pubs. The streets teem with dancers, and the houses vie with each other for the best and most politically incisive decorations.

16th October

Bad Trip at Woodstock

In 1649 the Parliamentarians were consolidating their victory over the Royalists. Commissioners were installed at the Manor House in Woodstock, Oxfordshire. Among several acts that angered locals, their most notorious was the uprooting of the local King's Oak, which was chopped up for firewood.

The woodpile was the first thing to be attacked following the arrival of **The Royalist Devil** on October 16th. This devil entered the house in the cunning disguise of a small black dog, and was first seen worrying the Commissioners' beds. Before you could say 'poltergeist' the firewood was scattered, the beds were jigging about, assorted household objects were flying willy-nilly, candles were being snuffed, glass was shattering, and occupants were being doused with ditchwater.

Matters came to a head when one of the Commissioners saw a disembodied hoof kicking a candle. He struck at the hoof with a sword, but his weapon was snatched from him. No mean feat for a hoof. The man was pummelled senseless, and the other Parliamentarians immediately fled, keen to keep their Roundheads round. The haunted Manor house was deemed a no-go zone for humans, and it was knocked down soon afterwards. A stone marking the site of the house can be seen in Blenheim Palace Park, Oxfordshire.

© Today at the church of St Katherine Cree in London, the **Lion Sermon** takes place; though if the 16th is a Saturday or Sunday, the sermon leaps on to the Monday. It celebrates the exploits of the 1646–7 Mayor of London, Sir John Gayer. During a trading trip in darkest Syria he became separated from his companions. Along loped a lion with a distinctly supper-time look on its face. Sir John prayed to Daniel for deliverance from a fate worse than wildebeest. The lion took a few sniffs, decided that Mayor Gayer was not suitable fare, and prowled off. So happy was Sir John with this turn of events that in his 1649 will he left a sizeable gift of £200 for the poor, on condition that his heroic story would be told every year in the Lion Sermon. The original endowment was spent long ago; but members of the Gayer family pool together to pay the lion's share of the costs.

Sir John was a Royalist, and spent 1647 in prison for refusing to let Parliament use London funds for their Cromwellian aims. Even Daniel had to pass on that particular problem. Gayer is buried at St Katherine Cree – an illustrated brass plaque marks the spot, and sings his praises at great length.

☀ A sliver of **weatherlore** applies to this day. If there is no rain, there will be a dry spring next year.

17th October
St Luke's Eve

North, South, East and Lost

At the **Battle of Neville's Cross** today in 1346 a Scots invasion force under King David II took on the English army of Edward III. To gee up the English troops during the mêlée the monks at nearby Durham Abbey sang Mass from their highest tower and rang their bells. The Abbot promised to make this an annual open-air event if the English won. They did, and true to his word the victory was and is commemorated with a singing, ringing free-for-all . . . on May 29th. This was the date in 1660 upon which Charles II rode back into London, ready to resume the monarchy and pre-Puritan fun. Many old customs, including this one, gravitated towards what became a nationwide day of celebrations.

© As well as changing date the ceremony has changed venue, moving to Durham Cathedral. On May 29th a different anthem is sung from each of three sides of the Cathedral tower. No one sings from the west side – it is said that a chorister, perhaps straining too hard for a high note, once fell over the edge there and was killed.

◉ The Neville's Cross anthems are annual one-offs; but six nights of the week, all year, Durham still rings the **curfew** at 9 pm. This is a survival from medieval times, summoning wayfarers back inside the city walls. The bells are not rung on a Saturday as a mark of respect to a bellringer who vanished in strange circumstances on that day several years ago.

The Battle of Neville's Cross was fought in the Red Hills near Durham. It took its name from a local landmark, an elaborate stone cross set up by a member of the powerful Neville family. The cross was smashed during the Reformation, and only its stump remains. It is said that anyone who walks nine time round the stump and then puts their ear to the ground will hear the clamour of the 14th-century battle.

The special service held on a mid-October Sunday at Flamborough in Humberside is a rare example of a **Harvest of the Sea Thanksgiving** which had not sunk without trace by the 1960s. The church of St Oswald – a patron saint of fishermen – was decorated with crab-pots and nets, and lines of fish were hung across the nave. But by the late 1980s Flamborough's fishing fleet had shrunk to three flat-bottomed cobles, and the service was abandoned.

Last century such services were an annual essential for most fishing communities, and the festivities along the Dorset coast went on for a whole week. At Abbotsbury, having dined on bread, cheese, fish and ale the fishermen's demanding prayer was: *'The god who gave us this can give us more.'* The local lord also stood to benefit if their prayers were answered, as he was entitled to claim a percentage of their catch, including 'The Prize Fish'.

Prayers always accompanied the launching of the fishing boats; but sometimes the god simply refused to fill the nets. When the ensuing catch was too small to interest buyers, the fishermen had a democratic way of dividing up their spoils. The catch was separated, and a blind-folded man doled out the fish prizes randomly.

◉ Tonight is St Luke's Eve, another in a series of popular divination opportunities. As well as being an advance chance to try out the methods detailed on Hallowe'en, there is one method linked specifically with tonight. Sleep with a sprig of rosemary and a crooked sixpence under your pillow, and you will dream of your future love.

18th October
St Luke's Day

Cuckoo, Ox,
Whipped-Dog and Giant Toad

At **Glamis Castle**, there are at least half a dozen active spectres – including Macbeth. There is also a 'monster' spirit, said to be a deformed Glamis heir born on October 18th 1821 and officially written off as dead at birth. He was locked away, but occasionally escaped for a spot of terrorising over the next hundred

years. There have been many sightings. Some reports describe him as resembling a giant toad with the strength of a dozen men (or of a thousand smaller amphibians). Others paint him as a huge egg-shaped mass with tiny arms and legs. His life was pretty miserable; but the after-life of another of the Glamis ghosts is not much fun either. He sits in a room in the castle playing cards with the Devil until Judgement Day.

King John was having a post-hunt rest at a miller's house in Charlton. Mutually randy, John and the miller's wife were soon giving a whole new meaning to the words Charlton Athletic. In burst a madder than Mad Max miller, threatening to do things only matched since in the history of regicide by the slaying of Edward II. But when he discovered that the intruding John Thomas was a King John Thomas, the miller realised that he was threatening above his station, and – fearing for his life, rather than his wife – begged royal forgiveness. John not only forgave the miller, he also made him lord of a new manor, the limits of which were marked with a stick and two ox horns. He also granted the new lord a fair charter.

One of the country's oldest and oddest fairs, **Charlton Horn Fair**, Greater London, had a strict dress code: everyone came as King, Queen or Miller, with a set of horns on their head. These symbolised the cuckolding of the original miller – an old saying has it that a cuckold or cuckoo 'wears the horns'. Men dressed as women at the Horn Fair, and whipped genuine females with bunches of furze. In 1872 the fair had degenerated into an all-out orgy, and was suppressed.

It is probable that the story of King John being caught *in flourgrante delicto* was dreamed up centuries after the fair was first held, to explain away the abundance of horns at the event. Duller, but more likely to pass the folklore lie-detector test, is the explanation that the horns stem from the ox, symbol of St Luke. Since Charlton held its fair on St Luke's Day, they used his symbols; although there is always the chance that the celebrations had simply ousted an older, animal-sacrifice-based feast.

There was a second outbreak of St Luke's Day flagellations, in York. The 18th was **Whip Dog Day**, when boys whipped all the dogs that they could find. Cruel but straightforward. It was said that a dog once ate some consecrated wafer in York Minster, and that an annual punishment must be meted out to the entire canine race. In reality packs of wild dogs were a genuine problem – in some cities they still are – and today may have been the once-yearly communal dog-drive.

In the West of Scotland, notably at Rutherglen in Glasgow, today was **Sour Cakes Day**. The cakes were made of fermented oat dough, and were all the rage at Rutherglen's St Luke Fair.

☼ Today traditionally heralds a spell of warm weather: **St Luke's Little Summer**.

19th October
St Frideswide's Day

Treacle Mining

On October 19th 1645, a wedding party was being ferried across **Lake Windermere** in Cumbria from the Nab to the Ferry Inn. Over went the ferry, and the guests all drowned. This may explain the origin of the **ghost** which used to shout mock-distress calls across the Nab. The first phantom call came in stormy weather. A lone ferryman braved the tempest to answer the summons. He returned to the inn all wobbly and curd-coloured. He died the next day.

From then on – and many people heard shouts when they knew no one was at the Nab – the ferrymen ignored the calls. But the cries became so incessant that a priest was summoned to lay the spirit. He rather poetically sentenced it to lie in nearby Claife Quarry until such a time as men can walk over Windermere without wetting their socks; until horses can walk through stone walls; and for as long as ivy remains green. The ghost has laid low ever since.

▥ The newly restored **St Margaret's Treacle Well** is at Binsey in Oxfordshire. For hundreds of years it was famous for its healing properties. It appeared when St Frideswide prayed to Margaret for healing waters to restore the sight of the 8th-century Mercian King. Ælfgar was struck blind for lustily pursuing the chaste Frideswide, which makes her miraculous attentions all the more touching: she took pity on the King, successfully prayed to Margaret, and used the magical waters to cure Ælfgar. St Frideswide's grave and shrine can be seen at Christ Church Cathedral in Oxford. Unfortunately, during the 16th-century Protestant desecration her bones were accidentally but inextricably mixed with those of the wife of a Regius Professor of Divinity.

Treacle, in the sense of St Margaret's Treacle Well, means a curative ointment. The most famous type was Venice Treacle, a mixture of drugs and honey. It was the popularity of this singular mixture which led to 'treacle' being used as a general term for sugary syrups. This medicinal origin explains an otherwise baffling alternative name for garlic, 'country folk's treacle'. It also clears up any possible misunderstandings inherent in a 17th-century book which declares: *'The chief use of Vipers is for the making of Treacle.'*

Binsey also had treacle mines – pools of water with treacle-like algae. Oxford students used to send freshmen to bring treacle from the well and mines, insisting that it was as tasty as Golden Syrup. When former chat-show host Russell Harty was a teacher at Giggleswick Grammar in Yorkshire, a favourite trick of his was to take new students on a search for treacle mines. Their excavations were always successful, as Harty led the children to where he had buried treacle on the previous night.

♀ ▥ When **King John** died on this day in 1216 after over-indulging on peaches and ale at Swineshead Abbey near Boston in Lincolnshire, assorted wild stories sprang up. The best of them says that he roams through Surrey as a **werewolf**. This may indeed be the origin of the numerous stories and sightings – mostly in the 1960s – of a beast which was christened 'The Surrey Puma'. The werewolf John does most of his howling around Runnymede, where in human form he was forced to sign the Magna Carta, and sign away many of his powers, in 1215. A rotunda marks the site of the signing. Runnymede meadow is just south of the A308 between Windsor and Staines.

20th October

Dudley (No) More

Skulking Dudley, Lord of Clopton Manor in Northamptonshire, had a reputation for irritability which extended beyond death. A Richard III look-alike, his most famous squabble was with Richard De Hazelbere in October

1349. In version one of the story he picks a fight with De Hazelbere and decapitates him with glee. In version two Skulking Dudley is a coward, who decides to feign illness rather than face the man in a duel. To save family honour Dudley's daughter dons her father's armour and prepares to fight. Seconds into the duel she is down and almost out; but as De Hazelbere moves to finish off his opponent he sees her through a chink in the armour, and spares her rather than spears her. To round the story off, they get married.

The story does not end so happily for Skulking Dudley. He died after whipping one of his harvesters – the man turned round and sliced off the Lord's head with his scythe. After that Dudley's skulking was confined to moonlit nights, when his twisted hunchback figure could be seen roaming from the moat at Clopton to a nearby coppice. This unambitious bit of haunting continued until 1900 when, over-excited at the prospect of a new century, Dudley upped his profile. He began turning up more regularly and with greater menace. In 1905 the Cloptonians petitioned the Bishop of Peterborough and as many clergymen as they could find to lay the ghost. They did, chucking their candles into the moat at the end of the proceedings. Since then things at the manor have been Dudley dull.

© **Yarm Cheese Fair** in Cleveland used to shift 500 tons of all things cheesy until the turn of the century – the streets resembled a Giant's Causeway of cheese. In 1665 local boy Peter Bazire, who was living in Rouen at the time, asked his mum to go to Yarm fair to get him cheese '*as bigge as the moone*'. 1820 was the record year, when 683 carts each brought 1¼ tons of cheese to the fair.

The Gypsy traders, who with some justification claim to have been ignored and undermined by the local authorities, mourn the passing of the livestock-trading, following an official curtailment of the auctioneering in 1979. In its heyday Yarm had three chief trading days: horses dominated the first, with local Cleveland Bays being a speciality; cattle appeared on the second day; and sheep and cheese shared the limelight on the third. Shop windows were barricaded to protect the glass from the animals' horns. Small boys used to earn a few pennies by 'bullock-walloping': keeping the animals under control with sticks. 🔟 In spite of persistent opposition from local traders, the fair still takes place, usually starting on the Wednesday after the 18th. It is now

mostly a funfair, and culminates in a Riding of the Fair parade on the Saturday, led by the town council, and marked by the blowing of a four-and-a-half-foot-long 18th-century horn. The horn can be seen in a glass case in the town hall for the rest of the year.

The third Sunday in October used to be **Winter Sunday** on Shetland, a day of feasting. Cattle were brought to the byres for overwintering, and it was a last blowout before the austerities of winter.

21st October
St John of Bridlington's Day/
St Ursula's Day

Victory Virgin on the Impossible

British **Princess Ursula** was a devout 4th-century Christian; but the prince who wanted to marry her was a devout 4th-century pagan. Ursula was keen to hang on to her virginity and so she turned the prince down. Knowing that he might become insistent if she seemed too negative, Ursula said that she would look very favourably on his offer once she had been on a short holiday – say, three years or so. Amazingly the love-sick prince agreed. Ursula decided to flee the country along with 10 of her equally virginal girlfriends. They each collected 999 virgin women apiece and set sail in 11 cramped boats, like a prototype Virgin Airlines.

Storms blew them up the Rhine, and they took advantage of their course by popping their 11,000 heads into Rome to see the tombs of the saints. On the way back the Huns waylaid them at Cologne. Once again Ursula found herself being asked by a pagan chieftain if she would marry him, and for the second time she said no. But, for the first time, she was killed, as were her 10,999 companions. Angels, witnessing the carnage, came to the virgins' aid. But their timing was appalling. They scattered the Huns but failed to save any of the women.

Ursula became a saint along with her unknown associates. The punchline is that the story has gained its cast of thousands thanks to a faded Latin inscription telling of '11 martyrs' being misread as '11 thousand'. Cast your saint upon the water and it shall increase a thousand fold, as virgin number 7,436 used to say.

🔟 Ursula and entourage were expunged from

the official calendar of saints in 1969. But she can still be seen in stained glass at Trinity Church in York.

© ☉ 🏛 This is the main day for **Lord Nelson** commemorations. Wreaths are laid at Trafalgar Square in London, and the decks of the HMS *Victory* in Portsmouth are garlanded for the occasion. One of the *Victory* wreaths, made from laurel shaped into an anchor, comes from descendants of men who served with Nelson. There is an 8 am naval service on board the ship, during which Nelson's famous signal 'England Expects that Every Man Will Do His Duty' is hoisted using all three masts. The flags are still flying when the *Victory* opens to the public at 10 am.

In his day Admiral Horatio Nelson was the highest of heroes. Devonians believed that he was the reincarnation of Francis Drake. His against-the-odds victory on this day in 1805 at the Battle of Trafalgar, where he routed a combined French-Spanish navy off the Portuguese coast, was a turning point in the Napoleonic wars. The success was assured when Nelson insisted on nailing a horse-shoe to his ship's mast. Admiral Horatio's image was untarnished despite playing postman's knock with Hardy, and despite having a name that sounds half-cheer, half-sneeze.

The Nelson festivities in London and Portsmouth are increasingly popular, and in the early 1990s a 'Nelson Day' came close to replacing the May Day Bank Holiday.

The 11,001st saint of the day is **John of Bridlington**, who died in 1329. A miracle worker, he cured scores of people, including five dead men. His most famous exploit came when he walked across the raging sea during a tempest and dragged some fishermen to safety. If only he had been around for Ursula and Co.

22nd October

Earth Birthday

This is the big one. According to Jewish folklore today, in 4004 BC, **God created the World**. There are different versions in the Judaic tradition of how he did it. One widespread line of thought has him speaking everything into existence over six days. It is said that his last acts of Creation were the miraculous aspects of the the Old Testament, including the

grave of Moses (forever concealed); Manna (candy-floss from Heaven); and the mouth of Balaam's Ass (the Bible's answer to Mr Ed).

The second theory is that from the original Godhead, existing on a higher plane of reality, there came emanations which leaked down to the more mortal planes of existence. From these emanations crystallised the more straightforward bits of the cosmos, including the World; even though these bits were still highly complex, built to mystical and often inscrutable specifications. The Earth itself started with a single foundation stone, the *shetiyyah*.

The theory that paints God in the worst light says that he had a go at Creation, but did not plant the way it turned out. He got annoyed with these first efforts and smashed up a job-lot of creation, making our universe from the rubble. God is also humanised in the idea of *Torah*, a blueprint from which He works. He figures it all out for Himself and writes it down in black fire upon white fire, having neglected to create higher-plane-of-existence durable ink.

According to many of the legends which grow in the gaps between theologies, Creation left behind it residual hints of the Creative process. These can be discovered upon the Earth, and once found they will yield fantastic power. Alchemists and mystics have searched; but not knowing quite what they are looking for the success rate has remained around the zero mark. There are reports that traces have occasionally been found at the bottom of the fourth pint of Old Peculier.

☉ In the weeks leading up to November the 5th, bonfires have to be built. Nicking gates is not the way to win a neighbour's affections; and so it was that the organised fuel-collecting tradition was born. **Cob-coaling** was the North's version of this. It survives around Stalybridge and Dukinfield, just east of Manchester.

Children go from door to door singing cob-coaling songs and asking for lumps of wood, as well as money for fireworks. The Cob-Coaling song has the complex and erudite chorus:

We've come a cob-coaling, cob-coaling, cob-coaling,
We've come a cob-coaling for Bonfire Night.

23rd October

Ghosts of the Civil Dead

The **Battle of Edgehill** was fought today in 1642. It was the first big showdown of the Civil War. Several thousand died, and only the staunching cold of the night prevented many others from bleeding to death. On Christmas Eve in the same year, the whole battle was re-enacted. By ghosts. This spectral Sealed Knot was witnessed by dozens of people, and a year later by hundreds. The one-night-only phanto became such a reliable Christmas Eve fixture that even the King came to watch, and the residents of nearby Kineton – sacked by the Royalists – all attested to its accuracy.

♰ The battle went to Cromwell's lot, the Parliamentarians. Prince Rupert had made a tactical error which left his infantry at the mercy of the enemy. Rupert's ghost, on a white horse with accompanying pet dog, still charges around this bit of Warwickshire as penance.

♰ Other spectres are occasionally seen at Edge Hill. Wraith horses gallop across the terrain searching for lost riders. An elusive building called **the Red Barn** is said to drip blood from its upper storey, marking the place where a wounded Royalist bled away. The whole site has an atmosphere renowned for putting the wind up people and dogs alike. And every Christmas Eve the phantom players re-enact the battle, although this claim appears to be a little half-hearted these days.

⌂ © A monument near Kineton in Warwickshire commemorates the Battle of Edgehill, and local thoroughfare Red Road is named after the stream of blood which ran afterwards. On the Sunday nearest the 23rd at 10.30 am some 500 pretend Civil War veterans, the Sealed Knot, march to Edgehill from an army car park near Radway on the B4086. All are in costume, led by a cavalry division and followed by spectators. At the battlefield there is a service, and a wreath is laid at the monument.

Church penances were commonplace for what was termed 'ante-marital incontinence'. In other words, tasting the oats before the porridge is made; licking the spoon before making the cake; sucking eggs before your grandmother has told you to. On this day in 1785, unmarried Susannah Philips of Bishops Caundle in Dorset was caught having sex. She was made to stand in church during the service, dressed only in her white linen bed-sheet. The rest of the congregation were encouraged to scrutinise the stains, on sheet and character alike.

24th October

Tie a Red Ribbon Round the Old Oak Cask

Jane Seymour, third and favourite Queen of Henry VIII, died on this day in 1537, 12 days after giving birth to Edward VI. The labour was long and troubled, but Edward eventually came out through the usual channels. When the songwriters of the time got to grips with Jane's death, they decided that this was all too straightforward. In the most famous ballad, from 1560, Jane asks to have her right side opened, insisting that this is the only way for the baby to be born. Her husband disagrees:

> 'Oh no' said King Henry, 'That's a thing I'll never do;
> If I lose the flower of England, I shall lose the branch too.'

Despite his protests, Jane is opened up, and the baby is removed. But the Queen dies, twelve days earlier than she did in real life. In the final verse:

> There was fiddling, aye, and dancing on the day the babe was born,
> But poor Queen Jane, beloved, lay cold as a stone.

♰ It is thought that bad post-natal surgery was what really killed Jane Seymour. Her ghost still walks at Hampton Court, west of London, on October 12th, the day of Edward's birth. The song's poignant tune and theme of tragedy in the midst of celebration ensured that it remained a favourite with singers, and it is still common on the folk scene today. Marwell Hall at Owslebury, near Eastleigh in Hampshire, also boasts a Jane Seymour ghost. Marwell is where Jane and Henry got married.

© It is still the season of the **Mop Fair**, and today was when Dalton-in-Furness, Cumbria, used to hold its. The fair was opened by the Steward. Standing in the market place accompanied by two javelin-bearers with halberds (half spear, half battle-axe), his proclamation included a command not to 'bear any habiliment of war, steel coats, bills or battle-axes'. Presumably the halberd-men were exceptions. Ale tasters were then elected. Competition was tough, as their sole task was to visit all the local pubs and drink loads of beer. A red ribbon was awarded for the best ale, and a blue one for the second best. The worst was used to sprinkle on chips. On October 24th 1925, the ale-tasters did the rounds for the last time, but since then the event has been held unofficially, as an organised pub-crawl.

© Stratford upon Avon has its Mop Fair on October 12th, and on the Friday of the following week the same town holds its **Runaway Mop**. Formerly, this gave those dissatisfied with their new employment a second chance to find jobs and happiness. These days it is yet another excuse for a funfair, smaller than the main Mop, and confined to the area around Stratford's Market Place.

25th October
St Crispin and
Crispinian's Day

England 10,000; France 29

St Crispin's Day comes once a year; but **St Crispin's Holiday** comes round every Monday. Crispin is the patron saint of shoemakers; and shoemakers – along with many other tradesmen – used to take Mondays off, claiming that they were celebrating St Crispin, or even **St Monday**. The reason for the slack Monday is explained by the improbable story that somewhere within Oliver Cromwell's army lurked a shoe-maker called Monday. One morning Monday woke up in a bad mood and hanged himself. Cromwell was mortified and offered a prize for the man who could pen the best lines on the shoe-maker's demise. The winner was:

Blessed be the Sabbath Day, and cursed by wordly pelf,
Tuesday will begin the week since Monday's hanged himself.

Cromwell was so impressed that he declared all Mondays henceforth to be a holiday.

The **shoe-makers'** celebrations of their patron saint were heavily based on drink, as can be divined from the rhymes:

The twenty fifth of October,
Cursed be the cobbler who goes to bed sober;

and:

Now shoemakers will have a Frisken,
All in honour of St Crispin.

St Crispin's Day itself gained in popularity as a holiday after the Battle of Agincourt in 1415, where his name was evoked to rally the British to victory. Henry V and 9,000 English troops defeated 20,000 French. Shakespeare's claim that 10,000 French were killed but only four English nobles '*and of all other men, but five-and-twenty*', was touchingly patriotic, if numerically made up.

Many of the key Agincourt soldiers' families hailed from Sussex. Bonfires and fireworks used to light the Sussex skies tonight well into the 19th century. Notable for such celebrations were the villages of Slaugham, Cuckfield and Hurstpierpoint.

At Horsham in Sussex the most unpopular person was strung up in effigy form from St Crispin's Day until November 5th, when they deputised for Guy Fawkes on the bonfire.

Perversely, given the Agincourt link, Crispin and his brother Crispinian were Frenchmen, martyred in the 3rd century. Popular tales about them shipping over to Faversham in Kent are the proverbial load of old cobblers.

✟ Today's ghost-fix comes from the Hanoverian **George II** who died on October 25th 1760. His spectre shuffles about Kensington Palace in London, eavesdropping on royal rows and supposedly gazing at the weather vane to check the winds. He is forever awaiting a favourable breeze, bringing ships and news from Hanover.

26th October

Alfred – the Grate

King Alfred died today in AD 899. Records indicate that he was a hypochondriac, but it is hard to escape being whacked across the back of the head with an impression of the man's brilliance. He inherited the Wessex throne in mid-war, in 871, and scrapped with countless Viking armies. In 878, after the **Battle of Edington** in Wiltshire, he forced principal Viking Guthrum to accept Wessex terms, including a compulsory conversion to Christianity. By 886, Alfred was King of all England, with the Vikings getting the title deeds to East Anglia, provided they behaved.

Freed from war, Alfred the Great organised land and sea defences; knocked existing laws into acceptable order; gave the go-ahead to an ongoing historical document later known as the Anglo-Saxon Chronicle; and founded a system of learning in a previously illiterate country.

It is ironic, and humbling, that after Alfred's death at 50 the legend that keeps his name alive is a probably apocryphal, certainly trivial yarn about burning some cakes. The incident 'occurred' during Alf's down-and-out pre-Edington days at the Isle of Athelney in Somerset. A fugitive from the Vikings, he and his army were holed up with a woodsman and his wife. One day Alfred's hostess asked him to watch over the oven, and gave him an earful when the carbonised cakes appeared. The story did not appear until several hundred years after Alfred's time, and whatever symbolism it contains remains impenetrable.

� **The Danes' Stream** at South Baddesley near Lymington, Hampshire runs red in memory of a thousand Vikings slain there during one of Alfred's battles. Cynics say that the colouring is more to do with the dyeing effect of iron present in the soil.

☰ The **Blowing Stone** in a private garden at Kingston Lisle in Oxfordshire is alleged to be the one with which Alfred mustered his army. A blast on the stone has a range of three miles. Alfred's statue can be seen at nearby Wantage, his birthplace. His exploits are commemorated at Athelney in Somerset, where a plaque marks his pre-victory call to arms.

© On the last Friday in October, Colchester in Essex has its invitation-only **Oyster Feast**, the climax of its oyster season (see September 1st). This civic feast celebrates the time when Richard I (1189–90) gave the people of Colchester sole oyster fishing rights on the River Colne. Each feast gets through around 12,000 shellfish.

If after this seafood orgy the diners dream of oysters, it is hardly surprising. It is also good luck. But to lovers the dream means imminent marriage. The linking of oysters to love, and to supposed aphrodisiac qualities, is down to crude observation, the same reason as for fresh figs: they reminded the ancients of a certain part of the female body.

At Ovingham in Cornwall this was **Gwonny**

Jokesane's Day. A mock mayor was elected with the usual bevvying and rowdiness, and carted through the streets. The origins of Gwonny Jokesane – whether animal, vegetable or mineral – are unknown.

27th October
St Odran's Day

One in the Eye for Odran

St Columba was having problems with his new church on the Scottish island of Iona. The walls kept falling down. He knew of only one remedy: a human sacrifice. Someone would have to be buried within the foundations of the church. In a surprise career move, St **Odran** volunteered himself for the job. Odran was an old friend of Columba, and the two had many times debated the nature of Heaven and Hell. Now Odran was going to find out who was right.

Three days after the burial, with the church walls at last remaining intact, the curious Columba decided to see how his old friend was doing. His monks dug around and soon exposed Odran's head. Which began speaking. '*There is no wonder in death,*' Odran declared. '*Heaven is not as it is said to be; Hell is not what it is said to be. The saved are not forever happy, the damned are not forever lost.*'

Columba acted quickly before Odran could spill any more of the divine beans. '*Pile earth on Odran's eye!*' he cried. The monks obeyed Columba's command, and Christianity was denied an early input of rational revelation.

This is one of the most astounding of all the stories of the saints. Although ritual human and animal killings to protect buildings were common in many cultures, including Britain, they were not a feature of Christianity. So to have St Columba endorsing such sacrifices hints at this being an updated retelling of some earlier pagan myth. Odran's depressing insights into the afterlife are also distinctly out of synch with the traditional heaven-is-good, hell-is-bad divide. There is another toned down version of the tale, in which Columba dreams of the soul of Odran being fought over by angels and devils; but he wakes up before he can see which of the opposing forces wins. The cemetery on Iona is still known as *Reilig Orain*: Odran's Crypt.

© **Founder's Day at Durham Cathedral** is

on the last Wednesday in October, having moved here from the more logical January 28th, death-date of its 'founder' Henry VIII. The church had been monastic since it was established in 1093 – Henry merely reinvented it as a cathedral. Founder's Day was instigated by Queen Mary to honour the various princes and prelates who had come to Durham with open hearts and wallets.

This was the month for brewing the formidable **October Ale**, a beer so strong that it needed locking up. Home brewers often stored it in the barn to prevent unfortunate drinking accidents.

This did not impress **Dick Turner**, the first teetotaller. He was a stammering abstainer from Preston in Lancashire who died on this day in 1846. The word 'teetotal' itself allegedly entered the English language in 1834 as a result of one of his stuttering outbursts. Speaking against a call for moderation in drinking – which he felt didn't go far enough – Turner shouted: '*I'll have nowt to do with the moderation botheration pledge; I'll be reet down t-total, that or nowt!*'

28th October
St Simon and St Jude's Day

A Pear of Saints

A joint saints' day, for two saints who worked as a team. **Simon and Jude** were 1st-century Apostles on the early missionary rounds. One day, speaking in tongues somewhere in Persia, they were set upon with a falchion and a club, and so died.

In art they were often made to look a little silly: Jude holding a boat and Simon clutching a fish, like a postcard from Skegness. For years no one prayed to Jude because his name looked too much like 'Judas', and so it was later assumed that anyone on the saintly hotline to him must have exhausted the rest of the canonised canon. For this touching reason he became the patron saint of lost causes.

☀ **Weather** takes a turn for the worse on St Simon and St Jude's Day. It marks the traditional last gasp of the tail-end of summer, and the onset of wet and windy winter. In Wales it is the day when Satan, having already ruined the brambles over the border last month, does the same in the Principality. But oxen are not bothered by any of this:

On St Jude's Day,
The oxen play

In Bedford and the surrounding area **baked Wardens** were sold on the streets today. Before drivers everywhere petition Parliament for this to be revived, they should note that the tradition pre-dates the motor car. All over Bedfordshire today the cry used to go up:

Who knows what I have got?
In a hot pot?
Baked Wardens, all hot!

The answer to the first bit must have been 'everybody'. *Wardens* are Warden pears, which originated at Old Warden in Bedfordshire. Warden Pie was a variation on the fruity theme. The basic recipe is simple enough. Cook the pears in red wine with cinnamon and cloves. Eat whole, or cut up and make into a pie.

Today used to herald the start of nocturnal emissions from **the Bellman in Stamford**, Lincolnshire. From now until Christmas, on three days of the week he drove the town insane with his early morning cry of: '*Good morning, worthy masters and mistresses all – past one – fine morning!*' On his nights off, the Waits were wheeled out to play their instruments and maintain the guarantee of a silence-free life in Stamford. Only the Sabbath was exempted. The bellman and musicians were a survival of the old winter curfew – there to remind locals that it was night-time. They were salaried as part of the Alderman's troop of officials. Stamford's Alderman wielded great authority, immune from the dictate of a Sheriff. He commanded his own militia and had other quirky privileges. His powers came to an end in 1835 under the regularising, reforming regime of the Municipal Corporation Act, which formed the roots of drab, efficient local goverment.

29th October

The Land that Time Faggot

Sir Walter Raleigh's golden years were behind him. He was released from prison for one last mission – to find *Eldorado*, a mythical land of boundless wealth which supposedly lay in the vicinity of Guyana. During the fruitless voyage his fleet attacked Spaniards in the

Americas. A few years earlier he had been rewarded for such bravura; but times had changed and James I was none too fond of Raleigh. Treason charges were trumped up when he returned Eldorado-less, and on the scaffold the smell of hypocrisy mingled with the whiff of burning tobacco. Raleigh smoked a last pipe before facing the hangman on this day in 1628.

🀆 Having introduced tobacco to the quivering lungs of the nation, Sir Walter had remained a great advocate of the pipe. In the stream at Greenway in Devon is Anchor Rock, where Raleigh used to stand and smoke, mulling over life and the universe. And at Henstridge in Wiltshire is the *Virginia Tavern*, where an alarmed barmaid once doused the smouldering Sir Walter with beer to extinguish him during an early puff. All this did nothing to endear Raleigh to James I. The King was so opposed to the evil weed that he took the trouble to write a pamphlet castigating its evils.

At one time Raleigh is supposed to have lived on the edge of Dartmoor at Fardel Hall in Devon, and to have deposited **treasure** somewhere nearby – presumably not gold from Eldorado. There is a local rhyme hinting at the hoard's location:

Between this stone and Fardell Hall
Lies as much money as the Devil can haul.

🀆 ♱ The *stone* was part of a bridge. It is carved with ancient Celtic *ogham* script and is now kept in the British Museum. The field containing the treasure is said to be barren, and guarded by a dark silk-clad woman who still haunts the area.

© At the end of October the Queen's Remembrancer receives the **Rendering of Quit Rents and Services** in a ceremony at the Royal Courts of Justice in the Strand in London. This Quit Rent is in respect of land once used as a forge at St Clements in the City; and – curiously – of land at Eardington in Shropshire, known as *The Moors*.

At the ceremony, the Remembrancer wields a sharp hatchet and a blunt billhook, on behalf of the Shropshire land. He ritually fails to cut a faggot of hazel twigs with the billhook, and then successfully hacks it in two with the hatchet. The implements are later given away on behalf of the Queen. The St Clements' forge is represented by six horseshoes and 61 nails, all of considerable antiquity. Adding to the general strangeness of the event, while The Moors

continues to generate its annual symbolic faggot rent, somewhere in the mists of time the actual location of the land has been forgotten.

30th October

Punk Gig

On the last Thursday in October **Chiselborough Fair** in Somerset provided a great excuse for drinking. Its chief wares were cloth, candles and cutlery. But to the women of Hinton St George and Lopen it represented potential tragedy. In order to return home from the revelries, their husbands had to cross a dangerous ford in what was likely to be a state of advanced inebriation. What they needed was illumination, which the women set about providing. They hollowed out some mangolds, and went to beg candles and money from the richer villagers. The candles were to make mangold-lanterns, and the money was to make their journey that little bit more worthwhile. They successfully rescued their late-travelling drunkards, and the lanterns proved such a boon that in the process they gave birth to a custom.

The male-dominated, less entertaining, version of the tale says that the men got lost in the fog on their way home, blundering through a turnip field before having a brainwave and improvising some lanterns from the vegetables and some candles which they had just bought at the fair. Again, once tried out, the lanterns became standard issue for all future trips to and from the festivities at Chiselborough.

◉ Chiselborough Fair is now defunct; but the two tales have arisen to explain the incandescent **Punkie Night** which still takes place at Hinton St George, near Ilminster in Somerset, on the last Thursday of the month. Local children go begging for candles, and it is very bad luck to refuse their requests. As in the stories, they use the candles to light up their hollowed mangolds (manglewurzels) or turnips; although these days pumpkins are allowed too. For several hours that night the children carry these *punkie* lanterns, dangling on strings, as they parade from house to house singing:

It's Punkie Night tonight, it's Punkie Night
*   tonight,*
Give us a candle, give us a light,
If you don't you'll get a fright (or If you
*   haven't a candle a penny's all right);*

*It's Punkie Night tonight, it's Punkie Night
tonight,
Adam and Eve would never believe it's
Punkie Night tonight.*

A Punkie King and Punkie Queen lead the proceedings, chosen on the strength of their lantern designs – flowers and animals are favourite motifs, and are far more intricately carved than the usual Hallowe'en-style jagged faces. The event survived a short-lived wartime ban – it is too awful to contemplate the kind of carnage that might have been caused by German bombers targeting glowing mangle-wurzels. Despite the rescuing-the-fairgoers stories, the real roots of Punkie Night are in the Celtic Festival of Samhain and in the light/dark rituals of the Hallowe'en season.

Newhaven in Derbyshire held a **Gig Fair** on the 30th, the end of October being a popular time for livestock and produce fairs. Attending the Gig at Newhaven were countless sheep, along with various quacks and shows, and stalls selling sweetmeats, toys and knick-knacks. It was a holiday for local farmworkers and servants. The name comes from the fun and merriment of the occasion, as in the old phrase *in high gig*, meaning a state of high, boisterous spirits.

31st October
Hallowe'en/All Hallows' Eve

The Night of the Living Dead

Hallowe'en is the eve of the Celtic New Year, the festival of **Samhain**, when witches stack up in the skies, and the dead, as well as the faeries, are able to gatecrash the world of us mere mortals. Tonight the past, present, and future collide, collude and coalesce.

With all the barriers down, Hallowe'en is the perfect night for those trapped in the wrong world to make a bid for freedom. Wandering knight **Tam Lin** had fallen from his horse one day and been captured by the **Queen of the Faeries**. Bound with magic, he was forced to remain in the Faerie Kingdom. He was posted as a guardian of one of the doorways which join the faerie lands to the world of mortals – the well at Carterhaugh, at the junction of the Ettrick and Yarrow rivers near Philiphaugh in the Borders. Parents warned their daughters to steer clear of the well, for every time a maiden plucked one of the roses that grew there, Tam Lin was able to demand in exchange either a green mantle, or her virginity.

Janet, a wily woman from Carterhaugh, decided to catch a glimpse of the man behind the myth, and plucked a rose from the well. Given her options, she sized up the knight carefully, and plumped for the sex. Soon she was returning for repeat performances, and Tam realised that after years as a captive of the faeries, with Janet's help he might be able to escape. He explained that the next night, Hallowe'en, gave them an opportunity that only came round once every seven years: the faeries' tithe to Hell was due, and to pay it they had to turn out on horseback in full regalia. Tam gave Janet several complicated instructions and warnings, and told her to wait for him at the crossroads at midnight on Hallowe'en.

The next night, at midnight, the faerie party appeared on time, decked out in all their finery. When Tam's white horse came past, Janet yanked him from the saddle and held tight. Just as he had warned, the Faerie Queen tried to make her let go, casting spells which turned Tam into a newt, a snake, a lion, a bear, and then a red-hot bar of iron. But Janet kept her grip, and when he became the burning iron, she plunged him into well water. The spell was broken, and out of the water emerged Tam, naked and once again in human form. The Queen ranted and raved, but her power over the mortal was at an end. The faeries retreated, leaving Janet and Tam to walk off into the sunrise together.

To gain entry into the **Other World** tonight, run nine times around a tumulus associated with faeries – the borders between their kingdom and the mortal plane are particularly hazy on Hallowe'en, as the Tam Lin yarn demonstrates.

Witches are also out in force at Hallowe'en, working all-purpose mischief. Numerous rhymes advise on where they can be found or how they can be avoided; but few create such a vivid picture as this one from Scotland:

*Halle'en! Halle'en!
This nicht at e'en,
Three witches on the green,
Ane black, ane greene,
Ane playing the tambourine!*

Witches ride their broomsticks or egg-shells this evening; though some prefer cats and horses, mounting the latter for the frenzied Hallowmas Ride north of the Border.

With covens of witches and legions of faeries on the march tonight, it is only to be expected that they sometimes meet up. In the ballad *Alison Gross* a man is transformed into a worm for refusing the sexual advances of Alison, '*the ugliest witch in the North Country*'. The Faerie Queen, this time the heroine of the story, comes to his rescue, getting rid of the witch and turning the man back into his old self.

For those wishing to avoid witches, faeries and any other other-worldly denizens at Hallowe'en, horseshoes are effective, as is anything made of **iron**. But the most effective charm tonight is **rowan**, as it is said:

If your whip-stock's made of rowan,
Your nag may ride through any town.

⚜ Fife suffers a Hallowe'en plague of carnivorous **water-bulls**, which leap from rivers to devour all and sundry; while **Pearlin Jean** is a witch-spirit who stalks up and down Scotland tonight. She has wild-cat's eyes, and haunts both countryside and homestead. She is a folk-memory of an old goddess.

Of similar ancient vintage, but better remembered, is the relationship between the islanders of Lewis in the Outer Hebrides and the **water-god Shony**, also known as Spony. In the weeks leading up to Hallowe'en, pocketfuls of malt were brought to the church of St Mulray on Lewis. They were combined and brewed into a batch of ale. Tonight before the church service a surrogate preacher used to wade up to his waist in the sea, carrying a cup of the strange brew, and saying the Gaelic equivalent of '*Shony, I give you this cup of ale, hoping that you'll be so kind as to send us plenty of sea-ware for enriching our ground for the ensuing year.*' Sea-ware refers to seaweed, a foodstuff vital to the island's economy. Songs and dances followed. This blatant hobnobbing with old gods came to an end only late last century.

Still with ancient deities, the winter goddess **Cailleach Bheur** wakes up tonight and starts blighting the land with her staff – see April 30th for more about her.

Hallowe'en was the night upon which animals were allowed back into the homestead for the winter, and so it was considered only polite to welcome humans back indoors too – even if they happened to be dead. In isolated areas, this **belief in the returning dead** survived even into the early part of this century, as underlined by a practical joke played on a folklorist visiting Barra in the Outer Hebrides.

Happy to blend in with what he was told was an island custom, he followed the locals' lead when they dressed up in Hallowe'en costumes, and knocked on the door of an old farmer. The door opened, and the locals did a runner, leaving the embarrassed visitor standing there in a gruesome mask and party frock. The farmer calmly bade the man come in, and made him some tea, but said nothing. Silence reigned as the folklorist drained cup after cup. Finally he could stand the tension no longer. He removed his mask and apologised for the high jinks of his companions. The farmer then showed surprise. '*Oh,*' he said, simply and honestly, '*I thought you were a dead man.*'

Having been stuck in Purgatory – or in some cases even further afield – the dead often needed help to make it back to the here and now. **Bells** used to be rung tonight to enable them to chart their course, and records survive of the annual ringings at places such as Blandford in Dorset. **Bonfires** fulfilled much the same purpose, acting as homing-beacons for short-sighted souls, and at the same time giving an unmistakable signal that all evil spirits should steer clear.

Because of their pagan and otherworldy connections, these fires were often built on ancient tumuli. In Wales and Scotland, where settlement was scattered, it was common for each family to light its own bonfire, whose blazes also protected homes from ill-fortune over the year ahead. A burning peat swiped from an enemy's bonfire was a great prize, and scattering a neighbour's fire – whether through enmity or incompetence – transferred their good luck to your own household. At Balquhidder in Central Region the last embers of this custom died out only this century.

There were many striking local variants of the tradition. On the White Cart River at Paisley in Strathclyde, platforms were assembled in the water, and the fire was built and lit mid-stream. Up at Balmoral, Grampian, they lit their Hallowe'en bonfire to the sound of pipers, and threw an effigy called **Shandy Dann** into the flames, gazumping Guy Fawkes. Queen Victoria was a great Shandy devotee, and often attended the proceedings.

In Lancashire the fiery foolery was called **teanlay** (alternatively, teanlas or tindles). Farmers tossed pitchforks of burning straw into the air, with prayers intoned as the burning bales scattered spectacularly in the evening breeze. This purified the land, drove out spirits, and was cheaper than a box of fireworks. Sometimes an old rhyme was chanted during the pitchforking:

> Fire and red low,
> Light on my teen low (as in 'teanlay').

In all areas **leaping over the flames** was an important part of the ceremony, bringing health and good luck. It was a relic of old human sacrifice rituals in which the person did not get to re-emerge from the flames.

Animals need a share of the fire's luck too. Hallowe'en flames 'purge' humans who jump through, and the fumes can do the same for animals if they are driven through the blaze. Cattle were given special attention as they underwent **lustration** tonight. This combined cure-all and pick-me-up involved chants and prayers, and the administering of a cocktail of fire, ammonia, salt and water; not a very pleasant experience for the poor animals.

In many parts of the north of Britain all household fires had to be extinguished on Hallowe'en. They could only be relit from a specially built magically-endowed central, communal blaze called the **Neid Fire**. The catch was that all financial and moral debts had to be sorted out before a home was allowed to claim a flame.

▥ Almost as common as this don't-keep-the-home-fires-burning custom is the tradition of the pyre-which-must-never-go-out. St Kilda, 45 miles west of Uist in the Outer Hebrides, has been uninhabited since 1930. But when the last farmers were ferried off the island they left behind them a peat fire which, so it was claimed, had never been doused and which they had tended continuously since the first occupation of St Kilda a thousand years earlier. Similarly at the *Warren House* inn near Postbridge on the edge of Dartmoor, customers warm themselves in front of a slow-burning peat hearth which, it is claimed, has not gone out, day or night, for the last 150 years.

Across mainland Britain, it was a common practice to race home once the fires had died down. In Wales, the sprint was enlivened by the firm belief that a **tail-less black pig** would appear and violently assault the slowest. Hence the saying: '*The cropped black sow take the hindmost*'. Since this pig was known to be the Devil in disguise, it all fits in neatly with the better known version of the saying. Welsh lore additionally insists that a black sow sits on every stile at Hallowe'en. When one of them

was caught, killed and butchered, it gave rise to the traditional song *Black Pudding on the Stile*.

While those suspended in Purgatory could fleetingly rejoin their families round the bonfire tonight, other less fortunate souls had to be content with a Hallowe'en haunting. The ether is thick with ectoplasm tonight, so here are just a few choice **Hallowe'en ghosts**.

✝ At Hawksdale Hall near Dalston just outside Carlisle in Cumbria, a hanged boy wanders outside and sinks gracefully into the River Caldew. At Hindlip Hall near Worcester a white calf and a woman go a-haunting, even though the Hall itself is no longer standing. In life the calf – which wears a wraith wreath of red roses round its neck – led the woman through a maze of secret doors and passages to the hiding place of two Catholic fugitives called Oldcorn and Gornet one Hallowe'en in the 17th century. The unlikely couple re-enact the circuitous trudge every year.

✝ Ned Pugh also met his fate in a secret tunnel. Taking with him a fiddle, food and candles, he set off to investigate a six-mile underground passageway said to lead from Chirk Castle in Clwyd to Morda, near Oswestry in Shropshire. He was never seen again in mortal form, but has been regularly spotted at Hallowe'en playing a tune now known as *Farewell Ned Pugh*. In an alternative version, multi-instrumentalist Ned plays the bugle, summoning hell-hounds to his side. He then leads the Hallowe'en Wild Hunt over the Black Mountains of Wales and around Aberdare in mid-Glamorgan.

✝ The **Wild Hunt** crops up in various other places tonight, and to see or hear it always spells bad news, usually instantaneous death. At Eagle's Crag on Cliviger Gorge, near Burnley in Lancashire, the huntsman leading the pack is Lord William Towneley. In ghostly form he re-enacts his wooing of a sorceress called Sybil. He trapped her while she was shape-shifting in the form of a doe, and forced her to cohabit. But she kept up her bad old ways. Sybil the Sorceress was later wounded in cat-shape and lost a paw/hand.

The last on-the-record sightings of the Wild Hunt were in the first years of the Second World War, a boom-time for doom-time omens of every kind.

👁 **Divination** was the chief entertainment in the days before Hallowe'en parties, and one of the best catalogues of such techniques remains Robert Burns' poem *Halloween*, written in 1786. Hallowe'en has several divination methods that are all its own, but also shares some with the handful of other key dates in the year when future-gazing is equally propitious. So tonight presents another occasion to have a go at baking a Dumb Cake (as detailed on St Agnes Eve, January 20th); hempseed (see Midsummer's Eve, June 23rd); or to try a bit of shoe-gazing – this involves putting your *footwear* into a T shape and chanting:

> Hoping this night my true love see,
> I leave my shoes in the shape of a T.

☉ Exclusive to Hallowe'en, seers can use **cabbages** (or kale) to anticipate amorous antics. Pick one at random – ideally from where it is planted, rather than at the supermarket – and its attributes will determine those of your **future lover**. Much mud at the root equals much wealth. Its taste – sweet or bitter – indicates their temperament; and the stalk, left over a door, will be first disturbed by someone with the same first name as this impending inamorato/a. If all these clues are not enough, you can dream of your future love by sleeping with the cabbage stalk under your pillow. For those using non-biological washing powders, the same personalised and predictive erotic dream can be conjured by substituting a garter which has been taken from your left leg and knotted three times. For an even simpler method, and tastier than cabbage, eat an apple whilst looking in the mirror: your true-love will appear, rather unnervingly, over your shoulder.

☉ Tonight if you dip your shirt in a **Dead and Living Ford** – one that crosses a stream regularly crossed by funeral parties – and let it dry overnight by the fire, the spirit of your true-love will come and turn the shirt for you. Some versions of this custom are more lenient, and say that a shirt soaked in any stream will do.

☉ **Nut Crack Night** is an alternative name for Hallowe'en and is a form of divination which doubles as a great party-game. First take some nuts. Hazelnuts and horse-chestnuts are ideal, but anything in its shell is acceptable, and in some areas even apple pips are given honourary nut-status for the night. Place them on the fire and name each one after a would-be lover. Having decided whether burning or bursting is the good omen (it differs across the country), sit back and watch how your future with each person will unravel. Alternatively, each nut can be made to represent one of the unattached people present in the room. Interpretations of what happens next

vary nationwide, but in Devon the strict formula is as follows: the first nut to catch fire will be the first to marry; the first one to crack is destined to be jilted; the first to burst and jump will never wed, but is destined for a long journey; the first one to smoulder moodily is going to lead a miserable, sickly life; and the one that flies vertically up the chimney and lustrates a passing witch will have to pay for the pizza.

All the above were nationwide customs, but **Whitby** in North Yorkshire has its own, unique way of future-gazing tonight. Locals are supposed to climb to the top of the church tower at Hallowe'en and shout the name of their true love across the sea. If they are to marry them, underwater bells will ring. The lagan bells formerly belonged to the church: sacrilegious sacking Vikings tried to make off with them, but a divinely hurled bolt from the blue dispatched raiders, longship and bells to a watery grave.

☉ Matters amorous are not the only subjects up for divination tonight. Concentrate on a specific question, and drip egg, hot lead or candle wax into water: the shape formed should in some way provide an answer. In Wales some families used to make a special **nine-ingredient** cake on Hallowe'en. The ninth ingredient was always a single bean or wheat grain. Finding it in your slice guaranteed prosperity in the year ahead.

Born gamblers can try their luck by **lating the witches**. Light a candle and go for a walk. The candle – a miniature version of the Hallowe'en bonfires – keeps evil forces at bay during the stroll. If it stays alight throughout the hike, fortune will grin broadly at you over the next 12 months. If the flame goes out, the grin turns into a very alarming grimace.

Apple-dooking/bobbing is a form of divining that has proved so much fun that it is now played largely just for entertainment, rather than enlightenment, value. An apple has to be grasped using only the mouth. To increase the difficulty and the likelihood of personal humiliation, the fruit dangles from string, or floats in a bucket of water. Sometimes the apple is stuck at one end of a spinning pole, with a lit candle at the other end – unsuccessful lunges lead to a coating of candle wax on your T-shirt. In Scotland, the apples are sometimes replaced with treacle-smeared bannocks, which leads to even more mess. The entire however-many-years-it-was run of *It's a Knockout* was an extrapolation of this one game.

Trick or Treat is a reimported American-isation of the notion that Hallowe'en is a Mischief Night, when all law is suspended and you can embark on expeditions of terrorism and extortion. But there is something ironically Establishment about mass-produced masks and costumes – a point neatly made in the film *Halloween Three – Season of the Witch*, scripted by Nigel 'Quatermass' Kneale.

The original reason for disguise tonight was to prevent lonely spirits from recognising you and snatching you away to their between-the-worlds home; and it was an additional bonus that the costumes allowed you to lead a mini-riot without being recognised by would-be human chastisers. The costumes were also an important part of a species of Celtic Hallowe'en mumming play called *Goloshan*.

Ancient Hallowe'en celebrations are alive and well on the Isle of Man tonight, most of them having migrated here from the traditional date of Hollantide: see November 12th.

From Hemswell in Lincolnshire comes the classic non-event quotation, noted down by a historian early this century. On the subject of Hallowe'en, a villager advised: '*If you are out of doors at midnight on All Hallows' Eve, and you keep still and listen hard, you will hear something, and it will probably frighten you, but you will not see anything.*' Thank you and goodnight.

NOVEMBER

1st November
All Saints' Day/
St Cadfan's Day

Love is Blind

November 1st was for centuries the date of the **Caernarfon Hiring Fair**, one of the biggest such fairs in north Wales. One year, so the old story goes, plain young Eilian stood in the line of women who clutched mops to show that they sought employment as maids. She caught the eye of an old couple – a farmer and his midwife wife – and they made her an offer which she immediately accepted. She proved an efficient maid, but a solitary one, keeping her own company and often going for long strolls at twilight. One day Eilian went for a walk and did not come back, and the couple were not particularly surprised.

A year or so later an opulent but agitated stranger came to call on the midwife. He said that his wife required her immediate ministrations, and he was prepared to pay an exorbitant rate for her services. The midwife packed her bag and followed the stranger to a grand hall full of riches: gold and silver plates, wallpaper studded with diamonds, and chairs that did not squeak when you sat on them. The stranger's dazzlingly beautiful wife had gone into labour, and the midwife helped deliver the baby. The stranger paid up, and offered more gold if the midwife would agree to stay on as nurse. She accepted the job, and was instructed that in addition to her normal duties, she must each day smear a special ointment on to the child's eyes.

All went swimmingly until the midwife accidentally rubbed her own eye with an ointment-smeared finger. She now saw the palace in a drastically different light: it was nothing but a dank cave furnished with wood and bark, and the gold that she had been paid was nothing but leaves. She realised that she was in faerieland, and that she had been deceived by faerie glamour. The baby was noticeably pointy-eared, and its beautiful mother was, she now saw, plain young Eilian. The girl had found no difficulty choosing between an out-of-this-world romance and the mundane drudgery of a maid's life.

After her mid-wife crisis the woman stuck to more reliable clients, and several months later she had almost forgotten how she had been diddled by the faeries. Then one day, as the midwife was walking through Caernarfon market, the still-lingering powers of the ointment enabled her to recognise the faerie who had hired her to tend to his human bride. '*How do*', said the midwife, politely. '*With which eye do you see me?*' growled the faerie in response. '*This one!*' said the midwife, rashly pointing to her all-seeing eye. Without hesitation the faerie grabbed a stick and poked out the eye.

All Saints, or All Hallows, is a celebration of all the redeemed, both the known and the unknown, just in case some saints had slipped through the net of the year unnoticed. But many of today's pursuits were less than devout.

November 1st was a day for pranks: pinching ploughs, smoking-out houses, loosing penned animals, and throwing things at doors. Cabbage stalks were a favourite projectile. So much so that in Scotland there were special **Kail Courts** to try people who had taken liberties with cabbage.

In Roman mythology **cabbages** have a peerless pedigree. Jupiter was over-exerting himself when, '*some drops of sweat happening to light on the earth produced what mortals call cabbage*' – as Rabelais succinctly put it when retelling the tale.

At Wootton Bassett Manor in Wiltshire the tenants had to pay up if they failed to get into the party spirit at the **Word Ale** today. They were exempt from their annual tithes as long as they followed certain customs, which involved singing and drinking lots of ale – nothing too taxing. They were also obliged to say a few prayers for the Cistercian monks who had instigated these remarkably frivolous proceedings. A different local acted as master of ceremonies each year.

✝ Hyde Hall at Sawbridgeworth near Bishop's Stortford in Hertfordshire is now a school. After today's lessons are over, **Sir Jocelyn Joyce** comes out to play, taking his horse for a ghostly night-time canter round the Hall. Sir Jocelyn insisted on being buried in his own unconsecrated ground, sitting on his horse. He was; and as a consequence of his single-mindedness he pays phantom penance each year on November 1st.

✝ **The Black Abbot** also calls this night his own. At Prestbury, on the outskirts of Cheltenham in Gloucestershire, he walks from the church to Reform Cottage, where he knocks and sets off much poltergeisting within. The cottage's garden is on the site of an old burial ground for monks. The Abbot can also be seen on Easter Sunday and Christmas Day, and is one of the many ghosts that crowd the ether around Prestbury: others include a girl playing a spinet, and the Phantom Strangler of Cleeve Corner.

☾ **All Hallows Summer** starts today, a traditional spell of unseasonable warmth. That said, this is also a day that brings its own fowl weather warnings:

> If ducks do slide at Hollantide, at Christmas they will swim;
> If ducks to swim at Hollantide, at Christmas they will slide.

That's ducks for you. This rhyme, by the way, is equally applicable to Old Samhain (Hollantide) on November 12th.

▥ Finally, imagine how poor **St Cadfan** feels. This is his feast day, and he shares it with every other saint who ever lived, and a good number who are pure fiction. Cadfan's Stone, thought to be his 5th-century gravestone, is in the church at Towyn near Rhyl in Clwyd; and his nearby well is good for rheumatic, scrofulous and cutaneous complaints. Wells in general are on top form today, their powers reaching a curative zenith.

2nd November
All Souls' Day/Souling Day

Flogging a Dead Horse

Souling Day presupposes that the dead do not depart this life with a first-class ticket to Heaven, but have to spend months, years or even an eternity in the cold, damp waiting room of **Purgatory**. Mortal sinners get the through-service to Hell, with no cheap day returns available. No returns whatsoever, in fact. Lesser, venial, sinners have to stay put in Purgatory awaiting their connection.

The only thing that can clear the unbelievers off the line and speed up the 7.15 to Paradise is prayer. On All Souls' Day the stay of all those in Purgatory can be shortened by prayers, preferably accompanied by mass and almsgiving. This is a Catholic tradition, not a Protestant one; and although today's prayers are directed at those in limbo, they are also an all-purpose SOS, going out to everyone who has ever died, from Abel to the lead item in that morning's obituary column.

Souling, or **Soul-caking**, on November 1st and 2nd, involved going from door to door singing a song in return for alms, in the form of food or money. Originally this was to pay for prayers for the dead; but after the Reformation and the disestablishment of Purgatory, soul-cakers came calling with a view to their own more immediate salvation and lubrication. It was particularly popular in north-west England.

Each household had to make loads of soul-cakes – or dirge cakes, as they were known in old Aberdeenshire – as it was customary to give one to every caller, whether or not they came begging. Milkmen could end their round with a floatful of buns. The cakes were usually small and spiced, and brought luck. They probably derived from the pagan practice of putting aside food for those who had recently died. Many families kept old soul cakes, sometimes for a hundred years or more.

Souling Songs varied across the country, but the core message behind them all is contained in these lines from the version sung at Uttoxeter, Staffordshire:

> You gentlemen of England I'd have you to draw near,
> For we have come a-Souling for your strong ale and beer.

© In Cheshire, soul-caking has not quite died out. As well as a few groups of children with blackened faces prising pennies from householders with their songs, there are the adult soul-cakers who have kept the **souling play** tradition alive. Cheshire is the home of Dick Tatton, the **Wild Horse of Antrobus**. Dick is the three-legged star of the play: two legs are human, and the third is a pole surmounted by a real horse's skull, painted black and with snapping jaws. In the narrative of the play, Dick is described as a dead horse, which may hint at a link with prehistoric horse cults and the ritual animal slaughter of Samhain, the Celtic New Year.

The play can be traced back over 400 years, and is a variant of Christmas mumming and hoodening plays. Its other characters include Beelzebub – who dresses as a tramp – and the village idiot Dairy Doubt. These days the play takes place on All Souls' Eve (yesterday) and the Thursday to Saturday of the following two weekends. The soulers perform the short plays about five times a night in pubs around Antrobus. The final performance is always in the *Antrobus Arms*. Even if there is no one in a bar, the play still goes ahead. Dick Tatton and Co. have encouraged other horse Cheshire-nuts; there are now revived plays at nearby Comberbach and Warburton, near Lymm. Perhaps the first of droves?

3rd November
St Winefride's/St Clydog's Day

There is Never a Constable Around When You Need One

The 7th-century St **Winefride** was being pursued by lusty Prince Caradoc at Holywell, Clwyd. She refused to participate in his advanced version of doctors and nurses, and so Caradoc sliced off her head. Winefride's uncle, St Beuno, witnessed the despicable deed, and melted Caradoc like a cheap candle. He then picked up his niece's head and placed it firmly back on her shoulders. A couple of breaths up each nostril, and he had revived her. All that showed of this ordeal was a Frankenstein-like red scar on Winefride's neck; but people held their breath every time she sneezed.

🏛 Where Winefride's head struck the ground at Holywell, a spring appeared. This became St **Winefride's Well**, once a five-star resort on the Costa del Pilgrim, and now the finest British example of a medieval well. It has a chapel and a bathing pool dating from the 15th century; and even after the Reformation royalty continued to visit, lured by stories of the hundreds who had shed diseases after a dip in its healing waters. In 1686 James II and his Queen were desperate for an heir. They visited the well, and it worked its magic: soon afterwards the Queen became pregnant.

St Winefride's is also a wishing well. Throwing in loose change is not necessary: instead, the faithful must duck under the water and kiss a stone near the steps, making sure that their wish is suitably devout and delivered with confidence.

The well was popular for baptisms. Even the bell in Holywell's ancient church, which is built on top of the well, was wrapped in a christening robe, blessed with the water, and given the name *Winefride*. To show its gratitude the Winefride bell continues to keep evil, lightning and tempest at bay.

For a saint whose principal base of operations is in Wales, Winefride has been known to exhibit anti-Welsh bias. When Richard the Lionheart was stranded and surrounded by the Welsh just north of Holywell, he offered a prayer to Winefride. Up rose a sandbank across the Dee, enabling the Constable of Chester to nip across the river and whisk the king away from the irate Welsh. The bank is still known as **Constable Sands**; although in another version of the story it gets its name after coming to the aid of a 13th-century Earl Richard.

St **Clydog** was 6th-century king of a mighty empire which now roughly corresponds to Hereford and Worcester. He was murdered on a hunting trip, and a cart and oxen were readied to take his body back home for burial. When the oxen reached the River Monnow their yoke broke and they ground to a halt, refusing to budge. This was no accident, mused the Clydog clan, but divine will. So they buried their King on the spot, adding a church for good measure, around which grew the village of Clodock.

♰ The museum at Bruce Castle, in north London, is filled with **ghostly screams** today. The castle, on Lordship Lane, was where 17th-century Lady Constantia was held captive. On November 3rd she jumped from the clock-tower to her death.

4th November
St Cleer's Day

The Hole Truth

On this day in 1820, William Hirons was travelling home to Stratford-upon-Avon, Warwickshire, when he was attacked by four men. The incident, at Littleham Bridge near Alveston, left him robbed and unconscious with his head in a hole. A servant discovered him later, and Hirons lived long enough to describe the four assailants and reveal that one of his stolen pound notes had the word 'one' written on it in red ink. Hirons' murderers were captured and executed after the marked money was located in one of their sweaty palms; but that was not the end of the case. The head-shaped hollow at the scene of the crime became known as **Hirons' Hole**. It was said to be haunted; and whenever it was filled, be it with rock, soil or water, it emptied itself within days.

It was only some years later that Hirons' servants confessed to having fuelled the legend with their own elbow grease. They had realised that once the hole disappeared, memories of their beloved boss would start to fade, and so each night they had emptied it to keep the story, and Hirons' name, alive. With no one left to excavate it, Hirons' Hole has now filled up; but Littleham Bridge is still in place.

▥ Hurling, that fine Celtic pursuit, is a rarity in Britain these days. This may have something to do with the implicit moral lesson of the three impressive stone circles known as **The Hurlers** which stand on Craddock Moor a few miles north of St Cleer, near Liskeard in Cornwall. St Cleer is named after the 6th-century hermit Cleer, whose holy well still stands in the village and whose feast is today. Out walking one Sunday, the hermit came upon a violation of the Sabbath no-games edict: a frenzied moortop hurling match. With the miraculous equivalent of a red-card, Cleer instantly zapped all the players into a series of tastefully arranged rings of rock. Another nearby stone formation, Trevethy Quoit, implies that the petrifying risks may have extended to other sports besides hurling.

◉ As well as being the day for collecting the final firewood for tomorrow's conflagrations, and the day for making such Fawkesian delicacies as Plot Toffee and gingerbread, this is also **Mischief Night** in certain parts of Yorkshire. Like other Mischiefs throughout history, law is thought to be temporarily suspended, and petty vandalism gets its paws on anything not securely nailed down. Gates have a habit of migrating, and street-numbers often swap houses to leave the next day's postie hopelessly befuddled. Top survival tips include sealing up letter-boxes to prevent indoor fireworks displays, and ignoring all doorbell-ringing and door-knocking. Favourite wizard wheezes include tying door-handles together so that householders are confined to quarters, and covering any available surface with treacle or whitewash.

✟ **Catherine Howard** escaped from her guards at Hampton Court on this day in 1541 and ran to the chapel to make husband Henry VIII change his mind about sentencing her to death. But her pleas fell on deaf ears and an axe soon fell on her neck. Catherine's ghost continues to make a break for it down the Haunted Gallery, and her screams are allegedly heard every now and then.

5th November
Guy Fawkes/Bonfire Night

Bonfire of the Insanities

▥ Shebbear, mid-way between Barnstaple and Launceston in Devon, has an enormous boulder known as the **Devil's Stone** outside its church. When vanquished Lucifer had been kicked out of Heaven and was plummeting hellwards, he checked his pockets for excess baggage. He found one small pebble, which he slung out as he was passing over Shebbear.

Another legend says that the boulder was the foundation stone for a church at Henscott over the river Torridge. Every night Satan stole it and plonked it down at Shebbear, and every day the masons sweated and strained to roll it back to Henscott. Eventually they hit upon a labour-saving plan and built the church at Shebbear instead.

◉ Legend number three says that Satan is actually under the stone, which must be turned annually to keep him prisoner. Just in case this is the correct version of the story, every November 5th at 8 pm the people of Shebbear, led by the vicar, leave *The Devil's Stone Inn* and take their sticks and crow-bars to turn the one-ton Devil's Stone, after a discordant peal of bells. If it is not turned completely, crops will fail and livestock will die.

The true origins of the custom are unknown, though there is a pre-Christian 'devil' of some sort involved. Turning stones was a way of gaining power over supernatural forces, and so Shebbear's stick-bearers may be keeping a malign god in check.

Bonfire Night has purloined most of the fire and noise formerly associated with Hallowe'en and Samhain. Guy Fawkes' ultimate contribution to the nation amounts to a delayed start for the Celtic New Year party.

Tonight, or on the nearest weeked, or whenever the school playing-field is free, millions of pounds go up in smoke across the country. Many displays have their own recent rituals, but a handful have been going their own bizarre way for centuries.

© In the 16th century Mary I burnt 17 Protestant martyrs at **Lewes** in Sussex, an inflammatory act which continues to ignite the town in annual protest. Each November 5th they **burn the Pope**. In fact they burn several Popes, as the town has six bonfire societies, each with its own massive display and each with its own giant firework-stuffed Pope – the original Roman (Catholic) Candle. Even odder are his human escorts, the four Cardinals, wearing welders' goggles and what soon turn out to be flame-proof vestments and mitres. Standing on a raised platform, they taunt the crowd, who respond with salvoes of fireworks all aimed squarely at the Cardinals. Burns are not uncommon, and with so many explosives whizzing past, even the flame-proof robes sometimes catch fire. This is an accepted part of the ritual, and adherence to the Firework Code seems to be suspended by mutual consent. However intense the assault, the Cardinals keep smiling and waving, leading the crowd in regular choruses of:

A rope, a rope, to hang the Pope, a piece of
cheese to toast him,
A barrel of beer to drink his health, and a
right good fire to roast him.

Usually this is condensed to the more readily chanted '*Burn the Pope*'. Images of local councillors and anyone out of favour with the townsfolk are also liable to be torched – 1993 being the year of *Jurassic Park* and supposed Euro-unity, a highlight was the detonation of an effigy of John Major riding a Tyrannosaurus labelled 'Maastricht'. There is a huge fancy-dress torchlight procession through the streets, with locals and spectators clutching flaming brands. A recent midnight curfew has curtailed the celebrations, but Lewes on 5th November remains one of Britain's wildest nights out.

© **Blazing tar-barrels** sometimes feature at Lewes; but the biggest and best such celebrations form the backbone of the November 5th **Ottery St Mary Carnival** in Devon. The day starts at 5.45 am with the (technically illegal) firing of hand-held gunpowder-filled pipes called 'rock cannons'. From 4 pm local men, women and children roll burning barrels and carry them on their backs, their only protection against scorching being greased faces, and gloves or layers of sacking on their hands. Once the lighted barrel is on their shoulders, the 'rollers' run up and down the street until their burden disintegrates. It is a feat of strength, endurance and foolhardiness. Burns and blisters are a regular consequence of these heroics. The ceremony drives out evil, brings in luck, and leaves stains that not even the whitest of whites washing powder can remove.

© Tar-barrels also roll at **Hatherleigh**, near Okehampton in Devon, on the Friday before its carnival, which is usually a week after Guy Fawkes' Night. In **Bridgewater** in Somerset, locals used to roll barrels too; but their carnival – on the Thursday nearest the 5th – has tamed its fires and now gets all its light and excitement from a parade of illuminated floats. On the following day there is a party known as Black Friday; but no longer because of the morning-after char marks.

Many November 5th celebrations used to get completely out of hand, with open warfare between the police and the gangs in charge – often known as the **Bonfire Boys**: see November 21st for details of the Guildford riots.

Citizens of **York** are not supposed to burn Guy today. He was a York-born soldier, roped into the 1605 plot as a mercenary. He was, ironically, born a Protestant.

In addition to the well-known '*Remember, remember the 5th of November, gunpowder treason and plot*', apposite **rhymes** today include:

Rumour, rumour, pump a derry,
Prick his heart and burn his body,
And send his soul to Purgatory,

and:

Gunpowder Plot shall ne'er be forgot
As long as Bella Brown makes good Tom
Trot.

Tom Trot was parkin, an oaty ginger and treacle cake. Thar or **Thor Cakes** are very similar, once a common delicacy today. Thar is probably from Anglo-Saxon *theorf*, meaning unleavened; but romantics like to pretend it is all to do with the god Thor, whose feast is said to have been on or about November 5th – presumably on the nearest Thors-day.

Free Warren came into force for the 24 hours of the 5th. It was an unofficial law that made all land common today, enabling poachers to work without the need for secrecy. The fleshy fruits of Free Warren were consumed at a slap-up evening feast.

6th November
St Leonard's Day

The Buck-Toothed Dragon

St Leonard's Forest, between Pease Pottage and Horsham in Sussex, has a long history of monster patronage. In the 6th century, Leonard came to the area hoping to qualify for membership of saint slayers, the exclusive club for virtuous **dragon** killers. He succeeded in his task, but ended up with a nasty wound. His blood splashed down, and lilies-of-the-valley sprang up with sanguine speed. The area is still known as The Lily Beds. In his pre-fight prayer session Leonard had been distracted by twittering nightingales, and for this indirect part in the saint's injury the birds were banished from the forest. Local adders, being the dragon's closest available relatives, were deprived of their stings.

This did not stop other dragons muscling in. In the 17th century, a nine-foot-high specimen appeared. Scaly, pot-bellied, and with vestigial wings, it ran as fast as a man, and spat poison with the sure eye of a Hollywood Robin Hood. The creature left a horrible smell in its wake, and although it poisoned a few people, it never ate them. According to a pamphlet which recorded the beast's movements, the dragon preferred to dine on rabbits.
☩ No one ever killed the rabbit-eating dragon of St Leonard's, and stories of strange things lurking in the trees linger still. Carrying the forest's flag for the humanoid school of ghostly manifestations is **Squire Paulett**. Like a phantom stunt-man he jumps down onto passing riders and hugs their torsos until they reach the forest edge. With fewer riders these days, sightings of the spectral squire are now rare.

☩ **Sibell Penn**, nurse to Edward VI, died on this day in 1562. She was enjoying her eternity of sweet oblivion until the events of 1829, when Hampton Church was pulled down, causing her tomb to be disturbed. In protest she began haunting her former home at Hampton Court, on the western edge of Greater London. The phantom is hard at work, appearing at a ghostly spinning wheel.

Until the church was destroyed by a bomb in the Second World War, the Sunday nearest the 2nd used to see a **celebration of fish** at St Dunstan's-in-the-East, London. Thirty-nine of the wide-eyed and legless denizens of the deep were brought into the church to represent the 39 Articles of Religion. They were blessed, and sent out to enliven hospital menus.

The ceremony featured the humble haddock, a fish said to have gained the two marks on its neck when St Peter grabbed it by the throat to prise out some money from its mouth. This all took place at Lake Gennesaret which, unfortunately for the story, is fresh-water and devoid of salty sea-faring haddocks.

7th November
St Willibrord's Day

Sittin' and Lying

St Willibrord had the difficult task of tackling pagan Europe head on, striding out across the heathen lands between 658 and 739. He was born in Yorkshire and educated at Ripon, but his muscle and mitre were flexed mainly on the continent. He once purchased 30 slave boys in Denmark. The Church held its breath; but Willibrord only wanted to convert and educate them. On the German island of Heligoland he was less subtle, slaughtering a herd of sacred heifers and serving up beef steaks to his converts. His final resting place and shrine is at Echternach, now in Luxembourg. This is the venue for the strange **Willibrord wiggle**, a formal dance performed by clergy and Bishops, of unknown origin but dating back at least 400 years.

Hornsea and Hedon in Humberside used to stage their hiring fairs today – or **Sittin's**, as they were known locally. The Sittin' was more than a local job market: it also set wages for the coming year, and acted as a local law court. The commonest crimes were committed by the officials themselves – the *petit constables* – who tended to bunk off their duties and were fined appropriately.

The custom of **crying** had nothing to do with sitting in front of a Sunday afternoon weepy with a box of tissues. Crying was the equivalent of a notice in the Post Office window: the crier shouted vociferously, alerting people to special events, missing articles, sales of obsolete computer software and suchlike. On this day in 1833, diary-keeper Samuel Hirst of Keele in Humberside noted: '*John Stacey the Pindar got the strange heifer cry'd at Pontefract.*' The 'strange heifer' was an impounded stray which went unclaimed after two cryings, and was bought by Mr Hirst for a knockdown price. In the same year at Pontefract in West Yorkshire, the daughter of a Mr Bootham was cry'd, having gone AWOL. She was discovered by vigilant locals a few fields away; although doing what and with whom, Samuel Hirst declined to reveal.

◉ The Thursday nearest the 23rd used to usher in **Driffield Hiring Fair** at Great Driffield, Humberside. The surviving fair at Driffield – the tail-end of Hull Fair – takes place early in the month. By the end of last century local papers would merely comment in passing on the occurrence of yet another riot at the notorious fair. The peace was not so much disturbed as ripped in half, chewed up and spat out in the face of authority. And even afterwards the drunkards were unrepentant. In 1905 after being fined £1 5s (£1.25p) for assault and disorderliness, a man amused the public gallery by eating a bun in court in spite of warnings from the bench. In the right hands, even a humble bun can become a symbol of anarchy.

Local man Reverend Eddowes wrote about the Hiring Fair late last century with something other than affection. He produced a pithy pamphlet condemning the event as the root of much of the world's evil:

Hiring Fair! The very name reminds us of scenes which we would willingly forget forever – the reeling men and drunken women . . . profanity and blasphemy and profligacy unchecked . . . every restraint seems loosened, and every feeling of shame forgotten . . .

Many a promising youth, now lingering in the felon's prison, may trace the first step in their course of crime to the temptations of the fair.

8th November
St Cybi's/St Tysilio's Day

Eels Heal Heels

The unimaginatively named **William Williams** of Peter Tavy, Devon, fancied Emma Doidge something rotten. But there was a rival for her affections, and Williams ended up at the sharp end of the love triangle when Emma decided that Williams was not her Mr Rightangle. On November 8th 1892 Emma stood at the altar, ready to marry a Mr Rowe. Williams sneaked into the service with a gun, and shot Emma, Rowe, and then himself. Everything went according to plan until the last bit. He managed to miss his own head. Staggering to his feet he had another try. He blew one eye away, but was still very much alive. Losing faith in his marksmanship he ran to the River Tavy and leaped in. In spite of his best efforts, he failed to drown. At the trial he pleaded insanity and inaccuracy, but was judged to be merely incompetent. The hangman needed only one go to finish Williams off.

The 6th-century **St Cybi of the Tawney Hue** and St Seiriol the Fair were Anglesey's two top saints. They were also best of friends, and acquired their nicknames because of their daily mid-island meetings. Cybi lived on an island just off the north-west of Anglesey, and Seiriol was based over in the east. To get to their regular tryst, Cybi walked (and presumably swam) facing the sun, while Seiriol walked with the sun at his back. In the absence of Factor 22, Cybi developed a hue that can best be described as tawny, hence the nickname. Apposite as it was, 'St Seiriol the Redneck' did not strike quite the right tone: given that his face was untanned, 'fair' was judged a more reverential appellation. Cybi was so righteous, pious and generally saintly that his island became known as Holy Island, and its main town came to be called Holyhead.

🏛 **St Cybi's Well** is at Llangybi near Porthmadog in Gwynedd. It is ruined, but still impressive with its baths and buildings. The curative well used to contain **eels**. They embodied the power of the water, and if they wrapped around your legs it was a sign of imminent recovery, particularly if you were suffering from a foot or leg ailment. If the eels failed to be lured by your lower limbs, it was bad news, or a hint to change your socks moray often.

St Cybi's Well can still be used to suss out the fidelity of your current sleeping partner. Drop a handkerchief into the eel-free water. If it floats to the south, your lover is inconstant; to the north, and he or she shows no signs of straying.

Today's other Welsh saint, 7th-century **St Tysilio**, gets top prize for being incorporated into a placename. He is the man to be found in the closing syllables of Anglesey's Llanfairpwllgwyngyllgogerychwyrndrobwllan*tysilio*gogogoch, which means St Mary's Church In The Hollow Of The White Hazel Near A Rapid Whirlpool And The Church Of St Tysilio Near The Red Cave.

🏠 The site of St Tysilio's cell is marked by a 15th-century church on a tiny island in the Menai Straits, Gwynedd.

9th November

The Mayor the Merrier

On November 9th 1674 Thomas Godard was walking near Ogbourne St George, Wiltshire, when he came upon his brother-in-law Edward Avon, leaning nonchalantly on a stile. This was made odd by the fact that Edward had been dead for quite a while. Unusually the phantom was aware of the likely effect that he was having, and considerately asked Thomas if he was frightened. The ghostly Edward then asked how the family were doing, and went on to explain that he was restless because in life he had denied his daughter certain cash which was rightfully hers. He handed Thomas some silver, but the man was too terrified to take the money. He ran off. Edward reappeared several times, and on the last occasion the persistent spirit urged Thomas to make Edward's son repay the debt, and to take Edward's sword to a spot where, in his former life, he had slain someone. Thomas passed on the details; Edward's son did his bit; and the ghost found its rest.

This used to be Lord Mayor's Day in London, and it was a traditional date for electing Mock

Mayors up and down England. Notable amongst the mock masses were the Mayor and Mayoress of Shamickshire, elected at Bideford in Devon. The Mayor's chief reponsibility was to visit every local pub and make a speech, until he lost that particular faculty in the course of his duties. Games and rowdiness were the order of the day. Some places had blazing tar barrels, a link with the Celtic fire festival, Samhain. The office of mayor was a Norman invention, superseding the Anglo-Saxon Portreeve. It is tempting to view the Mock Mayoring as a Saxon lampoon of Norman pomp.

© London's **Lord Mayor's Show** extravaganza has moved its tourist appeal and traffic chaos to the more user-friendly second Saturday after the second Friday in November. It is one of the few bits of genuine tradition to get its own year-in, year-out slot on television. The first election was instigated by a clause in the Magna Carta, which gave Londoners the right to choose their own mayor. The charter also stated that the elected person should be presented to the king or his justices – hence the start of what has become one of Britain's grandest annual parades.

The procession sets off from the Guildhall around 11 am, with the Lord Mayor joining in the pomp-up-the-volume floats, bands, troops and coaches parade just before mid-day. En route he is blessed at St Paul's Cathedral, before being sworn in by the Lord Chief Justice and the Master of the Rolls at the Royal Courts of Justice in the Strand. After lunch, the procession takes the scenic route to Mansion House, pausing for some rubbernecking as the RAF skim by on their now traditional fly-past. In the 15th century, part of the journey was by boat, the vessels being provided by the various London Companies. The Thames still features in the festivities, with the Lord Mayor usually travelling by boat to the early evening firework display which brings the show to a close.

🏠 When not on its annual outing in November, the Lord Mayor's coach and gear is on show in the Museum of London.

10th November
Martinmas Eve

You Can Lead a Horse to Water But You Can't Stop It From Disembowelling and Eating You

November is the favoured season of the **aughisky**, which live in the sea and Highland lochs. These water horses emerge from their lairs to gallop across beaches and fields. If you can catch and saddle one, it will run and work like Desert Orchid and a stableful of Shire horses rolled into one. But if it ever sees water again, it races away, with you on board, and disappears into the depths. The rider is powerless to dismount, and once he or she is drowned the aughisky will tuck in, as they are very fond of human flesh.

Sometimes the water-horse wants you for dinner from the onset. At Aberfeldy in Tayside an aughisky once lured seven sisters on to its back, but their brother refused to mount. It chased him, but got fed up and returned to the loch with the girls, who were glued to its back. Next morning their seven livers were washed ashore.

On Raasay, off the coast of Skye, a farmer saw his daughter being abducted by the horse, and found her heart and lungs the next morning. In a fit of vengeful grief, he and his son heated some iron hooks and lured the aughisky out with a roasting sheep. It could not resist, and they ripped it apart with their weapons.

Surprisingly, the Jockey Club says it has no records of anyone ever having risked Aughisky as the name for a horse.

ⓞ In Scotland, Martinmas Eve is a night for divining, via the **Trial of Three Dishes**. Fill one dish with clean water, one with dirty water, and one with nothing at all. Find someone who is curious about their future love life, blindfold them, and let them choose a dish at random. If the clean one is chosen, he or she will marry a maid or bachelor. If they opt for the dirty one, their partner will have previously been married. If they pick the third dish, it means that they will stay single. The ceremony must be performed three times. If all three results are the same, destiny beckons.

© Technically, **Diwali** is as moveable as Easter, taking place between mid-September and October; but in Leicester it is usually held in early November. The name means 'row of lights', and Belgrave Road becomes all aglow for this week-long Asian merchants' festival. Diwali celebrates, amongst other things, the outrageous physiognomy of Lakshmi, a four-armed goddess with an elephant trunk. The trunk represents both fertility and rain – see the nearest zoo for a demonstration of the origins of both bits of symbolism. Lakshmi always carries a lotus flower, making her a particularly lovable kind of goddess.

The Diwali lights are in remembrance of the day when **King Rama**, one of the many manifestations of the god Vishnu, came back from exile, having been ousted by Rama's stepmother. She had been rashly granted two wishes by the old King, and she used one of them to steal the crown for her son, Bharata. But Bharata felt guilty, and left a pair of sandals on the throne until the rightful heir returned. The sandals ruled in peace for many years.

Individual Hindu and Sikh households in Leicester, and elsewhere, put *divas* in their windows – not large loud women, but small earthenware oil-lamps. Rice and flour are made into edifying, edible patterns outside each house. Gambling is the done-thing during Diwali. Proper observance of the festival ensures health, wealth, and fertility.

11th November
Martinmas

Sacrificial Bulls, Pantomime Goats, Faerie Cows

In an unknown year at an unknown place in Scotland, an unnamed farmer had a unusual but named cow – she was called Hawkie and was not keen on any old bull. Hawkie insisted on being serviced by an elf-bull who lived in the local river. The water-bull was relatively small, with fur like an otter's, and the union produced fine calves each year. But one **Martinmas** the farmer decided that Hawkie was looking a bit lean and leathery, and decided to sell her at the local Martinmas Fair. Hawkie overheard his intentions and broke down the byre wall. She called her calves, and the whole herd trooped down to the river and disappeared into the water's depths. The farmer searched frantically for the moral.

© At dawn today **Wroth Silver** is still collected on Knightlow Hill, near Dunchurch. The hill is on the edge of Dunsmore Heath, close to Rugby in Warwickshire, and the extremely odd Saxon ceremony gives commoners from the local Knightlow Hundred the right to drive cattle over the Duke of Buccleuch's land. The ceremony must start as soon as it is light enough to read – should they ever miss the dawn (as nearly happened in 1992), the tradition must cease. As the names of the different parishes are read out, the representatives place their wroth money – about 15p, tops – into the base of an old cross, crying 'Wroth Silver!' as they do so. The whole procedure lasts under five minutes, and breakfast is then held at a local inn, with a traditional Buccleuch toast in rum and milk. This used to be paid for by the Duke, but is now an all-ticket affair.

Failure to pay the Wroth meant a fine of £1 for every penny; or handing over a white bull with red nose and ears. The last attempt to pay by cow was in 1893, but the proffered animal did not fit the necessary colour scheme. It was never likely to – white with red nose and ears is suspiciously close to the red ears and eyes livery of **faerie cattle**. Legend says that Dunsmore Heath was once crawling with the creatures, known locally as **dun cows**. In the 10th century, a certain dun cow was the bane of the countryside in Warwickshire, standing 18 feet by 24, with horns to match. It had given endless milk until someone got greedy and milked it into a sieve until it was dry. The cow then became a man-eater, running rampant until Guy of Warwick speared it.

The origin of these faerie cattle is likely to be the wild herds of white, red-eared beasts which once grazed freely across Britain. Overhunting and Roman imports of new breeds meant that even by Saxon times Jerseys and Friesians had taken over from the wild herds to such an extent that indigenous cows were already a rarity. Encounters with such animals generated the faerie-herd stories. Amazingly, they did not completely die out, and the last survivors of the wild herds now graze in the park around Chillingham Castle in Northumberland, as they have done since the 13th century, when they were already an extremely endangered species. The herd at Chillingham only milks tourists by prior appointment.

The **Horseman's Word** Ceremony used to take place around Martinmas, and still lingers in remote regions. It was centred on Huntly in Grampian, and was an initiation rite for horsemen once they had reached 18. Blindfolded, they had to fulfil various rituals, including entering the room with bread, whisky and jam, taking off their left sock, shaking the hoof of a live or pantomime goat, and swearing to keep all this nonsense secret. In return they were given a word which gave them power over horses. Like the Masons, only initiates are party to the modern form of these rituals. Enquiries are greeted with walls of misinformation and denial, but it is a safe bet that horsemen's societies still exist, and continue to exert great influence in some areas.

☺ The **Fenny Poppers** are set off today at Fenny Stratford, Buckinghamshire. These six unusual mini-cannons were used to commemorate the founding of the local church of St Martin's in 1730 by Dr Browne Willis, and have been fired on this day ever since. The diminutive detonations occur at 8 am, noon, 2 pm and 6 pm.

Before the ancient practice was snuffed out in 1924, everyone from Fortingall in Tayside used to go to the tumulus known as the **Mound of the Dead** tonight, and dance until dawn round a bonfire of furze and gorse. One ingredient which the bonfire ritually avoided was blackthorn. Today it is deeply unlucky to take so much as a twig from the shrub. The blackthorn is guarded by spirits called **Lunantishee**, and they are in vengeful mood at Martinmas, meeting any defoliation with all manner of misery.

Martinmas was the day when the land of **Lyonesse** sank. According to some legends it is the place of Arthur's birth, and was situated between Land's End and the Scilly Isles. In 1099, a huge wave washed it all away, including its cities and 140 churches. Only a man named Trevilian escaped, and the Trevilian coat of arms still depicts a horse rising from the waves. Until about 1000BC land did indeed stretch beyond what is now Land's End right through to the Scillys, and so Lyonesse may well be a folk-memory of such times. As late as the 1970s old fishermen went on record claiming to have sometimes glimpsed Lyonesse's drowned buildings in the waves beneath their boats.

St Martin was a 4th-century saint given the onerous task of replacing the original holder of the feast day of November 11th, the Graeco-Roman wine-and-wildness god Bacchus. The boozing traditions continued after the coming of Christianity, with a thin veneer of legend saying that Martin could cure drunkards. To be

'Martin Drunk' is to reach that strange state on the far side of drunkenness.

In one legend Martin meets his death in the form of a cow, which is why a bull, **the Mart**, was killed and eaten every year on this day. There were many sacrificial animals opening their throats today in the saint's name, making a ritual of the seasonal necessity of killing and salting down meat for the winter ahead.

Weatherwise, the direction of today's wind points the windy way for the rest of the year. If it is very cold, then winter will be gentle. But Martinmas is usually quite mild, the start of a short spell known as **St Martin's Summer**, or the November **Halcyon Days**. This is because Martin gave his cloak to a poor beggar, and God commemorates this charity every year with a burst of unseasonably warm weather.

This century most Martinmas observance disappeared when today became **Armistice Day**, with the accompanying Remembrance Sunday. The poppies (red or white) worn on this day mirror the vast crop which grew on the site of the old battlefield of Flanders. Poppy seeds lie dormant until disturbed, and there can never before have been such a dreadful disturbance as the one which those fields witnessed. The original Armistice was signed on the 11th hour of the 11th day of the 11th month, 1918.

12th November
Hollantide/Old Samhain

Practising the Royal Wave

King Cnut (Canute) died on this day in 1035 after a reign of 18 years as King of England and Denmark. Legend sometimes portrays him as a wet-behind-the-ears, wet-everywhere-else egomaniac, who got a deserved soaking when the tide ignored his command that it should turn. But Cnut knew what he was doing when he stood on the beach. It was an act of humility, designed to set an example to his toadying 'yes-men' courtiers. As the waves washed over him, he declared: '*Let all the world know that the power of monarchs is vain. No one deserves the name of King but He whose Will the Heavens, Earth and Seas do obey.*'

Cnut's demonstration is thought to have happened in the Trent at Gainsborough, Lincolnshire; but the man who wrote it all down in the mid-12th century, Henry of Huntingdon, was unspecific. The fens of Cambridgeshire claim the tale too. Here, after the lesson was over, Cnut wandered off to visit the monks of Ely. They were drunk, as usual, refusing to let him in; and so Cnut stayed instead with a man called Legres. Legres told the king how 18 years ago the same monks had ruined his life – they had raped his wife, and had flogged him when he tried to rescue her. His wife had died while giving birth to a girl nine months later. For the past 18 years, on the date of his wife's death, Legres had marked the anniversary by hunting down and killing a monk. Cnut was appalled by Legres' story, and he ordered his fleet immediately to destroy the dissolute monastery. The monks who survived were enlisted to build the new town of Littleport, north of Ely. Just in case they showed any inclination to revert to their old ways, Legres was installed as Littleport's first mayor.

St Dunstan faced problems at the same debauched monastery, 200 years earlier. His solution was to turn all the monks into eels – thus giving Ely its name.

On the Isle of Man this is **Hollantide**, the Celtic Samhain according to the old calendar, when cattle were brought down from the hills for winter and slaughter. The problem with the timing is that this is also the night which the Hogmen – local faeries – choose to up sticks and move on. This puts them in a foul mood, and they will attack anyone who gets in their way.

© The small hours of Hollantide and the evening before see the **Hop-tu-naa** processions. These consist of alms-seeking children with turnip lanterns and a song which, in Douglas, has the lines: '*Jinnee the witch goes over the house to fetch a stick to leather the mouse, Hop-tu-naa.*' This is the last remnant of old anti-witch charms. Even older versions of the Hop-tu-naa song read like an extended game of consequences, and usually involve food, a pole cat and a trip to Scotland. Hop-tu-naa is sometimes mutated into 'Hogunna', a word linked to *Hogmanay*, this being the old Celtic New Year. Hop-tu-naa is very much alive and hopping on Man; but only a handful of hamlets have resisted the enormous gravitational pull of Hallowe'en, and most of the customs have now moved to October 31st.

Stapag was eaten tonight on the Isle of Skye in Scotland. It is a creamy porridge with various knicks-knacks inside. Each member of the household takes a spoonful and examines the indigestible bits. A ring portends marriage; a thimble means prison; and a button means a bachelor.

13th November

Stamford Stampede

In the reign of King John, William the Earl of Warren was gazing from his castle window one day when he saw two bulls fighting in a meadow. The town butchers tried to capture the animals, driving one of them into the town where it went on a rampage. Gore-loving Earl Warren followed on his horse and was impressed by the devastation that the animal caused before capture. So impressed, in fact, that he gave the butchers the meadow in which the bulls had fought, on condition that they provided an annual 13th November bull to continue the dubious sport of **bull-running**. They did; and until it was banned in 1839 the bull-running was a red-letter red-rag day in Stamford, Lincolnshire. Fans of ritualised animal slaying were encouraged to *'Stump away to Stamford'* every year. These days they have to stump away to Spain, Portugal or South America instead.

Stamford's bull-running links with the bullish mood of Martinmas and its sacrificial cattle. The animal was hounded through the streets by **bullards**. Dung flew everywhere: a local proverb insisted: *'He that gets no bull-dirt gets no Christmas.'* The object was to drive the bull off the bridge into the River Welland before slaughtering him for the evening feast. The mood is immortalised in *The Song Of The Stamford Bullards*, a ditty that everyone in the town used to know by heart. The final verse gets under the skin of the pagan excitement with its poignant lines:

This is the rebel's riot feast, humanity must be debased,
And every man must do his best to bait the bull at Stamford.

Similarly, an old bullard's speech insisted: *'On this day there is no King in Stamford, we are every one of us high and mighty . . . a Lord Paramount, a Lord of Misrule, a King of Stamford . . . We are punishable for no crime but murder, and that only of our own and no other species.'*

♫ Still with old folksongs and blood-sports, November 13th 1854 was the death-date of fox-terroriser **John Peel**. The famous song *Do Ye Ken John Peel* was written in 1832 by his pal John Woodcock Graves following a hunting bout. After it was sung for the first time at *The Rising Sun* back home in Caldbeck, Graves said *'By Jove Peel! You'll be sung when we're both run to earth!'* There is a memorial plaque to Peel in Caldbeck, which is mid-way between Carlisle and Keswick in Cumbria, and the still-sung huntsman is buried beside his son Peter in the town's churchyard. Peter's coffin is said to contain a fox brush which his father put there as a tribute, having gone hunting for it on the day of the funeral.

♀ Charles II's mistress **Nell Gwyn** died today in 1687. Her ghost can still be seen at what used to be the Gargoyle Club on Dean Street, London. The building later became the first venue of the Comedy Store, and is now a recording studio. Nell used to live here, and still leaves an odour of gardenias after her manifestations. She also haunts her other home, Salisbury Hall in London Colney, near St Albans in Hertfordshire, where footsteps and the sound of ghostly laughter have been heard. Nell once dangled her illegitimate son from an upstairs window here, threatening to drop him unless his father, Charles II, promised to give him a title.

14th November
St Dyfrig's Day

King Dribbler's Indestructible Daughter

St Dyfrig, also known as Durbricius, had a particularly harrowing delivery. His mother was princess Eurddil, daughter of King Peibau, who was known as King Dribbler, thanks to a habit of foaming at the mouth uncontrollably. When King Dribbler realised that unmarried Eurddil was heavily pregnant, out came a torrent of saliva and abuse. He bundled his daughter into a sack and threw her into the river. After the current had thrown her back ashore three times, the King changed plans and chucked her onto a fire. Next morning Eurddil was discovered unsinged, nursing the newborn Dyfrig. Her father was placated, and Dyfrig touched him on the cheek. *Shazam!* King Dribbler foamed no more. Dyfrig went on to great things, and according to Geoffrey of Monmouth (whose scholastic recipe favoured one part history to five parts fantasy), he was the bishop who crowned King Arthur. Dyfrig died in AD 550.

Lying about your age is an old favourite. Then again, perhaps **Old Parr** of Shropshire was telling the truth. He married at the age of 80, remarried at 120, and died at 152 after an over-exciting visit to the court of Charles I. He was buried in Westminster Abbey in 1635.

Elaborate **epitaphs** made up for the fact that not everyone lasted as long as Old Parr. George Routleigh of Lydford in Devon has the following timely classic:

> *Here lies in a horizontal position the outward case of George Routleigh, Watchmaker, whose abilities in that line were an honour to his profession. Integrity was the main spring and prudence the regulator of all the actions of his life. Humane, generous and liberal, his hand never stopped till he had relieved distress. So nicely regulated were all his motions that he never went wrong except when set agoing by people who did not know his key. Even then he was easily set aright. He had the art of disposing of his time so well that his hours glided away in one continual round of pleasure and delight till an unlucky minute put a period to his existence. He departed this life November 14, 1802, aged 57. Wound up in hope of being taken in hand by his Maker and of being thoroughly cleaned and repaired and set agoing in the world to come.*

Those with time on their hands can see Routleigh's tombstone in the churchyard at Lydford near Okehampton in Devon.

15th November

No-Member

Alfred the Great was one of the stars of English history: patron of the arts, defender of the isle, burner of cakes. **Albert the Great** was a 13th-century Dominican friar-turned-saint, with little or no relevance to these islands. This is his feast day. What a difference a couple of letters can make.

This was job-changing time in the Yorkshire wolds around Howden and Holme, both of which held **hiring fairs** today. A rule in this part of the world was *Monday flit, never sit*. This means that leaving an old employer is fine that day, but starting with a new one goes against tradition.

Even **weatherlore** sometimes has to bear resemblance to reality, and so the predictions for November veer heavily towards bleakness and the big freeze:

> *Ice in November to bear a duck,*
> *Nothing afterwards but slush and muck.*

Thunder during the month points to a good fertile year to come. But a fine show of November flowers means a harsh winter; and a rainy month leads, logically enough, to flooding in December. No consolation in sailing either, for if the month is windy:

> *November take flail,*
> *Let ships no more sail.*

Last century the poet Thomas Hood summed up all his feelings towards the month in *November*, a sustained burst of negativity:

> *No sun, no moon, no morn, no noon,*
> *No dawn, no dusk, no proper time of day.*

He had obviously not heard of the Halcyon Days (see November 11th). Hood's most intimate detail is:

> *No warmth, no cheerfulness, no healthful ease,*
> *No comfortable feel in any member.*

The **Lying Contest** at Temple Sowerby in Cumbria used to award a whetstone to the best liar, with a razor-sharpener for the second best. The Bishop of Carlisle once dropped by and gave the revellers a sermon on the evils of lying, rounding off by saying that he never lied himself. The second prize was thrown into his carriage as he departed. Or is all this a lie too?

The spirit of the contest is kept alive by the **World's Biggest Liar** championships in the Lake District. Each year in mid-November truth economists descend on the *Bridge Inn* at Wasdale. It is an amateur competition, and so entries are not permitted from lawyers, journalists, salesmen, politicians and estate agents – all deemed to be professional liars.

Skyscraper-high tall stories are erected, with credibility stretched so that it can cover the entire edifice. Each year the judges face around 200 entries, and whittle them down to one absolute whopper. The contest claims to be 150 years old, and to have been inspired by Wordsworth and the Lakeland poets, who considered the locals to have the highest mendacity capacity in Britain.

November 15th used to be famous for the Pig Inflating Ceremony at Whitley Bay. Men dressed as badgers poured milk over each other and dissected a euphonium . . . damn, it's catching.

16th November
St Margaret of Scotland's Day

And a Hundred-Eyed Octopus Sang in Berkeley Square

Ludovic Greville was pressed to death on this day in 1588 – an unpleasant end for an unpleasant man. Greville had converted his home at Milcote near Stratford-upon-Avon into a mock-castle, pre-empting the later craze for follies. The building cost more than he had anticipated, and so he looked for alternative sources of wealth. One of his former employees, a man called Webb, had come into money. Greville invited him over to dinner, and had two servants strangle him. Webb was then placed in the guest room, with one of the murderers hiding under the bed. When the parson came to hear the 'dying' Webb's will, the servant croaked out the details, and the parson swallowed the ventriloquist act. 'Webb' gave all his worldly goods to Greville.

The murderers were not well recompensed, and after a while one of them grew rebellious, openly complaining about the Webb of deceit, and how Greville had sold the vicar a dummy. Bad move. Greville had him killed by the second hit-man. The surviving servant now realised that he alone knew Greville's secret, and that such knowledge had a tendency to impact negatively on life expectancy. So he revealed all to the authorities, who swiftly put the squeeze on Greville. Greville admitted to the murder, and was given a crushing sentence.

Today in 1878 The Folklore Society provoked a torrent of correspondence when their Notes and Queries mentioned: '*There is a house in Berkeley Square said to be haunted and long unoccupied on that account.*'

✝ Many people wrote in claiming to have seen the house's ghost, and from their descriptions it became clear that the **ghost of Berkeley Square** was like no other phantom in Britain. Some said it was a boneless, blubbery mass of seething unpleasantness with a horrendous stench, its ever-expanding foulness covered in hundreds of red eyes. Other tales described the creature as a multi-tentacled monster from the London sewers. More anthropomorphic descriptions talked of a shapeless-faced humanoid with a huge gaping red mouth. The whatever-it-is had supposedly frightened several people to death, including a sailor who was impaled on a railing after jumping from an upstairs room. These days the house, at 50 Berkeley Square, is the home of Maggs Booksellers, who say that the ghost still occasionally appears.

The **balm well** at Liberton in Edinburgh owes its fame to **St Margaret of Scotland**. She had received a phial of oil from the tomb of St Catherine of Siena, and had tipped it into the well with dramatic results. The water became black and oily, and cured all manner of ailments, notably leprosy. Liberton is said to have derived from *Leper-town*.

⛶ This etymology is, at best, dubious: the black colouration at the well is actually caused by a coal seam at the water's source. Nevertheless, its reputation lured hobbling columns of pilgrims from across the country, and James I/VI was so convinced of its powers that in 1617 he instigated a major upgrade of the facilities. The balm well, also known as St Katherine's Well, is at St Katherine's House, which is owned by the Regional Assessment Centre. Visits can be made only by prior arrangement.

The well's original benefactor Margaret, who died in 1093, was one of the last of the Anglo–Saxon monarchs, wife of King Malcolm III. It is this union that enables the current monarchy to trace a (circuitous) link back to the pre-Conquest monarchs.

17th November
St Hilda's Day

Heigh Ho, Heigh Ho, It's Off From Work We Go

St Hilda was of royal stock, and as pagan as pagan can be. But then along came St Paulinus in 627 and baptised her. Before she knew where she was, Hilda had become a wise woman of the Anglo-Saxon Church, eventually founding the Abbey at what was then known as Streanae-shalch, and is now – thankfully – Whitby, North Yorkshire. Hilda's mother was not surprised by all this: before the birth of her daughter she had dreamed that in her own undergarments there lurked a precious jewel whose brilliance, once extricated, would light the whole world. The jewel, needless to say, was a metaphor for our heroine.

Hilda presided over 663–4's epic Synod of Whitby, debating the vexed question of when Easter should be celebrated. Hilda favoured the Celtic way of calculating the date, though the Roman calendar won the day, and the date of Easter has been decided in the same convoluted way ever since. Hilda took the defeat serenely. She was mild mannered and sympathetic, having vented all her life's spleen in one fell blow earlier in her career. Deeply distressed by the abundance of snakes on the cliffs of Esk-dale, she rustled up a basilisk-style miracle, and turned them all to stone. The legend is all the more uncanny for bearing a striking resemblance to that of St Keyne.

▥ The petrified reptiles can still be seen in the cliffs around Whitby, though foolish palaeontologists claim that they are not snakes at all but fossilised ammonites.

In the year 680, at least two nuns witnessed Hilda's departing soul flying to Heaven, assisted by angels. After Whitby was roughed up by the Vikings in 800, the saint's relics went forth and mysteriously multiplied. Rival sets of Hilda's bones turned up at Glastonbury and Gloucester, helping to transform her into a cult of national proportions. Pilgrims oscillated between the two sites, but – as happened to many saint-related artefacts – both sets of relics disappeared during the Reformation.

November 17th used to be **Queen's Day**, or Queen Elizabeth's Holiday. Yes, it was a day off, and yes, it was instigated by Queen Elizabeth I. The event first took place in 1570, to commemorate the 12th anniversary of the Queen's accession. The festivities were marked by bonfires, bell-ringing, feasts and dances. These included such specially-composed classics as Anthony Holbourne's *Heigh Ho Holiday*, whose Eurovisionesque title does no justice to the blistering lute riff which it generates.

Long after it ceased to be a national holiday, Queen's Day remained a bank holiday – the Bank of England and The Exchequer traditionally do no business today.

© **The Court Leet and Court Baron** are held at Sidbury Manor near Sidmouth in Devon on the third Wednesday of the month. The Leet and Baron elects officers to the Manor, after which the newly-instated officials indulge in those fine old medieval rituals of bread-weighing, meat-tasting and ale-tasting. Originally the appointed officers had the task of checking that the produce going into the Manor was of top quality. These days it is an occasion for a bit of pomp, a touch of dressing up, and a skinful of the good stuff at the Leet-ale, the feast that follows the Court.

18th November

Sub-Merino

When Elizabeth I went to visit the lawyers at London's Middle Temple, they were so hospitable that she decided to make them a **Christmas Pudding**. The lawyers were so touched by the gesture that they left a little of Elizabeth's generous gift, and later added to the ingredients for the next year's pudding. Century after century a portion of each year's pudding was put aside, until the entire lot was scoffed in the 1960s.

● **The Queen's Pudding** was revived in 1971 when the Queen Mother briefly stirred a new pudding for the lawyers; but without the original atoms of that first gift from Elizabeth I, the tradition is shorn of its poignancy.

◉ The traditional time for *all* Christmas Puddings to be made is **Stir Up Sunday**, the Sunday before Advent Sunday, which is the final one in November. Each member of the family should help stir the mixture. The Suffolk method is to stir three times, sunwise, and make three wishes. Only one wish each will come true, so make sure that they are all good ones.

The name Stir Up Sunday, and the impetus

for the pud-mixing, comes from the Collect traditionally read on this day in church: '*Stir up we beseech thee, O Lord, the wills of thy faithful people.*' A children's alms-collecting song for the day echoes this:

Stir up we beseech thee the pudding in the pot,
And when we get home we'll eat the lot.

Puddings should be made from 13 ingredients, one for each Apostle and one for Jesus. They should be stirred with a wooden spoon – to recall the manger – and in a sunwise direction, retracing the route of the Magi. It is still the practice in some households to make 13 puddings, the last of which is known as the **Judas Pudding** and either given to a beggar or thrown out. And for a hat-trick on the 13-theme, anyone who manages to eat pudding in 13 different homes between Christmas Day and New Year's Day will wallow in joy over the next 12 months.

© The third Saturday in November is the date of the **Mardale Shepherds' Meet** in Cumbria. From time immemorial shepherds have gathered at Mardale to swap stray sheep and stories, and drink themselves into a stupor. The next morning it is traditional for shepherds to crawl out of the pub chairs in which they have passed out, and go on to the fell-top for the **foot hunt**: a high-altitude human-and-hound pursuit of foxes.

Mardale Meet still meets, but not at Mardale. In the late 1930s Manchester Corporation drowned the village when they flooded the valley to make Haweswater Reservoir, and after fruitless discussion about providing aqualungs for the sheep, the whole caboodle was moved up the road to the *St Patrick's Well Inn* at Bampton, near Penrith. The day starts with the foot-hunt, and always formally ends with *While Shepherds Watch*, sung in darkness.

© The ancient and continuously held Mardale Meet is the last of the big Cumbrian Shepherds' Meets over the autumn. Several of the other Meets are revivals, now as much geared to flocks of tourists as any other animal. Highlights often include sheep shows, dog trials and/or fell races. The main Meets are all in the west Lakes – at Wasdale Head on the second Saturday in October and Buttermere on the third; and at Walner Scar near Seathwaite on the first Saturday in November.

19th November
St Ermenburga's Day

Lighting the Saint's Hind-Quarters

The Returning Hero has taken many guises down the ages, most obviously in the shape of famous *Rex quondam Rexque futurus* candidates such as Jesus and King Arthur. One of the most obscure was **Judge Milton, The Promised Shiloh**. Prophetess Joanna Southcott had mentioned such a coming early in the 19th century (see December 20th). Judge Milton appeared at Wakefield on this day in 1898. He claimed to be Shiloh, the new Messiah, and demanded the rights to the property of one of Southcott's followers, John Wroe ('star' of the 1993 BBC TV series, *Mr Wroe's Virgins*). When he failed to provide any evidence to back up his grandiose claims, Milton was forced to drop the 'Son of God' and go back to plain 'Judge'.

The autumn of 1799 was ablaze with strange electrical storms and lights; and on this day at Huncoates in Lincolnshire a **ball of fire** flew across the heavens, leaving a trail of flashes behind it. Seven days earlier at Hereford, the moon had shone with a fierce glow, accompanied by short dazzling flashes and pulses. All the lights had suddenly coalesced, and then burst apart again, shooting trails of fire across the sky in the form of glowing red pillars. These natural fireworks were witnessed by hundreds. Many – with typical end-of-the-century-foreboding – saw them as apocalyptic omens.

St Ermenburga, who also liked to be called Domneva, was a Kentish princess whose uncle had usurped the local throne. Not only that, but he plotted with his own sons to kill the rightful heirs, Ermenburga's two brothers. The crime was carried out by Thunor, who became the new heir-apparent. In an act of weirdness, Thunor chose to bury the brothers beneath the King's throne. This already indiscreet location became even more conspicuous when the bodies began to glow, and light poured out from between the King's legs when he was in residence. Helped by this divine clue, the corpses were uncovered, and Ermenburga demanded the dead men's **wergild**.

Wergild was a monetary compensation which, in law, the next of kin could claim when members of their family were killed in unlawful circumstances. Being princes, the two wergilds were worth a packet. Ermenburga used the money to buy land so that she could fulfil her life's ambition: the founding of a nunnery. Estate agents did not have the same grasp of economics in the 7th century as they do today, and the size of Ermenburga's property was determined by unleashing a hind. All the ground that the animal was able to cover in a set time would be Ermenburga's to do with as she pleased. So the deer set off, with the crowd cheering it on its way. At one stage the unrepentantly villainous Thunor rode his horse in front of the hind to try and stop it, but to no avail. In fact he regretted his attempted intervention. As a medieval chronicler put it: '*This impiety so offended Heaven, that the earth opened and swallowed him up.*' Despite this hindrance, the hind somehow managed to cover 10,000 acres. The nunnery was built, and three of Ermenburga's four children became saints like their mum, who died in AD 700.

Anyone infringing the charter that gave Ermenburga her land at Minster, on the Isle of Thanet in Kent, runs the gauntlet of an inbuilt **curse**. And from the depths of Hell, Thunor's only consolation is that the name Thunor's Leap was given to the spot where he paid dearly for interfering with someone else's hind.

20th November
St Edmund's Day

Wolves 1, Spurs 0

Until both his reign and body were truncated after the Battle of Hoxne in Suffolk in 869, **St Edmund** was the King of East Anglia. The victorious Vikings had captured him and tried to make him carry on as a pagan puppet ruler. He refused, and so they tied him to a tree at Hellesden, Suffolk, and stuffed him full of arrows. An evocative Latin chronicler recorded the King as looking like '*a thistle, or a hedgehog*'.

When things had died down a bit, Edmund's men came searching for him. They found the body, but the head was elusive. That is, until one of the searchers got lost and shouted '*Where are you?*' The words '*Over here!*' came back in what sounded like the King's voice. The men followed the sound and found a huge grey wolf. Between the wolf's paws was Edmund's head. The beast followed the men

home and turned back only when they had reunited head and body, which miraculously glued together.

Edmund was buried at the Suffolk town which then became Bury St Edmunds – an appropriate name if ever there was one. But the ex-King's deeds did not end with death. A few years later he materialised in the middle of another battle against the Vikings, harpooned the Danish King, and then beamed straight back to Heaven.

☯ St Edmund remains popular across East Anglia, and in 1989 Southwold in Suffolk revived the old custom of giving schoolchildren a specially baked **St Edmund's Bun** on November 20th, or the nearest weekday. The origin of this bun bonus is unknown, but it appears to go back over a century, and died out when the local school was shut down during the Second World War. These days, after a short church service at 2.45 pm, the mayor of Southwold hands out sticky buns in the church porch. The celebration ends with the children planting a tree at a nearby site. Southwold has a long history of commemorative tree planting. In 1887 an oak was planted to mark the Jubilee of Queen Victoria. It died. Another was planted on the same spot to celebrate the marriage of George V and Queen Mary. It also died. But the idea took root, and from the 1920s Southwold introduced an annual **Arbor Day** tree-planting ceremony, as part of the St Edmund's celebrations at first, though it now takes place at the end of November, timed to coincide with National Tree Week.

☩ The one element that tarnishes Edmund's reputation as hero and martyr is a tale which says that before he was captured and killed, Edmund had fled the battlefield at Hoxne and hidden under Goldbrook Bridge. The glint of his golden spurs was spotted by some newly-weds, and the happy couple inadvertently gave away his hiding place. As Edmund was dragged away by the Danes, he cursed all married couples who crossed the bridge from that day on. The recently nuptialed must, even now, seek an alternative route or risk heading straight for the divorce courts. What is more, on moonlit nights Edmund's spurs can still be glimpsed, glinting in the water.

Still with Edmund but on a more bean-and-garlic sort of note:

Set garlic and beans on St Edmund the King,
The moon in the wane thereof hangeth a
thing.

If you can work out what it means, it is probably sound and sage advice.

21st November

Let's Go Foy a Kite

Today in 1863, Guildford belatedly celebrated Guy Fawkes Night with a riot. Even by the standards of the mid-19th century, the festivities on the 5th at Guildford in Surrey were wild. The **Guildford Guys** – a secret society led by the sons of wealthy locals – organised the huge bonfire, with the crowds making use of anything that came to hand for the blaze. Doors and fences were regularly torn down, and one year the entire grandstand from Merrow racecourse was ripped apart and thrown on the pyre.

Decoy beacons were lit to fool the police, and if officers were daft enough to tackle the mob they were pelted with stones. By the 1850s, it was usual for the Head Constable to lock his men in the cells on the night to protect them from the crowd.

In 1863 the town corporation got tough. Troops were called in, along with special constables armed with cutlasses. They patrolled the town every night from the 5th onwards. All remained calm, and – satisfied that the threat of anarchy was over – the soliders were withdrawn on the 21st. Two hours after they left, out came the Guys to take their vengeance. They wreaked havoc across the town, and threw patrolman PC Sutton on to their bonfire. He escaped with serious burns. Only after the mayor had read the Riot Act was a semblance of order restored. Guy Fawkes Night 1864 passed quietly, but it was not until several of the gang were arrested in the act of clubbing a policeman to death in 1865 that the power of the Guildford Guys was broken.

Henry Purcell died today in 1695. The 'Father of English Music', and the mother of all 17th century organists, he churned out great music for royal occasions. But with Purcell there is often a catch – for much of his life he turned his back on British traditions and influences. As well as frequently importing his myths from abroad – his opera *Dido and Aeneas* is based on an ancient Roman doomed-love legend – he had no truck with homegrown music, especially ballads. He described his work as no more than '*a just imitation of the most fam'd Italian masters*', which he had

written '*to bring the seriousness and gravity of that sort of Musique into vogue, and reputation among our Contry-men, whose humor 'tis time now, should begin to loath the levity, and balladry of our neighbours.*'

Today was **Old Martinmas Eve** in many peoples' diaries. In Scotland it marked the the end of seasonal employment, and formed an excuse to pig out. **The Foy**, as the feast was known, was for many the best meal of the year. The lucky had their Foy provided by their new or old employer; the very lucky would get one from each. There were other Foys too. The one that heralded the fishing season in coastal settlements had a traditional toast of: '*The Lord open the mouths of the gray fish.*'

From the same cookery class as the Foy, in East Yorkshire the Sunday nearest Old Michaelmas was called **Rahv-Kite Sunday**. *Rahv-Kite* means 'tear-stomach', a metaphor for eating far too much. It was a meal provided by the family after the prodigal offspring returned home between jobs. It was often the case that the Rahv-Kite nosh – usually a goose – was consolation for a hungry year in a bad situation. An East Yorkshire rhyme mentions the hiring fairs that followed Rahv-Kite Sunday, around Old Martinmas, which was often the one and only pay day in the year:

> Good Morning, Mister Martinmas, you've
>   come to set me free,
> For I don't care for Master, and he don't
>   care for me.

22nd November
St Cecilia's Day

Cecilia – The First Organ Donor

St Cecilia was a 3rd-century Roman Christian who, despite having a husband, took a vow of chastity, and declined to consummate the marriage. Cecilia's other claim to fame – and the reason why she is the patron of musicians – is that she is said to have invented the organ. She began passing the time of day with an angel, as the amorous heavenly spirit had fallen in love with Cecilia and her wondrous musical charms. These were most thrilling '*When to her organ vocal breath was giv'n*', as Dryden wrote.

Cecilia was sentenced to death after refusing to sacrifice to pagan gods, and was put in a dry bath for roasting. A bizarre execution, and one which failed. She remained cool and collected; so they tried to chop her head off. After several blows, she was merely bleeding profusely. She died three days later. Her body survived intact for over a thousand years, but when her tomb was opened in 1599 her corpse began to decay rapidly and was replaced by a hastily fashioned stone replica.

Like those of many other saints, Cecilia's celebrations were damped down by the Puritans. But after the Restoration, her links with music were such that in 1683 a society was set up with the sole aim of celebrating St Cecilia's Day with songs and sermons. Purcell wrote a special inaugural Ode, and added several more down the years. In 1686, Dryden weighed in with his *Song for Saint Cecilia's Day*. This perceives music as the wool that knits together the universe, concluding with a wonderful End Of Time epitaph that rivals Michael Moorcock:

So when the last and dreadful hour
This crumbling pageant shall devour,
The trumpet shall be heard on high,
The dead shall live, the living die,
And Musick shall untune the sky.

As well as the contributions of Purcell and Dryden, there is also Pope's *Ode For Music on St Cecilia's Day*; and, much earlier, Chaucer's *Second Nun's Tale* in *The Canterbury Tales*, which deals with Cecilia's life and death. © By the 20th century, all had again gone quiet on St Cecilia's Day; but the festivities were revived in 1946. Benjamin Britten wrote some new music – today was his birthday, which gave him added impetus. It is still the custom to commission big league composers to write an ode or anthem for the concert. The venue for the day's service was St Sepulchre in London, until 1990 when the church closed for restoration. The service now alternates between Westminster Abbey, Westminster Cathedral and St Paul's on the Wednesday nearest the 22nd. The royal concert in the evening alternates between the Barbican, The Albert Hall and the Royal Festival Hall, featuring the massed choirs of the three alternating churches. There are other St Cecilia concerts throughout the country – notably at Rochester, Edinburgh, York, Bournemouth, Norwich, Brighton and Wakefield.

Today used to be a hatters' holiday, being the eve of their patron **Saint Clement**. Like Cecilia, he was both saint and inventor, having stumbled upon **hat-felt** after a long and tiring walk. To prevent chafing, Clement stuffed wool between his foot and sandal, and the combination of sweat and compaction resulted in the first felt.

23rd November
St Clement's Day/
Old Martinmas

Smiths and Legends

St Clement was tied to an anchor in AD 100, and drowned. Angels then made an under-sea tomb for him, which was said to be uncovered once a year by an exceptionally low tide. The fact that the fatal anchor was made of iron was reason enough for **blacksmiths** to forge links with Clement and make him their patron, ousting Wayland, the Saxon smith-god, who was himself a recast version of the Roman god Vulcan. Smiths, after all, dealt with fire and metal, gifts from the gods.

Blacksmiths were a proud clan in those days. When King Alfred had a competition to see who was the best craftsman, the smith felt certain of victory. But the tailor slipped Alfred a new coat, and that swayed him. Incensed at this corruption, the smith went on strike, and soon all the iron weapons and implements were falling apart with no one to mend them. At this stage Alfred's men tried to do the smithying themselves but made a pig's ear of the job, knocking over the anvil and shattering it.

It was only when Clement appeared in ghostly form that Alfred admitted to being bribed, and he belatedly awarded the smith first prize. In a final act of pique, the tailor nipped under the table and slashed the smith's apron. This is said to be why blacksmiths have ever since worn ragged aprons.

Today was once a mega-bash for blacksmiths everywhere. **Clementing** took to the streets – parades with torches, mock anvils, axes and Old Clem, who was either an effigy or a smith dressed in apron, false grey wig and beard. The gang used to be seen at Woolwich in Kent, parading from pub to pub to pub to oblivion.

The best celebrations took place at Twyford, Hampshire. Old Clem and his team did the rounds for a feast in the *Bugle Inn*, before the heavy metal climax of **Firing the Anvil**. Gunpowder was crammed into a hole in the side of the anvil, and lit. The explosion lifted the anvil off the ground, and could be heard over a mile away.

In the Midlands, Clement himself somehow dropped out of the Clementing, which became a simple alms-collecting mission for fruit and money. At Walsall in the West Midlands, the mayor used to throw apples and pennies at the children in the name of Clem; while at Ripon in North Yorkshire, choristers handed out apples stuck through with a sprig from a box tree, much to the bemusement of the recipients.

For **seamen** to embrace a saint who drowned may seem a bit odd. But, because of his anchor connection, Clement was once popular with sailors, and even now is patron of lighthousemen. At Tenby in Dyfed, the fishing-crews rounded off their Clementing with a meal of roast goose and rice pudding, provided by the boatowners.

Along with the hatters' celebrations (see yesterday) all the Clem clamour died out at the end of the 19th century. The one recent revival was in 1961 at Enville, Staffordshire. Locals dusted down the local Clemeny Song, and schoolchildren took part in a penny and apple scramble. Unfortunately, the school itself closed down in the mid-1980s, bringing the custom to an inclement end.

Appropriately, given all the Twyford gunpowder, this was the day in 1605 upon which the **Gunpowder Plotters** confessed to hiring a certain Guy Fawkes to carry out their abortive plan.

24th November
St Catherine's Eve

Coaching Ghosts in Teme Work

There are two impressive **coach-driving ghosts** in villages just west of Worcester. At Leigh, long-deceased local JP Richard Colles used to return to Leigh Court every St Catherine's Eve, his eerie entry heralded by tinkling bells. He then swept in with his coach and eight black horses, careering round the Court 13 times. For the finale Old Colles, as he was fondly known, headed over the top of the tithe barn, and into the River Teme without even a sploosh.

This yearly exercise was exorcised by 12 parsons who, armed only with a short candle, laid Old Colles in a nearby pool. The ghost was told that it could not rise again until the candle had burned down. To make this event highly unlikely, the exorcists then threw the candle into the pool, which was subsequently filled in.

☥ The other ghost-coach can be seen in Little Shelsley, and belongs to Lady Lightfoot, who was murdered at the Court House. At irregular intervals she drives round the house, then nips through the wall for a brief but impressive spot of indoor shrieking, before hurtling out again and into the moat, where she sinks with a hiss and a cloud of smoke.

For many centuries it was believed that storms were a manifestation of a monarch's illness, and that he or she would die when the winds were at their wildest and the isobars were most densely packed. In 1928, **George V** was ill while a great storm raged. On November 24th the storm peaked, and an old beater of the King's on the Isle of Skye came down from the hills and into Kingsburgh to listen to the latest bulletin on the hamlet's one radio. He heard news that the King was still alive, and went away satisfied. When told a few days later that George was recovering, the old man shrugged and nodded. George had not passed away at the height of the storm, and so would obviously survive – the old man did not need a radio to tell him that.

It has long been polite practice to cover the face of the recently deceased with a **handkerchief** or piece of muslin. In 1880 on this day a murderer called Pavey was sentenced at the Old Bailey. He had killed a child, but had still done the decent thing and covered his victim's face with a hanky. *His* hanky. It was personalised and was easily traced back to Pavey, who admitted his crime and was sent to the gallows.

Rotherham Statutes, at Rotherham in South Yorkshire, used to be well into its stride by today. They began on St Edmund's Eve (the 19th), and continued for the following week. There is an old song about the *Stattis*, as they were known locally. In it, the merrymaking mob drink hot ale and gin and dance while a fiddler '*played 'em* Farewell Manchester *and warbled until dark*'. One of the dancers then treads on the fiddle, ending the dance, and the song. The Stattis died out in the 1920s, and even before then they had lost one of their highlights, **the flagellations**. In 1879, writer

John Guest lamented their passing: '*Where are now the robust farming men with the long wagon whips, the emulative cracking of which in the church yard was one of the sights (and sounds) of the day?*'

25th November
St Catherine's Day

Catterns and Patterns

In the 13th century, Sir Guy Saucimer decapitated Sir Everard Bevercotes. He loved Isabell de Caldwell, and killed Bevercotes because he was the obtuse angle in a love triangle. This happened near Newark-on-Trent in Nottinghamshire, at an earthwork called the Queen's Sconce by the river in Devon Park. When Bevercotes' head left his shoulders and hit the ground, a spring gushed forth. Sensing divine intervention, Saucimer fled. Isabell then died of grief, and Saucimer came down with a sudden, unexplained and very large dose of leprosy.

It was at this sorry stage that St Catherine appeared, telling the by now comprehensively repentant Saucimer to bathe in the spring. He did, and was cured. It became known as **St Catherine's Well**. Saucimer built a chapel over it and spent the rest of his life there in constant prayer. The well is now in a private garden, and at least one GP recently claimed that the waters had retained their powers.

Wheels wrapped in burning straw were a symbol of the ancient sun-god, and were regularly rolled around the fields in his honour, a supplication on behalf of good weather or fertility. When sun gods fell from fashion, the wheels became associated with St Catherine, who was tortured on one. The **Catherine Wheels** of Guy Fawkes Night are miniatures of the sun-god and saint emblems. As for our heroine, she survived the blades and stretchings of the wheel when it burst apart, killing several wicked bystanders, including its inventor. But her pagan persecutors chopped off her head instead, and out sprang gushing, gory streams of frothy, bubbling . . . milk. For this reason Catherine is patron of wet-nurses.

A favourite game during the St Catherine festivities involved the **Cattern Candle**. This was about two feet high with a large flame. The goal was to jump over it. If it went out as you leaped, farewell good luck. Catching fire was

not good news either. One accompanying rhyme has outlasted the game:

> *Kit (or Jack) be nimble, Kit be quick,*
> *Kit jump over the candlestick.*

An alternative, less familiar, version challenges us with a game of spot-the-rhythm:

> *The tailor of Bister he has but one eye,*
> *He cannot cut a pair of green galagaskins, if*
> *he were to die.*

All this flame-leaping is another example of the fire-and-fertility sun-god muscling in on a supposedly Christian festival.

On the food front, Catterners could look forward to **Cattern Cakes** made from sweet dough; and wigs, light buns flavoured with caraway. Somerset farmers ate Cattern Pies, shaped like a Catherine Wheel, filled with mince, honey and breadcrumbs, and harking back again to the sun-image. And no one left home without their iron stomach-linings, as the drink of the day was hot pot: not a liquidised mixture of lamb and potatoes, but a flagon of hot beer, rum, and eggs.

Some areas went in for **Catterning**, which was a simple procession, often with a white-robed Cattern Queen, begging for money. Catherine went arm in alm with St Clement (whose feast is the 23rd), as seen in the traditional rhyme for the occasion:

> *Cattern and Clemen be here, be here,*
> *Some of your apples and some of your beer.*

🗌 At Abbotsbury, near Weymouth in Dorset, those seeking bolt-from-the-blue romance used to trek to **St Catherine's Well** today, put one knee and their hands in three holes inside the chapel (one bit of the body per hole), and wish aloud for a tall dark stranger to engulf them. Only female applicants are accepted at the still-visible well, and legend has it that results are swift.

As well as by wet-nurses, Catherine was adopted as patron by **lacemakers**, whose main holiday was today. But this patronage resulted from a mix-up in Catherines. The lace-champion was not the woman who went her separate ways on the spinning wheel, but **Katherine of Aragon**, first wife of Henry VIII. Katherine moved to Ampthill Park, Bedfordshire, after the divorce, bringing with her all the Spanish skills of lace-making. She passed on her craft to the locals, and the trade was thus established. Bedfordshire and Hertfordshire have ever since been the main bases for ace lacemakers, with an isolated pocket in Nottinghamshire. Another legend says that Katherine burned all her old lace and ordered replacements, giving the lacemakers a bonanza of work and cash. Ms Aragon's name is perpetuated by a traditional lace pattern that is named after her.

☗ If planning holidays for next February, check the **weather** today: '*As at Catherine foul or fair, so will be the next February.*'

26th November

Double Decker Sandwich

The fortnight-long storm of November 1703 killed thousands of seamen, the largest death toll ever suffered by the navy at that point, in battle or otherwise. At **Goodwin Sands** off Deal and Sandwich in Kent, 1,190 perished. On November 26th there were 160 vessels moored around Deal. Some 24 cataclysmic hours later, more than half had sunk. One of the luckier sailors was Thomas Atkins. He found himself sole survivor of the *Mary* as he clung to a section of the shattered ship and watched his Admiral go down with the rest of the wreckage. A wave then carried Atkins high in the air and deposited him on the deck of the sinking *Stirling Castle*. So he had the misfortune to be shipwrecked a second time. As the vessel went down, another wave miraculously plonked the man into the one intact ship's boat, and the wind drove him ashore.

British folklore has several tales in which a miner or geologist hacks into a previously undisturbed, millenia-old stratum of rock and is amazed when a **toad** nonchalantly hops out. On this day in 1825, geologist William Buckland put these stories to the test. He took two dozen toads – 12 large, 12 small – and encased each in its own lump of sandstone or limestone. There were glass panels through which all the victims could be viewed. After 13 months there was not much to watch. The small toads were all stone dead, as were the large ones embedded in the sandstone. The large toads wedged into the limestone hung on for a few more months, but that was all.

So, observed Buckland, permeable limestone lets in air and water, perhaps even tiny animals, and large toads can survive for quite a while on their fat reserves. Not that hanging in there for just over a year – impressive as that is – explains the proposed phenomenon of toads sitting tight through aeons. Rather than inferring that the fabulous rock-dwelling toad was no more than a pleasing myth, Buckland concluded that in yet-to-be-determined ideal conditions it might be possible for toads to survive for a yet-to-be-determined number of years. Sounds suspiciously like a man angling for a further research grant.

© The four evenings before the last Friday in November constitute the **Court Leet** at Wareham in Dorset. Strangely dressed men wander from shop to pub to shop with their secret weapons for fighting crime: an 18th-century pewter ale-measure, and a clapped-out pair of ancient scales. The pewter is for the ale-tasters, and the scales are for the bread-weighers. Some bakers used to skimp on the flour but used extra yeast to achieve a uniform size in the loaf: the weighers made sure that there was bulk, not just air. The old song *Rigs of the Time* bemoans this crime in its lines about the baker:

When he do bring it in it's no bigger than your fist,
And the top of the bread is popped off with the yeast.

The Court Leet also has a Leather Sealer, two Scavengers – who check rubbish – a Hayward, and Surveyors and Searchers of Mantles and Chimneys. Also known as the Chimney Peepers, these last officials check flues and ventilation, seeking out any soot that might lead to fires. If soot is found, the landlord is fined a double measure of whisky or the equivalent. Such rare, surviving inspections hark back to Norman times, when every town had an annual Court Leet to install a large dollop of law, order, weights and measures for the coming year.

27th November

My Typo Woman

Today in 1582, William **Shakespeare** obtained a licence to marry **Anne Whateley**. The following day a legal bond was signed by two friends of the Hathaway family, promising £40 to Shakespeare after his marriage to Anne *Hathaway*. Now, in days when a giant of literature could sign his name not just as *Shakespeare*, but *Shakspear* and *Shaxper*, it does not take an earth-girdling leap of imagination to realise that Hathaway and Whateley are the same woman.

But no, legend is not going to take this lying down. Drawing on the known fact that Ms Hathaway gave birth six months after the wedding, we have the yarn that she was a maidservant to Anne Whateley. Shakespeare was betrothed to Whateley, but it was Hathaway, his mistress, who got pregnant. But all's well when Anne swells, and the maidservant had persuasive relatives who made Shakespeare do the decent thing.

✝ The myth-making does not stop there. It claims that Anne Whateley had a second identity as the poet Elizabeth Anne Beck, the Whateley tag having being supposedly taken from the family who had owned her father's land years before. Beck ended her days as a nun, dying in 1600. At her home, Hillborough Manor near Temple Grafton, just west of Stratford in Warwickshire, the **ghost** of a glowing nun is sometimes seen. Hillborough is the only house to be haunted by a printing error.

Premonitions and forewarnings are a favourite subject in the spirit world. Much less common is the sport of **bilking the ghost**.

Lord Lyttelton died on this day in 1779 at his house, Pitt Place, at Epsom in Surrey, after receiving a forewarning and unsuccessfully attempting to bilk. Seventy-two hours prior to his death Lyttelton had heard wings fluttering at his bedside, and had looked up to see the pale but familiar form of Mrs Amphlett. The mother of three young girls, she had allowed Lord Lyttelton to have his way, or ways, with her daughters. Mrs Amphlett had just died from a broken heart, and at the instant of her death her ghost had manifested in Lyttelton's bedroom to advise him of his own demise. She informed the bane of her ex-life that in just three days he too would be no more.

Three days later he was still feeling fine, and talked of 'bilking' the ghost – thwarting its prophecy. But in what he thought was mid-bilk, he keeled over and passed away. At that exact moment, over at Dartford in Kent, Lyttelton's friend Miles Andrews saw Lyttelton enter his room and say '*It's all over with me, Andrews*'. Andrews was momentarily flabbergasted by his ghostly visitor, but then he attacked in a way which no phantom could

have anticipated: he threw his slippers at it, and followed its retreat into the drawing room. Even though there was no one there, and all the doors were locked, it took Andrews a long time to realise that he had seen the wraith of Lyttelton at the exact moment of his death.

◉ ⬛ Today in 1703 the **tempest** which devastated the ships at Goodwin Sands (see yesterday) continued on its path, destroying Eddystone Lighthouse in Devon, and killing 15,000 sheep in Gloucestershire. Among the human dead was Rowland Briggs of Swallowmire in Cumbria. He left money in his will to provide bread for the poor of the parish. He is buried at Cartmel priory, and to this day there is a special cupboard in the church which all year round is kept supplied with buns for the needy.

28th November
St Juthwara's Day

Cheesed Off

After the Restoration in England, the **Covenanters** – the Scottish pro-Parliament, anti-English-Monarchy, anti-Catholic, pro-Presbyterianism, back-to-basics religious and political movement – came in for some heavy duty persecution and imprisonment. This lowered their numbers but strengthened their resolve, and in 1666 the Covenanters had a last fling against authority. They mustered an army of 3,000 and marched on Edinburgh. Today, at Rullion Green in the Pentland Hills just four miles outside the Scottish capital, they took on the forces of the Crown. The Covenanters were crushed, despite singing Psalms 74 and 78 as they fought. Many were captured: the lucky ones were deported to Barbados; the less lucky were gibbeted. The even less fortunate were tortured first, their feet smashed horribly in contracting iron boots. But they still refused to renounce the Covenant.

⬛ A monument in the churchyard at Hamilton in Strathclyde commemorates four Covenanters executed and dismembered in Edinburgh after the Covenanters' defeat at Rullion Green. Carved beneath four stone skulls is the verse:

Stay, passenger take notice what thou reads:
At Edinburgh lie our bodies, here our heads:
Our right hands stood at Lanark, these we
*   want.*
Because with them we sware the Covenant.

Pious young **Juthwara**, having just lost her father, complained to her wicked stepmother of chest pains. The stepmother serendipitously realised that she could turn Juthwara's ailment to her advantage, and convinced the girl that the best remedy was for her to cover her breasts in cheese. The stepmother then sneaked off and told her son that his step-sister was pregnant. The son noticed the damp patches on Juthwara's vest, and concluded that it was breast milk. He confronted the girl and her bra-full of cheese and cut off her head. A spring arose on the spot, and despite having got it in the neck, Juthwara carried her own head to the local church. Based on this legend, St Juthwara's unusual religious emblem is two cream cheeses, making her a rival to St Ivel (who is even more fictional than St Juthwara).

The life story of the historical Juthwara is all holes and no substance, like a giant Emmental. The only half-fact is that she probably died at Lanteglos in Cornwall. At Halstock, near Yeovil in Dorset, there is a tale of a St Juthware which is similar to the cheesy one. Here, the saint keeps an open house for local pilgrims, much to the chagrin of her mother and brother. When the queue for the bathroom becomes too much to bear, her brother slays Juthware by cutting off her head. She then carries it to Halstock church, and dies. Nice story; but it could do with a bit of cheese.

♱ A swift mention for Juthwara/Juthware (whose alternative name was Judith)'s **headless ghost**, which wanders around Judith Hill in Halstock. And, sadly, we have to mention *The Quiet Woman* pub in Halstock, which shows Juthware carrying her head in the crook of her arm: the ultimate misogynist joke.

29th November

Cardinal's Shadowy Fate

♱ In the cellars of England's oldest pub, *The Trip to Jerusalem* in Nottingham, is a passage called **Mortimer's Hole**, which leads up to Nottingham Castle. Rebel and regent Roger de Mortimer was apprehended and sent to Tyburn for a severe hanging on November 29th 1330 after **Edward III** crept through the Hole and surprised him in mid-misdeed. Treacherous Mortimer – the mole in the Hole – haunts the passage to this day.

Edward was 14 when his mother Isabella led a rebellion with Mortimer and forced her husband King Edward II to step down, in 1327. After murdering the deposed Edward senior, Mortimer and Isabella ruled the country and hoped that young Edward III would be too busy with growing up to interfere. But in 1330, at the age of 17, Edward decided that Mortimer was a crook, sent him to Tyburn, and forced his mother to go and twiddle her thumbs in the country on a pension of £3,000.

🍺 *The Trip To Jerusalem* is still pulling pints. It was originally the spot where pilgrims to the Holy Land stopped for ale. After all, if you aim for the Holy Land and end up in Nottingham, you need some kind of consolation.

There is a hill in the Malverns that casts a nasty shadow. Find yourself in the shade of **Ragged Stone Hill**, and it is more bad luck than a trip under a ladder factory or a jack-knifed Acme Mirrors juggernaut. **Cardinal Wolsey** once dozed off near the hill and woke to find himself under its shadow. He was horrified, for he knew of the hill's reputation. Despite rising to the position of Cardinal, Archbishop of York and Lord Chancellor under Henry VIII, the Ragged Stone Hill curse eventually caught up with him. He fell from grace after failing to obtain Henry's first divorce, and was accused of treason. Old and sick, he died on this day in 1530 en route to his trial, on the road from York to London, at Leicester Abbey, which is now a ruin.

🍺 A symbol of Wolsey's fall sits in the churchyard at East Bergholt near Ipswich in Suffolk. There is a wooden bell-house, separate from the church. It is said to have been erected late in the 15th century by Wolsey to hang the bells temporarily while he built a grand tower on the church. The tower was not finished at the time of the Cardinal's fall and demise, and so the wooden building still stands.

© On the Saturday nearest St Andrew's Day, Eton College in Berkshire stages the **Eton Wall Game**. Scrums of players – known as bullies – engage in a messy mêlée across a pitch, which measures 125 feet by five yards. A goal has not been scored since 1911. With so much going for it, it is no wonder that the Wall Game is unique to Eton. The all-mud, no-action spectacle can be watched by anyone with time to kill, and the thrills start just before 11 am.

30th November
St Andrew's Day/Andermass

Sheep's Head, Squirrels' End, and Assorted Bits of Andrew

When St Andrew was martyred in the 1st century AD he opted for an X-shaped cross, as he felt unworthy of being killed in the same way as Jesus. When his time came to be crucified, he amazed his detractors by saying: '*I come to thee exulting and full of joy.*' Followers were impressed by this Adoration of the Cross, as it came to be called, and Andrew became the second Christian to gain a cross as his symbol.

Meanwhile, in 8th-century Scotland, a giant X appeared in the sky just before the Pictish High King Angus went into battle. He won, and from then on the St Andrew's Cross or saltire was to be the Scottish flag. To remind people of his Caledonian inclinations, Andrew also appeared to Robert the Bruce before the Battle of Bannockburn in 1314.

Andrew's actual connection with Scotland is tenuous. It is said that St Rule brought some of the saint's relics – teeth, kneecap, arm-bone and three fingers – with him on a wild sea voyage. Angels had told Rule to set sail at the mercy of the elements. These elements had tossed him on to the shores of Fife. Rule and the relics came to rest at what is now St Andrews. A few miracles, a churchful of pilgrims, and 18 holes of golf later, St Andrews was a rich and thriving holy town.

© All over the world Scots raise the following toast today: '*To the memory of St Andrew and Scotland yet*.' Rather late on the scene, since 1980 the Fife town of St Andrews' own St Andrew's Society has organised a day of religious services, music and drama on the 30th. In former times the north of the border St Andrew's Day celebrations were all about slaughter and feasting, as harvest came later in Scotland than in the south, and this was the time for thinking about winter and the killing of surplus stock.

In Northamptonshire tonight was Mischief Night, when no gate or window in the county was safe. As a consolation there were traditional Tander Cakes to be eaten. Some recipes tart up a basic bread dough with fruit, sugar, eggs and copious lard. In Bedfordshire the cakes were called Tandry Wigs, or St Andrew's Buns – which sounds like something particularly disgusting amongst St Rule's box of relics.

The day's other name was Andermass. And no Andermass was complete without a bout of squirrel-hunting. In Scotland the hunt was known as Andra-ing, a squirrel (and rabbit) massacre to bolster the Andermass casserole later in the day. But in England – especially Kent and Sussex – the legal squirrel purge was cover for widespread illegal activity. Marching to the woods and fields with guns and snares, locals would often ignore the small furry things with the long tails, and spend the day poaching as many pheasant, partridge, rabbit and hare as they could find.

These days, apart from the occasional Tander Cake, St Andrew's food has changed. Squirrel has moved aside on the Scottish menu for the robust delights of haggis and singed sheep's head.

DECEMBER

1st December

What a Waist

How many men can you squeeze into a single waistcoat? Today in 1750 at Maldon in Essex seven men won a wager by proving that they could all fit at once into the waistcoat of **Edward Bright**. He had recently died aged 29, height five foot nine, and weight 51½ stone.

Maldon's other famous corpse was that of Ealdorman Byrhtnoth (also known as Bertnoth or Britnoth), killed in AD 991. He was the archetypal English gentleman, even when confronting the Vikings at Maldon. The enemy were trapped on an offshore island, and the only way to the mainland was via a narrow causeway where they would be easy pickings for the English archers lined up onshore. Byrhtnoth decided that the Vikings' dilemma stacked the odds rather too much in his favour, and so – most sportingly – he allowed the enemy to cross before commencing battle. A surviving poem, *The Battle of Maldon*, is laden with grand speeches in honour of noble, courageous Byrhtnoth. Noble, courageous, killed-by-the-Vikings Byrhtnoth.

The invaders had appreciated his gesture, but did not let it affect their capacity for carnage. They wiped the floor with the Essex army, creating a lot of stiff upper-lipped stiffs. This marked the re-emergence of the Vikings as the bane of England, culminating in the ascension in 1016 of Danish King Cnut to the English throne. And all because Essexman wanted to see fair play.

The issuing of an oddly-valued new coin today, back in 1797, was reason enough to inflict a new ballad on the world. The **seven shilling piece** was the size of a modern penny, and replaced the paper English dollar in the pockets of the rich. The song's jingling verse was a low-pay paean to small change, curse of modern times:

The swaggering blade who has spent all his
  money
First searches his pockets, then looks very
  funny,
But his horrid perplexities suddenly cease,
Should there lurk in his fob a seven-shilling
  piece.

All together with the rousing chorus:

Yet barring all pother, the one and the other,
'Tis a snug little seven shilling piece.

The authors did not spend much time coining a title for their ballad: it gained currency as *A New Song Called Seven Shilling Piece*.

☀ '*December cold with snow, good for rye*' so they say, which is good news for hard-core Ryvita fans. Other December **weatherlore** has it that thunder means fine weather ahead, and – most shocking of all – that frost means problems for farmers.

This is the first day on most shop-bought **Advent Calendars**, although Advent formally begins on the last Sunday in November. It is the traditional countdown to the birth of Christ, with the simultaneous anticipation of His second coming. Christ's return is imminent . . . but first, will it be a candle, bauble or small chicken behing the exciting '1' on the cardboard window?

2nd December

Mayors Eat Does

Thomas Paine, supporter of revolting Americans and French, was a major influence on English Radicals late in the 18th century. His *The Rights of Man* (published 1791–2) defended the French Revolution, and championed the causes of freedom and democracy.

He asked why his countrymen should fight against their innocent counterparts in other countries at the whim of the Government of the day, and for no personal gain. This reasonable query was far too dangerous for those in power. Thomas had become a Paine in the neck. While he was fulfilling his duties in the French Convention, the authorities condemned him in his absence for sedition, declaring him an outlaw on December 2nd 1792. Up and down the country, everyone was encouraged to burn Paine effigies. For a few years in the West Country he ousted Guy Fawkes as the most inflammatory and inflammable figure to leap into their annual bonfires.

The second volley of anti-Paineite feeling came in a barrage of jingoistic sloganeering, including the ballad *Down With Tom Paine*, with its dismal refrain:

God save George our king, Tom Paine, let him swing;
Let us for ever sing – down with Tom Paine.

The **Cinque Ports** were prestigious seaports which had to furnish a large part of the Navy, and were therefore granted special privileges in the Middle Ages. The original five were Sandwich, Hastings, Dover, Romney and Hythe. Winchelsea and Rye were later allowed to join the elite group. After being made a 'limb of Sandwich' in 1360, special associate Cinque Port status was granted to one town neither in Kent nor Sussex – Brightlingsea in Essex.

© In commemoration of this singular honour, on the first Monday in December Brightlingsea still elects its Deputy. His formal title is **Deputy of the Cinque Port Liberty**, and after a swearing-in up in the belfry of All Saints Church, he pays for the privilege by handing the Mayor of Sandwich 50p Ship Money, the vestigial loose change from an old tax. The Deputy's role is now mostly charitable, but he does get to wear a solid silver chain of office depicting the source of what was once the town's main industry – it is made of alternate links of oyster shells and crossed sprats.

Apart from this, Brightlingsea's main claim to fame is that in 1884 it suffered one of the most serious British earthquakes in modern times.

© During December, in accordance with the 15th-century **Venison Warrant**, the Lord Mayor of London is entitled to a gift of four does, having enjoyed four bucks in July – that's about £3 in British money (boom boom). This all started after Dick Whittington, of cat and U-turn fame, lent Henry V a substantial sum of money to help finance the wars in France. After the King's Agincourt victory, Dick went to Henry and tore up an IOU for £30,000. Impressed, the King instigated the venison benison. Deer at any price, it is a medium-rare example of food being more expensive 500 years ago than it is now.

3rd December
St Birinus' Day

The Snail in the Coffin

St Birinus was at the cutting edge of Christianity in the 7th century. From his base in Dorchester-on-Thames, near Abingdon in Oxfordshire, his original intention was to make evangelical inroads into the unbaptised Midlands. But he found things in Dark Age Oxfordshire so pagan that he decided to stay put and concentrate his efforts there instead. At first everything went without a hiccup: he became the first Bishop of Dorchester (a thriving Romano-British town in those days) and built a fine church. But in 650 an adder bit him, and he died. Though he was not quite in St Patrick's league, before expiring Birinus declared that all people of Dorchester would be forever protected from snake-bite as long as they stayed within earshot of the church bells. Ever since, locals have been able to drink vast quantities of mixed cider and lager without fear of falling over.

▥ The tall gabled shrine of St Birinus, now restored to its former glory, can be seen in Dorchester's Abbey of St Peter and St Paul. Next to it is the wildly twisted and striated 13th-century effigy of a knight – a very odd bonus for visitors.

It is still believed that **snakes** will continue to by-pass the village as long as its tenor bell still rings regularly; but should it cease chiming, then adders, pythons, vipers – in fact anaconda snakes – will come slithering into Dorchester.

Snails, not snakes, traditionally cause most concern in December. Impractical as it may be, superstition has it that unless the local population is culled this month, vegetable patches will suffer a snail Armageddon come the spring.

Snails leave a glistening trail over the surface of superstition. It was once thought that they were born without shells, and had to go crawl-about to find their separately created homes. Depending on their choice of shelter, some snails are bringers of good fortune. If you throw a stripy snail over your head and say:

Lucky snail, go over my head
And bring me a penny before I go to bed,

it is a no-lose situation – except possibly for the snail.

The prosperity diminishes if you happen to be a tin miner. Snails mean bad luck in that particular industry. Miners can offset the misfortune by offering the snail a morsel of food or a piece of tallow candle. The chemical symbol for tin is *Sn*, so snail equals 'Sn' + 'ail'. Probably not an explanation for the superstition, but an odd coincidence nonetheless.

Invasions of black snails mean that a front of rain clouds is on its way. Do not attempt to seek consolation in the following cruel, possibly occult-origin cure for warts: stalk and capture a black snail, wake it up, make it crawl over the wart, and then impale it on a thorn. When the new moon appears, wave to it and blow across your warts in a lunar direction.

4th December
St Barbara's Day/
St Osmund's Day

Candid Peal

Today in 1154 **Nicholas Breakspear** achieved what no other British person has managed either before or since. He became Pope. Adrian IV, to be precise. His glory days lasted five years, and his chief act was to issue a Papal Bull allowing Henry II to invade and conquer the Irish. When Adrian died in 1159, the Bull was taken by the horns and removed from the statute books. Adrian's other claim to fame was his dress sense. His sandals and mitre had been embroidered by St Christina of Markyate, an English virgin who founded a nunnery in Hertfordshire. But this was as far as she went in embroidering Adrian's threadbare life-story.

Becoming Pope is tricky; getting all the way to sainthood is even trickier. When man-of-God, man-of-the-people Bishop of Salisbury Os-mund died in 1099, his huge supporters club started raising cash to get him bumped up to a saint. Despite all their well-formulated pro-canonisation arguments, it was not until 1456, at a cost of £731 13s (a sum which in those days would buy you a cathedral and still leave change for the embossed notepaper), that Osmund had the magical 'St' stuck in front of his name. Osmund can be invoked for curing toothache, rupture, madness and paralysis.

Osmund shares his feast day with **Barbara**, the saint invoked by artillerymen and miners to ward off explosions. Legend says that she was locked in a tower by her father to keep the pulsating loins of suitors at bay. Imprisoned, Barbara became a Christian, and moved into her father's bath-house. There she added a third window in honour of the Trinity. Her father not only hated the idea of his daughter dating, he also despised modern architecture. So he tortured Barbara and handed her over to the pagan authorities, who chopped off her head. The father was immediately struck by lightning and blown apart. Hence Barbara is associated with detonations of all kinds. It is a shame to explode a great myth like Barbara's, but she is almost certainly apocryphal.

Today used to see the shivering sheep gather at Lambourn in Berkshire for the **Sheep Fair**. The date was Old St Clement's Day. Stallholders sold sweets and toys, but the chief attraction was the Clementy Cake. These were spiced fruit buns made in Wantage and delivered to Lambourn in a make-shift baker's cart.

Three weeks before Christmas the **Curfew bells** at Scarcliffe church near Chesterfield in Derbyshire traditionally began their nightly peal, which lasted until three weeks after the 25th. The bell-ringing was paid for by land purchased posthumously by Lady Constantia de Frecheville, via her will of 1200. She was eternally grateful to the bells for saving her from a fate worse than scandal. Her tabloid-headline story tells how she became pregnant out of wedlock, but was abandoned by her lover. In shame she rode away after the birth, taking herself and the baby into the wilds of Scarliffe Wood. By the time she decided that acute embarrassment was insufficient reason to die, she was hopelessly lost and hypothermia beckoned. But at the last minute she heard the bells of the church and was able to navigate back to the village.

🔲 Lady Constantia's impressive statue, complete with child, is in Scarliffe church. The Curfew bell has not done as it was tolled since the end of the last war.

5th December
St Justinian's Day

You Only Live Twice, Twice

A Parliamentarian until 1642, **Baron Ralph Hopton** switched sides in the Civil War that year, and copped it. On December 5th he was declared *'either dead or dangerously sicke'*. Which says much for the state of medical diagnoses in the 17th century. The following year he leaped from obscurity again to lead a skirmish on Roborough Down, clearly not entirely dead. However, the post-battle reports declared that this time Ralph really had perished on the field, on May 6th. But the good Baron was not one to be deterred – or interred – that easily. After leading the King's forces in Cornwall nine days later he was again written off as well and truly dead. But before you could say 'cross your heart and Hopton die', he was out fighting again in July, this time at Lansdown, where he was badly wounded. Again he recovered, and managed to last the best part of the next decade before passing away for good in exile in 1652. All of which led to the cynical Civil War saying, *'When in doubt, kill Hopton'*.

On December 5th 1664, a ship foundered and sank off the coast of north Wales. Eighty-one passengers died, the only survivor being a man called **Hugh Williams**. On December 5th 1785, another ship went down – 60 people died and there was just one survivor, a man called Hugh Williams. When a third ship with a December 5th problem went down on this day in 1860, 25 passengers were lost, and once again the sole survivor was a Mr Hugh Williams.

St Justinian's Spring used to be on Ramsey Island, off the Dyfed coast near St David's. It was a run-of-the-mill healing spring formed in the time-honoured way, by the saint's decapitated head.

Justinian, whose feast day is today, was a Breton hermit who cantankerously came to Ramsey. Once established there he asked resident holy man Honorious to banish his sister and her handmaid so that the lads could live together without the distraction of women. Honorious complied, and in the climate of the times Justinian earned a reputation for purity, rather than misogyny. His spiritual mentor was St David, who lived across Ramsey Sound on the mainland.

One day two sailors came to the island and told Justinian that David was dying. They offered to row him over to see the great saint. Justinian gratefully accepted, but half way across he suddenly decided that the sailors were demons, luring him to his demise. He belted out Psalm 79, and sure enough, the two sailors turned into demons, then into crows, and flew away. David, it later transpired, was still as fit as a fiddle.

Later the demons returned, possessing Justinian's servants. When the saint told them to knuckle down to work, they tossed him in the air and lopped off his head. Which is where we, and the spring, came in . . . Decapitated Justinian picked up his head and carried it to his favourite bit of the island – or to the mainland, in some versions of the legend – where he was buried. A church was built over him for good measure. The servants were exorcised and forced to spend the rest of their lives as lepers on Ramsey Island's Leper's Rock.

December 6th
St Nicholas' Day

Santa Gets His Nickars in a Twist

St Nicholas was Bishop of 4th-century Myra in south-west Turkey. One day while out do-gooding, Nicholas came upon an inn. The innkeeper, seeing that his guest was a bishop, offered him meat and drink. Nicholas accepted, but was suspicious – there was famine throughout the land, so how had the innkeeper come by the meat? Nicholas slipped into the kitchen and found the dismembered bodies of three young boys, stuffed into a barrel of pork and pickle. The bishop miraculously managed to turn the macabre Spam back into three live boys. This was one of several good deeds which led to Nicholas becoming patron saint of children, especially boys.

He is also patron of single women. Once upon a time a poor family decided that the youngest of their three daughters would have to take up prostitution to finance the dowries of the other two. To prevent this, Nicholas slipped into their house on three successive nights, each time leaving a bag of gold. Saint

Nicholas' anonymous gold-giving would later give rise to legends of a certain Santa (Nick) Claus.

This in turn led to Nicholas becoming patron saint of pawnbrokers – their three gold balls derive from the three bags of gold in the story – apothecaries, bankers, clerks, captives, perfumiers (his shrine allegedly emitted a pungent myrrh), and sailors.

St Nicholas' sea-connections are somewhat spurious. Scandinavian sailors used to live in fear of a sea god called **Hold Nickar**, and they gave offerings to prevent him from devouring them. Under the influence of Christianity, the similar-sounding St Nick took the place of the old monster in the hearts of the sailors, swapping the malign with the benign. Meanwhile, the name *Hold Nickar* survives as 'Old Nick', no longer an autonomous sea-god, but one of Satan's many alter egos. Thieves used to be called 'St Nicholas' Clerks', and this is another example of the Saint/Devil being confused.

St Nicholas' role as patron of children gave rise to the tradition of **boy bishops**, who were elected in cathedrals, parish churches and schools today. The boy, in full regalia and with a train of minors, ruled until Holy Innocents' on December 28th, officiating in all a bishop's duties except Mass. If a boy died in office he was given all ceremony due to a grown-up bishop – an effigy in Salisbury Cathedral, Wiltshire, supposedly represents such a casualty.

There have been revivals this century of boy bishops, though most of them simply turn up as extras on the back of the May Queen's float. The genuine custom lingered longest at Eton in Berkshire. Not everyone agrees, but it seems that the school's **Montem Day** developed from the real thing, with the boy bishop evolving into a different youthful figure of authority, The Captain, by the 18th century. His men solicited money, giving out salt in exchange (an oblique reference to the origins of the word *salary*), and everyone trooped up Salt Hill. There, a boy chaplain read Latin prayers with his clerk. The chaplain then kicked the clerk downhill. In 1793, by which time Montem Day had moved to Whit Tuesday, the Saltbearers collected the vast sum of £1,000 for their Captain. So there was more at stake than simple custom and ceremony. The tradition came to an end in 1847, despite an outcry, and despite having the support of Queen Victoria and Albert, who were Montem regulars.

In the spirit of the boy-in-charge figure, many schools today staged a **Barring-out**, which involved the children locking out the teacher and granting themselves a bonus day off. Shrove Tuesday was the other big day for these extended free periods.

7th December
St Diuma's Day

Jeffrey the Headless Badger

By December 7th 1716, the Wesley household at Epworth Rectory, near Scunthorpe in Humberside, were adapting to the attentions of the poltergeist who became known as **Old Jeffrey**. At the beginning of the month the hauntings had kicked off with a loud knocking on the door, followed by a groan. This was the forerunner of more thumping, moaning, rustling, stamping, invisible bottle smashing and coin dropping. Other ear-catching noises included a rocking cradle, a gobbling turkey, and Jeffrey's speciality, described by the Wesleys as a '*dead hollow note*', which marked the ghost's presence in any given room. The entity appeared once as a man in a night-gown, but usually darted about in the shape of either a white rabbit, or a creature which the Wesleys described as '*like a badger, only without any head that was discernible*'.

The girls got used to Jeffrey – the youngest even chased the noise from room to room for fun. Samuel Wesley was more concerned. He decided to level the spirit with his pistol. At the eleventh hour his friend Mr Hoole, rector of nearby Haxey, pointed out the folly of his plan. Guns seldom kill ghosts, and all he was likely to achieve was the turning of a noisy but harmless apparition into a vengeful ghoul. Distraught but powerless, Samuel issued a challenge to Jeffrey: '*Thou deaf and dumb devil, why dost thou frighten children that cannot answer thee? Come to me in my study, that am a man.*' Jeffrey did not respond, opting to continue ploughing steadily through his collection of horror sound effects.

Old Jeffrey played with the latches and beat his tattoos on the walls throughout that December, and into the following month. The main haunting then ceased; although one of the daughters, Emilia, claimed that the ghost visited her throughout her adult life, and in the mid-19th century the rector of Epworth did a runner on account of being badgered by renewed ghostly activity in the parsonage.

🔟 Modern theories, linking poltergeist activity with the traumas of puberty, tend to blame the teenage children in the Wesley brood. John, 13 at the time, later wrote about the haunting, but gained more lasting fame as the driving force of Methodism. It is due to the Wesleyan connection rather than the ghost story that the Old Rectory is still a popular tourist attraction.

Venerating a saint usually presupposes a knowledge of the sanctified one's sex. Not so St Diuma. A 7th-century bishop doing lots of converting in the pagan Midlands, he was revered for centuries 'not as a pious and noble man, but as a pious and noble woman. The evidence for this was that s/he was also known as Dimma, which – the feminist lobby argued – was clearly a women's name.' This raised further technical difficulties, for if Diuma was a woman how could she have been a bishop? And if she was not a bishop, how did she get to be a saint? Eventually logic prevailed, and it was realised that although Diuma/Dimma had a girly name, he was not a girl.

8th December
Feast of the Conception/
St Budoc's Day

Rayne Now, Son (or Daughter) Later

On this day in 1824, *The Times* reported a disturbance in Hampshire. Residents of Chichester had seen buildings shake and had watched bells oscillate and ring with the shock. In Portsmouth floorboards heaved and furniture wobbled. Hardly something to break the needle on the Richter scale, but in these parts **earthquakes** are not exactly common, and it kept the shaken locals talking for weeks.

An earthquake across Glasgow, in December 1978, damaged buildings and kept the newspapers happy with its very own celebrity, a self-styled Welsh prophet who had recently been arrested. Having had a premonition that Strathclyde was about to suffer imminent structural damage, the man had hopped on a southbound train from Inverness hoping to warn the Glasgow authorities that they should shore up everything in sight. Sadly, he failed to buy a ticket and was duly arrested. The earthquake occurred three weeks after the *Dundee Courier and Advertiser*'s moving headline 'Prophet Didn't Have a Ticket'.

Customs '*Go and say your prayers at Rayne*' was the traditional retort in Essex if anyone said 'By the way, I'm pregnant'. Rayne, near Braintree, was famous for its altar to the **Virgin Mary**, especially efficacious on her feast days, including this, the Feast of Her Conception in the womb of St Anne. Mary would ensure the women safe deliverance if they prayed at her altar.

And still with pregnant women, Azenor, the mother of 6th-century **St Budoc**, had a rough confinement. Her husband falsely accused her of sleeping around, and chucked her into the English Channel in a barrel. She gave birth in mid-voyage to Budoc, after enlisting the aid, via prayers, of St Bride. The barrel, complete with Azenor and the newborn Budoc, eventually washed up on the Irish coast, and Azenor secured her son's future by becoming the washerwoman at Beau Port monastery, near Waterford. In later life Budoc became big in south-west England, leaving his name at Budock Water in Cornwall, and St Budeaux in Devon.

A brief round of applause for Mr Cracker of Fleet in Dorset, 18th-century UFO spotter and master of the written word. His account of a flying saucer seen on December 8th 1733 makes you wish that he had written a few novels for posterity. He saw:

> . . . *something in the sky which appeared in the north, but vanished from my sight, as it was intercepted by trees, from my vision. I was standing in a valley. The weather was warm, the sun shone brightly. On a sudden it reappeared, darting in and out of my sight with an amazing coruscation. The colour of the phenomenon was like burnished, or new washed silver. It shot with speed like a star falling in the night.*

9th December

Lions, Maid

Today in 1165, **William the Lion** became King of Scotland, and reigned with tooth and claw for 49 years. On good terms with Henry II of England at first, he later fought the English with might and mane, marching to war behind a magical **Speckled Banner**, carried at the head of his army by a priest. The tradition came from Rob Roy's clan, the MacGregors, who had a speckled banner believed to have been captured from the faeries. Whenever they carried it, the MacGregors were victorious. So the habit spread and the Scots army marched to battle behind the mystic banner. But at Alnwick in Northumberland in 1174 its magic failed and William, captured by the English, was forced to declare that Henry was the true king of the jungle. In 1189 William paid Richard the Lionheart (what was this 12th-century fixation with *Panthera Leo*?) 10,000 marks – a mark, post-Conquest, being two-thirds of £1 – to shake off the feudal tie to the English throne and restore Scottish pride, followed by another 15,000 marks to King John to stop the latter embarking on more big game hunting.

🏰 Dunvegan Castle on the Isle of Skye, home of the **Clan Macleod** since 1200, has what is claimed to be a faerie flag. The silken speckled banner is now discoloured with age, and the current clan chief maintains that it was given to one of his predecessors by the man's faerie wife. Having married into the mortal world, she came to miss her own people, and gave the flag to her husband as a parting gift. The site where the couple said farewell to each other is still known as the Faerie Bridge. Before the woman crossed back into faerieland, she told Chief Macleod that the flag would save his clan three times.

Twice the MacLeods have followed the speckled banner into battle and won out against overwhelming odds, but the clan is keeping the flag's third and final dose of magic for some as-yet unspecified future time of crisis.

Some of the best **Maids' Garlands** (also known as Crants or Crowns) survive in Derbyshire. The garlands, a favourite device of the 18th century, commemorated young women of the parish who died after they were engaged but before they could wed. The usual construction was a wooden frame resembling an old bird-cage, on to which ribbons and flowers were fastened, along with tokens of purity such as gloves and handkerchiefs – all made of paper. A girl of the same age as the deceased maid, and preferably of similar build and looks, brought the garland into the church for a blessing, after which it was hung over the bereaved parents' pew. There it remained, and was only removed if it fell apart. One of the finest of the garlands at Ashford-on-the-Water, near Bakewell, is in memory of Ann Swindel, who died today in 1798. It is inscribed:

Be always ready, no time to delay,
I in my youth was called away.
Great grief to those that's left behind,
But I hope I'm great joy to find.

🏰 It is poignant and appropriate that the garlands, pretty and colourful when first made, are now warped and faded. There are several more Maids' Garlands alongside Ann's; and there are other good examples in churches at Ilam, near Leek in Staffordshire, and Abbots Ann just outside Andover in Hampshire.

10th December

Walkies on the Wild Side

One cold, moonlit December night last century a man was walking across Dartmoor on the road from Princetown to Plymouth. Having crossed Roborough Down he stopped for a quick dram. Recommencing his desolate journey, he heard noises behind him. Each time he looked back, there was nothing there; though the sound continued as soon as he turned away. Then from the mist a huge **black dog** appeared on his right. The traveller, a dog-lover, innocently spoke to it and patted it on the head. Or at least, he tried to. His hand went through the apparition, which gazed at him with huge unblinking eyes and yawned its mouth wide, belching out sulphurous breath.

The man rapidly deduced that this was no Saint Bernard. He scarpered, but the dog followed, keeping pace with him until they reached a crossroads near some old fortifications. The hell hound had been gaining on the traveller; but then there was an explosion and a flash of light. The next thing the man knew it was morning and he was being helped from a ditch by a postman. As a notorious enemy of dogs everywhere, a postman must have been a very reassuring sight.

👻 This particular ghostly dog has often been seen on the moor. It is said to have belonged to a murdered man, and is compelled to prowl the moors until justice is done. Until that day comes, the dog has to kill everyone it meets. Close observers of the plot will notice that in this particular case it failed to fulfil its brief.

The many Dartmoor legends of ghostly dogs inspired Conan Doyle to write *The Hound of the Baskervilles*, and black dogs have lingered in the popular imagination through to modern times. Large phantom black creatures are still regularly glimpsed on moors and in isolated spots, though the current trend is to report them as being some kind of huge cat.

On this night in 1883, the country faced all those things which occur once in a blue moon. Freak atmospheric conditions meant that there was indeed a **blue moon** in the sky. December 1200 had even more moonshine. In Raphael Holinshed's *Chronicles* (Shakespeare's favourite source-book) he describes how '*there were seen in the province of York five moons, one in the east, the second in the west, the third in the north, the fourth in the south, and the fifth as it were set in the middle of the others*'. Shakespeare uses the five moons story to brighten up *King John* (in Act IV, Scene II).

© **Boston Beast Mart** takes place today in Lincolnshire. It used to last for a week, and was first authorised in 1576. These days the proceedings are somewhat diminished. The traditional proclamation is read aloud with or without the presence of beasts – it is now a self-conscious tradition rather than a functional market-cum-fair. The old mart yard is now the playground of Boston Grammar School, so the pupils get a half day holiday while the mayor, chief constable and assorted dignitaries go through the short ceremony.

The festival of **St Obert's Play** at Perth, Tayside is long gone. It commemorated Obert, an obscure saint who was a local hero and patron of Perth's bakers. The bakers wandered the streets in outrageous costumes, one of them playing the part of Obert in a kind of mumming play. It was all far too much fun for later, austere church thinking. The play's Obertuary came soon after the demise of Scottish Catholicism.

11th December

Kingfishers and King Fissures

In spite of the fact that **James II** was head of the Church of England, his wife, life and decrees showed an ever-increasing Catholic bias. Fortunately for the strong anti-Catholic lobby, but unfortunately for James, years of trying yielded no offspring. But then in 1688 a Catholic heir was born to the King and Queen, and people began to panic. Rumour insisted that the child was a con, planted in the palace following nine months of pillows stuffed up the

barren Mary Beatrice's skirts. The couple themselves put the sudden fertility down to magic waters, including those at Holywell.

But the royal celebrations were short-lived. Protestant forces mustered against the King, and today in 1688 James saw that the game was up. He kept watching his weathervane on the Banqueting Hall in Whitehall, to see if the wind was 'Protestant or Popish'. A 'Protestant' wind was one that would blow ashore the fleet of William of Orange to claim the throne in the name of Protestantism. The wind must have been unambiguous on this day, for James abandoned the ship of state, chucking his Great Seal into the Thames. It was never found, unlike James, who was captured and brought back to London before formal banishment.

🗒 Kirton-in-Lindsey, near Scunthorpe in Lincolnshire, used to hold its **T'Andra Fair** today, Old St Andrew's Day. Only locals and guest celebrities were encouraged to drink from the village's Ash-well, which still continues to attract visitors. The well's enchanted waters were thought to be so powerful that no one who imbibed there would want to leave – one sip and it was Kirton's for you, forever.

This is not Kirton's only eccentricity. The village is home to a curious donkey-shaped ghost, the **Shag-Foal**; and an even odder local law, which allowed any woman coming to a marriage in debt to take steps to clear her future husband's liability. All she had to do was leave her old house in the nude and walk to her new husband's abode. This altogether strange way of disclosing your remaining assets was last successfully invoked over a century ago, when a desperate but discreet woman streaked down a ladder from her bedroom, then donned a gown for the rest of the journey. See December 14th for more nude nuptials.

In Northamptonshire today was the lacemakers' holiday, being Old St Andrew's Day. Last century the festivities – enjoyed by everyone, not just lacemakers – were described temptingly as '*unbridled licence*'. It was customary for men and women to dress in each other's clothes and drink vast quantities of hot elderberry wine.

👄 December 11th is the beginning of the **Halcyon Days** of December, a spell of traditionally fine weather. *Halcyon* is another name for the kingfisher. They were supposed to build their nests on the sea at this time of year, calming the waves with their song. This piece of Greek mythology is the ancestor of a some-what forced piece of British weatherlore. It is said that if kingfishers' nests are washed from the river bank and carried out to sea without capsizing, it means a long spell of fine weather. Equally unlikely and cruel, a stuffed kingfisher can be utilised as an indoor wind-vane (Protestant, Popish and otherwise). Suspended from string, the hanging halcyon points its beak in the direction from which the wind is coming.

12th December
St Finnian's Day/
St Lucia's Eve

Fasten your safety-belts, loosen your underwear

Hannah Baddaley died today in 1764, aged 26. It was tragically young; especially as she had spectacularly survived a suicide attempt only two years earlier. In love with fickle William Barnsley, she despaired when he deserted her. There was only one thing to do. She went to the limestone crags of Stoney Middleton, near Bakewell in Derbyshire, and jumped off. But she was improperly dressed for suicide. Her petticoats opened and she parachuted down to the ground virtually unharmed. That was her official story anyway, and one that turned her from jilted lover to 18th-century celebrity. In fact her early death was probably due to her being more Baddaley injured in the jump than was generally realised. The site of her deed is now known as Lover's Leap, and the foot of the cliff is marked by a wayside café called, funnily enough, the Lover's Leap. Its sign depicts Hannah in mid-flight. Tales of forlorn leaping lovers are common – there are at least three other examples in Derbyshire alone – but few showed Hannah's para-suicidal tendencies.

In Scandinavian countries St Lucy – or Lucia – is much higher in the saintly hierarchy than she is in Britain. But the northern British islands remained under Scandinavian influence for several centuries, and she has not been entirely forgotten. Tonight, St Lucia's Eve, is the night when Lucian witches and faeries are abroad, ready to snatch away anyone foolish enough to have gone to bed without supper. This general belief survives across the Scottish Highlands and Islands tonight, but has become associated with the Celtic St Finnian. The tradition sounds more like a nursery threat than a genuine belief in wayfaring faeries.

Perhaps these faeries are yellow. It would make sense of an otherwise enigmatic statement by Finnian's 6th-century biographer that the saint 'died at Clonard for the sake of the people of the Gael, that they might not all perish of the yellow pest'. Clonard is in Ireland, though Finnian spent his formative years in Wales.

In schoolyards and backstreets up and down the country, Christmas season games used to get under way at this time of year. Just as football belongs to winter and cricket to summer, so the Christmas season is the only time to try your hand at such epics as My Lady's Toilet, Fox and Geese and Hawld Hard (see tomorrow for more past pastimes).

In My Lady's Toilet – or Turn Trencher – each player represents an item of a woman's toiletry. The caller spins a plate or tray, the trencher, on his hand and calls out an item of the toilet. Whoever 'is' that particular item has to catch the tray before it falls, or else suffer a forfeit.

Fox and Geese is a game of chase-and-catch. After a ritualistic round of words and rhymes the fox chases the geese, simple as that. The chants include such lines as 'Geese, geese, gannio; fox, fox, fannio'; and the immortal 'My mother sits in yonder chimney and says she must have a chicken'.

To play Hawld Hard, everyone grips a handkerchief, and the leader says either 'Hawld hard!' or 'Let go!' Whichever is said, the players must do the opposite or suffer the forfeits. Ah, happy forfeiting memories of wet rags in the face, peppermint and curry cocktails, gherkins and ginger biscuits in tomato sauce . . .

13th December
St Lucy's Day

Hairry my bossie with hot cockles

St Lucy was a devout virgin who gave all her worldly goods to the poor. But the poverty did not deter a persistent suitor, who had fallen in love with her beautiful eyes. Lucy at first rebuffed his advances; and then in desperation she plucked out her own eyes, handed them over and said *'Now let me live to God'*. God restored her vision a little later, but the suitor was not amused. He had Lucy arrested, in AD 304, and she was sentenced to be violated in a brothel. However, God rooted her to the spot, and no amount of dragging and winching could budge her. So the authorities set her on fire. But Lucy would not burn. Desperate, the executioner stabbed her through the neck, and she promptly died, having used up her quota of miracles.

Lucy's fire episode is the only link between her and the festivities of **Lucia Day** in Scandinavia. Girls dress as Lucy, with crowns of candles. This ties in with pagan winter-sun festivities – before the calendar was changed Lucia Day fell in the Norse Yule festival, near the solstice. Hence the unrepentant inaccuracy of the old rhyme: *'Lucy light, the shortest day and longest night.'* Shetland and Orkney used to celebrate Lucia Day; and more recently she has migrated into those British cities with large Scandinavian populations.

Lucy can be invoked by people suffering from poor eyesight. This is a double-edged patronage, as it not only harks back – with black humour – to the eye-pulling incident, but also refers to the long dark night of the original St Lucy's Day.

This is the season when Christmas games even older than Monopoly are played (see also yesterday). **Headicks and Pinticks** – also known as Headim and Corsim – involves a pin, which one player lays on his palm and conceals with a finger. The other has to guess which way the pin-head is pointing by saying either *'headick!'* (up) or *'pintick!'* (down). The winner leaves the arena with an enviable prize – loads of pins.

Hairry My Bossie is similar to Headicks and Pinticks. A boy conceals a number of objects in his hand, and a girl has to guess how many, and what they are. She does this by carefully listening to the sound they make when shaken up and down in the boy's fist. If she is correct, she wins the objects; if wrong she has to make up the difference. The name is more interesting than the actual game, which does not stick rigidly to these gender divisions – it just makes the rules easier to explain.

Hot Cockles is a weird one. In the Sheffield version one boy stands with his back to the wall, and another bends so that his head is in the other's stomach. The other players all put one finger in the second boy's upturned cap, which is put on his back, and sing:

> The wind blows east, the wind blows west,
> The wind blows o'er the cuckoo's nest.
> Where is this poor man to go?
> Over yon cuckoo's hill, I-O!

More commonly, the bending boy has his own hand upturned on his back. The players each put their hand on his, and he has to guess to whom each piece of clammy flesh belongs. If correct, he is released; if wrong, there is a forfeit. The Sheffield version is said to be closest to the original game, which was played at funerals. Game and song were to help the soul on its way to the afterlife, or else to see who would die next.

14th December

Stark Ballengeich naked

On this day in 1542, one of Scotland's best-loved monarchs, **King James V**, died. Known as The Commons King, he liked to hob-nob with the peasantry. Highlanders called him *The King in the Grey Coat*; whereas the King himself preferred the more user-friendly title *The Goodman of Ballengeich*. Using this pseudonym, he enjoyed wandering the countryside in dowdy disguise. On one occasion he was attacked by four thieves, but managed to fight them off with the aid of a passing farmer. The farmer, Jock Howieson, gave the King water to wash his cuts and bruises, and then escorted him back to Edinburgh, still unaware of the Goodman's true identity.

James said that he worked in the royal palace at Holyrood, and took Jock on a tour. James also added that they would recognise the King if he appeared, as His Majesty would be the only one wearing a hat. Sure enough, they came to a room of courtiers, and Jock noticed that only he and the Goodman of Ballengeich were wearing hats. One of them had to be King, and he was pretty sure that it was not him. He began bowing and scraping; but James thought all this was a hoot, and he granted Jock's dearest wish – to own the farm on which he worked. For rent Jock and his descendants had to present a bowl and ewer of water every time they were near Holyrood. Even by the standards of daft folkloric rentals, this was cheap.

Exploits such as this led to King James V's

immortalisation in folk song, the commonest of which is *The Jolly Beggar* (or *The Gaberlunzie Man*). The song *King Jamie and the Tinkler* has the same basic plot as the story recounted above, and is also the name of a pub at Enfield in North London.

Getting married in the altogether is a rare but invigorating custom. In assorted parts of the country, a woman of wealth marrying a man in debt could keep her own money secure from the creditors' sweaty paws by stripping at the altar. Such a wedding was recorded at Birmingham in 1797, with a watered down version taking place on this day in 1842 at Gedney in Lincolnshire. In the latter case, the woman could not bring herself to go all the way, and married in a loose sheet instead. In some places a similar law applied if the woman was the debtor (see December 11th), but once again it is the bride-to-be, never the groom, that asset-strips.

15th December

Cunning and Canning

Cunning Murrell, self-proclaimed Devil's Master, was the last witchdoctor of Essex. He moved to Hadleigh in 1812 and lived there until his death on this day in 1860. He was the seventh son of a seventh son, and fulfilled all the legendary expectations of such a child. His favourite tools were a magic telescope which could see through walls; a magic mirror which could detect lost objects; and an umbrella, which had no magic power whatsoever, but was Murrell's constant companion wherever he went. His chief areas were predictions and cures for bewitchment. Cunning's witch-remedy involved taking the hair, nails, blood and urine of the bewitched, putting it into his iron witch-bottle, and boiling the concoction. The witch then began to burn and, in theory, would reverse the evil spell rather than get completely frazzled.

One night Cunning Murrell heard barking outside his door. It was not the dog returning with his evening newspaper, but a panting girl on all fours. The lassie had been cursed by a witch, and so Murrell got his bottle out. The stuff heated so spectacularly that the iron burst apart. The next morning an exploded witch was found lying messily by the roadside.

For his last trick, Murrell predicted his own death to within the minute, 24 hours before it took place. The Devil could breathe again at last. Murrell is buried in Hadleigh churchyard: to make the search more challenging, the grave is unmarked.

© On the first Sunday after the 12th December, just after the chimes of midnight, the **Broughton Tin Can Band** strike up outside St Andrew's church at Broughton, near Kettering in Northamptonshire. Up to 100 bandsmen, plus spectators, turn up, using anything they can get their hands on to make as much din as possible. This is an obscure custom linked with Old St Andrew's Day, but whether it is meant to drive out evil spirits with noise or is simply a means of beating the bounds of the parish, no one knows or cares. A feeble and non-PC story says that it all started when villagers threw cans at gipsies to move them on. The whole thing was slowly dying out until 1929 when the local council made a fatal mistake. They attempted to ban it. On the next relevant Sunday the biggest turn out for centuries congregated in front of the Rectory before midnight with their tins in hand and their faces blackened to avoid recognition. The racket was heard several miles away, and – despite the disguise – faces were recognised several streets away. The participants were all charged with breaching the peace.

A few weeks later, the offending Canners were cheered as they drove to court in Kettering to be sentenced. A band played for them; and that evening's supper and dance raised much more than the 10-shilling-a-piece fine which the judge had imposed. Next year, because they had all been bound over to keep the peace, the offenders merely held the cans while newcomers beat them (the cans, that is, not the offenders). The council eventually conceded defeat, and the band is still going strong today, organised by a committee since the watershed year 1929. They set out just after midnight outside the Rectory.

Local superstition says that if the Tin Canners should fail to turn out, the event must cease forever. One December during the last war a lone Canner trudged his way through the snow at midnight, thumping out a can-solo to keep the custom alive.

16th December
O Sapientia

Lambe Gets Man Pregnant

John Lambe the **Wizard of Worcester** was a five-star celebrity, and his aristocratic pals ensured that he did not go the way of other witches. Lambe claimed to converse with spirits and predict the future – all for a healthy fee, of course. High-society new-agers lapped up his performances, but eventually he pushed his luck too far. Lambe was charged with various crimes, including having bewitched Lord Windsor on 16th December 1607 at Tardebigg near Bromsgrove, by *'certain evil, diabolical and execrable arts called witchcraft etc'*. Rather than denying the charges, Lambe offered to demonstrate his powers. He commanded an angel to appear in a glass placed on top of his hat. No angel appeared, but Lambe bluffed his way onwards. He boasted of knowing the ex-directory numbers of jobbing spirits who could locate lost objects or hidden treasure, and he listed a few spells, one of which could make men pregnant.

While he was confined at Worcester jail, there was a mysterious outbreak of fever and 40 men died, including the High Sheriff of Worcester and the chief of the jury. Lambe was blamed but not condemned, and was allowed to relocate to London. He resumed the good-life for a while, but after committing rape he was sentenced to hang. Yet again his influential fans came to the rescue and Lambe was released. Rough justice was eventually done by a gang who mugged the wizard and clubbed him to death in 1628.

It appears that Lambe's only genuine powers were the non-magical skills of juggling, sleight-of-hand tricks and hypnosis. The level of his art and humour is revealed by an incident in which he made a handsome young woman expose her lower portions in the middle of the street. These days he would be given his own prime-time weekend TV show.

December 16th is known as *O Sapientia*, after the anthem traditionally sung today. It heralds the official start of the **Mince Pie Season**. This is better news these days than it was a few years ago, when the pies were made with real meat whose rottenness had to be disguised with sugar and spice, not at all nice.

The seriousness of the grand old custom of marriage was drilled home to Rector Joseph Hunt of Eyam, just north of Bakewell in Derbyshire, in 1684. He visited publican Matthew Ferns at *The Miner's Arms* and engaged in what a contemporary report described as '*a drunken freak*'. The rector took an intoxicated, irreverent fancy to Matthew's daughter Anne, and underwent a **mock-marriage** on the spot, capitalising on the clerical powers vested in him, and his pocket Prayer Book. He sobered up later when the Bishop of Derby told him to marry Anne properly as soon as possible. Unfortunately Joseph was engaged to someone else. Acrimony, alimony and lawsuits were bandied about, but Hunt eventually married the girl from *The Miner's Arms*. He died, renowned as a carouser rather than a clergyman, on this day in 1709.

🔲 The story of Hunt's clerical errors is told in full on the walls of *The Miner's Arms* which is still pulling fine pints in Eyam.

17th December
Saturnalia/Sow Day

Cross-Channel Faerie

During Saturnalia a Cornish tin-streamer – a down-market version of a gold-panner – attended the pre-Christmas tinners' feast near Luxulyan in Cornwall. After a decent but unmemorable session, he trudged back home over Tregarden Down. Here he met a company of faeries, having a much wilder time near a granite tor. The man sidled over for a bit of unsubtle gate-crashing, and heard the company shout in unison: '*Ho! And away to Par beach!*' The man repeated the cry and materialised on far-away Par beach, joining the faeries in a dance. The troop then yelled '*Ho! And away to Squire Tremain's cellar!*' The man shouted the same; and there he was, in one of the best cellars in the county. Barrels were broached and brains were poached with wine. When the faeries again cried '*Ho! And away to Par beach!*' all the drunken man could manage was '*Yag sponge froth gibber*', and he passed out.

Next morning the interloper was found by the Squire's butler. Far from impressed with the streamer's stream of consciousness, he dragged the man into the arms of the law. The court also found his 'beam me up, faerie' story hard to swallow, and condemned him to death for burglary. As in all the best adventure films, he was standing on the gallows with the rope around his neck, when the cavalry arrived. A twinkling-eyed woman glided to the front of the crowd and shouted '*Ho! And away to France!*' The not-quite-hanged man repeated the words, and before he could mention his lack of passport, he was spirited away to start a new life abroad.

This **faerie mode of transport** is wonderful, if you can get the hang of the controls. A popular version of the command is '*Horse and hattock! Away to . . .*', appended by the place-name of your dreams.

The 17th was the start of the seven-day Roman **Saturnalia**, ancestor of modern Christmas. The Romans took the festival with them wherever they settled, and such was its popularity that few who had tasted it were willing to forsake it. Christians soon realised this, and were forced to absorb many Saturnalian elements into their own festivities. These include the use of greenery in decorations – Saturn being a god of vegetation and crops – and the giving of presents. Saturnalia was a time of orgy and excess, elements far from uncommon in modern Christmas parties. Slaves used to become masters today, and everything was turned topsy-turvy (arsy-versy, if you are reading this after the 9 pm watershed).

In Scottish feasting halls the **Lord of Misrule** held sway during the season, a figure of parody and anarchy imported during the court's Mary Queen of Scots-inspired French phase in the 16th century. He was soon popular in England too. Unlike the sacrificial Saturnalian King, he usually survived the festivities, MC-ing the debauchery with an eye to chaos and mockery of the usual feudal order of things.

The 17th is also **Sow Day** – as in pigs. Sows were butchered today on Orkney in preparation for another pre-Christmas precursor, Yule. Sow Day was observed most religiously in the parish of Sandwick. But it is not wise – even on Sow Day – to kill the pig if the moon is on the wane. This means that the meat will shrink in the pot, and no one wants to pour poor pork from the pot.

When not being stuck and eaten, **pigs** are said to be able to see the wind. Equally plausibly, a pig's bite causes cancer, and their brains contain a truth drug – snack on one and you are incapable of telling porkies. It is unlucky to meet a sow and a boar together; but pulling a boar backwards from a sow after they have finished mating ensures a healthy sackful of piglets.

The flesh of boars was the food of heroes in Germanic and Norse traditions – it was top of the menu in Valhalla. Boars were earthly echoes of the sacred golden boar *Gulliburstin*, who represented the sun. It was a sacred beast to the Celts too, who thought that it originated in the land of the faeries. No banquet was complete without pork, hams and boar's head, until well into the 17th century. The disconsolate Christmas chipolata is the vestigial end of this tradition. In Nottinghamshire, Mince-pigs, a further echo of the pig tradition, were made during the festive season: sweetmeats shaped like boars, with currant eyes.

◉ The **boar's head** is a symbol of prosperity. The orange or apple stuffed into its mouth is a piece of solar imagery. But usually, from the Middle Ages onwards, the dish livened up the dining table. The butchers of Smithfield present a mock-boar's head to the Lord Mayor at Christmas, a revival of a tradition which started in the 12th century. Many 'heads' were in fact meat-loaves shaped into boars.

◉ The best survival is the **Boar's Head Dinner** at Queen's College, Oxford, formerly on Christmas Day itself, but now at the end of the Michaelmas term in mid-December. Here a real, cooked and decorated head is carried in by the cooks on a silver platter, accompanied by choristers who pause during the procession to sing the three verses of *The Boar's Head Carol*. The tradition seems to have begun soon after the founding of the College in 1341. The lead singer is presented with the fruit from the pig's mouth (a humble sow from the butcher these days), and the garnishes of rosemary, holly and bay are handed out to the guests. During the enforced austerities of the Second World War, a papier-mâché head was used instead. Tongue-in-cheek legend says that the custom began when a Queen's student named Copcot met a savage boar on Shotover Hill outside Oxford. Copcot's only weapon was a copy of Aristotle, and he shoved the book down the beast's throat, saying '*Swallow that if you can*'. The boar muttered '*Graecum est*', and died. Copcot carried its head home in triumph.

18th December

Mum's the Word

On this day in 1844, Champion of the Tyne Clasper and Champion of the Thames Coombes met in an epic **rowing battle** on the River Tyne. This meeting of giants was such a big event that a song was written, anonymously, and printed for sale before the boat-race. Being of Newcastle origin, it did not hide its bias:

> And now if Clasper gains the day you'll all
>   with me agree, sir,
> In Durham and Northumberland too there'll
>   be a glorious spree, sir;
> They'll fill their glass and drink this toast,
>   with hands together joined, sir.
> Success to Clasper if he wins the race upon
>   the Tyne, sir.

The optimistic song had much the same positive effect on Clasper as *'We're on the March with Ally's Army'* had on the Scotland football team in 1978. Clasper started well, then collided with a moored keel, lost an oar, lost the lead and lost the race.

© In 1688, James II's army, with the collusion of the town's governor Lundy, prepared to enter Londonderry/Derry and give the locals a bad time. But just in time 13 apprentices closed the Ferryquay Gate and blew raspberries at the thwarted soldiers. On December 18th every year Stroke City (as Derry/Londonderry has been nick-named) celebrates the victory with the **Closing the Gates Ceremony**. New apprentices are installed in the Apprentice Boys' Hall, and there is a procession to the Cathedral followed by a symbolic burning of a Governor Lundy effigy.

In days of yore, wildly-dressed **Morris-mummers** across the country began to tour their plays in the week before Christmas. The custom was so widespread, and the costumes so outrageous, that a plot to murder Henry IV by a gang disguised as mummers was only narrowly foiled. Henry VIII later tried to ban mumming, but although often sneered at by the well-to-do, the custom limped on into the early 20th century. It was often the case that by the time someone took the trouble to record their words last century, most of the original dramatic thrust had faded from the plays, leaving a sort of nonsense panto. Of the extensive lines noted from the Mumby Mummers' performances at Mumby in Lincolnshire, there is no hint of light-versus-dark and spring-versus-winter, the themes of the original dramas. The key scene, in the Mumby version, is between Tom Fool and a Dandy, fighting for the attentions of a trans-

vestite. Tom greeted the household, who had to be rich to make the fuss worthwhile, with:

> Here comes I that's niver been yet,
> With my great head and little wit.
> I know what my wife and me likes best,
> And we'll have it too: a leg of a lark, and
>   the limb of a louse,
> And cut a great thumpin' toast offen a farden
>   loaf.

He then settled down to his love-battle. At one stage he promises that the 'woman' *'should have bacon fliks, and flour i' the bin, and everything, if you won't take notice of that chap with his ruffles and danglements.'* So when Tom *does* marry her, the hosts are compelled to bring out the food and drink. The other players then go through their own lines, most of them tongue-twisters, or 'isrums', such as:

> As I sat i' me titterty tatterty looking out've
> me hazy-gazy I saw rueri run away wi'
> randy pipes. If I'd had me striddlestripes on,
> I'd've made rueri put randy pipes doon.

Sadly, the Lincolnshire plays are no more. The last recorded performance was at Brattleby in 1984: no one has yet taken up the mantle of the organisers, who have since left the village.

© These days, most surviving or revived mumming plays have moved to Boxing Day, (see, funnily enough, December 26th). But since their play was resurrected in the 1970s, the **White Boys** on the Isle of Man have performed it before Christmas, usually on the preceding Saturday. From 10 am to 5 pm several different groups do the rounds in Peel, Ramsey and Douglas, and some of the smaller towns and villages along the way.

During the action St Denis kills St George, only to be killed by St Patrick. As is common in many mumming plays, they are brought back from the dead by the magical ministrations of The Doctor and his potions:

> I carry a little bottle in my pocket
> Of rixum-raxum, prixum-praxum, with cock-
>   o-lory
> A little of this to his nostrils soon their vigour
>   will restore
> And make them sound and active as before.

The patter then assumes a culinary angle as the revived saints join Patrick in a song which promises:

*With hostile bands confronted, to fight we are
    not slack,
On roast beef and plum pudding we make a
    stout attack.*

The Doctor then asks for his fee, but everyone is skint – a cue for the audience to lend a hand with the reimbursement. The performance, which lasts around 15 minutes, ends with a sword dance.

© Long before even the Manx players put on their whites, there is a flurry of mumming activity in east Kent. There are various times of the year when the **Hooden Horse** gets put through his paces – notably at the Whit Monday service in Charing, and the Hop Hoodening at Canterbury. But for the period from early December until Twelfth Night, and at no other time, he features in **Hoodening** plays. Like the show involving the Richmond Poor Horse (see tomorrow) these dramas are related to mumming plays, and feature a snapping-jawed hobby horse, the Hooden Horse, and a jockey who attempts to ride him. In the course of the short play, the jockey is thrown several times, sometimes quite violently. Injuries are not uncommon, and the only thing guaranteed not to be broken is the hooden horse itself. People used to go hoodening from house to house, extorting money and drink in the time-honoured fashion; but these days nearly all performances take place in pubs, with the morris-men playing bars in their immediate area in the approach to, and aftermath of, Christmas.

Hoodening, which looked to be on its last legs half a century ago, has proved to be a real dark horse. Few customs have made such a strong comeback, and there are now established groups of Kentish hoodeners at Whitstable; at Sandgate on the outskirts of Folkestone; at Charing near Ashford; and on the Isle of Thanet near Margate and Ramsgate. The Hooden Horse used to be peculiar to the Isle of Thanet, before hoodening died out in 1910. Since its revival in the 1950s it has become a county-wide phenomenon. As well as the Richmond Poor Horse, the Hooden Horse's stable-mates include The Wild Horse of Antrobus, Mari Lwyd and the May 'Obby 'Osses of Padstow and Minehead.

19th December

Touch of Evil

🎵 **Henry II** was crowned today in 1154. His two chief legacies are the jury system, installed as part of no-nonsense reforms following the anarchy of King Stephen's reign; and a still-visible big hole in Offa's Dyke at Chirk in Clwyd. It is known as *Adwy'r Beddau*, The Gap of the Graves, and marks the post-slaughter corpse pit of the Battle of Crogen which Henry lost to the Welsh, mainly – he claimed – due to lousy weather. A nearby meadow belonging to Crogen Wladus Farm must never be ploughed, otherwise the bones of the dead troops will be revealed, bringing acres of rotten luck.

🎵 Henry also bursts into a song, as joint hero of the 'based-on-a-true-story' ballad *The Miller of Mansfield*. Separated from his hunt, Henry lodges incognito with miller John Cockle, who serves him some wonderful venison recently poached at the King's private hunting park. Oops – this is a hanging offence. When Henry reveals himself as King, the miller falls to his knees and prepares for his head and body to begin a trial separation. But Henry has revelled in the deed and the down-to-earth company. He dubs the miller a knight and makes him forest overseer on £300 a year. If you fail to track down the song, the full tale can be seen in *The Miller of Mansfield* pub, located not in Nottinghamshire but, bizarrely, in Streatley, Berkshire.

Another King came into his own today. Protestant **William III**, invited over by disaffected politicians to oust the increasingly Catholic James II, strode unopposed into London on December 19th 1688, and was crowned the following year. William of Orange was the grandson of Charles I, and the son-in-law of James II through his daughter Mary. Very incestuous in one sense; though politically it was a break and a turning point in history: royalty would never again rule without parliamentary sanction. On the downside, William made many enemies after the messy massacre of Glencoe in 1692, and helped create the current political mess known as the Irish Problem. William has also stymied centuries of pro- and anti-Catholic song-writers searching in vain for something to rhyme with 'Orange'.

William's main contribution to tradition was a negative one. It was long held that a touch from the reigning monarch could help cure the glandular disease scrofula, which for this reason was known as **The King's Evil**. But towards the end of his reign William refused to attend the then customary laying-on of hands. One early sufferer with whom William had reluctantly made bodily contact was told: '*God give you better health and more sense.*' William's sister Queen Anne was the last monarch to attempt a hands-on remedy for The King's Evil.

In the mid 19th-century the Disraeli-led Tory splinter group, **Young England**, sought a return to feudalism: they wanted to rename the working classes the 'Order of the Peasantry', and to bring back monarchs touching the sick to 'cure' the King's Evil.

© From the week before Christmas, pubs and parties around Richmond, North Yorkshire are the main targets of the **Richmond Poor Horse** players. These mummers perform and sing *Poor Old Horse* which describes a horse's life and death. One man, dressed in garish mock-horse guise – complete with a decorated horse skull – mimes the appropriate actions. The creature dies, and rises again; at which point you realise that you have strayed into totem-beast-as-Celtic-god territory.

20th December
St Thomas' Eve

Close Shave with God the Cat

Joanna Southcott, born in Gittisham, Devon, claimed to be the Lamb's Bride, aka The Woman Clothed In The Sun. In other words, she and God were like *that*. Among the many forms which God took for his chats were a cat, and a cup which Joanna peevishly smashed. The principal message received via her hotline to Heaven was that she was to give birth to the next Messiah, to be known as Shiloh. Despite Joanna's clearly advancing years, her followers vowed not to shave until Shiloh was born. Unfortunately the new Messiah was not God's number one priority, and the Southcottians gradually acquired a new name – The Bearded Men.

In 1814 it began to look as if Joanna's prophecy might come to pass. Despite eschewing intimacy with mortals, she was diagnosed as pregnant, and swelled accordingly. Alas, it was a tumour in the womb, and Joanna Southcott died on December 20th 1814, aged 64. Strangely, this only seemed to make her more popular. Joanna had long promised that Shiloh's mother would be '*as one dead*' for four days before the birth, so her followers treated her death as just a phase. Long after the four days were up, amid the odd untransubstantiated rumour that Joanna had indeed resurrected, these fans continued to grow in numbers and fervour. Sounds familiar?

In the absence of Shiloh, succeeding generations of Southcottians put their faith in **Joanna's box**. This was said to contain magical items that would end all war, plague, famine and dischord. However, it could only be opened in the presence of a minimum of 24 bishops, otherwise all its powers would fade away. In 1927 the box was sent to psychic investigater Harry Price, who X-rayed it and then, on the 11th of July, with an attack of excitement usually confined to small children at dawn on Christmas Day, ripped it open. He had invited 88 bishops and archbishops. Only the Bishop of Grantham turned up. The box contained books, a pistol, a night-cap, a dice box, a purse of loose change and a lottery ticket.

◉ The Panacea Society remained undeterred. They are the surviving rump of the Southcottians, and claim to keep the *real* box at their HQ in Bedford. They also maintain that Joanna *did* give birth to Shiloh, but that only believers can see him. Look out for the small ads which they still regularly place in national newspapers – a popular form depicts an innocuous looking trunk, with the banner headline: '*Crime and Banditry, Distress and Perplexity will increase in England until the Bishops open THIS box*'. The members maintain that if they are wrong, and that if the box proves powerless when opened with 24 or more bishops in attendance, then they will shut up and go away. But as they not unreasonably point out, is it not worth going through with the ceremony just in case they are right?

The Bearded Men would not have got on with **Lanfranc**, Archbishop of Canterbury. In 1070 he wrote: '*On the Vigil of St Thomas*' – tonight – '*the brethren shall be shaved, and let those who will take a bath.*' The bathing instructions were: '*Sit in silence in the bath.*' That was it. And not for too long. After all, as St Benedict had written: '*To those in health, and especially to the young, baths shall be seldom permitted.*' Lanfranc was more liberal, recommending five baths and changes of clothes per annum.

⊙ If after a year of **love-divination** your romance quota is so persistently low that you are tempted to try carbon-dating, give the following a whirl tonight, St Thomas' Eve. Take an onion, peel it, stick pins in it, and retire to bed with the words:

> Good St Thomas, do me right,
> Send me my true love tonight.

On Guernsey an apple should be used instead of the onion. Alternatively, if passion is on the back burner and you are seeking a more long-term strategy, stick pins into onions to denote an eligible lover, one onion per contestant. Hang the bunch in the chimney until spring. The person linked to the first one to sprout will win the jackpot – you.

The 20th-century version of the Christmas story has had all the awkward bits hacked off and filed down. The **old Christmas songs** which came a cropper during the Puritanical 17th century told some now unfamiliar tales. In the *Cherry Tree Carol*, sore-footed Mary en route to Nazareth asks for some cherries from a nearby tree. Joseph declines, all grumpy after the long trek, and hints that he does not find her imminent virgin-birth story very convincing: '*it was not a cherry that got thee with child*', he adds sarcastically. From within the womb Jesus speaks out and commands the tree to bow down and give his mother-to-be some fruit. He then goes on to predict his own birth-date:

> On the 6th of January my birthday shall be,
> When the stars in the elements shall tremble
>   with glee,

which puts him in agreement with the Eastern churches.

In *The Carnal and the Crane*, the carnal (a crow, from the French *corneille*) tells a crane (a common country name for the heron in England) about the Nativity, as a bizarre device for some colourful stories. King Herod is dining on chicken, and after hearing news of the Messiah's birth he declares that if it is true his dinner will poulet itself together and crow in the pot. Sure enough, the bird ups, sprouts feathers and crows three times, and so Herod sends assassins to slay the Nazarene. Meanwhile Jesus, precocious infant, tells a farmer to sow his corn and reap it at once. The miracle occurs, and the man is taking in his instant crop when Herod's men arrive. They ask if he has seen the Holy family, and the man replies,

honestly, that he has not seen them since he sowed his corn. Noticing that the crop is being harvested, the thugs assume that they have missed the Messiah by several months, and give up their pursuit.

Another Christmas song from the folk tradition, called *The Bitter Withy*, depicts the Christ-child asking his mother if he can join his friends in a game of ball. Mary warns him to keep out of trouble, and off he goes. But his three playmates mock, saying that they are lords and ladies' sons, while he is a lowly Jew's child born in an ox's stall. So Jesus builds a bridge from the rays of the sun and runs over. The other children chase after him, the bridge disappears, and the three are drowned. The mothers come screaming to Mary, and she punishes Jesus by laying him across her knee and thrashing him with a bundle of withies from the willow tree. Jesus, smarting at the pain, declares that the willow will be '*the very first tree to perish at the heart*'. Which probably accounts for its disgruntled habit, in superstition, of wandering the countryside at night to mislead or mug travellers.

Many of these **old carols** were rescued last century and printed in song collections; but the High Church has never been very keen on their ragbag of lyrical mysticism, common-place imagery and glorious apocrypha. Most contemporary family favourites are Victorian and Edwardian compositions, with an ever-increasing stock of new songs. Carols, originally, were not the strict preserve of Christmas. A *carol* was a song with a refrain, sung to an accompanying round-dance, popular at all the year's major festivals. The verb *to carol* means to dance and make merry. The custom of singing for alms has managed to survive in a reduced form, with door-to-door singers now favouring carol-sampling: a short burst of a Christmas classic, followed by a long burst on the doorbell and a raid on the household's small change.

The Coventry Carol – which dates from the 15th century at the latest – has remained immune to the vagaries of musical fashion. It gained renewed poignance in 1940 when BBC Radio broadcast it being sung from the bombed-out shell of Coventry Cathedral, and what was once a local favourite is now a staple feature of carol concerts up and down the country.

© In selected villages of South Yorkshire and North Derbyshire, including Castleton, Oughtibridge, Bradfield, Ecclesfield and Worrall, the weekend before Christmas is the time for traditional carols. These songs are unique to the area or even to the individual village, with distinctive and sometimes impregnably complicated tunes. The tradition has been going for at least a couple of hundred years, and the atmosphere is terrific.

21st December
St Thomas the Apostle's Day

A Mumping Frumentation

✝ Tonight the **witches of Dorrington** near Sleaford in Lincolnshire come out to play at the village church. Even early this century, a wry local fondly remembered the unusually friendly witches and the '*rare owd games they 'ad there! Now there was some goin's on!*' They have a chat and a sing-song; but despite regular manifestations down the centuries on this night, there have been no reports of unpalatable potions or of small children being turned into voles. The explanation for this Neighbourly Witch Scheme may be the presence of an occult superior. This is the very church in which, legend has it, you can witness the Devil himself having a bit of harmless fun. Peer through the church door keyhole on any bright moonlit night, and you will see Satan playing with glass marbles.

© If yesterday's onion tricks have failed to boost relationship confidence, go tell it to the **chickens**. Sneak up on the henhouse in the wee small hours tonight, and your marital arrangements will be made. If the cock crows before the hens cackle, you will be married within the year. If the hens strike up first, forget it.

Today is the **Winter Solstice**, good news for nocturnal creatures. The rhyme says it all, and yet says nothing:

St Thomas gray, St Thomas gray,
The longest night and the shortest day.

A frosty St Thomas' means a big bad winter ahead. Whatever the weather, it is an opportune time for human activities, and a not-so-opportune time for pigs:

St Thomas divine,
Brewing, baking, and killing of fat swine.

Cynics, meanwhile, argue that today is ideal for **weddings**. The solstice is the shortest day of the year, and so there is less time to repent. Geddit?

The commonest St Thomas tradition was **mumping**, also known as Thomassing, gooding or corning. A woman or child from each household was entitled to knock on doors and ask for largesse. Ideally this was in the form of food. Corn and milk were amongst the commonest goodies, being made into Christmas loaves or frumenty, a dish of grains baked in milk, with fruit, sugar and spice. Alms for this latter purpose were called a *frumentation*.

It was not just poor people who went mumping. In some areas quite wealthy women were out and about, on a sort of social call with a catch. And some places had a diminished concept of goodwill-and-plenty. In Grimsby, Humberside, large crowds of mumpers used to go on a grumpy mump and fight over the money and provisions. The strongest, not the most needy, usually ended up with all the booty.

Mumping declined early this century. One of the last bouts was at Haddenham, Buckinghamshire, in 1942: a single old woman did the rounds just for the fun of it.

Today the tenants of Thornford in Dorset had to leave their annual five shilling **tithe** in the hollow of a certain gravestone in Thornton churchyard. If it was not in place before noon, the Lord of the Manor could claim his ancient rights to a hay tithe.

22nd December

Anarchy in the UK

King Stephen prepared to sit on the uncomfortable English throne today in 1135, having fought off the rival claim of his uncle Henry I's daughter, Empress Matilda. Stephen's reign was far from happy. It became known as The Anarchy, a time of civil war and rampant nobles who knew no fear. They imposed a reign of terror on the countryside, torturing and pillaging, ransacking homes and churches. People had to hand over protection money, and the sums which they came up with were never enough. *The Anglo-Saxon Chronicle* – which ceased publication soon after Stephen's death – is consistently appalled by the goings-on. It contrasts the mess of Stephen's years with the previous reign of Henry I, of whom it says: '*He was a good man and held in great awe. In his days no man dared to wrong another. He made peace* *for man and beast.*' As opposed to the rampaging nobles: '*I know not how to, nor am I able to tell of, all the atrocities nor all the cruelties which they wrought upon the unhappy people of this country.*'

It was said that during the Anarchy's 19 years, crops refused to grow; and that Christ and the saints slept. Things were pretty grim. '*Evil reigned in the land*', said the Chronicle. Eventually Stephen turned up his toes, and the old war-horse Matilda got her own son Henry II on the throne, following the death of Eustace, the heir.

Hiring some jobbing builders to fix your extension is a fine old British tradition. In 1545 Sir Thomas Moyle brought in a bunch of likely lads during the construction of his mansion at Eastwell Park, near Boughton Aluph in Kent. During the first tea break he was surprised to find his foreman reading – not the sports pages, but a book of Latin. After a few polite inquiries, Sir Thomas found that the man was none other than **Richard Plantagenet**, son of Richard III, and the last member of the House of York. Richard Junior had fled the field after his father was defeated at Bosworth in 1485, and had become a bricklayer to evade discovery and capture. He hid behind the hod for a number of years, and then got to like the work; though he could not shake off the habit of reading weighty tomes. Moyle was impressed by all this, and ensured that Richard lived out his life comfortably at Eastwell. He died on this day in 1550, and is, according to legend, buried in an unmarked grave on the north side of the church – anyone positively identifying it deserves a free claim to the English throne and a cut-price extension. It is not known if Richard ever learned to wolf-whistle.

◉ Richmond's **Mayor's Audit Money** is linked with the St Thomas Doles which used to be given out up and down the country near the feast of St Thomas on the 21st. It is handed out shortly before Christmas at Richmond in North Yorkshire to any local pensioner who cares to turn up at the mayor's house. The money started out as a Norman land-tax called 'fee rent'. In 1576 this money went into a fund, later the mayor's purse, to be handed out to the poor, originally on the 22nd. The dole is not going to make anyone rich, and so to make it all worthwhile modern mayors announce an open house with tea and biscuits. Specially minted 'Richmond Shilling' coins have been produced

in recent years, in lieu of the real thing. This is all part of a conscious decision to keep the custom alive, following its near-demise in the mid-1980s.

23rd December

Merry Multitude's Idle Day

Watched over by three carers, **Harriet Pearson** was on her sick-bed in 1864 at 19 St James' Place, London. On the evening of December 23rd, Harriet's sister Ann called round and went in to see the invalid. This caused some surprise as Ann had been dead for several years. One of the carers understood the mythic significance of such an after-life visitation, and tactlessly cried out: '*Then Aunt Harriet will die today!*' In fact Harriet held on until the next day, Christmas Eve.

© On the Channel Islands, tonight is traditionally known as *La Longue Veille*, **The Long Knitting Evening**, although *Longue Veille* gatherings now take place throughout the Christmas season. Thrilling as it sounds, the *Veille* has become an informal gathering of neighbours for a chat and a drink. Originally this was the night of the big knit: the last chance to finish goods destined for the market; a long hard session of woolly thinking with everyone pulling together, then sitting down together afterwards for a traditional supper of mulled wine, cheese and biscuits.

Finishing work before Christmas is a traditional goal. So you can really annoy a Channel Island builder by preventing the completion of his work with the **Clameur de Haro**. This is done by shouting (in French): '*Haro! Haro! Haro! Help me, Prince, I have been misused!*' Building then has to cease until your complaint has been heard in court. This is an ancient right if you have any grievance about the work. *Haro* is thought to be Rollo, the first Duke of Normandy, a squat brown man filled with toffee.

✝ One of the Channel Islands, Jersey, is home to a shape-shifting cat. Take the **Black Cat of Carrefour a Cendre** away from town and it grows in size. Return it and it shrinks. If you get too close it disappears altogether; and presumably if you go too far it either crushes you or swallows you whole. Whether it is a ghost, a goblin or the tail-end of some half-forgotten legend, it keeps the local mice confused.

On this day in 1882 a farmer's wife who lived near Bridport in Dorset took a gamble with four quid. She entrusted the cash to two travelling women who claimed that they could **treble money**, and who asked for just a few shillings in return for their financial acumen. They marked the coins with astrological symbols, and hid them. The farmer was having none of this and demanded to know where they had put the loot. Despite his wife's warnings that it must be left undisturbed until Easter Sunday, the farmer dragged the truth from her and discovered that the two strangers had stuck something up the chimney. The something turned out to be a cloth-wrapped, pin-stuck smoked pig's heart stuffed with polished farthings. That was that: the spell was broken, and so the four quid was never trebled. That is the non-cynic's way of viewing it.

1652 was **the year they cancelled Christmas**. Having already stamped out lesser customs, the Puritan Parliament of Oliver Cromwell declared that '*No Observation shall be had of the five and twentieth day of December, commonly called Christ-mass Day*.' It was not the sure-fire way to popularity. There were riots when officers tried to confiscate holly and other greenery from the churches. Christmas remained a non-event until the Restoration in 1660; though the old 12-day celebration was gone for good. The Puritans' alternative names for Christmas also vanished – such pithy tags as The Old Heathens' Feasting Day, Multitude's Idle Day, and Satan's Working Day.

24th December
Christmas Eve

The Toad Queen and the Half-Fish Half-Ouzel Boggart

The '*not a creature was stirring*' bit of the poem *The Night Before Christmas* does not apply to ghosts. Tonight they are at their busiest, perhaps due to the large numbers of people wandering the streets late at night in an advanced state of impressionability.

♱ At Rainham in Kent at midnight tonight a coach with a headless array of horses, coachman and passenger, leaves the church, heading for Queen's Court. When it reaches the site of the Court (now Berengrave Lane in the middle of a housing estate), the horses are watered. The fact that they have no heads, and therefore no mouths, does not seem to deter the ghostly charade. The passenger is Christopher Bloor, and the final stop for the coach is his former home, Bloor's Place. Bloor is said to have been a notorious Tudor womaniser. One night jealous husbands waylaid him and cut off his head, sticking it on a church tower spike. The **phantom coach**'s appearances on Christmas Eve have been so reliable that later owners of Bloor's Place used to leave a glass of brandy for the former occupant. In spite of Bloor having the same problem as the horses, on Christmas morning the glass was always found empty.

♱ Boughton churchyard in Northamptonshire has a unique ghost, the combined spirit of a dead bride and groom. In one guise or the other the spirit favours Christmas Eve above all other nights. It appears to wayfarers as whichever gender they find attractive, and arranges a tryst. These are evidently sexy ghosts, as the tryst is usually kept by the willing mortal. The ghost turns up, but hurries away after giving the traveller a quick kiss to consummate the brief affair. It is the **kiss of death**, and the jilted person always dies soon afterwards. This kiss'n'toll story closely parallels Celtic legends of a faerie-spirit called the *Ganconer*, or Love Talker, who wins the hearts of poor young women, and then disappears, leaving the mortal to pine to death with a broken heart. Today in 1875 a farmer called William Parker, passing Boughton churchyard, was inveigled by a flirtatious red-haired woman. When she dashed off after a quick peck on the cheek, her footsteps making no sound, Parker realised that he had succumbed to the charms of the bride from hell. He told everyone in the village that his number was up and, sure enough, exactly one month later he died.

♱ Even more bizarre is the wonderful ghost known as the **Lumb Boggart** which once laid siege to a house at Bradwell in Derbyshire. It started its roaming after the bones of a woman were found under a staircase in the village in 1760; and as time went by the haunting became noisier and more unpleasant. At last the villagers called in an exorcist. After a great deal of effort he shouted: '*Beroald, beroald, gab gabor agaba!*' – which for some reason conjured up the ghost. The exorcist commanded the boggart to cease its haunting forever, and to assume the form of a small fish and live at Lumb Mouth, the source of Bradwell Beck. As a reminder of its former freedom, or perhaps just for show, once a year on Christmas Eve the exorcist allowed the fish to take the shape of a white ouzel and fly the two miles to Lumbley Pool, between Brough and Bamford. Fish-ghosts and phantom ouzels are not easy to spot; but boggart-memory is long, and well into this century the pool was still considered a fearful, spooky place.

🕆 The old troopers of the Civil War armies that met at **Edgehill** in Warwickshire stage their annual re-enactment of the battle today – see October 23rd for the details.

🕆 The ghosts in the tale of John Turner are noticeably absent; though one explanation of his fate suggests that he had tangled with a type of **hobgoblin** well known for appearing in tempting guises and luring innocents to their deaths. Turner ran pack horses between Chester and Derby, and today in 1735 he travelled through a snowstorm to reach festive home and hearth at Saltersford near Rainow in Cheshire. He never made it, and his body was found the following day, just a mile from home and with an inexplicable single female footprint beside him. The tale is retold on a stone which marks the site of Turner's death.

When the King of Northumberland remarried, it had dire consequences for his daughter. The stepmother took a dislike to the girl, and transformed her into a huge snake-like dragon, the **Laidley Worm**. The creature took up residence near Bamburgh, wreaking havoc and poisoning the earth with its fetid breath, until it was challenged by the King's son, fighting under the grand title of the Childe of Wynde. He was unaware that the dragon was really a princess with acute halitosis and serious complexion problems, and was all set to put the creature to the sword. But the Worm deflected his blow by telling the sad story of its bewitchment, and the soft-hearted prince kissed the monster three times. This broke the spell, and the Worm turned back into the princess. The unbinding of so much black magic then backfired on the evil stepmother, who was transformed into a toad the size of a chicken and banished to the bowels of Bamburgh Castle. Every seven years on Christmas Eve a secret door opens into the lair of the **Toad Queen**; but she can only be freed if someone enters, unsheathes the Childe of Wynde's sword three times, blows thrice on his horn, and then kisses the amphibian.

📖 It is not as much legend as leg-pull, but a commemorative stone in Kirklees Park, Brig-house, West Yorkshire, claims to mark the grave of **Robin Hood** who died there on this day in 1247. Its cod-medieval verse makes McGonagal blush:

> *Hear Underneath dis laitl stean, Laz robert*
> *of Huntingtun;*
> *Ne'er arcir ver az hie sa geud, An pipl*
> *Kauld im robin heud;*
> *Sick utlawz az hi an iz men, Vil england*
> *nivr si agen.*

📖 Tonight is a grand time for seeing **faeries** at countless sites all over the islands. They tend to be very elusive; but there can surely be no mistaking the lumbering exercises of the **Robber's Stone**, Carreg Lleidr, south of Llandyfrydog on Anglesey in Gwynedd. It is the petrified remains of a man who once stole a bible from the local church. Every Christmas Eve as the clock strikes midnight the stone circumnavigates the field three times.

📖 The **Odin Stone**, one of the Stones at Stenness near Stromness on Mainland, Orkney, used to be visited by lovers who wished to plight their troth. Tonight was especially auspicious; but one young couple met with tragedy after their Christmas Eve liaison. They travelled home separately, and the young man was ambushed and murdered by a rival suitor. The woman learned of this when she heard a cry, and saw a fleeting apparition of her lover pointing heavenward with a hopeful arm. The Odin Stone – which was destroyed last century – had a hole in it, through which lovers used to join hands and swear the Odin Oath, said to be more binding than a church wedding. When a woman's pirate lover was hanged in London, she trekked down from the north so that she could grip his dead hand – only then could she be considered released from the oath.

📖 **Old Palm**, another lump of stone, also goes walkabout tonight. But in this case the stone is a small statue on an overly ornate plinth in the woods at Mapledurham House in Oxfordshire. Old Palm walks through the village in Father Christmas-like mood, dispensing festive jollity.

Somewhere off the coast in the Fylde region around Blackpool in Lancashire is the site of **Kilgrimol**, a town lost to the sea many centuries ago. If you visit the beach and put your ear to the sand, it is said that you will hear the muffled sound of the lost town's bells ringing.

According to legend, in the 13th-century Sir

Thomas de Soothill murdered one of his servants in Dewsbury, West Yorkshire. Overcome with remorse, Soothill later decided to make a clean sweep, and he purchased a tenor bell for the church of All Saints, hoping that its tolling would help atone for his crimes.

© The bell, known as Black Tom, is still rung every Christmas Eve in a ceremony called the **Devil's Knell**, or the Old Lad's Passing Bell. It celebrates the symbolic defeat of Satan when Jesus was born, and also keeps the Devil out of Dewsbury for the next 12 months. Each Christmas Eve it is rung once for each year since the Nativity, the tally being kept by a man with pen and paper. The Knell, which will soon be passing the 2,000 toll mark, lasts about two hours, and is always timed to end bong on midnight. It was brought to national attention in 1986 when it featured as one of the five Christmas customs on that year's commemorative stamps from the Post Office.

© The ringing-in of Christmas Day remains a climax of **Midnight Masses** across the land – for many people the one time of year when they voluntarily enter a church. Drunks seem to get particular pleasure from these occasions, and sadly some churches have taken to moving these traditional services away from midnight.

© **Ash Faggots**, just to confuse American readers, used to be a key element of' the Christmas Eve festivities in the south-west of England. Ash burns well, even when it is still green, and huge bundles of the stuff bound with withies were often ceremonially dragged to the hearth by four oxen, regardless of the weight of the bundle. Sometimes these faggots were supposed to burn – or at least glow – for the entire Christmas season, during which it was unlucky to kindle new fire. A fragment of the burned-out faggot was put aside and was used 11-and-a-bit months later to torch the next year's festive fuel.

The bringing-in of the faggot was sometimes celebrated with an **Ashen Faggot Ball**. At Taunton in Somerset these were said to have been instigated by King Alfred. During the lean years of Viking warring in the 9th century, Alfred sought shelter in the town, and was eternally grateful to the easy-burning green ash which warmed him and his weary men. It is also said that the infant Jesus was warmed by an ash fire, an attempt to kindle a spark of Christianity in this ancient tradition.

© The Faggot survives at Dunster near Minehead in Somerset, where, at *The Luttrell Arms*, a modest bundle is brought in this evening.

Twelve stout sticks are bound with green ash withies, and while the bundle burns the rousing *Dunster Carol* is sung. As each withie bursts, rounds of drinks are ordered. And there is divination to be had too: couples can nominate a withy, and the first to break denotes the first to marry. The green ash burns quickly, and if you can formulate a wish as one of the thin sticks catches, completing it before it burns out, then the wish will come true. The custom here was revived in 1935, and the landlord believes that his pub was chosen above all others simply because it has the largest fireplace.

The Ash Faggot was a Saxon version of the Norse **Yule Log** tradition which still lingers in those northern areas that fell under Viking influence. Also known as the Yule Clog or Block, it was dragged from the woods and brought in by an ox or horse. The log had to be found, not bought. Corn and ale/cider were sometimes sprinkled on the wood before lighting. The log, like the faggot, was a means of using light and heat to rout temporarily the forces of winter and darkness. In Cornwall a human figure was chalked on to the bark, an apparent echo of sacrificial antecedents. In the Highlands of Scotland the sacrifice was made more explicit. A log was carved into rough human shape and called *Cailleach Noillaich*, or **The Christmas Old Wife**. She was burned solemnly tonight before the festivities were allowed to begin. Sadly the main form in which these Yule Clog traditions survive is the log-shaped chocolate cake (plastic robin optional), piled by the dozen on supermarket shelves from early November.

Yule, the Vikings' Winter Solstice festival, roughly corresponding with the Christmas season, also featured huge **Yule Candles**. These were to be seen in the Christian church for many centuries, a tradition in which size was important: entire rhinoceros-worths of tallow were formed into candles which towered over the congregation. They were relit for each day of the festival, and if they were doused by accident during this time, calamity was sure to follow. These Yule lights survive in the much-reduced shape of the Advent Candle, and the mock-candles of Christmas tree decorations.

On the Isle of Man dreams of giant candles were what sustained many churchgoers during the long Christmas Eve service. Islanders had to sit through the **Oei'l Voirrey**, during which dirge-like carols on the themes of death, sin and repentance were chanted. The consolation came afterwards, with decent amounts of pepper-spiced ale consumed until a pre-lit candle had burned itself out.

In the lead-mining district of Derbyshire a candle was left burning tonight on a lump of best-quality ore, in honour of a legendary miner's guardian called T'Owd Man.

Once the Faggot or Log was alight, the feast could begin. In many places Christmas Eve, sprawling into the early hours of the 25th, was the key festive day of the season. Various spiced cakes and mince pies were produced, along with mulled beer or cider. At St Peter Port in Guernsey country folk used to flock into town for a seasonal treat of oranges and chestnuts. At Grimsby in Humberside, the fun took to the streets. In 1724 the party was in full swing with an ale-swigging crowd watching the Plough Ship pageant, a mixture of mumming play and Morris dancing. But a storm whipped up and put the fear of God into the revellers, who deduced that their unbridled antics had met with divine wrath on the eve of such a hallowed day.

Of the countless games played at the Christmas Eve parties, two survivors unique to the season are Snapdragon and Flapdragon. In Snapdragon, players try to snatch and eat raisins which have been set alight with brandy, and each dried fruit successfully removed and consumed brings luck for one of the coming months. Popular last century, and still played in some areas, Flapdragon involved participants drinking from a cider jug in which a lighted candle was doing its best to compromise the excesses of Victorian facial hair.

♀ Some games were even more hazardous. At Marwell Hall in Owlesbury, Hampshire, a woman called Maud married Sir John Lovell on Christmas Eve, some time in the Middle Ages. During the party a bout of hide-and-seek proved her downfall. Still clad in her wedding regalia, she climbed into a trunk in the attic, and won the game. In other words, the chest locked when she closed the lid and nobody ever found her. The body was only discovered centuries later, in its dusty wedding gown. Maud's ghost still haunts the Hall. The events were set down in the 19th century by Thomas Haynes Bayley, in a poem called The Mistletoe Bough. Undermining this legend, the same events are also said to have occurred at Bramshill in the same county; at Titchmarsh Manor in Northamptonshire; at Minster Lovell Hall in Oxfordshire; at Bawdrip in Somerset; and at Brockdish Hall in Norfolk.

◉ There are various means of gazing into the future tonight, including many of the ones mentioned on Hallowe'en and Midsummer Eve. To decipher the marital stakes you can go to the chicken coop and knock three times. If the cock crows first, you will marry within the year. If the hens beat him to it with a bit of cackling, marriage has no place in next year's diary.

◉ Another way of angling for marriage, and/or wealth, is with the help of a Christmas Eve posset. The posset is made by curdling milk with hot ale, adding eggs, spice and dried fruit, and inserting a ring and a coin into the mixture. Whoever gets the ring will soon marry, and the one who gets the coin will come into money. Once the prospect of marriage is established, bear in mind the following: at midnight if you manage to pluck 12 sage leaves without breaking the stalks, the wraith of your future companion-at-the-altar will appear.

◉ This is also an auspicious night for making a dumb-cake, which must be baked in silence with a nearby door kept constantly open. Recipes are endlessly variable, but try to include at least one unpalatable item such as soot or egg-shell. Having fasted all day, which is a bit of downer at the Christmas Eve party, prick your name in the top of the cake and shove it in the oven, still remembering to keep mum. Once baked, it should then be placed on the hearthstone, and at midnight the ghostly form of the person who holds the key to your wedlock will stroll in through the open door, lured by the cake's aroma. In another version the unpalatable cake has to be eaten, and in still another the dumb-cake has to be wedged under your pillow overnight, before the ghost of romance-yet-to-come will appear.

Care must be taken with cooking and all other activities today. In Scotland, if any bannock baked on Christmas Eve falls apart during the process, the cook will die within the year. And any yarn left on a spinning wheel tonight will be finished by the Devil, which brings bad luck.

The sanctity of the season affects all creatures great and small. Tonight at midnight bees hum the 100th Psalm. Many parts of the country knew this superstition to be rubbish – it was the 23rd Psalm, or another tune altogether. But there was widespread agreement across Britain, and in parts of Europe and America, that tonight every hive hummed musically.

Bees do not like to let any important occasion

pass unobserved. Fail to tell the hive of important family news – such as marriage and death – and they will desert, or die, or produce sub-standard honey. The correct form of bee-address is to tap three times on top of the hive and make the announcement in a clear voice. One formula recorded at Stallingborough in Humberside – for use if the farm owner had died – involves the rattling of keys at the hive, and then the rhyme:

> *Honey bees! Honey bees! Hear what I say!*
> *Your master, X, has passed away.*
> *But his wife now begs you freely stay,*
> *And still gather honey for many a day.*
> *Bonny bees, bonny bees, hear what I say.*

In Flora Thompson's *Lark Rise to Candleford*, Queenie tells her industrious insects: '*Bees, bees, your master's dead, an' now you must work for your missis.*'

If the bees have been informed of a wedding, they should be invited along: a bee on the bouquet is thought to be good luck, as is a swarm of bees on the day of the ceremony – though at a distance, presumably. The hive should be decorated with a ribbon. At a funeral a hive should be given a token of mourning, as well as a piece of funeral cake. Again, they can be invited to attend; though this courtesy backfired at Cullompton, Devon in the 18th century. After a family death, the hives had been moved incorrectly, and the bees flew out in a rage, routing the mourners. It was several hours before the burial could be completed. Any rheumatism sufferers in attendance may have found some consolation in the fact that bee stings are supposed to be a cure for the ailment.

The other Christmas insect is the somewhat unlikely **cricket**. The sound of one chirping in the house tonight brings good luck, and is the embodiment of home, hearth and happiness. The idea is still popular in Ireland; and Charles Dickens seized upon the notion, expanding it and adding a big dollop of sentimentality, as the central image of his Christmas story *The Cricket on the Hearth*.

While the bees are busy singing their psalms, the **cattle kneel** and **sheep face east** – in remembrance of the Nativity and the attendant animals away in the manger. In Herefordshire it was said that only seven-year-old cattle – supposedly the age of the beasts in the Holy Stall – took part in the kneeling. For the duration of the night all the farmyard animals can talk; but to overhear what they say brings

inordinate amounts of bad luck – a brilliant way of discouraging the sceptical from sounding out the superstition.

◉ With squadrons of evil spirits abroad tonight, Dorset cocks went on night shift, crowing from dusk to dawn to keep them at bay. Crowing or not, it was usual to give poultry an extra good feed on Christmas Eve. Other animals got special rations too; and birds were sometimes given a special cake of fat and grain known as the **Christmas Sheaf**. At Walmer in Kent the ducks on the local pond still look forward to their slice of Christmas Sheaf today. But the usual modern form of all these seasonal creature comforts is the pet-present industry, by which cats and dogs receive unlikely shaped treats in ludicrously shaped Christmas stockings from a doting Santa Claws.

25th December
Christmas Day

Myths, Mithras and Mistletoe

The ancient sun-god **Attis** was born on December 25th in Phrygia – part of modern Turkey – and was worshipped far and wide. It was therefore no coincidence when another god was born on that same day. But this one proved even more popular, spreading throughout Europe with the Roman soldiers who worshipped him. The god was born of a virgin in lowly surroundings, and after his death he was miraculously resurrected. The chief tenets of his faith were fraternity and moral purity, with a hope of everlasting life. The good god, ruler of the universe, guarded his followers during their fleshly incarnation, and kept a benign eye on them after death. The deity was **Mithras**, the Persian sun-god.

So close were these underlying themes to the basic yarn of the Christian myth that the early church could only get its head round the problem by saying that Mithras and his parallel life were the work of Satan, a demonic device to lure men away from the one true faith by bastardising a few holy truths.

But Mithras was there centuries before Jesus, and had a head start. His Roman soldiers had allies in high places, and when Jupiter and the pantheon of old gods were swamped by the waves of new religions, the final showdown for the official new religion of the Roman Empire was a godhead-to-head between Jesus and Mithras. We all know who won, and so farewell to December 25th, *Dies Natali Invicti Solis*, the Birthday of the Unconquered Sun.

The Resurrection motif – in Mithraism a simple myth dealing with the rise and fall of the sun – is linked with spring rather than winter festivities in Christianity; but the flames of Mithras remain in the blazing puddings and logs of the Christmas season, reinforced by the parallel fire-and-light imagery of the Vikings' Yule. The fire strengthens the old god in his weak and weary winter phase. The fleeting gospel references (in St Luke and St Matthew) to the infant Jesus were mined and padded heavily to provide the seasonal Christ-child imagery needed to counter the popular Mithraic practice of carrying effigies of the child god (born of the earth-virgin) through the streets: babes in arms have always guaranteed broad market appeal.

The most complete surviving example of a British temple to Mithras – which was unearthed in 1950 complete with marvellously preserved altar stones – is just south of the fort of Brocolitia on Hadrian's Wall, near Hexham. Temples dedicated to Jesus Christ are more abundant.

It was only in AD 354 that the **birth of Christ** fell into step with Mithras and Attis, and was fixed as December 25th, though January 6th remained the favourite choice in the east. As for the actual year, Christ was probably born sometime between 12 and 4 BC. King Herod died in 4 BC, so the events cannot post-date that. The census that drew Joseph to No-Vacancies-Bethlehem in the first place is thought to have been issued between 11 and 7 BC. If the star in the east was Halley's Comet as some claim, then that would make it 12 BC. If the star, as others claim, was the bright lights of Saturn and Jupiter in conjunction with Pisces, then it would have been 7 BC, that event only occurring every 257 years. Whatever, from the evidence of surviving records, it was not until 1123 that the birth celebrations had become important enough to merit their own handy name, 'Christmas'.

For a certain sad, banished **trow** on Shetland, Christmas was one time in the year when friends and family could be visited back in the old country of Trowland. Trows are the Shetland version of the Norse trolls, and the worst crime which one of their kind can perpetrate is to steal from his or her elders. The banished trow had done just that, and was only allowed home today, Yule Day, spending the rest of his time moping up and down the islands. And even when he made it home, all he received were pinches, punches and abuse.

The long nights of the Christmas season are the trows' favourite time for wandering in mortal realms; though if not back underground by daybreak they are trapped on earth until sunset. This is a scaled-down version of the old legends in which trolls turn to stone if touched by sunlight: a fact familiar to readers of Tolkien's *The Hobbit*. Trows are fond of fiddle music, live under green hills, and sometimes give a helping hand on mortal farms. There was generally an uneasy peace between human and trow; but at Christmas Shetlanders marked their property with crosses of iron to deter faerie fingers. Anyone straying near one of the trow-hills at this season was liable to spend a year and a day in Trowland. '*Trow take thee*' is still yelled at Shetland children who are being especially irritating. It is unlucky to spy the creatures; though to overhear them brings good fortune. Anyone with a mysterious ailment was thought to have been trow-struck, and was known as *trowie*, an adjective that has come to mean any sickly person.

Shetland used to have another Christmas faerie interloper, known simply as *It*. No one knew exactly what *It* was, as *It* could change its shape at will. The thing has been described as a headless man, a huge shapeless jellyfish, a sack of wool, and a legless beast. Legs or not, *It* was able to run very quickly, and could also fly. One particular islander was plagued by *It* every Christmas, until one year when he decided to have a show-down. *It* made its presence known by appearing with a sound like that of wet meat hitting a stone slab. Bible in one hand, axe in the other, the man chased *It* from the house and on to the clifftops. Before the thing could jump into the sea, the man said holy words and flung his axe at the shapeless mass. He then ran back to summon his friends, and when they returned each person saw *It* differently, in a chaos of illusion. But *It* appeared to be dead, and so they buried the blubber where it lay and dug a deep trench around the site. All was well until a person, his curiosity keeping him awake at nights, sneaked to the clifftop to investigate the grave. When he probed, a light-emitting mist rose from the ground – just like in John Carpenter's film *The Fog* – and *It* slithered from the earth and rolled over into sea and well-deserved retirement.

Like *It*, **Father Christmas** is a creature of many conflicting identities, and with an even longer and more convoluted history. In Britain the starting point is the Saxon god **Woden** (the Vikings' Odin), who rewarded his followers at Yule, which corresponded roughly to the modern Christmas season. Woden rode through the skies on his eight-legged horse *Sleipnir*, showering gifts on the faithful. This benison arrived in the household via the huts' smoke-holes, which opened to the sky – the precursors of chimneys. With a dose of the Roman Bacchus for good measure, a figure of robust mid-winter jollity was firmly established at an early stage.

The British Father Christmas first seems to have appeared as a central character in many of the season's mumming plays, where he embodied festive mirth and merriment. After his Puritan 'exile' – dealt with on December 23rd – there were celebrations for Father Christmas' triumphant return in 1660 with the Restoration. He was often called Sir Christmas as a mark of respect, a well-established, larger-than-life figure of benevolence; though he was flexible enough to take on many aspects of the equally lovable St Nicholas.

St Nicholas was for many years a parallel, separate development (see December 6th). The two were never completely amalgamated; but the spirit of goodwill and gift-giving made them obvious brothers. Nicholas is said to have once thrown gold coins down the chimney of a poor household, which landed in their drying stockings. This handy story simultaneously accounts for the place in the festive ritual of both chimneys and gift-receiving footwear.

St Nicholas is mythologicially schizophrenic, one part becoming happily absorbed within the thoroughly British Father Christmas, another fragment spinning off into the more European **Santa Claus** (as in Saint Ni-claus). It was this latter aspect of St Nick that took root in America, and even in the middle of the 19th century there were enough clear distinctions between Santa and Father Christmas to enable the two guardians of the season to co-exist peacefully.

Father Christmas, in early Victorian illustrations, wears a long fur-trimmed robe with attached hood, usually red, but sometimes green, blue, whatever colour the artist fancied. He was generally shown wearing a crown of greenery, or carrying a rough cross – strange blurrings between pagan and Christian imagery. His Bacchus-nature came to the fore in many prints, depicting him surrounded by food and wine – this Woden-cum-Bacchus figure was the basis of the Ghost of Christmas Present in Charles Dickens' *A Christmas Carol*.

Santa Claus, meanwhile, wore a tight red buttoned jacket and hat, a wide black belt, and rather dinky boots. This was the wardrobe used by Thomas Nast in his 1863 illustrations of Santa, setting his dress-code for all time. All that has been lost is the clay pipe smoked by Nast's man. What further helped secure Santa in the public imagination as indelibly and inflexibly clad in red was when, in the early years of this century, Coca-Cola made him the centre of a huge worldwide advertising campaign, and naturally kitted him out top to toe in the corporate colours of red and white.

As regards his famous magnanimity, Father Christmas, prior to this century, only ever delivered simple items such as nuts and oranges: a scenario far from alien to the childhood of many of today's pensioners. Some houses had no stocking traditions at all, and received nothing, unless a moneyed relative deigned to send a few items to the poor end of the family. In these days of high commerce Father Christmas/Santa now has an official postal address: it is Arctic Circle, SF 96930, Rovaniemi, Finland (although Sweden, Iceland and Greenland also claim him). He always writes back.

After the stroke of midnight, homes in Sussex would throw open their doors shouting '*Welcome old Father Christmas*', a way of ushering out bad luck and inviting in good. Rather than let Midnight Mass hog all the chiming, it was and is customary to go in for some self-service ringing, celebrating the start of this most holy and happy of days with whatever **bells** come to hand.

✦ There are the body-bells of the Morris dancers; the hand-bells which now seem to be enjoying something of a renaissance; and, thanks to the merciless pen of J. Pierpont last century, there are sleigh bells, dashing through the snow on one-horse open sleighs in *Jingle Bells*. And there are even underground bells. In what is almost a dead-ringer for yesterday's tale of submerged chiming at Kilgromel, tonight in darkest Nottinghamshire it is supposed to be possible to hear a strange clanging echoing up from the ground. It is the sound of the church bells of the lost town of Raleigh, swallowed up by the earth long ago for reasons which are now forgotten. The same vagueness also applies to the precise former location of Raleigh.

◉ Some of the day's ringing and singing was more formal. Money was often left to encourage memorial bells to sound at a set hour: at

Ruardean in Gloucestershire a female benefactor left £5 for a two-hour Virgin Peal on Christmas Day. Belting out hymns from cathedral and church-towers was a nationwide habit today, and across Wales large male choirs raised the rafters at carol services called *plygeiniau*. These still take place in some areas, notably at Llanrhaeadr-ym-Mochnant and elsewhere in the Tanad Valley on the Clwyd-Powys border.

Plygain was another Welsh church tradition, meaning 'crowing of the cock'. At some time between 3 and 6 am the household would drag itself from bed or all-night party and attend a short service with extended carol-singing. The old and infirm often said prayers and sang songs at the same hour from the confines of home, as the next best thing. The sturdier souls sometimes walked through the streets with burning torches, singing and blowing on cow horns – most spectacularly at Tenby in Dyfed. Another custom of the *plygain* was to bring a candle, so that the church was ablaze with light.

The singing spilled out from churches and on to the streets. The modern tradition of belting out carols gets into full swing several days before Christmas Day itself. This seasonal carolling has its origins in the old town Waits: hired musicians who played at key dates throughout the year and hoped for financial contributions at Christmas. Lincoln's Waits used to go **Crying Christmas** today, performing a narrative poem which warned against breaking the 'rules of Christmas'. The chief rule was mirth, in remembrance of the joyful holy birth. The miserable were to receive no mercy according to the Elizabethan text:

> Whatsoever oppressor will be cruel and not
> merry make
> Shall be sore fettered in a dungeon full deep
> Wherein is toads and mites and many a great
> snake,
> That place is so dark you shall not see your
> feet.

'Mites' was used to denote any crawling arthropod. The only other rules were to fear God, be charitable, and give alms to anyone who called for them. All this by command of the merry mayor. Sometimes today's carollers carried decorated boxes with wax effigies of Mary and/or Jesus. Those who went for this approach, revealing the dolls to prompt the alms, sometimes called the custom *Milly Box*, from 'My Lady's Box'. But it was more often

known as **vesselling**, or besselling. This can be taken to refer to the vessel in which the dolls were carried; though it is in fact a corrupted form of wassailing – sometimes it was corrupted even further to *Wesley-Bob*, a Chinese-whispers version of 'wassail cup'.

Wassailing comes in two forms: the visiting wassail, and the wassailing of objects, such as the apple-trees solicitations of mid-January. The word *wassail* means be hale/cheery. The **visiting wassail** went on its rounds throughout the Christmas period, usually starting today. A wassail bowl was ferried from house to house, originally full of drink to offer at the doorstep, but later used as a receptacle for the alms. Often a decorated wassail-bough was carried instead of the bowl. There was, invariably, music to accompany all this – songs of food, drink and conviviality, the pagan cousin of the Christmas alms-carol. There are endless variations on the basic formula of:

> A wassail, a wassail, throughout all the town,
> Our cup it is white and our ale it is brown,
> Our wassail is made of the good ale and true,
> Some nutmeg and ginger, the best we could
> brew.

These songs often offered reassurance, such as the Yorkshire lines:

> We are not daily beggars that beg from door
> to door,
> But we are neighbours' children who you have
> seen before.

In Somerset they offered the broad directive: '. . . and a little more cider will do us no harm'. Appealing for the sympathy vote, the warm, generous houses of the prospective alms-givers were often contrasted in the songs with '*us poor wassail boys that's wandered in the mire*'. Some of the lines were more esoteric:

> We know by the moon that we are not too
> soon,
> And we know by the sky that we are not too
> high;

or the Shepton Beauchamp, Somerset, couplet:

> And to the mare and to her right eye
> God send our Missis an old Christmas pie.

The traditional wassailing drink was **lambs-wool**, made from ale or cider mixed with spices, sugar, eggs and cream, with a froth of roasted apples or crab-apples. 'Lambswool' derives from the Irish apple-gathering festival of *la mas ubhal*. Wassailing, and the Waits, along with the devotional church music, sired the Advent custom of carol-singing.

Occasionally the wassailers were accompanied by a man dressed as a **bull**. At Kingscote in Gloucestershire he was called the Broad, a leftover from some pagan revelry of the past. At Tetbury in the same county a white wooden bull's head was wrapped in sacking and carried on a pole from door to door to solicit money. When each door was opened the sacking was pulled away to reveal the face – like a giant 3-D advent calendar. This is a pagan version of *vesselling*, and the horned figure may be an echo of some long-forgotten priest, or a representation of the horny god himself.

Bulls are native to the British Isles, **reindeer** are not; and yet there is no contest in this or any other country when it comes to naming the animal of the season. Casting **reindeer** as best supporting actors in the Christmas story is largely down to Clement Clarke and his 1822 poem *A Visit From St Nicholas*. It was this poem, with its familiar *'Twas the night before Christmas'* beginning, that Thomas Nast was illustrating when he drew what became the role model for all future Santas. The poem's reindeer – one for each leg of their precursor, Woden's steed Sleipnir – answered to Dasher, Dancer, Prancer, Vixen, Comet, Cupid, Donder and Blitzen. Rudolph, of red-nosed fame, only appeared in 1939 with the publication of a certain song.

Clarke's poem stitched reindeer into the fabric of Christmas worldwide, but long before his time many European versions of the story had reindeer pulling Santa's sleigh, and hovering over roofs while the big man slipped into homes with his sack. One appealing theory, which attempts to account for both the flying reindeer and the problems of getting a fat man down a chimney, traces everything back to a Lapland virility ceremony. Men drank reindeer urine as part of an elaborate ritual, unaware that the key chemical ingredients of that urine were derived from the various mosses, lichen and fungi upon which reindeer subsist. And up towards the frozen tundra, some of the hardiest of those plants are rich in an hallucinogenic drug known to induce illusions which show a strong bias towards flying and shape-changing. Hence the skybound reindeer and the incredible shrinking Santa. Like we say, it is just a theory.

A less well-publicised seasonal mammal is the **mole**. One of the odder Christmas superstitions maintains that moles can be banished today by sharpening a scythe in a field which is troubled by the creatures: it will never be molested again. But if the problem lies at a crossroads, then it is best to leave the moles alone, for **ghosts** wander disconsolately at the nation's crossroads on Christmas Day, compromising anyone who dares to cross their path. The spirits belong to the many unfortunates – suicides, the unbaptised and the unidentified – who were laid to rest in these unconsecrated places. None of which stopped many people from going first-footing – the custom is now wholly associated with New Year; but the Christmas footer, the **Lucky Bird**, used to be a common feature today.

Anyone **born on Christmas Day** is able to see spirits – and not just moody ones at crossroads. Today's babies are also immune to hanging or drowning; and if the day happens to be a Sunday, 'of great worship he shall be'. In some places it was said that a Christmas baby would have the power to talk to the animals, grunt and squeak and squawk to the animals. Regarding **marriage**, a piece of very practical-minded pregnancy advice: '*He's a fool that marries at Yule, for when the bairn's near, the corn's to shear.*' Girls used to go to the woodpile and bring in an armful of logs in the wee hours. In daylight the logs were counted: an even number meant that she would marry soon; an odd number meant that all knots would remain unspliced for the forseeable future. And to complete the ages-of-man cycle, turning a mattress at Christmas can result in a family **death**. Even more morbidly, if anyone does die between New and Old Christmas – January 5th – it means that the family will provide a good harvest for the Grim Reaper during the coming year.

☕ Death is also in the air if the weather turns mild: '*a green Christmas, a full churchyard.*'

Dipping toes further into the welter of Christmas **weatherlore**, a pleasantly specific piece of whimsy maintains: '*If a Christmas ice hangs on the willow, clover may be cut at Easter.*'

Sunshine on the afternoon of Christmas Day presages a good apple crop; but at all other times of day it indicates fires in the coming year. Snow means a good hay crop; rain means a bad grain harvest; and a stormy wind before sunset means sickness and disease. And consolation for sun-haters:

If Christmas Day be bright and clear,
There'll be two winters in the year.

The way to keep out thoughts of winter – whether single or plural – was with a big fire, and plenty of evergreen symbols of the soon-to-come spring. Of all the greenery abounding at this time of year, the most recent addition to the British lounge is the **Christmas tree**. It is well established that Prince Albert had a hand in popularising this country's seasonal spruce-up when he imported a tree for the royals' Windsor bash of 1841, to remind him of the Christmas tree custom with which he had grown up in Germany. Albert was not actually the *first* festive lumberjack. Manchester had a long tradition of Christmas trees, due to its large German merchant population; and in 1821 Queen Caroline's household erected a tree (she being the consort of King George IV from 1820–1). If she had not separated from the king, the tradition of Hoovers overloaded with pine-needles might have pre-empted Albert. The most celebrated modern Christmas tree is the 70-footer sent each year by Norway to adorn Trafalgar Square in London.

Charles Dickens called the 19th-century craze for Christmas trees '*the new German toy*', but it was simply a new species grafted onto an ancient tradition of festive **greenery**. Houses were overrun with almost anything which manages to show a leaf here at the beginning of winter, including box, fir, bay, laurel, and **rosemary**. Rosemary grows in bush-form, not just as green nail-clippings on the herb-and-spice rack. It is said to grow upwards for 33 years, after which time it has attained the height of the adult Jesus; and then it merely puts on a good deal of middle-age spread. In some parts of the country yew also joined the festive flora, but in other areas it was avoided, as to have yew in the house was a sure way to precipitate a family death.

The greenery was not just brought indoors: it was lashed to ships' masts, and was also used to festoon tall poles in public places, a decoration which resembled the offspring of a maypole and a Christmas tree.

There is one plant which outranks all others at Christmas. According to *The Sans Day Carol*, '*the first tree in the greenwood, it was the holly*'. **Holly** is used as a bower by good spirits. It can only be cut at this time of year, and must not be brought in before the 24th: a rule which applies to most greenery apart from the post-pagan spruces.

Holly protects houses and stables from malign forces – fire, lightning, witches and faeries – and was formed into wreaths for animals to wear, as well as being a popular wood for thresholds, to keep first-footing nasties at bay. Thrown after a fleeing cow, holly can summon the beast back to the fold. Its fumes can also cure toothache. Simply open your mouth over a bowl full of hot-steeped holly, and the worms – which, as everyone knows, cause the toothache – drop into the water and drown. Only one branch of the family shows signs of malevolence: a **Dancing Holly Bush** hangs out in the woods near Claonaig, south of Tarbert in the Kintyre peninsula of Strathclyde. It dances on the B8001 to prevent travellers from finding their way home. There are delinquent faeries around here too, so avoidance would seem to be the sensible policy.

As a decoration, holly, like ivy and most other items of seasonal foliage, has its origins with the Roman *Saturnalia*. It was Christianised by some ingenious, if forced, carols, which tie its various attributes to the Christian story: red berries for the blood of Christ, and white blossom for the white sheet in which Mary wrapped the infant. When direct symbolism proves elusive the carols turn to simple rhymes, such as:

> *The holly bears a berry as sharp as any*
> *thorn,*
> *And Mary bore sweet Jesus Christ on*
> *Christmas Day in the morn.*

Ivy suffers in the old **holly and ivy songs**, which are about the battle of the sexes. Brash, prickly holly is male, and clinging ivy is female. The chauvinistic victory appears only in the first verse of the most famous of these carols:

> *The holly and the ivy when they are both full*
> *grown,*
> *Of all the trees that are in the wood the holly*
> *tree bears the crown.*

Others are more upfront, such as the 15th-century *Holly and Ivy*:

> *Nay! Ivy, nay; it shall not be, iwis:*
> *Let Holy have the maistry, as the maner is.*

A 16th-century rewrite of this carol describes wood-pigeons devouring ivy's berries, lifting their tails, and defecating on the plant – an act which, says the song, they would never inflict upon holly. But all these songs are degraded forms of earlier medieval troubadour versions, which had an evenly matched holly and ivy coming to the arena with different virtues. Another 15th-century carol redresses the balance with a one-sided argument, *In Praise of Ivy*:

Ivy, chefe of trees it is,
Veni, coronaberis (come, you shall be
  crowned).

In the battle between the two plants, what finally tips the balance – and balances the tipsy – in favour of ivy is the fact that it can cure one of the season's greatest dangers, drunkenness. This stems from the plant's link with bibulous god Bacchus, one of Saturnalia's stars. If you drink from an ivy-wood bowl, the effects of any amount of booze is supposedly nullified. One of the year's great pieces of wishful thinking.

The femaleness of ivy can be used to influence the fickle heart. Single girls in Scotland used to put an ivy leaf to their hearts and sigh:

Ivy, ivy, I love you, in my bosom I put you;
The first young man who speaks to me, my
  future husband he shall be.

The Christianisation of the plant plumbs the depths of ingenuity. Ivy – or, rather I.V.E. – was said to be an acronym, derived from the initials of Iesus/Jesus; Vife/Wife, *ie* Mary; and Emmanuel.

The one plant that remained Christianity-proof was that lusty pagan favourite, **mistletoe**. To the Celts it was a sacred herb which could cure almost anything; and after a few thousand pages of closely-worded theorising, James Frazer proposed that mistletoe was *The Golden Bough* – the title of his 12-volume study of classical and Celtic mythology – a plant equally cherished by the ancient Greeks and Romans.

For Celts the best time to harvest mistletoe was on the sixth day of the moon. It had to be cut from an oak tree with a golden sickle, and allowed to fall into a blanket without touching the ground. Afterwards **bulls** were sacrificed in thanks. The fluid in the mistletoe's berries, the source of its power, was the semen of the tree-god, containing the life of the 'dead' host tree. The fact that mistletoe is uncommon on oaks, preferring apple trees, made the prize all the greater. Its rootless appearance made it an enigmatic plant; though the link between

thrushes and the propagation of seeds through droppings was common knowledge by the early 17th century – the missel, or mistle, **thrush** gets its name from a perceived culinary preference. The downside for the thrush was that mistletoe was used to make sticky bird-lime, spread on branches to capture birds:

The thrush when he pollutes the bough
Sows for himself the seeds of woe.

The Latin name for a thrush, appropriately, is *Turdus*.

Mistletoe can bring fertility to barren humans and animals, and has all the anti-evil powers of holly when used in the homestead. It was often fed to cattle after being taken down at the end of the Christmas festivities. It is widespread – in all counties except Devon, where, according to legend it was long ago banned, for reasons which are now forgotten. One orchard straddling the Devon and Somerset border had mistletoe in the Somerset trees, but none on the Devon side, so they say. It was a pre-requisite at all seasonal gatherings in Wales, where they maintain '*No mistletoe, no luck*'.

Churches would not allow mistletoe under their roofs, and most still hold to this 'ban'. The only exception is York Minster, where the plant has always been welcome. This is probably something to do with the Viking domination of that city. Mistletoe was used to kill the Norse god **Balder**. All things in heaven and on earth swore an oath not to harm him; but mistletoe, in the opinion of the adjudicating goddess Frigga, was too young to swear. Nasty Loki used the plant to fashion an arrow with which Balder was slain. Perhaps anything which had laid low a leading pagan god was deemed acceptable by the church authorities in York. But the custom is probably a simple survival of Viking tradition: for them the mistletoe was a symbol of peace; and in York, as long as the plant was in the Minster, there was a general pardon for all local miscreants.

⊙ The tradition of **kissing under the mistletoe** seems, surprisingly, to be uniquely British in origin. To observe correct formalities, a kisser should pluck one of the berries before demanding lip service, the plant only being 'usable' while berries remain. To refuse a kiss means that you will die single; or, at the very least, it indicates no marriage for at least 12 months.

Formerly the mistletoe was the central item

in an elaborate **Kissing Bough** or Bunch: a decoration of evergreens, fruits and ribbons, often shaped like a crown, or made of intersecting hoops. Candles were attached to its extremities – a catch-all Yule symbol if ever there was one.

Candles remain a regular feature of the Christmas dinner-table, but they are not fixed; and until very recently nor was any other component of the traditional **Christmas menu**. The only thing that you could be sure of was plenty of meat. Swans, bustards and peacocks, all dressed in their original plumage, were the top poultry dishes in rich households. Goose was a good greasy perennial too, and it remained pre-eminent for many years after the introduction of **turkey** into the 1542 stomach of Henry VIII. The name *turkey* comes from the bird's gobbling cry of *turk, turk* – they are from Mexico, not Turkey. Traditional cooking advice spurns the hour-for-every-pound stuff, and states:

A turkey boiled is a turkey spoiled,
A turkey roast is a turkey lost,
But a turkey braised, the Lord be praised!

Christmas pies came in all manner of guises. One cooked for Sir Henry Gray in 1770 consisted of seven blackbirds, six pigeons, six snipe, four partridges, four geese, four ducks, two turkeys, two rabbits, two curlews, two woodcock, two ox tongues, with 20 pounds of butter and two bushels of wheat for pastry. An 1800 Christmas menu from Bristol's *Bush Inn* tempts the diner with 16 different types of fish and 39 species of fowl. But on that same menu there is no room for Christmas pudding, now an integral part of any restaurant's festive table.

Other favourite meats included sirloin of beef and, in the north of Britain, haggis, usually as a breakfast dish. **Yule brose** was common in Scotland too, a gory cauldron of bullocks' heads and/or knee joints simmered overnight to make a heady broth, into which oatmeal was tipped on Christmas Day. The family dipped their spoons into the pot as it simmered.

From the Dark Ages onwards, the non-poultry meat synonymous with the season was **pig**. Royal and poor households alike enjoyed a dish of pork – apart from James I who hated pig products and went for turkey instead. Until the second half of the 19th century at Hornchurch in Essex a boar's head was carried on a pole or pitchfork to Mill Field

today, and used in a game of rugby-cum-wrestling, which probably goes closer to the old traditions than the surviving seasonal pig customs detailed on Sow Day, December 17th.

The other main area of Christmas food is strictly for the sweet-toothed. **Christmas puddings** appeared in their present form in the 17th century, spherical things boiled in pudding-bags. Prior to that the dish had been plum-porridge, a thick mixture of fruit and spices cooked in meat broth and thickened with bread. It was a culinary cousin of frumenty, that porridgey sweet dish made with creed grains of wheat, barley or oats which put in an appearance at many of the year's fairs and festivities – including Christmas. Suffolk had a tradition of leaving out a portion of frumenty for the faeries tonight – presumably they managed to get there before the all-drinking all-guzzling Father Christmas.

Christmas puddings, also known as fig (or figgy) puddings, were a favourite dish of George I, who was called the Pudding King after his predilections and shape. The dying custom of putting money and charms in the pud mixture was carried over from the earlier plum-porridge. Originally different items denoted different fates. For example, finding a coin in the pudding meant marriage, while a thimble meant a single but happy life. For the rituals of making Christmas pudding, see Stir Up Sunday on November 18th.

Christmas Cake was originally associated with Twelfth Night, though there was a long-standing tradition of plum cakes and plum breads, which were often dunked in hot ale before consumption. **Yule Babies**, small human-shaped cakes, were also popular, and may be an echo of human sacrifice like the gingerbread man.

Nibble-wise, Christmas has long been a time for exotica: dates, satsumas and tangerines, chocolate and all kinds of nuts. Although all are commonplace these days, they are still in many ways a seasonal treat. At Lustleigh Cleave in Devon Christmas nuts were cracked using a logan stone known as the **Nutcrackers**, a natural formation in which the top rock could be rocked just enough to gently crack nutshells. But in May 1950 the Nutcrackers fell over and rolled 40 feet down the hillside. All attempts to winch them back failed, and they ended up a further hundred feet down. Time and the elements have since shattered the rock and erased all trace of it, bringing a dramatic end to an ancient tradition with a completeness that the Puritans would have envied.

⊚ **Mince pies** were originally mixtures of eggs, fruit, spice and meat. Mincemeat was real minced meat. In Lincolnshire a line was drawn between the meatless mince pie and the meaty *minch-pie*. The earliest ones seem to have been coffin-shaped, suggesting some ritual significance; and some had pastry babies on the top to represent the holy infant in the manger. It is lucky to eat 12 mince pies, made by 12 different cooks, ideally in 12 different houses, one for each month of the year ahead. Any month 'missed' will be grim. In some areas this feat has to be accomplished before Christmas Day; in others it is done between today and January 1st. A similar tradition maintains that you must eat the twelve pies today, in one sitting. To refuse a mince pie brings bad luck.

Mince pies were sometimes called Christmas pies – not to be confused with the savoury multi-meated ones mentioned earlier. It was into one of these that **Little Jack Horner** stuck his famous thumb and proceded to sing his own plum-fed praises. The nursery rhyme started life as a political comment on the acquisitive habits of Jack Horner, steward of the last Abbot of Glastonbury during the Reformation in the 16th century. He was sent by the Abbot to Henry VII with a large Christmas pie, inside which were deeds to a dozen manors owned by the Abbey. The Abbot was making a vain attempt to save his own skin at a time when abbey asset-stripping was all the rage. Safe in the knowledge that the King did not know the ingredients of the bribe, Jack stuck his entire hand into the pie and siphoned off one of the deeds for himself: the rights to the Manor of Mells in Somerset. Or so the story goes. The more prosaic truth is that Jack was involved in the suppression of the Abbey, and bought some of its lands – without the aid of a purloining thumb – including the ripe plum of the Mells estate.

The various foods of the day have been washed down with all manner of **drinks** throughout the ages. Strong Christmas Ale is traditionally brewed for the occasion, and although it once came close to extinction, year by year more breweries are bottling it and more pubs are stocking it. But whatever the meal, and however it is drowned afterwards, the digestive system will have the last say. An old proverb makes this perpetual prediction: '*Christmas feastings are the physician's harvest.*'

26th December
Boxing Day/St Stephen's Day

Devilish Santa

Apart from Jesus himself, **St Stephen** was the first person to die for the Christian faith, gaining him the title *Protomartyr*. He had argued that the new Christian Law must come before the old Mosaic Law, implying that the Messianic Age had indeed begun. The Elders' response was to have him stoned to death in 35 AD. But before this, the Apostles had hired Stephen as a keeper of alms for the poor. For this reason St Stephen's Day has always been associated with the doling of alms.

It was usual to open the church **alms**-boxes today for the benefit of the needy, and this is one of the origins of the name *Boxing Day*. Alms-seekers also often went from house to house with personal boxes, like piggy-banks. When one-to-one gifts became the norm, employers handed out 'Christmas boxes' – sums of money – to their workers; and the phrase came to mean any gift given in the festive season, especially to milkmen, dustmen and others whose trade brought them regularly to people's homes. The actual name Boxing Day only appears to have been coined last century; though the Romans also had a money-giving custom at this time of year.

Sometimes food was doled out instead of money. Large households sent their leftovers to the poor, and in days of huge meals and wastage this was often a substantial amount. At Bampton-in-the-Bush, Oxfordshire, the parish's three vicars served **St Stephen's Breakfast** – boiled beef and beer – to all comers.

Collecting alms today was sometimes known as **Stephening**, a custom that was vigorously observed in Drayton Beauchamp, Buckinghamshire. Locals used to call at the rectory, and could claim as much bread, cheese and ale as they could carry. The dole was transmuted into a fixed sum of money in 1808 by the latest in a line of sorely-pressed vicars; and in 1834 the Charity Commissioners ruled that the locals had no legal claim to the dole, which ended there and then. A few years earlier a less official attempt to stop the dole had ended in violence. A militant vicar opposed to such hand-outs kept his doors locked on St Stephen's Day. Locals broke through his roof and looted his larder and cellar.

Somewhere along the way, St Stephen became

associated with **horses**, and his feast day became a key date for horse-racing, and for hunting with horse and hounds. In Cleveland the importance of the day also stretched to those hunting on foot and without permit. It was an unwritten rule that hunting laws were suspended today, and anyone could catch what they liked without fear of getting caught themselves.

The day's sporting cue was later taken up by other games. These days the headlining games are the various Boxing Day football fixtures, and the 100-yard dash in the Serpentine at Hyde Park in London. Swimmers here have been competing since the 19th century, though the prize is now the Peter Pan Cup, instigated by J. M. Barrie in 1903, a year before his play *Peter Pan* was staged for the first time.

Horses also suffered more insidious attentions today. Along with cattle, they had their jugulars pierced for a good **bleeding**. The saying ran:

> *If you bleed your nag on St Stephen's Day*
> *He'll work your wark for ever and aye.*

Bleeding animals today was thought to secure their health and stamina for the coming year. They also had a few days' holiday in which to recover from the incisive tradition.

This stems from the ancient belief that draining off sickly blood – be it with leeches or the knife – aids the patient. Never mind the dangers of anaemia and infection. When horses fell ill, they were often bled by making a deep incision in the gum. A full two to three pints of blood-loss was considered helpful.

Some humans suffered a similar fate today. **Holming** lingered longest in the Tenby area of Dyfed, with children attempting to whip each other's legs with holly until blood was drawn. Sometimes women were hunted down for the same treatment. In Scotland this sort of thing never flailed to take place on New Year's Day, when it was said that every drop of blood shed represented a healthy year to come.

© In Norfolk, St Stephen's was called **Handbell Day**, and troops of handbell-ringers would jingle the neighbourhood to the point of insanity. To avoid this sort of noise, Runwell in Essex has a tradition, revived in 1983, of getting out into the wilds. There is an annual walk along the local footpaths, ending at the Running Well a mile or two from the village. At Melrose, Borders, the walking is undertaken by men with top hats, white wands, and optional strange trouser arrangements. **The Mason's Walk** steps out in honour not of St Stephen, but of St John the Apostle, whose eve this is. They parade by torchlight from the market square to the ruined Cistercian abbey, alleged to be the final resting place of Robert the Bruce's roving heart.

☺ In the Middle Ages, the country as a whole was a couple of degrees warmer than it is now, on average. **Vineyards** in those days were not just a few ambitious southern and south-facing hillsides. Vines even made it into national weatherlore, and it was said that '*St Stephen's Day windy, bad for next year's grapes.*'

As detailed on December 18th, **Mumming plays** used to be common to the whole Christmas season. But the few which are still performed have now established Boxing Day as their base camp (the mummers at Symondsbury in Dorset are a notable exception, putting on their play on New Year's Day). Almost all mumming plays had died out by the middle of this century, and most stayed dead. With each year that passed, the number of people still alive who had first-hand memories of mumming grew fewer and fewer. But just as the whole tradition seemed about to teeter over the edge of living history, people began talking to old performers, writing down what they remembered, and reviving several of the old plays. Sometimes there was even a script around to help. It is not unlike the common theme in mumming plays, where one of the principal characters dies but is not so dead that the doctor cannot bring him back to life with a bit of quack magic.

© Marshfield near Bath in Avon still has its Boxing Day play in the classic old mumming costumes made of paper ribbons. The **Paper Boys**, as they are known, wear head-dresses of elevated crowns with coloured paper streamers hanging down, making their heads look like a school of huge jellyfishes. The chief mummer wears an ornate pagan tea-cosy, and the overall appearance is reminiscent of tribal chiefs and witchdoctors in old Tarzan films. There are usually four performances of the brief play, which has a cast of eight and features characters called Tenpenny Nit and Mince Pie as well as many of the more familiar mumming play regulars – St George (sometimes King George), Father Christmas, Beelzebub (who also appears under his stage names the Devil or Old Nick), a Turkish Knight, and the Doctor. As usual in such plays, the characters all brag, squabble, fight and request money or beer from the audience.

© Every year on Boxing Day, **Father Christmas is killed** on the mean streets of Crookham near Fleet in Hampshire. The murder of the familiar chubby red-and-white garbed Santa comes at the climax of the play performed by the Crookham Mummers at various sites around the area, starting outside the *Chequers* pub (or the *Canal Wharf*) at noon. Like Marshfield's team, they favour costumes made from hundreds of tiny paper ribbons, but here the effect more closely resembles psychedelic Wombles. King George, Bold Roamer and Bold Slasher feature prominently in the play, but it is Little Johnny Jack who commits the ho-ho-homicide. There is no potion-packing Doctor character to bring Father Christmas back to life, and amid the weeping of bemused toddlers in the audience, Jack delivers the final lines sitting on Santa's prostrate corpse:

> *Ladies and Gentlemen, see what I have done,*
> *I've killed my father Abraham before the*
> *   setting sun.*
> *As I sit taking my ease,*
> *Ladies and Gentlemen, give what you please!*

What nerve. The most plausible explanation for this outrage is that somewhere back down the line Old Nick and Saint Nick – Satan and Santa – got mixed up. Evidence to back this up comes from the fact that some of the lines given to Father Christmas at Crookham are identical to ones spoken by Old Nick in Cotswold mumming plays.

© Revived mumming plays are also performed today at various other venues, including Headington just outside Oxford and St Albans in Hertfordshire. From 10 am to 3 pm the **Headington Quarry Mummers** and other mumming groups tour from pub to pub in the village. The **mummers of St Albans** are not so lucky, working mostly in the open air, starting outside the old Town Hall at lunchtime. They always call in on the Bishop's Palace, and once even managed to involve the bishop in the action of the play. They report that their call is usually met with the news that the bishop is not at home.

Other seasonal mumming plays survive at Moulton just outside Northampton and Coventry in the West Midlands where Boxing Day is also the preferred performance time. See also December 18th.

Another old form of mumming associated with Boxing Day – and New Year's Eve – was the Midlands custom of **Tupping**. A man dressed as a tup – a castrated ram – in sheepskin and decorated ram's head. He was then 'sacrificed' by the other players, and resurrected by the ever-ready mumming character, a mad doctor. The usual song to accompany this tupper-wear party was *The Derby Ram*, which tells of a beast so huge that it covers an acre of land with each stride, while eagles build their eyries in its horns. The ram is finally slain, and several onlookers drown in the torrent of blood; its gall stones are rolled away like boulders; and its eyes are used as footballs. There are several variations on these basic themes, which have many similarities with the Norse myth of the giant **Ymir**. He was slain by the sons of Bor, and his blood drowned all the Frost Giants and formed the oceans of the world. His flesh became the earth, his teeth the rocks, and his skull the firmament of the heavens. Tupping appears to be a drama based on a myth of Creation itself. It is also a logically extravagant ritual sacrifice: since the killing is not real, the make-believe victim may as well be the biggest and the best of rams, a gesture designed to honour the powers-that-be all the more.

Dorset mummers often did the rounds accompanied by a figure that was part ram, part bull, part god, part fool. The ooser wore a horned, snapping-jawed, woolly mask with human and yet savage features. He was a rough and tumble Fool-figure, relying more on shock and fear than pig-bladder slapstick. The ooser had a mock 'keeper', and drank vast amounts of alcohol. By the end of the evening he was genuinely dangerous, and yet the ooser had to be admitted to any house at which he knocked. One of the final oosers was still lurking in dark places at Melbury Osmond in Dorset at the tail-end of last century. With less emphasis on menace, there have been several recent ooser revivals, with old photographs used to provide the basis for the modern masks.

© Like mumming plays, **Morris dancing** on Boxing Day went through a lean period, but with little in the way of outside coaching it somehow rallied itself, and in many areas modern teams still go the distance today. Handsworth and Grenoside, both on the outskirts of Sheffield, have traditional **sword-dancing** on Boxing Day, a robust form of the Morris. Their swords are not panto-style bits of plank, but two and a half feet of flexible, locally-forged steel.

© The Grenoside **Longsword Dancers** dress in garish paisley-patterned tunics and rosettes; and the leader of team wears a rabbit-skin hat. At 11 am they meet outside *The Old Harrow Inn*, then parade to Old Harrow on the Turnpike Road (blocked off for the occasion). After their calling-on song the convoluted swordplay begins. The men grip the handle of their own and the tip of their neighbour's weapon to perform intricate weaving dances with various knots and jumps, never letting go of the swords or breaking the circle. At the climax of what even die-hard Morris-bashers grudgingly admit to be an impressive performance, the swords are formed into a star-shaped 'lock' around the leader's head. When raised, his rabbit-hat is perched on top of the mock-blades, and the man has thus been ritually decapitated. Giving away the dance's mumming-play origins, the leader falls 'dead', and a quack-doctor from the accompanying pack of mummers comes forward to revive him with a potion. These days a few other dance teams turn up to make the event into more of a festival.

© The **Handsworth** dance is very similar to the one at Grenoside. The dancers' garb is based on the uniform of the Light Dragoons of the early 19th century: braided black jackets, white breeches, leather gaiters, and maroon caps with pom-poms, ribbons and rosettes. Their first Boxing Day performance is outside Handsworth church, and the team of eight men then go on to dance at nearby Woodhouse.

● At **Flamborough**, in one of the bits of Humberside nicked from the East Riding of Yorkshire, sword-dancing also takes place today, around lunchtime. There is no official team, simply a group cobbled together on the day, and venues and precise times tend to vary from year to year. The dances are common currency in the village thanks to the efforts of the local schools; and what the occasion lacks in formal splendour it makes up for in impromptu exuberance.

It smacks of something that should long ago have been dispatched to the customs knacker's yard, but **Hunting the Wren** is still with us, albeit in a highly symbolic form. The wren was King of the Birds, and an old tale explains that it claimed the title after winning a contest to see which bird could fly the highest. The wren cheated by hiding in the eagle's feathers, and just as the exhausted eagle reached maximum

altitude the tiny hitch-hiker nipped out and flew up an extra few feet.

To the Celts the wren was the bird of the underworld, a theory deduced from its habit of nesting in tombs, where it was believed to commune with the dead; and in caves, which were held to be entrances to the twilit lands of the Other World. Its Latin name, *Troglodytes troglodytes*, means cave dweller – said twice just in case you missed it the first time. As the confidant of the King of the underworld, the wren was a representative of winter and darkness. So killing it was deemed to be necessary in order to displace winter and allow spring to return. This, and the notion that as King of the Birds it was a royal sacrifice, made the tradition of wren-hunting a very potent one, thought by some to date back to Neolithic times.

These days the once nationwide Hunt is largely limited to rural areas of Ireland, and the Isle of Man. It was carried out at various dates during the Christmas season, depending on the location. New Year's Day and Twelfth Night were common; and in Suffolk the Hunters waited until Valentine's Day. But the usual date was Boxing Day – known as Wrenning Day. Stealth was not a key tactic in the hunt, and the assailants dressed liked the Eurodisney division of the Home Guard. The Manx hunts always featured someone with a blackened face, draped in a fishing net and with a bunch of leeks for a tail. Amazingly the hunters usually succeeded in catching their quarry; though substitute small birds were not unknown. In Ireland the Wren Boys, as they were known there, sometimes resorted to carving a small potato and sticking it with feathers.

Once trapped, the bird (or tuber) was placed in a wren-box, or strung on the end of a garlanded pole. It was usually dead; though in Wales it was sometimes allowed to hop around in a glass-fronted box, and was later released. At Kirkmaiden south of Stranraer in Dumfries and Galloway, the wren was caught, decorated with ribbons, and released afterwards with minimum fuss. But elsewhere, alive or dead, the bird was paraded through the streets as '*the smallest, yet the king*'. The goldcrest is actually a whole centimetre smaller; but, wisely, its PR people suppressed the facts, leaving the wren to cope with the media onslaught alone.

At each house, the Wren Boys gave a voiciferous cry of '*Please to see the King!*' (also the title of one of Steeleye Span's best records), and launched into one of the many **wrenning carols**. In one widespread version,

The Cutty Wren, the words describe a huge beast, like a flying Derby-Ram, which is hunted with cannons, hacked to bits with cleavers and boiled in large cauldrons. Afterwards the King and Queen attend a wren-feast, and the bird's bones are fed to the poor. To play up this imagery, the wrenners would sometimes affect mock-straining under the weight of their load. But more often than not the wren carol was simply a straightforward plea for alms. A common first-verse manages to proclaim, describe and beg in the space of four lines:

> *The wren, the wren, the King of the Birds,*
> *St Stephen's Day was caught in the furze,*
> *Although he is little, his family is great;*
> *I pray you good landlady, give us a treat!*

© On the Isle of Man, whoever caught the first wren was King for the day. However, modern Wrenning on the island has a notable absence – the wren. The garlanded wren-pole has a fake bird, which is only marginally better than a potato, but is politically correct. Very *very* occasionally the locals might use a dead wren – but only if someone finds its diminutive corpse by chance. Starting at 10 am in Douglas the Wren Boys go round the town performing a circle dance called *Shelg yn Drean*, 'Hunt the Wren', and singing the epic *Hunting of the Wren*, which weighs in at 30-odd verses.

Wren feathers plucked from a St Stephen's Day bird can protect sailors from shipwreck and drowning. This seems to stem from a Norse legend which tells of a beautiful faerie-siren who lured countless men to a watery grave. Eventually the desperate villagers managed to capture her; but she escaped in wren-form. Every year she had to resume the guise, and men hunted her annually to keep the land and sea safe for another year. A simplified alternative says that wrens are spirits which haunt the herring-fishing grounds. To have one, or bits of one, on board offsets disaster. Once St Stephen's Day wrens had been hunted and plucked, what was left was often buried on the beach. In the absence of a beach the wren qualified for a place in the churchyard, a custom which lasted until the late 18th century on Man. Some of the wren-carols ask for money for the specific purpose of giving the bird a decent burial.

In Scotland the wren was called the **Lady of Heaven's Hen**. But in spite of this lofty title, the bird suffered an unenviable reputation. Scots claimed that it was a wren's piercing song that alerted the Roman guards to the presence of Jesus in the Garden of Gethsemane, and that the same bird later alighted on a jailer's face and stirred him just in time to prevent poor St Stephen from making a get-away. In Ireland, the wren also comes in for some stick – legend says that its singing alerted either the Vikings or Cromwell's army to the presence of a tiptoeing Irish troop which was just about to get the upper hand by making a surprise attack. As a final justification for the church-condoned annual persecution of the wren, it was also said to have been the messenger bird of the pagan druids.

St Stephen's Day was a one-off licence to kill. At any other time of year a dead wren means **bad luck**, and is said to induce blood in cows' milk. The same is also said of the robin. The nests are similarly taboo – if you touch a wren's egg your finger is supposed to wither and drop off. To wreck the nest will subject your family to both fire and broken bones. Once again, the same goes for the robin. As an old rhyme says:

> *Robinets and Jenny Wrens*
> *Are God Almighty's cocks and hens.*

The wren may be king of the birds, but the **robin** is king of the festive season, beating even the turkey into second place. It is protected by the same taboos as the wren, with the added advantage of having no customs hingeing on its death. The conspicuous song and breast of the mate-seeking male in December may explain why the robin is so tied up with Christmas imagery; though scenes depicting groups of robins on cards are unsound – the bird is too territorial to allow another of its species anywhere near without a brawl, even when posing for an artist.

The redbreast's red feathers were made by the blood of Christ: the robin either tried to peck at the gory crown of thorns, or else attempted to cover the corpse of Christ with leaves and moss, thus getting stained. Then again, it is said that the robin got singed bringing fire to mankind; or, after the wren had brought fire from Hell, the robin doused the forbidden blaze, getting scalded in the process. Alternatively, the bird was said to have visited Hell to fetch water to alleviate mankind's suffering, and burned itself in situ. Whatever, the bird is said to have a drop of God's blood in it. The only bad news is if a robin comes indoors or taps on the window: it means more death.

27th December
St John the Evangelist's Day

A-Liver Lie-O

Richard Trevithick was raising steam for the first time on British roads back in 1801. On Christmas Eve he gave his passenger-carrying steam carriage a maiden run. James Watt, steam pioneer in the mid to late 18th century, warned the cocky Trevithick that there was too much pressure in the engine. Trevithick ignored the advice, and on the 27th he took a few of his mates down to the local pub. They could have walked there just as quickly, but no matter. Trevithick left the engine running and they all went in for a celebratory pint or two. Ka-boom. The steam carriage exploded – a leading contender for the first-ever powered vehicle accident.

Undeterred by the big bang theory, Trevithick went on to terrify James Watt with the first steam locomotive in 1804, 25 years before Stephenson's Rocket. And where did all this ingenuity and creative hot air get him? A room over a squalid inn in Dartford, and a pauper's death in 1833.

A certain **Charles Darwin** paved the way for another Big Bang theory today when he set off from Plymouth on board the HMS *Beagle* to put an end to the longest running folkloric belief of them all. Five years later he came back to *The Origin of the Species*, fame, notoriety, endless angels-or-apes-ancestry discussions, a bald head and a huge white beard. His barber was out of work, but scientific, philosophical and religious thought would never be the same again.

St John the Evangelist was a first-generation saint. A close friend, some even say brother, of Jesus, he was one of the Bible's co-authors. For this reason he is patron of theologians, writers and booksellers. His emblems are numerous, but the commonest is an **eagle**, because he used to have one as a pet. Eagles flew close to the sun, and John metaphysically speaking, did the same.

⌧ The eagle was included in the coat of arms of Liverpool in the 13th century. There it stayed, and in 1910 the sculptor involved in the building of the Royal Liver Building intended to continue the tradition. His offering was a brace of eagles that sadly had more of the duck/pigeon/cassowary about them. Exit embarrassed sculptor, and enter myth-making. The sculptures were not of eagles – never had been, went the story – they were depictions of the birds that used to paddle about eating lava (a kind of seaweed) in the salty lagoons that existed before the city was built. Lava-bird became **Liver Bird**; and the rest is history and an endless string of Carla Lane sitcoms. The non-species specific Liver Birds still nest on top of the Royal Liver Building, and they crop up on the crest of Liverpool Football Club.

☙ On a shutting-the-stable-door-after-the-horse-has-exploded note, bear in mind that *Never rued the man that laid in his fuel before St John* – in other words, act now while stick stocks last, as there is frosty weather ahead.

As well as the cold, St John can also help stave off the forces of darkness. Faeries and malign spells will not molest anyone wearing a decorative piece of St John's Gospel. However, none of this will save you from the saint's **axe**. To feel the weight of St John's axe is to face the onslaught of God's judgement.

28th December
Holy Innocents' Day/ Childermas

Some Enceinted Evening

Folklore defeated folk law today in 1880. A woman was due to appear at Bow Street courts to give evidence in the case of some Irish men accused of miscellaneous misdemeanours. However, on account of the fact that she was *enceinte*, she refused to take the oath. The judge pointed out that no oath meant no admissable evidence. But the ancient *enceinte* custom won the day, and the evidence – crucial to the fates of the men, perhaps – was not given.

It was widely held that an *enceinte* woman – one who is pregnant – should not give an oath, otherwise she would come to grief. So, similarly, if you find yourself in this condition, you are not supposed to become a godmother. To do so will result in your premature demise.

Did you fall out of the bed this morning, choke on the toothbrush, tumble down the stairs, kill the cat by spilling scalding coffee on it, and wind up in hospital with cornflake poisoning? Well, this is hardly surprising, as **Childermas** claims to be the **unluckiest day of the year** (though other days also vie for this distinction). No new enterprise should be undertaken, and if possible no work should be done at all. Especially not washing. As they say in Northamptonshire: '*What is begun on Dyzemas Day will never be finished.*' As can be inferred from this, in Northamptonshire the 28th is known as Dyzemas Day.

Mindful of the day's ill bodings, Edward IV, realising that his 1461 coronation was scheduled to take place on Sunday the 28th, postponed the event until the Monday. And to underline the unluckiness further, Scots point to the fact that on December 28th 1879 the Tay Bridge blew down; a disaster in itself, but a double disaster in that it inspired William McGonagall's epic, chronic poem. Optimists can always call on Edward the Confessor. He laid the foundation stone of Westminster Abbey today in 1065, and that's still doing OK. On the other hand, Edward died the following year and England was plunged into the chaos of the Norman Conquest.

To make things even more exciting, the last Monday in December is also **Judas' Birthday**, another incredibly unlucky day. So if the Monday is the 28th, your shopping bags will burst, your bananas will all be empty; and don't even think about trying to programme the video.

Making the most of a bad time, Boy Bishops used to hold their sermons today, the last in their pre-Christmas reign – see December 6th. Bells were rung in many parish churches and cathedrals in memory of the Holy Innocents, the children slain by Herod on the off-chance that they might be Jesus. More to the penitial point, children were whipped today, to remind them of the suffering of the Innocents. The know-all customs-police, however, argue that this fledgling flagellation derives from the blood-letting of St Stephen's Day two days ago.

☕ As work is out, and as everything else is fraught with danger today, everyone may as well sit around in their unwashed clothes and watch the **weather**. A drizzly, yucky sort of day means scarcity, whereas a fine day implies plenty.

29th December
St Thomas Beckett's Day

Pilgrims' Tail

On this day in 1669 Captain Michael Mansfield helped see off seven Algerian ships on the south coast, in his ship *Marigold*. But folksong being folksong, the ditty based on the occasion told of a Captain Wellfounder routing seven Turkish men-of-war in his vessel *The Royal Oak*. Well, what are a few names between friends? The irony is that the man from whom this song – *The Royal Oak* – was collected early this century was called Mansfield, little realising that his namesake was the original hero of the ditty. To give you a brief flavour of the jingo involved:

> *Oh three we sank and three we burned,*
> *And three we caused to run away,*
> *And one we brought into Portsmouth harbour*
> *For to let them know we had won the day.*

Thomas Beckett and young Henry II were best of mates, and in 1162 Henry made Beckett Archbishop of Canterbury. But Beckett took his job seriously and refused to be a pawn of the King, who wanted to limit the power of the church by making it answerable to the crown court. In 1170 the breach had been artificially healed, and the Archbishop returned from exile in France. But the new bonhomie was a sham. Behind closed doors Henry still fumed, and made his now-famous aside, '*Will no one rid me of this turbulent priest?*' Four knights took him at his word and sloped off to the cathedral in Canterbury. That was the end of Beckett.

Or rather it was the start of Beckett. Henry did penance, being whipped in front of his tomb, and pilgrims flooded in. By 1173 Thomas was a saint, and within a decade a record-breaking 703 miracles had been reported at his tomb.

Beckett became an entire legend industry. Pilgrims trekked to Canterbury from all over Europe. This is best recorded in Chaucer's door-stopping and yet unfinished *Canterbury Tales*, whose characters are hot-footing it to Thomas' still much-frequented shrine: the long distance footpath called The Pilgrims' Way, running from Winchester via London, leads there.

It was 17th-century poet Andrew Marvell who said: '*For Beckett's sake, Kent always shall have tails.*' The legend says that it was Kentish Men (or was it Men of Kent?) who killed the saint, and the tails were their punishment. A toned-down version says that in Strood, where the locals supported the King, Beckett's horse had its tail cut off by the mob. He cursed the descendants of the culprits, saying that they would be born with tails. These tales of tails used to be the ultimate in witty slander.

On an earlier, friendlier jaunt through Kent, Beckett came to Otford and drank the water. It tasted like week-old dishwater and draught lard. So he struck his crozier in the ground, and up sprang Beckett's Well. On this same visit he was disturbed by nightingales. He banished the birds, and they have never reappeared thereabouts.

In a similar feat, Beckett purified the water at Deanshanger in Northamptonshire. He had been hiding at the Gilbertine Monastery there, and was unrecognised by all except a single farm labourer, who, knowing of Beckett's skills, asked him if he could sort out the water supply. Beckett was impressed at the man's sharp eyesight, and complied.

30th December
St Egwin's Day

A Baboon, a Goldspink and a Lobster in a Pear Tree

St Egwin was falsely denounced as a crook by his enemies in the late 7th century. To prove his innocence, he locked his feet in fetters, threw the key into the River Avon, and shuffled off to Rome. Just before reaching his destination, he bought a fish. At the Vatican he unzipped his purchase, and out popped the key to his fetters. It certainly impressed the Pope, and Egwin was vindicated on the spot.

After this he got to work. Evesham Abbey in Hereford and Worcester was his coup de grace. At a crucial stage of the building, Satan hurled a huge clod of earth at the edifice. Egwin deflected the missile with a well-aimed prayer. The earth fell instead on Warwickshire, and became what is now Meon Hill – see tomorrow for its ghost.

The ungodly Meon Hill was matched by the ungodly blacksmiths of Alcester in the same county. They worked on Sundays, and when reprimanded by Egwin, they sang loudly to drown him out. Afterwards they all felt an odd swelling in their trousers. To their disappointment, each blacksmith discovered that he had sprouted a tail. The smiths were so ashamed

that they fled the forge, and the trade died out in the town.

The first of the *The Twelve Days of Christmas* is not Christmas Day, it is Boxing Day, which makes today the fifth – where the tune slows down and even amnesiacs shout along with '*Five go-old rings!*'

The song originated as a Christmas game, and originally there were dozens of alternative versions. The one that has passed into mass-produced history comes complete with mishearings: '*A Partridge in a pear tree*' should read '*A part of a juniper* (or *June-apple) tree*'. Juniper gives a sweet smell when burnt, keeps away demons, and lasts a long time in the grate, attributes which make it an ideal Christmas gift. As for the game itself, each person says a line of the song, and the next person repeats their line and adds the next, or undergoes a forfeit. One excessive version runs to 13 Days, and all the gifts come in threes:

> The King sent his lady on the thirteenth Yule Day,
> Three stalks o'merry corn, three maids a-merry dancing,
> Three hinds a-merry hunting, An Arabian baboon,
> Three swans a-merry swimming, three ducks a-merry laying,
> A bull that was brown, three goldspinks, three starlings,
> A goose that was grey, three plovers, three partriges, a papingo-aye.

Another splendid remix offers 12 huntsmen, eleven ships, ten comets, nine peacocks, eight joiners, seven lobsters, six beetles, five puppies, four horses, three monkeys, two pudding ends, and a gaping wide-mouthed waddling frog – all in tongue-twisting predicaments. At the ambitious end of the scale, one of the songs ends with:

> Ten Italian dancing masters going to teach ten Arabian magpies how to dance;
> Eleven guests going to celebrate the marriage of the Princess Baldroulbadour with the Prince of Terra-del-Fuego,
> Twelve triumphant trumpeters triumphantly trumpeting the tragical tradition of Telemachus.

☕ The events and weather of the Twelve Days are, bizarrely, said to mirror the coming 12 months – so expect a September full of lobsters.

31st December
New Year's Eve/Hogmanay

Great Balls of Fire: It's the Flambeaux Rambos

✝ **Great night for ghosts.** The 16th-century Chief Justice **Sir John Popham** pops from the ground at Wellington church in Somerset, and each year his spectre is said to move one cock's-stride towards the tomb of his wife. She saved his soul with her prayers after he fell down a bottomless pit into Hell during a hunting trip; but at this rate it will be past Doomsday before he reaches her.

✝ Making much smoother progress is **Granny Austin**, a ghost who floats footless and fancy-free tonight around Upper and Lower Brailes, south of Stratford in Warwickshire. During the last war she panicked the Home Guard in the area when, without the aid or presence of legs, her dark form drifted past one of their patrols.

William Pell was murdered on New Year's Eve 1407, and was immediately 'laid' – not quite an exorcism, but still a damper of spirits – by a friar, for 250 years. When this time had elapsed he appeared to the new owners of Old Pell farmhouse on New Year's Eve and commanded one of them to accompany him to Southwark in London to help recover the lost Pell treasure. The man eventually complied, fed up with the earwigging which Pell's ghost was giving him. He went to the house of Pell's descendants, introduced them to the ghost of their ancestor, and helped dig up the booty. Once the spoils were divvied up, Pell was happy. He has not reappeared since.

✝ Equally bossy is the **phantom huntsman** of Meon Hill – see yesterday for the Hill's own story. In life he delighted in hunting, until one day he was eaten by his own dogs: it was no accident, but very likely a divinely humorous punishment, as the man regularly hunted on the Sabbath. Tonight his ghost does the rounds across Warwickshire along with his phantom pack, the Hooters. When mortals are encountered, the Huntsman attempts to persuade them to open the gates to their homes, and then asks all sorts of questions. Keep the gates locked and do not attempt to answer. Any response and Beelzebob Monkhouse will give out the ultimate booby prize – a one-way ticket to Hell.

© **New Year's Eve fire** customs, ritually burning out the old year, have survived in a few places. Allendale, near Haltwhistle in Northumberland, has a parade of wildly-attired flame-haired **Guisers** this evening. Shortly before midnight the leaders (men only, as usual) don their better-than-Ascot outrageous hats: half-barrels filled with 40 pounds of blazing tar. After the march past, the barrels are thrown on to a bonfire, and the Allendalers sing and dance until midnight heralds the first-footing.

© Stonehaven in Grampian goes one better by making its **fireballs** airborne. Wood and cloth, with a bit of paraffin here and there, are enmeshed in wire, and the finished product has to be perfectly round. The procession begins at 11.30 pm, during which the fireballs are whirled around the participants' heads on wire strings. Half an hour later the pageant has reached the beach, and the blazing balls are hurled into the sea. This all originated as a fishermen's festival, assuming its present form in the middle of last century.

◉ The **Flambeaux Procession** at Comrie in Tayside is another lucky survivor; though it is very much a locals-only affair. Three 10-foot birch poles topped with burning hessian sacking are paraded in a pipe-led procession at midnight, with three to five more pole-pyres being lit during the course of the evening. All are later thrown into a heap to burn amidst a carnival atmosphere of bonfire, food, fancy-dress and nifty footwork. In former days, with an echo of the ritual's herd-purifying-and-protecting origins, the participants dressed as animals.

© Equally combustible, Biggar in Strathclyde lights a New Year's Eve **bonfire** of wood and fireworks in the town square, and then stands well back during the drinking and dancing. After midnight the event becomes a **Mischief Night**: lock your doors and tie your goats down – all laws are suspended and almost anything goes. Various places used to 'Burn Out the Old Year' in similar fashion, or shoot the year out with guns. Wick in the north-east Scottish Highlands still builds a huge bonfire for the occasion.

© Considerably further south, Guernsey constructs a personification of **The Old Year's End** – *La Vieux Bout De L'An* – a monstrous effigy in the Guy Fawkes mould. It is carried ceremoniously to a bonfire for the inevitable sacrificial act.

All this fire is meant to drive out evil, purify the air for the coming New Year, and act as a boost to the weak winter sun. **Fire**, in general, must be kept burning tonight in order to ensure the survival of the household during the coming year. On no account must anyone be 'lent' the flame – do not give coals away or let folk light their candles at your hearth. If your fire *does* go out, it cannot be re-lit or replaced until noon on New Year's Day.

Dressing up as bulls, deer or goats used to be a favourite pastime today and tomorrow. It was all to do with pagan horned-god worship. Not surprisingly, the Church took a dim view of this, imposing a penance of three years' fasting as punishment. Nevertheless, until early this century a tradition survived in remoter parts of Scotland in which a man in a bull's hide was led from door to door and symbolically beaten before each. The bull-man brought luck to those households that he passed. Sometimes he handed out sticks with the bull hide or other animal skins wrapped around the end. These had to be singed and passed round the family from hand to hand like a sort of prehistoric spliff, then taken three times round the house sunwise. This being done, it was whisky, cakes and cheese all round. Eating any kind of cheese brings luck at New Year; but cheese with holes in it doubles up as a mystic torch – peer through the hole and you can see through darkness or mist.

Tonight **Mari Lwyd** rides out in Wales. The fun and games are sometimes called *Y Warsel*, a Welsh form of 'wassail'; or *Y March*, 'The Horse'. Mari Lwyd (meaning Grey Mare/ Mary/Death – no one is too sure which) is a horse's skull wrapped in tight white cloth and decorated. It is held on the end of a pole by a man covered in a white sheet. Mari and her party used to go on their rounds throughout the Christmas season, wandering from farmhouse to farmhouse, gaining entry and refreshment by out-singing the householders. The songs are verses of challenge, insult, parody, some of them traditional and others improvised on the night. The battle of bards is a fine old Celtic concept; and after the wordy prologue, Mari is allowed indoors where cake and drink are handed round.

© Mari Lwyd still performs her cantering cantos at midnight tonight in and around the gorgeous thatched 12th-century *Yr Hen Dy (Old House)* pub at Llangynwyd near Bridgend in Mid Glamorgan. The annual appearance is masterminded by octogenarian Cynwyd Evans, said to be the only man who still knows how to carry out the Mari Lwyd ceremony correctly. Early on New Year's Day a second, more primitive, horse turns up to take

the strain. This Mari is from the Welsh Folklore Museum in Cardiff, and appears all over Glamorgan throughout the Christmas season, with a special sneak preview at the Museum early in December. Other Mari Lwyds are more intermittent, but most years between late December and the middle of January she is a regular sight around Llantrisant and Pontypridd in Mid Glamorgan, Ystradgynlais on the West Glamorgan-Powys border, and Ammanford in Dyfed.

This is all linked to ancient mumming and wassailing traditions, Mari being a relative of the Antrobus Horse, the Richmond Old Horse, and the humble Pantomime Horse. To the Celts the horse was a sacred animal: one of the notable features of an Iron Age hoard of almost a thousand gold and silver pieces unearthed near Worcester in the Summer of 1993 was the familiar horse motif struck on to the coins.

© The Christian reaction to all tonight's headlong paganism was to introduce a note of serenity. In the 18th century Methodists made New Year's Eve their **Watchnight,** an idea that soon spread to rival denominations. Everyone sings hymns until a few minutes before midnight. There is then silence until the bells strike the New Year. Cue joyous hymns, more bell-ringing, and sometimes a special hymn sung from the church tower. St Paul's in London, and Ripon Cathedral in North Yorkshire – where there is also a torchlight procession – hold two of the biggest Watchnight services.

Bellringers up and down the country used to have their main revels tonight. At Over in Cambridgeshire they feasted in *The Swan*, swilling pints of a spectacular hot-pot consisting of beer, spirits, sugar, spice, eggs and milk. This was quaffed from *Long Tom*, an old cow's horn. At Tewin in Hertfordshire, the bellringers ran round the church seven times. This was not merely due to too much hot pot. Local tradition maintains that to do so, on any night of the year, will summon the Devil to the gravestone of Lady Anne Grimston. However, on New Year's Eve he normally turned up there anyway, whether bidden to or not. The bellringers did the seven circuits, and claimed to have summoned Old Nick.

👁 The future yawns before us on New Year's Eve, and it is an ideal time for **divinations.** If you throw **fruit peel** over your shoulder, it will form the initial of your loved one. For more fun

– and recommended for that Hogmanay party hiatus – drip **candle wax** (or, ideally, melted lead) into water, and the ensuing shapes will reveal what lies ahead in the coming year. Or for women fancying a little more of a build up, place a key on chapter eight, verse seven ('*Many waters cannot quench love . . .*') of the *Song of Solomon* in the **Bible**, then suspend the Bible in your garter. Twirl the lot round with your ring-finger while the audience goes through the alphabet. When the Bible drops, the last letter chanted is the initial of your true love. If the book does not drop by 'Z', you will be celibate forever.

◉ Even weirder, use the following Borders custom to get the lowdown on your current beau or belle. Put three buckets of water in the bedroom, and pin three leaves of holly to your night gown in the proximity of your heart. In the middle of the night three bears will roar; but do not worry – you have not been on a nocturnal porridge raid. This will be followed by three hoarse laughs; then the apparition of your loved one will appear. If his intentions are sound, he will, in some way, tamper with the buckets. If he is a fly-by-night, he will leave the room undisturbed and pail into insignificance.

Spinning and weaving should all be finished before bedtime tonight. If not – in Fife, at least – **the Gyre-carlin** will abscond with all your flax. The Gyre-carlin, also known as Habetrot, is a powerful faerie woman, and a dab hand at spinning. She once came to the aid of a hopeless weaver-girl by doing her work and producing seven pieces of perfect cloth. To celebrate, the girl went downstairs and ate seven black puddings. Her mother, amazed at this dual feat of weaving and pudding-guzzling, went outside and improvised a quick song about her daughter's skills. A passing laird overheard, and whisked the lucky girl off to a posh wedding. But he now expected her to keep making equally marvellous cloth. Panicking, the girl called on Habetrot, and the faerie invited the newly-weds round to her place for tea. When they arrived they found the household full of grotesquely deformed monsters. The laird ingenuously asked what had happened, and Habetrot replied that all weavers ended up looking that way. The laird opted for love over linen, and forbade his new wife from ever touching flax again.

🔟 The Rollright Stones in Oxfordshire (see June 23rd for their full story) are said to leave their field and wander down to the stream to drink water tonight. Perhaps Stonehenge was trying to do something similar in 1900 on this day, when one of its stone lintels fell off.

☕ If you end the year in poverty, tradition says that – surprise, surprise – you will spend the coming year in poverty. The only consolations are that, in Scotland, this is traditionally an auspicious day for weddings; and if you go **weather**-watching you will be able to sort out the entire year ahead:

> *If New Year's Eve night wind blows south,*
> *It betokeneth warmth and growth;*
> *If West, much milk and fish in the sea;*
> *If North, much cold and storms there will be;*
> *If East, the trees will bear much fruit;*
> *If North-east, flee it, man and brute.*

The Hogmanay hog-fondling and first-footing fun continues, of course, on January 1st.

APPENDIX

Days for main moveable feasts until the year 2000

	1996	1997	1998	1999	2000
Chinese New Year	Feb 19	Feb 7	Jan 28	Feb 16	Feb 5
Shrove Tuesday	Feb 20	Feb 11	Feb 24	Feb 16	Mar 7
Ash Wednesday	Feb 21	Feb 12	Feb 25	Feb 17	Mar 8
Purim	Mar 5	Mar 21	Mar 12	Mar 2	Mar 20
Mothering Sunday	Mar 17	Mar 9	Mar 22	Mar 14	Apr 2
Easter Sunday	Apr 7	Mar 30	Apr 12	Apr 4	Apr 23
Hock Sunday	Apr 14	Apr 6	Apr 19	Apr 11	Apr 30
Rogation Sunday	May 12	May 4	May 17	May 9	May 28
Ascension Day	May 16	May 8	May 21	May 13	June 1
Whit Sunday	May 26	May 18	May 31	May 23	June 11
Trinity Sunday	June 2	May 25	June 7	May 30	June 18
Corpus Christi	June 6	May 29	June 11	June 3	June 22

For *Chinese New Year* see 31st January

For *Purim* see 26th February

Shrove Tuesday is situated under **Shrovetide** and *Ash Wednesday* and *Mothering Sunday* under **Lent**, both of which can be found between **February** and **March**

Easter Sunday is in the **Easter** section and *Hock Sunday* under **Hocktide**, both of which can be found between **March** and **April**

Rogation Sunday and *Ascension Day* are situated in **Rogationtide**, which can be found between **April** and **May**

Whit Sunday is under **Whitsuntide**, *Trinity Sunday* under **Trinity** and *Corpus Christi* under **Corpus Christi**, all of which are situated between **May** and **June**

ACKNOWLEDGEMENTS

The vast majority of people who helped us – notably tourist-board staff, parish councillors, publicans, village librarians, area archivists, local historians, regional-newspaper reporters and church officials – did so without us ever discovering their names. Many thanks for your time, trouble and specialist knowledge. We are particularly grateful to:

Lawrence Adams
Robin Ansell
Revd. Christopher Atkinson
Eric Barnes
Penny Bayer
John Beresford
Pamela Booth
Dr Powell Brett
June Brown
B. Burton
Arthur Capers
Andrew Cheek
Rosemary Clarke
Yvonne Creswell
Pauline Davey
Peter Dence
Revd. H.A.R. Edgell
Jane Fairney
Canon Finney
John Franklin
G.E. Garfield
Iain Grant
John Hadman
E.S. Harban
Tom Henderson
Jenny Hirsall
Martin Hollingsworth
Michael Houghton
Revd. David James
Revd. R.B. Jenkyns
Ann Kilbey
Stan Knight
Father Korniotis
Mark Lawson
Revd. Peter Lewis
Harry Lovell
John Maggs
Revd. Nicholas Martin
Jimmy McEwan
Bill Meek
Anne Morton
Gordon Newton
Kay O'Brien
Ros Palmer
Alex Parks
Fraser Pithy
William Porre
Ivan Rabey
Robyn Read
John Reynolds
Christine Roberts
Kathy Rooney
David Saint

Peter Allan
Paul Archibald
Richard Bachelor
Dick Barton
Revd. R. Beardall
Joan Bird
J. Bottrill
George Britton
Jackie Bruce-Jones
Peter Chivers
Les Casey
Lt. Commander M. Cheshire
Revd. Michael Clayton
Lynne Cunningham
Peter Davies
Peter Dicks
G.S. Elliott
Karin Farnworth
Kathy Fishwick
Willy Freckleton
Revd. Peter Gilks
Geoff Green
Roy Halsall
Lorna Haycock
Fiona Hepworth
Jonathan Hilderstadt
Robyn Hitchcock
Heather Holden-Brown
Adrienne House
Chris Jaques
Janet Johnson
Terry Knight
Brian Lambie
Joan Leach
Nick Linus
Revd. Keith Lovell
Frank Mansfield
Revd. Peter Martin
Revd. McGuffie
Sid Merry
Gordon Myland
Roger Norris
Catriona Organ
Barry Parker
Jenny Parrott
J.R. Pitt
E.M. Preston
Jim Railton
Dr D. Reader
Jean Rhymer
J.G.W. Roberts
Colonel Christopher Ross
R.C.H. Saunders

Alison Andrew
Tony Ashcroft
Ethel Baker
Phyllis Barton
John Beech
Barbara Blanchard
John Boundy
David Bromwich
Dr Francis Burns
Revd. J. Campbell
Castleton Primary School
S.M. Child
Jill Collard
Angela Cutting
Revd. David Davis
Margaret Dixon
Eileen Ellis
Hugh Featherstone
Wendy Fitzgerald
John Fuller
Revd. Simon Godfrey
Sue Griffiths
Michael Handley
Barbara Heathcote
Revd. Lewis Higdon
Geoff Hodkinson
Revd. John Holder
Deborah Hulbert
Stan Jarvis
Annie Jones
William Humphreys-Jones
F.J. Knights
A.E. Lattimore
Keith Leech
Eleanor Lockyer
Fiona McArdle
M. Marino
Sheena McCulloch
Helen McMurray
Joyce Messner
Roxburgh Nairn
Revd. North
Clive Paine
Mick Parker
Ray Paul
Kathleen Pitt
Russell Preston
Gary Rainbow
Dr Ben Rees
Charles Richard
Revd. Chris Rogers
Barbara Rothwell
D. Seddon

Revd. Howard Ansell
John Ashdown
Mary Baldwin
Michael Basson
Colin Bell
Nicholas Blandy
J. Braid
Joyce Brown
Bob Burns-Murdoch
Revd. Caney
M.E. Chapman
D.G. Clark
Tim Collier
Tom Dale
Lorraine Deacon
S.M. Draper
Angela English
Barnett Field
Sally Flatman
Peter Gant
Canon Alder Gofton
C. Grimsey
Richard Hankinson
Mrs P. Helmes
Joanne Hillman
Isobel Holborn
Len Hoskins
Tony Innes
G. Jeffrey
Eileen Jones
Revd. George King
Helen Knox
Martin Lawrence
Martin Leftwitch
Anne Loudon
Edwin Macnamara
Revd. D. Marr
Paula McDonnell
Martin McKenna
Christine Mitchell
Eleanor Nanestad
Revd. Peter Norton
Sue Painter
John Parkes
Peter Percival
Kate Pleydell-Bouverie
Kate Quarry
Dave Rayner
Mary Reid
Ian Rickerby
Revd. Hugh Rom
Doc Rowe
Colonel Henry Shellard

Francis Shergold
Barbara Smith
Roland Smith
A.G. Storey
Jenny Tansley
John Thirks
Revd. S.J. Trott
Jane Twist
Rachel Watson
Shirley Wickham
E.M. Willmott
Revd. Keith Wood

Pat Shurmur
Harry Smith
Tracey Smith
Martin Stray
Gerald Tatum
Pete Thomas
Revd. Alan Turner
A.L. Ward
Len Weaver
Mrs Wilborne
David Wilson
Christine Wright

Edith Sidall
Janet Smith
Sheila Steffans
E. Swales
John Taylor
David Tomlinson
Cannon Turner
Charles Warmingham
Joan Weir
Revd. Steve Williams
James Wilson
Nigel Wright

Revd. Michael Silley
Norman Smith
Pru Stokes
John Symonds
R.F. Tennant
Harry Tomlinson
David Turner
P. Watkins
Revd. Richard Wheeler
Revd. Wilmold
Barry Wood

INDEX